A-Level Year 2

Chemistry

The Complete Course for OCR A

Let's face it, Chemistry is a tough subject. You'll need to get to grips with a lot of difficult concepts, and have plenty of practical skills up your lab-coat sleeve.

But don't worry — this brilliant CGP book covers everything you'll need for the new OCR A course. It's packed with clear explanations, exam practice, advice on maths skills and practical investigations... and much more!

It even includes a free Online Edition to read on your PC, Mac or tablet.

How to get your free Online Edition

Go to **cgpbooks.co.uk/extras** and enter this code...

3339 0622 2195 4284

This code will only work once. If someone has used this book before you, they may have already claimed the Online Edition.

Contents

Introduction

How Science Works

HOW SCIENCE WORKS

Practical Skills

PRACTICAL SKILLS

Practical Skills for the Practical Endorsement

Module 5

Section 1: Reaction Rates

Section 2: Equilibrium

Section 3: Acids, Bases and pH

Section 4: Enthalpy, Entropy and Free Energy

Section 5: Redox and Electrode Potentials

Section 6: Transition Elements

Module 6

Section 1: Aromatic Compounds and Carbonyls

Section 2: Nitrogen Compounds and Polymers

Section 3: Organic Synthesis and Practical Techniques

Section 4: Analysis

Maths Skills

MATHS SKILLS

Exam Help

EXAM HELP

Reference

How to use this book

Learning Objectives

- These tell you exactly what you need to learn, or be able to do, for the exam.
- There's a specification reference at the bottom that links to the OCR A specification.

Learning Objective:

- Be able to describe the electrophilic substitution of aromatic compounds with a haloalkane or acyl chloride in the presence of a halogen carrier (Friedel-Crafts reaction) and its importance to synthesis by formation of a C–C bond to an aromatic ring.

Specification Reference 6.1.1

3. Friedel-Crafts

Because benzene is so stable, it's fairly unreactive. Friedel-Crafts is a useful process for overcoming this problem.

Acylation

Friedel-Crafts acylation is used to add an acyl group (–C(=O)–R) to the benzene ring. It results in the formation of a new C–C bond, which are difficult to make, and so this reaction is important in organic synthesis. Once an acyl group has been added, the side chains can be modified by further reactions to produce useful products, making this a very versatile reaction in organic synthesis. The products of the reaction are HCl and a phenylketone. The reactants need to be heated under reflux in a non-aqueous environment for the reaction to occur. Here's the equation for the reaction:

$$R{-}C({=}O){-}Cl + C_6H_6 \xrightarrow[\text{reflux}]{AlCl_3} C_6H_5{-}C({=}O){-}R + HCl$$

Acyl chloride — Benzene — Phenylketone

An electrophile has to have a pretty strong positive charge to be able to attack the stable benzene ring — most just aren't polarised enough. But some can be made into stronger electrophiles using a catalyst called a **halogen carrier**.

Friedel-Crafts acylation uses an acyl chloride to provide the electrophile and a halogen carrier such as $AlCl_3$. $AlCl_3$ accepts a lone pair of electrons from the acyl chloride. As the lone pair of electrons is pulled away, the polarisation in the acyl chloride increases and it forms a carbocation. This makes it a much, much stronger electrophile, and gives it a strong enough charge to react with the benzene ring. The formation of the carbocation is the first step in the reaction mechanism and is shown below:

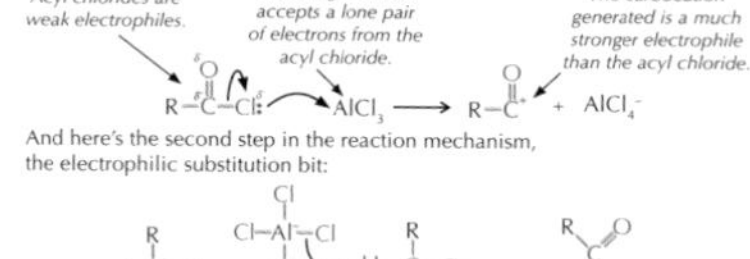

Acyl chlorides are weak electrophiles.
The halogen carrier accepts a lone pair of electrons from the acyl chloride.
The carbocation generated is a much stronger electrophile than the acyl chloride.
AlCl₃
AlCl₄⁻

And here's the second step in the reaction mechanism, the electrophilic substitution bit:

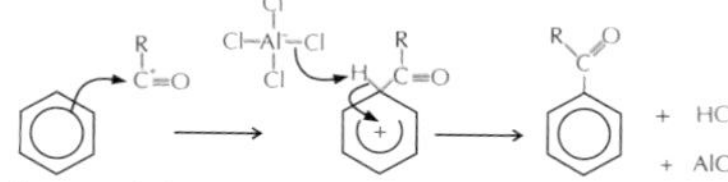

+ HCl
+ AlCl₃

Electrons in the benzene ring are attracted to the positively charged carbocation. Two electrons from the benzene bond with the carbocation. This partially breaks the delocalised ring and gives it a positive charge.

The negatively charged $AlCl_4^-$ ion is attracted to the positively charged ring. One chloride ion breaks away from the aluminium chloride ion and bonds with the hydrogen. This removes the hydrogen from the ring, forming HCl. It also allows the catalyst to reform. Any acyl chloride can react with benzene in this way.

Figure 1: Charles Friedel — co-developer of Friedel-Crafts acylation.

Tip: A phenylketone is produced, unless R is just H, in which case an aldehyde called benzenecarbaldehyde, or benzaldehyde, is formed.

Exam Tip
You could draw out the full structure of benzene when writing out this equation — but these simplified diagrams are a lot quicker and could save you valuable time in your exam.

Tips

These are here to help you understand the theory.

Exam Tips

There are tips throughout the book to help with all sorts of things to do with answering exam questions.

Brady's reagent

PRACTICAL ACTIVITY GROUP 7

Brady's reagent is 2,4-dinitrophenylhydrazine (2,4-DNPH) (see Figure 2) dissolved in methanol and concentrated sulfuric acid.

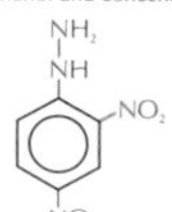

NH₂
NH
NO₂
NO₂

Figure 2: Brady's reagent (2,4-dinitrophenylhydrazine).

The 2,4-dinitrophenylhydrazine forms a bright orange precipitate if a carbonyl group is present (see Figure 3). This only happens with C=O groups, not with ones like COOH, so it only tests for aldehydes and ketones.

Figure 3: Brady's reagent reacting with propanone.

Using melting points to identify unknown carbonyls

The orange precipitate is a derivative of the carbonyl compound. Each different carbonyl compound produces a crystalline derivative with a different melting point. So if you measure the melting point of the crystals and compare it against the known melting points of the derivatives, you can identify the carbonyl compound.

Tip: A derivative of a compound is a similar compound to the original or one that has been made from it.

Example

An unknown carbonyl compound, molecule **J**, is reacted with Brady's reagent and an orange precipitate is formed. The melting point of the product was found to be 115.3 °C. Use the table below to identify molecule **J**.

Carbonyl compound	Melting point of 2,4-DNPH derivative (°C)
Propanal	156
Methylpropanal	182
Butan-2-one	115
3-methylbutan-2-one	124

Butan-2-one has a 2,4-DNPH derivative with a melting point of 115 °C. So molecule **J** must be butan-2-one.

Tip: There's more about how to find the melting point of a substance on page 228.

Tollens' reagent

PRACTICAL ACTIVITY GROUP 7

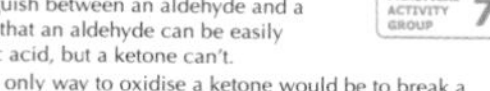

This test lets you distinguish between an aldehyde and a ketone. It uses the fact that an aldehyde can be easily oxidised to a carboxylic acid, but a ketone can't.

Remember, the only way to oxidise a ketone would be to break a carbon-carbon bond so ketones are not easily oxidised (see pages 178-179).

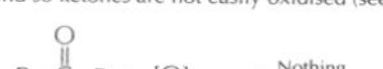

R–C(=O)–R + [O] ⟶ Nothing happens

Tip: Remember to carry out a risk assessment before starting any experiment. A risk assessment involves reviewing the hazards of the reacting chemicals, the products and any conditions needed, such as heat.

183

Practical Activity Groups

You need to show you've mastered some key practical skills in your Practical Endorsement. Information on the skills you need and opportunities to apply them are marked up throughout the book.

Examples

These are here to help you understand the theory.

How Science Works

- You need to know about How Science Works. There's a section on it at the front of the book.
- How Science Works is also covered throughout the book wherever you see this symbol.

HOW SCIENCE WORKS

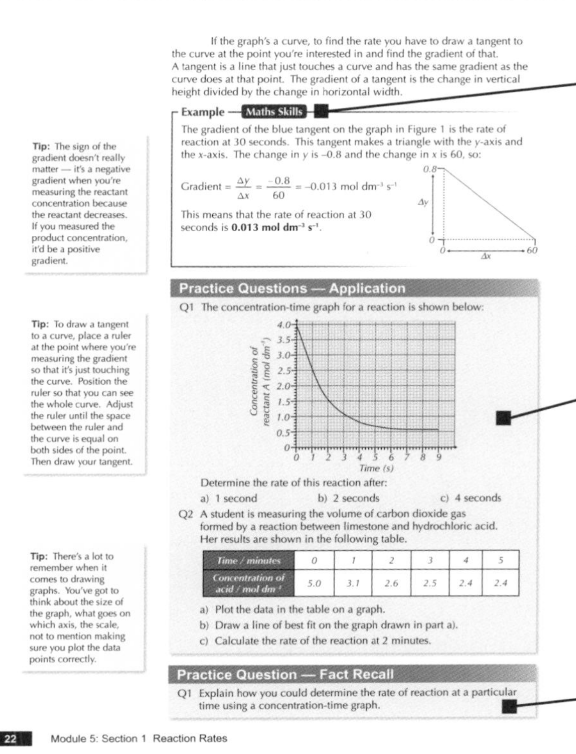

If the graph's a curve, to find the rate you have to draw a tangent to the curve at the point you're interested in and find the gradient of that. A tangent is a line that just touches a curve and has the same gradient as the curve does at that point. The gradient of a tangent is the change in vertical height divided by the change in horizontal width.

Example — Maths Skills

The gradient of the blue tangent on the graph in Figure 1 is the rate of reaction at 30 seconds. This tangent makes a triangle with the y-axis and the x-axis. The change in y is –0.8 and the change in x is 60, so:

$$\text{Gradient} = \frac{\Delta y}{\Delta x} = \frac{-0.8}{60} = -0.013 \text{ mol dm}^{-3}\text{ s}^{-1}$$

This means that the rate of reaction at 30 seconds is **0.013 mol dm⁻³ s⁻¹**.

Tip: The sign of the gradient doesn't really matter — it's a negative gradient when you're measuring the reactant concentration because the reactant decreases. If you measured the product concentration, it'd be a positive gradient.

Practice Questions — Application

Q1 The concentration-time graph for a reaction is shown below:

Determine the rate of this reaction after:
a) 1 second b) 2 seconds c) 4 seconds

Q2 A student is measuring the volume of carbon dioxide gas formed by a reaction between limestone and hydrochloric acid. Her results are shown in the following table.

Time / minutes	0	1	2	3	4	5
Concentration of acid / mol dm⁻³	5.0	3.1	2.6	2.5	2.4	2.4

a) Plot the data in the table on a graph.
b) Draw a line of best fit on the graph drawn in part a).
c) Calculate the rate of the reaction at 2 minutes.

Tip: To draw a tangent to a curve, place a ruler at the point where you're measuring the gradient so that it's just touching the curve. Position the ruler so that you can see the whole curve. Adjust the ruler until the space between the ruler and the curve is equal on both sides of the point. Then draw your tangent.

Tip: There's a lot to remember when it comes to drawing graphs. You've got to think about the size of the graph, what goes on which axis, the scale, not to mention making sure you plot the data points correctly.

Practice Question — Fact Recall

Q1 Explain how you could determine the rate of reaction at a particular time using a concentration-time graph.

22 Module 5: Section 1 Reaction Rates

Maths Skills

There's a range of maths skills you could be expected to apply in your exams. Examples that show these maths skills in action are marked up like this. There's also a maths skills section at the back of the book.

Practice Questions — Application

- Annoyingly, the examiners expect you to be able to apply your knowledge to new situations — these questions are here to give you plenty of practice at doing this.
- All the answers are in the back of the book (including any calculation workings).

Practice Questions — Fact Recall

- There are a lot of facts you need to learn — these questions are here to test that you know them.
- All the answers are in the back of the book.

Exam-style Questions

- Practising exam-style questions is really important — you'll find some at the end of each section.
- They're the same style as the ones you'll get in the real exams — some will test your knowledge and understanding and some will test that you can apply your knowledge.
- All the answers are in the back of the book, along with a mark scheme to show you how you get the marks.

Exam Help

There's a section at the back of the book stuffed full of things to help with your exams.

Glossary

There's a glossary at the back of the book full of useful words — perfect for looking up key words and their meanings.

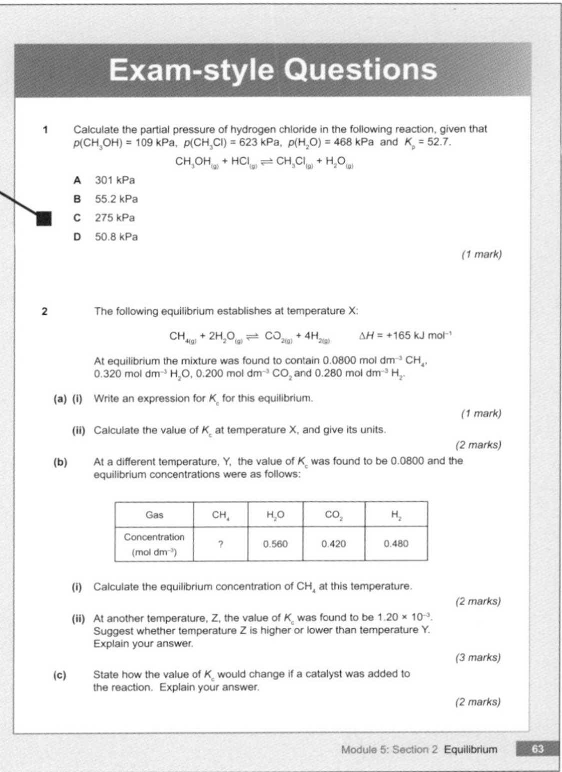

Exam-style Questions

1 Calculate the partial pressure of hydrogen chloride in the following reaction, given that $p(CH_3OH)$ = 109 kPa, $p(CH_3Cl)$ = 623 kPa, $p(H_2O)$ = 468 kPa and K_p = 52.7.

$$CH_3OH_{(g)} + HCl_{(g)} \rightleftharpoons CH_3Cl_{(g)} + H_2O_{(g)}$$

A 301 kPa
B 55.2 kPa
C 275 kPa
D 50.8 kPa

(1 mark)

2 The following equilibrium establishes at temperature X:

$$CH_{4(g)} + 2H_2O_{(g)} \rightleftharpoons CO_{2(g)} + 4H_{2(g)} \qquad \Delta H = +165 \text{ kJ mol}^{-1}$$

At equilibrium the mixture was found to contain 0.0800 mol dm⁻³ CH_4, 0.320 mol dm⁻³ H_2O, 0.200 mol dm⁻³ CO_2 and 0.280 mol dm⁻³ H_2.

(a) (i) Write an expression for K_c for this equilibrium.

(1 mark)

(ii) Calculate the value of K_c at temperature X, and give its units.

(2 marks)

(b) At a different temperature, Y, the value of K_c was found to be 0.0800 and the equilibrium concentrations were as follows:

Gas	CH_4	H_2O	CO_2	H_2
Concentration (mol dm⁻³)	?	0.560	0.420	0.480

(i) Calculate the equilibrium concentration of CH_4 at this temperature.

(2 marks)

(ii) At another temperature, Z, the value of K_c was found to be 1.20×10^{-3}. Suggest whether temperature Z is higher or lower than temperature Y. Explain your answer.

(3 marks)

(c) State how the value of K_c would change if a catalyst was added to the reaction. Explain your answer.

(2 marks)

Module 5: Section 2 Equilibrium 63

Published by CGP

Editors:
Katie Braid, Mary Falkner, Katherine Faudemer, Gordon Henderson, Emily Howe, Paul Jordin, Rachel Kordan, Sophie Scott, Ben Train.

Contributors:
Mike Bossart, Robert Clarke, Ian H. Davis, John Duffy, Lucy Muncaster, Paul Warren.

ISBN: 978 1 78294 327 3

With thanks to Kate Reid for the proofreading.
With thanks to Jan Greenway for the copyright research.

OCR Specification reference points and the IR data table on page 320 are adapted and reproduced by permission of OCR.

Printed by Elanders Ltd, Newcastle upon Tyne.
Clipart from Corel®

The Scientific Process

Science tries to explain how and why things happen. It's all about seeking and gaining knowledge about the world around us. Scientists do this by asking questions and suggesting answers and then testing them to see if they're correct — this is the scientific process.

Developing and testing theories

A **theory** is a possible explanation for something. Theories usually come about when scientists observe something and wonder why or how it happens. (Scientists also sometimes form a **model** too — a simplified picture or representation of a real physical situation.) Scientific theories and models are developed and tested in the following way:

- Ask a question — make an observation and ask why or how whatever you've observed happens.
- Suggest an answer, or part of an answer, by forming a theory or a model.
- Make a prediction or **hypothesis** — a specific testable statement, based on the theory, about what will happen in a test situation.
- Carry out tests — to provide evidence that will support the prediction or refute it.

Tip: A theory is only scientific if it can be tested.

Tip: The results of one test can't prove that a theory is true — they can only suggest that it's true. They can however disprove a theory — show that it's wrong.

Examples

Question: Why does bromine water react easily with cyclohexene but not with benzene?

Theory: Benzene has a ring of carbon atoms with delocalised electrons, so the negative charge is spread over the whole molecule. This makes it more stable than if it contained three double bonds, with a region of high electron density at each double bond.

Hypothesis: The enthalpy change for the hydrogenation of benzene (an exothermic reaction — see pages 165-166) will be less than three times the enthalpy change of the hydrogenation of cyclohexene, which contains one double bond.

Test: Use a calorimeter to measure the enthalpies of hydrogenation of benzene and cyclohexene. If the value for benzene is less than three times the value for cyclohexene, then the evidence supports the hypothesis.

Question: How do substances change during a redox reaction?

Theory: During a redox reaction electrons move from one substance to another.

Hypothesis: When electrons move, a current flows. So a current will flow between the electrodes of an electrochemical cell when an oxidation reaction takes place at one electrode and a reduction reaction at the other.

Test: Set up an electrochemical cell using substances with different electrode potentials. Put an ammeter in the circuit and observe whether a current is flowing. If it is, then this evidence supports the hypothesis.

Tip: You couldn't carry out this test in your school or college lab — you'd need specialist equipment.

Tip: Hydrogenation of 1 mole of cyclohexene is the addition of 1 mole of hydrogen. Hydrogenation of 1 mole of benzene is the addition of 3 moles of hydrogen.

Tip: See pages 165-166 for more on the stability of benzene compared to alkenes.

PHILOSOPHICAL
TRANSACTIONS:
GIVING SOME
ACCOMPT
OF THE PRESENT
Undertakings, Studies, and Labours
OF THE
INGENIOUS
IN MANY
CONSIDERABLE PARTS
OF THE
WORLD.

Vol I.
For Anno 1665, and 1666.

In the SAVOY,
Printed by T. N. for John Martyn at the Bell, a little without Temple-Bar, and James Allestry in Duck-Lane, Printers to the Royal Society.

***Figure 1:** The first British scientific journal, 'Philosophical Transactions of the Royal Society', published in 1665.*

Tip: Scientific research is often funded by companies who have a vested interest in its outcomes. Scientists are ethically obliged to make sure that this does not bias their results.

Communicating results

The results of testing a scientific theory are published — scientists need to let others know about their work. Scientists publish their results in scientific journals (see Figure 1). These are just like normal magazines, only they contain scientific reports (called papers) instead of the latest celebrity gossip.

Scientists use standard terminology when writing their reports. This way they know that other scientists will understand them. For instance, there are internationally agreed rules for naming organic compounds, so that scientists across the world will know exactly what substance is being referred to.

Scientific reports are similar to the lab write-ups you do in school. And just as a lab write-up is reviewed (marked) by your teacher, reports in scientific journals undergo **peer review** before they're published. The report is sent out to peers — other scientists who are experts in the same area. They go through it bit by bit, examining the methods and data, and checking it's all clear and logical. Thorough evaluation allows decisions to be made about what makes a good methodology or experimental technique. Individual scientists may have their own ethical codes (based on their personal moral or religious beliefs), but having their work scrutinised by other scientists helps to reduce the effect of personal bias on the conclusions drawn from the results.

When the report is approved, it's published. This makes sure that work published in scientific journals is of a good standard. But peer review can't guarantee the science is correct — other scientists still need to reproduce it. Sometimes mistakes are made and bad work is published. Peer review isn't perfect but it's probably the best way for scientists to self-regulate their work and to publish quality reports.

Validating theories

Tip: Once an experimental method is found to give good evidence it becomes a protocol — an accepted method to test that particular thing that all scientists can use.

Other scientists read the published theories and results, and try to test the theory themselves. This involves repeating the exact same experiments, using the theory to make new predictions, and then testing them with new experiments. This is known as **validation**. If all the experiments in the world provide evidence to back it up, the theory is thought of as scientific 'fact' (for now). If new evidence comes to light that conflicts with the current evidence, the theory is questioned all over again. More rounds of testing will be carried out to try to find out where the theory falls down. This is how the scientific process works — evidence supports a theory, loads of other scientists read it and test it for themselves, eventually all the scientists in the world agree with it and then bingo, you get to learn it.

Example

The structure of benzene

Benzene is an organic molecule with the formula C_6H_6. It was first purified in 1825, but nobody knew back then what its structure was like.

In 1865, Kekulé suggested a possible structure for the benzene molecule. His idea was a ring of six carbon atoms with alternate double and single bonds between them, with one hydrogen atom bonded to each carbon.

But in the 20th century, data from X-ray diffraction studies and enthalpy experiments suggested that the Kekulé model was wrong. So scientists came up with a new model (the delocalised electron model — see Figure 2) that fitted the new data better. (There's lots more about this on pages 164 and 165). This is the model of the benzene molecule that we use today.

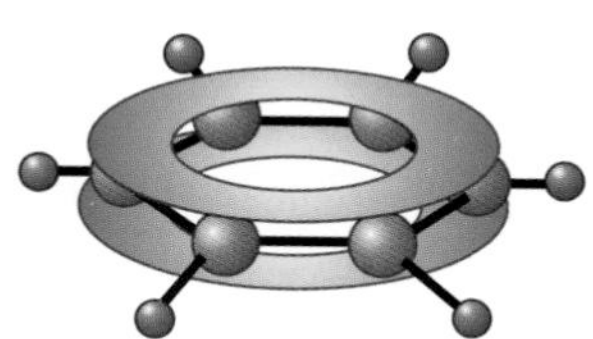

***Figure 2:** A representation of the delocalised electron model of benzene.*

How do theories evolve?

Our currently accepted theories have survived this 'trial by evidence'. They've been tested over and over again and each time the results have backed them up. But they never become totally indisputable fact. Scientific breakthroughs or advances could provide new ways to question and test a theory, which may lead to changes and challenges to it. Then the testing starts all over again. This is the tentative nature of scientific knowledge. It's always changing and evolving.

Tip: Sometimes data from one experiment can be the starting point for developing a new theory.

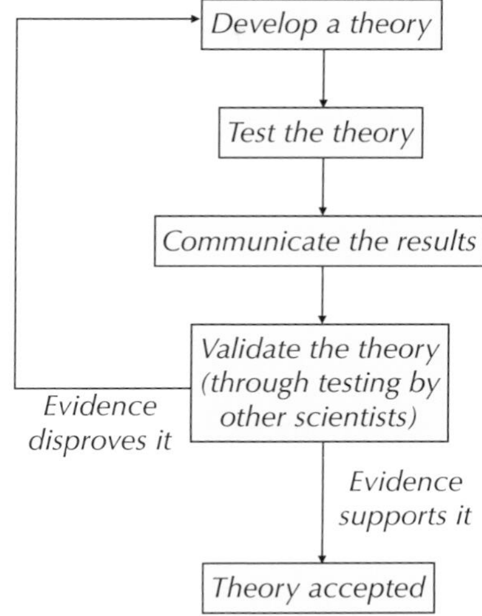

Figure 3: *Flow diagram summarising the scientific process.*

Example

CFCs and the ozone layer

When CFCs were first used in fridges in the 1930s, scientists thought they were problem-free — well, why not? There was no evidence to say otherwise. It was decades before anyone found out that CFCs were actually making a whopping great hole in the ozone layer.

A couple of scientists developed a theory that CFCs were destroying ozone in the stratosphere, and this was tested, shared and validated by other scientists worldwide. The rigour of the scientific process meant that there was strong enough evidence against CFCs that governments could impose bans and restrictions in order to protect the ozone layer.

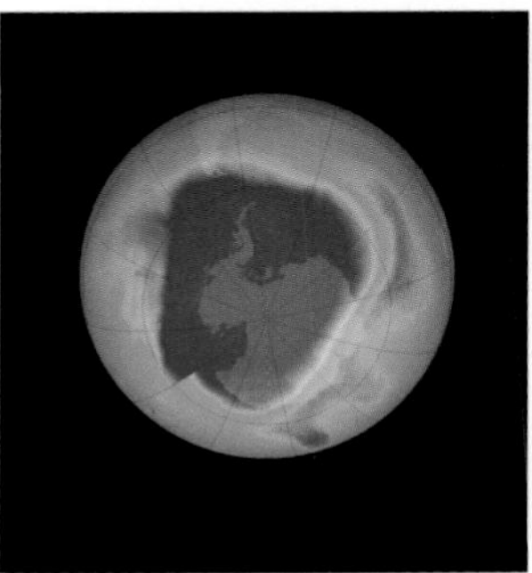

Figure 4: *The Antarctic ozone hole.*

Collecting evidence

1. Evidence from lab experiments

Results from controlled experiments in laboratories are great. A lab is the easiest place to control **variables** so that they're all kept constant (except for the one you're investigating). This means you can draw meaningful conclusions.

Example

Reaction yields

If you're investigating how the concentration of a reactant affects the yield of a reaction, you need to keep everything constant except for the concentration. This means controlling things like the temperature of the reaction mixture, the volumes used, etc. Otherwise you won't know if it's the change in concentration that's affecting the yield, or something else.

2. Investigations outside the lab

There are things you can't study in a lab. And outside the lab controlling the variables is tricky, if not impossible.

Example

How effective is cisplatin as an anti-cancer drug?

There are always differences between groups of people. The best you can do is to have a well-designed study using matched groups of people — choose two groups of patients (those who are being treated with cisplatin and those who aren't) which are as similar as possible (same type of cancer, same stage of cancer, same combinations of treatments, etc.). But you still can't rule out every possibility. There are always variables that can't be controlled so it's never a completely fair test. The size of the groups that you study is also important — the more people involved in the study the more reliable the results will be. And as with any study that's to do with people's health, there are ethical issues that have to be taken into consideration.

Science and decision-making

Lots of scientific work eventually leads to important discoveries that could benefit humankind and improve everyone's quality of life. But there are often risks attached (and almost always financial costs). Society (that's you, me and everyone else) must weigh up the information in order to make decisions — about the way we live, what we eat, what we drive, and so on. Information can also be used by politicians to devise policies and laws. However, there is not always enough information available for society and politicians to be certain about the decisions made. The scientific evidence we do have can also be overshadowed by other influences such as personal bias and beliefs, public opinion, and the media. Decisions are also affected by social, ethical and economic factors.

Tip: Don't get mixed up — it's not the scientists who make the decisions, it's society. Scientists just produce evidence to help society make the decisions.

Examples

Fuel cells

Hydrogen-oxygen fuel cells are an alternative to traditional fuel cells (see page 135). They're better for the environment than batteries, because their only waste product is water. But energy from another source is needed to produce the hydrogen and oxygen. And hydrogen is flammable, so it's tricky to store safely.

Developing drugs

Pharmaceutical drugs are expensive to develop and drug companies want to make money. So they put lots of effort into developing drugs that they can sell for a good price. Society has to consider the cost of buying drugs — the NHS can't afford the most expensive drugs without sacrificing other things.

Disposal of plastics

Synthetic polymers are very useful — they're cheap to produce and very durable. But they're hard to dispose of (they don't break down easily). So we need to make choices about how we can best dispose of plastics and whether we should try to reduce the amount that we use, or work to develop more biodegradable plastics.

Figure 5: *Waste plastic on a landfill site.*

What is the Practical Endorsement?

The Practical Endorsement is assessed slightly differently to the rest of your course. Unlike the exams, you don't get a mark for the Practical Endorsement — you just have to get a pass grade. The Practical Endorsement is split into twelve categories, called Practical Activity Groups (PAGs). Each PAG covers a variety of practical techniques, for example, measuring mass or heating under reflux. In order to pass the Practical Endorsement, you'll have to carry out at least one experiment for each PAG, and demonstrate that you can carry out each of the required techniques. You'll do the experiments in class, and your teacher will assess you as you're doing them.

You'll need to keep a record of all your assessed practical activities. You may have already done some experiments that count towards the Practical Endorsement in Year 1 of the course. For example, moles determination (PAG 1) and acid-base titrations (PAG 2) fit in with the material you learned in Year 1, so it's quite likely you carried out these practical activities then.

This section takes you through some of the techniques you'll meet during Year 2 of the course, as well as tips for keeping an accurate record of the experiments you've carried out for your Practical Endorsement.

Tip: Throughout this book, experiments and skills that you could use for your Practical Endorsement are marked with a big PAG stamp, like this one:

PRACTICAL ACTIVITY GROUP 4

1. General Practical Skills

The way you do an experiment is important. You may be given a method, or you may have to plan it yourself. It's important that you follow all the steps in a method — this ensures that you work safely, and also that your results will be precise.

Solving problems in a practical context

Practical experiments are used to solve problems or test whether a theoretical model works in a practical setting. If you're given a method to follow for an experiment, you should carry out each step, as described, in the correct order.

It's possible you'll be given a problem and asked to solve it using your own knowledge. In Module 1, there's loads of information about how to plan and carry out experiments correctly. Have a look back at your Year 1 book if it's all a bit hazy. Here's a quick round-up of some of the things you'll need to think about when you plan an experiment:

- First, identify the aim of your experiment.
- Next, work out how to achieve the aim. You'll often need to identify a variable that you'll change (the independent variable) and the variable you'll measure (the dependent variable) in order to gather data that meets the aim of your experiment.
- Identify all the variables that will need to be controlled during your experiment, and how to control them.
- Think about how to make your data as precise and accurate as possible. This could include repeating your experiment a number of times, or choosing equipment with a scale that has the right sensitivity for the data you're trying to collect.

Tip: Experiments are often used to test scientific theories to see if they are true in a practical context.

Tip: Variables include things like temperature, time, mass, volume and colour.

Tip: Precise results are reproducible and repeatable. Accurate results are close to the true value.

Recording observations and analysing data

Once your experiment is planned, you can carry it out, working carefully to make sure your results are precise. There's loads of information about how to carry out some general techniques you may come across on pages 11-16, and other techniques are covered as they come up during the course. You'll also have already come across some techniques in Year 1. As you carry out your experiment, you should record your results in a well laid-out table, leaving space for any data analysis you might want to do later. This may include finding averages or using your table of data to draw a graph of your results.

Tip: If you need more information about analysing data, including the maths you'll need to know and how to draw and interpret graphs, have a look back at your Year 1 notes — it's all covered in Module 1.

Uncertainties and error

An important part of your data analysis is to work out the percentage error and uncertainties in the apparatus you've used.

Uncertainty

For any piece of equipment you use, the uncertainty will be half the smallest increment the equipment can measure, in either direction.

Tip: Uncertainty tells you how much the value of a measurement could be out by. Percentage error gives this uncertainty as a percentage of the measurement you made.

Example — Maths Skills

In a titration using a burette that measures to the nearest 0.05 cm^3, the initial reading is 12.15 cm^3 and the final reading is 26.75 cm^3.

The uncertainty in each reading will be 0.05 cm^3 ÷ 2 = ±0.025 cm^3.

So the total uncertainty will be 0.025 cm^3 + 0.025 cm^3 = **±0.05 cm^3**.

Percentage error

You can calculate the percentage error of a measurement using this equation:

$$\text{percentage error} = \frac{\text{uncertainty}}{\text{reading}} \times 100$$

Tip: In science, error doesn't mean things have gone wrong — instead it's a measure of how different your results could be to their true value based on how sensitive the equipment you used is.

Example — Maths Skills

In the titration measurement above, the total volume of liquid measured is 26.75 – 12.15 = 14.60 cm^3

The total uncertainty in the reading is ±0.05 cm^3, so the percentage error is:

$\frac{0.05}{14.60} \times 100 = \mathbf{0.34\%}$

Tip: If two variables are correlated, then as one of the variables changes, so will the other.

Conclusions and evaluations

When you've collected and analysed your data, it's time to wrap up your experiment with some conclusions and an evaluation. Conclusions explain what your results showed. They need to be supported by the data you collected, and shouldn't make sweeping generalisations. Sometimes, you'll be looking to see if there is a correlation between two variables, but you should be cautious before claiming that the change in one is what causes the change in the other — there may be another factor that is causing both variables to change.

An evaluation is a chance for you to look at what you did and think about how you could have improved your method to improve the validity, accuracy and precision of your results. You should consider how well your results address the original aim of your experiment, how you could reduce errors in your results, and whether you need to repeat your experiment further to show your results can be reproduced.

Tip: Some results won't fit the trend of your data at all — these are anomalous results, and you tend to get them if something went wrong as you carried out your experiment. You should ignore anomalous results when calculating averages or drawing lines of best fit.

2. Working Safely

When you do an experiment, you need to carry out a risk assessment and work safely at all times. This reduces the risk of anyone being hurt.

Risks and hazards

HOW SCIENCE WORKS

Many chemistry experiments have risks associated with them. These can include risks associated with the equipment you're using, such as the risk of burning from a hot plate, as well as risks associated with chemicals. When you're planning an experiment, you need to identify all the hazards and what the risk is from each hazard. This includes working out how likely it is that something could go wrong, and how serious it would be if it did go wrong. You then need to think of ways to reduce these risks. Any hazardous chemicals you use should come with a list of dangers associated with them — this can be found on the bottle they come in, or looked up on something called a Material Safety Data Sheet.

Hazard word	Potential harm	Examples of how to reduce the risk
Corrosive	May cause chemical burns to tissues such as skin and eyes.	Use as little of the substance as possible. If the chemical is a solution, use it in low concentrations. If the chemical is a gas, carry out the experiment in a fume cupboard. Wear a lab coat, goggles and gloves when handling the chemical.
Irritant	May cause inflammation and discomfort.	Use as little of the substance as possible. If the chemical is a solution, use it in low concentrations. If the chemical is a gas, carry out the experiment in a fume cupboard. Wear a lab coat, goggles and gloves when handling the chemical.
Flammable	May catch fire.	Keep the chemical away from any naked flames. If you have to heat it, use a water bath, an electric heater or a sand bath instead of a Bunsen burner.
Toxic	May cause illness or even death.	Use as little of the substance as possible. If the chemical is a solution, use it in low concentrations. If the chemical is a gas, carry out the experiment in a fume cupboard. Wear a lab coat, goggles and gloves when handling the chemical.
Oxidising	Reacts to form oxygen, so other substances may burn more easily in its presence.	Use as little of the substance as possible. Use it in solution rather than as a solid powder. Use in clean, well-ventilated areas. Keep away from combustible materials, such as wood or paper.

Figure 1: *Some common types of hazard and how to reduce the risks they present.*

Tip: A <u>hazard</u> is anything that has the potential to cause harm or damage. The <u>risk</u> associated with that hazard is the probability of someone (or something) being harmed if they are exposed to the hazard.

Tip: The CLEAPSS® website has a database with details of the potential harm lots of the hazardous chemicals you're likely to come across could cause. It also has student safety sheets, and your school or college may have CLEAPSS® hazcards® you can use. These are all good sources of information if you're writing a risk assessment.

Tip: This isn't a comprehensive list of all the types of hazard you may encounter — just some of the more common ones.

Figure 2: *The hazard symbols for flammable (top left), oxidising (top middle), toxic (top right), corrosive (bottom left) and irritant (bottom right).*

Tip: Esters are organic compounds made by reacting carboxylic acids with alcohols. There's more about how to synthesise them and how they react on pages 190-192.

Tip: The hazard symbols in Figure 2 are quite new, so you may come across the old-style ones on bottles in your laboratory. The symbols are very similar, but they're in orange squares instead of red and white diamonds (see Figure 4).

Figure 4: *A bottle of ethanoic acid with a 'corrosive' hazard symbol.*

Tip: The risk associated with a solution might change depending on how concentrated it is. So whilst concentrated sulfuric acid is corrosive, dilute sulfuric acid is an irritant.

Example

A student plans to carry out an experiment to synthesise the ester propylethanoate using the following procedure:

- Add some propan-1-ol and concentrated ethanoic acid to a test tube containing concentrated sulfuric acid.
- Gently heat the mixture for 1 minute.
- Cool the mixture.
- Pour the mixture into a solution of sodium carbonate and mix to neutralise any remaining acid.

This experiment involves hazards in both the procedure and the chemicals used. For example, one hazard in the procedure comes from heating. The risks associated with the chemicals in the experiment are summarised in the table below:

Hazard	Type of hazard	Ways to reduce the risk
Propan-1-ol	Flammable	Keep away from naked flames — carry out the experiment using a water bath to heat the reaction mixture.
	Irritant	Use as little propan-1-ol as possible. Wear a lab coat, goggles and gloves when handling it.
Concentrated ethanoic acid	Corrosive	Use as little concentrated ethanoic acid as possible. Wear a lab coat, goggles and gloves when handling it.
Concentrated sulfuric acid	Corrosive	Use as little concentrated sulfuric acid as possible. Wear a lab coat, goggles and gloves when handling it.
Sodium carbonate solution	Irritant	Use as little sodium carbonate solution as possible, in a low concentration. Wear a lab coat, goggles and gloves when handling it.

Figure 3: *Chemical hazards in an experiment to synthesise propylethanoate.*

To reduce the risk of being burnt by any equipment, you shouldn't touch the apparatus whilst it is being heated. You should use tongs to remove the test tube from the heating apparatus and allow it to cool completely before continuing with the experiment.

The procedure can now be rewritten, taking into account the steps that should be taken to reduce the risks in this experiment:

- Add 1 cm^3 propan-1-ol and 1 cm^3 concentrated ethanoic acid to a test-tube containing 0.5 cm^3 concentrated sulfuric acid.
- Gently heat the mixture in a water bath for 1 minute.
- Remove the test tube from the water bath using tongs, and leave it in a test tube rack on a heat-proof mat to cool.
- Pour the mixture into 5 cm^3 of sodium carbonate solution and mix.

3. Keeping Scientific Records

When you carry out experiments, it's important to keep records of everything you do. The records should be detailed and clear enough that a complete stranger would be able to read them and understand what you did.

Records of scientific experiments

Throughout your A Level Chemistry course, you should keep a record of all the experiments you carry out, the results you obtain and the solutions to any data analysis you do. This could be done in a physical lab book, or kept in folders on a computer. However you choose to keep your records, the information for each experiment should include:

- The aim of the experiment.
- A detailed method for how you carried out the experiment, including the quantities of all the chemicals and any safety precautions you had to take.
- The results of your experiment, clearly set out in a table. The results may be hand-written, or a print-out of data collected by a data logger.
- Any other important observations you made whilst carrying out your experiment, for example, anything that went wrong or anything you did slightly differently from how it was described in the method.
- The solutions to any analysis you did on your results, or any graphs drawn using your results. These should be clearly labelled to show what analysis has been done or what graph has been drawn.
- Citations of any references you used.

Tip: Try to keep all your lab reports in the same place — write them in the same book, or keep them in the same folder on your computer. That way you'll know where everything is.

Tip: You'll have learned about making observations, recording data and analysing your results in Module 1, so look back at your Year 1 notes if you need a reminder of these.

Sources of information

PRACTICAL ACTIVITY GROUP 12

It's possible you'll have to do some research to find out information before you get started with an experiment. Useful sources of information include:

Websites

Using the Internet for research is really convenient, but you have to be slightly wary as not all the information you find will be true. It's hard to know where information comes from on forums, blogs and websites that can be edited by the general public, so you should avoid using these. Websites of organisations such as the Royal Society of Chemistry and the National Institute of Standards and Technology (NIST) provide lots of information that comes from reliable scientific sources. To decide whether a website gives reliable information, think about the following things:

- Who has written the information — was it a scientist, a teacher, or just a member of the public?
- Whether or not anyone will have checked the source — articles on websites for scientific organisations will have people reading through the information and checking all the facts. Information on forums or blogs is likely to have been written by an individual, and won't necessarily have been thoroughly checked.
- What the purpose of the website is — if it's a website all about Chemistry, then it's likely whoever has written it will know quite a lot. If it's a website where you can also find out how to make a plant pot from an old teacup and some PVA glue, then the depth and quality of the information may not be enough.

Tip: If you're unsure whether the information on a website is true or not, try and find the same piece of information in a different place. The more sources you can find for the information, the more likely it is to be correct.

Textbooks

Your school or public library is likely to have textbooks covering specific areas of Chemistry in a lot of detail.

Scientific papers

You can find papers in online catalogues, such as SciFinder or PubMed, as well as in journals that are often available in public libraries.

Tip: Scientific papers are checked by other scientists who are experts in the subject of the paper. This is called peer review (see page 2).

The source you do your research from needs to give the right level of information. It's no good trawling through a scientific paper if you're just looking for the boiling point of a compound — the information will be far too detailed, and you'll probably end up wading through lots of complicated information that you don't need to understand. Equally, if you're researching the theory behind an experiment, you want a source that gives enough detail. A GCSE textbook will probably be too simplistic — you're better off finding a book that deals specifically with the subject in a library instead.

Using references and making citations

PRACTICAL ACTIVITY GROUP 12

It's going to sound obvious, but when you're using the information that you've found during your research, you can't just copy it down word for word. Any data you're looking up should be copied accurately, but you should rewrite everything else in your own words.

When you've used information from a source, you need to cite the reference properly. Citations allow someone else to go back and find the source of your information. This means they can check your information and see you're not making things up out of thin air. Citations also mean you've properly credited other people's data that you've used in your work.

Citations for each piece of information may include the title of the book, paper or website where you found the information, the author and/or the publisher of the document and the date the document was published.

Tip: There are lots of slightly different ways of referencing sources, but the important thing is that it's clear where you found the information.

Examples

The boiling point of butan-1-ol is 390.6 K. (http://webbook.nist.gov/chemistry)

The boiling point of butan-1-ol is 390.3 K. (Harrison R.D., Ellis H; Nuffield Advanced Science Book of Data Revised Edition; 1984)

4. Practical Techniques

This section is an introduction to some of the techniques you'll be expected to know for A Level Chemistry. You'll have met many of them before, and others will be covered in more detail as they crop up throughout the book.

Making measurements

Almost every experiment you carry out in Chemistry involves some sort of measurement. You'll probably have met a number of techniques for making measurements back in Year 1 Chemistry. These will have included measuring things such as mass, time, volumes of liquids and gases, and temperature. During the Year 2 course, you may also need to measure the pH of a solution.

Tip: Make sure you do a risk assessment before you carry out any of the techniques in this topic.

Measuring pH

PRACTICAL ACTIVITY GROUP 11

The pH of a solution is a measure of how acidic or basic it is. There's more than one way of measuring this — you can use pH charts, pH meters or pH probes.

pH charts

Universal indicator is a substance that changes colour according to the pH of a solution. A pH chart tells you what colour Universal indicator will be at different pHs (see Figure 1). So, if you add a few drops of Universal indicator to a solution, you can compare the resulting colour to a pH chart and determine the pH of the solution. pH charts are good for giving a rough value of the pH of the solution, but since the colour of a solution is a qualitative observation (it's based on opinion), the data won't be accurate or precise.

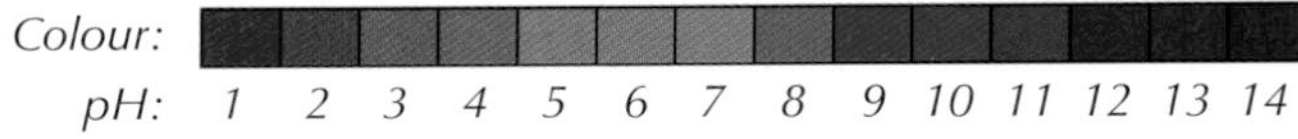

Figure 1: *The pH chart of Universal indicator*

pH meters

A pH meter is an electronic gadget that can be used to give a precise and accurate value for the pH of a solution (see page 84). They are made up of a probe attached to a digital display. The probe is placed in the solution, and the pH reading is shown on the display.

pH probes on a data logger

A pH probe can be attached to something called a data logger. A data logger could be a piece of software on a computer or tablet. It records the pH readings from the pH probe and stores them so you can look back at them later. This makes them useful for experiments where you're measuring how pH changes, as the data logger will record the results, meaning you don't have to write them down separately. You may need to print the results once the experiment is complete, so you can keep a record of them in your lab book.

Tip: Organic compounds are generally flammable, so you might use these methods for heating them when carrying out tests for organic functional groups (see pages 238-241).

Heating substances

PRACTICAL ACTIVITY GROUP 7

Many chemical substances are flammable, so are at risk of catching fire if they're heated with a naked flame, e.g. with a Bunsen burner. Luckily, there are a number of other techniques you can use to heat a reaction mixture.

Figure 2: *An electric heater.*

Electric heaters

Electric heaters are often made up of a dish of metal that can be heated to a specified temperature. The reaction vessel is placed on top of the hot plate (see Figure 2). The mixture is only heated from below, so you'll usually have to stir the reaction mixture to make sure it's heated evenly.

Water baths

A water bath is a container filled with water that can be heated to a specific temperature (Figure 3). You place the reaction vessel in the water bath until the reaction mixture is completely submerged. The mixture will then be warmed to the same temperature as the water. As the reaction mixture is surrounded by water, the heating is very even. However, water boils at 100 °C, so you can't use a water bath to heat the reaction mixture to a higher temperature than this.

Figure 3: *A water bath.*

Sand baths

Sand baths are similar to water baths, but the container is filled with sand. Sand can be heated to a much higher temperature than water, so sand baths are useful for heating reaction mixtures to temperatures above 100 °C.

Acid-base titrations

PRACTICAL ACTIVITY GROUP 2

Titrations are used to find the concentration of an unknown solution. In acid-base titrations, the concentration of an acid can be determined by finding how much base of a known concentration is required to neutralise a given volume of it, or vice versa. The mixture is shown to be neutralised by the colour change of an **indicator**. The indicator you use for a particular titration needs to change colour at a pH that falls in the range in which the pH of the mixture changes rapidly upon addition of a small amount of acid or base.

Tip: Titrations between weak acids and weak bases can't be carried out using an indicator, as there's no clear end point.

Strength of acid	Strength of base	Range in which pH changes rapidly
Strong	Strong	2-12
Strong	Weak	2-8
Weak	Strong	8-11
Weak	Weak	Only gradual change

Two common indicators are methyl orange and phenolphthalein. Methyl orange changes colour from red to yellow as the pH changes from about 3.1-4.4. So it's suitable as an indicator in titrations between strong acids and either weak or strong bases. Phenolphthalein changes colour from colourless to purple as pH changes from about 8.3-10, so you can use it in titrations between strong or weak acids and strong bases.

Measuring rates of reactions

There are two common ways of measuring how the rate of reaction changes when you vary the concentration of one of the reactants.

1. Continuous monitoring

PRACTICAL ACTIVITY GROUP 9

Continuous monitoring experiments show you how the rate of a reaction changes over the course of the entire reaction. They're done by taking regular measurements of the amount of one of the reactants or products over the course of the reaction. For example, if a gas is produced you could measure the volume of gas formed at regular intervals, or if there is a colour change you could use colorimetry to measure how the absorbance of a particular frequency of light changes over time. The results can be used to plot a graph of the variable you measured against time, for example, a volume-time graph or a concentration-time graph. The rate of the reaction at any point is given by the gradient of these graphs at that point, with units of the variable you measured against time (for example, $cm^3\ s^{-1}$ for a volume-time graph or $mol\ dm^{-3}\ s^{-1}$ for a concentration-time graph).

Sometimes, you may have collected data such as volume or pH, and want to convert it into concentration in order to plot a concentration-time graph. This can be done with a few calculations, such as on pages 18-19. You may also have found the change in concentration of one of the products, and want to determine how the concentration of one of the reactants changes over time. You can do this using your information about the product formation and the reaction equation. There's more detail on how to do this on page 19.

Tip: There's loads more about finding the rate of a reaction from a concentration-time graph on pages 21-22.

2. Initial rates

PRACTICAL ACTIVITY GROUP 10

The initial rates method is used to investigate the order of a reaction with respect to each of the reactants. You carry out a series of experiments that let you work out the rate at the beginning of the reaction for different starting concentrations of one reactant. For example, you could measure the volume of gas that's produced in the first 30 seconds of a reaction for four different starting concentrations of one reactant.

You can also use a **clock reaction** to give you an approximation of the initial rate of the reaction. Here, at a set concentration of one of the products, a visual change such as a colour change is seen in the reaction mixture. You carry out a series of experiments, each with a different starting concentration of one of the reactants, and measure the time taken for this change to occur.

Once you've carried out these experiments at different reactant concentrations, you can work out the initial rate for each reaction and plot a graph of rate against the initial concentration of the reactant you investigated. The numerical data you've got and the shape of the graph both tell you the order of the reaction with respect to the reactant you've investigated.

Tip: The order of a reaction with respect to a reactant tells you how much the rate will change if you vary the concentration of that reactant (see page 27).

Tip: Orders of reactions and initial rates experiments are quite hard to get your head around, so don't worry if it all seems a bit strange at the moment. There's loads more information in Module 5 on pages 23-29.

Tip: The iodine clock reaction is the most famous clock reaction. See page 25 for more detail.

Setting up electrochemical cells

PRACTICAL ACTIVITY GROUP 8

Electrochemical cells use redox reactions to generate electricity. For example, batteries are electrochemical cells. You can make your own electrochemical cell from two half cells — metal electrodes dipped in separate flasks containing a solution of their own metal ions. The electrodes are connected by a wire that runs though a voltmeter, which can be used to measure the voltage of the cell. To complete the circuit, the two flasks are connected by a salt bridge — normally a strip of paper dipped in a solution of inert ions, such as KNO_3. The salt bridge allows ions to pass between the half cells, but doesn't interfere with the reaction happening at either electrode.

Tip: There's loads more about electrochemical cells and the reactions that occur at the electrodes in Module 5 Section 5.

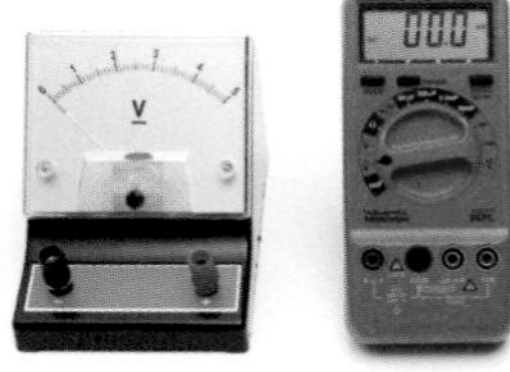

Figure 4: *An analogue and a digital voltmeter.*

Tip: Measuring the voltage of an electrochemical cell tells you the difference in reduction potentials between the two metals at each of your electrodes.

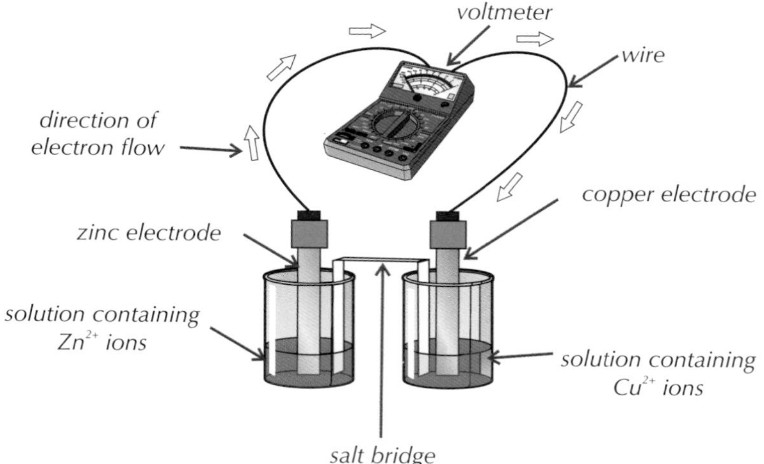

Figure 5: *An electrochemical cell made up of zinc and copper electrodes.*

Organic techniques

PRACTICAL ACTIVITY GROUP 6

In Year 1 Chemistry, you learnt some techniques for synthesising and purifying organic liquids. This year, you'll have to synthesise and purify an organic solid. The synthesis techniques are the same, but there are some more techniques you need to know about for purifying organic solids — filtration and recrystallisation, for example.

Filtration

PRACTICAL ACTIVITY GROUP 6

Filtration is used to separate a solid from a liquid.
There are two types of filtration you need to know about:

1. Filtration under reduced pressure

Filtration under reduced pressure is normally used when you want to keep the solid and discard the filtrate. You use a piece of equipment called a Büchner funnel — a flat-bottomed funnel with holes in the base. The Büchner funnel is attached to the top of a side-arm flask, which is secured with a stand-and-clamp to stop it from falling over. The side-arm flask is attached to a vacuum line, which, when it is switched on, causes the flask to be under reduced pressure.

Here's how you carry out the filtration:

- Place a piece of filter paper, slightly smaller than the diameter of the funnel, on the bottom of the Büchner funnel so that it lies flat and covers all the holes.
- Wet the paper with a little solvent, so that it sticks to the bottom of the funnel, and doesn't slip around when you pour in your mixture.
- Turn the vacuum on, and then pour your mixture into the funnel. As the flask is under reduced pressure, the liquid is sucked through the funnel into the flask, leaving the solid behind.
- Rinse the solid with a little of the solvent that your mixture was in. This will wash any of the original liquid from the mixture (and so any soluble impurities) that has stayed on your wet, solid crystals into the flask, and leave you with a more pure solid.
- Disconnect the vacuum line from the side-arm flask and then turn off the vacuum.
- The solid will be a bit wet from the solvent, so leave it to dry completely.

Tip: There's more detail about these organic techniques on pages 226-228.

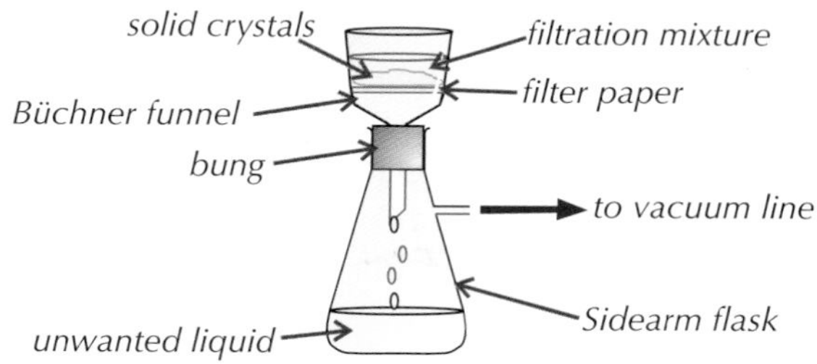

***Figure 6:** Apparatus for filtration under reduced pressure.*

2. Filtration using fluted filter paper

Filtration using fluted filter paper is normally used when you want to keep the liquid (the filtrate) and discard the solid. For example, it can be used to remove the solid drying agent from the organic layer of a liquid that has been purified by separation. A piece of fluted filter paper is placed in a funnel that feeds into a conical flask. The mixture to be separated is poured gently into the filter paper. The solution will pass through the filter paper into the conical flask, and the solid will be trapped. A pure sample of the solvent present in the solution can be used to rinse the solid left in the filter paper. This makes sure that all the soluble material has passed through the filter paper and collected in the conical flask.

Tip: If you're doing a filtration using fluted filter paper, take care not to fill the funnel above the top of the filter paper when you're pouring in your mixture.

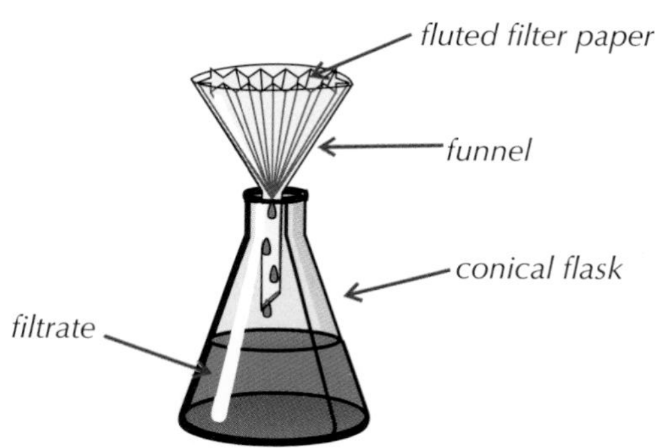

***Figure 7:** Filtration using fluted filter paper.*

Tip: Fluted filter paper is a cone with a concertinaed edge. The concertina gives the paper a greater surface area than if the paper were smooth, so the solution is filtered faster.

Filter paper normally comes as a flat disc. To make fluted filter paper, follow the steps in Figure 8.

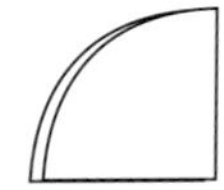

1. Fold the paper in half, then in quarters.

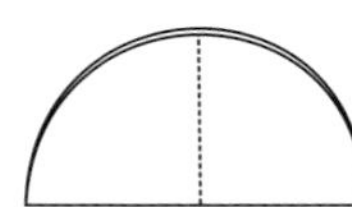

2. Unfold the paper so it's in half.

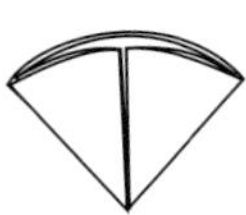

3. Fold each side into the centre.

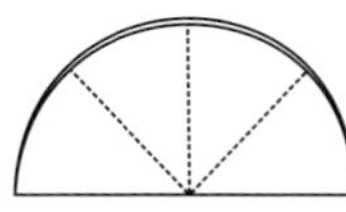

4. Unfold the paper again so that it's in half.

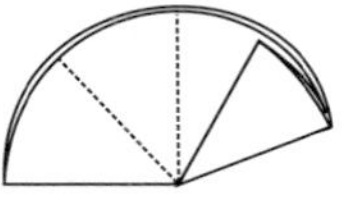
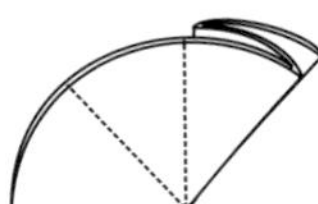
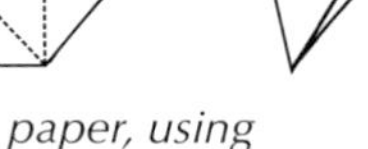

5. Concertina the paper, using the folds as guidelines.

6. Unfold the paper, and make it into a cone.

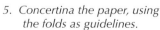

***Figure 8:** Making fluted filter paper.*

Recrystallisation

PRACTICAL ACTIVITY GROUP 6

> **Tip:** The solvent you choose for a recrystallisation is important — see page 227 for more on this and more information on recrystallisation.

Recrystallisation is used to purify an organic solid. A solvent is chosen in which the organic product is soluble when the solvent is hot, and insoluble when the solvent is cold. The impure solid is dissolved in a minimal amount of hot solvent. The solution is then left to cool, and the pure product should crystallise out of the solution whilst any soluble impurities stay in solution. The pure crystals can be removed from the solvent containing the impurities by filtration under reduced pressure.

Testing the purity of an organic solid

The purity of an organic solid can be assessed in a couple of different ways.

> **Tip:** See page 228 for more detail on how to measure the melting points of organic solids.

1. Melting point

If you measure the melting point of a pure solid, you should get the same value as stated in a data book. The range in temperature over which the solid melts should also be very small. An impure solid will have a melting point that is lower than the recorded value, and it will melt over a wider range in temperature. So, you can determine how pure a solid sample is by measuring its melting point and comparing it to the recorded value. You can find the melting point of a solid using a piece of equipment called a melting point apparatus. The lower the melting point is than the standard value, and the greater the range of the melting point, the less pure the solid is.

> **Tip:** Chromatography plates can be made of paper or they might be a piece of glass or plastic coated with a thin solid layer such as silica gel or aluminium powder.

2. Thin layer or paper chromatography

Thin layer or paper chromatography separates a liquid mixture into its component parts based on how well each component dissolves in a particular solvent. Each component in a mixture will show up as a spot at a different point on a chromatography plate. By looking at how many points are on a chromatography plate, you can determine how many components are in your mixture, and so how pure your sample is.

Figure 9: *Using paper chromatography to separate the components of different coloured inks.*

In a chromatography experiment, a solid is dissolved into a solution, and a drop of the mixture is put near the bottom of a plate. The plate is then placed in a beaker containing a small amount of a solvent, so that the solvent sits below the spot of mixture. The solvent moves slowly up the plate, and the components of the mixture move with it at different speeds depending on how well they dissolve in the solvent. At the end of the experiment, each component part of the mixture will be separated into spots positioned at different places along the plate.

> **Tip:** See pages 242-243 for more on chromatography.

1. Monitoring Reactions

Understanding all about the rates of chemical reactions is a really important part of A Level Chemistry. You've already learnt a bit about reaction rates in Year 1, but now it's time to cover things in a bit more detail.

Learning Objectives:
- Be able to explain and use the term rate of reaction.
- Understand the techniques and procedures used to investigate reaction rates by continuous monitoring, including use of colorimetry (PAG 9).

Specification Reference 5.1.1

What are reaction rates?

The **reaction rate** is the change in the amount of reactants or products per unit time (normally per second). For example, if the reactants are in solution, the rate will be the change in concentration per second — the units will be mol dm^{-3} s^{-1}.

Continuous monitoring

PRACTICAL ACTIVITY GROUP 9

You might want to know how the rate of a reaction changes during the course of a reaction. One way of doing this is to measure how the amount of a product or reactant changes over the complete course of the reaction. This is called **continuous monitoring**. There are quite a few ways to follow reactions, but not every method works for every reaction. You've got to study a property that changes as the reaction goes on. Here are a few examples:

Measuring the formation of a gas

If a gas is given off, you could collect it in a gas syringe and record how much you've got at regular time intervals.

Example

This would work for the reaction between an acid and a carbonate in which carbon dioxide gas is given off.

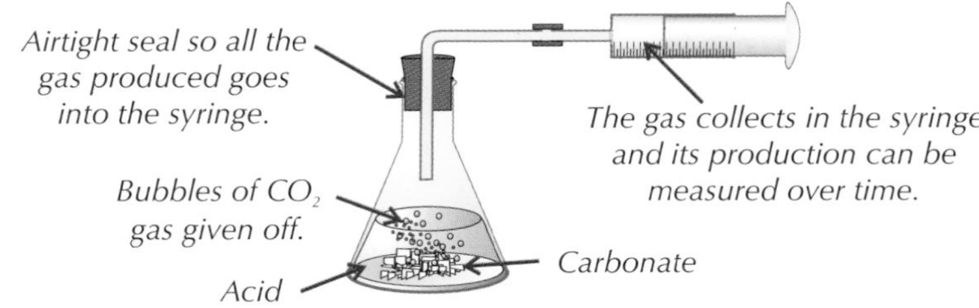
Airtight seal so all the gas produced goes into the syringe.
The gas collects in the syringe and its production can be measured over time.
Bubbles of CO_2 gas given off.
Carbonate
Acid

Tip: As well as continuous monitoring, you can also measure the rate of a reaction using a technique called the 'initial rates method'. See pages 23-24 for more on this.

You could also measure the change in mass of the reaction vessel at regular intervals as the gas is lost, using a mass balance.

Example

The reaction between sodium hydrogen carbonate and an acid can be monitored by measuring the mass lost as carbon dioxide gas is evolved:

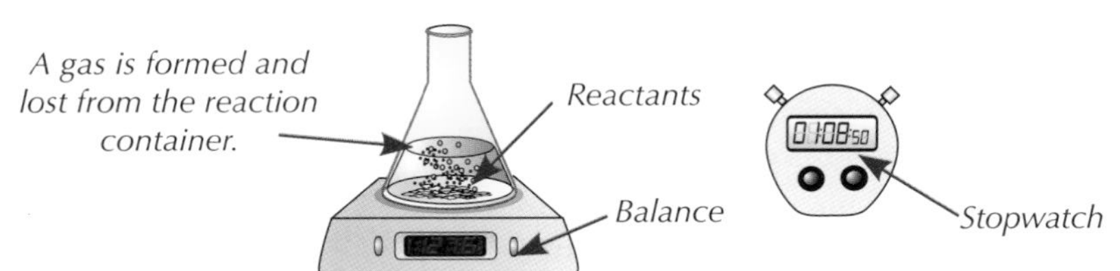
A gas is formed and lost from the reaction container.
Reactants
Balance
Stopwatch

Tip: Both of these methods for monitoring the formation of a gas are covered in more detail in the first year of the course, so have a look back at your Year 1 notes for more information.

Figure 1: *A student using a colorimeter as part of a colorimetry experiment. A digital display shows the absorbance value of a sample at any given moment.*

Measuring a colour change

Sometimes you can track a colour change of a reaction using a gadget called a colorimeter. Colorimeters measure the absorbance of a particular wavelength of light by a solution. If they're set to measure the absorbance of a wavelength that is absorbed by one of the reactants but not by the products (or vice versa), then the change in absorbance over the course of the reaction can be used to measure the rate. Here's how you use a colorimeter:

- First, set the colorimeter to measure the wavelength of light that you're interested in measuring.
- Next, calibrate the colorimeter. Place a sample of distilled water in a sample tube, known as a cuvette, and place it in the colorimeter. Set the absorbance to zero.
- Carry out your reaction. You should take samples from the reaction mixture at regular intervals, and measure the absorbance of each one using the colorimeter.

Example

You could monitor the reaction between propanone and iodine using colorimetry. As the reaction progresses, the brown colour fades.

$$\underbrace{CH_3COCH_{3\,(aq)}}_{\text{colourless}} + \underbrace{I_{2\,(aq)}}_{\text{brown}} \rightarrow \underbrace{CH_3COCH_2I_{(aq)} + H^+_{(aq)} + I^-_{(aq)}}_{\text{colourless}}$$

Tip: Before you carry out any of these techniques for monitoring the progress of a reaction, make sure you do a risk assessment.

Measuring a change in pH

If either hydrogen or hydroxide ions are produced or used up in a reaction, then you can monitor the progress of the reaction by measuring the change in the pH.

Example

In the reaction between propanone and iodine above, H^+ ions are produced, so you can monitor the progress of the reaction by measuring the change in pH.

Tip: You can measure the pH of a mixture using a pH meter.

Processing data

Once you've carried out your experiment, you may want to draw a concentration-time graph of your results to work out more information about the reaction and its rate. To do this, you may first have to process your data to get it into units of concentration. Here are some examples to show you how it's done.

Tip: You don't always monitor the amount of product produced — sometimes it's easier to monitor the consumption of a reactant instead.

Examples

Colorimetry

A student follows the rate of the following reaction by measuring the change in absorbance of a wavelength of light that is absorbed by I_2:

$$CH_3COCH_3 + I_2 \rightarrow CH_3COCH_2I + H^+ + I^-$$

For each data point, the student will have to convert the absorbance reading into a concentration of I_2. He can do this using a calibration curve for the absorbance of a wavelength of light by solutions of different concentrations of I_2.

So, if at any point the absorbance of the reaction solution was 1.3, the concentration of I_2 was $\mathbf{9.0 \times 10^{-3}}$ **mol dm^{-3}**.

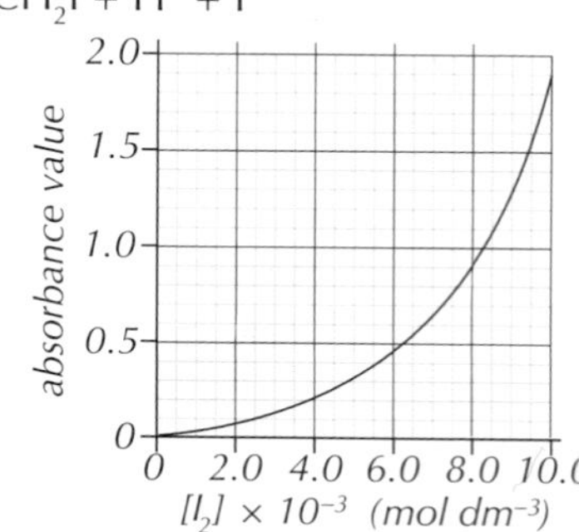

Tip: To plot a calibration curve like the one on the right, you'll need to measure the absorbances of some standard solutions of I_2 of various concentrations.

pH

A student follows the rate of the following reaction by measuring the change in pH:

$$NaHCO_3 + HCl \rightarrow NaCl + H_2O + CO_2$$

For each data point, the student will have to convert the pH into a concentration in order to plot a concentration-time graph for HCl.
She can do this by rearranging the equation:

$$pH = -\log[H^+] \text{ to } [H^+] = 10^{-pH}.$$

Since HCl is a strong, monobasic acid, the concentration of H^+ is equal to the concentration of HCl.

So if, for example, after 20 seconds the pH was 5.20, the concentration of H^+ ions (and therefore the concentration of HCl) would be:

$$10^{-5.20} = \mathbf{0.0000063\ mol\ dm^{-3}}$$

Tip: Don't worry if all this pH stuff looks unfamiliar. There's loads more about calculating the concentration of H^+ ions or OH^- ions in solution from the pH on pages 69 and 73.

If you've measured the formation of a product, but you want to draw a concentration-time graph to follow one of the reactants to, for example, work out the reaction order (see page 29), then you'll have to carry out the following steps for each of your data points:

- Use the initial concentration of the reactant you're interested in to work out how many moles of it there were at the start of the reaction.
- For each data point, work out how many moles of product have formed (how you do this will vary, depending on what the experimental data is).
- Use the balanced reaction equation to work out how many moles of the reactant you're interested in have been used.
- Subtract the number of moles of reactant used from the initial number of moles of the reactant to find the number of moles of reactant at that time point.
- Divide the number of moles of that reactant by the volume of the reaction mixture to find the concentration of the reactant at that time.

Tip: Doing this sort of data processing can take an absolute age if you do it all by hand, and there's lots of potential for making mistakes. Using computer software, such as Microsoft Excel®, can make the whole process much quicker and less painful.

Example

A student follows the rate of the following reaction by measuring the volume of carbon dioxide gas evolved over time:

$$NaHCO_{3(s)} + HCl_{(aq)} \rightarrow NaCl_{(aq)} + H_2O_{(l)} + CO_{2\,(g)}$$

The reaction mixture starts with 25.0 cm^3 of 1.50 mol dm^{-3} HCl, and the reaction takes place at 298 K. After 40 s, 0.490 cm^3 gas has been evolved.

- The initial concentration of HCl is 1.50 mol dm^{-3}, and the reaction mixture has a volume of 25.0 cm^3.
  So, initial number of moles of HCl = volume × concentration
  = (25.0 ÷ 1000) × 1.50 = 0.0375 moles.
- To find the number of moles of gas evolved after 40 seconds, rearrange the equation $pV = nRT$ to give $n = (pV) \div (RT)$.
  So $n = (1.0 \times 10^5 \times 0.490 \times 10^{-3}) \div (8.31 \times 298) = 0.0197...$ moles
- From the reaction equation, you can see that 1 mole of HCl reacts to form 1 mole of CO_2, so given that after 40 s, 0.0197... mol CO_2 has been produced, 0.0197... moles of HCl will have been used.
- The number of moles left of HCl is 0.0375 – 0.0197... = 0.0177... moles.
  So [HCl] after 40 seconds is 0.0177... ÷ (25.0 ÷ 1000) = **0.709 mol dm^{-3}**.

Tip: The equation $pV = nRT$ is the ideal gas equation. Have a look back at your Year 1 notes if your memory of it is a bit fuzzy. Under standard conditions, $p = 1.0 \times 10^5$ Pa, $T = 298$ K and $R = 8.31$ J K^{-1} mol^{-1}. V is the volume in m^3.

Tip: You could also monitor this reaction by measuring the change in mass of the reaction vessel as CO_2 was lost. If this was the case, you'd first have to work out the change in mass of the reaction vessel at each data point. Then, to find the number of moles of CO_2 corresponding to this change in mass, you could use the equation moles = mass ÷ M_r.

Tip: Think carefully about the reactants and products present in each of these reactions.
It may help you to write out a chemical equation.

Tip: Don't panic if you're asked to convert multiple experimental data points into concentration data. Just follow the same method for each step and you'll be fine.

Tip: You'll need the ideal gas equation for this question.
It's: $pV = nRT$.

Practice Questions — Application

Q1 Suggest a technique you could use to follow the progress of each of the following reactions.

a) The reaction between chromate(VI) ions (CrO_4^{2-}) and an acid to form dichromate(VI) ions ($Cr_2O_7^{2-}$) and water.

b) The reaction between zinc metal and hydrochloric acid.

c) The reaction between thiosulfate ($S_2O_3^{2-}$) and acid to produce sulfur dioxide gas, water and a yellow precipitate of solid sulfur.

Q2 A student is monitoring the rate of a reaction between an acid and a metal by collecting gas in a gas syringe. How would her calculated rate be affected if there was a leak in the system?

Q3 A student is using a balance to monitor the loss of mass over the course of the following reaction between zinc sulfide and 250 cm³ of 1.50 mol dm⁻³ hydrochloric acid.

$$ZnS_{(s)} + 2HCl_{(aq)} \rightarrow ZnCl_{2\,(aq)} + H_2S_{(g)}$$

She records the mass of the reaction vessel at various time intervals. Calculate the concentration of HCl at each time interval shown below.

Time / seconds	*0*	*10*	*20*	*30*	*40*	*50*	*60*
Mass of vessel / g	*411.02*	*410.42*	*409.84*	*409.25*	*408.65*	*408.08*	*407.51*

Q4 A student is following the reaction between 100 cm³ 1.00 mol dm⁻³ sulfuric acid and 15.0 g of solid sodium carbonate,
by monitoring the volume of gas produced at r.t.p.. She takes measurements at 15 second intervals. Her results are recorded in the table below.
Calculate the concentration of H_2SO_4 at each time point.

Time / seconds	*0*	*15*	*30*	*45*	*60*	*75*
Volume of gas produced / cm³	*0.00*	*3.20*	*6.51*	*9.94*	*13.0*	*15.9*

Practice Questions — Fact Recall

Q1 What is meant by the term 'continuous monitoring'?

Q2 Draw and label the set-up you would use to measure the volume of gas produced over the course of a reaction.

Q3 What does a colorimeter measure?

Q4 Describe how you could follow the rate of reaction for a reaction where a gas is lost from the reaction container.

2. Concentration-Time Graphs

Once you've converted the data you've collected from continuously monitoring a reaction into concentration data, you can plot a concentration-time graph. You can use the gradient of the line of this graph to work out the reaction rate.

Learning Objectives:

- Be able to calculate the rate of a reaction from the measurement of the gradient of a concentration-time graph.

Specification Reference 5.1.1

Gradients of straight-line graphs

You can use the data from a continuous monitoring experiment to plot a graph of concentration against time. The rate at any point is given by the gradient at that point on this concentration-time graph.

You work out the gradient using this equation:

gradient = change in y ÷ change in x

Tip: Don't forget, the x-axis is the horizontal axis and the y-axis is the vertical axis.

Example — Maths Skills

A concentration-time graph for a reactant, X, is shown below. Work out the rate of the reaction.

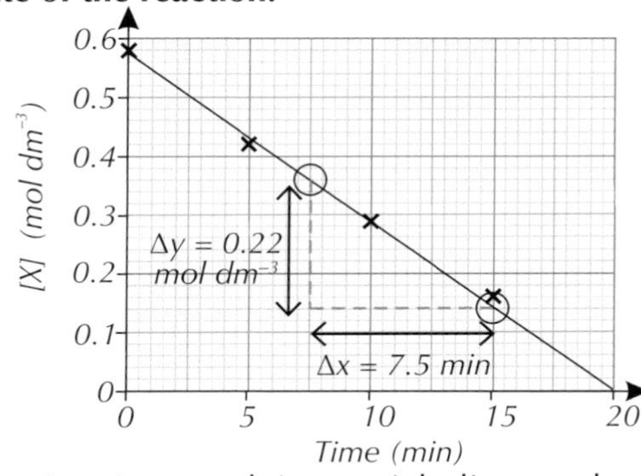

1. The concentration-time graph is a straight-line graph, so the gradient is the same at all points on the line.
2. Pick two points on the line of best fit that pass through the corners of the squares, and so are easy to read.
3. Use the equation, gradient = change in y ÷ change in x, to work out the gradient of the graph.
   gradient = 0.22 ÷ 7.5 = 0.029 mol dm^{-3} min^{-1}
4. So the rate of reaction is 0.029 mol dm^{-3} min^{-1}.

Tip: 'Δ' means 'the change in', so Δx is the change in x, and Δy is the change in y.

Tip: Square brackets, [ ], mean something is a concentration, so [X] is the concentration of reactant X.

Tip: You learnt how to calculate gradients from concentration-time graphs back in Year 1. Have a look back at your notes if you need a reminder on how it all works.

Gradients of curved graphs

If the rate of a reaction changes over time, then the concentration-time graph will be a curve, like the one in Figure 1.

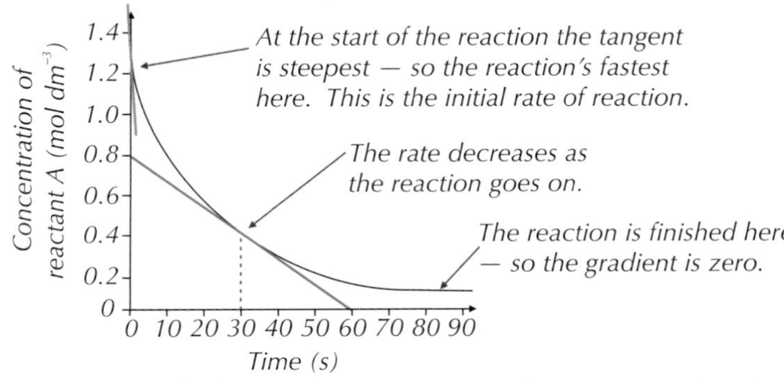

Figure 1: *Graph showing the concentration of a reactant against time.*

Tip: For the reaction in Figure 1, the rate of reaction slows down as time progresses. This is because the reactants get used up, and so collisions between reactant molecules become less likely.

If the graph's a curve, to find the rate you have to draw a tangent to the curve at the point you're interested in and find the gradient of that. A tangent is a line that just touches a curve and has the same gradient as the curve does at that point. The gradient of a tangent is the change in vertical height divided by the change in horizontal width.

Tip: The sign of the gradient doesn't really matter — it's a negative gradient when you're measuring the reactant concentration because the reactant decreases. If you measured the product concentration, it'd be a positive gradient.

Example — Maths Skills

The gradient of the blue tangent on the graph in Figure 1 is the rate of reaction at 30 seconds. This tangent makes a triangle with the *y*-axis and the *x*-axis. The change in *y* is –0.8 and the change in *x* is 60, so:

$$\text{Gradient} = \frac{\Delta y}{\Delta x} = \frac{-0.8}{60} = -0.013 \text{ mol dm}^{-3}\text{ s}^{-1}$$

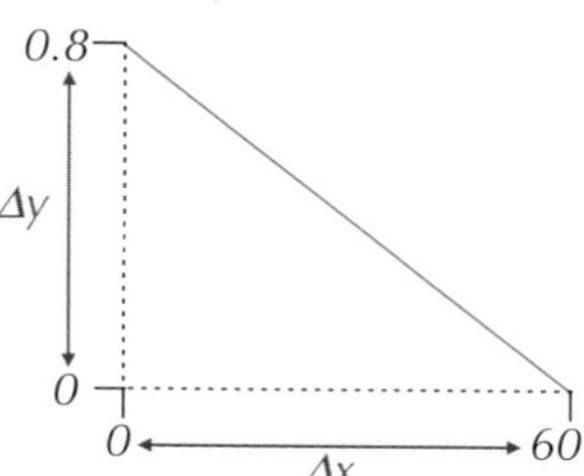

This means that the rate of reaction at 30 seconds is **0.013 mol dm^{-3} s^{-1}**.

Practice Questions — Application

Q1 The concentration-time graph for a reaction is shown below:

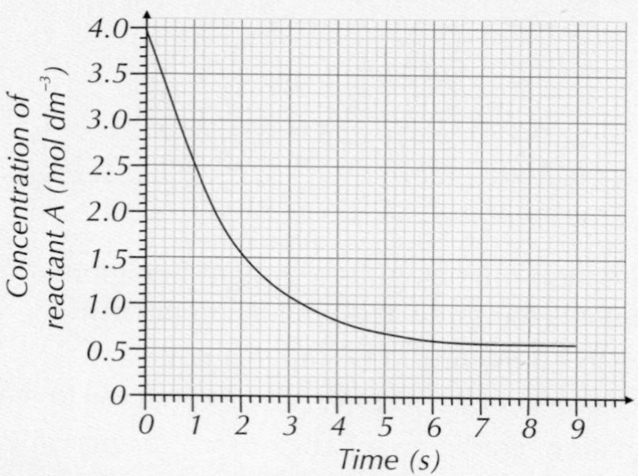

Tip: To draw a tangent to a curve, place a ruler at the point where you're measuring the gradient so that it's just touching the curve. Position the ruler so that you can see the whole curve. Adjust the ruler until the space between the ruler and the curve is equal on both sides of the point. Then draw your tangent.

Determine the rate of this reaction after:

a) 1 second b) 2 seconds c) 4 seconds

Q2 A student is measuring the volume of carbon dioxide gas formed by a reaction between limestone and hydrochloric acid. Her results are shown in the following table.

Time / minutes	0	1	2	3	4	5
Concentration of acid / mol dm^{-3}	5.0	3.1	2.6	2.5	2.4	2.4

a) Plot the data in the table on a graph.

b) Draw a line of best fit on the graph drawn in part a).

c) Calculate the rate of the reaction at 2 minutes.

Tip: There's a lot to remember when it comes to drawing graphs. You've got to think about the size of the graph, what goes on which axis, the scale, not to mention making sure you plot the data points correctly.

Practice Question — Fact Recall

Q1 Explain how you could determine the rate of reaction at a particular time using a concentration-time graph.

3. Initial Rates

You can find the initial rate of a reaction from a concentration-time graph. This is a faff if you want to find how the initial rate changes with initial concentrations of the reactants, so the initial rates method is often used instead.

Learning Objective:

- Understand the techniques and procedures used to investigate reaction rates using the initial rates method (PAG 10).

Specification Reference 5.1.1

Finding the initial rate

The initial rate of a reaction is the rate right at the start of the reaction. You can find this from a concentration-time graph by calculating the gradient of the tangent at time = 0 (see Figure 1).

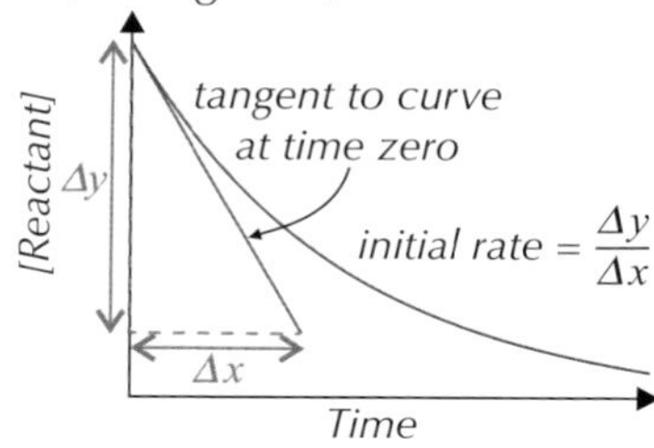

Figure 1: *Graph showing how to calculate the initial rate of reaction.*

Example — Maths Skills

The graph on the right shows the change in concentration of H^+ ions over time in a reaction between a metal and an acid. To work out the initial rate, you need to work out the gradient of the curve right at the start of the reaction.

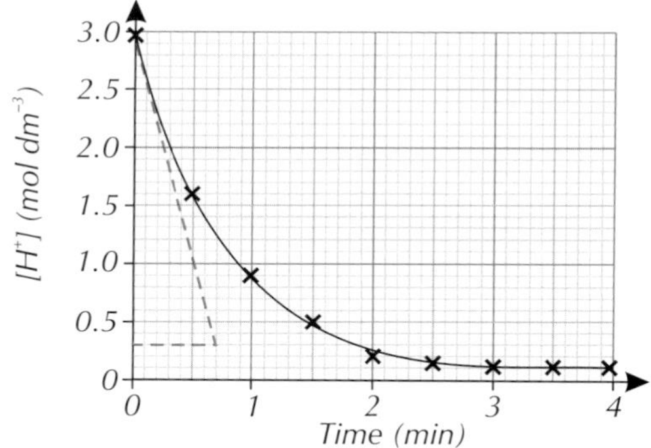

- Draw a tangent to the curve at time = 0.
- Work out the gradient of the tangent using the method on page 21-22.
  gradient = change in y ÷ change in x = (0.3 – 3.0) ÷ (0.7 – 0.0)
  = –2.7 mol dm^{-3} ÷ 0.7 mins = –3.875... mol dm^{-3} min^{-1}
- So the initial rate of reaction was **3.9 mol dm^{-3} min^{-1}**.

Tip: The gradient of the tangent is negative as it slopes down from left to right. You can ignore this when writing down what the rate of the reaction is though — you don't get negative rates of reaction.

The initial rates method

PRACTICAL ACTIVITY GROUP 10

Another way of finding the initial rate of a reaction is the **initial rates method**. This method is often used to find how the initial rate varies as you change the initial concentration of one of the reactants, as it's easier than doing multiple continuous monitoring experiments and finding each initial rate from a concentration-time graph. In the initial rates method, you time how long it takes for a set amount of product to form at the beginning of the reaction in order to calculate an initial rate for a reaction. For example, for reactions that produce a precipitate, you can measure the time it takes for a mark underneath the reaction vessel to disappear from view at varying concentrations of the reactants. Or, for a reaction that produces a gas, you could time how long it takes for a set amount of the gas to form. When you plan an experiment like this, you need to ensure that the rate won't change much over the time period of your experiment — otherwise you can't assume that your results give you an indication of the initial rate of your experiment.

Tip: If you're using the initial rates method, you don't have to keep measuring until the reaction is completely over — you just need enough data to be able to work out the rate at the beginning of the reaction.

Once you've collected your data, you can work out the initial rate of the reaction by doing the following calculations:

- Work out how many moles of product there are in the set amount that you measure in each reaction. This will be the same for each of your experiments, as the same amount of product always forms.
- Use the reaction equation to work out how many moles of the reactant you're interested in will have been used up when the set amount of product has formed. Again, this will be the same for each of the experiments.
- Divide this by the volume of the reaction mixture to calculate the change in concentration of your reactant.
- Divide the change in concentration of the reactant by the time taken for the set amount of product to form. This is the initial rate of your reaction.

By changing the initial concentrations of each reactant, and working out each initial rate, you'll get data similar to that shown in the example below. This can be used to work out reaction orders and rate constants.

Tip: If you're going to do an initial rates experiment, don't forget to carry out a risk assessment first.

Figure 2: *Students measuring the rate of a reaction that has a gaseous product.*

Tip: In the ideal gas equation, pressure is in Pa, volume is in m^3, temperature is in K and the gas constant is 8.31 J mol^{-1} K^{-1}.

Tip: The rate of production of H_2 for each experiment is just 10 cm^3 (the volume produced) divided by the time taken to produce this volume in units of cm^3 s^{-1}.

Tip: 1/time is proportional to the reaction rate. You can therefore use (1 ÷ time) to give you a measure of the rate in units of, e.g. s^{-1}.

Tip: You can use this data to draw a rate-concentration graph which can tell you lots about the reaction (see pages 29 and 34).

Example

A student is investigating how the initial rate of the following reaction changes as he varies the concentration of hydrochloric acid:

$$Mg_{(s)} + 2HCl_{(aq)} \rightarrow MgCl_{2(aq)} + H_{2(g)}$$

For each concentration of HCl, he starts with 15 cm^3 acid and a 5 cm length of magnesium ribbon. He times how long it takes for 10 cm^3 of $H_{2(g)}$ to be produced at each concentration of HCl. His results are shown in the table.

Initial concentration HCl / mol dm^{-3}	Time to produce 10 cm^3 $H_{2(g)}$ / s
3.00	79
2.00	131
1.50	144
0.800	222

- The number of moles of H_2 formed in each reaction can be calculated by rearranging the ideal gas equation:

$$pV = nRT \longrightarrow n = (pV) \div (RT)$$

So $n = [(1.0 \times 10^5) \times (10 \div 10\,000)] \div (8.31 \times 298) = 0.0403...$ moles.

- From the reaction equation, you can see that for every mole of $H_{2(g)}$ that forms, 2 moles of $HCl_{(aq)}$ will have reacted.
So the number of moles of $HCl_{(aq)}$ that react to form 10 cm^3 of $H_{2(g)}$ is $0.0403... \times 2 = 0.0807...$ moles.
- The reaction mixture is always 15 cm^3, so the change in concentration for each experiment is $0.0807... \div (15 \div 1000) = 5.38...$ mol dm^{-3}.
- The initial rate of each reaction can now be calculated by dividing 5.38... mol dm^{-3} by the time taken for the reaction to finish.

Initial concentration HCl / mol dm^{-3}	Time to produce 10 cm^3 $H_{2(g)}$ / s	Initial rate / mol dm^{-3} s^{-1}
3.00	79	0.0682
2.00	131	0.0411
1.50	144	0.0374
0.800	222	0.0243

Clock reactions

A particular type of initial rates reactions are **clock reactions**. Here, the formation of a set amount of product is shown by a sudden, visual change in the reaction mixture. This works by adding a known amount of a substance that reacts with the product you're interested in to the reaction vessel. To begin with, this substance reacts immediately with the product as it forms. As soon as the substance is used up, the presence of unreacted product in the reaction vessel causes a sudden change, such as a colour change. This is the endpoint of the reaction. The quicker the endpoint is reached, the faster the initial rate of the reaction.

PRACTICAL ACTIVITY GROUP 10

When carrying out a clock reaction, you need to make the following assumptions:

- The concentration of each reactant doesn't change significantly over the time period of your clock reaction.
- The temperature stays constant.
- When the endpoint is seen, the reaction has not proceeded too far.

As long as these assumptions are reasonable for your experiment, you can assume that the rate of reaction stays constant during the time period of your measurement. So the rate of your clock reaction will be a good estimate for the initial rate of your reaction.

Tip: When carrying out clock reactions, the data you collect will be in units of time, rather than units of rate. You can use 1/time as a measure of the rate.

Example

The most famous clock reaction is the iodine clock reaction. The reaction you're monitoring is:

$$H_2O_{2\,(aq)} + 2I^-_{(aq)} + 2H^+_{(aq)} \rightarrow 2H_2O_{(l)} + I_{2\,(aq)}$$

- Small amounts of sodium thiosulfate solution and starch are added to an excess of hydrogen peroxide and iodide ions in acid solution. Starch is used as an indicator — it turns blue-black in the presence of iodine.
- The sodium thiosulfate that is added to the reaction mixture reacts instantaneously with any iodine that forms:

$$2S_2O_3^{2-}{}_{(aq)} + I_{2\,(aq)} \rightarrow 2I^-_{(aq)} + S_4O_6^{2-}{}_{(aq)}$$

- To begin with, all the iodine that forms in the first reaction is used up straight away in the second reaction. But once all the sodium thiosulfate is used up, any more iodine that forms will stay in solution, so the starch indicator will suddenly turn the solution blue-black. This is the end of the clock reaction.
- Varying iodide or hydrogen peroxide concentration while keeping the others constant will give different times for the colour change.

Tip: These are ionic equations — they only show the reacting particles. You met them in Year 1 of the course.

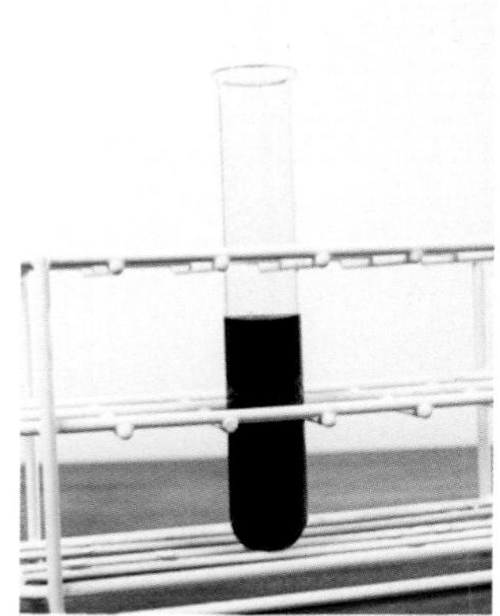

Figure 3: *A solution containing starch turns blue-black when iodine is present.*

Tip: Colorimetry is a great way of monitoring the iodine clock reaction due to the change in colour of the starch indicator when iodine is present. Since this change is very sudden, you could also monitor the reaction by eye.

Practice Questions — Application

Q1 The data on the graph below was obtained experimentally from the decomposition of SO_2Cl_2. Work out the initial rate of the reaction.

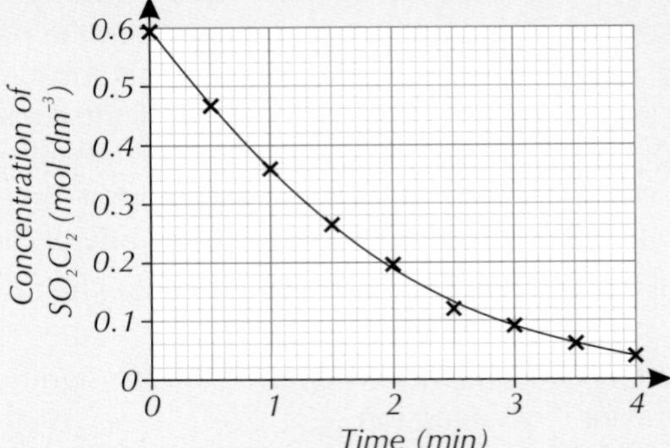

Q2 A student is carrying out an initial rates reaction to try and work out how the rate of the following reaction depends on the initial concentrations of the reactants:

$$Mg_{(s)} + 2HCl_{(aq)} \rightarrow MgCl_{2\,(aq)} + H_{2\,(g)}$$

He times how long it takes for 20 cm³ of hydrogen gas to be formed at varying concentrations of HCl. His results are in the table below.

Trial number	[HCl] / mol dm^{-3}	Time to produce 20 cm³ $H_{2(g)}$ / s
1	1.25	5.1
2	0.800	15.3
3	0.500	31.5

Work out the initial rate of each reaction in cm³ s^{-1}.

Tip: If you need some help calculating the gradients of graphs, have a look back at pages 21-22, or pages 278-279 in the Maths Skills section.

Practice Questions — Fact Recall

Q1 How do you find out the initial rate of a reaction from a concentration-time graph?

Q2 Give three assumptions you need to make when calculating the initial rate of reaction using a clock reaction.

4. Reaction Orders

Reaction orders tell you how the rate of a reaction will be affected if you change the concentration of a reactant. Each reactant has its own order, and you can work them out with the help of a few experiments.

Learning Objectives:

- Be able to explain and use the terms order and overall order.
- Be able to deduce orders from experimental data.
- Be able to deduce the order (0 or 1) with respect to a reactant from the shape of the concentration-time graph of that reactant.
- Be able to deduce the order (0, 1 or 2) with respect to a reactant from the shape of the rate-concentration graph of that reactant.

Specification Reference 5.1.1

What are reaction orders?

The **reaction order**, or **order of reaction** with respect to a particular reactant tells you how the reactant's concentration affects the rate.

- If you double the reactant's concentration and the rate stays the same, the order with respect to that reactant is 0 (the reaction is zero order with respect to the reactant).
- If you double the reactant's concentration and the rate also doubles, the order with respect to that reactant is 1 (the reaction is first order with respect to the reactant).
- If you double the reactant's concentration and the rate quadruples, the order with respect to that reactant is 2 (the reaction is second order with respect to the reactant).

A reaction will also have an **overall order**. This is the sum of the orders of all the different reactants. So if there are two reactants in an reaction, and one has an order of 1 and another has an order of 2, then the overall order of the reaction will be 3.

Tip: If reactant B is ten times more concentrated than reactant A, and they react in a 1:1 ratio, then in the time it takes for the concentration of reactant A to half, the concentration of reactant B will only have fallen by (50% ÷ 10) = 5%. This change will have a negligible effect on the rate compared to the change in concentration of reactant A.

Finding the orders of reactants in a reaction

You can only find orders of reaction from experiments.
You can't work them out from chemical equations.
Think about the generic reaction:

$$A + B \rightarrow C$$

To find the order of each reactant in a reaction, you have to monitor how each reactant affects the rate one by one. So first, you would want to find out the order of the reaction with respect to the concentration of A. You have to use experimental data to work out the order, and you've got two options. You could continuously monitor the change in concentration of A against time to construct a concentration-time graph and then a rate-concentration graph (see pages 28-29), or you could use the initial rates method (see pages 23-24) to find out how the initial rate changes as you vary the concentration of A.

Tip: If you're using the initial rates method, then remember to keep all the variables other than the concentration of the reactant constant, for example the temperature and the reaction volume.

If you decide to monitor your reactions using continuous monitoring, you have to make sure that the concentrations of any reactants you're not investigating, here it's just B, are in excess — there's loads more B than there is A. This means the concentration of B won't change much during the reaction (it will be pretty much constant, and the reaction is effectively zero order with respect to B). Any change in the rate can therefore only be due to the change in concentration of A (the reactant you're investigating). To find the order of the reaction with respect to reactant B, you repeat the experiments, but this time varying the concentration of B and having reactant A in excess.

Tip: There's information about different techniques you can use to follow reactions on pages 17-18.

Tip: Don't forget — if doubling the concentration doesn't affect the rate it's zero order, if doubling the concentration doubles the rate it's first order and if doubling the concentration quadruples the rate it's second order.

Reaction orders from experimental data

You met the initial rates method on pages 23-24 — it's used to see how the rate right at the start of a reaction changes if you change the starting concentration of one of the reactants. The initial rates method is a great way of working out the orders of different reactants in a reaction. To do this, you have to compare how the initial rate of the reaction changes as you change the initial concentration of one of the reactants using the steps on page 24. You then use this to work out the order for that reactant. You can then repeat the process for each reactant (different reactants may have different orders).

Example — Maths Skills

The table below shows the results of a series of initial rate experiments for the reaction $NO_{(g)} + CO_{(g)} + O_{2(g)} \rightarrow NO_{2(g)} + CO_{2(g)}$. Work out the reaction orders with respect to each reactant.

Experiment number	[NO] / mol dm^{-3}	[CO] / mol dm^{-3}	[O_2] / mol dm^{-3}	Initial rate / mol dm^{-3} s^{-1}
1	2.0×10^{-2}	1.0×10^{-2}	1.0×10^{-2}	0.16
2	1.0×10^{-2}	1.0×10^{-2}	1.0×10^{-2}	0.04
3	2.0×10^{-2}	2.0×10^{-2}	1.0×10^{-2}	0.16
4	4.0×10^{-2}	1.0×10^{-2}	2.0×10^{-2}	0.64

- Look at experiments 1 and 2 — when [NO] doubles (and all the other concentrations stay constant) the rate is four times faster. So the reaction is second order with respect to NO.
- Look at experiments 1 and 3 — when [CO] doubles (but all the other concentrations stay constant), the rate stays the same. So the reaction is zero order with respect to CO.
- Look at experiments 1 and 4 — the rate of experiment 4 is four times faster than experiment 1. The reaction is second order with respect to NO, so the rate will quadruple when you double [NO]. But in experiment 4, [O_2] has also been doubled. As doubling [O_2] hasn't had any additional effect on the rate, the reaction must be zero order with respect to O_2.

So, this reaction is second order with respect to NO, zero order with respect to CO and zero order with respect to O_2.

Exam Tip
You would usually only change one concentration at a time between experiments, but you could get a question where more than one concentration changes — don't get confused, the principle is the same.

Exam Tip
You need to be able to work out orders of reaction from initial rates data in the exam, so make sure you understand this example.

Finding reaction orders using graphs

You can work out the reaction order with respect to a particular reactant using a concentration-time graph, or a rate-concentration graph. Concentration-time graphs can be made by taking repeated measurements of the concentration of the reactant you are investigating during a reaction (continuous monitoring, page 17). You can make a rate-concentration graph using a concentration-time graph. Here's how:

- Find the gradient (which is the rate) at various points along the concentration-time graph (see pages 21-22 for a reminder of how to do this). This gives you a set of points for the rate-concentration graph.
- Then just plot the points and join them up with a line or smooth curve.

You can also plot a rate-concentration graph using data obtained from initial rates experiments.

Tip: If you've measured something else other than concentration in your experiment (such as volume) you can either use your data along with the reaction equation to calculate the concentrations of the reactants left behind, or just plot a graph of the data you've measured against time (e.g. a volume-time graph). The shape should be the same as a concentration-time graph.

The shapes of rate-concentration graphs and concentration-time graphs tell you the order of the reaction with respect to the reactant you're investigating. This is because rate and concentration are correlated — changing the concentration of one of the reactants can have a direct effect on the rate of the reaction. This is a causal link, as reducing the concentration of a reactant will cause fewer collisions to occur, and so, unless the reactant is zero order, the rate of the reaction will decrease. How much the rate decreases as the concentration decreases (the order) is what determines the shape of rate-concentration or concentration-time graph.

HOW SCIENCE WORKS

Zero order

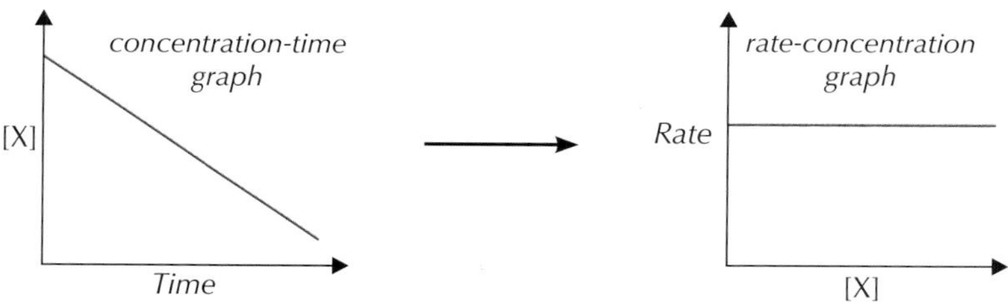

A horizontal line on a rate-concentration graph means that changing the concentration doesn't change the rate, so the reaction is zero order.

Tip: If something is in [square brackets] it's a concentration. So [X] means the concentration of reactant X.

First order

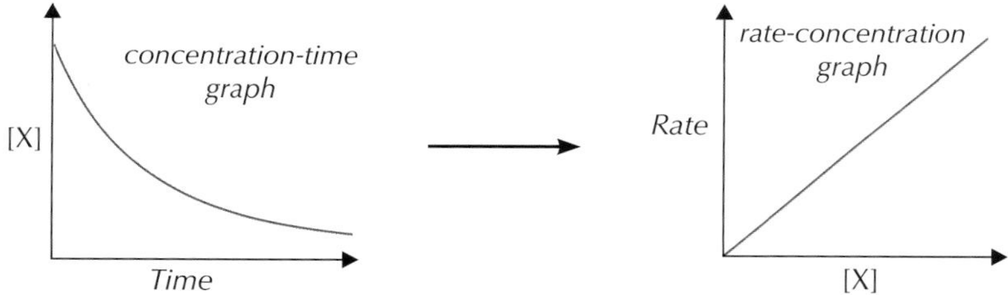

If the rate-concentration graph is a straight line through the origin, then the reaction is first order. The rate is proportional to [X]. For example, if the concentration of X triples, the rate will triple. If it halves, the rate will halve.

Tip: You don't need to be able to recognise the shape of a concentration-time graph for a reaction that is second order with respect to one of its reactants. So if you're given a concentration-time graph of a reactant that is curved and asked to predict its order, it'll probably be first order.

Second order

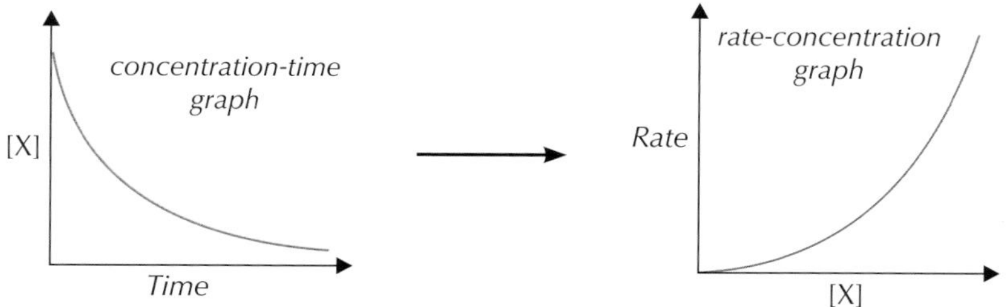

A curved rate-concentration graph means that the reaction is second order. The rate is proportional to $[X]^2$. For example, if the concentration of X triples, the rate will be nine times as fast (because $3^2 = 9$).

Tip: In theory, a curved rate-concentration graph could mean a higher order than 2. But you won't be asked about any with a higher order than 2 in the exams — so if you see a curve, always say order 2.

> **Exam Tip**
> Rate-concentration graphs and concentration-time graphs look similar, so if you're given one in the exam, make sure you double-check which it is before you start answering the question. You can tell the difference by looking at what's plotted on each of the axes.

Practice Questions — Application

Q1 The results of a series of initial rate experiments for the following reaction are shown below: $O_3 + C_2H_4 \rightarrow 2CH_2O + \frac{1}{2}O_2$

Experiment number	$[O_3]$ / mol dm^{-3}	$[C_2H_4]$ / mol dm^{-3}	Initial rate / mol dm^{-3} s^{-1}
1	8.0×10^{-4}	8.0×10^{-4}	0.053
2	1.6×10^{-3}	8.0×10^{-4}	0.106
3	1.6×10^{-3}	2.4×10^{-3}	0.318

a) Determine the orders of reaction with respect to O_3 and C_2H_4.

b) What is the overall order of the reaction?

Q2 Below are the rate-concentration graphs produced as the concentrations of three different reactants (A, B and C) changed during a reaction.

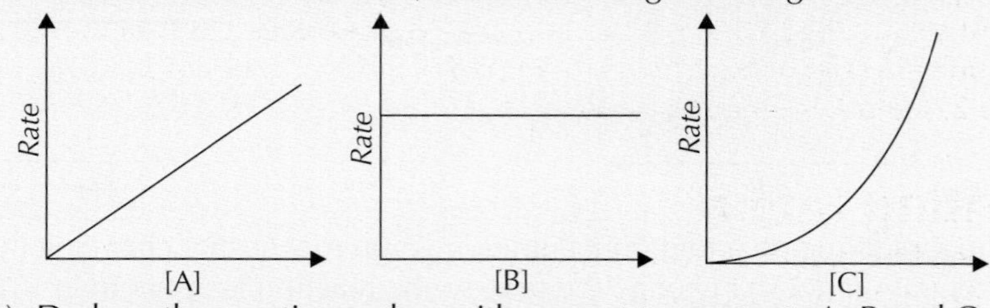

a) Deduce the reaction orders with respect to reactants A, B and C.

b) State how you would expect the rate of reaction to change if the concentration of:

(i) A was halved (ii) B was tripled (iii) C was doubled

Q3 The results of a continuous monitoring experiment investigating the change in concentration of sodium hydroxide for the following reaction are shown below: $(CH_3)_3CBr + NaOH \rightarrow (CH_3)_3COH + NaBr$

Time / s	0	30	60	90	120
[NaOH] / mol dm^{-3}	0.500	0.465	0.429	0.382	0.349

Use the table to draw a concentration-time graph and determine the order of the reaction with respect to sodium hydroxide.

> **Exam Tip**
> Make sure you get as much practice as you can with working out reaction orders using the initial rates method — you need to be confident with it if it comes up in the exams.

Q4 The table below shows the results of a series of initial rate experiments for the reaction: $2A + B + C \rightarrow AB + AC$

Experiment number	[A] / mol dm^{-3}	[B] / mol dm^{-3}	[C] / mol dm^{-3}	Initial rate / mol dm^{-3} s^{-1}
1	1.2	1.2	1.2	0.25
2	1.2	2.4	1.2	1.00
3	1.2	2.4	3.6	3.00
4	0.60	2.4	2.4	1.00

Determine the orders of reaction with respect to reactants A, B and C.

> **Tip:** If you're given the time the reaction took, rather than the initial rate of the reaction, then 1/time is proportional to the rate, so you can compare these values to work out the order of the reaction with respect to a reactant.

Practice Questions — Fact Recall

Q1 Explain what is meant by the term 'reaction order'.

Q2 a) Describe two methods you could use to produce a rate-concentration graph.

b) Explain how you could determine the order of reaction with respect to a reactant using a rate-concentration graph.

5. Rate Equations

The rate of a reaction is linked to the concentrations of the reactants by something called a rate equation. This topic is all about rate equations and why they are useful. Have fun...

Learning Objectives:

- Be able to explain and use the term rate constant.
- Be able to deduce a rate equation from orders of the form: rate = $k[A]^m[B]^n$, where m and n are 0, 1 or 2.

Specification Reference 5.1.1

What are rate equations?

Rate equations look ghastly, but all they're really telling you is how the rate is affected by the concentrations of reactants. For a general reaction: A + B $\rightarrow$ C + D, the rate equation is:

$$\textbf{Rate} = k[A]^m[B]^n$$

The square brackets mean the concentration of whatever's inside them. So [A] means the concentration of A and [B] means the concentration of B. The units of rate are mol $dm^{-3}\,s^{-1}$. m and n are the **orders of reaction** (see page 27) and k is the **rate constant** — the bigger k is, the faster the reaction.

Tip: There are only two reactants in this general equation, but you can write rate equations for equations with any number of reactants. E.g. if there are three reactants the equation is:

$$\text{Rate} = k[A]^m[B]^n[C]^x$$

Writing rate equations

You need to know how to write rate equations for reactions. This example shows you how:

Example — Maths Skills

The chemical equation below shows the acid–catalysed reaction between propanone and iodine.

$$CH_3COCH_{3(aq)} + I_{2(aq)} \xrightarrow{H^+_{(aq)}} CH_3COCH_2I_{(aq)} + H^+_{(aq)} + I^-_{(aq)}$$

This reaction is first order with respect to propanone, first order with respect to $H^+_{(aq)}$ and zero order with respect to iodine. Write the rate equation for this reaction.

In this example there are three things that you need to think about — the orders of reaction of propanone (CH_3COCH_3), iodine (I_2) and hydrogen ions (H^+). (Even though H^+ is a catalyst, rather than a reactant, it can still be in the rate equation because it affects the rate of reaction.) So the rate equation will be in the form:

$$\text{Rate} = k[A]^m[B]^n[C]^x$$

You're told the reaction orders with respect to each reactant in the question so just use that information to construct the rate equation:

$$\text{Rate} = k[CH_3COCH_3]^1[H^+]^1[I_2]^0$$

But $[X]^1$ is usually written as [X], and $[X]^0$ equals 1 so is usually left out of the rate equation. So you can simplify the rate equation to:

$$\text{Rate} = k[CH_3COCH_3][H^+]$$

This rate equation shows that the rate of reaction is proportional to the concentrations of propanone and H^+. So doubling the concentration of either propanone or H^+ will double the rate of the reaction.

Exam Tip

m and n could take any value, but in the exam you'll only have to deal with rate equations where m and n are 0, 1 or 2.

Tip: The rate equation is a standard way of showing how rates relate to reactant concentrations and their orders. So, scientists all over the world understand its meaning.

HOW SCIENCE WORKS

Tip: When simplifying rate equations think about the indices laws from maths (see page 276) — the same rules apply here. Anything to the power of zero is one (e.g. $[X]^0 = 1$) and anything to the power of one doesn't change (e.g. $[X]^1 = [X]$).

Tip: Remember, you can only find the order of reactions, and so rate equations, by doing experiments. You can't work them out from a balanced chemical equation.

Exam Tip
In the exams, you might be asked to predict a rate of reaction after having written the rate equation and calculated a value for k — so make sure you know how to do it.

Tip: Before you calculate the rate of a reaction, you may first have to determine the value of the rate constant. See pages 33-35 for how to do this.

Figure 1: The reaction between $Na_2S_2O_3$ and HCl. The solution turns cloudy as the reaction progresses which allows the rate of reaction to be measured.

Predicting the rate of a reaction

If you know the rate constant and the rate equation for a particular reaction at a certain temperature, you can use them to predict the rate of reaction for given reactant concentrations at this temperature. All you have to do is substitute values into the rate equation and solve to find the rate.

Example — Maths Skills

The reaction $2HI \rightarrow H_2 + I_2$ is second order with respect to hydrogen iodide. Construct a rate equation for this reaction and calculate the rate when the concentration of HI is 0.0200 mol dm^{-3} given that at the reaction temperature, the rate constant, k = 1.11 × 10^{-19} mol dm^{-3} s^{-1}.

The reaction is second order with respect to HI, so the rate equation is:

$$\text{Rate} = k[\text{HI}]^2$$

To calculate the rate of the reaction when [HI] = 0.0200 mol dm^{-3}, you just have to substitute the value of the concentration of HI and the value of the rate constant into the expression for the rate equation:

$$\text{Rate} = 1.11 \times 10^{-19} \times (0.0200)^2 = \mathbf{4.44 \times 10^{-23}\ mol\ dm^{-3}\ s^{-1}}$$

Practice Question — Application

Q1 The following reaction occurs between sodium thiosulfate ($Na_2S_2O_3$) and hydrochloric acid:

$$Na_2S_2O_{3(aq)} + 2HCl_{(aq)} \rightarrow 2NaCl_{(aq)} + S_{(s)} + SO_{2(g)} + H_2O_{(l)}$$

This reaction is first order with respect to $Na_2S_2O_3$ and zero order with respect to HCl.

a) Construct the rate equation for this reaction.

b) Given that the rate constant, k = 4.67 × 10^{-1} s^{-1} at 298 K, calculate the rate of the reaction when the concentration of sodium thiosulfate is 0.45 mol dm^{-3} and the concentration of hydrochloric acid is 0.60 mol dm^{-3}.

Practice Questions — Fact Recall

Q1 What does the rate equation tell you?

Q2 In the rate equation, Rate = $k[A]^m[B]^n$, what do the following represent:

a) k? b) [A]? c) m?

Q3 Write the general rate equation for a reaction which has 3 reactants.

6. The Rate Constant

The rate constant, k, is the value in the rate equation that links the concentration and the order of each of the reactants to the rate of the reaction. To start, you need to know how to find it using experimental data.

Learning Objectives:

- Be able to calculate the rate constant, k, and related quantities from a rate equation, including determination of units.
- Be able to determine the rate constant for a first order reaction from the gradient of a rate-concentration graph.
- Be able to explain and use the term half-life.
- Be able to measure the constant half-life, $t_{½}$, from the concentration-time graph of a first order reaction.
- Be able to determine the rate constant, k, for a first order reaction from the constant half-life, $t_{½}$, using the relationship: $k = \ln 2/t_{½}$.

Specification Reference 5.1.1

Using the rate equation to find k

If you know the orders of a reaction, you can use the rate equation and experimental data to work out the rate constant, k. The units of k vary, so you'll need to work them out too.

Example — Maths Skills

The reaction below is second order with respect to NO and zero order with respect to CO and O_2.

$$NO_{(g)} + CO_{(g)} + O_{2(g)} \rightarrow NO_{2(g)} + CO_{2(g)}$$

At a certain temperature, the rate is 1.76×10^{-3} mol dm^{-3} s^{-1}, when $[NO_{(g)}] = [CO_{(g)}] = [O_{2(g)}] = 2.00 \times 10^{-3}$ mol dm^{-3}.
Find the value of the rate constant, k, at this temperature.

- To answer this question you first need to write out the rate equation:

$$\text{Rate} = k[NO]^2[CO]^0[O_2]^0$$
$$= k[NO]^2$$

- Next insert the concentration and the rate, which were given to you in the question:

$$\text{Rate} = k[NO]^2$$
$$1.76 \times 10^{-3} = k \times (2.00 \times 10^{-3})^2$$

- Rearrange the equation and calculate the value of k:

$$k = \frac{1.76 \times 10^{-3}}{(2.00 \times 10^{-3})^2} = 440$$

- Find the units of k by putting the other units in the rate equation:

$$\text{Rate} = k[NO]^2 \quad \text{so} \quad \text{mol dm}^{-3}\text{ s}^{-1} = k \times (\text{mol dm}^{-3})^2$$

- Rearrange the equation to get k:

$$k = \frac{\text{mol dm}^{-3}\text{ s}^{-1}}{(\text{mol dm}^{-3})^2}$$

- Cancel out units wherever possible. In this example you can cancel out a mol dm^{-3} from the top and bottom lines of the fraction:

$$k = \frac{\cancel{\text{mol dm}^{-3}}\text{ s}^{-1}}{(\cancel{\text{mol dm}^{-3}})(\text{mol dm}^{-3})} = \frac{\text{s}^{-1}}{\text{mol dm}^{-3}}$$

- Get rid of the fraction using index laws:

$$k = \frac{\text{s}^{-1}}{\text{mol dm}^{-3}} = \text{mol}^{-1}\text{ dm}^{3}\text{ s}^{-1}$$

- So the answer is:

$$k = 440 \text{ mol}^{-1}\text{ dm}^{3}\text{ s}^{-1}$$

Tip: You need to know how to work out what units your answer is in — it crops up a lot in this section so it's important that you understand how to do it. Have a look at page 275 for more on finding units.

Tip: Index laws state that to move a number from the bottom of a fraction to the top of a fraction, you just have to change the signs of the powers. So if you've got a mol^2 dm^{-6} on the bottom of the fraction it becomes mol^{-2} dm^6 when it's on the top.

Tip: The value of k depends on the temperature (see pages 41-42), so predicted rates of reaction will only be accurate if the reaction is performed at the same temperature as the reaction used to calculate k.

Once you've found the rate constant for a reaction, you can use it in the rate equation to predict the rate of the reaction at the same temperature but with different concentrations of reactants.

Example — Maths Skills

On the previous page, you saw that the rate equation for the reaction $NO_{(g)} + CO_{(g)} + O_{2(g)} \rightarrow NO_{2(g)} + CO_{2(g)}$ is rate = $k[NO]^2$ and you worked out that the rate constant for the reaction is 440 $mol^{-1}\ dm^3\ s^{-1}$.

Calculate the rate of reaction if the concentration of NO is 0.00500 mol dm^{-3}.

$$\text{Rate} = k[NO]^2$$
$$= 440 \times (0.00500)^2$$
$$= \mathbf{0.0110\ mol\ dm^{-3}\ s^{-1}}$$

Rate constants of first order reactions

If you're asked to calculate the rate constant of a first order reaction, there are a few special methods you can use that won't work for reactions with different orders.

Calculating the rate constant from a rate-concentration graph

If the overall reaction is first order, then the rate constant is equal to the gradient of the rate-concentration graph of that reactant.

Tip: Rate-concentration graphs of a first order reactions are straight-line graphs (see page 29).

Example — Maths Skills

The graph below shows how the rate of the following reaction depends on the concentration of 2-chloro-2-methylpropane $[(CH_3)_3CCl]$ in the following reaction:

$$(CH_3)_3CCl + NaOH \rightarrow (CH_3)_3COH + NaCl$$

Use the graph to calculate the rate constant, k, of this reaction.

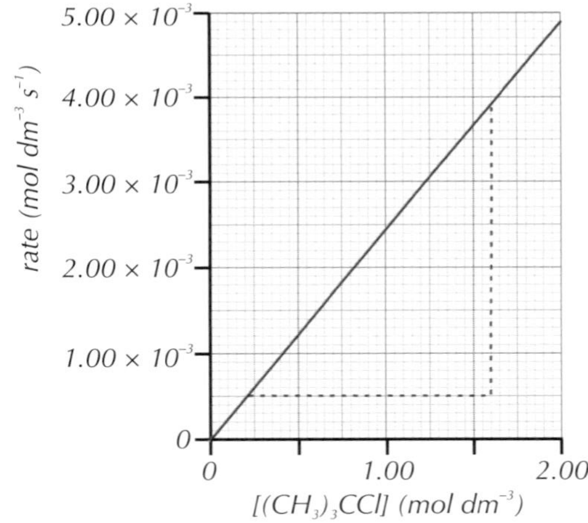

Tip: The rate equation of a first order reaction is: rate = k[X], so a graph of rate against [X] has a gradient equal to the rate constant, k.

The rate-concentration graph is a straight line, so the reaction is first order and the rate constant is equal to the gradient of the graph.

$$\text{Gradient} = \frac{\text{change in } y}{\text{change in } x} = \frac{(3.90 \times 10^{-3}) - (0.50 \times 10^{-3})}{1.60 - 0.20} = \frac{3.40 \times 10^{-3}}{1.40}$$
$$= 2.43 \times 10^{-3}$$

The units of y are mol $dm^3\ s^{-1}$, and the units of x are mol dm^{-3}.

So the units of k are $\frac{\text{mol dm}^3\ \text{s}^{-1}}{\text{mol dm}^3} = \text{s}^{-1}$.

So k = $\mathbf{2.43 \times 10^{-3}\ s^{-1}}$

Calculating the rate constant from the half-life

The **half-life** of a reaction is the time it takes for half of the reactant to be used up. You can work out the half-life from a concentration-time graph (see Figure 1). All you have to do is read off the graph how long it takes for the concentration of the reactant to halve.

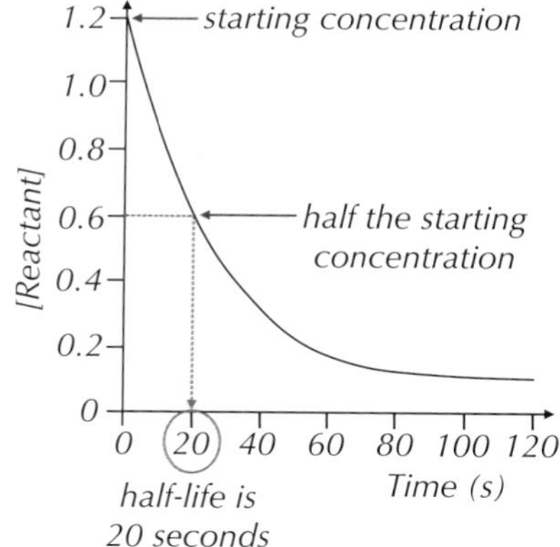

Figure 1: Graph showing how to work out the half-life of a reaction.

The half-life of a first order reaction is independent of the concentration. This means that the half life is constant (the same) no matter what the concentration is. This is only true for first order reactions — so if you see a reaction with a constant half-life, you know it must be first order. If you know the half-life of a first order reaction you can work out the rate constant using the equation:

$$k = \frac{\ln 2}{t_{1/2}}$$

The units of k are: $\frac{\text{no units}}{\text{s}} = \text{s}^{-1}$

Example — Maths Skills

This graph shows the decomposition of hydrogen peroxide, H_2O_2. Use the graph to measure the half-life at various points and work out the rate constant of the reaction.

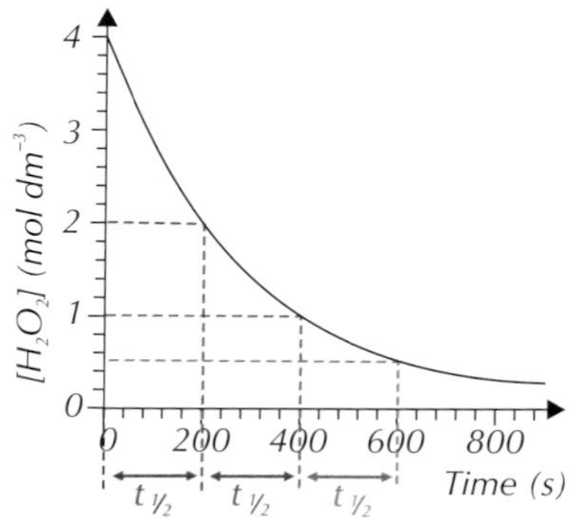

$[H_2O_2]$ from 4 to 2 mol dm^{-3} = 200 s,
$[H_2O_2]$ from 2 to 1 mol dm^{-3} = 200 s,
$[H_2O_2]$ from 1 to 0.5 mol dm^{-3} = 200 s.

The half-life is always 200 s, regardless of the concentration, so it's a first order reaction with respect to $[H_2O_2]$.

The rate constant is: $k = \frac{\ln 2}{t_{1/2}} = \frac{\ln 2}{200 \text{ s}} =$ $\mathbf{3.47 \times 10^{-3}\ s^{-1}}$

Tip: Half-life can also be written as $t_{1/2}$.

Tip: Lots of natural processes are first order reactions and so have a constant half-life. E.g. when a radioactive substance decays or a drug is broken down in the body the half-life is usually constant.

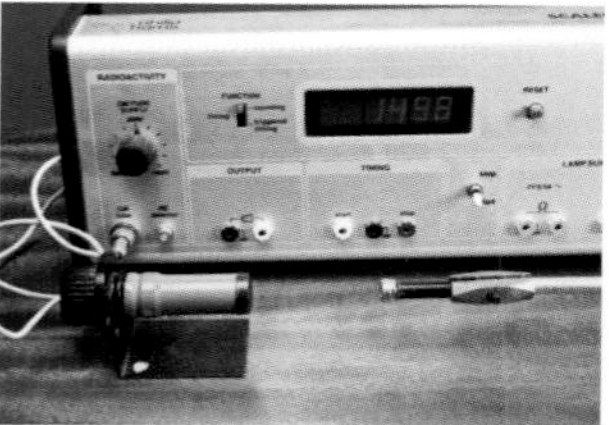

Figure 2: A Geiger counter measuring radioactive decay, which is a first order reaction.

Tip: 'ln x' means the natural logarithm of x. It's the opposite of 'e^x'. You'll need a scientific calculator to work it out. See pages 276-277 in the Maths Skills section for more on logs and powers.

Tip: You can measure the half-life between any two concentrations as long as the concentration halves — for example, you could also measure the half-life from 3 to 1.5 mol dm^{-3} and it should be the same.

Exam Tip
When answering calculation questions like these always remember to give the units for your answer.

Tip: Remember to convert all your values into standard units (seconds for time, mol dm^{-3} for concentration) before you start any calculations.

Practice Questions — Application

Q1 The reaction below is second order with respect to NO and first order with respect to Cl_2:

$$2NO_{(g)} + Cl_{2(g)} \rightarrow 2NOCl_{(g)}$$

The rate of reaction is 5.85×10^{-6} mol dm^{-3} s^{-1} at 50 °C, when the concentration of both NO and Cl_2 is 0.400 mol dm^{-3}.

a) Write the rate equation for this reaction.

b) Calculate the rate constant (k) for this reaction at 50 °C.

c) Calculate the expected rate of reaction if 0.500 mol dm^{-3} NO were mixed with 0.200 mol dm^{-3} Cl_2 at 50 °C.

Q2 The following graph shows a plot of rate against concentration for a first order reaction. Calculate the rate constant of the reaction.

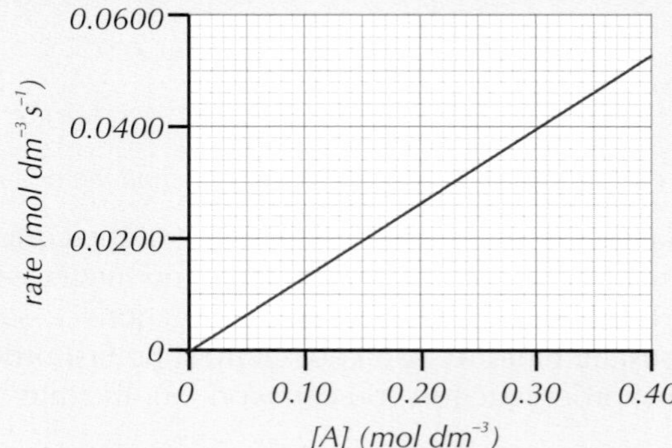

Q3 The table below shows the results of an experiment to investigate the decomposition of ozone: $O_3 \rightarrow O_2 + O$

Time / min	0.0	3.0	6.0	9.0	12.0	15.0	18.0
Concentration / mol dm^{-3}	0.24	0.14	0.085	0.050	0.035	0.020	0.015

a) Plot a graph of these results, and determine the first three half-lives of the reaction.

b) What is the rate constant of this reaction?

Practice Questions — Fact Recall

Q1 How could you find the rate constant of a first order reaction from a rate-concentration graph?

Q2 Define the half-life of a reaction.

Q3 Give the equation that links the half-life of a first order reaction to its rate constant.

7. The Rate-Determining Step

Reaction mechanisms show step by step how a chemical reaction takes place. The most important step is the rate-determining step — that's what these pages are all about.

What is the rate-determining step?

Reaction mechanisms can have one step or a series of steps. In a series of steps, each step can have a different rate. The overall rate is decided by the step with the slowest rate — the **rate-determining step**.

The rate equation is handy for working out the mechanism of a chemical reaction. You need to be able to pick out which reactants from the chemical equation are involved in the rate-determining step. Here's how:

- If a reactant appears in the rate equation, it must affect the rate. So this reactant, or something derived from it, must be in the rate-determining step.
- If a reactant doesn't appear in the rate equation, then it won't be involved in the rate-determining step and neither will anything derived from it.

An important point to remember about rate-determining steps and mechanisms is that the rate-determining step doesn't have to be the first step in a mechanism. Also, the reaction mechanism can't usually be predicted from just the chemical equation — you need information about the orders of the reactants as well, which you can only get from doing experiments.

Predicting rate equations

The order of a reaction with respect to a reactant shows the number of molecules of that reactant that are involved in the rate-determining step. So, if a reaction's second order with respect to X, there'll be two molecules of X in the rate-determining step. This link means that if you know the rate determining step of a reaction, you can predict the rate equation.

Example

The mechanism for the reaction between chlorine radicals (Cl•) and ozone (O_3) consists of two steps:

$Cl\bullet_{(g)} + O_{3(g)} \rightarrow ClO\bullet + O_{2(g)}$ *This step is slow — it's the rate determining step.*

$ClO\bullet_{(g)} + O\bullet_{(g)} \rightarrow Cl\bullet + O_{2(g)}$ *This step is fast.*

Cl• and O_3 are both in the rate-determining step so must both be in the rate equation. So, the rate equation will be:

$$\text{Rate} = k[Cl\bullet]^m[O_3]^n$$

There's only one Cl• and one O_3 molecule in the rate-determining step, so the orders, m and n, are both 1. So the rate equation is:

$$\text{Rate} = k[Cl\bullet][O_3]$$

Predicting reaction mechanisms

If you know the rate equation you can predict which reactants are in the rate-determining step, and if you know which reactants are in the rate-determining step, you can work out the reaction mechanism. There's an example coming up on the next page to show you how.

Learning Objectives:

- Be able to explain and use the term rate-determining step.
- Be able to predict a rate equation for a multi-step reaction that is consistent with the rate-determining step.
- Be able to predict possible steps in a reaction mechanism of a multi-step reaction from the rate equation and the balanced equation for the overall reaction.

Specification Reference 5.1.1

Tip: You might also see the rate-determining step being called the rate-limiting step.

Tip: Catalysts can appear in rate equations, so they can be part of the rate-determining step too.

Tip: Have a look back at your Year 1 notes for more detail on how chlorine radicals catalyse the break-down of ozone in the stratosphere.

Exam Tip
In the exams, you might be asked to write the rate equation for a reaction from the rate-determining step so make sure you know what you're doing.

Tip: Experimental evidence about reaction orders is often used to develop theories for what the mechanism of a reaction will be. HOW SCIENCE WORKS

Tip: You need to be sure that you understand rate equations before tackling this, or it won't make sense. If you need a reminder, flip back to page 31 and have a quick glance over the relevant bits.

Tip: This reaction is zero order with respect to OH^-. Changing the concentration of OH^- ions won't change the reaction rate.

Tip: When you've come up with a mechanism, don't forget to double check that the steps add up to give you the overall equation. If they don't, it can't be right. (The steps add up fine in this example — I've just checked. Phew.)

Example

2-bromo-2-methylpropane can react with the nucleophile OH^- to give 2-methylpropan-2-ol and bromide ions (Br^-).

There are two possible mechanisms for this reaction. Here's one...

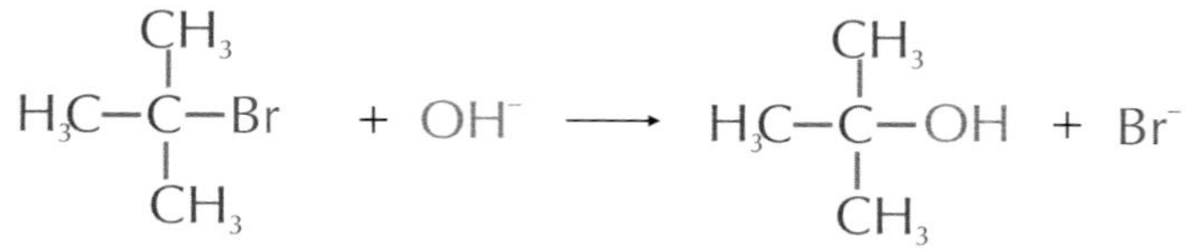

$$H_3C-C(CH_3)_2-Br + OH^- \longrightarrow H_3C-C(CH_3)_2-OH + Br^-$$

... and here's the other one:

$$H_3C-C(CH_3)_2-Br \longrightarrow H_3C-C^+(CH_3)_2 + Br^-$$

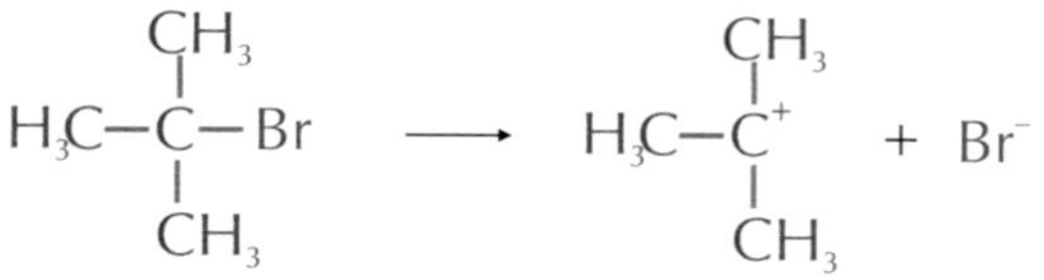

This step is slow — it's the rate-determining step.

$$H_3C-C^+(CH_3)_2 + OH^- \longrightarrow H_3C-C(CH_3)_2-OH$$

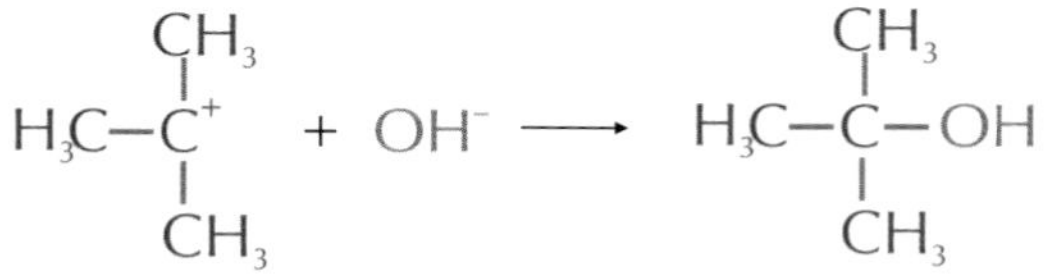

This step is fast.

The actual rate equation was worked out using rate experiments. It is:

$$\text{Rate} = k[(CH_3)_3CBr]$$

OH^- isn't in the rate equation, so it can't be involved in the rate-determining step. The second mechanism is likely to be correct because there is one molecule of $(CH_3)CBr$ and no molecules of OH^- in the rate-determining step — just like the rate equation suggests.

If you're suggesting a mechanism, watch out — the most obvious answer might not always be the right one.

Example

When nitrogen(V) oxide, N_2O_5, decomposes, it forms nitrogen(IV) oxide and oxygen:

$$2N_2O_{5(g)} \rightarrow 4NO_{2(g)} + O_{2(g)}$$

From the chemical equation, it looks like two N_2O_5 molecules react with each other. So that might be your first idea — a simple one-step mechanism. The rate equation for this mechanism would be: rate = $k[N_2O_5]^2$.

But, experimentally, it's been found that the reaction is first order with respect to N_2O_5 — the rate equation is: rate = $k[N_2O_5]$.

This shows that there's only one molecule of N_2O_5 in the rate-determining step. So a one-step mechanism can't be right (a one-step mechanism would have two molecules of N_2O_5 in the rate-determining step).

One possible mechanism that fits the rate equation is:

$$N_2O_{5(g)} \rightarrow NO_{2(g)} + NO_{3(g)}$$ *slow (rate-determining step)*

$$NO_{3(g)} + N_2O_{5(g)} \rightarrow 3NO_{2(g)} + O_{2(g)}$$ *fast*

In this mechanism, only one molecule of N_2O_5 is in the rate-determining step — this fits in with the rate equation.

Suggesting a mechanism

In the exams, you won't always be given a selection of possible mechanisms and asked to pick the right one. You could be given the overall equation and rate equation for a reaction and be asked to suggest a mechanism yourself. If this happens there are three rules you have to stick to:

- The rate-determining step of the reaction must fit with the rate equation.
- All of the equations in the mechanism must balance.
- The different steps of the reaction must add up to the overall equation.

Often there is more than one correct answer you could give, but as long as you stick to the rules above you should get the marks in the exam.

Exam Tip
If the reaction you're given involves a catalyst, you need to make sure that the catalyst is regenerated at the end.

Example

Nitrogen dioxide can react with fluorine to produce nitryl fluoride (NO_2F):

$$2NO_{2\,(g)} + F_{2\,(g)} \rightarrow 2NO_2F_{(g)}$$

The rate equation for this reaction is: rate = $k[NO_2][F_2]$. Suggest a possible two-step mechanism for this reaction. The first step is the slowest step.

The first step is the slowest step so this must be the rate-determining step. From the rate equation you can see that the rate determining step involves one molecule of NO_2 and one molecule of F_2. So the first step in the reaction must be:

$$NO_{2\,(g)} + F_{2\,(g)} \rightarrow ???$$

The second molecule of NO_2 isn't involved in the rate-determining step so it must be involved in the second step. This means that the second step in the reaction mechanism must be:

$$NO_{2\,(g)} + ??? \rightarrow ???$$

After that it's just a case of filling in the blanks, making sure that both equations balance and that you only end up with two molecules of NO_2F at the end. One possible solution is shown below:

$$NO_{2\,(g)} + F_{2\,(g)} \rightarrow NO_2F_{(g)} + F\bullet_{(g)}$$
$$NO_{2\,(g)} + F\bullet_{(g)} \rightarrow NO_2F_{(g)}$$

In this example, the F• is an intermediate species — it is generated in the first step and consumed in the second step to leave you with the overall products of the reaction.

Another possible mechanism would be:

$$NO_{2\,(g)} + F_{2\,(g)} \rightarrow NO_2F_{2\,(g)}$$
$$NO_{2\,(g)} + NO_2F_{2\,(g)} \rightarrow 2NO_2F_{(g)}$$

This time NO_2F_2 is the intermediate species.

The correct mechanism is the first one, but in the exam you would get the marks for either answer because both answers fit the information that's given in the question.

Exam Tip
The rate-determining step won't necessarily be the first step in the reaction — but don't worry, you should be told which one is the slowest step.

Tip: F• is a fluorine radical. See your Year 1 notes for more on radicals.

Exam Tip
You could also have suggested a mechanism like this:

$NO_2 + F_2 \rightarrow NO + F_2O$

$NO_2 + NO + F_2O \rightarrow 2NO_2F$

But reactions happens when molecules collide, and it's very unlikely that 3 molecules would collide simultaneously. So try and avoid reaction mechanisms which involve more than two molecules reacting at a time.

Don't panic if you're asked to propose a mechanism in the exam. It sounds hard but as long as you follow the rules above you'll be just fine.

Practice Questions — Application

Q1 The rate-determining step for a reaction between two reactants (A and B) is $2A + B \rightarrow X + Y$. Predict the rate equation for this reaction.

Q2 The reaction $Br_{2\,(g)} + 2NO_{(g)} \rightarrow 2BrNO_{(g)}$ has a two step mechanism:

Step 1: $Br_{2\,(g)} + NO_{(g)} \rightarrow Br_2NO_{(g)}$

Step 2: $Br_2NO_{(g)} + NO_{(g)} \rightarrow 2BrNO_{(g)}$

Step 1 is the rate-determining step.
Write down the rate equation for this reaction.

Q3 The reaction $NO_{2\,(g)} + CO_{(g)} \rightarrow NO_{(g)} + CO_{2\,(g)}$ has a two-step mechanism:

Step 1: $2NO_{2\,(g)} \rightarrow NO_{(g)} + NO_{3\,(g)}$

Step 2: $NO_{3\,(g)} + CO_{(g)} \rightarrow NO_{2\,(g)} + CO_{2\,(g)}$

The rate equation for this reaction is rate = $k[NO_2]^2$.

a) What is the rate-determining step of this reaction? Explain your answer.

b) A one-step mechanism was also proposed for this reaction. How can you tell that this reaction isn't a one-step mechanism?

Q4 Under certain conditions, two molecules of ozone gas (O_3) will decompose to give oxygen gas (O_2):

$$2O_{3\,(g)} \rightarrow 3O_{2\,(g)}$$

The rate equation for this reaction was found to be rate = $k[O_3]$. Suggest a possible two-step mechanism for this reaction, given that the first step is the rate-determining step.

Q5 In the presence of an iodide (I^-) catalyst, hydrogen peroxide decomposes to give oxygen and water, as shown below:

$$2H_2O_{2\,(aq)} \rightarrow 2H_2O_{(l)} + O_{2\,(g)}$$

The rate equation for this reaction is rate = $k[H_2O_2][I^-]$.
The first step is the rate-determining step.
Suggest a possible two-step mechanism for this reaction.

Exam Tip
These mechanism questions can feel quite tricky, but don't despair — once you've had a go at all these practice questions you'll feel a lot more confident tackling the ones that come up in the exams.

Tip: Remember that you can use free radicals in possible reaction mechanisms.

Tip: Don't forget — catalysts affect the rate of a reaction so they can be included in the rate equations too.

Figure 1: *Hydrogen peroxide decomposing in the presence of an iodide ion catalyst. The bubbles are oxygen gas forming.*

Practice Questions — Fact Recall

Q1 What is the rate-determining step of a chemical reaction?

Q2 A reaction is second order with respect to oxygen. How many molecules of oxygen are involved in the rate-determining step?

Q3 One molecule of a particular reactant is involved in the rate-determining step of a reaction. What is the order of reaction with respect to that reactant?

8. The Arrhenius Equation

Changing the temperature of a reaction changes the rate constant. There's a handy equation that links the rate constant to the temperature and the activation energy of the reaction. It's time to meet the Arrhenius equation...

Learning Objectives:

- Be able to give a qualitative explanation of the effect of temperature change on the rate of a reaction and hence the rate constant.
- Know that the exponential relationship between the rate constant, k, and temperature, T, is given by the Arrhenius equation, $k = Ae^{\frac{-Ea}{RT}}$.
- Be able to determine E_a and A graphically using the equation $\ln k = \frac{-E_a}{RT} + \ln A$ derived from the Arrhenius equation.

Specification Reference 5.1.1

Rate and temperature

You learnt in the first year of the course that increasing the temperature of a reaction will increase its rate. This is because, for a reaction to happen, the particles need to collide with each other, have enough energy to react (i.e. have at least the activation energy) and have the right orientation. Increasing the temperature gives the reactant particles more kinetic energy. This means the particles speed up, so they collide more often. Increasing the temperature also means more reactant particles will have the required activation energy for the reaction, so a greater proportion of the collisions will result in the reaction actually happening. In other words, increasing temperature increases the reaction rate.

According to the rate equation, reaction rate depends only on the rate constant and reactant concentrations:

$$\text{Rate} = k[\text{A}]^m[\text{B}]^n$$

Changing the temperature won't have any effect on the concentration of the reactants, so instead it must change the rate constant. The rate constant and the temperature are correlated so the rate constant only applies to a particular reaction at a certain temperature. At a higher temperature, the reaction will have a higher rate constant.

HOW SCIENCE WORKS

Tip: The higher the rate constant, the faster the rate.

The Arrhenius equation

The **Arrhenius equation** (nasty-looking thing in the purple box) links the rate constant (k) with activation energy (E_a, the minimum amount of kinetic energy particles need to react) and temperature (T). This is probably the worst equation you're going to meet in A Level Chemistry. Luckily, it'll be on your data sheet in the exams, so you don't have to learn it off by heart. But you do need to know what all the different bits mean, and how it works.
Here it is:

$$k = Ae^{\frac{-E_a}{RT}}$$

Tip: The Arrhenius equation is an exponential relationship. The 'e' is the e^x button on your calculator.

Where:

k = rate constant

E_a = activation energy (J mol^{-1})

T = temperature (K)

R = gas constant ($8.31\ \text{J K}^{-1}\ \text{mol}^{-1}$)

A = the pre-exponential factor (another constant. The units are the same as the rate constant.)

You can use the Arrhenius equation to predict how the rate constant (and so the rate of a reaction) will change if you change certain parameters, such as the activation energy or the temperature of the reaction.

Exam Tip
Always double-check the units of any values you're given in the exams, as you may need to convert them before you use them in the Arrhenius equation. Temperature needs to be in kelvin, and the activation energy needs to be in joules per mole.

The rate constant and activation energy

As the activation energy, E_a, gets bigger, k gets smaller. You can test this out by trying different numbers for E_a in the equation... ahh go on, have a go.

Tip: e^{-x} is the same as '$1 \div e^x$', so as x gets bigger, e^{-x} gets smaller.

Tip: The term $e^{-E_a/RT}$ is called the exponential.

Examples — Maths Skills

If you increase the activation energy, then this fraction becomes a larger, more negative number...

$$k = Ae^{\frac{-E_a}{RT}}$$

...which results in the value of the exponential becoming smaller, and so k also gets smaller.

If you decrease the activation energy, then this fraction becomes a smaller, less negative number...

$$k = Ae^{\frac{-E_a}{RT}}$$

...which results in the value of the exponential becoming larger, and so k also increases.

Tip: Increasing A will also increase the rate constant. R, the gas constant, never changes.

So, a large E_a will mean a slow rate. This makes sense when you think about it. If a reaction has a high activation energy, then not many of the reactant particles will have enough energy to react. So only a few of the collisions will result in the reaction actually happening, and the rate will be slow.

Tip: R, the gas constant, is a defined physical constant and never changes. By contrast, even though k and A are called constants, they are only constant for a particular reaction under certain conditions.

The rate constant and temperature

The equation also shows that as the temperature rises, k increases.

Examples — Maths Skills

If you increase the temperature, then this fraction becomes a smaller, less negative number...

$$k = Ae^{\frac{-E_a}{RT}}$$

...which results in the value of the exponential increasing, and so k increases.

If you decrease the temperature, then this fraction becomes a larger, more negative number...

$$k = Ae^{\frac{-E_a}{RT}}$$

...which results in the value of the exponential becoming smaller, and so k also decreases.

The temperature dependence makes sense too. Higher temperatures mean reactant particles move around faster and with more energy, so they're more likely to collide and more likely to collide with at least the activation energy, so the reaction rate increases.

Figure 1: *Svante Arrhenius, the chemist who came up with the Arrhenius equation.*

Rearranging the Arrhenius equation

Putting the Arrhenius equation into logarithmic form makes it a bit easier to use.

Example — Maths Skills

- The exponential form of the Arrhenius equation is:

$$k = Ae^{\frac{-E_a}{RT}}$$

- If you take the natural logarithm of each side of this equation you get:

$$\ln(k) = \ln(Ae^{\frac{-E_a}{RT}})$$

- The logarithm of two numbers that are multiplied together is equal to the sum of their logs:

$$= \ln(A) + \ln(e^{\frac{-E_a}{RT}})$$

- $\ln(x)$ and e^x are inverses of each other, so $\ln(e^x) = x$. Therefore,

$$\ln k = \frac{-E_a}{RT} + \ln A$$

Tip: Here, you can use the log rule that log (AB) = log A + log B. There's more about log rules in the Maths Skills section on page 277.

Tip: There's a handy 'ln' button on your calculator that you can use for finding the natural logarithm of a number.

Arrhenius plots

You can use the logarithmic form of the Arrhenius equation to create an **Arrhenius plot** by plotting ln k against $\frac{1}{T}$. This will produce a graph with a gradient of $\frac{-E_a}{R}$ and a y-intercept of ln A. So once you've plotted the graph, you can find both the activation energy and the pre-exponential factor.

Tip: The logarithmic version of the Arrhenius equation, $\ln(k) = \frac{-E_a}{RT} + \ln A$ is in the form $y = mx + c$, the equation for a straight-line graph.

Example — Maths Skills

The graph below shows an Arrhenius plot for the decomposition of hydrogen iodide (an overall second order reaction). Calculate the activation energy and the pre-exponential factor for this reaction. R = 8.31 J K^{-1} mol^{-1}.

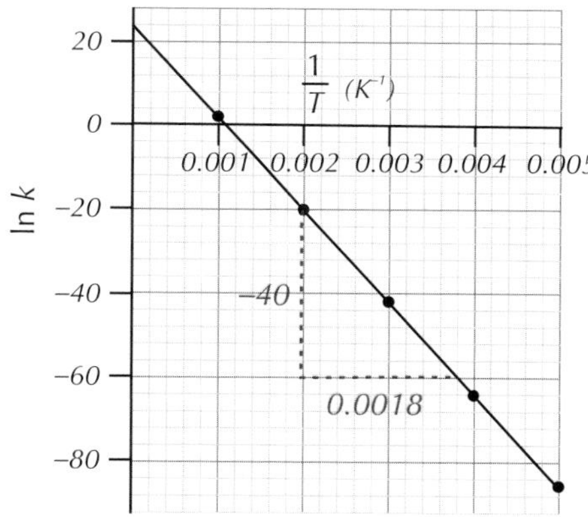

- To find the value of E_a, find the gradient of the line of best fit from the Arrhenius plot:

  The gradient, $\frac{-E_a}{R} = \frac{-40}{0.0018} = -22\,222...$

  Now rearrange the equation $\frac{-E_a}{R} = -22\,222...$ to find the value of E_a:

  $E_a = -(-22\,222... \times R) = -(-22\,222... \times 8.31)$

  $= 184\,666...$ J mol^{-1} = **185 kJ mol^{-1}**

- The value of ln A is found from the y-intercept:

  ln A = 24

  So, $A = e^{24}$ = **3 × 10^{10} dm^3 mol^{-1} s^{-1}**

Exam Tip

E_a should always be a positive answer, so if you get a negative result, check your calculation to see where you've slipped up.

Tip: The value for A might vary a bit depending on whether you calculate it from the intercept or by substituting values into the logarithmic form of the Arrhenius equation. As long as they're in the same order of magnitude (raised to the same power of ten), then you don't need to worry.

- You could also find A by substituting values back into the logarithmic form of the Arrhenius equation now that you know E_a. You can use any data point from your graph to give you a value for k and T.

  When $\ln k = -20$, $\frac{1}{T} = 0.002$

  So $-20 = \frac{-184\,666...}{8.31} \times 0.002 + \ln A$

  $\ln A = -20 + 44.4... = 24.4...$

  $A = e^{24.4...} = \mathbf{4 \times 10^{10}\ dm^3\ mol^{-1}\ s^{-1}}$

  You can use the value of $\ln A$ calculated by substitution to check the value you obtained from the intercept. Here, they're both very similar (24.0 and 24.4), so both calculations have been done correctly.

Tip: If the axes are drawn so that you can't find the y-intercept, then you have to find A by substituting values into the logarithmic form of the Arrhenius equation.

Practice Questions — Application

Q1 Two reactions, reaction A and reaction B, are carried out at a temperature of 30 °C. Reaction A has an activation energy of 141.9 kJ mol^{-1}, and Reaction B has an activation energy of 132.9 kJ mol^{-1}.

a) Predict which reaction will have a larger rate constant. Explain your answer using the Arrhenius equation.

b) Reaction A is carried out again using the same concentration of reactants as before, but this time at a temperature of 45 °C. Predict whether this reaction will occur at a faster or slower rate than before, using the Arrhenius equation to explain your answer.

Q2 The table below shows how the rate constant of the following second order reaction changes with temperature:

$$H_2 + I_2 \rightarrow 2HI$$

Temperature / K	k / dm^3 mol^{-1} s^{-1}
280	1.25×10^{-21}
300	1.79×10^{-19}
320	1.38×10^{-17}
340	6.34×10^{-14}
360	1.91×10^{-14}
380	4.02×10^{-13}

a) Use the data to draw an Arrhenius plot.

b) Calculate the activation energy, E_a, for this reaction.

c) Calculate the pre-exponential factor, A, for this reaction.

Exam Tip
You'll be given the Arrhenius equation in the exam. It's:

$$k = Ae^{\frac{-E_a}{RT}}$$

Tip: Before you draw the graph in Question 2, you'll have to work out $1/T$ and $\ln k$ at each point.

Practice Questions — Fact Recall

Q1 Define each of the following terms in the Arrhenius equation, and state their units:

a) k b) E_a c) T d) A

Q2 Write the logarithmic form of the Arrhenius equation.

Q3 What is the significance of the gradient of the line given by a plot of $\ln k$ against $1/T$?

Section Summary

Make sure you know...

- That reaction rate is the change in the amount of reactants or products per unit time.
- The techniques and procedures used to investigate reaction rates, such as measuring volumes of gases or using colorimetry.
- How to convert data collected from continuous monitoring experiments into concentration-time data.
- How to work out reaction rates from concentration-time graphs.
- How to measure the initial rate of a reaction using the initial rates method.
- How to measure the initial rate of a reaction using a clock reaction.
- That reaction orders tell you how a reactant's concentration affects the rate of reaction.
- That the overall order of a reaction is the sum of the orders of all the reactants.
- How to use the initial rates method to work out reaction orders.
- How to deduce reaction orders from rate-concentration and concentration-time graphs.
- That the rate equation for the reaction $A + B \rightarrow C + D$ is rate = $k[A]^m[B]^n$.
- What each of the terms in the rate equation means.
- How to use the rate equation to predict the rate of a reaction.
- How to calculate the rate constant and its units, using the rate equation and experimental data.
- How to calculate the rate constant of a first order reaction from a rate-concentration graph.
- That the half-life of a reaction is the time taken for the amount of reactant to halve.
- How to deduce half-lives from concentration-time graphs.
- That the half-lives of first order reactions don't vary with concentration (the half-life is constant).
- How to find the rate constant of a first order reaction from the half-life.
- That the rate-determining step is the slowest step in a reaction mechanism.
- How to use the rate equation to determine which step in a reaction is the rate-determining step.
- How to propose a reaction mechanism from the rate equation and the overall equation for a reaction.
- That the rate constant, k, is always the same for a certain reaction at a particular temperature.
- That the Arrhenius equation links the rate constant to the activation energy and the temperature.
- That increasing the temperature increases the rate constant.
- That the Arrhenius equation can be rearranged into a logarithmic form, $\ln k = \ln A - E_a/RT$
- That the gradient of a graph of $1/T$ against $\ln k$ gives a straight line graph where the gradient is equal to $-E_a/R$, and the y-intercept is equivalent to $\ln A$.

Exam-style Questions

1 Increasing the value of which of the following variables will result in a decrease in rate, given that $k = Ae^{\frac{-E_a}{RT}}$?

A The Arrhenius constant.

B The temperature.

C The activation energy.

D The pressure.

(1 mark)

2 A reaction, A + B → C, is first order with respect to A and second order with respect to B. When [A] = 0.426 mol dm^{-3} and [B] = 0.775 mol dm^{-3}, the rate of the reaction is 0.00238 mol dm^{-3} s^{-1}. What is the rate constant?

A 0.00930 mol^{-2} dm^6 s^{-1}

B 0.00721 mol^{-1} dm^3 s^{-1}

C 0.00360 mol^{-1} dm^3 s^{-1}

D 0.00169 mol^{-2} dm^6 s^{-1}

(1 mark)

3 What is the pre-exponential factor, A, of the first order reaction in the Arrhenius plot on the right, given that the logarithmic form of the Arrhenius equation is $\ln k = \frac{-E_a}{RT} + \ln A$?

A 1.38 s^{-1}

B 4.0 s^{-1}

C 0.60 s^{-1}

D 54.6 s^{-1}

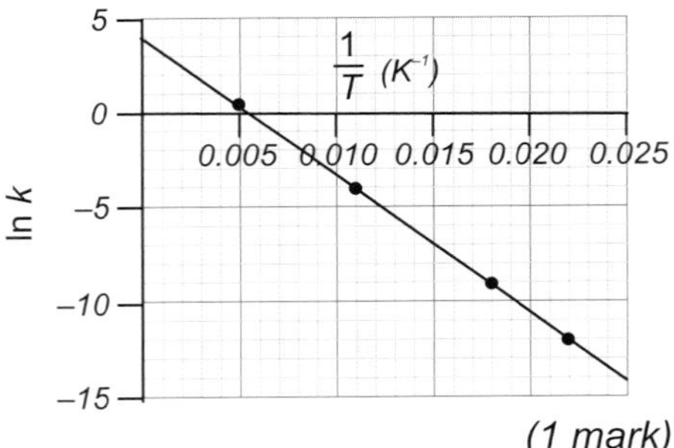

(1 mark)

4 Which of these experiments uses a continuous monitoring method?

A Measuring the time taken for 50 cm^3 of a gas to be produced at varying concentrations of one of the reactants.

B Measuring the pH of a reaction every 10 seconds from the start of the reaction until the time when the pH no longer changes.

C Measuring the time taken for a reaction that produces a gas to stop bubbling.

D Measuring how long it takes for a reaction mixture where a precipitate forms to go cloudy.

(1 mark)

5 Under certain conditions the following reaction occurs between nitrogen monoxide (NO) and hydrogen (H_2):

$$2NO_{(g)} + 2H_{2(g)} \rightarrow N_{2(g)} + 2H_2O_{(g)}$$

The table below shows the results of a series of initial rate experiments for this reaction.

Experiment	[NO] (mol dm^{-3})	[H_2](mol dm^{-3})	Initial rate (mol dm^{-3} s^{-1})
1	3.0×10^{-3}	6.0×10^{-3}	4.50×10^{-3}
2	3.0×10^{-3}	3.0×10^{-3}	2.25×10^{-3}
3	6.0×10^{-3}	1.5×10^{-3}	4.50×10^{-3}

(a) Determine the orders of reaction with respect to NO and H_2.

(2 marks)

(b) Write out the rate equation for this reaction.

(1 mark)

(c) Using the data above, calculate the rate constant (k) for this reaction and give its units.

(3 marks)

(d) What would the rate of reaction be if 4.5×10^{-3} mol dm^{-3} NO were mixed with 2.5×10^{-3} mol dm^{-3} H_2 under the same conditions as the experiment above?

(2 marks)

(e) (i) Using the rate equation, explain why a one-step mechanism is not possible for this reaction.

(2 marks)

(ii) Suggest a possible two step mechanism for this reaction. The first step is the slowest step.

(2 marks)

6 The table below shows how the rate constant, k, varies with temperature for the second order reaction:

$$CF_3Cl + Cl\bullet \rightarrow \bullet CF_3 + Cl_2$$

Temperature / °C	50	100	150	250	300
k / mol^{-1} dm^3 s^{-1}	1.96×10^{-31}	1.36×10^{-28}	2.01×10^{-26}	2.50×10^{-23}	3.47×10^{-22}

(a) Draw an Arrhenius plot of $1/T$ against $\ln k$.

(5 marks)

(b) Use the equation; $\ln k = \frac{-E_a}{RT} + \ln A$, to find:

(i) The activation energy, E_a, of the reaction.

(2 marks)

(ii) The pre-exponential factor, A, of the reaction.

(2 marks)

7 Under certain conditions, 2-chloro-2-methylpropane, $(CH_3)_3CCl$, will react with hydroxide ions as shown below:

$$(CH_3)_3CCl_{(aq)} + OH^-_{(aq)} \rightarrow (CH_3)_3COH_{(aq)} + Cl^-_{(aq)}$$

The reaction is zero order with respect to hydroxide ions. The graph below shows how the concentration of $(CH_3)_3CCl$ changes over time:

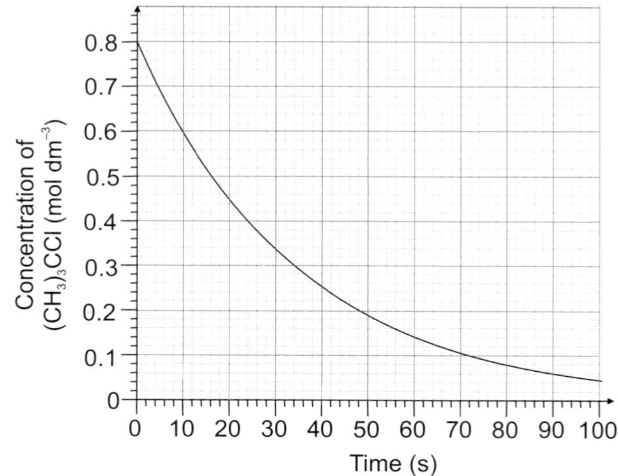

(a) (i) Given that the overall reaction is either zero or first order, what is the order of reaction with respect to $(CH_3)_3CCl$?

(1 mark)

(ii) Sketch a graph to show the shape of the rate-concentration graph for this reaction with respect to the concentration of $(CH_3)_3CCl$.

(1 mark)

(b) Write a rate equation for this reaction.

(1 mark)

(c) Calculate the rate of the reaction after:

(i) 20 seconds

(1 mark)

(ii) 40 seconds

(1 mark)

(d) What is the half-life of the reaction?

(1 mark)

(e) Find the rate constant, *k*, for this reaction.

(1 mark)

(f) Use your value of the rate constant to predict the rate of the reaction when the concentration of 2-chloro-2-methylpropane is 1.35 mol dm^{-3} and the concentration of hydroxide ions is 0.725 mol dm^{-3}.

(1 mark)

(g) Given that this reaction occurs in two steps, and the first step is the rate-determining step, predict a mechanism for this reaction.

(2 marks)

1. The Equilibrium Constant

Hopefully you should remember a bit about reversible reactions and equilibrium constants from Year 1. For Year 2 you need to learn a bit more detail. But first, a quick recap of dynamic equilibrium.

Learning Objectives:

- Be able to calculate K_c, or related quantities, including determination of units.
- Be able to calculate quantities present at equilibrium, given appropriate data.
- Be able to describe the techniques and procedures used to determine quantities present at equilibrium.
- Be able to deduce expressions for K_c for homogeneous and heterogeneous equilibria.

Specification Reference 5.1.2

Dynamic equilibrium

When a reversible reaction reaches dynamic equilibrium, the forward and reverse reactions are going at the same rate and there's no overall change in the concentrations of the reactants and products. A dynamic equilibrium can only happen in a **closed system** (a system where nothing can get in or out) at a constant temperature. Equilibria can be set up in physical systems and chemical systems:

Examples

Physical Systems

When liquid bromine is shaken in a closed flask, some of it changes to orange bromine gas. After a while, equilibrium is reached — bromine liquid is still changing to bromine gas and bromine gas is still changing to bromine liquid, but they are changing at the same rate.

$$Br_{2(l)} \rightleftharpoons Br_{2(g)}$$

Chemical Systems

If hydrogen gas and iodine gas are mixed together in a closed flask, hydrogen iodide is formed.

$$H_{2(g)} + I_{2(g)} \rightleftharpoons 2HI_{(g)}$$

Imagine that 1.0 mole of hydrogen gas is mixed with 1.0 mole of iodine gas at a constant temperature of 640 K. When this mixture reaches equilibrium, there will be 1.6 moles of hydrogen iodide and 0.2 moles of both hydrogen gas and iodine gas. No matter how long you leave them at this temperature, the equilibrium amounts never change. As with the physical system, it's all a matter of the forward and backward rates being equal.

Figure 1: A flask containing bromine at equilibrium.

The equilibrium constant, K_c

You'll have encountered the expression for the **equilibrium constant**, K_c, in Year 1 but you'll be using it a lot over the next couple of pages so it never hurts to recap:

The lower-case letters a, b, d and e are the number of moles of each substance in the equation.

For the general reaction $aA + bB \rightleftharpoons dD + eE$:

$$K_c = \frac{[D]^d[E]^e}{[A]^a[B]^b}$$

The square brackets, [ ], mean concentration in mol dm^{-3}.

The products go on the top line and the reactants go on the bottom line.

Tip: The superscript numbers look like the orders of reaction that you saw in rate equations. But they're not — they're the numbers of moles in the equation.

Tip: If K_c is large, at equilibrium there will be lots of product and not much reactant. If K_c is small, it's the other way around — at equilibrium there'll be lots of reactant but not much product.

Exam Tip
In exam questions on K_c you'll often be told the temperature. You don't need this value for your calculation — it's just so you know the temperature is constant.

Calculating K_c

If you know the equilibrium concentrations, just bung them in your expression. Then with a bit of help from the old calculator, you can work out the value of K_c. The units are a bit trickier though — they vary, so you have to work them out after each calculation.

Example — Maths Skills

Calculate K_c, including units, for the reaction:

$$N_2O_{4(g)} \rightleftharpoons 2NO_{2(g)}$$

At 298 K, the equilibrium concentrations are:
$[N_2O_4] = 4.17 \times 10^{-2}$ mol dm^{-3}, $[NO_2] = 1.41 \times 10^{-3}$ mol dm^{-3}

Just stick the concentrations into the expression for K_c:

$$K_c = \frac{[NO_2]^2}{[N_2O_4]} = \frac{(0.00141)^2}{0.0417} = 4.77 \times 10^{-5}$$

Now work out the units for the equilibrium constant by substituting the units for each component into the expression for K_c:

$$K_c = \frac{(\text{mol dm}^{-3})\cancel{(\text{mol dm}^{-3})}}{\cancel{\text{mol dm}^{-3}}} = \text{mol dm}^{-3}$$

So K_c = **4.77×10^{-5} mol dm^{-3}**

Tip: K_c has units of mol dm^{-3} in this example but this won't always be the case, so always work the units out — there's often a mark for giving the correct units in the exam.

You might have to figure out some of the equilibrium concentrations before you can find K_c. To do this follow these steps:

Step 1: Find out how many moles of each reactant and product there are at equilibrium.
(You'll usually be given the number of moles at equilibrium for one of the reactants. You can then use the balanced reaction equation to work out the number of moles of all the others.)

Step 2: Calculate the molar concentrations of each reactant and product by dividing each number of moles by the volume of the reaction.
(You'll be told the volume in the question but you may have to convert it into different units. To work out molar concentrations you need the volume to be in dm^3.)

Tip: The molar concentration is just the concentration in mol dm^{-3}.

Once you've done this you're ready to substitute your values into the expression for K_c and calculate it.

Example — Maths Skills

0.20 moles of phosphorus(V) chloride decomposes at 600 K in a vessel of 5.00 dm^3. The equilibrium mixture is found to contain 0.080 moles of chlorine. Write the expression for K_c and calculate its value, including units.

$$PCl_{5(g)} \rightleftharpoons PCl_{3(g)} + Cl_{2(g)}$$

1. Find out how many moles of PCl_5 and PCl_3 there are at equilibrium:
   - The equation tells you that when 1 mole of PCl_5 decomposes, 1 mole of PCl_3 and 1 mole of Cl_2 are formed.
   - So if 0.080 moles of chlorine are produced at equilibrium, then there will be 0.080 moles of PCl_3 as well.

Exam Tip
For long wordy questions like this it can help to highlight any important bits of information before you start — e.g. any concentrations or volumes you're given.

- 0.080 moles of PCl_5 must have decomposed to form 0.080 moles of Cl_2 and PCl_3, so there will be 0.12 moles of PCl_5 left at equilibrium (0.20 – 0.080 = 0.12).

2. Divide each number of moles by the volume of the flask to give the molar concentrations:

$$[PCl_3] = [Cl_2] = \frac{0.080}{5.00} = 0.016 \text{ mol dm}^{-3}$$

$$[PCl_5] = \frac{0.12}{5.00} = 0.024 \text{ mol dm}^{-3}$$

3. Put the concentrations in the expression for K_c and calculate it:

$$K_c = \frac{[PCl_3][Cl_2]}{[PCl_5]} = \frac{[0.016][0.016]}{[0.024]} = 0.011$$

4. Now find the units of K_c:

$$K_c = \frac{(\text{mol dm}^{-3})\cancel{(\text{mol dm}^{-3})}}{\cancel{\text{mol dm}^{-3}}} = \text{mol dm}^{-3}$$

So K_c = **0.011 mol dm^{-3}**

Exam Tip
You may be asked to calculate the molar amounts of some substances in an earlier part of the question — if this happens you can reuse your answers to find K_c. Handy.

Exam Tip
When you're writing expressions for K_c make sure you use [square brackets]. If you use (rounded brackets) you won't get the marks.

Here's one more example.

Example — Maths Skills

0.100 mol dm^{-3} Cu^{2+} ions are mixed with 0.300 mol dm^{-3} HCl to form the following equilibrium: $Cu^{2+}_{(aq)} + 4Cl^-_{(aq)} \rightleftharpoons [CuCl_4]^{2-}_{(aq)}$
At equilibrium, the concentration of $[CuCl_4]^{2-}_{(aq)}$ is x mol dm^{-3}.
Write an expression for K_c in terms of x.

From the equation, for every mole of $[CuCl_4]^{2-}_{(aq)}$ formed, you will lose 1 mole $Cu^{2+}_{(aq)}$ and 4 moles $Cl^-_{(aq)}$ from your initial reactant concentrations. So if x moles of $[CuCl_4]^{2-}_{(aq)}$ have formed, you will have lost x moles $Cu^{2+}_{(aq)}$ and $4x$ moles $Cl^-_{(aq)}$. So the equilibrium concentrations will be:

- $Cu^{2+}_{(aq)}$ = (initial $Cu^{2+}_{(aq)}$ concentration) – x
- $Cl^-_{(aq)}$ = (initial $Cl^-_{(aq)}$ concentration) – $4x$

You can use this information to construct a table:

Equilibrium component	$Cu^{2+}_{(aq)}$	$Cl^-_{(aq)}$	$[CuCl_4]^{2-}_{(aq)}$
Initial conc. (mol dm^{-3})	0.100	0.300	0
Equilibrium conc. (mol dm^{-3})	$0.100 - x$	$0.300 - 4x$	x

From your equilibrium concentrations, you can see that:

$$K_c = \frac{[[CuCl_4]^{2-}]}{[Cu^{2+}][Cl^-]^4} = \frac{\boldsymbol{x}}{\mathbf{(0.100 - \boldsymbol{x})(0.300 - 4\boldsymbol{x})^4}}$$

Tip: The square brackets in $[CuCl_4]^{2-}_{(aq)}$ in this example show that the species is a complex ion — it has nothing to do with concentration.

At 291 K, the equilibrium concentration of $[CuCl_4]^{2-}$ for the equilibrium shown above is 0.0637 mol dm^{-3}. Calculate K_c.

Substitute the concentration of $[CuCl_4]^{2-}$ at equilibrium for x:

$$x = 0.0637 \text{ mol dm}^{-3}, \text{ so } K_c = \frac{0.0637}{(0.100 - 0.0637)(0.300 - 4 \times 0.0637)^4}$$

= **4.20 × 10^5 mol^{-4} dm^{12}**

Using K_c

If you know the value of K_c you can use it to find unknown equilibrium concentrations. Here's how you do it:

Step 1: Put all the values you know into the expression for K_c.

Step 2: Rearrange the equation and solve it to find the unknown values.

Tip: Equilibrium concentrations can be determined experimentally by measuring pH, if the equilibrium involves an acid or base (see page 84). A colorimeter can be used to determine equilibrium concentrations if the equilibrium species are coloured (see page 18).

Example — Maths Skills

When ethanoic acid was allowed to reach equilibrium with ethanol at 25 °C, it was found that the equilibrium mixture contained 2.0 mol dm^{-3} ethanoic acid and 3.5 mol dm^{-3} ethanol. The K_c of the equilibrium is 4.0 at 25 °C. What are the concentrations of the other components?

$$CH_3COOH_{(l)} + C_2H_5OH_{(l)} \rightleftharpoons CH_3COOC_2H_{5(l)} + H_2O_{(l)}$$

1. Put all the values you know in the K_c expression:

$$K_c = \frac{[CH_3COOC_2H_5][H_2O]}{[CH_3COOH][C_2H_5OH]} \quad \text{so} \quad 4.0 = \frac{[CH_3COOC_2H_5][H_2O]}{2.0 \times 3.5}$$

2. Rearranging this gives:

$$[CH_3COOC_2H_5][H_2O] = 4.0 \times 2.0 \times 3.5 = 28.0$$

From the equation, you know that $[CH_3COOC_2H_5] = [H_2O]$, so:

$$[CH_3COOC_2H_5] = [H_2O] = \sqrt{28} = 5.3 \text{ mol dm}^{-3}$$

The concentration of $CH_3COOC_2H_5$ and H_2O is **5.3 mol dm^{-3}**.

Tip: The units of concentration should always be mol dm^{-3}. If your answer doesn't give you this then go back and check your calculation to see where you've gone wrong.

Calculating K_c for heterogeneous equilibria

If all the reactants and products in a reaction are in the same state (e.g. they're all gases, or all in solution) then the reaction is homogeneous. All the calculations in this topic so far have involved homogeneous equilibria. But if the reactants and products in a reaction are in different states the reaction is heterogeneous. A heterogeneous reaction can change what you put in the equilibrium constant expression. The rule is:

- If the mixture is homogeneous, all the reactants and products are put into the expression for the equilibrium constant.
- If the mixture is heterogeneous, only gases and aqueous substances go into the expression for the equilibrium constant (any solids or liquids get left out).

Example — Maths Skills

Write an expression for the equilibrium constant of the following reaction:

$$Cu_{(s)} + 2Ag^+_{(aq)} \rightleftharpoons Cu^{2+}_{(aq)} + 2Ag_{(s)}$$

The reactants and products are a mixture of aqueous and solid. So the reaction is heterogeneous. Only the aqueous substances go into the equilibrium constant.

$$\text{So } K_c = \frac{[Cu^{2+}]}{[Ag^+]^2}$$

At a certain temperature, there are 0.431 mol dm^{-3} Ag^+ and 0.193 mol dm^{-3} Cu^{2+} at equilibrium. Calculate K_c and give its units.

$$K_c = \frac{[Cu^{2+}]}{[Ag^+]^2} = \frac{0.193}{(0.431)^2} = 1.04$$

The units are $\frac{(\text{mol dm}^{-3})}{(\text{mol dm}^{-3})^2} = \frac{1}{\text{mol dm}^{-3}} = \text{mol}^{-1}\,\text{dm}^3$

So K_c = **1.04 mol^{-1} dm^3**

Tip: If the units end up as (1 / mol dm^{-3}), you write that as mol^{-1} dm^3.

Practice Questions — Application

Q1 The following equilibrium exists under certain conditions:

$$C_2H_{4(g)} + H_2O_{(g)} \rightleftharpoons C_2H_5OH_{(g)}$$

a) Write out the expression for the equilibrium constant, K_c, for this reaction.

5.00 moles of C_2H_5OH was placed in a container and allowed to reach equilibrium. At a certain temperature and pressure the equilibrium mixture was found to contain 1.85 moles of C_2H_4, and have a total volume of 15.0 dm^3.

b) Determine the number of moles of each substance at equilibrium.

c) Calculate the molar concentrations (in mol dm^{-3}) of all the reagents at equilibrium.

d) Calculate K_c for this equilibrium.

At a different temperature and pressure, the value of K_c = 3.8 and the equilibrium mixture contained 0.80 mol dm^{-3} C_2H_5OH.

e) Determine the equilibrium concentrations of C_2H_4 and H_2O under these conditions.

Tip: Don't forget — you need to work out the units of K_c too.

Q2 Under certain conditions the following equilibrium is established:

$$2SO_{2(g)} + O_{2(g)} \rightleftharpoons 2SO_{3(g)}$$

a) Write out an expression for K_c for this reaction.

At a certain temperature, the equilibrium concentrations for the three reagents were found to be:

SO_2 = 0.250 mol dm^{-3} O_2 = 0.180 mol dm^{-3} SO_3 = 0.360 mol dm^{-3}

b) Calculate K_c for this equilibrium.

c) If all other conditions (including the concentrations of O_2 and SO_3) were to stay the same, what would the equilibrium concentration of SO_2 have to be for K_c to be 15?

Q3 250 cm³ 0.500 mol dm^{-3} iron(II) sulfate solution is added to 250 cm³ 0.500 mol dm^{-3} silver(I) nitrate at 298 K to set up the following equilibrium reaction:

$$Fe^{2+}_{(aq)} + Ag^{+}_{(aq)} \rightleftharpoons Fe^{3+}_{(aq)} + Ag_{(s)}$$

Once the solution has reached equilibrium, a sample is taken and titrated to calculate the concentration of Fe^{2+} ions. Given that at equilibrium, $[Fe^{2+}_{(aq)}]$ = 0.0844 mol dm^{-3}, calculate K_c.

Practice Questions — Fact Recall

Q1 Explain what is meant by the term 'dynamic equilibrium'.

Q2 Describe the conditions that are needed for a dynamic equilibrium to be established.

Q3 Write out an expression for K_c for the general reaction:

$$aA + bB \rightleftharpoons dD + eE$$

Q4 What are the units of K_c?

2. Gas Equilibria

When you're dealing with equilibrium reactions involving gases, it's easier to think in terms of pressure than in terms of concentrations. A gaseous equilibrium system will have a total pressure, but there will also be individual pressures for each of the individual gases. These are called partial pressures.

Learning Objectives:

- Be able to use the terms partial pressure and mole fraction.
- Be able to calculate K_p, or related quantities, including determination of units.
- Be able to deduce expressions for K_p for homogeneous and heterogeneous equilibria.

Specification Reference 5.1.2

Partial pressures

In a mixture of gases, each individual gas exerts its own pressure — this is called its **partial pressure**.

Example

The reaction between hydrogen and iodine vapour is an example of a gaseous equilibrium reaction.

$$H_{2(g)} + I_{2(g)} \rightleftharpoons 2HI_{(g)}$$

In this reaction, the total pressure can be expressed as:

Total pressure = $p(H_2) + p(I_2) + p(HI)$

In the example above, hydrogen, iodine and hydrogen iodide are all gases and will all exert a pressure on the system. The size of the pressure exerted by each gas doesn't have to be the same. Partial pressures are often written as $p(X)$ — this just means the partial pressure of X. The partial pressure of X depends on the number of moles of X present.

The total pressure of a gas mixture is the sum of all the partial pressures of the individual gases. You can put this fact into use when dealing with pressure calculations, such as the one below.

Figure 1: John Dalton, the English chemist, who came up with the theory that the total pressure of a mixture of gases is equal to the sum of the partial pressures of the gases in the mixture. This theory is also known as Dalton's Law.

Example — Maths Skills

When 3.00 moles of the gas PCl_5 is heated, it decomposes into PCl_3 and Cl_2:

$$PCl_{5(g)} \rightleftharpoons PCl_{3(g)} + Cl_{2(g)}$$

In a sealed vessel at 500 K, the equilibrium mixture contains chlorine with a partial pressure of 263 kPa. If the total pressure of the mixture is 714 kPa, what is the partial pressure of PCl_5?

From the equation, you know that PCl_3 and Cl_2 are produced in equal amounts, so the partial pressures of these two gases are the same at equilibrium — they're both 263 kPa.

Total pressure = $p(PCl_5) + p(PCl_3) + p(Cl_2)$

$$714 = p(PCl_5) + 263 + 263$$

So the partial pressure of PCl_5 = 714 – 263 – 263 = **188 kPa**

Mole fractions

Partial pressures can be worked out from mole fractions. A '**mole fraction**' is just the proportion of a gas mixture that is a made up of a particular gas. So if you have four moles of gas in total and two of them are gas A, the mole fraction of gas A is 0.5. There are two formulas you need on the next page.

Exam Tip
You won't be given these equations in the exam — make sure you learn them off by heart so you can handle any K_p calculations the examiners could throw at you.

Mole fraction of a gas in a mixture = $\frac{\textbf{number of moles of gas}}{\textbf{total number of moles of gas in the mixture}}$

Partial pressure of a gas in a mixture = mole fraction of gas × total pressure of the mixture

Example — Maths Skills

When 3.00 moles of PCl_5 is heated in a sealed vessel, the equilibrium mixture contains 1.75 moles of chlorine. If the total pressure of the mixture is 714 kPa, what is the partial pressure of PCl_5?

First, write out a chemical equation so you can see what's happening:

$$PCl_{5(g)} \rightleftharpoons PCl_{3(g)} + Cl_{2(g)}$$

From the equation, PCl_3 and Cl_2 are produced in equal amounts, so there'll be 1.75 moles of PCl_3 too.

1.75 moles of PCl_5 must have decomposed, so (3.00 – 1.75) = 1.25 moles of PCl_5 must be left at equilibrium.

This means that the total number of moles of gas at equilibrium = 1.75 + 1.75 + 1.25 = 4.75.

So the mole fraction of $PCl_5 = \frac{1.25}{4.75} = 0.263...$

The partial pressure of PCl_5 = mole fraction × total pressure
= 0.263... × 714 = **188 kPa**

Tip: You need to use a balanced chemical equation when working out mole fractions — you have to take into account the ratio of the number of moles of each gas when working out the mole fraction of a particular reactant or product.

The gas equilibrium constant, K_p

K_p is the equilibrium constant for a reversible reaction where some, or all, of the reactants and products are gases. The expression for K_p is just like the one for K_c, except you use partial pressures instead of concentrations.

Tip: K_c and K_p work in pretty much exactly the same way — K_p is just specifically for gases.

For the equilibrium
$aA_{(g)} + bB_{(g)} \rightleftharpoons dD_{(g)} + eE_{(g)}$ $\quad K_p = \frac{p(D)^d p(E)^e}{p(A)^a p(B)^b}$

Example

Write an expression for K_p for the following reaction.

$$O_{3(g)} + H_2O_{(g)} \rightleftharpoons H_{2(g)} + 2O_{2(g)}$$

There are two moles of O_2 in the balanced equation, so the partial pressure of O_2 needs to be raised to the power of 2.

$$K_p = \frac{p(O_2)^2 \times p(H_2)}{p(O_3) \times p(H_2O)}$$

The reactants go on the bottom of the expression.

The products go on the top of the expression.

Tip: Solid, liquid and aqueous substances don't appear in the expression for K_p. They also don't contribute to the total pressure of a system (see page 60).

Tip: Make sure your chemical equation is balanced — otherwise you'll get your expression for K_p wrong.

To calculate K_p you put the partial pressures in the expression. Then you work out the units like you did for K_c.

Tip: If you're given an equation that contains a non-gaseous chemical, then don't include it in your equation for K_p. For example:
$H_2O_{(g)} + C_{(s)} \rightleftharpoons H_{2(g)} + CO_{(g)}$

$$K_p = \frac{p(H_2) \times p(CO)}{p(H_2O)}$$

C is not included in the expression for K_p because it's a solid — not a gas. There's more about this on the next page.

Example — Maths Skills

Calculate K_p for the decomposition of PCl_5 gas at 500 K. The partial pressures of each gas are:
$p(PCl_5)$ = 188 kPa, $p(PCl_3)$ = 263 kPa, $p(Cl_2)$ = 263 kPa

Start by writing out a balanced chemical equation:
$PCl_{5\,(g)} \rightleftharpoons PCl_{3\,(g)} + Cl_{2\,(g)}$

Now, write an expression for K_p. Remember, the reactants go on the bottom of the expression, and the products go on the top.

$$K_p = \frac{p(Cl_2) \times p(PCl_2)}{p(PCl_5)}$$

Then just substitute in all the partial pressure values you were given in the question.

$$K_p = \frac{263 \times 263}{188} = 368$$

To find the units, substitute all the partial pressure units into your expression for K_p, then cancel down as much as you can.

$$K_p = \frac{\cancel{kPa} \times kPa}{\cancel{kPa}} = kPa \qquad \text{So } K_p = \mathbf{368\ kPa}$$

Tip: K_p is temperature dependent (see page 59). So, a particular value of K_p is only valid at a given temperature.

You might be given K_p for a reaction and have to use it to calculate equilibrium partial pressures.

Example — Maths Skills

An equilibrium exists between ethanoic acid monomers, CH_3COOH, and dimers, $(CH_3COOH)_2$. At 160 °C the K_p for the reaction

$$(CH_3COOH)_{2(g)} \rightleftharpoons 2CH_3COOH_{(g)}$$

is 180 kPa. At this temperature the partial pressure of the dimer, $(CH_3COOH)_2$, is 28.5 kPa. Calculate the partial pressure of the monomer in this equilibrium and state the total pressure exerted by the equilibrium mixture.

First, use the chemical equilibrium to write an expression for K_p:

$$K_p = \frac{p(CH_3COOH)^2}{p((CH_3COOH)_2)}$$

This rearranges to give: $p(CH_3COOH)^2 = K_p \times p((CH_3COOH)_2)$

$$= 180 \times 28.5 = 5130$$

$$p(CH_3COOH) = \sqrt{5130} = 71.6 \text{ kPa}$$

So the total pressure of the equilibrium mixture = 28.5 + 71.6 = **100 kPa**

K_p for heterogeneous equilibria

You met the idea of homogeneous and heterogeneous equilibria on page 52. Up until now we've only thought about K_p expressions for homogeneous equilibria. If you're writing an expression for K_p for a heterogeneous equilibrium, you don't include solids or liquids.

Example

Write an expression for K_p for the following reaction:

$$NH_4HS_{(s)} \rightleftharpoons NH_{3(g)} + H_2S_{(g)}$$

The equilibrium is heterogeneous — a solid decomposes to form two gases. Solids don't get included in K_p, so $\boldsymbol{K_p = p(NH_3)\, p(H_2S)}$.

Tip: Being able to write balanced chemical equations is a really important skill in chemistry. It will help you solve loads of questions. Look back at your Year 1 notes for more details.

Practice Questions — Application

Q1 Ammonia gas is reacted with oxygen gas in a reversible reaction. The products are nitrogen gas and water vapour.

a) Write out a balanced chemical equation for this reaction.

b) Write out an expression for the total pressure of the system.

c) $p(O_2)$ = 85 kPa, $p(NH_3)$ = 42 kPa, $p(N_2)$ = 21 kPa, and $p(H_2O)$ = 12 kPa.
Calculate the total pressure of the system.

d) What is the mole fraction of water vapour in the system?

Q2 A sealed container holds 4.00 g of helium gas (He) and 2.81 g of oxygen gas. Given that the total pressure of the container is 8.12 kPa, what is the partial pressure of oxygen?

Tip: Remember — moles = mass ÷ M_r.

Q3 The following equation shows the reaction between benzene and hydrogen to create cyclohexane:

$$C_6H_{6\,(g)} + 3H_{2\,(g)} \rightleftharpoons C_6H_{12\,(g)}$$

a) Write an equation for K_p for the reaction above.

b) At equilibrium, the partial pressures of the three gases are all equal. Given that $K_p = 4.80 \times 10^{-13}$ kPa^{-3}, what is the partial pressure of hydrogen?

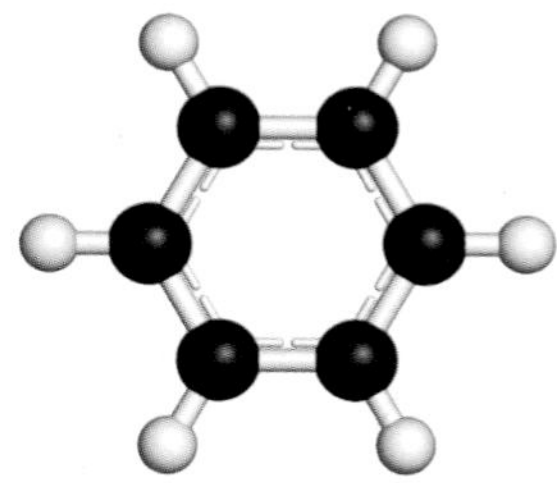

Figure 2: A molecular model of benzene (C_6H_6). In the hydrogenation of benzene, hydrogen is added to the aromatic ring to create a saturated alkane — cyclohexane.

Q4 When 24.32 moles of hydrogen fluoride are heated in a sealed vessel, the equilibrium mixture contains 9.340 moles of fluorine gas.

a) If the total pressure of the mixture is 2313 kPa, what is the partial pressure of hydrogen?

b) Calculate the gas equilibrium constant for this reaction.

Practice Questions — Fact Recall

Q1 What is meant by the term 'partial pressure'?

Q2 What equation links the mole fraction of a gas, the number of moles of that gas and the total number of moles of gas in a mixture?

Q3 What is K_p?

Q4 Write an expression for K_p for the equation: $aA_{(g)} + bB_{(g)} \rightleftharpoons dD_{(g)} + eE_{(g)}$.

3. Changing the Equilibrium

The position of equilibrium for a reaction can change if conditions change, but not all changes in conditions result in a change in the value of K_c.

Learning Objectives:

- Be able to explain the qualitative effect on equilibrium constants of changing temperature for exothermic and endothermic reactions.
- Be able to explain the constancy of equilibrium constants with changes in concentration, pressure or in the presence of a catalyst.
- Be able to explain how an equilibrium constant controls the position of equilibrium on changing concentration, pressure and temperature.

Specification Reference 5.1.2

Changing the position of equilibrium

If you change the concentration, pressure or temperature of a reversible reaction, you're going to alter the position of equilibrium. This just means you'll end up with different amounts of reactants and products at equilibrium.

- If the position of equilibrium moves to the left, you'll get more reactants.

$$H_{2(g)} + I_{2(g)} \rightleftharpoons 2HI_{(g)}$$

- If the position of equilibrium moves to the right, you'll get more products.

$$H_{2(g)} + I_{2(g)} \rightleftharpoons 2HI_{(g)}$$

There's a rule that lets you predict how the position of equilibrium will change if a condition changes. This rule is known as **Le Chatelier's Principle**:

> Le Chatelier's Principle: If there's a change in concentration, pressure or temperature, the equilibrium will move to help counteract the change.

So, basically, if you raise the temperature, the position of equilibrium will shift to try to cool things down. And if you raise the pressure or concentration, the position of equilibrium will shift to try to reduce it. Although changes in temperature and changes in concentration both affect the position of the equilibrium, only changing the temperature affects the value of K_c. The size of the equilibrium constant tells you where the equilibrium lies:

- If the equilibrium constant is greater than 1, then there will be more products than reactants (the equilibrium will lie to the right). The larger the value of K_c, the further to the right the equilibrium lies.
- If the equilibrium constant is less than 1, then there will be more reactants than products (the equilibrium will lie to the left). The smaller the value of K_c, the further to the left the equilibrium lies.

Tip: You've come across Le Chatelier's Principle before — in Module 3 of Year 1 Chemistry.

Figure 1: *Henri Le Chatelier.*

Changing the temperature

If you increase the temperature, you add heat. The equilibrium shifts in the **endothermic** (positive ΔH) direction to absorb the heat. Decreasing the temperature removes heat energy. The equilibrium shifts in the **exothermic** (negative ΔH) direction to try to replace the heat. If the forward reaction's endothermic, the reverse reaction will be exothermic, and vice versa. If the change means more product is formed, K_c will rise. If it means less product is formed, then K_c will decrease. So, changing the temperature alters the position of equilibrium and therefore the value of the equilibrium constant.

Tip: The ΔH values given for reversible reactions show the ΔH of the forward reaction.

Examples

The reaction below is exothermic in the forward direction:

Exothermic →

$$2SO_{2(g)} + O_{2(g)} \rightleftharpoons 2SO_{3(g)} \qquad \Delta H = -197 \text{ kJ mol}^{-1}$$

← *Endothermic*

Tip: If the temperature <u>decreases</u> the opposite happens — for reactions that are exothermic in the forward direction K_c will increase and for reactions that are endothermic in the forward direction K_c will decrease.

If you increase the temperature, the equilibrium shifts to the left (in the endothermic direction) to absorb some of the extra heat energy. This means that less product's formed so the concentration of product ($[SO_3]$) will be less.

$$K_c = \frac{[SO_3]^2}{[SO_2]^2[O_2]}$$

There's less product and more reactant, so the number on the top gets smaller and the number on the bottom gets bigger. This means K_c must have decreased.

The reaction below is endothermic in the forward direction:

Endothermic →

$$CH_{4(g)} \rightleftharpoons 2H_{2(g)} + C_{(s)} \qquad \Delta H = +90 \text{ kJ mol}^{-1}$$

← *Exothermic*

This time increasing the temperature shifts the equilibrium to the right. This means more product's formed, so K_c increases.

Changing the concentration

Tip: Don't get confused — the position of the equilibrium can change without affecting the value of K_c.

The value of the equilibrium constant, K_c, is fixed at a given temperature. So if the concentration of one thing in the equilibrium mixture changes then the concentrations of the others must change to keep the value of K_c the same.

Example

$$CH_3COOH_{(l)} + C_2H_5OH_{(l)} \rightleftharpoons CH_3COOC_2H_{5(l)} + H_2O_{(l)}$$

If you increase the concentration of CH_3COOH then the equilibrium will move to the right to get rid of some of the extra CH_3COOH — so more $CH_3COOC_2H_5$ and H_2O are produced. This keeps the equilibrium constant the same.

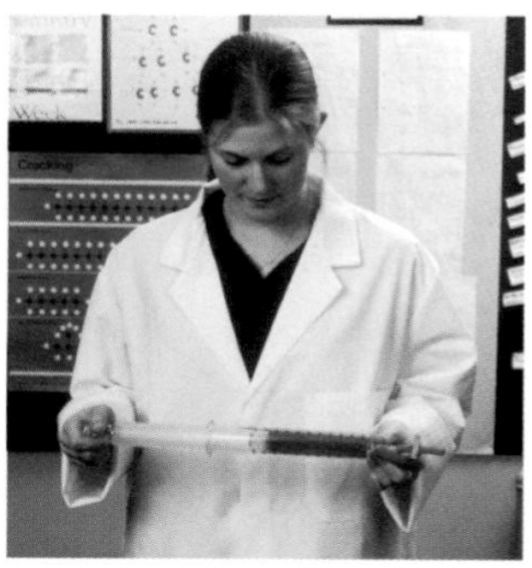

Figure 2a: Equilibrium between $NO_{2(g)}$ (brown) and $N_2O_{4(l)}$ (colourless).

Changing the pressure

Changing the pressure only really affects equilibria involving gases. Increasing the pressure shifts the equilibrium to the side with fewer gas molecules — this reduces the pressure. Decreasing the pressure shifts the equilibrium to the side with more gas molecules. This raises the pressure again. K_p and K_c stay the same, no matter what you do to the pressure.

Example

The following equilibrium exists between nitrogen dioxide (NO_2) and nitrogen tetroxide (N_2O_4):

$$2NO_{2(g)} \rightleftharpoons N_2O_{4(g)}$$

There are 2 moles of gas on the left, but only 1 mole of gas on the right. So an increase in pressure would shift the equilibrium to the right.

This shift in equilibrium can be seen because NO_2 is a brown gas (see Figure 2a). If pressure is applied to the gas (e.g. in a syringe), the colour becomes paler (see Figure 2b). This is because the equilibrium has shifted to the right and some of the brown NO_2 has been converted to N_2O_4 which is colourless.

So, the equilibrium shifts to the right. However, the values of K_p and K_c stay the same.

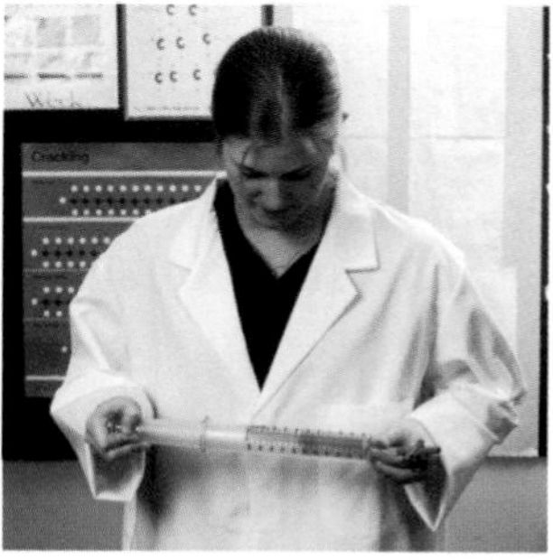

Figure 2b: When pressure is applied the colour changes because the equilibrium shifts in favour of $N_2O_{4(l)}$.

Adding a catalyst

Catalysts have no effect on the position of equilibrium or on the value of K_c or K_p. This is because a catalyst will increase the rate of both the forward and backward reactions by the same amount. As a result, the equilibrium position will be the same as the uncatalysed reaction, but equilibrium will be reached faster. So catalysts can't increase yield (the amount of product produced) — but they do decrease the time taken to reach equilibrium.

Example

The Haber process is used to synthesise ammonia:

$$N_{2(g)} + 3H_{2(g)} \rightleftharpoons 2NH_{3(g)}$$

This reaction uses an iron catalyst. Adding the iron catalyst decreases the amount of time taken for this reaction to reach equilibrium, but it has no effect on the equilibrium position or on the value of K_p or K_c.

Exam Tip
Don't be thrown if a reaction you're given in the exam has a catalyst. Catalysts don't affect the equilibrium constants.

Practice Questions — Application

Q1 The following equilibrium is established under certain conditions:

$$2CHClF_{2(g)} \rightleftharpoons C_2F_{4(g)} + 2HCl_{(g)} \qquad \Delta H = +128 \text{ kJ mol}^{-1}$$

State and explain how you would expect the following to affect the value of K_c for this equilibrium:

a) Increasing the concentration of C_2F_4.

b) Increasing the temperature.

c) Adding a catalyst.

Q2 The value of K_c for the following equilibrium increases if the temperature is decreased:

$$2SO_{2(g)} + O_{2(g)} \rightleftharpoons 2SO_{3(g)}$$

a) Is the forward reaction endothermic or exothermic? Explain your answer.

b) How would decreasing the pressure of this reaction affect:

(i) the position of equilibrium?

(ii) the value of K_p?

Q3 The reaction below occurs between methane and steam:

$$CH_{4(g)} + H_2O_{(g)} \rightleftharpoons CO_{(g)} + 3H_{2(g)}$$

The forward reaction is endothermic.

a) How could you increase the value of K_p for this equilibrium?

b) How could you increase production of $H_{2(g)}$ without affecting the value of K_p?

Exam Tip
In the exam, make sure you read the question really carefully and pay attention to whether concentrations and temperatures are increasing or decreasing — one slip up could cause you trouble...

Practice Questions — Fact Recall

Q1 State Le Chatelier's principle.

Q2 How will increasing the temperature affect K_c if:

a) the forward reaction is endothermic?

b) the forward reaction is exothermic?

Q3 Explain why changing the concentration of a reagent does not affect K_c.

Q4 How does increasing the pressure of a reaction affect the value of K_p?

Q5 How does adding a catalyst affect an equilibrium?

Section Summary

Make sure you know...

- How to calculate K_c and its units from the equilibrium concentrations and molar ratios for a reaction.
- How to use K_c to find unknown equilibrium concentrations for a reaction.
- How to deduce expressions for K_c for homogeneous and heterogeneous equilibria.
- That partial pressure is the pressure an individual gas in a mixture exerts.
- That a mole fraction is the proportion of a gas mixture that is a made up of a particular gas.
- How to calculate K_p and its units from the equilibrium partial pressures for a reaction.
- How to use K_p to calculate unknown partial pressures for an equilibrium system.
- How to deduce expressions for K_p for homogeneous and heterogeneous equilibria.
- How changing the temperature will affect the value of the equilibrium constants for endothermic and exothermic reactions.
- That changing the concentration or pressure of reactants or adding a catalyst has no effect on the equilibrium constants.

Exam-style Questions

1 Calculate the partial pressure of hydrogen chloride in the following reaction, given that $p(CH_3OH)$ = 109 kPa, $p(CH_3Cl)$ = 623 kPa, $p(H_2O)$ = 468 kPa and K_p = 52.7.

$$CH_3OH_{(g)} + HCl_{(g)} \rightleftharpoons CH_3Cl_{(g)} + H_2O_{(g)}$$

A 301 kPa

B 55.2 kPa

C 275 kPa

D 50.8 kPa

(1 mark)

2 The following equilibrium establishes at temperature X:

$$CH_{4(g)} + 2H_2O_{(g)} \rightleftharpoons CO_{2(g)} + 4H_{2(g)} \qquad \Delta H = +165 \text{ kJ mol}^{-1}$$

At equilibrium the mixture was found to contain 0.0800 mol dm^{-3} CH_4, 0.320 mol dm^{-3} H_2O, 0.200 mol dm^{-3} CO_2 and 0.280 mol dm^{-3} H_2.

(a) (i) Write an expression for K_c for this equilibrium.

(1 mark)

(ii) Calculate the value of K_c at temperature X, and give its units.

(2 marks)

(b) At a different temperature, Y, the value of K_c was found to be 0.0800 and the equilibrium concentrations were as follows:

Gas	CH_4	H_2O	CO_2	H_2
Concentration (mol dm^{-3})	?	0.560	0.420	0.480

(i) Calculate the equilibrium concentration of CH_4 at this temperature.

(2 marks)

(ii) At another temperature, Z, the value of K_c was found to be 1.20×10^{-3}. Suggest whether temperature Z is higher or lower than temperature Y. Explain your answer.

(3 marks)

(c) State how the value of K_c would change if a catalyst was added to the reaction. Explain your answer.

(2 marks)

1. Acids and Bases

Learning Objectives:

- Be able to describe a Brønsted-Lowry acid as a species that donates a proton and a Brønsted-Lowry base as a species that accepts a proton.
- Understand the differences between monobasic, dibasic and tribasic acids.
- Be able to use the term conjugate acid-base pairs.
- Be able to describe the role of H^+ in the reactions of acids with metals and bases (including carbonates, metal oxides and alkalis), using ionic equations.
- Be able to describe how different models developed over time to explain acid–base behaviour.

Specification Reference 5.1.3

There are a few different theories that describe acids and bases. One of those theories is the Brønsted–Lowry theory. Here it is...

Brønsted–Lowry acids and bases

Brønsted–Lowry acids are proton donors — they release hydrogen ions (H^+) when they're mixed with water. For example, for the general acid HA:

$$HA_{(aq)} \rightleftharpoons H^+_{(aq)} + A^-_{(aq)}$$

You never get H^+ ions by themselves in water though — they're always combined with H_2O to form hydroxonium ions, H_3O^+:

$$HA_{(aq)} + H_2O_{(l)} \rightleftharpoons H_3O^+_{(aq)} + A^-_{(aq)}$$

Brønsted–Lowry bases do the opposite — they're proton acceptors. When they're in solution, they grab hydrogen ions from water molecules. For example, for the general base B:

$$B_{(aq)} + H_2O_{(l)} \rightleftharpoons BH^+_{(aq)} + OH^-_{(aq)}$$

Dissociation in water

Acids and bases dissociate in water. This just means they break up into positively and negatively charged ions. The amount of dissociation depends on how weak or strong the acid or base is. **Strong acids** dissociate (or ionise) almost completely in water — nearly all the H^+ ions will be released. **Strong bases** (like sodium hydroxide) ionise almost completely in water too.

Examples

Hydrochloric acid is a strong acid: $HCl_{(g)} \rightarrow H^+_{(aq)} + Cl^-_{(aq)}$

Sodium hydroxide is a strong base: $NaOH_{(s)} \rightarrow Na^+_{(aq)} + OH^-_{(aq)}$

These reactions are actually reversible reactions but the equilibrium lies very far to the right, so only the forward reaction is shown in the equation.

Tip: Don't forget — H^+ ions and protons are the same thing.

Weak acids (e.g. ethanoic or citric) dissociate only very slightly in water — so only small numbers of H^+ ions are formed. An equilibrium is set up which lies well over to the left. **Weak bases** (such as ammonia) only slightly dissociate in water too. Just like with weak acids, the equilibrium lies well over to the left.

Examples

Ethanoic acid is a weak acid: $CH_3COOH_{(aq)} + H_2O_{(l)} \rightleftharpoons CH_3COO^-_{(aq)} + H_3O^+_{(aq)}$

Ammonia is a weak base: $NH_{3(aq)} + H_2O_{(l)} \rightleftharpoons NH_4^+{}_{(aq)} + OH^-_{(aq)}$

Monobasic, dibasic and tribasic acids

Acids like HCl and HNO_3 only have one proton per molecule that they can release into solution. These are **monobasic** acids. But some acids, such as sulfuric acid (H_2SO_4) or phosphoric acid (H_3PO_4), have more than one proton per molecule that they can release into solution. Acids that can release two protons into solution are called **dibasic** acids, and acids that can release three protons into solution are **tribasic** acids.

Examples

Sulfuric acid can release two protons, so it's a dibasic acid:

$$H_2SO_{4(aq)} \rightleftharpoons 2H^+_{(aq)} + SO_4^{2-}{}_{(aq)}$$

Phosphoric acid can release three protons, so it's a tribasic acid.

$$H_3PO_{4(aq)} \rightleftharpoons 3H^+_{(aq)} + PO_4^{3-}{}_{(aq)}$$

Tip: Acids that can release more than one proton into solution are also known by the general term 'polyprotic acids'.

Conjugate pairs

Conjugate pairs are species that are linked by the transfer of a proton. They're always on opposite sides of the reaction equation. The species that has lost a proton is the conjugate base and the species that has gained a proton is the conjugate acid. When Brønsted-Lowry acids and bases react together, the equilibrium below is set up:

$$HA + B \rightleftharpoons BH^+ + A^-$$

Tip: A species is just any type of chemical — it could be an atom, a molecule, an ion...

When HA loses a proton it forms A^- and when A^- gains a proton it forms HA — HA and A^- are linked by proton transfer so are a conjugate pair. HA has gained a proton so is the conjugate acid of A^-. A^- has lost a proton so is the conjugate base of HA.

$$HA \rightleftharpoons H^+ + A^-$$

conjugate acid → HA; *conjugate base* → A^-; *linked by proton transfer*

The base, B, takes a proton from the acid, HA, to form BH^+ — so B is the conjugate base of BH^+, and BH^+ is the conjugate acid of B.

$$B + H^+ \rightleftharpoons BH^+$$

conjugate base → B; *conjugate acid* → BH^+; *linked by proton transfer*

So, you get two conjugate pairs when an acid, HA, reacts with a base, B:

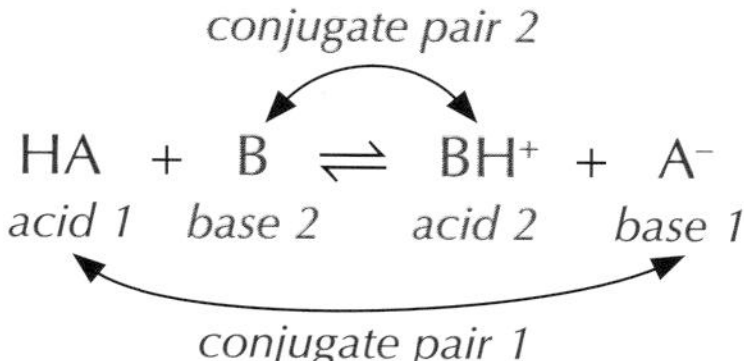

Conjugate pairs when acids and bases dissolve in water

Water is a special case — it reacts with acids to form a conjugate acid (H_3O^+), and reacts with bases to form a conjugate base (OH^-).

Here's the general equation for the reaction when an acid dissolves in water:

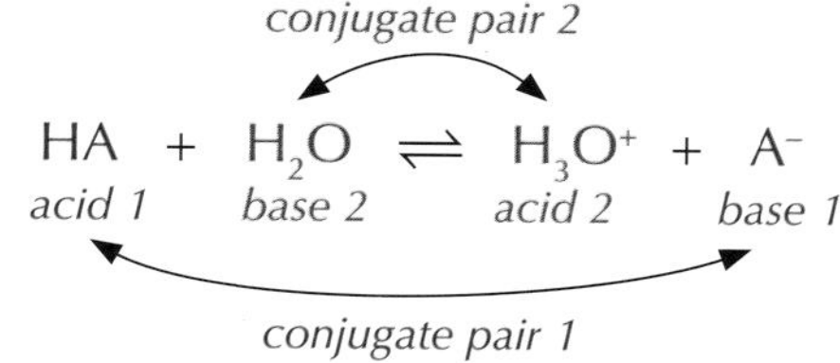

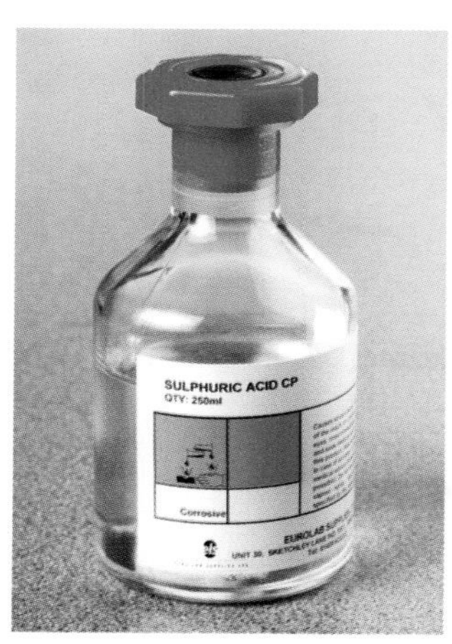

Figure 1: *A bottle of aqueous sulfuric acid. In this bottle the following equilibrium is established:*

$$H_2SO_4 + H_2O \rightleftharpoons H_3O^+ + HSO_4^-$$

H_2SO_4 and HSO_4^- are a conjugate pair — H_2SO_4 is an acid and HSO_4^- is a base.

Tip: In this reaction, water is acting as a base and is accepting a proton from the acid.

Tip: H_3O^+ is also known as the hydroxonium ion.

Example

Here's the equilibrium for aqueous HCl. Cl^- is the conjugate base of HCl.

conjugate pair 2

$$\underset{\text{acid 1}}{HCl} + \underset{\text{base 2}}{H_2O} \rightleftharpoons \underset{\text{acid 2}}{H_3O^+} + \underset{\text{base 1}}{Cl^-}$$

conjugate pair 1

This is the general equation for the reaction when a base dissolves in water:

conjugate pair 2

$$\underset{\text{base 1}}{B} + \underset{\text{acid 2}}{H_2O} \rightleftharpoons \underset{\text{acid 1}}{BH^+} + \underset{\text{base 2}}{OH^-}$$

conjugate pair 1

Tip: Alkalis like NaOH and KOH produce hydroxide ions (OH^-). The conjugate acid of hydroxide ions is water.

Example

Here's the equilibrium when NH_3 is dissolved in water. NH_4^+ is the conjugate acid of NH_3.

conjugate pair 2

$$\underset{\text{base 1}}{NH_3} + \underset{\text{acid 2}}{H_2O} \rightleftharpoons \underset{\text{acid 1}}{NH_4^+} + \underset{\text{base 2}}{OH^-}$$

conjugate pair 1

Identifying conjugate pairs

In your exams, you need to be able to identify the conjugate pairs formed in a reaction. It's easy enough to do — just find the species that are linked by proton transfer and work out which one is the acid and which one is the base.

Tip: Two species can't be a conjugate pair if they are on the same side of the equation — they have to be on opposite sides.

Example

When ammonium nitrate, NH_4NO_3 is dissolved in water the following equilibrium is set up: $NH_4^+ + NO_3^- \rightleftharpoons HNO_3 + NH_3$

Identify the conjugate pairs in this reaction.

NH_4^+ and NH_3 are linked by proton transfer so they must form one conjugate pair.

NO_3^- and HNO_3 are also linked by proton transfer so they must be the other conjugate pair.

In the NH_4^+/NH_3 conjugate pair, NH_4^+ donates a proton so must be the conjugate acid — NH_3 accepts a proton so must be the conjugate base.

In the NO_3^-/HNO_3 pair, NO_3^- accepts a proton so must be the conjugate base — HNO_3 donates a proton so must be the conjugate acid.

So the conjugate pairs in this reaction are:

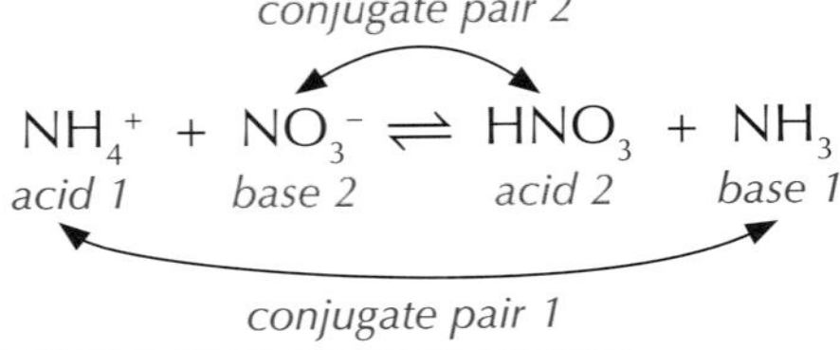

Reactions of acids

There are a few reactions of acids that you need to know about.

Reactions with metals

Reactive metals react with acids forming a salt and releasing hydrogen gas. The metal atoms donate electrons to the H^+ ions in the acid solution. The metal atoms are oxidised and the H^+ ions are reduced.

Example

Magnesium reacts with hydrochloric acid to produce magnesium chloride and hydrogen:

Full equation: $Mg_{(s)} + 2HCl_{(aq)} \rightarrow MgCl_{2(aq)} + H_{2(g)}$

Ionic equation: $Mg_{(s)} + 2H^+_{(aq)} \rightarrow Mg^{2+}_{(aq)} + H_{2(g)}$

Oxidation states: 0   +1   +2   0

Oxidation   *Reduction*

Tip: Don't forget — oxidation is the loss of electrons, reduction is the gain of electrons. You met this in Year 1, so have a skim over your notes if you've forgotten.

Reactions with carbonates

Carbonates react with acids to produce carbon dioxide, water and a salt.

Example

Sodium carbonate reacts with sulfuric acid to produce carbon dioxide, water and sodium sulfate:

Full equation: $Na_2CO_{3(s)} + H_2SO_{4(aq)} \rightarrow Na_2SO_{4(aq)} + CO_{2(g)} + H_2O_{(l)}$

Ionic equation: $CO_3^{2-}{}_{(aq)} + 2H^+_{(aq)} \rightarrow H_2O_{(l)} + CO_{2(g)}$

Figure 2: Sodium carbonate reacting with acid. The bubbles are the CO_2 gas that's being given off.

Reactions with bases and alkalis

Acids produce H^+ ions when dissolved in water and alkalis produce OH^- ions. Acids and alkalis neutralise each other to form water. The other ions present form a salt. The ionic equation for the reaction of an acid with an alkali is:

$$H^+_{(aq)} + OH^-_{(aq)} \rightarrow H_2O_{(l)}$$

Example

Hydrochloric acid reacts with potassium hydroxide to produce potassium chloride and water:

Full equation: $HCl_{(aq)} + KOH_{(aq)} \rightarrow KCl_{(aq)} + H_2O_{(l)}$

Ionic equation: $H^+_{(aq)} + OH^-_{(aq)} \rightarrow H_2O_{(l)}$

Tip: Alkalis are bases that release hydroxide ions (OH^-) when they dissolve in water.

Acids can react with insoluble bases in a similar way. Here's how an acid neutralises an insoluble base:

$$2H^+_{(aq)} + O^{2-}_{(s)} \rightarrow H_2O_{(l)}$$

Tip: Lots of metal oxides are insoluble bases.

Example

Hydrochloric acid reacts with solid copper oxide to produce copper chloride and water:

Full equation: $2HCl_{(aq)} + CuO_{(s)} \rightarrow CuCl_{2(aq)} + H_2O_{(l)}$

Ionic equation: $2H^+_{(aq)} + CuO_{(s)} \rightarrow H_2O_{(l)} + Cu^{2+}_{(aq)}$

Exam Tip

Make sure you can write full and ionic equations for the reactions of acids with metals, carbonates, bases and alkalis — you could be asked about any of these in your exams.

Development of acid-base theory

Scientific theories can take years to develop. A scientist will come up with an idea, and then someone else will find holes in the theory and make changes to improve it. This is how the Brønsted-Lowry theory of acids and bases came about.

Lavoisier came up with the first theory of acids and bases in the 18th century. He didn't know the formulas of compounds like hydrochloric acid but he did know that sulfuric acid had the formula H_2SO_4 and nitric acid had the formula HNO_3. So he proposed that acids had to have oxygen in them. It was later shown that acids like hydrochloric acid (HCl) and hydrogen sulfide (H_2S) don't have any oxygen in them at all.

At the end of the 19th century, a chemist called Arrhenius suggested that acids release protons in aqueous solution, whilst bases release hydroxide ions. He said that when acids and bases react together they form water and a salt. This is true for loads of examples, but doesn't work for bases such as ammonia (NH_3), which don't contain any hydroxide ions.

Figure 3: *J.N. Brønsted — co-author of the Brønsted–Lowry theory.*

Brønsted and Lowry came up with their definition of acids and bases independently of one another. It's clearly based on Arrhenius' theory, but broadens the definition of a base to be a proton acceptor. They also came up with the idea that acids and bases react to form conjugate pairs, rather than a salt and water. This definition currently explains most of our observations, so is one of the theories we still use today — around 100 years later.

Practice Questions — Application

Q1 Write full and ionic equations for the reaction of:

a) hydrochloric acid (HCl) with sodium metal (Na).

b) sulfuric acid (H_2SO_4) with solid calcium carbonate ($CaCO_3$).

c) nitric acid (HNO_3) with potassium hydroxide solution (KOH).

d) hydrocyanic acid (HCN) with solid sodium oxide (Na_2O).

Q2 Identify the conjugate acid-base pairs in the following reactions by labelling them 'acid 1' and 'base 1' and 'acid 2' and 'base 2':

a) $H_2CO_{3(aq)} + H_2O_{(l)} \rightleftharpoons H_3O^+_{(aq)} + HCO_3^-{}_{(aq)}$

b) $CH_3NH_{2(aq)} + H_2O_{(l)} \rightleftharpoons CH_3NH_3^+{}_{(aq)} + OH^-_{(aq)}$

c) $CH_3COO^-_{(aq)} + NH_4^+{}_{(aq)} \rightleftharpoons CH_3COOH_{(aq)} + NH_{3(aq)}$

d) $HCl_{(aq)} + OH^-_{(aq)} \rightleftharpoons Cl^-_{(aq)} + H_2O_{(l)}$

Practice Questions — Fact Recall

Q1 What is the definition of:

a) a Brønsted-Lowry acid? b) a Brønsted-Lowry base?

Q2 Give both the definition and an example of the following substances:

a) a monobasic acid b) a dibasic acid c) a tribasic acid

Q3 a) What type of acid dissociates almost completely in water?

b) What type of base dissociates only slightly in water?

Q4 What is a conjugate pair?

Q5 What products are formed when an acid reacts with:

a) a metal? b) a carbonate? c) a base?

2. pH Calculations

There are lots of pH calculations that you need to know how to do for your exams. The next few pages tell you everything you need to know to get started.

Learning Objectives:

- Be able to use the expressions $pH = -\log[H^+]$ and $[H^+] = 10^{-pH}$
- Be able to calculate pH and related quantities for strong, monobasic acids.

Specification Reference 5.1.3

The pH scale

pH is a measure of the hydrogen ion concentration in a solution. The concentration of hydrogen ions in a solution can vary enormously, so those wise chemists of old decided to express the concentration on a logarithmic scale, called the pH scale.

pH can be calculated using the following equation:

$$pH = -\log_{10}[H^+]$$

$[H^+]$ is the concentration of hydrogen ions in a solution, measured in mol dm^{-3}. So, if you know the hydrogen ion concentration of a solution, you can calculate its pH by sticking the numbers into the formula.

Tip: To calculate logarithms you need to use the 'log' button on your calculator. Different calculators work differently so make sure you know how to calculate logs on yours.

Example — Maths Skills

A solution of hydrochloric acid has a hydrogen ion concentration of 0.010 mol dm^{-3}. What is the pH of the solution?

$pH = -\log_{10}[H^+]$

$= -\log_{10}[0.010] = \mathbf{2.00}$

Just substitute the [H⁺] value into the pH formula and solve.

Exam Tip
In the exam, always give your calculated pH values to the same number of decimal places as there are significant figures in your original value. If you're unsure, give your answer to 2 d.p.

The pH scale normally goes from 0 (very acidic) to 14 (very alkaline). pH 7 is regarded as being neutral. Solutions that have a very low pH include strong acids such as HCl and H_2SO_4. Strong bases such as NaOH and KOH have a very high pH. Pure water has a pH of 7 and is neutral.

Calculating $[H^+]$ from pH

If you've got the pH of a solution, and you want to know its hydrogen ion concentration, then you need the inverse of the pH formula:

$$[H^+] = 10^{-pH}$$

Now you can use this formula to find $[H^+]$.

Example — Maths Skills

A solution of nitric acid has a pH of 1.52.
What is the hydrogen ion concentration of this solution?

$[H^+] = 10^{-pH}$

$= 10^{-1.52}$

$= 0.030$ mol dm^{-3}

$= \mathbf{3.0 \times 10^{-2}}$ **mol dm^{-3}**

Just substitute the pH value into the inverse pH formula and solve.

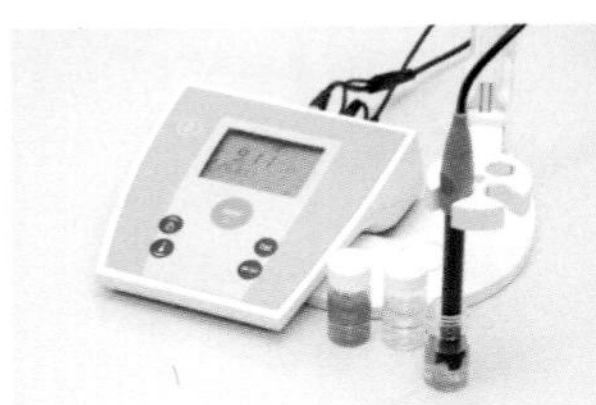

Figure 1: *pH can be measured using a pH meter like this one* *(see page 84).*

Exam Tip
If your calculation involves a power, like 10^x, your answer should be to the same number of significant figures as the number of decimal places in x. This is a bit different to the normal significant figures rules.

Practice Questions — Application

Q1 A solution of hydrochloric acid (HCl) has a hydrogen ion concentration of 0.05 mol dm^{-3}. Calculate the pH of this solution.

Q2 A solution of nitric acid (HNO_3) has a pH of 2.86. Calculate the concentration of hydrogen ions in this solution.

Q3 Calculate the pH of a solution of hydrochloric acid (HCl) with a hydrogen ion concentration of 0.02 mol dm^{-3}.

Tip: The strength of an acid has nothing to do with its concentration. How strong an acid is depends on how much it dissociates in water. The concentration is just how diluted the acid is.

Tip: Monobasic acids are also known as monoprotic acids — meaning they release one proton.

Exam Tip
Acids like H_2SO_4 are dibasic — they release two protons when they dissociate. Don't worry though, you won't have to do pH calculations for dibasic acids in the exam.

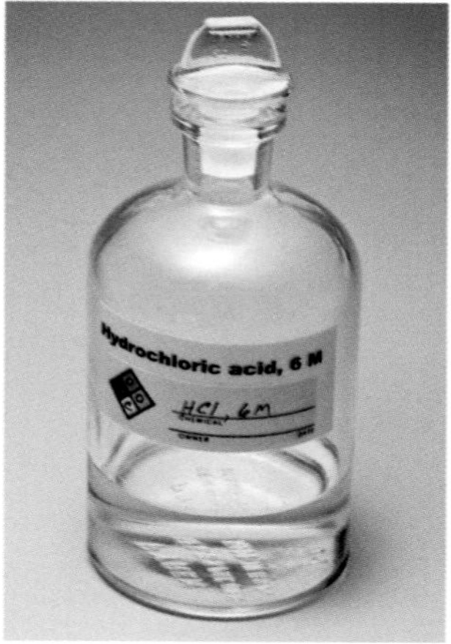

Figure 2: *Hydrochloric acid is a strong acid.*

Exam Tip
Calculating the pH of acids from their concentrations comes up in loads of calculations so you need to be really confident that you know how to do it.

pH of strong, monobasic acids

Monobasic means that each molecule of an acid will release one proton when it dissociates. Hydrochloric acid (HCl) and nitric acid (HNO_3) are strong acids so they ionise fully:

$$HCl_{(aq)} \rightarrow H^+_{(aq)} + Cl^-_{(aq)}$$

HCl and HNO_3 are also monobasic, so each mole of acid produces one mole of hydrogen ions. This means the H^+ concentration is the same as the acid concentration. So, if you know the concentration of the acid you know the H^+ concentration and you can calculate the pH.

Examples — Maths Skills

Calculate the pH of 0.10 mol dm^{-3} hydrochloric acid:

$[HCl] = [H^+] = 0.10$ mol dm^{-3}. So:

$$\begin{aligned} pH &= -\log_{10}[H^+] \\ &= -\log_{10} 0.10 \\ &= 1.00 \end{aligned}$$

Calculate the pH of 0.050 mol dm^{-3} nitric acid:

$[HNO_3] = [H^+] = 0.050$ mol dm^{-3}. So:

$$\begin{aligned} pH &= -\log_{10} 0.050 \\ &= 1.30 \end{aligned}$$

If a solution of hydrochloric acid has a pH of 2.45, what is the concentration of the acid?

$[HCl] = [H^+] = 10^{-pH}$. So:

$$\begin{aligned} [HCl] &= 10^{-2.45} \\ &= 3.5 \times 10^{-3} \text{ mol dm}^{-3} \end{aligned}$$

Practice Questions — Application

Q1 Hydrochloric acid (HCl) is a strong monobasic acid.
Calculate the pH of a 0.08 mol dm^{-3} solution of HCl.

Q2 Nitric acid (HNO_3) is a strong monobasic acid.
Calculate the pH of a 0.12 mol dm^{-3} solution of HNO_3.

Q3 A solution of hydrochloric acid has a pH of 0.96.
Calculate the concentration of this hydrochloric acid solution.

Q4 A solution of nitric acid has a pH of 1.28.
Calculate the concentration of this nitric acid solution.

Practice Questions — Fact Recall

Q1 Write out the expression that defines pH.

Q2 Write out the equation that you would need to calculate the hydrogen ion concentration of an acid, given its pH.

Q3 Explain what is meant by the term monobasic.

Q4 What is the relationship between the concentration of H^+ ions and the acid concentration in strong monobasic acids?

3. The Ionic Product of Water

The ionic product of water (also known as K_w) is really just another equilibrium constant. "So why do I need to know about it?", I hear you cry. Well, mainly because it comes in handy for calculating the pH of strong bases. Read on...

What is K_w?

Water dissociates into hydroxonium ions and hydroxide ions. So this equilibrium exists in water:

$$H_2O_{(l)} + H_2O_{(l)} \rightleftharpoons H_3O^+_{(aq)} + OH^-_{(aq)}$$

If you remove an H_2O from both sides, this simplifies to:

$$H_2O_{(l)} \rightleftharpoons H^+_{(aq)} + OH^-_{(aq)}$$

And, just like for any other equilibrium reaction, you can apply the equilibrium law and write an expression for the equilibrium constant:

$$K_c = \frac{[H^+][OH^-]}{[H_2O]}$$

Water only dissociates a tiny amount, so the equilibrium lies well over to the left. There's so much water compared to the amounts of H^+ and OH^- ions that the concentration of water is considered to have a constant value. So if you multiply the expression you wrote for K_c (which is a constant) by $[H_2O]$ (another constant), you get a constant. This new constant is called the **ionic product of water** and it is given the symbol K_w.

$$K_w = K_c \times [H_2O] = \frac{[H^+][OH^-]}{\cancel{[H_2O]}} \times \cancel{[H_2O]}$$

So... $K_w = [H^+][OH^-]$

K_w always has the same value for an aqueous solution at a given temperature. For example, at 298 K (25 °C), K_w has a value of 1.00×10^{-14} mol^2 dm^{-6}.

K_w behaves like other equilibrium constants:

- The value of K_w is fixed at a given temperature. So if the concentration of one thing in the equilibrium mixture changes then the concentrations of the others must change to keep the value of K_w the same.
- Changing the temperature of the solution changes the value of K_w — dissociation of water is an endothermic process, so warming the solution shifts the equilibrium to the right (it dissociates more), and the value of K_w increases. Cooling the solution shifts the equilibrium to the right (there is less dissociation), and the value of K_w decreases.

Finding the pH of water

The pH of water is not always exactly 7 — it actually varies depending on the temperature. You can calculate the pH of water using K_w. The expression for K_w is $K_w = [H^+][OH^-]$. But in pure water, there is always one H^+ ion for each OH^- ion. So $[H^+] = [OH^-]$. That means if you are dealing with pure water, you can say that:

$$K_w = [H^+]^2$$

If you want to find the pH of water at a particular temperature, substitute the value for K_w at that temperature into the equation above, solve it to find $[H^+]$ by taking the square root of both sides, then use $pH = -\log_{10}[H^+]$ to find the pH.

Learning Objectives:

- Be able to state and use the expression for the ionic product of water, K_w.
- Be able to describe the constancy of K_w with changes in concentration.
- Be able to describe the qualitative effect on K_w of changing temperature for exothermic and endothermic reactions.
- Be able to explain how K_w controls the position of equilibrium on changing concentration and temperature.
- Be able to calculate pH and related quantities for strong bases, using K_w.

Specification Reference 5.1.2, 5.1.3

Tip: See page 49 for more on the equilibrium constant, K_c.

Tip: The units of K_w are <u>always</u> mol^2 dm^{-6} because mol dm^{-3} × mol dm^{-3} = mol^2 dm^{-6}.

Exam Tip
Remember — K_w only equals $[H^+]^2$ in <u>pure water</u>. If you're asked to write an expression for K_w, always give $K_w = [H^+][OH^-]$.

Tip: Although the pH of water changes with temperature, water is always described as neutral (not acidic or alkaline) because $[H^+]$ always equals $[OH^-]$.

Example — Maths Skills

At 50 °C, the value of K_w is 5.48×10^{-14} mol² dm⁻⁶. Calculate the pH of pure water at this temperature.

- Substituting in K_w gives $5.48 \times 10^{-14} = [H^+]^2$
- So $[H^+] = \sqrt{5.48 \times 10^{-14}} = 2.34... \times 10^{-7}$
- $pH = -\log_{10}[H^+] = -\log_{10}(2.34... \times 10^{-7}) = 6.631$

So the pH of pure water at 50 °C is **6.631**.

Practice Questions — Application

Q1 Calculate the pH of pure water at 30 °C.
The value of K_w at 30 °C is 1.47×10^{-14} mol² dm⁻⁶.

Q2 Calculate the pH of pure water at 40 °C.
The value of K_w at 40 °C is 2.92×10^{-14} mol² dm⁻⁶.

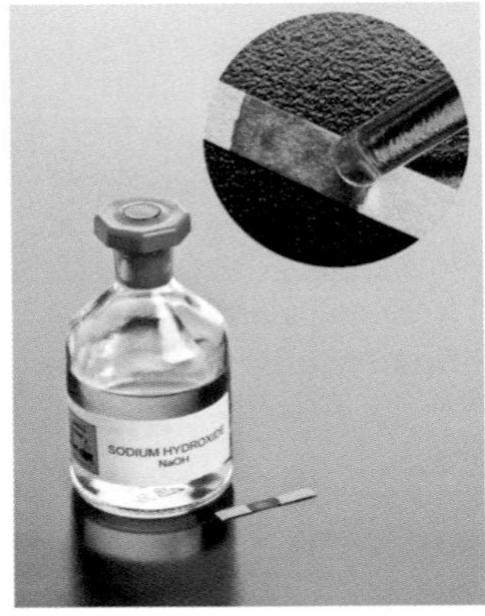

Figure 1: Sodium hydroxide turns this Universal indicator paper dark blue, which shows that it has a high pH.

Finding the pH of strong bases

Sodium hydroxide (NaOH) and potassium hydroxide (KOH) are strong bases that fully ionise in water — they donate one mole of OH^- ions per mole of base. This means that the concentration of OH^- ions is the same as the concentration of the base. So for 0.02 mol dm⁻³ sodium hydroxide solution, $[OH^-]$ is also 0.02 mol dm⁻³. But to work out the pH you need to know $[H^+]$ — luckily this is linked to $[OH^-]$ through the ionic product of water, K_w:

$$K_w = [H^+][OH^-]$$

If you know $[OH^-]$ for a strong aqueous base and K_w at a certain temperature, you can work out $[H^+]$ and then the pH. Just follow these steps:

Step 1: Find the values of K_w and $[OH^-]$. You may be told these in the question or you may have to work them out.

Step 2: Rearrange the equation, substitute the values for K_w and $[OH^-]$ into the equation, and solve it to find $[H^+]$.

Step 3: Once you know $[H^+]$, substitute this into the pH equation ($pH = -\log_{10}[H^+]$) and solve it to find out the pH.

Tip: It doesn't matter whether water is pure or part of a solution — K_w is always the same at the same temperature.

Example — Maths Skills

The value of K_w at 298 K is 1.0×10^{-14} mol² dm⁻⁶.
Find the pH of 0.100 mol dm⁻³ NaOH at 298 K.

1. Find the values of K_w and $[OH^-]$:
   - The value of K_w is given in the question as 1.0×10^{-14} mol² dm⁻⁶
   - NaOH is a strong base so will donate one mole of OH^- ions per mole of base. The concentration of NaOH is 0.100 mol dm⁻³ so $[OH^-]$ must be 0.100 mol dm⁻³.
2. Substitute the values of K_w and $[OH^-]$ into the K_w equation:
   $$K_w = [H^+][OH^-] \text{ so } [H^+] = \frac{K_w}{[OH^-]} = \frac{1.0 \times 10^{-14}}{0.100} = 1.0 \times 10^{-13} \text{ mol dm}^{-3}$$
3. Substitute the value of $[H^+]$ into the pH equation:
   $$pH = -\log_{10}(1.0 \times 10^{-13}) = \mathbf{13.00}$$

Exam Tip
Don't worry — you don't have to memorise any values of K_w. You'll always be told K_w in the question if you need to use it.

Practice Questions — Application

Q1 Calculate the pH of a 0.200 mol dm^{-3} solution of KOH at 50 °C. The value of K_w at 50 °C is 5.48×10^{-14} mol^2 dm^{-6}.

Q2 Calculate the pH of a 0.155 mol dm^{-3} solution of NaOH at 20 °C. The value of K_w at 20 °C is 6.81×10^{-15} mol^2 dm^{-6}.

Q3 Calculate the pH of a 0.0840 mol dm^{-3} solution of KOH at 10 °C. The value of K_w at 10 °C is 2.93×10^{-15} mol^2 dm^{-6}.

Finding the concentration of strong bases

If you know the pH of a strong base you can use K_w to find its concentration. Here's what you have to do:

Step 1: Use the equation $[H^+] = 10^{-pH}$ to find the value of $[H^+]$ in the solution.

Step 2: Substitute your value for $[H^+]$ along with the value of K_w into the K_w equation and solve it to find $[OH^-]$.

Step 3: Because strong bases fully dissociate, $[OH^-]$ is the same as the concentration of the base.

Tip: This is very similar to finding the pH of strong bases — you just have to do the steps in reverse.

Example — Maths Skills

A solution of NaOH has a pH of 12.50 at 30 °C. The value of K_w at 30 °C is 1.47×10^{-14} mol^2 dm^{-6}. Calculate the concentration of this NaOH solution.

1. Find $[H^+]$:

$$[H^+] = 10^{-pH} = 10^{-12.50} = 3.16... \times 10^{-13}$$

2. Substitute $[H^+]$ and the value for K_w into the K_w equation:

$$K_w = [H^+][OH^-] \text{ so } [OH^-] = \frac{K_w}{[H^+]} = \frac{1.47 \times 10^{-14}}{3.16... \times 10^{-13}} = 0.046 \text{ mol dm}^{-3}$$

3. Because NaOH is a strong base [NaOH] = $[OH^-]$ so the concentration of the NaOH solution is **0.046 mol dm^{-3}**.

Exam Tip
Make sure you know how to find the pH and the concentration of a strong base — you could be asked to do either in the exams.

Tip: The temperature at which measurements are taken and the temperature of K_w have to match — otherwise the calculation won't be valid.

Practice Questions — Application

Q4 Find the concentration of a solution of KOH that has a pH of 12.40 at 20 °C. The value of K_w at 20 °C is 6.8×10^{-15} mol^2 dm^{-6}.

Q5 Find the concentration of a solution of NaOH that has a pH of 13.98 at 40 °C. The value of K_w at 40 °C is 2.92×10^{-14} mol^2 dm^{-6}.

Q6 Find the concentration of a solution of KOH that has a pH of 13.25 at 30 °C. The value of K_w at 30 °C is 1.47×10^{-14} mol^2 dm^{-6}.

Practice Questions — Fact Recall

Q1 Write an expression for K_w.

Q2 What are the units of K_w?

Q3 Explain why $K_w = [H^+]^2$ for pure water.

4. The Acid Dissociation Constant

Learning Objectives:

- Be able to define and use the acid dissociation constant, K_a, for the extent of acid dissociation.
- Understand the limitations of using approximations to K_a related calculations for 'stronger' weak acids.
- Be able to describe the constancy of K_a with changes in concentration.
- Be able to describe the qualitative effect on K_a of changing temperature for exothermic and endothermic reactions.
- Be able to explain how K_a controls the position of equilibrium on changing concentration and temperature.
- Be able to carry out calculations of pH, K_a or related quantities, for a weak monobasic acid using approximations.
- Understand the relationship between K_a and pK_a.

Specification Reference
5.1.2, 5.1.3

You've already seen how to calculate the pH of strong acids and strong bases. Now get ready for part three: calculating the pH of weak acids.

What is the acid dissociation constant?

Weak acids don't ionise fully in solution, so the $[H^+]$ isn't the same as the acid concentration. This makes it a bit trickier to find their pH. You have to use yet another equilibrium constant — the **acid dissociation constant**, K_a. The units of K_a are mol dm^{-3} and the equation for K_a is derived as follows:

For a weak monobasic aqueous acid, HA, you get the equilibrium:

$$HA_{(aq)} \rightleftharpoons H^+_{(aq)} + A^-_{(aq)}$$

As only a tiny amount of HA dissociates, you can assume that [HA] at the start of the reaction is the same as [HA] at equilibrium, i.e.

$$[HA] \gg [H^+], \text{ so } [HA]_{(start)} \approx [HA]_{(equilibrium)}$$

So if you apply the equilibrium law, you get:

$$K_a = \frac{[H^+][A^-]}{[HA]_{start}}$$

When dealing with weak acids, you can assume that dissociation of the acid is much greater than dissociation of water. This means you can assume that all the H^+ ions come from the acid, so for a monobasic acid, $[H^+] \approx [A^-]$.

So the formula for K_a can be simplified to: $K_a = \frac{[H^+]^2}{[HA]}$

HOW SCIENCE WORKS

In order to use the expression for K_a properly, you need to know the limitations under which it works. The assumptions made to find K_a only work for **weak acids**. Stronger acids **dissociate more** in solution, so the difference between $[HA]_{start}$ and $[HA]_{equilibrium}$ becomes significant, and the assumption that $[HA]_{start} \approx [HA]_{equilibrium}$ is no longer valid.

K_a behaves like other equilibrium constants:

- The value of K_a is fixed at a given temperature. So if the concentration of one thing in the equilibrium mixture changes then the concentrations of the others must change to keep the value of K_a the same.
- Changing the temperature of the solution changes the value of K_a.
  If dissociation is endothermic, warming the solution shifts the equilibrium to the right (it dissociates more), so K_a increases, and vice versa.
  If dissociation is exothermic, warming the solution shifts the equilibrium to the left, so K_a decreases, and vice versa.

Tip: K_a is a type of equilibrium constant, so the formula for K_a is based on the one for K_c. It applies to a particular acid at a specific temperature, regardless of the concentration.

Calculations using K_a

You can rearrange the expression of K_a in order to find the concentration of a weak acid, and hence its pH. You can also use the pH and concentration of a weak acid to find K_a for that acid at a particular temperature.

Finding the pH of weak acids

You can use K_a to find the pH of a weak acid. Just follow these steps.

Step 1: Write an expression for K_a for the weak acid. (You can write out the equilibrium equation first if it helps you write this expression.)

Step 2: Rearrange the equation and substitute in the values for K_a and [HA] to find $[H^+]^2$.

Step 3: Take the square root of the number to find $[H^+]$.

Step 4: Substitute $[H^+]$ into the pH equation to find the pH.

Example — Maths Skills

Find the pH of a 0.020 mol dm^{-3} solution of propanoic acid (CH_3CH_2COOH) at 298 K. K_a for propanoic acid at this temperature is 1.30 × 10^{-5} mol dm^{-3}.

1. First write an expression for K_a for the weak acid.
   Propanoic acid equilibrium: $CH_3CH_2COOH \rightleftharpoons H^+ + CH_3CH_2COO^-$

$$\text{So, } K_a = \frac{[H^+][CH_3CH_2COO^-]}{[CH_3CH_2COOH]} = \frac{[H^+]^2}{[CH_3CH_2COOH]}$$

2. Rearrange the equation to find $[H^+]^2$:

$$[H^+]^2 = K_a[CH_3CH_2COOH]$$
$$= (1.30 \times 10^{-5}) \times 0.020 = 2.60 \times 10^{-7}$$

3. Take the square root of this number to find $[H^+]$:

$$[H^+] = \sqrt{2.60 \times 10^{-7}}$$
$$= 5.09... \times 10^{-4} \text{ mol dm}^{-3}$$

4. Use $[H^+]$ to find the pH of the acid:

$$pH = -\log_{10} [H^+]$$
$$= -\log_{10} 5.09... \times 10^{-4} = \mathbf{3.29}$$

Figure 1: Lemon juice contains citric acid. It turns this universal indicator paper orange, which shows that it's a weak acid.

Exam Tip
It's really important to show all the steps of your working in exam questions — that way the examiner can give you some marks for your method even if your final answer is wrong.

Finding the concentration of weak acids

If you already know the pH you can use K_a to find the concentration of the acid. You don't need to know anything new for this type of calculation — you use the same formulas you used to find the pH.

Step 1: Substitute the pH into the inverse pH equation to calculate $[H^+]$.
Step 2: Write an expression for K_a.
Step 3: Rearrange the equation to give the concentration of the acid.
Step 4: Substitute the values for K_a and $[H^+]$ into the equation and solve it.

Example — Maths Skills

The pH of an ethanoic acid (CH_3COOH) solution is 3.02 at 298 K. Calculate the molar concentration of this solution. The K_a of ethanoic acid is 1.75 × 10^{-5} mol dm^{-3} at 298 K.

1. Use the pH of the acid to find $[H^+]$:

$$[H^+] = 10^{-pH}$$
$$= 10^{-3.02}$$
$$= 9.5... \times 10^{-4} \text{ mol dm}^{-3}$$

2. Write an expression for K_a:

$$K_a = \frac{[H^+][CH_3COO^-]}{[CH_3COOH]} = \frac{[H^+]^2}{[CH_3COOH]}$$

3. Rearrange it to give $[CH_3COOH]$:

$$[CH_3COOH] = \frac{[H^+]^2}{K_a}$$

4. Substitute in K_a and $[H^+]$ and solve the equation to find $[CH_3COOH]$:

$$[CH_3COOH] = \frac{(9.5... \times 10^{-4})^2}{1.75 \times 10^{-5}} = \mathbf{0.052 \text{ mol dm}^{-3}}$$

Tip: Remember, you can write out the equilibrium equation to help with Step 2 if you like.

Exam Tip
If you can't work out the chemical formula of an acid, just use HA instead and you might still get the marks.

Exam Tip
You need to be able to do all three types of calculation in the exams — any one of them could crop up so make sure you understand these examples.

Finding the K_a of weak acids

If you know both the concentration and the pH, you can use them to find the K_a of the weak acid. Just find $[H^+]$ (as shown in the previous example), substitute the values you know into the expression for K_a and solve.

Example — Maths Skills

A solution of 0.162 mol dm^{-3} HCN has a pH of 5.05 at 298 K. What is the value of K_a for HCN at 298 K?

1. Use the pH of the acid to find $[H^+]$:

$$[H^+] = 10^{-pH} = 10^{-5.05} = 8.9... \times 10^{-6} \text{ mol dm}^{-3}$$

2. Write an expression for K_a:

$$K_a = \frac{[H^+][CN^-]}{[HCN]} = \frac{[H^+]^2}{[HCN]}$$

3. Substitute in the values for $[H^+]$ and $[HCN]$:

$$K_a = \frac{[H^+]^2}{[HCN]} = \frac{(8.9... \times 10^{-6})^2}{0.162} = \mathbf{4.9 \times 10^{-10} \text{ mol dm}^{-3}}$$

The logarithmic constant, pK_a

The value of K_a varies massively from one acid to the next. This can sometimes make the numbers difficult to manage so to make life easier, scientists often use the pK_a instead. pK_a is calculated from K_a in exactly the same way as pH is calculated from $[H^+]$ — and vice versa:

$$pK_a = -\log_{10}(K_a) \qquad K_a = 10^{-pKa}$$

So if an acid has a K_a value of 1.5×10^{-7} mol dm^{-3}, then:

$$pK_a = -\log_{10}(K_a) = -\log_{10}(1.5 \times 10^{-7}) = 6.82$$

Tip: Notice how pK_a values aren't annoyingly tiny like K_a values.

And if an acid has a pK_a value of 4.32, then:

$$K_a = 10^{-pKa} = 10^{-4.32} = 4.8 \times 10^{-5} \text{ mol dm}^{-3}$$

Tip: The larger the pK_a, the weaker the acid. Strong acids have very small pK_a values.

Just to make things that bit more complicated, there might be a pK_a value in a 'find the pH' type of question. If so, you need to convert it to K_a so that you can use the K_a expression.

Example — Maths Skills

Calculate the pH of 0.050 mol dm^{-3} methanoic acid (HCOOH). Methanoic acid has a pK_a of 3.75 at 298 K.

1. Convert the pK_a value to a K_a value:

$$K_a = 10^{-pKa} = 10^{-3.75} = 1.7... \times 10^{-4} \text{ mol dm}^{-3}$$

Tip: These are the same steps as you followed on page 74 but with an extra step (converting the pK_a into K_a) at the beginning.

2. Write out an expression for K_a:

$$K_a = \frac{[H^+][HCOO^-]}{[HCOOH]} = \frac{[H^+]^2}{[HCOOH]}$$

3. Rearrange it to give $[H^+]^2$:

$$[H^+]^2 = K_a[HCOOH]$$
$$= 1.7... \times 10^{-4} \times 0.050$$
$$= 8.8... \times 10^{-6}$$

4. Take the square root to get $[H^+]$:

$$[H^+] = \sqrt{8.8... \times 10^{-6}}$$
$$= 2.9... \times 10^{-3} \text{ mol dm}^{-3}$$

5. Substitute $[H^+]$ into the pH equation and solve:

$$\text{pH} = -\log (2.9... \times 10^{-3}) = \mathbf{2.53}$$

It works the other way round too. Sometimes you are asked to calculate K_a but have to give your answer as a pK_a value. In this case, you just work out the K_a value as usual and then convert it to pK_a — and Bob's your pet hamster.

Exam Tip
pH values for weak acids are usually between 2 and 5. If you get an answer much bigger or smaller than this in your exam, double-check your calculation — you may have gone wrong somewhere.

Practice Questions — Application

Q1 A solution of the weak acid, hydrocyanic acid (HCN) has a concentration of 2.0 mol dm^{-3}. The K_a of this acid at 25 °C is 4.9×10^{-10} mol dm^{-3}.
  a) Write down an expression for the K_a of this acid.
  b) Calculate the pH of this solution at 25 °C.

Q2 A sample of the weak acid nitrous acid (HNO_2) has a pH of 3.80 in solution at 25 °C. The K_a of this acid at 25 °C is 4.0×10^{-4} mol dm^{-3}. Determine the concentration of this solution at 25 °C.

Q3 A 0.280 mol dm^{-3} solution of a weak acid (HA) has a pH of 4.11 at 25 °C. Calculate the K_a of this acid at 25 °C.

Q4 Methanoic acid (HCOOH) has a K_a of 1.8×10^{-4} mol dm^{-3} at 298 K. The pH of a solution of methanoic acid was measured to be 3.67 at 298 K. Determine the concentration of this solution of HCOOH.

Q5 Ethanoic acid has a pK_a of 4.78 at 298 K. Determine the K_a of ethanoic acid at 298 K.

Q6 A 0.154 mol dm^{-3} weak acid solution has a pH of 4.50 at 45 °C. Calculate the pK_a of this acid at 45 °C.

Q7 The pK_a of hydrofluoric acid (HF) is 3.14 at a certain temperature. Calculate the concentration of a solution of hydrofluoric acid that has a pH of 3.20 at this temperature.

Q8 A weak acid (HX) has a pK_a of 4.50 at 25 °C. Calculate the pH of a 0.60 mol dm^{-3} solution of this acid at 25 °C.

Exam Tip
You'll almost certainly have to use expressions for terms like pH and pK_a in the exam so you really, really need to make sure that you know the formulas. Have a look at page 272 for a summary of all the formulas in this section.

Practice Questions — Fact Recall

Q1 What are the units for K_a?

Q2 a) Write an expression for the K_a of a general weak acid (HA).
  b) Rearrange this equation to give an expression for calculating [HA].

Q3 a) Write out the expression that defines pK_a.
  b) Rearrange this equation to give an expression for K_a.

5. Buffer Action

Sometimes, it's useful to have a solution that doesn't change pH when small amounts of acid or base are added to it. That's where buffers come in handy.

Learning Objectives:

- Be able to describe a buffer solution as a system that minimises pH changes on addition of small amounts of an acid or a base.
- Be able to describe the formation of a buffer solution from a weak acid and a salt of the weak acid, e.g. CH_3COOH/ CH_3COONa, or from an excess of a weak acid and a strong alkali, e.g. excess CH_3COOH/NaOH
- Be able to explain the role of the conjugate acid-base pair in an acid buffer solution, e.g. CH_3COOH/ CH_3COO^-, in the control of pH.
- Be able to explain the control of blood pH by the carbonic acid–hydrogencarbonate buffer system.

Specification Reference 5.1.3

What is a buffer?

A **buffer** is a solution that minimises changes in pH when small amounts of acid or base are added. A buffer doesn't stop the pH from changing completely — it does make the changes very slight though. Buffers only work when you add small amounts of acid or base — put too much in and they won't be able to cope. You get acidic buffers and basic buffers — but you only need to know about acidic ones.

Acidic buffers

Acidic buffers have a pH of less than 7 — they're made by setting up an equilibrium between a weak acid and its conjugate base. They can resist a change in pH when either an acid or a base is added to the solution. There are two ways of preparing acidic buffers that you need to know about.

Tip: The acid has to be a weak acid — you can't make an acidic buffer with a strong acid.

1. Making a buffer from a weak acid and the salt of its conjugate base

If you mix a weak acid with a salt of its conjugate base, then a small amount of the acid will dissociate, but some will remain undissociated. The salt will fully dissociate to form the conjugate base of the acid in the solution. So the solution will contain a mixture of a weak acid and its conjugate base, and can act as an acidic buffer.

Example

A mixture of ethanoic acid (CH_3COOH) and sodium ethanoate ($CH_3COO^-Na^+$) is an **acidic buffer**. Ethanoic acid is a weak acid, so it only slightly dissociates:

$$CH_3COOH_{(aq)} \rightleftharpoons H^+_{(aq)} + CH_3COO^-_{(aq)}$$

But the salt fully dissociates into its ions when it dissolves:

$$CH_3COONa_{(s)} \xrightarrow{water} CH_3COO^-_{(aq)} + Na^+_{(aq)}$$

So in the solution you've got heaps of undissociated ethanoic acid molecules ($CH_3COOH_{(aq)}$), and heaps of ethanoate ions ($CH_3COO^-_{(aq)}$) from the salt.

2. Making a buffer from an excess of weak acid and some strong alkali

If you mix an excess of a weak acid with a small amount of a strong alkali then some of the acid is neutralised to make a salt, but some is left un-neutralised. The reaction mixture would then contain a weak acid and its conjugate base, and so would act as an acidic buffer.

Example

You could make an acidic buffer by mixing an excess of ethanoic acid (CH_3COOH) with sodium hydroxide (NaOH). Some of the ethanoic acid would react with the sodium hydroxide to form its conjugate base:

$$CH_3COOH + OH^- \rightleftharpoons CH_3COO^- + H_2O$$

But because the acid is in excess, some of the ethanoic acid will remain un-neutralised. This means the solution contains some ethanoic acid and some of its conjugate base, so is an acidic buffer.

Tip: When preparing buffer solutions in this way, you have to make sure the acid is in excess. If the alkali is in excess, all the acid will react and there will be no acid left.

How acidic buffers work

Whichever way you prepare an acidic buffer, the following equilibrium is set up between the weak acid and its conjugate base:

$$HA_{(aq)} \rightleftharpoons H^+_{(aq)} + A^-_{(aq)}$$

Lots of undissociated weak acid (→ HA) — *Lots of conjugate base* (→ A^-)

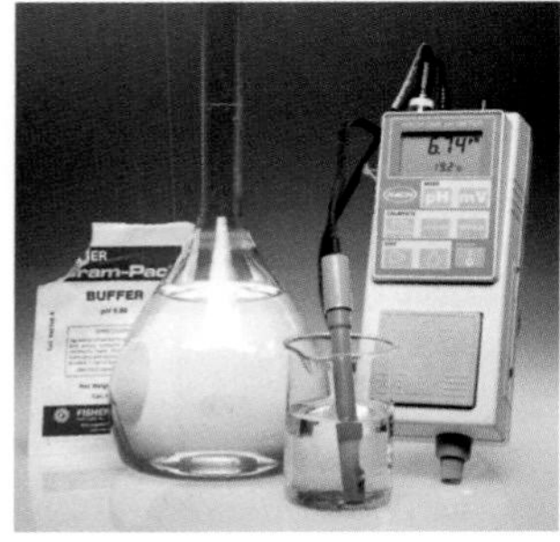

Figure 1: *An acidic buffer solution.*

The buffer solution contains lots of undissociated acid (HA), lots of the acid's conjugate base (A^-) and enough H^+ ions to make the solution acidic. When you alter the concentration of H^+ or OH^- ions in the buffer solution the equilibrium position between the conjugate pair moves to counteract the change (this is down to Le Chatelier's principle — see page 59). The conjugate base can react to mop up any excess H^+ ions, and the conjugate acid can dissociate and release H^+ ions if there's too much base around.

Resisting an acid

The large number of A^- ions make the buffer able to cope with the addition of acid. If you add a small amount of acid (e.g. $HCl_{(aq)}$) the H^+ concentration increases. Most of the extra H^+ ions join with A^- ions to form HA. This shifts the equilibrium to the left, reducing the H^+ concentration to almost its original value. So the pH doesn't change much.

Resisting a base

If a small amount of base (e.g. NaOH) is added to the buffer solution, the OH^- concentration increases. Most of the extra OH^- ions react with H^+ ions to form water — removing H^+ ions from the solution. This causes more of the weak acid, HA, to dissociate to form H^+ ions — shifting the equilibrium to the right. There's no problem doing this as there's loads of spare undissociated HA molecules. The H^+ concentration increases until it's close to its original value, so the pH doesn't change much.

Example

If you mix ethanoic acid with sodium ethanoate, the following equilibrium is set up:

$$CH_3COOH_{(aq)} \rightleftharpoons H^+_{(aq)} + CH_3COO^-_{(aq)}$$

If you add some acid to this mixture, then the extra H^+ ions can react with the CH_3COO^- ions, and the equilibrium shifts to the left, reducing the H^+ concentration to almost its original value. So the pH doesn't change much.

Addition of H^+ (acid) ←

$$CH_3COOH_{(aq)} \rightleftharpoons H^+_{(aq)} + CH_3COO^-_{(aq)}$$

If you add some base to this mixture, then the OH^- ions react with the H^+ ions to form water. This reduces the concentration of H^+, so more of the CH_3COOH molecules will dissociate to counteract this change, and the equilibrium moves to the right. This causes the H^+ concentration to rise back to almost its original value. So the pH doesn't change much.

Addition of OH^- (base) →

$$CH_3COOH_{(aq)} \rightleftharpoons H^+_{(aq)} + CH_3COO^-_{(aq)}$$

Tip: CH_3COOH and CH_3COO^- are a conjugate pair. See page 65 for more on conjugate pairs.

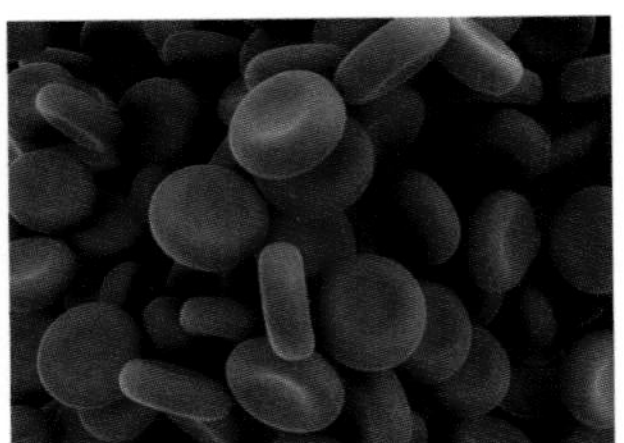

Figure 2: Red blood cells. Blood has to be kept at a pH of between 7.35 and 7.45 so is buffered by carbonic acid.

Buffer action in blood

Blood needs to be kept at between pH 7.35 and 7.45. The pH is controlled using a carbonic acid-hydrogencarbonate buffer system. Carbonic acid dissociates into H^+ ions and HCO_3^- ions as shown below:

$$H_2CO_{3(aq)} \rightleftharpoons H^+_{(aq)} + HCO_3^-{}_{(aq)}$$

If the concentration of H^+ rises in blood, then HCO_3^- ions from the carbonic acid-hydrogencarbonate buffer system will react with the excess H^+ ions, and the equilibrium will shift to the left, reducing the H^+ concentration to almost its original value. This stops the pH of blood from dropping. Meanwhile, if the concentration of H^+ ions falls in blood, then more H_2CO_3 molecules from the carbonic acid-hydrogencarbonate buffer system will dissociate, and the equilibrium will shift to the right, increasing the H^+ concentration to almost its original value. This stops the pH of blood from rising.

The levels of H_2CO_3 are controlled by respiration. By breathing out CO_2, the level of H_2CO_3 is reduced, as it moves this equilibrium to the right:

$$H_2CO_{3(aq)} \rightleftharpoons H_2O_{(l)} + CO_{2(aq)}$$

The levels of HCO_3^- are controlled by the kidneys, with excess being excreted in the urine.

Practice Questions — Fact Recall

Q1 What is a buffer?

Q2 State two ways of making an acidic buffer.

Q3 Explain how an acidic buffer resists changes in pH when:
a) a small amount of acid is added.
b) a small amount of base is added.

Q4 What buffer system is used to keep the pH of blood between 7.35 and 7.45?

6. Calculating the pH of Buffers

You need to be able to calculate the pH of buffer solutions. These calculations look scary, but don't worry — they're not nearly as bad as they look.

Learning Objective:

- Be able to calculate the pH of a buffer solution, from the K_a value of a weak acid and the equilibrium concentrations of the conjugate acid-base pair, and be able to calculate related quantities.

Specification Reference 5.1.3

Calculations using known concentrations

If you know the K_a of the weak acid and the equilibrium concentrations of the weak acid and its salt, calculating the pH of an **acidic buffer** isn't too tricky. To do any calculations, you need to make the following assumptions:

- The salt of the conjugate base is fully dissociated, so the equilibrium concentration of A^- is the same as the initial concentration of the salt.
- HA is only slightly dissociated, so its equilibrium concentration is the same as its initial concentration.

If these assumptions are valid, then here's how you calculate the pH of an acidic buffer:

Step 1: Write out the expression for the K_a of the weak acid.

Step 2: Rearrange the equation to give an expression for $[H^+]$.

Step 3: Substitute the value for K_a and the equilibrium concentrations of the acid and salt into the equation.

Step 4: Solve the equation to find a value for $[H^+]$.

Step 5: Substitute your value for $[H^+]$ into the pH equation ($pH = -\log_{10} [H^+]$) and solve it to calculate the pH.

Tip: Writing expressions for K_a was covered on page 74. Have a look back if you need a recap.

Example — **Maths Skills**

A buffer solution contains 0.400 mol dm^{-3} methanoic acid, HCOOH, and 0.600 mol dm^{-3} sodium methanoate, $HCOO^-Na^+$. For methanoic acid, $K_a = 1.6 \times 10^{-4}$ mol dm^{-3}. What is the pH of this buffer?

1. Write the expression for K_a of the weak acid:

$$HCOOH_{(aq)} \rightleftharpoons H^+_{(aq)} + HCOO^-_{(aq)} \quad \text{so} \quad K_a = \frac{[H^+][HCOO^-]}{[HCOOH]}$$

2. Rearrange the equation to get $[H^+]$:

$$[H^+] = \frac{K_a \times [HCOOH]}{[HCOO^-]}$$

3. Substitute in the value of K_a and the concentrations given in the question: From the assumptions above:

- The equilibrium concentration of $HCOO^-$ is the same as the initial concentration of $HCOO^- Na^+$.
- The equilibrium concentration of HCOOH is the same as its initial concentration.

$$[H^+] = \frac{K_a \times [HCOOH]}{[HCOO^-]} = \frac{(1.6 \times 10^{-4}) \times 0.400}{0.600}$$

4. Solve to find H^+:

$$[H^+] = \frac{(1.6 \times 10^{-4}) \times 0.400}{0.600} = 1.0... \times 10^{-4} \text{ mol dm}^{-3}$$

5. Use your value of $[H^+]$ to calculate the pH:

$$pH = -\log_{10} [H^+] = -\log(1.0... \times 10^{-4})$$
$$= \mathbf{3.97}$$

Tip: Remember — the concentrations in the expression for K_a all have to be equilibrium concentrations.

Tip: See page 69 for a reminder on how to calculate pH.

Tip: See page 78 for more on how a buffer can be prepared by mixing an acid and a base.

Tip: The molar ratios tell you how many moles of acid will react with a certain number of moles of base, and how many moles of salt are produced. These numbers will always be in the same ratio for a given reaction.

Tip: It's really important that you know formulas like:

$$\text{moles} = \frac{\text{conc.} \times \text{vol. (cm}^3\text{)}}{1000}$$

You won't be able to do the harder calculations if you haven't got your head around the basics. Check out pages 271-273 for a summary of the formulas that you need to know for your A Level Chemistry exams.

Finding the equilibrium concentrations

If a buffer has been prepared by mixing an acid with a base, you might have to work out the equilibrium concentrations of the acid and its salt before you can calculate the pH. Here's what to do:

Step 1: Write out the equation for the neutralisation reaction — remember acid + base → salt + water.

Step 2: Calculate the number of moles of acid and base at the start of the reaction using the volumes and concentrations given in the question.

Step 3: Use the molar ratios in the equation to work out the moles of acid and salt left at the end of the reaction.

Step 4: Calculate the concentration of the acid and salt in the buffer solution by dividing by the volume of the solution — this is the volume of the acid and the base added together.

Step 5: Then you're ready to calculate the pH.

Example — Maths Skills

A buffer is formed by mixing 15 cm³ of 0.10 mol dm⁻³ sodium hydroxide (NaOH) and 30 cm³ of 0.60 mol dm⁻³ propanoic acid (CH_3CH_2COOH). Calculate the pH of this buffer solution (K_a = 1.35 × 10⁻⁵ mol dm⁻³).

1. Write out the equation for the reaction:

$$CH_3CH_2COOH + NaOH \rightarrow CH_3CH_2COO^-Na^+ + H_2O$$

2. Calculate the number of moles of acid and base:

$$\text{Moles } CH_3CH_2COOH = \frac{\text{Conc. (mol dm}^3\text{)} \times \text{Vol. (cm}^3\text{)}}{1000} = \frac{0.60 \times 30}{1000}$$
$$= 0.018 \text{ moles}$$

$$\text{Moles NaOH} = \frac{\text{Conc. (mol dm}^3\text{)} \times \text{Vol. (cm}^3\text{)}}{1000} = \frac{0.10 \times 15}{1000}$$
$$= 0.0015 \text{ moles}$$

3. The acid is in excess, so all the base reacts. There's 0.0015 moles of NaOH at the start of the reaction. If it all reacts there will be 0.0015 moles of salt at the end of the reaction.

   The equation shows us that 1 mole of base will react with 1 mole of acid to give 1 mole of salt. So if there are 0.0015 moles of salt, 0.0015 moles of acid must have been used up.
   This leaves 0.018 – 0.0015 = 0.0165 moles of acid.

   So, the buffer solution contains 0.0015 moles of $CH_3CH_2COO^-Na^+$ and 0.0165 moles of CH_3CH_2COOH.

4. Calculate the concentration of acid and salt in the buffer solution:

   The total volume of the solution is 15 + 30 = 45 cm³

$$\text{Conc. } CH_3CH_2COOH = \frac{\text{moles} \times 1000}{\text{volume (cm}^3\text{)}} = \frac{0.0165 \times 1000}{45}$$
$$= 0.37 \text{ mol dm}^{-3}$$

$$\text{Conc. } CH_3CH_2COO^-Na^+ = \frac{\text{moles} \times 1000}{\text{volume (cm}^3\text{)}} = \frac{0.0015 \times 1000}{45}$$
$$= 0.033 \text{ mol dm}^{-3}$$

5. Work out the pH as before:

$$CH_3CH_2COOH \rightleftharpoons H^+ + CH_3CH_2COO^- \text{ so } K_a = \frac{[H^+][CH_3CH_2COO^-]}{[CH_3CH_2COOH]}$$

$$[H^+] = \frac{K_a \times [CH_3CH_2COOH]}{[CH_3CH_2COO^-]} = \frac{(1.35 \times 10^{-5}) \times 0.37}{0.033}$$
$$= 1.5... \times 10^{-4} \text{ mol dm}^{-3}$$

$$pH = -\log_{10}[H^+] = -\log_{10}(1.5... \times 10^{-4}) = \mathbf{3.82}$$

Tip: This bit was covered in much more detail on page 81 — have a look back if you need a quick reminder of what's going on.

Practice Questions — Application

Q1 An acidic buffer solution contains 0.200 mol dm^{-3} propanoic acid (CH_3CH_2COOH) and 0.350 mol dm^{-3} potassium propanoate. For propanoic acid, $K_a = 1.35 \times 10^{-5}$ mol dm^{-3}.

a) Write an expression for the K_a of propanoic acid.

b) Calculate the concentration of H^+ ions in this buffer solution.

c) Calculate the pH of this buffer solution.

Q2 A buffer solution contains 0.150 mol dm^{-3} ethanoic acid and 0.250 mol dm^{-3} potassium ethanoate. For ethanoic acid $K_a = 1.74 \times 10^{-5}$ mol dm^{-3}. Calculate the pH of this buffer.

Q3 A buffer is made by mixing 30.0 cm^3 of 0.500 mol dm^{-3} propanoic acid (CH_3CH_2COOH) with 20.0 cm^3 of 0.250 mol dm^{-3} potassium hydroxide (KOH). For propanoic acid, $K_a = 1.35 \times 10^{-5}$ mol dm^{-3}.

a) Write an equation to show the reaction of propanoic acid with potassium hydroxide.

b) Calculate the number of moles of propanoic acid and potassium hydroxide at the beginning of the reaction.

c) Calculate the concentration of propanoic acid and potassium propanoate in the buffer solution.

d) Calculate the concentration of H^+ ions in this buffer solution.

e) Calculate the pH of the buffer solution.

Q4 A buffer is formed by mixing together 25.0 cm^3 of 0.200 mol dm^{-3} methanoic acid (HCOOH) and 15.0 cm^3 of 0.100 mol dm^{-3} sodium hydroxide (NaOH). For methanoic acid, $K_a = 1.60 \times 10^{-4}$ mol dm^{-3}. Calculate the pH of this buffer.

7. pH Curves and Titrations

When acids and bases are mixed together a neutralisation reaction occurs — H^+ ions from the acid join with OH^- ions from the base to create water. If there are equal numbers of H^+ and OH^- ions the mixture will be neutral (pH 7). What do pH curves and titrations have to do with this? Read on...

Learning Objectives:

- Understand the techniques and procedures used when measuring pH with a pH meter (PAG 11).
- Be able to sketch and interpret the shapes of pH titration curves for combinations of strong and weak acids with strong and weak bases.
- Be able to explain indicator colour changes in terms of equilibrium shift between the HA and A^- forms of the indicator.
- Be able to use pH titration curves to explain the choice of suitable indicators, given the pH range of the indicator.

Specification Reference 5.1.3

Measuring pH

PRACTICAL ACTIVITY GROUP 11

A **pH meter** does what it says on the tin — it's an electronic gadget you can use to tell you the pH of a solution (see Figure 1). pH meters have a probe that you put into your solution and a digital display that shows the reading. At the bottom of the probe is a bulb that's very delicate, so be careful when handling it.

Before you use a pH meter, you need to make sure it's calibrated correctly. Here's how you do this:

1. Place the bulb of the pH meter into distilled water and allow the reading to settle. Now adjust the reading so that it reads **7.0**.
2. Do the same with a standard solution of pH 4.0 and another of pH 10.0. Make sure you rinse the probe with distilled water in-between each reading.

You're now ready to take your actual measurement. To do this, place the probe in the liquid you're measuring and let the reading settle before you record the result. After each measurement, you should rinse the probe in distilled water.

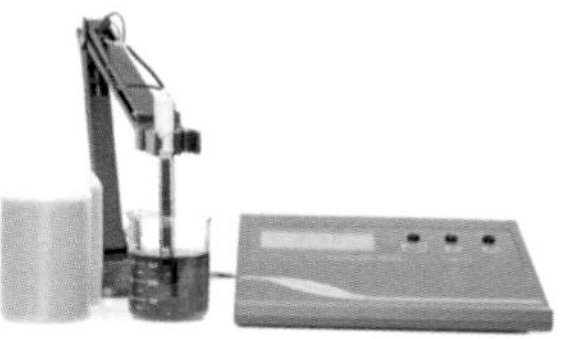

Figure 1: A pH meter.

Tip: If you're going to do a titration experiment, remember to carry out a risk assessment first.

Tip: There are more details on how you can measure the pH of a solution in the Practical Skills for the Practical Endorsement section, on page 11.

pH curves

pH curves show the results of titration experiments. They can be made by plotting the pH of the titration mixture against the amount of base added as the titration goes on. The pH of the mixture can be measured using a pH meter and the scale on the burette can be used to see how much base has been added.

The shape of the curve looks a bit different depending on the strengths of the acid and base that are used. The graphs below and on the next page show the pH curves for the different combinations of strong and weak monobasic acids and bases:

Strong acid/strong base

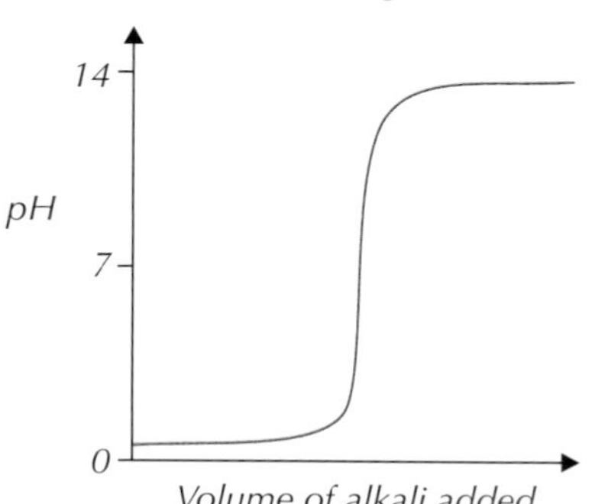

The pH starts around 1, as there's an excess of strong acid.
It finishes up around pH 13, when you have an excess of strong base.

Strong acid/weak base

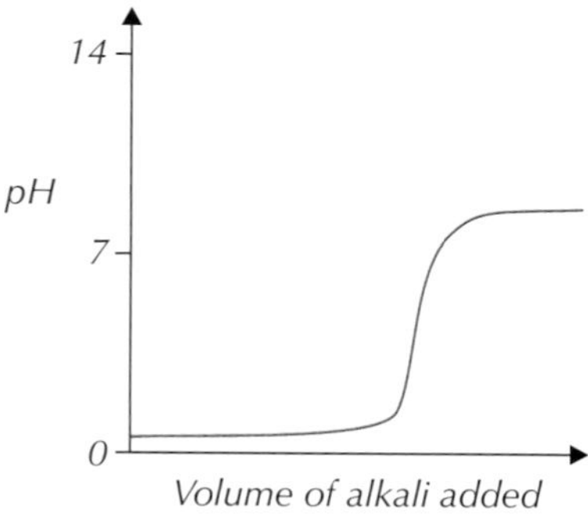

The pH starts around 1, as there's an excess of strong acid.
It finishes up around pH 9, when you have an excess of weak base.

Weak acid/strong base

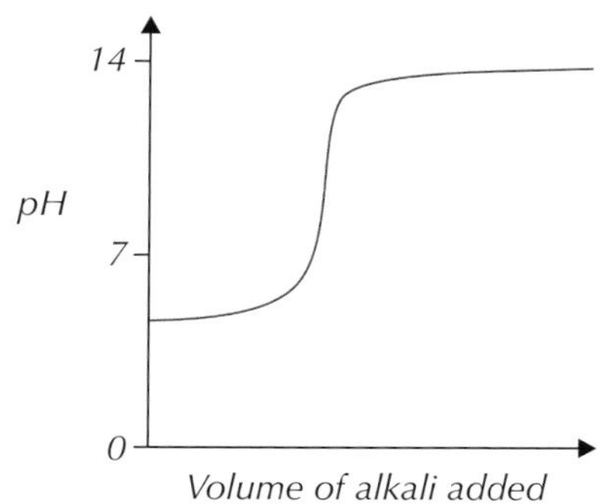

The pH starts around 5, as there's an excess of weak acid.
It finishes up around pH 13, when you have an excess of strong base.

Weak acid/weak base

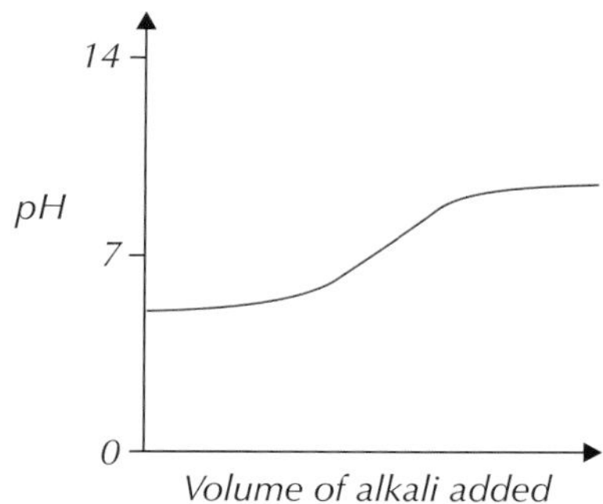

The pH starts around 5, as there's an excess of weak acid.
It finishes up around pH 9, when you have an excess of weak base.

You can explain why each graph has a particular shape:

- The initial pH depends on the strength of the acid. So a strong acid titration will start at a much lower pH than a weak acid titration.
- To start with, addition of small amounts of base have little impact on the pH of the solution.
- All the graphs (apart from the weak acid/weak base graph) have a bit that's almost vertical — the mid-point of this vertical section is the equivalence point or end point. At this point $[H^+] \approx [OH^-]$ — it's here that all the acid is just neutralised. When this is the case, a tiny amount of base causes a sudden, big change in pH.
- You need to add more weak base than strong base to a strong acid to cause a pH change, and the change is less pronounced. On the other hand, you need to add less strong base to a weak acid to see a large change in pH.
- The final pH depends on the strength of the base — the stronger the base, the higher the final pH.

Tip: If you titrate a base with an acid instead, the shapes of the curves stay the same, but they're reversed. For example:

Strong base/strong acid

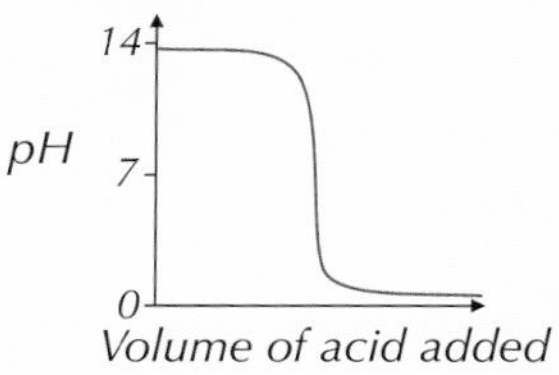

Strong base/weak acid

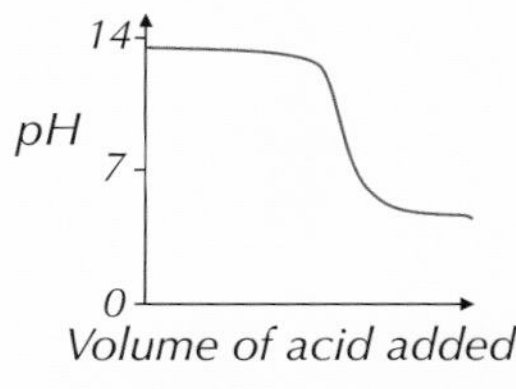

Weak base/strong acid

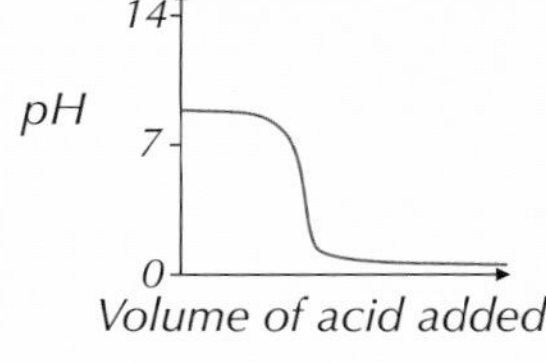

Weak base/weak acid

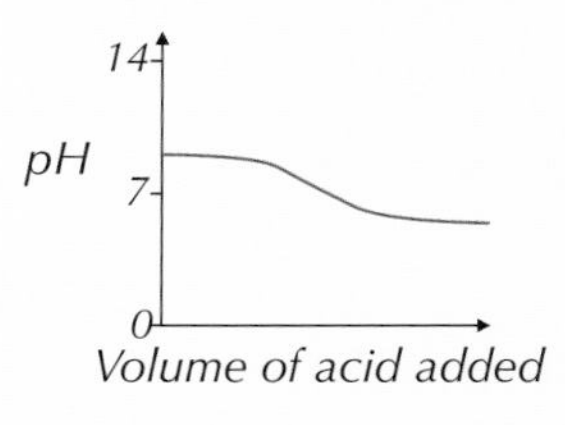

Indicators

You can use titrations instead of pH meters to work out the concentration of an acid or base. You'll need an **indicator** that changes colour to show you when your sample has been neutralised.

Indicators can be thought of as weak acids. They work because they have differently coloured conjugate pairs. As the pH of the solution changes during a titration, the equilibrium concentrations of the conjugate pairs will also change. The colour will change depending on whether the indicator is mainly protonated or deprotonated.

Tip: Have a look back at your Year 1 notes if you're not sure how to calculate the concentration of an acid or base from titration data.

Examples

Methyl orange and **phenolphthalein** are indicators that are often used for acid-base titrations.

Phenolphthalein as an indicator

The protonated form of phenolphthalein is colourless, whilst its conjugate base is pink:

$$\text{Phenolphthalein-H} \rightleftharpoons \text{Phenolphthalein}^- + H^+$$

colourless — *pink*

Figure 2: The colourless to pink colour change of phenolphthalein.

At low pH, there are lots of H^+ ions in solution, so most of the phenolphthalein is protonated and the indicator is colourless. As the pH rises, and the concentration of H^+ ions decreases, the equilibrium shifts to the right, and more of the phenolphthalein deprotonates. So, at high pH, the indicator is pink.

Methyl orange as an indicator

The protonated form of methyl orange is red, whilst its conjugate base is yellow:

$$\underset{\textit{red}}{\text{Methyl orange-H}} \rightleftharpoons \underset{\textit{yellow}}{\text{Methyl orange}^-} + H^+$$

At low pH, there are lots of H^+ ions in solution, so most of the methyl orange is protonated and the indicator is red. As the pH rises, and the concentration of H^+ ions decreases, the equilibrium shifts to the right, and more of the methyl orange deprotonates. At high pH, the indicator is yellow.

Figure 3: The red to yellow colour change of methyl orange.

Choosing indicators

When you use an indicator, you need it to change colour exactly at the end point of your titration. So you need to pick one that changes colour over a narrow pH range that lies entirely on the vertical part of the pH curve. So for the titration shown in Figure 4 (below) you'd want an indicator that changed colour somewhere between pH 8 and pH 11:

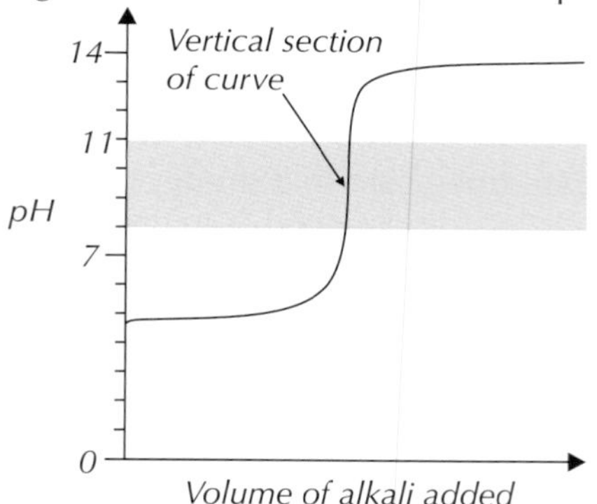

The curve is vertical between pH 8 and pH 11— so a very small amount of alkali will cause the pH to change from 8 to 11.

So, an indicator that changes colour between pH 8 and pH 11 is needed.

Figure 4: *Graph showing how to select an indicator.*

Methyl orange and phenolphthalein each change colour over a different pH range:

Name of indicator	Colour at low pH	Approx. pH of colour change	Colour at high pH
Methyl orange	red	3.1 – 4.4	yellow
Phenolphthalein	colourless	8.3 – 10	pink

Exam Tip
Don't worry, you don't have to learn the pH ranges of any indicators. You'll always be told them in the question if you need to use them.

- For a strong acid/strong alkali titration, you can use either of these indicators — there's a rapid pH change over the range for both indicators.
- For a strong acid/weak alkali only methyl orange will do. The pH changes rapidly across the range for methyl orange, but not for phenolphthalein.
- For a weak acid/strong alkali, phenolphthalein is the stuff to use. The pH changes rapidly over phenolphthalein's range, but not over methyl orange's.
- For weak acid/weak alkali titrations there's no sharp pH change, so no indicator will work.

Tip: To find the end point of a weak acid/weak base titration, you can't use an indicator — you have to use a pH meter instead.

You need to be able to use a pH curve to explain a choice of indicator:

Example — Maths Skills

The graph to the right shows the pH curve produced when a strong acid is added to a weak base. Bromophenol blue, which has a pH range of 3.0 – 4.6, was used as an indicator. Explain why bromophenol blue is a suitable indicator to use.

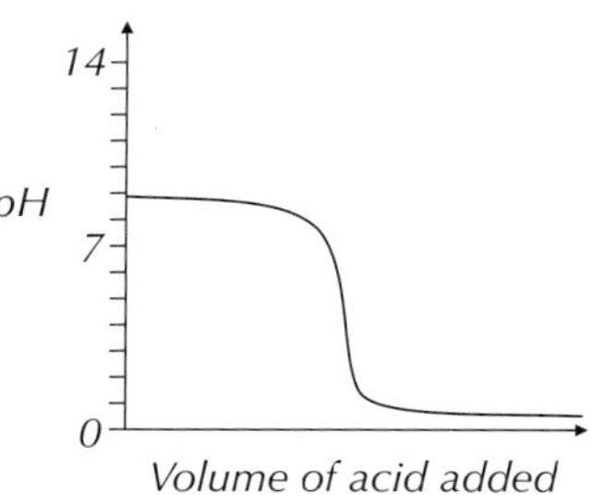

The graph shows that the vertical part of the pH curve is between about pH 2 and pH 6. So you need an indicator with a pH range between 2 and 6. Bromophenol blue changes colour within this range so bromophenol blue is a suitable indicator to choose.

Tip: The pH range of an indicator is the range in which the colour changes.

Practice Questions — Application

Q1 The graphs below show the pH curves for four different acid–base titrations. For each reaction state what type of acid and base were used and select an appropriate indicator from the table below.

Indicator	pH range
Thymol blue	1.2 – 2.8
Methyl orange	3.1 – 4.4
Litmus	5.0 – 8.0
Cresol purple	7.6 – 9.2
Phenolphthalein	8.3 – 10

a)

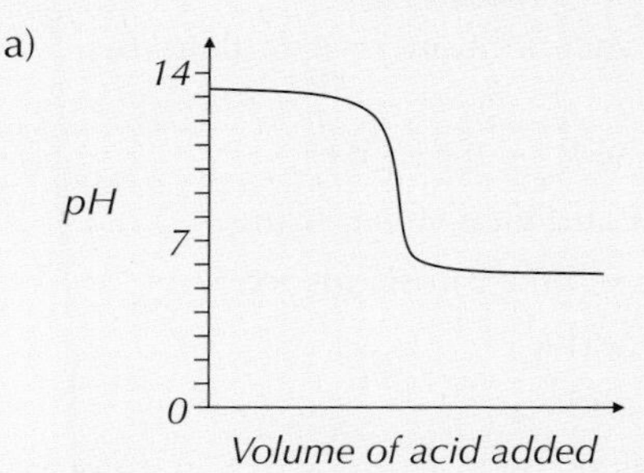

b)

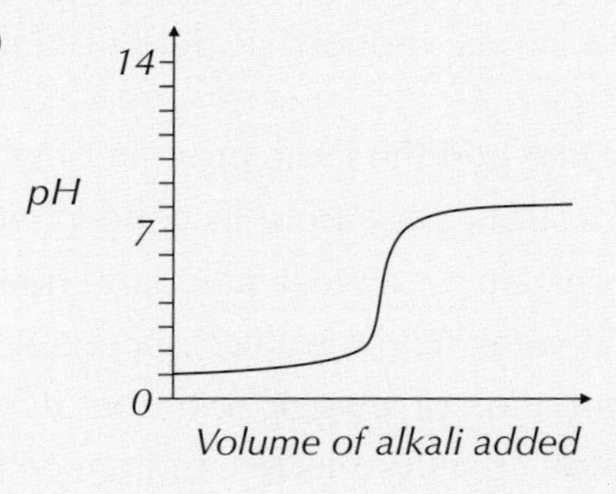

c)

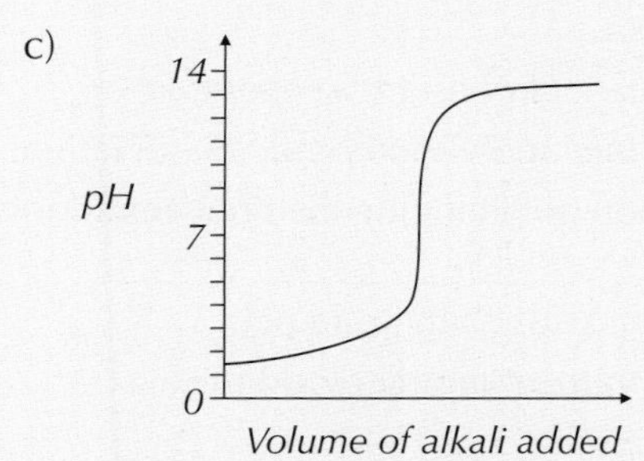

d)

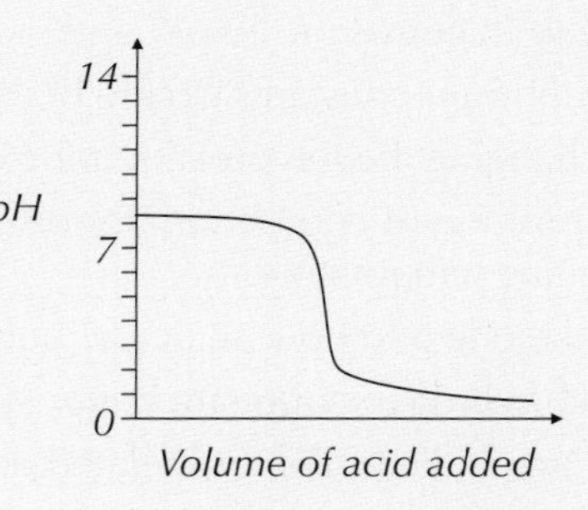

Tip: You need to look at where the curves start and finish to work out if you've got an acid neutralising a base or a base neutralising an acid.

Q2 Neutral red changes colour from red to yellow between pH 6.8 and pH 8.0. Sketch the pH curve for a titration reaction that this indicator could be used for.

Practice Questions — Fact Recall

Q1 Sketch the pH curve produced when:
a) A strong acid neutralises a weak base.
b) A strong base neutralises a strong acid.
c) A weak acid neutralises a strong base.

Q2 a) What happens at the end point of a titration reaction?
b) How can you see that the end point has been reached when you're carrying out a titration?
c) How can you tell the end point has been reached using a pH curve?

Q3 How would you know if an indicator is suitable for a particular titration reaction?

Tip: Don't forget — acids have low pHs and bases have high pHs.

Section Summary

Make sure you know...

- That a Brønsted-Lowry acid is a species that can donate a proton and a Brønsted-Lowry base is a species that can accept a proton.
- That strong acids/bases dissociate fully in water while weak acids/bases only partially dissociate.
- That monobasic acids donate one proton per molecule into solution, dibasic acids can donate two protons per molecule and tribasic acids can donate three protons per molecule into solution.
- What conjugate acid-base pairs are and how to identify them.
- How acids react with metals, carbonates, alkalis and metal oxides.
- That pH = $-\log_{10}$ $[H^+]$ where $[H^+]$is the concentration of H^+ ions in mol dm^{-3}.
- How to convert pH into $[H^+]$ and vice versa.
- How to calculate the pH of a strong, monobasic acid from its concentration, or calculate its concentration from the pH.
- That water is weakly dissociated and the ionic product of water is $K_w = [H^+][OH^-]$.
- How to calculate the pH of a strong base from its concentration and vice versa, using K_w.
- That K_a is the dissociation constant for a weak acid, and how to write expressions for K_a.
- How to calculate the pH of a weak acid from its concentration and K_a.
- How to calculate the concentration of a weak acid from its pH and K_a.
- How to calculate K_a for a weak acid from its pH and concentration.
- That $pK_a = -\log_{10}(K_a)$ and how to convert K_a to pK_a and vice versa.
- That K_w and K_a are both equilibrium constants, so are both constant at constant temperature.
- The effect on K_w and K_a of changing the temperature for exothermic and endothermic dissociation.
- How K_w and K_a control the position of equilibrium for dissociation on changing the concentrations of H^+, OH^- or A^-, and on changing temperature.
- What a buffer is, how to make one and how an acidic buffer can resist changes in pH.
- The role of the carbonic acid-hydrogencarbonate buffer system in maintaining blood pH.
- How to calculate the pH of an acidic buffer and related quantities.
- How to measure pH using a pH meter.
- What the pH curves for all the different combinations of weak and strong acids and bases look like.
- That indicators change colour due to changes in the equilibrium between the differently coloured HA and A^- forms of the indicator.
- How to use pH curves to select an appropriate pH indicator to use in a titration.

Exam-style Questions

1 A 0.375 mol dm^{-3} solution of lactic acid, a weak acid, has a pH of 2.14 at 25 °C. What is K_a of lactic acid at this temperature?

A 0.019 mol dm^{-3}

B 1.4×10^{-4} mol dm^{-3}

C 3.85

D 7.24×10^{-3} mol dm^{-3}

(1 mark)

2 What is the pH of a 0.012 mol dm^{-3} solution of the strong base potassium hydroxide, KOH, at 15 °C? K_w at this temperature is 0.457×10^{-14} mol^2 dm^{-6}.

A 7.17

B 14.34

C 1.82

D 12.42

(1 mark)

3 Methanoic acid (HCOOH) is a weak acid. A 0.240 mol dm^{-3} solution of HCOOH has a pH of 2.18 at 25 °C.

(a) (i) Write out the equation for the dissociation of HCOOH.

(1 mark)

(ii) Write out an expression for K_a for this acid.

(1 mark)

(iii) Calculate the pK_a of methanoic acid at 25 °C.

(3 marks)

(b) A buffer solution contains 0.0840 mol dm^{-3} methanoic acid (HCOOH) and 0.0600 mol dm^{-3} ammonium methanoate ($HCOONH_4$)

(i) Calculate the pH of this buffer.

(2 marks)

(ii) This buffer can be prepared by reacting methanoic acid with ammonia.

- Write an equation for the reaction of methanoic acid with ammonia.
- Label one conjugate acid/base pair 'Acid 1' and 'Base 1'.
- Label the other conjugate acid/base pair 'Acid 2' and 'Base 2'.

(3 marks)

(iii) Explain how this buffer resists changes in pH when an acid is added.

(3 marks)

4 The concentrations of strong acids and strong bases can be found by carrying out titrations. Titrations are usually done at room temperature (25.0 °C). The value of K_w at 25.0 °C is 1.00×10^{-14} mol dm^{-3}.

(a) (i) Give the expression for K_w.

(1 mark)

(ii) Give the expression for pH.

(1 mark)

(b) Calculate the pH of a 0.150 mol dm^{-3} solution of NaOH at 25.0 °C.

(3 marks)

(c) In a titration reaction at 25.0 °C, 25.0 cm^3 of this 0.150 mol dm^{-3} solution of NaOH was neutralised by 18.5 cm^3 of a 0.203 mol dm^{-3} solution of HCl.

(i) Which of the graphs below (A, B and C) shows the pH curve for this reaction?

A

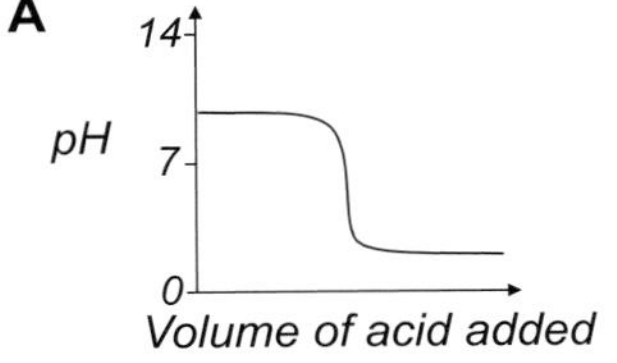

B

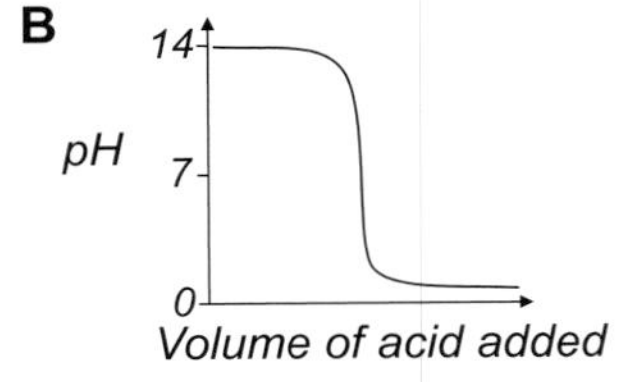

C

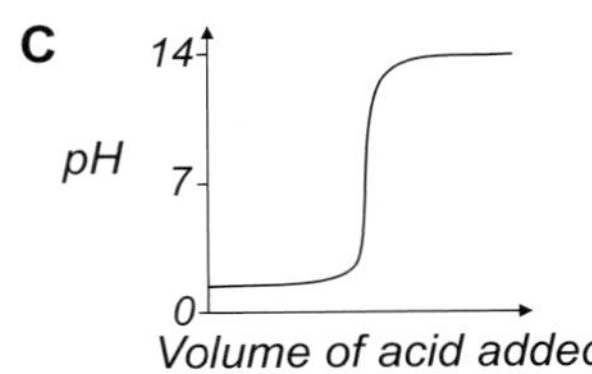

(1 mark)

(ii) Calculate the pH of the HCl solution.

(2 marks)

(d) The pH curve for another titration is shown below.

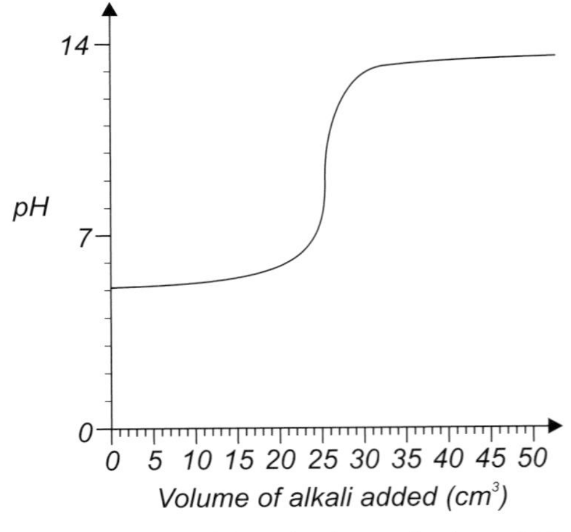

Indicator	pH range
Thymol blue	1.2 – 2.8
Bromophenol blue	3.0 – 4.6
Litmus	5.0 – 8.0
Phenolphthalein	8.3 – 10

(i) Suggest an acid and a base that could have been used in this titration.

(2 marks)

(ii) From the table above, suggest an indicator that would be suitable for this titration.

(1 mark)

1. Enthalpy Changes

Some of this stuff may ring a few bells from Year 1. Make sure you understand all the definitions in this topic because they're really important for the rest of the section.

The basics

Enthalpy notation

Enthalpy change, ΔH (delta H), is the heat energy transferred in a reaction at constant pressure. The units of ΔH are kJ mol^{-1}. You write ΔH° to show that the substances were in their standard states and that the measurements were made under **standard conditions**. Standard conditions are 100 kPa (about 1 atm) pressure and a stated temperature (e.g. ΔH°_{298}). In this book, all the enthalpy changes are measured at 298 K (25 °C). Sometimes the notation will also include a subscript, for example to signify whether the enthalpy change is for a reaction (r), for combustion (c), or for the formation of a new compound (f).

Tip: You covered enthalpy notation in Year 1 so if you need a reminder, get your old notes out.

Exothermic and endothermic reactions

Exothermic reactions have a negative ΔH value, because heat energy is given out (the chemicals lose energy). **Endothermic reactions** have a positive ΔH value, because heat energy is absorbed (the chemicals gain energy).

Tip: HOW SCIENCE WORKS According to the first law of thermodynamics, energy is always conserved (it is never created or destroyed). So if the products of a reaction have less energy than the reactants, the extra energy has to go somewhere. It is transferred to the surroundings as heat energy — this is the enthalpy change.

Enthalpy and energy definitions

There are lots of different enthalpy and energy terms you need to know on the next few pages. Unfortunately, each specific type of change has its own definition and you need to learn them all.

- **Enthalpy change of formation**, $\Delta_f H$, is the enthalpy change when 1 mole of a compound is formed from its elements, e.g. $Ca_{(s)} + Cl_{2(g)} \rightarrow CaCl_{2(s)}$
- **Enthalpy change of atomisation of an element**, $\Delta_{at} H$, is the enthalpy change when 1 mole of gaseous atoms is formed from an element, e.g. $\frac{1}{2}Cl_{2(g)} \rightarrow Cl_{(g)}$
- **Enthalpy change of atomisation of a compound**, $\Delta_{at} H$, is the enthalpy change when 1 mole of a compound is converted to gaseous atoms, e.g. $NaCl_{(s)} \rightarrow Na_{(g)} + Cl_{(g)}$
- The **first ionisation energy** is the energy needed to change 1 mole of gaseous atoms into 1 mole of gaseous 1+ ions, e.g. $Mg_{(g)} \rightarrow Mg^{+}_{(g)} + e^{-}$
- The **second ionisation energy** is the energy needed to change 1 mole of gaseous 1+ ions atoms into 1 mole of gaseous 2+ ions, e.g. $Mg^{+}_{(g)} \rightarrow Mg^{2+}_{(g)} + e^{-}$
- **First electron affinity** is the energy needed to change 1 mole of gaseous atoms into 1 mole of gaseous 1– ions, e.g. $O_{(g)} + e^{-} \rightarrow O^{-}_{(g)}$
- **Second electron affinity** is the energy needed to change 1 mole of gaseous 1– ions into 1 mole of gaseous 2– ions, e.g. $O^{-}_{(g)} + e^{-} \rightarrow O^{2-}_{(g)}$

Exam Tip
You'll have to understand all of these definitions for the exam, so make sure you've learned them all.

Tip: There's lots more on lattice enthalpy on page 93, and more on enthalpy change of hydration and enthalpy change of solution on page 99.

Tip: These terms will crop up a lot in this section so don't move on until you understand what each one means — you might want to fold this page over so you can find it again if you need to.

- **Lattice enthalpy**, $\Delta_{LE}H$, is the enthalpy change when 1 mole of a solid ionic compound is formed from its gaseous ions, e.g. $Na^+_{(g)} + Cl^-_{(g)} \rightarrow NaCl_{(s)}$
- The **enthalpy change of hydration**, $\Delta_{hyd}H$, is the enthalpy change when 1 mole of gaseous ions is dissolved in water, e.g. $Na^+_{(g)} \rightarrow Na^+_{(aq)}$
- The **enthalpy change of solution**, $\Delta_{sol}H$, is the enthalpy change when 1 mole of solute is dissolved in a solvent, such as water, e.g. $NaCl_{(s)} \rightarrow NaCl_{(aq)}$

Practice Questions — Fact Recall

Q1 What is meant by the term enthalpy change?

Q2 Give the symbol for enthalpy change.

Q3 Define the following:

a) enthalpy change of formation,

b) second electron affinity,

c) enthalpy change of hydration.

Q4 Name the enthalpy or energy changes defined below:

a) The enthalpy change when 1 mole of gaseous atoms is formed from an element.

b) The energy needed to change 1 mole of gaseous atoms into 1 mole of gaseous 1– ions.

Q5 Write the symbol for the following enthalpy changes:

a) the enthalpy change of hydration,

b) the enthalpy change of solution.

2. Lattice Enthalpy

As you might have guessed from the title, this topic is all about lattice enthalpies. Read on to find out what lattice enthalpies are, why they are useful and what affects the lattice enthalpy of an ionic compound.

What is lattice enthalpy?

Ionic compounds can form regular structures called giant ionic lattices, where the positive and negative ions are held together by electrostatic attractions. When gaseous ions combine to make a solid ionic lattice, energy is given out — this is called the **lattice enthalpy**. So, lattice enthalpy is a measure of ionic bond strength. Here's the definition of lattice enthalpy that you need to know:

> The **lattice enthalpy**, $\Delta_{LE}H$, is the enthalpy change when 1 mole of a solid ionic lattice is formed from its gaseous ions.

Example

Sodium chloride (NaCl) is an example of an ionic lattice. The diagram below shows how NaCl is formed from gaseous Na^+ and Cl^- ions.

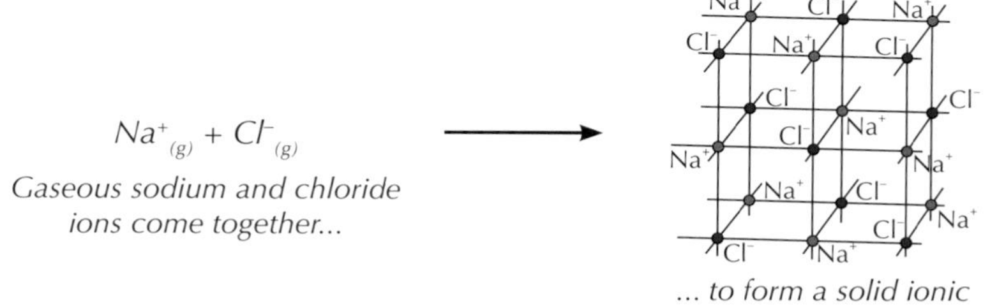
$Na^+_{(g)} + Cl^-_{(g)}$
Gaseous sodium and chloride ions come together...
Na⁺
Cl⁻
... to form a solid ionic lattice of sodium chloride.

The standard lattice enthalpy, $\Delta_{LE}H^\circ$, for this reaction is –787 kJ mol^{-1}. The negative ΔH value shows that lattice formation is an exothermic process.

Lattice enthalpies are quite handy because they tell you how strong the ionic bonding is. The more negative the lattice enthalpy, the stronger the bonding.

Example

The lattice enthalpies of NaCl and MgO are:

$$Na^+_{(g)} + Cl^-_{(g)} \rightarrow NaCl_{(s)} \qquad \Delta_{LE}H^\circ = -787 \text{ kJ mol}^{-1}$$
$$Mg^{2+}_{(g)} + O^{2-}_{(g)} \rightarrow MgO_{(s)} \qquad \Delta_{LE}H^\circ = -3791 \text{ kJ mol}^{-1}$$

Out of NaCl and MgO, MgO has the more negative lattice enthalpy so the MgO lattice is held together by stronger ionic bonds.

Factors affecting lattice enthalpy

Lattice enthalpies have specific values that differ depending on the ions involved. There are two main factors which influence the lattice enthalpy:

1. Ionic charge

The higher the charges on the ions, the stronger the electrostatic attractions between the ions so the more energy is released when an ionic lattice forms. More energy released means that the lattice enthalpy will be more negative. So the lattice enthalpies for compounds with 2+ or 2– ions (e.g. Mg^{2+} or S^{2-}) are more negative than those with 1+ or 1– ions (e.g. Na^+ or Cl^-).

Learning Objectives:

- Be able to explain the term lattice enthalpy (formation of 1 mole of ionic lattice from gaseous ions, $\Delta_{LE}H$) and know that it is used as a measure of the strength of ionic bonding in a giant ionic lattice.
- Be able to give a qualitative explanation of the effect of ionic charge and ionic radius on the exothermic value of a lattice enthalpy.

Specification Reference 5.2.1

Figure 1: *A 3D model of a sodium chloride lattice.*

Tip: Ionic compounds with two 1+ (or 1–) ions and one 2– (or 2+) ion, like Na_2O, have intermediate lattice enthalpies.

Tip: You can work out the charge on an ion from the periodic table — elements in Group 1 form 1+ ions, elements in Group 2 form 2+ ions, elements in Group 6 form 2– ions and elements in Group 7 form 1– ions.

Example

The standard lattice enthalpy of NaCl is only –787 kJ mol^{-1}, but the standard lattice enthalpy of $MgCl_2$ is –2526 kJ mol^{-1}.

MgS has an even higher standard lattice enthalpy (–3299 kJ mol^{-1}) because both magnesium and sulfur ions have double charges.

2. Ionic radius

The smaller the ionic radii of the ions involved, the higher the charge density of the ion. This means the electrostatic attraction between the ions is greater so the lattice enthalpy is more exothermic (more negative).

Tip: Li, Na, K and Rb are all in Group 1 of the periodic table.

Example

Here are the standard lattice enthalpies of some chloride compounds:

Compound	*Standard lattice enthalpy (kJ mol^{-1})*
LiCl	*–861*
NaCl	*–787*
KCl	*–701*
RbCl	*–692*

Of all the positive ions, Li^+ has the smallest ionic radius. This means that LiCl has the most exothermic lattice enthalpy because the smaller Li^+ ions are more strongly attracted to the Cl^- ions than larger ions like Rb^+.

Exam Tip
Don't worry — you don't need to remember any of these standard lattice enthalpy values. You'll always be told them in the exam if you need to use them.

You should remember from Year 1 that ionic radius increases down a group — so have a look at the periodic table if you're unsure about which ions have the largest ionic radii.

Exam Tip
In the exam, you need to be able to explain why one ionic compound has a higher or lower lattice enthalpy than another ionic compound — so make sure you understand why these two factors affect the standard lattice enthalpy.

Practice Questions — Application

Q1 The table below shows the standard lattice enthalpies of some sodium containing compounds.

Compound	*Standard lattice enthalpy (kJ mol^{-1})*
NaCl	*–787*
NaBr	*–747*
NaI	*–704*

a) Explain why the standard lattice enthalpy becomes less exothermic from NaCl to NaI.

b) Which of these compounds contains the strongest ionic bonds?

Q2 The standard lattice enthalpy of K_2O is –2238 kJ mol^{-1}. Would you expect the standard lattice enthalpy of CaO to be more or less negative than this? Explain your answer.

Practice Questions — Fact Recall

Q1 a) Define the term 'lattice enthalpy'.

b) What is the symbol for lattice enthalpy?

Q2 What is the relationship between the lattice enthalpy of an ionic compound and the ionic bond strength?

Q3 Name two factors that affect the lattice enthalpy of an ionic compound.

3. Born-Haber Cycles

Get those rulers and pencils out — it's time to draw some Born-Haber cycles.

Learning Objective:

- Be able to use the lattice enthalpy of a simple ionic solid (e.g. NaCl, $MgCl_2$) and relevant energy terms to construct Born–Haber cycles and carry out related calculations.

Specification Reference 5.2.1

Forming ionic lattices

The lattice enthalpy is the enthalpy change when an ionic lattice is formed from its gaseous ions. But when an ionic lattice forms, you won't usually start with gaseous ions — you'll probably start with elements in their standard states. There are two routes you can follow to get from the elements in their standard states to an ionic lattice:

- A direct route, which involves converting the elements in their standard states directly into an ionic lattice. The enthalpy change for this reaction is given by the enthalpy of formation ($\Delta_f H$) of the lattice.
- An indirect route, which involves forming gaseous atoms, converting these into gaseous ions and then forming the ionic lattice. Each of the steps in this route has its own energy change — see Figure 1.

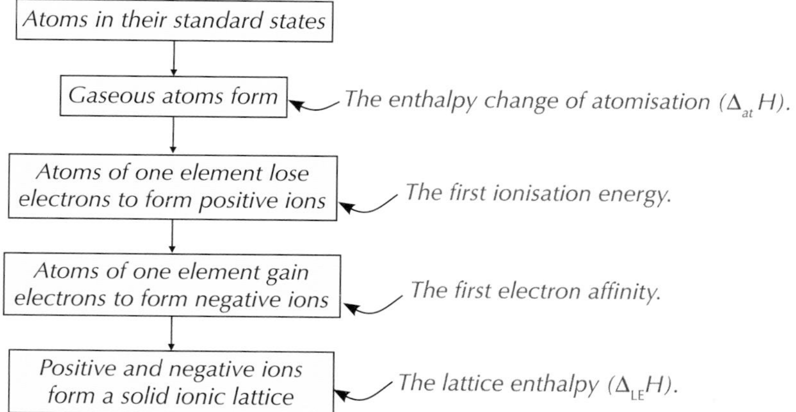

Figure 1: *The indirect route for forming an ionic lattice.*

Tip: See pages 91-92 for a recap on the definitions of all these different energy changes.

Born-Haber cycles

The two different routes for forming an ionic lattice and the energy changes involved can be illustrated using a **Born-Haber cycle**. Here's how to draw a Born-Haber cycle:

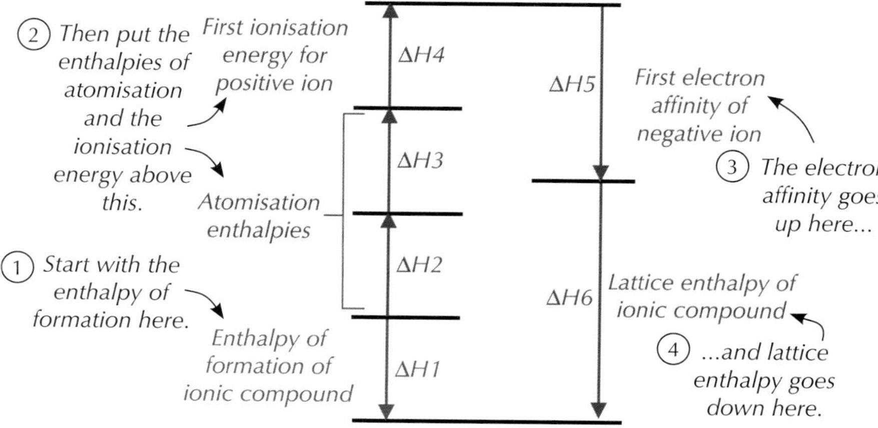

On the diagram above, the blue arrow shows the direct route and the red arrows show the indirect route.

Figure 2: *German physicist, Max Born, who, along with Fritz Haber, developed Born-Haber cycles.*

Tip: The Haber who helped develop Born-Haber cycles is the same Haber who invented the Haber process for synthesising ammonia.

Calculating lattice enthalpies using Born-Haber cycles

Lattice enthalpies can't be measured directly, but **Hess's law** states that:

> The total enthalpy change of a reaction is always the same, no matter which route is taken.

Figure 3: *Victor Franz Hess — the scientist who proposed Hess's law.*

This means that if you know all the other enthalpy changes, you can use a Born-Haber cycle to calculate the lattice enthalpy via an indirect route. All you have to do is use an alternative route around the diagram — for example, route 2 on the diagram below:

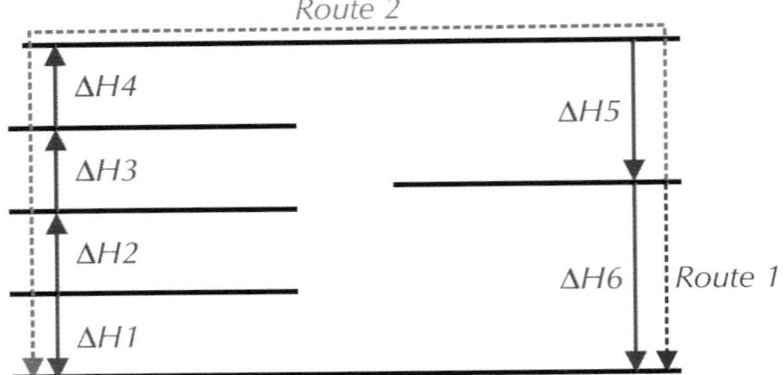

According to Hess's law, the enthalpy change of route 1 (the lattice enthalpy) is the same as the enthalpy change of route 2.

You can find the ΔH of route 2 by adding all the enthalpy changes in this route together and adding in a minus sign whenever you go the wrong way along an arrow. So...

$$\Delta H_{route\ 2} = (-\Delta H5) + (-\Delta H4) + (-\Delta H3) + (-\Delta H2) + \Delta H1$$

Add all the enthalpy changes in route 2 together.

Add a minus sign if you go the wrong way along an arrow.

$\Delta H_{route\ 2} = \Delta H_{route\ 1} = \Delta H6$ so...

$$\Delta H6 = -\Delta H5 - \Delta H4 - \Delta H3 - \Delta H2 + \Delta H1$$

Tip: You can use this technique to find any unknown enthalpy change on the diagram, as long as you know all the rest — just use an alternative route round the diagram.

Tip: Don't forget — ΔH is the symbol for enthalpy change. See page 91 for more.

Tip: You can also get the equation above by re-arranging this equation: $\Delta H1 = \Delta H2 + \Delta H3 + \Delta H4 + \Delta H5 + \Delta H6$.

Tip: Be really careful with your + and – signs in these calculations. You could end up minusing a minus number which is the same as adding it.

Example — Maths Skills

This is the Born-Haber cycle for the formation of sodium chloride:

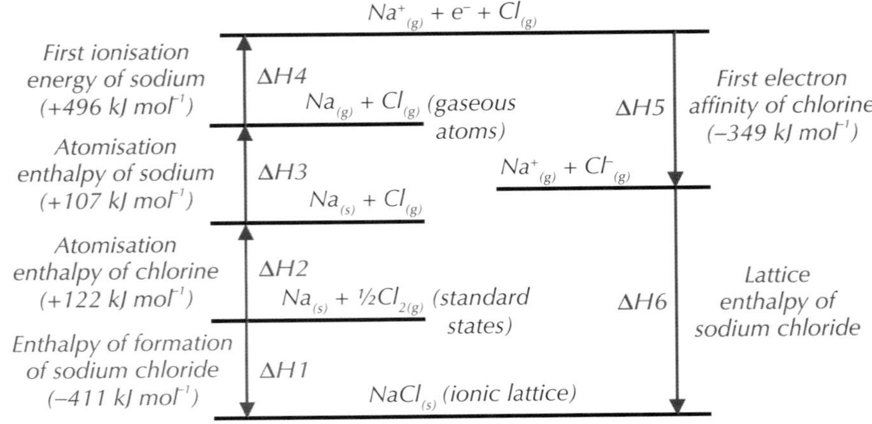

Hess's law says that the total enthalpy change of a reaction is always the same, no matter which route is taken. So...

$$\Delta_{LE}H = \Delta H6 = -\Delta H5 - \Delta H4 - \Delta H3 - \Delta H2 + \Delta H1$$
$$= -(-349) - (+496) - (+107) - (+122) + (-411) = \mathbf{-787\ kJ\ mol^{-1}}$$

Born-Haber cycles for compounds containing Group 2 elements have a few changes from the ones on the previous page. Here's a Born-Haber cycle for a compound containing a Group 2 element:

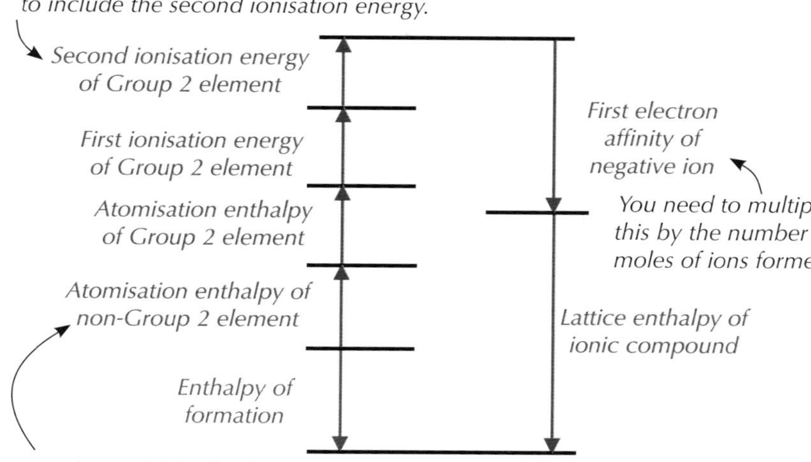

Exam Tip
Make sure you understand what's going on with these Group 2 elements so you can handle whatever compound they throw at you in the exam.

Tip: Remember, enthalpy change of formation, $\Delta_f H$, is the enthalpy change when one mole of a compound is formed from its elements.

Example — Maths Skills

Magnesium can react with chlorine to form magnesium chloride. Here's how you calculate the lattice enthalpy of magnesium chloride ($MgCl_2$).

$$Mg_{(g)} + Cl_{2(g)} \rightarrow MgCl_{2(s)}$$

Magnesium forms 2+ ions — so you've got to include the second ionisation energy.

You need to multiply the electron affinity of chlorine by 2 because two moles of ions form.

You need to multiply the atomisation enthalpy of chlorine by 2 because there are two moles of Cl in one mole of $MgCl_2$.

Here's the Born-Haber cycle:

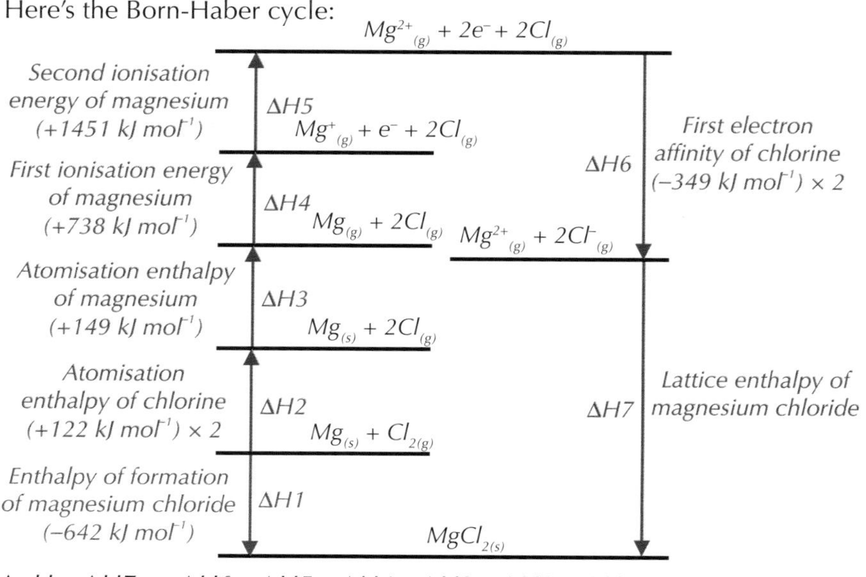

$\Delta_{LE}H = \Delta H7 = -\Delta H6 - \Delta H5 - \Delta H4 - \Delta H3 - \Delta H2 + \Delta H1$
$= -(-349 \times 2) - (+1451) - (+738) - (+149) - (+122 \times 2) + (-642)$
$= \mathbf{-2526\ kJ\ mol^{-1}}$

Figure 4: *Dry magnesium chloride.*

Tip: State symbols are really important here. If you're not sure of which state symbols go with which steps, check the definitions on pages 91-92.

Exam Tip
If you're asked to complete a Born-Haber cycle, it just means fill in the blank bits on the diagram — you don't have to write out what each stage is unless it specifically asks you to.

Tip: Calcium is a Group 2 element.

Exam Tip
Always double-check that you've got the plus and minus signs right when you're doing calculations using a Born-Haber cycle. It's really easy to make a mistake and get it wrong in the exam — and you will lose precious marks.

Exam Tip
When completing Born-Haber cycles in the exam, make sure you get the enthalpy changes in the right order. Atomisation always comes before ionisation, and they always come before electron affinity.

Practice Questions — Application

Q1 Complete the following Born-Haber cycle for the formation of $CaBr_2$.

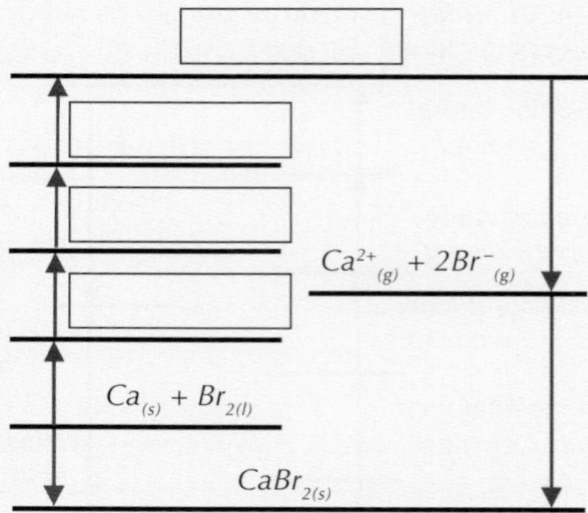

Q2 Look at the table below.

Enthalpy change	ΔH° / kJ mol^{-1}
Enthalpy change of atomisation of chlorine	+122
Enthalpy change of atomisation of lithium	+159
First ionisation energy of lithium	+520
First electron affinity of chlorine	−349
Lattice enthalpy of lithium chloride	−861

a) Draw the Born-Haber cycle for the formation of LiCl.

b) Use Hess's law to calculate the enthalpy of formation of LiCl.

Q3 Look at the table below.

Enthalpy change	ΔH° / kJ mol^{-1}
Enthalpy change of atomisation of potassium	+89
Enthalpy change of atomisation of fluorine	+79
First ionisation energy of potassium	+419
First electron affinity of fluorine	−328
Enthalpy of formation of potassium fluoride	−563

a) Draw the Born-Haber cycle for the formation of KF.

b) Use Hess's law to calculate the lattice enthalpy of KF.

4. Enthalpies of Solution

Lattice enthalpies aren't the only enthalpies you can calculate using Hess's law. You can work out enthalpies of solution too. You'll need to remind yourself of the definition of lattice enthalpy (page 93) before you start.

Learning Objectives:

- Be able to explain and use the terms enthalpy change of solution and enthalpy change of hydration.
- Be able to use the enthalpy change of solution of a simple ionic solid (e.g. NaCl, $MgCl_2$) and relevant energy terms (enthalpy change of hydration and lattice enthalpy) to construct enthalpy cycles and carry out related calculations.
- Be able to explain, in qualitative terms, the effect of ionic charge and ionic radius on the exothermic value of an enthalpy change of hydration.

Specification Reference 5.2.1

Dissolving ionic lattices

When a solid ionic lattice dissolves in water these two things happen:

- The bonds between the ions break to give gaseous ions — this is endothermic. This enthalpy change is the opposite of the **lattice enthalpy**.
- Bonds between the ions and the water are made — this is exothermic. The enthalpy change here is called the **enthalpy change of hydration**.

Water can form bonds with the ions because it is a polar molecule. Oxygen is more electronegative than hydrogen, so it draws the bonding electrons toward itself, creating a dipole. Consequently, positive ions form weak bonds with the partial negative charge on the oxygen atom and negative ions form weak bonds with the partial positive charge on the hydrogen atoms (see Figure 1).

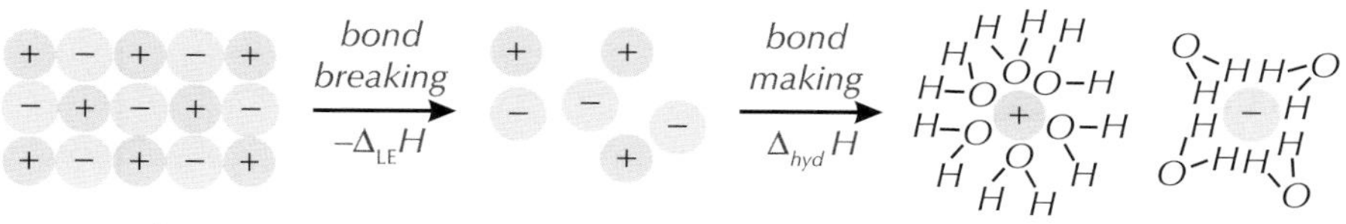

***Figure 1:** A solid ionic lattice dissolving in water.*

Tip: Take a look back at your Year 1 notes if you need a reminder about electronegativity and the δ^+ and δ^- charges on polar molecules such as water:

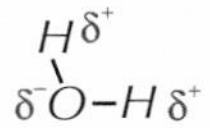

The **enthalpy change of solution** is the overall effect on the enthalpy of bond breaking and bond making. Here are the definitions you need to know:

> The **enthalpy change of hydration**, $\Delta_{hyd}H$, is the enthalpy change when 1 mole of gaseous ions is dissolved in water, e.g. $Na^+_{(g)} \rightarrow Na^+_{(aq)}$

> The **enthalpy change of solution**, $\Delta_{sol}H$, is the enthalpy change when 1 mole of solute is dissolved in a solvent, such as water, e.g. $NaCl_{(s)} \rightarrow NaCl_{(aq)}$

Tip: If these definitions look familiar, it's because you've seen them before on page 92.

Entropy and dissolving ionic lattices

Substances generally only dissolve if the energy released is roughly the same, or greater than the energy taken in. But enthalpy change isn't the only thing that decides if something will dissolve — **entropy** change is important too.

A reaction or state change is more likely when there is a positive entropy change. Dissolving normally causes an increase in entropy. But for small, highly charged ions there may be a decrease because when water molecules surround the ions, it makes things more orderly. The entropy changes are usually pretty small but they can sometimes make the difference between something being soluble or insoluble.

Tip: Entropy is a measure of the disorder of a system. It's covered in loads of detail on pages 103-104 so don't worry about it too much just yet.

Figure 2: Copper(II) sulfate ($CuSO_4$) dissolved in water.

Tip: You don't have to draw your enthalpy cycles in this triangular shape — you could use a square shape, like the Born-Haber cycles on pages 95-97.

Calculating enthalpy change of solution

You can work out the enthalpy change of solution using an enthalpy cycle. You just need to know the lattice enthalpy of the compound and the enthalpy changes of hydration of the ions. Here's how to draw an enthalpy cycle for calculating the enthalpy change of solution:

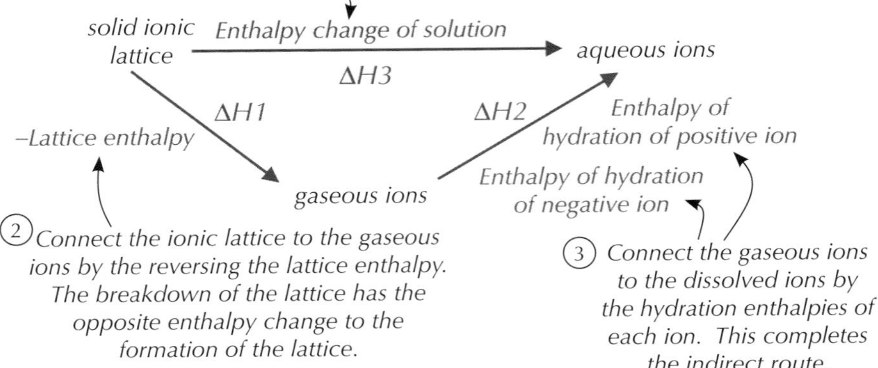

Example — Maths Skills

Here's the enthalpy cycle for working out the enthalpy change of solution for sodium chloride.

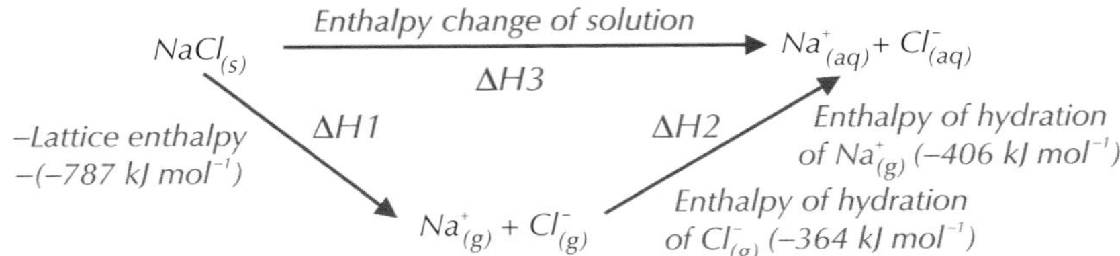

Tip: For this enthalpy cycle, $\Delta H2$ is equal to the two enthalpies of hydration added together.

From Hess's law: $\Delta_{sol} H = \Delta H3 = \Delta H1 + \Delta H2$

$= -(-787) + (-406 + -364) = \mathbf{+17\ kJ\ mol^{-1}}$

Tip: Take a look back at page 96 for more on Hess's law.

The enthalpy change of solution is slightly endothermic, but this is compensated for by a small increase in entropy, so sodium chloride still dissolves in water.

And here's another example. This enthalpy cycle is for working out the enthalpy change of solution for silver chloride.

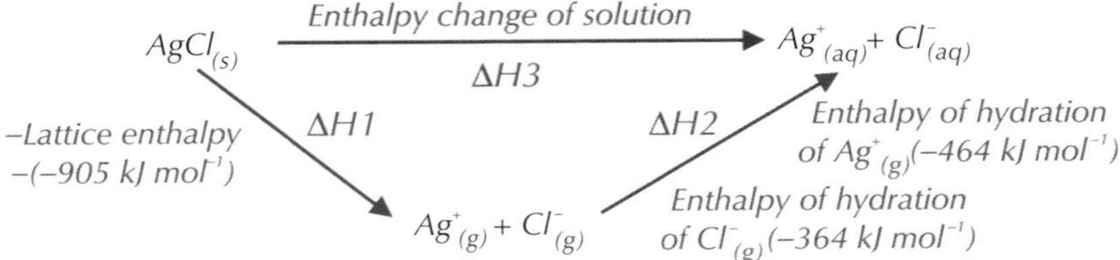

From Hess's law: $\Delta_{sol} H = \Delta H3 = \Delta H1 + \Delta H2$

$= -(-905) + (-464 + -364) = \mathbf{+77\ kJ\ mol^{-1}}$

Tip: A positive enthalpy value means that a reaction is endothermic.

This is much more endothermic than the enthalpy change of solution for sodium chloride. There is an increase in entropy, but it's pretty small and not enough to make a difference — so silver chloride is insoluble in water.

If 2+ or 2– ions are involved, you need to multiply the enthalpies of hydration by the number of moles of the ions that are reacting.

Example — Maths Skills

Here's the enthalpy cycle for working out the enthalpy change of solution for magnesium chloride ($MgCl_2$).

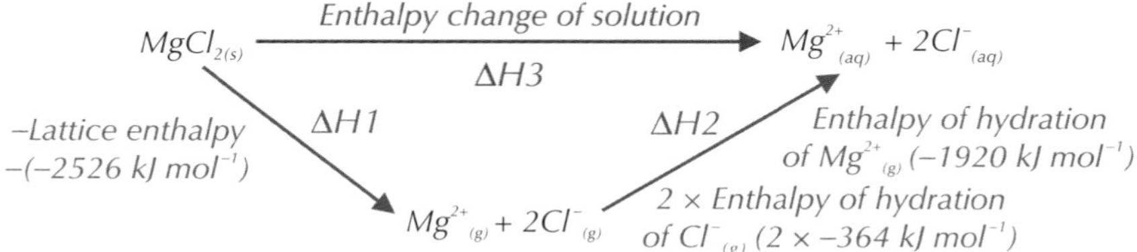

In this example, there are two moles of Cl^- ions in the ionic lattice, so you have to multiply the enthalpy of hydration of Cl^- by two when you're calculating the enthalpy change of solution. So...

From Hess's law: $\Delta_{sol}H = \Delta H3 = \Delta H1 + \Delta H2$

$$= -(-2526) + [-1920 + (2 \times -364)] = \mathbf{-122\ kJ\ mol^{-1}}$$

$\Delta_{sol}H$ is negative, so $MgCl_2$ dissolving in water is an exothermic processes and $MgCl_2$ is soluble.

Tip: If there were three moles of an ion present in an ionic lattice you'd have to multiply the enthalpy of hydration for that ion by three to calculate the enthalpy change of solution.

Tip: If you know the enthalpy change of solution you can calculate the lattice enthalpy or an enthalpy of hydration — you just have to rearrange the equation.

Factors affecting the enthalpy of hydration

The two things that can affect the lattice enthalpy (see pages 93-94) can also affect the enthalpy of hydration. They are the charge and the size of the ions.

1. Ionic charge

Ions with a greater charge have a greater enthalpy of hydration. This is because ions with a higher charge are better at attracting water molecules than those with lower charges. More energy is released when the bonds are made, giving them a more exothermic enthalpy of hydration.

Tip: Remember — more exothermic processes have more negative enthalpy changes, more endothermic processes have more positive enthalpy changes.

2. Ionic radius

Smaller ions have a greater enthalpy of hydration. This is because smaller ions have a higher charge density than bigger ions. They attract the water molecules better and have a more exothermic enthalpy of hydration.

Example

The diagram below shows aqueous Na^+ and Mg^{2+} ions:

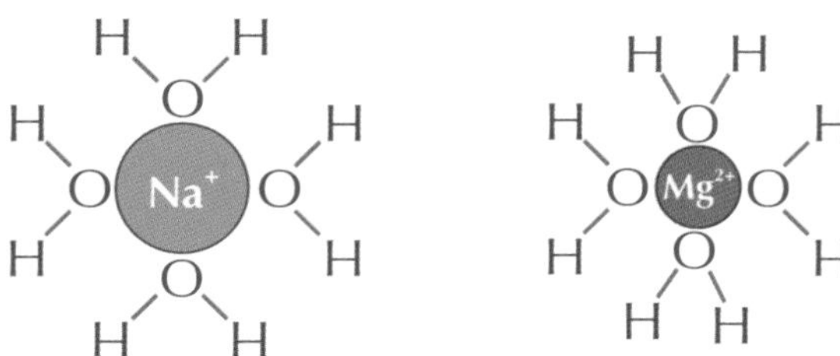

The magnesium ion is smaller and has a higher charge than the sodium ion. The higher charge and smaller size create a higher charge density. This creates a stronger attraction for the water molecules and gives it a much more negative enthalpy of hydration. The enthalpies of hydration of Mg^{2+} and Na^+ ions are: $Mg^{2+} = -1927$ kJ mol⁻¹, $Na^+ = -406$ kJ mol⁻¹

Figure 3: *Hydration of copper(II) sulfate. Because the Cu^{2+} ions are small and highly charged, this reaction is exothermic enough to produce steam.*

Practice Questions — Application

Q1 The cycle below shows the enthalpy change of solution for LiCl.

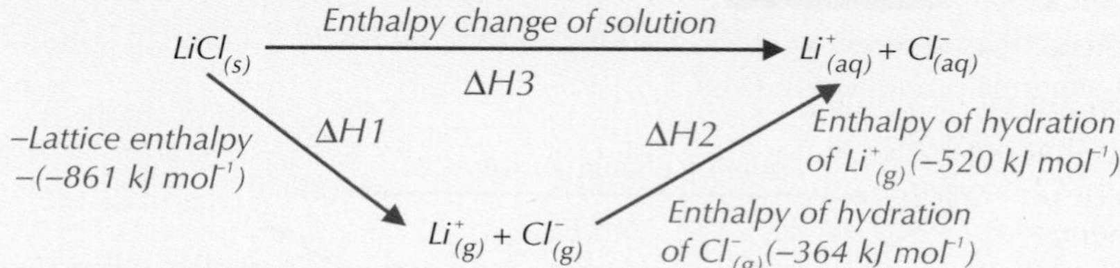

Calculate the enthalpy change of solution for LiCl.

Q2 a) Draw a cycle to show the enthalpy change of solution for sodium bromide. Use the following values:

Lattice enthalpy of NaBr = –747 kJ mol^{-1}
Enthalpy of hydration of Na^+ = –406 kJ mol^{-1}
Enthalpy of hydration of Br^- = –336 kJ mol^{-1}

b) Calculate the enthalpy change of solution for sodium bromide.

Q3 Use the data given in Q1 and Q2 a) and the data below to calculate enthalpy changes of solution for the following compounds:

a) lithium bromide.

b) potassium chloride.

c) magnesium bromide.

Lattice enthalpy of LiBr = –807 kJ mol^{-1}
Lattice enthalpy of KCl = –701 kJ mol^{-1}
Lattice enthalpy of $MgBr_2$ = –2440 kJ mol^{-1}
Enthalpy of hydration of K^+ = –322 kJ mol^{-1}
Enthalpy of hydration of Mg^{2+} = –1921 kJ mol^{-1}

Q4 Explain why the enthalpy of hydration of Mg^{2+} is more negative than the enthalpy of hydration of K^+.

Exam Tip
Don't be afraid to draw out an enthalpy cycle in the exam if you think it will help you answer the question.

Practice Questions — Fact Recall

Q1 a) What two processes happen when a solid ionic lattice dissolves in water?

b) State whether each of these processes is exothermic or endothermic.

Q2 The enthalpy change of solution is the combined effect of two enthalpy changes. Name them.

Q3 Give two factors which influence the enthalpy of hydration of an ion.

5. Entropy

Left alone, things generally tend towards disorder — that's entropy.

What is entropy?

Entropy tells you how much disorder there is. It's a measure of the number of ways that particles can be arranged and the number of ways that the energy can be shared out between the particles — so entropy is also a measure of the dispersal of energy in a system. Substances are actually more energetically stable when there's more disorder. So the particles move to try to increase the entropy. Entropy is represented by the symbol S. There are a few things that affect entropy, such as:

Physical state

Physical state affects entropy. You have to go back to the old 'solid-liquid-gas particle explanation thingy' to understand this. Solid particles just wobble about a fixed point — there's hardly any disorder, so they have the lowest entropy. Gas particles whizz around wherever they like. They've got the most disordered arrangements of particles, so they have the highest entropy.

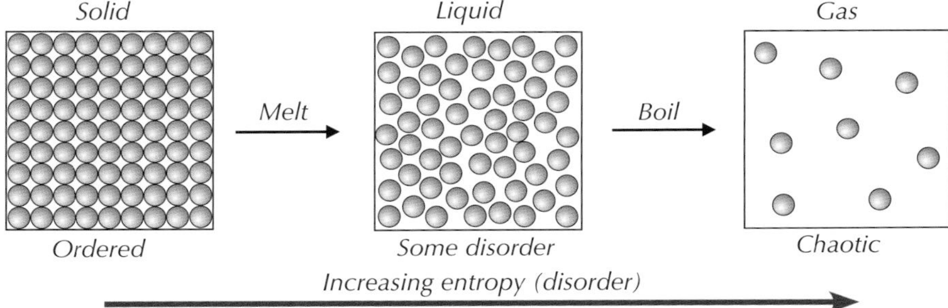

Dissolution

Dissolving a solid also increases its entropy — dissolved particles can move freely as they're no longer held in one place:

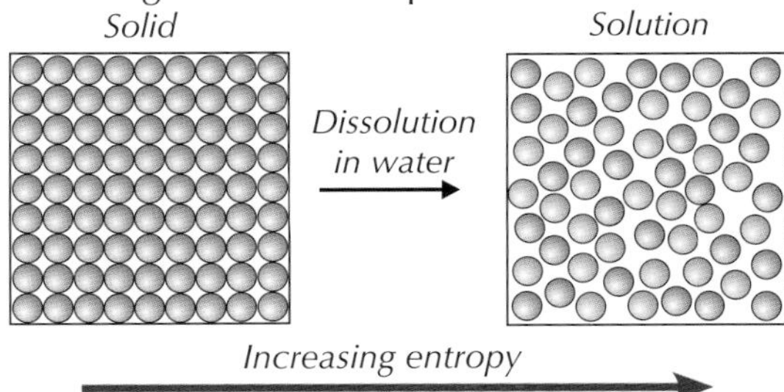

Number of gaseous particles

More gaseous particles means more entropy. It makes sense — the more gaseous particles you've got, the more ways they and their energy can be arranged. So in a reaction like $N_2O_{4(g)} \rightarrow 2NO_{2(g)}$, entropy increases because the number of gaseous moles increases:

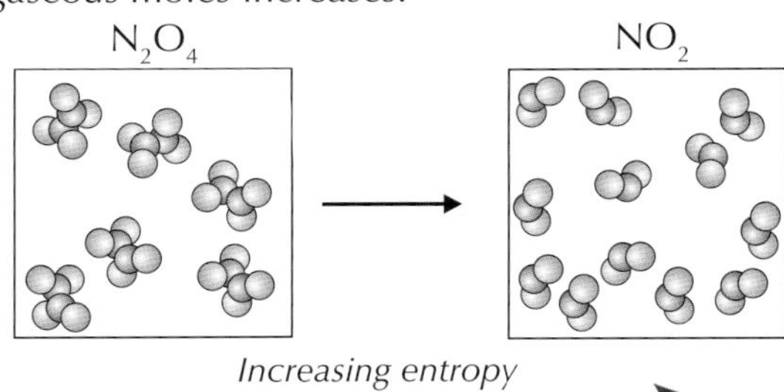

Learning Objectives:

- Be able to explain that entropy is a measure of the dispersal of energy in a system which is greater, the more disordered a system is.
- Be able to explain the difference in magnitude of the entropy of a system: (i) of solids, liquids and gases, (ii) for a reaction in which there is a change in the number of gaseous molecules.
- Be able to calculate the entropy change of a system, ΔS, and related quantities for a reaction, given the entropies of the reactants and products.

Specification Reference 5.2.2

Figure 1: *Melting ice. When ice melts its entropy increases.*

Figure 2: *The evaporation of water to form clouds involves an increase in entropy.*

Examples

Evaporation of water

When water evaporates, there is an increase in entropy because there's a change in physical state from liquid to gas.

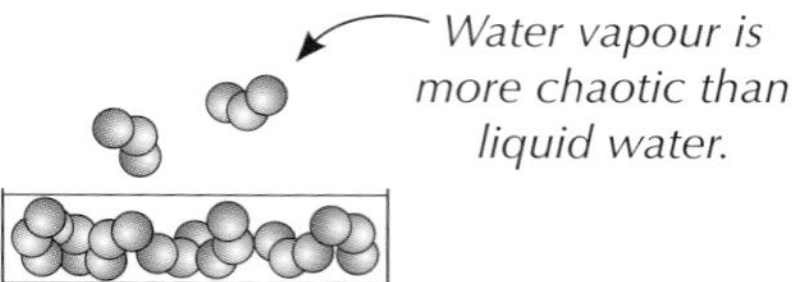

Water vapour is more chaotic than liquid water.

Reaction of $NaHCO_3$ and HCl

When sodium hydrogen carbonate reacts with hydrochloric acid there is an increase in entropy.

$$NaHCO_{3(s)} + H^+_{(aq)} \rightarrow Na^+_{(aq)} + CO_{2(g)} + H_2O_{(l)}$$

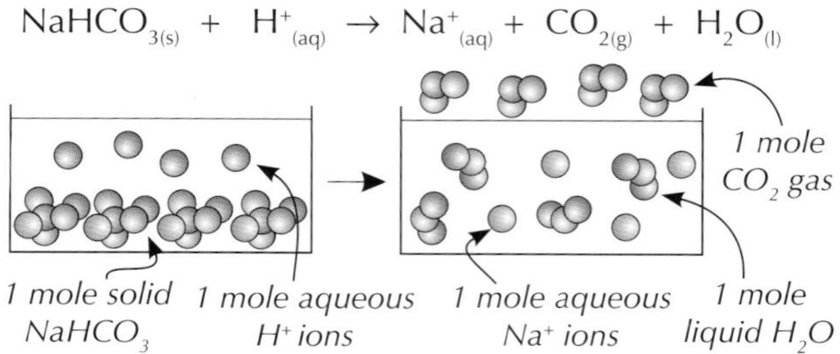

There are more particles in the products — and gases and liquids have more entropy than solids too.

Exam Tip
You need to be able to calculate entropy changes in your exam so make sure you learn this equation.

Calculating entropy changes

Most reactions won't happen unless the entropy change is positive. During a reaction, there's an entropy change (ΔS) between the reactants and products.

This is just the difference between the entropies of the reactants and products.

$$\Delta S = S_{products} - S_{reactants}$$

Tip: $S^\ominus$ is the standard entropy. The $S^\ominus$ value of a substance is the entropy of one mole of that substance, measured under standard conditions.

Example — Maths Skills

Calculate the entropy change for the reaction of ammonia and hydrogen chloride under standard conditions.

$$NH_{3(g)} + HCl_{(g)} \rightarrow NH_4Cl_{(s)}$$

$S^\ominus[NH_{3(g)}]$ = **192.3 J K⁻¹ mol⁻¹**

$S^\ominus[HCl_{(g)}]$ = **186.8 J K⁻¹ mol⁻¹**

$S^\ominus[NH_4Cl_{(s)}]$ = **94.6 J K⁻¹ mol⁻¹**

First find the entropy change of the system:

$$\Delta S = S_{products} - S_{reactants} = 94.6 - (192.3 + 186.8)$$

$$= \mathbf{-284.5\ J\ K^{-1}\ mol^{-1}}$$

This reaction has a negative change in entropy. It's not surprising, as 2 moles of gas have combined to form 1 mole of solid.

Tip: When you calculate an entropy change, don't forget to give the units — they're always J K^{-1} mol^{-1}.

Practice Questions — Application

Q1 Solid sodium hydroxide is added to aqueous hydrogen chloride. The reaction produces sodium chloride solution. The solution is heated to produce solid sodium chloride and water vapour.

Describe the entropy changes that take place during these processes.

Q2 Using the data from Figure 3, work out the entropy change for this reaction under standard conditions:

$$CH_{4(g)} + 2O_{2(g)} \rightarrow CO_{2(g)} + 2H_2O_{(l)} \qquad \Delta H^{\ominus} = -730 \text{ kJ mol}^{-1}$$

Q3 Using the data in Figure 3 work out the entropy change for this reaction under standard conditions:

$$SO_{2(g)} + 2H_2S_{(g)} \rightarrow 3S_{(s)} + 2H_2O_{(l)} \qquad \Delta H^{\ominus} = -235 \text{ kJ mol}^{-1}$$

Practice Questions — Fact Recall

Q1 a) What is entropy?

b) Give the symbol for entropy change.

Q2 Explain how the following affect the entropy of a system:

a) a substance changing from a liquid to a gas.

b) a solid dissolving in water.

c) a reaction that results in an increased number of gaseous particles.

Substance	*Standard entropy of substance, $S^{\ominus}$ ($J\ K^{-1}\ mol^{-1}$)*
$CH_{4(g)}$	186
$O_{2(g)}$	205
$CO_{2(g)}$	214
$H_2O_{(l)}$	69.9
$SO_{2(g)}$	248
$H_2S_{(g)}$	206
$S_{(s)}$	31.6

Figure 3: *Standard entropy values for different substances.*

6. Free Energy Change

Everyone likes free things, so I can almost guarantee you'll like free energy.

Learning Objectives:

- Be able to explain that the feasibility of a process depends upon the entropy change and temperature in the system, $T\Delta S$, and the enthalpy change of the system, ΔH.
- Be able to explain and carry out calculations of the free energy change, ΔG, as: $\Delta G = \Delta H - T\Delta S$ (the Gibbs equation) and know that a process is feasible when ΔG has a negative value.
- Be able to explain the limitations of predictions made by ΔG about feasibility, in terms of kinetics.

Specification Reference 5.2.2

What is free energy change?

Free energy change, ΔG, is a measure used to predict whether a reaction is **feasible**. A feasible reaction is one that, once started, will carry on to completion, without any energy being supplied to it. If ΔG is negative or equal to zero, then the reaction is feasible. Free energy change takes into account the changes in enthalpy and entropy in the system. And of course, there's a formula for it:

$$\Delta G = \Delta H - T\Delta S$$

Free energy change (in J mol⁻¹) — ΔG; *Enthalpy change (in J mol⁻¹)* — ΔH; *Temperature (in K)* — T; *Entropy change (in J K⁻¹ mol⁻¹)* — ΔS

A negative ΔG doesn't guarantee a reaction will happen or tell you about its rate. Even if ΔG shows that a reaction is theoretically feasible, it might have a really high activation energy or be so slow that you wouldn't notice it happening at all. Here's an example of calculating free energy change.

Example — Maths Skills

Calculate the free energy change for the following reaction at 298 K.

$MgCO_{3(s)} \rightarrow MgO_{(s)} + CO_{2(g)}$ $\Delta H^{\ominus} = +117 \text{ kJ mol}^{-1}$ $\Delta S^{\ominus} = +175 \text{ J K}^{-1}\text{ mol}^{-1}$

$\Delta G = \Delta H - T\Delta S = +117 \times 10^3 - [298 \times (+175)]$

$= \mathbf{+64\,900 \text{ J mol}^{-1}}$ (3 s.f.)

ΔG is positive — so the reaction isn't feasible at this temperature.

Tip: The units of ΔH and ΔS must be the same. So, if you're given a value for ΔH in kJ, multiply it by 10^3 to get in J. If you want ΔG in kJ mol⁻¹, divide ΔS by 10^3 instead.

Tip: You might see free energy referred to as 'Gibbs free energy'. They're the same thing.

Effect of temperature

If a reaction is exothermic (negative ΔH) and has a positive entropy change, then ΔG is always negative since $\Delta G = \Delta H - T\Delta S$. These reactions are feasible at any temperature.

If a reaction is endothermic (positive ΔH) and has a negative entropy change, then ΔG is always positive. These reactions are not feasible at any temperature. But for other combinations, temperature has an effect.

If ΔH is positive (endothermic) and ΔS is positive, then the reaction will only be feasible above a certain temperature.

Example

The decomposition of calcium carbonate is endothermic but results in an increase in entropy (the number of molecules increases and CO_2 is a gas).

$$CaCO_{3(s)} \rightarrow CaO_{(s)} + CO_{2(g)}$$

The reaction only occurs when $CaCO_3$ is heated — it isn't feasible at 298 K.

Figure 1: *Calcium carbonate ($CaCO_3$) being heated to produce CaO and CO_2.*

If ΔH is negative (exothermic) and ΔS is negative then the reaction will only be feasible below a certain temperature.

Example

The process of turning water from a liquid to a solid is exothermic but results in a decrease in entropy (a solid is more ordered than a liquid). So it will only occur at certain temperatures (i.e. at 0 °C or below).

Here are some examples of how to decide if a reaction is feasible at different temperatures.

Examples — Maths Skills

Reaction 1: $\Delta H = +10$ kJ mol^{-1}, $\Delta S = +10$ J K^{-1} mol^{-1}

At 300 K:

$$\Delta G = \Delta H - T\Delta S$$
$$= +10 \times 10^3 - (300 \times +10)$$
$$= \mathbf{+7000\ J\ mol^{-1}}$$

At 1500 K:

$$\Delta G = \Delta H - T\Delta S$$
$$= +10 \times 10^3 - (1500 \times +10)$$
$$= \mathbf{-5000\ J\ mol^{-1}}$$

So this reaction is feasible at 1500 K, but not at 300 K.

Reaction 2: $\Delta H = -10$ kJ mol^{-1}, $\Delta S = -10$ J K^{-1} mol^{-1}

At 300 K:

$$\Delta G = \Delta H - T\Delta S$$
$$= -10 \times 10^3 - (300 \times -10)$$
$$= \mathbf{-7000\ J\ mol^{-1}}$$

At 1500 K:

$$\Delta G = \Delta H - T\Delta S$$
$$= -10 \times 10^3 - (1500 \times -10)$$
$$= \mathbf{+5000\ J\ mol^{-1}}$$

So this reaction is feasible at 300 K, but not at 1500 K.

Tip: Don't forget — the value of ΔG has to be less than or equal to zero for a reaction to be feasible.

When ΔG is zero, a reaction is just feasible. You can find the temperature when ΔG is zero by rearranging the free energy equation.

$\Delta G = \Delta H - T\Delta S$, so when $\Delta G = 0$, $T\Delta S = \Delta H$. So:

$$T = \frac{\Delta H}{\Delta S}$$

temperature at which a reaction becomes feasible (in K) → T; *enthalpy change (in J mol^{-1})* → ΔH; *entropy change (in J K^{-1} mol^{-1})* → ΔS

Substance	Standard entropy of substance, S° (J K^{-1} mol^{-1})
$WO_{3(s)}$	76.0
$H_{2(g)}$	65.0
$W_{(s)}$	33.0
$H_2O_{(g)}$	189.0

Figure 2: *Standard entropy values for different substances.*

Example — Maths Skills

Tungsten, W, can be extracted from its ore, WO_3, by reduction using hydrogen.

$$WO_{3(s)} + 3H_{2(g)} \rightarrow W_{(s)} + 3H_2O_{(g)} \qquad \Delta H^\circ = +117 \text{ kJ mol}^{-1}$$

Use the data in Figure 2 to find the minimum temperature at which the reaction becomes feasible.

First, convert the enthalpy change, ΔH, to joules per mole:

$$\Delta H = 117 \times 10^3 \text{ J mol}^{-1} = 117\ 000 \text{ J mol}^{-1}$$

Then find the entropy change, ΔS:

$$\Delta S = S_{products} - S_{reactants} = [33.0 + (3 \times 189.0)] - [76.0 + (3 \times 65.0)]$$
$$= +329 \text{ J K}^{-1} \text{ mol}^{-1}$$

Then divide ΔH by ΔS to find the temperature at which the reaction just becomes feasible:

$$T = \frac{\Delta H}{\Delta S} = \frac{117\ 000}{329} = \mathbf{356\ K}$$

Tip: For more on the ΔS formula, see page 104.

Substance	Standard entropy of substance, S° ($J\ K^{-1}\ mol^{-1}$)
$Al_2O_{3(s)}$	51.0
$Mg_{(s)}$	32.5
$Al_{(s)}$	28.3
$MgO_{(s)}$	27.0

Figure 3: *Standard entropy values for different substances.*

Tip: When calculating free energy changes, be really careful with your units. The temperature must be in K (add 273 if it's given in °C) and the enthalpy and entropy values should involve J not kJ.

Practice Questions — Application

Q1 Using the data from Figure 3 for this reaction under standard conditions: $Al_2O_{3(s)} + 3Mg_{(s)} \rightarrow 2Al_{(s)} + 3MgO_{(s)}$ $\Delta H^\circ = -130\ kJ\ mol^{-1}$

a) calculate ΔS.

b) calculate ΔG.

c) explain whether the reaction is feasible at 298 K.

Q2 Consider the reaction below:

$$ZnCO_{3(s)} \rightarrow ZnO_{(s)} + CO_{2(g)}$$

$\Delta H^\circ = +71.0\ kJ\ mol^{-1}$ $\quad$ $\Delta S = +176\ J\ K^{-1}\ mol^{-1}$

a) Determine whether or not this reaction is feasible at:

(i) 298 K $\quad$ (ii) 600 K

b) Calculate the temperature at which this reaction becomes feasible.

Q3 Calculate the temperature at which this reaction becomes feasible:

$$CaCO_{3(s)} \rightarrow CaO_{(s)} + CO_{2(g)}$$

$\Delta H^\circ = +178\ kJ\ mol^{-1}$ $\quad$ $\Delta S = +165\ J\ K^{-1}\ mol^{-1}$

Practice Questions — Fact Recall

Q1 a) What is free energy change?

b) Give the symbol for free energy change.

Q2 Give the formula needed to work out free energy change.

Q3 Suggest two reasons why a reaction might not happen, even if it has a negative free energy change value.

Q4 A reaction is endothermic, has a negative entropy change and so has a positive value for free energy. Is this reaction feasible?

Q5 Give the formula that you'd use to calculate the temperature at which a reaction becomes feasible.

Section Summary

Make sure you know...

- That enthalpy change is the heat energy transferred in a reaction at constant pressure, and the symbol for it is ΔH.
- That exothermic reactions have negative ΔH values and endothermic reactions have positive ΔH values.
- The definitions of enthalpy change of formation, enthalpy change of atomisation for elements and for compounds, ionisation energy, and electron affinity.
- The definition of the lattice enthalpy, $\Delta_{LE}H$.
- How lattice enthalpy is affected by ionic charge and ionic radius.
- How to construct Born-Haber cycles and use them to calculate lattice enthalpies and related values.
- The definitions of enthalpy change of hydration, $\Delta_{hyd}H$, and enthalpy change of solution, $\Delta_{sol}H$.
- The different enthalpy changes that take place when a solid ionic lattice dissolves.
- How to use enthalpy cycles to calculate enthalpies of solution and related values.
- How enthalpy of hydration is influenced by ionic charge and ionic radius.
- That entropy, S, is a measure of the dispersal of energy in a system and that a system becomes energetically more stable when it becomes more disordered.
- How entropy is affected by physical state and number of particles.
- How to calculate the entropy change, and related values, for a reaction.
- That the tendency of a reaction to happen depends on temperature, entropy and enthalpy.
- That it's the balance between entropy and enthalpy that determines the feasibility of a reaction.
- What free energy change is and how to calculate it using $\Delta G = \Delta H - T\Delta S$.
- That the feasibility of some reactions depends on temperature, and how to calculate the temperature at which a reaction becomes feasible.
- That feasibility predictions, based on the free energy change value, are limited because reactions may have a very high activation energy or very slow rate of reaction.

Exam-style Questions

1 Which of the following ionic compounds would you expect to have the most negative standard lattice enthalpy?

A BeO

B NaCl

C KBr

D MgS

(1 mark)

2 The following reaction is feasible at any temperature:

$$H_{2(g)} + \frac{1}{2}O_{2(g)} \rightarrow H_2O_{(g)}$$

Which statement about this reaction is true?

A The enthalpy change is positive and the entropy change is positive.

B The enthalpy change is positive and the entropy change is negative.

C The enthalpy change is negative and the entropy change is positive.

D The enthalpy change is negative and the entropy change is negative.

(1 mark)

3 Strontium fluoride is a solid ionic lattice which dissolves in water and can be used as an optical coating for lenses.

(a) Draw an enthalpy cycle for the enthalpy change of solution of $SrF_{2(s)}$. Label each enthalpy change.

(2 marks)

(b) Calculate the enthalpy change of solution for SrF_2, using the data in the table below.

(2 marks)

Enthalpy change	ΔH° / kJ mol^{-1}
Lattice enthalpy of $SrF_{2(s)}$	–2492
Enthalpy change of hydration of Sr^{2+} ions	–1480
Enthalpy change of hydration of F^- ions	–506

4 Manganese can be extracted from its ore manganese(IV) oxide, MnO_2, by reduction using carbon at 1473 K. The reaction is shown in the equation below.

$$MnO_{2\,(s)} + C_{(s)} \rightarrow Mn_{(s)} + CO_{2\,(g)} \qquad \Delta H^{\circ} = +127 \text{ kJ mol}^{-1}$$

	$MnO_{2\,(s)}$	$C_{(s)}$	$Mn_{(s)}$	$CO_{2\,(g)}$
S°/ J K^{-1}mol^{-1}	53.0	5.70	32.0	214

(a) Use the balanced equation to explain whether you would expect entropy to decrease or increase during this reaction.

(1 mark)

(b) Calculate the free energy change for the extraction of manganese from its ore.

(4 marks)

(c) Explain how the free energy change of a reaction relates to the feasibility of that reaction.

(1 mark)

(d) Give the equation which links the temperature at which a reaction becomes feasible, T, the enthalpy change for the reaction, ΔH, and the entropy change, ΔS.

(1 mark)

(e) Calculate the temperature at which the reduction of manganese oxide using carbon becomes feasible.

(2 marks)

The standard enthalpy of change formation of MnO_2 is –521 kJ mol^{-1}.

(f) Define the term enthalpy change of formation.

(1 mark)

(g) State whether the formation of manganese(IV) oxide from manganese and oxygen will be endothermic or exothermic.

(1 mark)

5 Rubidium chloride is an ionic compound that dissolves easily in water and can be used as a cell marker in laboratories. The table below shows thermodynamic data for rubidium chloride.

Enthalpy change	ΔH° / kJ mol^{-1}
Enthalpy change of atomisation of rubidium	+81
First ionisation enthalpy of rubidium	+403
Enthalpy change of hydration of Rb^+ ions	–296
Enthalpy change of atomisation of chlorine	+122
Electron affinity of chlorine	–349
Enthalpy change of hydration of Cl^- ions	–364
Enthalpy change of formation of rubidium chloride	–435

(a) Define the term lattice enthalpy.

(1 mark)

(b) Complete the Born-Haber cycle for the formation of rubidium chloride by filling in the blank lines. You should include chemical symbols and state symbols.

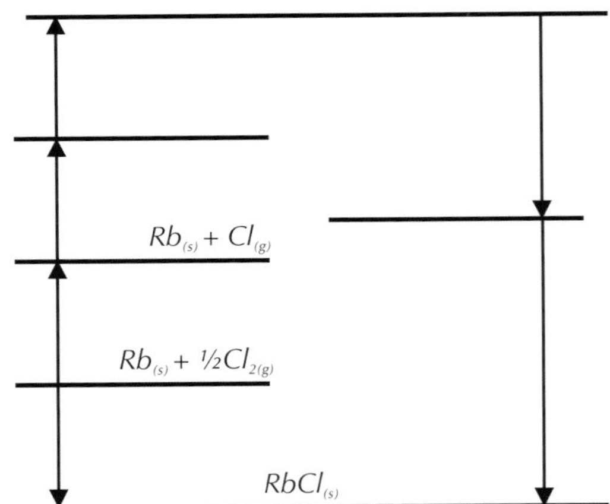

(3 marks)

(c) Use the data in the table to calculate the standard lattice enthalpy of rubidium chloride.

(3 marks)

(d) The standard lattice enthalpy of sodium chloride is more exothermic than that of rubidium chloride. Explain why.

(3 marks)

(e) Calculate the enthalpy change of solution for rubidium chloride.
(If you have not been able to answer **(c)** use the value of –300 kJ mol^{-1} for the standard lattice enthalpy of rubidium chloride. This value is incorrect.)

(2 marks)

1. Redox Reactions

You've already done a bit about redox reactions in the first year of the course. Here's a reminder, plus a bit more about writing equations for redox reactions.

What is a redox reaction?

A loss of electrons is called **oxidation**. A gain of electrons is called **reduction**. Reduction and oxidation happen simultaneously — hence the term 'redox' reaction. An **oxidising agent** accepts electrons and gets reduced. A **reducing agent** donates electrons and gets oxidised.

Example

In the reaction between potassium and chlorine:

Potassium is the reducing agent — it donates electrons and gets oxidised.

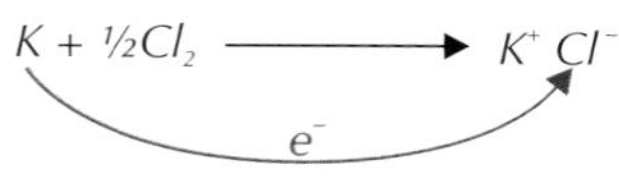

K + ½Cl2 → K+ Cl−
e−

Chlorine is the oxidising agent — it accepts electrons and gets reduced.

Learning Objectives:

- Be able to explain and use the terms *oxidising agent* and *reducing agent*.
- Be able to construct redox equations using half-equations and oxidation numbers.
- Be able to interpret and predict reactions involving electron transfer.

Specification Reference 5.2.3

Half-equations

A redox reaction is made up of an oxidation half-reaction and a reduction half-reaction. You can write an ionic **half-equation** for each half-reaction.

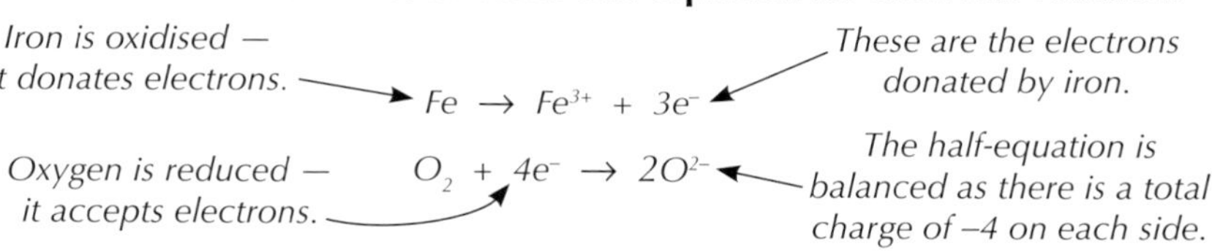

Iron is oxidised — it donates electrons.
Fe → Fe3+ + 3e−
These are the electrons donated by iron.
Oxygen is reduced — it accepts electrons.
O2 + 4e− → 2O2−
The half-equation is balanced as there is a total charge of –4 on each side.

Figure 1: *Half-equations for the oxidation of iron and the reduction of oxygen.*

An oxidation half-equation can be combined with a reduction half-equation to make a full redox equation.

Example — Maths Skills

Zinc metal displaces silver ions from silver nitrate solution to form a solution of zinc ions and a deposit of silver metal.

The zinc atoms each lose 2 electrons (oxidation): $Zn_{(s)} \rightarrow Zn^{2+}_{(aq)} + 2e^-$

The silver ions each gain 1 electron (reduction): $Ag^+_{(aq)} + e^- \rightarrow Ag_{(s)}$

Two silver ions are needed to accept the two electrons released by each zinc atom. So you need to double the silver half-equation before the two half-equations can be combined:

$$2Ag^+_{(aq)} + 2e^- \rightarrow 2Ag_{(s)}$$

Now the number of electrons lost and gained balance, so the half-equations can be combined:

$$Zn_{(s)} + 2Ag^+_{(aq)} + 2e^- \rightarrow Zn^{2+}_{(aq)} + 2e^- + 2Ag_{(s)}$$

The electrons cancel each other out, so this is the overall redox equation:

$$Zn_{(s)} + 2Ag^+_{(aq)} \rightarrow Zn^{2+}_{(aq)} + 2Ag_{(s)}$$

Tip: Don't forget:
OIL RIG
Oxidation Is Loss
Reduction Is Gain
(...of electrons)

Tip: Electrons are shown in half-equations so that the charges balance.

Tip: It's a good idea to check that the charges balance in your final redox equation. If they don't, you've probably done something wrong somewhere...

Tip: If you see Roman numerals in a chemical name, it's an oxidation number (see below). For example, in dichromate(VI) ions, chromium has an oxidation number of +6.

Tip: 'Acidified' just means that some acid has been added to the oxidising agent. It's telling you that the reaction is taking place under acidic conditions.

Tip: You could also balance this reaction by looking at the changes in oxidation numbers (see next page).

Tip: You might see oxidation numbers called oxidation states. They're the same thing though.

Tip: Check your Year 1 notes for the rules on how to assign oxidation numbers.

Balancing more complex half-equations

Sometimes you might have to write a half-equation for a more complicated reaction where the oxidising or reducing agent contains oxygen or hydrogen (for example dichromate(VI) ions, $Cr_2O_7^{2-}$). In this case you might have to add water and either H^+ or OH^- ions to make the half-equations balance.

You can always add electrons and water (H_2O) to your half-equations to balance them. If the reaction is taking place under acidic conditions, then you can also add H^+ ions. If the reaction is taking place under alkaline conditions, then you can add OH^- ions to balance your half-equation. But that's it — those are the only things that you're allowed to add.

Example — Maths Skills

As part of a redox reaction, acidified dichromate(VI) ions, $Cr_2O_7^{2-}$, are reduced to Cr^{3+} ions. Write a half-equation for this reaction.

Start by balancing all the elements in the reaction except for O and H. Here, this just means balancing the number of Cr atoms in the dichromate(VI) ions on the left-hand side of the reaction and the Cr^{3+} ions on the right-hand side:

$$Cr_2O_7^{2-} \rightarrow 2Cr^{3+}$$

Now balance the oxygen atoms. Since the reaction is taking place under acidic conditions there won't be any OH^- ions around. So you add seven H_2O molecules to the right-hand side to balance the oxygen in $Cr_2O_7^{2-}$:

$$Cr_2O_7^{2-} \rightarrow 2Cr^{3+} + 7H_2O$$

Then balance the hydrogen atoms from the water by adding some H^+ ions (from the acid) to the left-hand side:

$$Cr_2O_7^{2-} + 14H^+ \rightarrow 2Cr^{3+} + 7H_2O$$

Finally, add some electrons to balance the charges:

$$Cr_2O_7^{2-} + 14H^+ + 6e^- \rightarrow 2Cr^{3+} + 7H_2O$$

Charges: $(-2)\ (+1 \times 14)\ (-6) \rightarrow (+3 \times 2)\ (0 \times 7)$

Total: $+6 \rightarrow +6$

Oxidation numbers

The **oxidation number** of an element tells you the total number of electrons it has donated or accepted. Oxidation numbers go up or down as electrons are lost or gained. To work out which atoms are oxidised and which are reduced in a reaction, you need to look at the oxidation numbers.
The oxidation number for an atom will increase by one for each electron lost.
The oxidation number will decrease by one for each electron gained.

Example

The reaction between vanadium(V) oxide and sulfur dioxide is shown below:

$$V_2O_5 + SO_2 \rightarrow V_2O_4 + SO_3$$

	V_2O_5	SO_2		V_2O_4	SO_3	
Oxidation number of V:	+5		→	+4		*reduction*
Oxidation number of S:		+4	→		+6	*oxidation*

In this reaction, vanadium is reduced from +5 to +4 (it gains 1 electron) and sulfur is oxidised from +4 to +6 (it loses two electrons).

You can also use changes in oxidation numbers to write redox equations.

Example — Maths Skills

Acidified manganate(VII) ions (MnO_4^-) can be reduced to manganese(II) ions by iron(II) ions. The iron(II) ions are oxidised to iron(III) ions. Write an overall redox equation for this reaction.

1. In the question you're told that iron changes from iron(II) to iron(III) — its oxidation number has increased by 1, so it must have lost one electron:

$$Fe^{2+} \rightarrow Fe^{3+} + e^-$$

2. You're also told that manganate(VII) is reduced to manganese(II) — its oxidation number has decreased by 5, so it must have gained 5 electrons:

$$MnO_4^- + 5e^- \rightarrow Mn^{2+}$$

But this half-equation isn't balanced — you need to add some water to the right-hand side and then some hydrogen ions to the left-hand side:

$$MnO_4^- + 8H^+ + 5e^- \rightarrow Mn^{2+} + 4H_2O$$

3. Five iron ions are required to release the five electrons needed by each manganate ion, so you need to multiply the first half-equation by 5:

$$5Fe^{2+} \rightarrow 5Fe^{3+} + 5e^-$$

4. Now you can combine the half-equations:

$$MnO_4^- + 8H^+ + 5Fe^{2+} \rightarrow Mn^{2+} + 4H_2O + 5Fe^{3+}$$

Tip: Remember to finish by checking that the charges balance — that way you know you haven't made a mistake.

Practice Questions — Application

Q1 Metallic iron can displace copper(II) ions in solution to form a solution of iron(III) ions and a deposit of copper metal. The half-equations are:

$$Fe_{(s)} \rightarrow Fe^{3+}_{(aq)} + 3e^- \qquad Cu^{2+}_{(aq)} + 2e^- \rightarrow Cu_{(s)}$$

Combine these half-equations to give the full redox equation for this reaction.

Q2 The following reaction occurs between iron and chlorine:

$$Cl_{2(g)} + 2Fe^{2+}_{(aq)} \rightarrow 2Cl^-_{(aq)} + 2Fe^{3+}_{(aq)}$$

One of the half-equations is $Fe^{2+}_{(aq)} \rightarrow Fe^{3+}_{(aq)} + e^-$. Write out the other.

Q3 Dichromate ions ($Cr_2O_7^{2-}$) are reduced by zinc.
The unbalanced half-equations for this reaction are:

$$Zn \rightarrow Zn^{2+} + e^- \quad \text{and} \quad Cr_2O_7^{2-} + H^+ + e^- \rightarrow Cr^{3+} + H_2O$$

a) Balance both of these half-equations

b) Give the full redox equation for this reaction.

Q4 Ethanol, CH_3CH_2OH, can be oxidised to ethanoic acid, CH_3COOH, using an acidified solution of dichromate(VI) ions, $Cr_2O_7^{2-}{}_{(aq)}$.

a) What is the oxidation state of chromium in dichromate(VI) ions?

b) Write out half-equations for the oxidation and reduction reactions.

c) Write a balanced redox equation for this reaction.

Tip: Writing the half-equation for the oxidation of ethanol in Q4 is a bit tricky, but don't panic — just use the method from the last page. First check that the carbons are balanced. Then add some water to balance the oxygens. Then add some H^+ ions to balance the hydrogens. Finally, balance the charges by adding some electrons.

Practice Questions — Fact Recall

Q1 a) What is an oxidising agent?

b) What is a reducing agent?

Q2 What happens to the oxidation number of an element that is reduced as part of a redox reaction?

Tip: The oxidation of alcohols by dichromate(VI) ions can be used as a test for primary or secondary alcohols. It's all covered in your Year 1 notes.

2. Redox Titrations

You learnt all about redox reactions on pages 113-115 (and if you haven't, you should). Now here's a nice topic all about how you can use redox reactions in experimental chemistry.

Learning Objectives:

- Know the techniques and procedures used when carrying out redox titrations including those involving Fe^{2+}/MnO_4^-.
- Be able to perform structured and non-structured titration calculations, based on experimental results of redox titrations involving Fe^{2+}/MnO_4^- and non-familiar redox systems.

Specification Reference 5.2.3

Oxidising and reducing agents

Transition (d-block) elements can exist in many different **oxidation numbers** (see page 144). They can change oxidation number by gaining or losing electrons in redox reactions (see pages 156-157). The ability to gain or lose electrons easily makes transition metal ions good oxidising or reducing agents. What's more, as they change oxidation number, transition elements often also change colour, so it's easy to spot when they've been oxidised or reduced. Here are a couple of examples:

Examples

The oxidation of Fe^{2+} to Fe^{3+} by manganate(VII) ions in solution.

Acidified potassium manganate(VII) solution, $KMnO_{4(aq)}$, is used as an oxidising agent. It contains manganate(VII) ions (MnO_4^-), in which manganese has an oxidation number of +7. They can be reduced to Mn^{2+} ions during a redox reaction with Fe^{2+} ions.

Half equations:

$$MnO_4^- + 8H^+ + 5e^- \rightarrow Mn^{2+} + 4H_2O$$

$$5Fe^{2+} \rightarrow 5Fe^{3+} + 5e^-$$

$$MnO_4^- + 8H^+ + 5Fe^{2+} \rightarrow Mn^{2+} + 4H_2O + 5Fe^{3+}$$

In this reaction the manganese is reduced and the iron is oxidised.

$MnO_{4\,(aq)}^-$ is purple and $[Mn(H_2O)_6]^{2+}_{(aq)}$ is colourless so, during this reaction, you'll see a colour change from purple to colourless — see Figure 1.

Figure 1: *The colour change seen during the reaction of potassium manganate(VII) solution with iron(II) ions. The solution goes from purple to colourless as the manganate(VII) ions are reduced to Mn^{2+} ions.*

The oxidation of Zn to Zn^{2+} by dichromate(VI) ions in solution.

Acidified potassium dichromate(VI) solution, $K_2Cr_2O_{7(aq)}$, is another oxidising agent. It contains dichromate(VI) ions ($Cr_2O_7^{2-}$), in which chromium has an oxidation number of +6. They can be reduced to Cr^{3+} ions during a redox reaction with Zn metal.

Half equations:

$$Cr_2O_7^{2-} + 14H^+ + 6e^- \rightarrow 2Cr^{3+} + 7H_2O$$

$$3Zn \rightarrow 3Zn^{2+} + 6e^-$$

$$Cr_2O_7^{2-} + 14H^+ + 3Zn \rightarrow 2Cr^{3+} + 7H_2O + 3Zn^{2+}$$

In this reaction the chromium is reduced and the zinc is oxidised.

$Cr_2O_{7\,(aq)}^{2-}$ is orange and $[Cr(H_2O)_6]^{3+}_{(aq)}$ looks green so, during this reaction, you'll see a colour change from orange to green — see Figure 2.

Figure 2: *The colour change seen during the reaction of potassium dichromate(VI) solution with zinc. The solution goes from orange to green as the dichromate(VI) ions are reduced to Cr^{3+} ions.*

The pretty colours of transition metal ion solutions make them really useful as indicators. The sharp colour changes let you know when a reaction has taken place. This characteristic of transition metal ions is especially useful in titrations, as you'll see on the next few pages...

Performing titrations

Titrations using transition element ions let you find out how much oxidising agent is needed to exactly react with a quantity of reducing agent — they're **redox titrations**. If you know the concentration of either the oxidising agent or the reducing agent, you can use the titration results to work out the concentration of the other. Here's how.

- First, measure out a quantity of reducing agent, e.g. aqueous Fe^{2+} ions, using a pipette, and put it in a conical flask.
- Use a measuring cylinder to measure out about 20 cm^3 of dilute sulfuric acid and add it to the flask — this is in excess, so you don't have to be too exact. (The acid is added to make sure there are plenty of H^+ ions to allow the oxidising agent to be reduced.)
- Add some oxidising agent (e.g. potassium manganate(VII) solution) to a burette and take a reading of the initial volume.
- Now gradually add the oxidising agent to the reducing agent. Swirl the flask as you go.
- The oxidising agent you are adding will react with the reducing agent. This reaction will continue until all of the reducing agent is used up.
- At this point, the very next drop that you add will give the mixture the colour of the oxidising agent.
- Stop when the mixture in the flask becomes just tainted with the colour of the oxidising agent (the end point) and note down the volume of oxidising agent that you added. This is the rough titration.
- Now do some accurate titrations. Measure out the solutions and take an initial reading. Run the oxidising agent into the reducing agent until you are within 2 cm^3 of the end point from your rough titration. Then add the oxidising agent drop by drop until you reach the exact end point.
- Record the final volume of oxidising agent in the burette. Subtract this from the initial reading to find the exact volume of oxidising agent needed to react with the reducing agent — this is called the titre.
- Repeat until you get at least three readings within 0.10 cm^3 of each other.

The equipment you'll need to do a titration is shown in Figure 3.

Burette
Oxidising agent
The scale on the burette means you can see exactly how much oxidising agent has been added.
Tap on the burette means the oxidising agent can be added one drop at a time.
Conical flask
Reducing agent and dilute sulfuric acid.

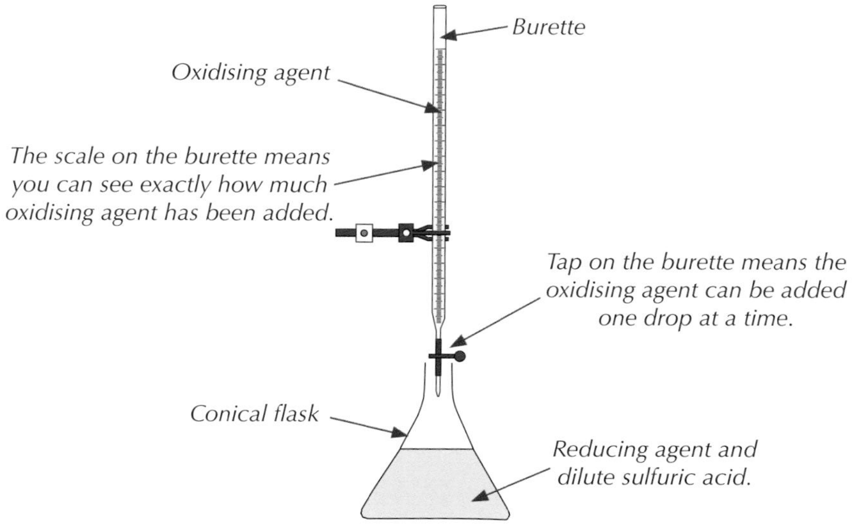

Figure 3: *The equipment needed to perform a redox titration.*

Tip: Before carrying out any experiment, do a full risk assessment and take any necessary safety precautions.

Tip: You've already seen how to do acid-base titrations and accurately measure out volumes of liquids in the first year of the course. So look back at your Year 1 notes if you need a reminder.

Tip: You can also do titrations the other way round — adding the reducing agent to the oxidising agent.

Tip: You could use a coloured reducing agent and a colourless oxidising agent instead — then you'd be watching for the moment that the colour in the flask disappears.

Tip: Readings that are within a small range are known as concordant results.

Tip: Remember to read any volume measurements from the bottom of the meniscus, and at eye-level.

Figure 4: *$KMnO_4$ being added to Fe^{2+} ions. The solution in the flask is just tinted purple, so the titration is at the end point.*

Tip: These calculations are the same as the ones for acid-base titrations (which you should have covered in Year 1).

Tip: The molar ratio is the ratio of one ion (or compound) to another ion (or compound) in the balanced equation.

Exam Tip
In your exams, you could be asked to carry out titration calculations using chemicals and systems you've not met before. If this happens, don't panic. Just follow the method above and you should be fine.

Tip: In these calculations the units of concentration should always be mol dm^{-3}.

Titrations using $KMnO_4$

Manganate(VII) ions (MnO_4^-) in aqueous potassium manganate(VII) ($KMnO_4$) are purple. When they're added to the reducing agent, they start reacting. This reaction will continue until all of the reducing agent is used up. At this point the solution in the flask will start to turn purple. The exact point at which the solution turns from colourless to purple is the end point of the reaction. The trick is to spot exactly when this happens. Doing the reaction in front of a white surface (for example, by putting the flask on a white tile, as in Figure 4) can make the colour change much easier to spot.

Calculating the concentration of a reagent

Once you've done a titration you can use your results to calculate the concentration of either the oxidising agent or the reducing agent. To do this:

Step 1: Write out a balanced equation for the redox reaction that's happening in the conical flask.

Step 2: Decide what you know already and what you need to know — usually you'll know the two volumes and the concentration of one of the reagents and want to find the concentration of the other reagent.

Step 3: For the reagent you know both the concentration and the volume of, calculate the number of moles present using the equation:

$$\text{moles} = \frac{\text{concentration (mol dm}^{-3}) \times \text{volume (cm}^3)}{1000}$$

Step 4: Use the molar ratios in the balanced equation to find out how many moles of the other reagent were present in the solution.

Step 5: Calculate the unknown concentration using the equation:

$$\text{concentration (mol dm}^{-3}) = \frac{\text{moles} \times 1000}{\text{volume (cm}^3)}$$

Example — Maths Skills

27.5 cm^3 of 0.0200 mol dm^{-3} aqueous potassium manganate(VII) reacted with 25.0 cm^3 of acidified iron(II) sulfate solution.
Calculate the concentration of Fe^{2+} ions in the solution.

1. The balanced equation for this titration reaction is:

$$MnO_{4\,(aq)}^- + 8H^+_{(aq)} + 5Fe^{2+}_{(aq)} \rightarrow Mn^{2+}_{(aq)} + 4H_2O_{(l)} + 5Fe^{3+}_{(aq)}$$

2. You know the concentration and the volume of the MnO_4^- ion solution (0.0200 mol dm^{-3} and 27.5 cm^3) and the volume of the Fe^{2+} solution (25.0 cm^3). You need to know the concentration of the Fe^{2+} solution.

3. Work out the number of moles of MnO_4^- ions added to the flask.

$$\text{moles } MnO_4^- = \frac{\text{conc.} \times \text{volume}}{1000} = \frac{0.0200 \times 27.5}{1000} = 5.50 \times 10^{-4} \text{ moles}$$

4. From the molar ratios in the equation, you know 1 mole of MnO_4^- reacts with 5 moles of Fe^{2+}. So 5.50×10^{-4} moles of MnO_4^- must react with $(5.50 \times 10^{-4}) \times 5 = 2.75 \times 10^{-3}$ moles of Fe^{2+}.

5. Calculate the concentration of Fe^{2+}:

$$\text{conc. } Fe^{2+} = \frac{\text{moles} \times 1000}{\text{volume}} = \frac{(2.75 \times 10^{-3}) \times 1000}{25.0} = \mathbf{0.110 \text{ mol dm}^{-3}}$$

Practice Questions — Application

Q1 28.2 cm^3 of a 0.0500 mol dm^{-3} acidified iron(II) sulfate solution reacted exactly with 30.0 cm^3 of aqueous potassium manganate(VII).

a) Write an ionic equation for the reaction between Fe^{2+} ions and MnO_4^- ions.

b) Calculate the number of moles of acidified iron(II) sulfate solution that reacted with the aqueous potassium manganate(VII).

c) Use your answer from part b) to calculate the concentration of the potassium manganate(VII) solution.

Q2 Aqueous potassium manganate(VII) with a concentration of 0.0750 mol dm^{-3} was used to completely react with 28.0 cm^3 of a 0.600 mol dm^{-3} solution of acidified iron(II) sulfate. Calculate the volume of potassium manganate(VII) solution that reacted.

Q3 22.2 cm^3 of 0.150 mol dm^{-3} aqueous potassium dichromate(VI) was needed to completely react with 20.0 cm^3 of an acidified iron(II) sulfate solution.

a) Write down the balanced ionic equation for the reaction between Fe^{2+} ions and $Cr_2O_7^{2-}$ ions.

b) Calculate the number of moles of aqueous potassium dichromate(VI) that reacted with the acidified iron(II) sulfate solution.

c) Calculate the concentration of Fe^{2+} ions in the solution.

Q4 A 0.450 mol dm^{-3} solution of acidified iron(II) sulfate completely reacted with 24.0 cm^3 of a 0.0550 mol dm^{-3} solution of aqueous potassium dichromate(VI). Calculate the volume of iron(II) sulfate solution used.

Q5 A lump of zinc metal was dropped into 30.0 cm^3 of a 0.230 mol dm^{-3} solution of acidified dichromate(VI) ions.

a) Write a balanced ionic equation for this reaction.

b) Calculate the number of moles of dichromate(VI) ions present in the solution.

c) The lump of zinc fully dissolved in the solution. Calculate the mass of zinc that was added to the solution. Assume that all of the acidified dichromate(VI) solution reacted. (You will need to use the equation mass = moles × M_r).

Exam Tip
These questions are quite wordy. In the exams, you might find it helpful to underline the key bits of information in the question.

Tip: It may help to swot up on your acid-base titration calculations before you start these. They're all covered in your Year 1 notes.

Tip: Question 5 is a bit different because there's a solid and a solution involved. But you still start your calculations by following the same steps.

Practice Questions — Fact Recall

Q1 Give an example of an oxidising agent.

Q2 Why is acid added to the reducing agent in redox titrations?

Q3 How do you know when you've reached the end point of a titration?

3. More on Titrations

More titrations... hurrah. As well as knowing all about acid-base titrations (which you studied in Year 1) and Fe^{2+}/MnO_4^- titrations (pages 116-118), you also need to know about iodine-sodium thiosulfate titrations. Keep learning...

Learning Objectives:

- Know the techniques and procedures used when carrying out redox titrations including those involving $I_2/S_2O_3^{2-}$.
- Be able to perform structured and non-structured titration calculations, based on experimental results of redox titrations involving $I_2/S_2O_3^{2-}$ and non-familiar redox systems.

Specification Reference 5.2.3

Iodine-sodium thiosulfate titrations

Iodine-sodium thiosulfate titrations are a way of finding the amount of iodine in a solution. If the iodine has been formed in a redox reaction, knowing the amount of iodine allows you to work out the amount of other substances involved in the reaction too — for example, the amount of oxidising agent present. So here's how you can find out the concentration of a solution of the oxidising agent potassium iodate(V):

Step 1: Oxidise the iodide ions to iodine

Measure out a certain volume of potassium iodate(V) solution (KIO_3) (the oxidising agent) — say 25 cm³. Add this to an excess of acidified potassium iodide solution (KI). The iodate(V) ions in the potassium iodate(V) solution oxidise some of the iodide ions to iodine — the solution will be red-brown.

$$IO_3^-{}_{(aq)} + 5I^-{}_{(aq)} + 6H^+{}_{(aq)} \rightarrow 3I_{2\,(aq)} + 3H_2O_{(l)}$$

Step 2: Titrate the iodine solution with sodium thiosulfate

You need to titrate the solution formed in step 1 with sodium thiosulfate ($Na_2S_2O_3$) of a known concentration. The iodine in the solution reacts with thiosulfate ions like this:

$$I_{2\,(aq)} + 2S_2O_3^{2-}{}_{(aq)} \rightarrow 2I^-{}_{(aq)} + S_4O_6^{2-}{}_{(aq)}$$

The set-up for this titration is shown in Figure 1. Here's how you carry it out:

- Take the flask containing the solution that was produced in Stage 1.
- From a burette, add sodium thiosulfate solution to the flask drop by drop.
- It's hard to see the end point, so when the iodine colour fades to a pale yellow, add 2 cm³ of starch solution (to detect the presence of iodine). The solution in the conical flask will go dark blue, showing there's still some iodine there.
- Add sodium thiosulfate one drop at a time until the blue colour disappears.
- When this happens, it means all the iodine has just reacted.
- Record the volume of sodium thiosulfate added to the solution.

Ideally, you should repeat steps 1 and 2 until you get three concordant results. Then you can work out a mean titre value to use in steps 3 and 4.

Tip: Make sure you carry out a risk assessment before starting any experiment.

Exam Tip
If you have to write out these equations in the exams, make sure they're balanced. You'll lose easy marks if they're not.

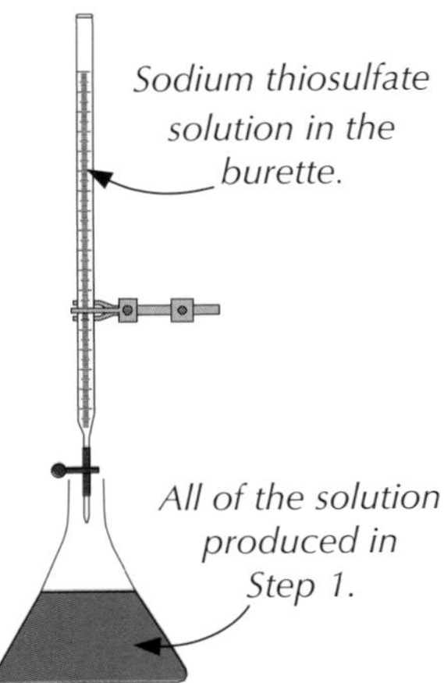

***Figure 1:** The apparatus used to perform an iodine-sodium thiosulfate titration.*

Step 3: Calculate the number of moles of iodine present

To do this you need to:

- Calculate the number of moles of thiosulfate ions used in the titration.
- Then use the 1 : 2 molar ratio of $I_2 : S_2O_3^{2-}$ in the balanced equation for the reaction (shown in Step 2) to work out how many moles of iodine were present in the solution.

Step 4: Calculate the concentration of the oxidising agent

This bit's the same as the last few steps for a redox titration (see page 118).

- Use the 3 : 1 molar ratio of $I_2 : IO_3^-$ from the balanced equation in step 1 to work out how many moles of iodate(V) ions were present in the solution.
- You can then use this to work out the concentration of potassium iodate(V).

Example — Maths Skills

25.0 cm³ of potassium iodate(V) solution was added to an excess of acidified potassium iodide. This solution was then titrated against a 0.120 mol dm⁻³ solution of sodium thiosulfate. 11.1 cm³ of thiosulfate solution was required to react fully with the solution.
Find the concentration of the potassium iodate(V) solution.

Because you're given the titration data in the question you can start at step 3 for this one:

First calculate the number of moles of thiosulfate ions used in the titration...

$$\text{Number of moles of thiosulfate} = \frac{\text{concentration} \times \text{volume (cm}^3)}{1000}$$

$$= \frac{0.120 \times 11.1}{1000}$$

$$= 1.332 \times 10^{-3} \text{ moles}$$

Then use the balanced equation and the molar ratio to calculate the number of moles of iodine in the solution.

Balanced equation: $\mathbf{I_2 + 2S_2O_3^{2-} \rightarrow 2I^- + S_4O_6^{2-}}$

1 mole of iodine reacts with 2 moles of thiosulfate. So,

Number of moles of iodine in the solution = $1.332 \times 10^{-3} \div 2$

$= 6.66 \times 10^{-4}$ moles

Now do step 4: Look at the balanced equation for the reaction of iodate ions with acidified iodide ions. Use the molar ratio from this equation to calculate the number of moles of potassium iodate(V) present in the solution.

Balanced equation: $\mathbf{IO_3^-{}_{(aq)} + 5I^-{}_{(aq)} + 6H^+{}_{(aq)} \rightarrow 3I_{2\,(aq)} + 3H_2O}$

25.0 cm³ of potassium iodate(V) solution produced 6.66×10^{-4} moles of iodine. The equation shows that one mole of iodate(V) ions will produce three moles of iodine.

That means there must have been $(6.66 \times 10^{-4}) \div 3 = 2.22 \times 10^{-4}$ moles of iodate(V) ions in the original solution. So now it's straightforward to find the concentration of the potassium iodate(V) solution, which is what you're after:

$$\text{concentration of iodate(V) ions} = \frac{\text{number of moles} \times 1000}{\text{volume (cm}^3)}$$

$$= \frac{2.22 \times 10^{-4} \times 1000}{25.0}$$

concentration of KIO_3 = **0.00888 mol dm⁻³**

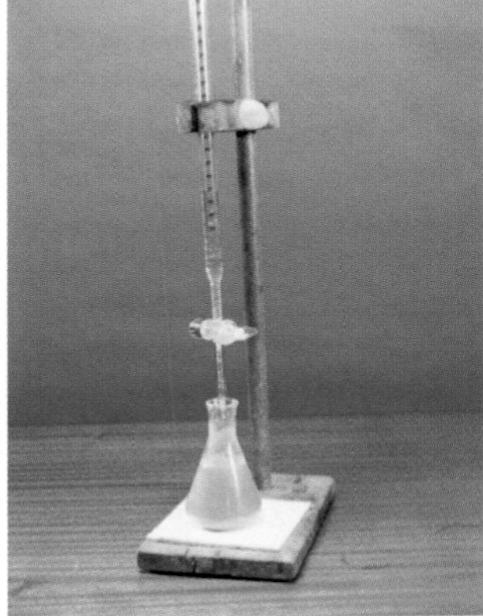

Figure 2: Titrating iodine with sodium thiosulfate.

Tip: Don't forget that in step 3 and step 4 you are using different balanced equations and different molar ratios. First you need to calculate the number of moles of iodine then you can use this information to calculate the moles of iodate(V) ions.

Tip: This is just the formula:
moles = conc. × volume
rearranged to give:
conc. = moles ÷ volume

Tip: Always remember to give units with your answer. It'd be crazy to get through all those steps just to lose marks 'cause you didn't put down your units.

You don't have to use potassium iodate(V) solution (KIO_3) as the oxidising agent for this reaction — the method works the same way with any oxidising agent.

In fact, you may have to answer questions in the exams involving redox titration systems you've not met before. Just follow the same method as shown on the last few pages, and you'll be fine.

Practice Questions — Application

Q1 13.2 cm^3 of potassium iodate(V) solution was added to an excess of acidified potassium iodide, and the following reaction occurred: $IO_3^-{}_{(aq)} + 5I^-{}_{(aq)} + 6H^+{}_{(aq)} \rightarrow 3I_{2\,(aq)} + 3H_2O_{(l)}$.
The solution formed by this reaction was then titrated against a 0.200 mol dm^{-3} solution of sodium thiosulfate. 41.1 cm^3 of thiosulfate solution was required to react fully with the solution. Here's the equation for this reaction: $I_{2\,(aq)} + 2Na_2S_2O_{3\,(aq)} \rightarrow 2NaI_{(aq)} + Na_2S_4O_{6\,(aq)}$

a) Calculate the number of moles of sodium thiosulfate used in the reaction.

b) Calculate the number of moles of iodine formed by adding the potassium iodate(V) solution to the acidified potassium iodide.

c) Work out the number of moles of potassium iodate present.

d) Work out the concentration of the potassium iodate(V) solution used in this experiment.

Q2 39.0 cm^3 of potassium manganate(VII) solution was added to 61.0 cm^3 (an excess) of acidified potassium iodide. 25.0 cm^3 of this solution was then titrated against a 0.750 mol dm^{-3} solution of sodium thiosulfate. 4.00 cm^3 of thiosulfate solution was required to react fully with the solution. Here are the reactions that occur in this experiment:

$$2MnO_4^-{}_{(aq)} + 10I^-{}_{(aq)} + 16H^+{}_{(aq)} \rightarrow 5I_{2\,(aq)} + 8H_2O_{(l)} + 2Mn^{2+}{}_{(aq)}$$
$$I_{2\,(aq)} + 2Na_2S_2O_{3\,(aq)} \rightarrow 2NaI_{(aq)} + Na_2S_4O_{6\,(aq)}$$

a) Calculate the number of moles of sodium thiosulfate used in the reaction.

b) Calculate the total number of moles of iodine formed by adding the potassium manganate(VII) solution to the acidified potassium iodide.

c) Work out the concentration of the potassium manganate(VII) solution used in this experiment.

Tip: For Q2 b) it's important to remember that the total volume of the reaction mixture was 39.0 + 61.0 = 100 cm^3, but that only 25 cm^3 of this solution was then used in the titration.

Q3 15.0 cm^3 of potassium dichromate(VI) solution was added to an excess of acidified potassium iodide. This solution was then titrated against a 0.0600 mol dm^{-3} solution of sodium thiosulfate.
If 22.3 cm^3 of sodium thiosulfate solution was required to react fully with the solution, what was the concentration of the potassium dichromate(VI) solution?

Here are the equations for the two steps of the experiment:

$$Cr_2O_7^{2-}{}_{(aq)} + 6I^-{}_{(aq)} + 14H^+{}_{(aq)} \rightarrow 2Cr^{3+}{}_{(aq)} + 3I_{2\,(aq)} + 7H_2O_{(l)}$$
$$I_{2\,(aq)} + 2S_2O_3^{2-}{}_{(aq)} \rightarrow 2I^-{}_{(aq)} + S_4O_6^{2-}{}_{(aq)}$$

Exam Tip
In your exams you could be asked to complete a calculation like this one step at a time, or you could be dumped in at the deep end and asked to do the whole calculation (like in Q3). So you need to be really clear on how to work through them.

Practice Questions — Fact Recall

Q1 Write out the ionic equation for a reaction between iodate(V) ions, and acidified potassium iodide solution.

Q2 Write down the ionic equation for the reaction between iodine and thiosulfate ions.

Q3 Describe how you would carry out a titration between an iodine solution and sodium thiosulfate.

Tip: Remember, you need to know how to carry out the titrations as well as how to do all the titration calculations.

4. Electrochemical Cells

In redox reactions, electrons move from one atom to another. When electrons move, you get an electrical current. So redox reactions can be used to generate electricity.

Learning Objectives:

- Know the techniques and procedures used for the measurement of cell potentials of metals or non-metals in contact with their ions in aqueous solution (PAG 8).
- Know the techniques and procedures used for the measurement of cell potentials of ions of the same element in different oxidation states in contact with a Pt electrode (PAG 8).

Specification Reference 5.2.3

What are electrochemical cells?

Electrochemical cells can be made from two different metals dipped in salt solutions of their own ions and connected by a wire (the external circuit). There are always two reactions within an electrochemical cell — one's an oxidation and one's a reduction — so it's a **redox** process.

Example

The diagram below shows an electrochemical cell made using copper and zinc.

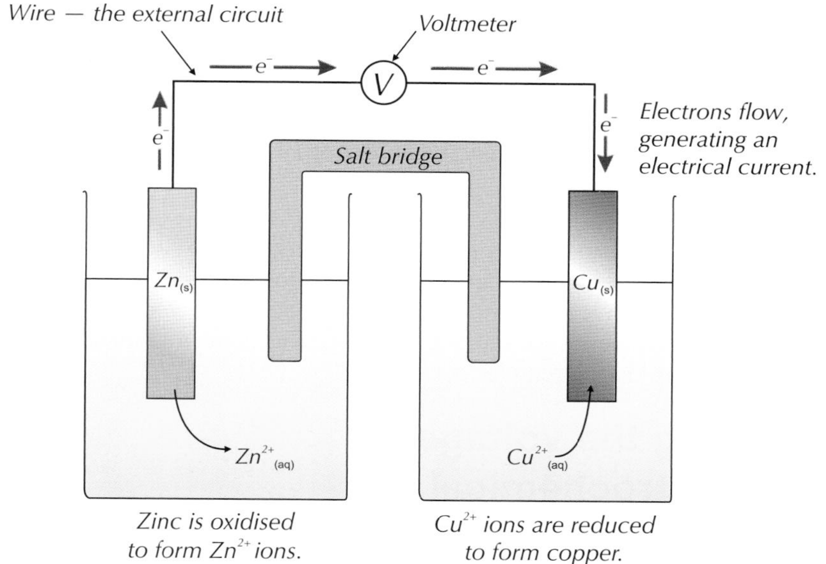

Wire — the external circuit
Voltmeter
V
e⁻
Electrons flow, generating an electrical current.
Salt bridge
$Zn_{(s)}$
$Cu_{(s)}$
$Zn^{2+}_{(aq)}$
$Cu^{2+}_{(aq)}$
Zinc is oxidised to form Zn^{2+} ions.
Cu^{2+} ions are reduced to form copper.

A copper electrode is dipped in a solution of Cu^{2+} ions and a zinc electrode is dipped in a solution of Zn^{2+} ions. Zinc loses electrons more easily than copper. So in the half-cell on the left, zinc (from the zinc electrode) is oxidised to form $Zn^{2+}_{(aq)}$ ions. This releases electrons into the external circuit. In the other half-cell, the same number of electrons are taken from the external circuit, reducing the Cu^{2+} ions to copper atoms.

The solutions are connected by a **salt bridge**, e.g. a strip of filter paper soaked in $KNO_{3(aq)}$. This allows ions to flow through and balance out the charges — it completes the circuit.

Tip: See pages 113-115 for more on redox reactions.

Figure 1: *An electrochemical cell.*

Tip: The two different sides of the electrochemical cell are called half-cells — two half-cells make a whole.

Electrons flow through the wire from the more reactive metal to the less reactive metal. A voltmeter in the external circuit shows the voltage between the two half-cells. This is the **cell potential** or e.m.f., E_{cell}.

You can also have half-cells involving solutions of aqueous ions of the same element with different oxidation numbers.

Tip: e.m.f. stands for electromotive force.

Tip: An electrode has to be a solid that conducts electricity. If a half-cell doesn't contain anything like this, as in this example, you can use something else as the electrode. But it must be inert too — this means it won't react with any of the solutions in the cell. You'd usually use an electrode made from platinum or graphite.

Example

You can make an electrochemical half-cell using solutions of Fe^{2+} and Fe^{3+} ions. A platinum electrode is dipped into the solution.

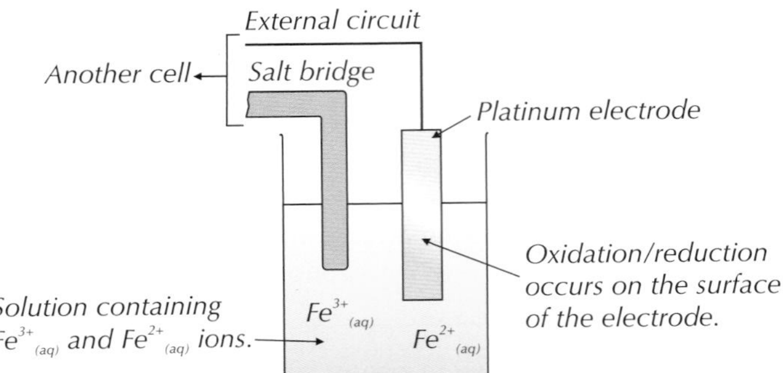

When this half-cell is connected to another half-cell, a current will flow and $Fe^{2+}_{(aq)}$ will be converted to $Fe^{3+}_{(aq)}$ or vice versa. The conversion of $Fe^{2+}_{(aq)}$ to $Fe^{3+}_{(aq)}$ (or Fe^{3+} to Fe^{2+}) happens on the surface of the platinum electrode.

The direction of the conversion depends on the other half-cell in the circuit. If the other cell contains a metal that is less reactive than iron then Fe^{2+} will be oxidised to Fe^{3+} at the electrode. But if the other cell contains a metal that is more reactive than iron, then Fe^{3+} will be reduced to Fe^{2+} at the electrode.

Tip: Remember to carry out a risk assessment before starting any experiment.

You can also use non-metals, like chlorine or hydrogen, as reactants in electrochemical cells. For systems involving a gas, the gas can be bubbled over an inert electrode (for example, a platinum electrode) sitting in a solution of its aqueous ions (e.g. Cl^- or H^+). This is the technique used to create a standard hydrogen electrode (see page 127).

Measuring the voltage of an electrochemical cell

PRACTICAL ACTIVITY GROUP 8

Tip: Setting up an electrochemical cell involving non-metals can be a bit harder. You may need a platinum or graphite electrode and a stream of gas of the non-metal you're investigating.

You need to know how to set up an electrochemical cell and use it to take measurements of voltage. Here's a method you can use to construct an electrochemical cell involving two metals.

1. Get a strip of each of the metals you're investigating. These are your electrodes. Clean the surfaces of the metals using a piece of emery paper (or sandpaper).
2. Clean any grease or oil from the electrodes using some propanone. From this point on, be careful not to touch the surfaces of the metals with your hands — you could transfer grease back onto the strips.
3. Place each electrode into a beaker filled with a solution containing ions of that metal. For example, if you had an electrode made of zinc metal, you could place it in a beaker of $ZnSO_{4\,(aq)}$. If you had an electrode made of copper, you could use a solution of $CuSO_{4\,(aq)}$.
4. Create a salt bridge to link the two solutions together. You can do this by simply soaking a piece of filter paper in a salt solution, e.g. $KCl_{(aq)}$ or $KNO_{3\,(aq)}$, and draping it between the two beakers. The ends of the filter paper should be immersed in the solutions.
5. Connect the electrodes to a voltmeter, using crocodile clips and wires. If you've set up your circuit correctly, you'll get a reading on your voltmeter.

Tip: If you're creating an electrochemical cell where one of the species you're investigating involves two ions (e.g. $Fe^{3+} + e^- \rightleftharpoons Fe^{2+}$), then you'll need to use a platinum electrode and a solution containing both ions.

You can carry out various investigations using this basic set-up. By changing the materials the electrodes are made of and the solutions which they sit in, or varying the concentration of the solutions used, you can measure how the cell potential varies.

If you perform your experiment under **standard conditions**, the voltage that you measure will be the standard cell potential (E°_{cell}) for that cell. There's more about the standard conditions used for measuring electrode potentials on page 127. For now, just remember that if you're asked how you would set up an experiment to measure standard cell potential, you must say that the experiment would be performed at 298 K, a pressure of 100 kPa and with all the solutions at a concentration of 1.00 mol dm^{-3}.

Electrode potentials

The reactions that occur at each electrode in a cell are reversible.

Example

The reactions that occur at each electrode in the zinc/copper cell are:

$$Zn^{2+}_{(aq)} + 2e^- \rightleftharpoons Zn_{(s)}$$

$$Cu^{2+}_{(aq)} + 2e^- \rightleftharpoons Cu_{(s)}$$

The reversible arrows show that both reactions can go in either direction.

Tip: These are half-equations for the reactions occurring in the electrochemical cell. See pages 113-114 for more on half-equations.

Which direction each reaction goes in depends on how easily each metal loses electrons (i.e. how easily it's oxidised). How easily a metal is oxidised is measured using **electrode potentials**. A metal that's easily oxidised has a very negative electrode potential, while one that's harder to oxidise has a less negative (or positive) electrode potential.

Example

The table below shows the electrode potentials for the copper and zinc half-cells:

Half-cell	Electrode potential / V
$Zn^{2+}_{(aq)}/Zn_{(s)}$	*−0.76*
$Cu^{2+}_{(aq)}/Cu_{(s)}$	*+0.34*

The zinc half-cell has a more negative electrode potential, so in a zinc/copper cell, zinc is oxidised (the reaction goes backwards), while copper is reduced (the reaction goes forwards).

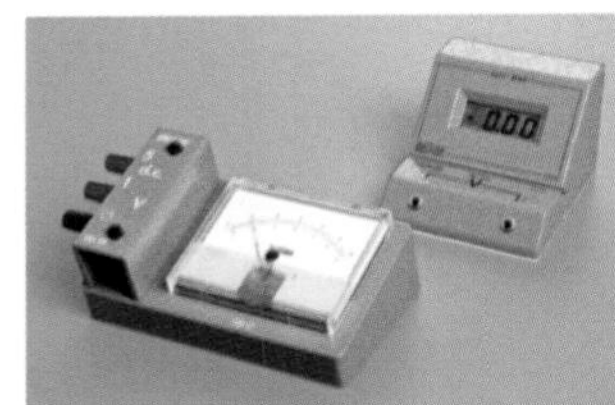

Figure 2: *Analogue or digital voltmeters can be used to measure electrode potentials.*

Tip: There's more on how standard electrode potentials are measured coming up.

Practice Questions — Application

Q1 The following reactions occur in an electrochemical cell:

$$Ni^{2+}_{(aq)} + 2e^- \rightleftharpoons Ni_{(s)} \qquad E^\circ = -0.25$$

$$Cu^{2+}_{(aq)} + 2e^- \rightleftharpoons Cu_{(s)} \qquad E^\circ = +0.34$$

a) Draw and label a diagram showing how this electrochemical cell could be set up.

b) Which of the reactions above will go in the direction of oxidation in this electrochemical cell?

Exam Tip
You don't have to memorise values for electrode potentials. You'll always be told them in the question.

Q2 An electrochemical cell containing a calcium half-cell and a silver half-cell was set up using a salt bridge.

Half-cell	Electrode potential / V
$Ca^{2+}_{(aq)}/Ca_{(s)}$	–2.87
$Ag^{+}_{(aq)}/Ag_{(s)}$	+0.80

a) Write a half-equation for the reduction reaction that will happen in this cell.

b) Write a half-equation for the oxidation reaction that will happen in this cell.

Q3 In an electrochemical cell with a $Mg^{2+}_{(aq)}/Mg_{(s)}$ half-cell and a $Fe^{3+}_{(aq)}/Fe^{2+}_{(aq)}$ half-cell (using a Pt electrode), oxidation occurs in the $Mg^{2+}_{(aq)}/Mg_{(s)}$ half-cell and reduction in the $Fe^{3+}_{(aq)}/Fe^{2+}_{(aq)}$ half-cell. State which half-cell has the more negative electrode potential.

Practice Questions — Fact Recall

Q1 a) Suggest a substance that could be used for the electrode in a half-cell involving solutions of two aqueous ions of the same element.

b) Explain why the substance you have named is suitable for this use.

Q2 Two half-cells are joined to form an electrochemical cell. A salt bridge, made from filter paper soaked in $KNO_{3(aq)}$, is put between the half-cells. A voltmeter is placed in the external circuit of the cell.

a) What is the purpose of the salt bridge?

b) What does the reading on the voltmeter tell you?

Q3 In an electrochemical cell, will oxidation or reduction occur in the half-cell with the more positive electrode potential?

Q4 If you have two metals, one of which is very easy to oxidise and the other of which is difficult to oxidise, which metal will have the more negative electrode potential?

5. Standard Electrode Potentials

Electrode potentials are influenced by things like temperature and pressure. So if you want to compare electrode potentials, they need to be standardised. This is done using a standard hydrogen electrode.

Learning Objectives:

- Be able to use the term *standard electrode* (redox) *potential,* $E^{\ominus}$.
- Know how to measure the standard electrode (redox) potential, $E^{\ominus}$, using a hydrogen electrode.

Specification Reference 5.2.3

Factors affecting the electrode potential

Half-cell reactions are reversible. So just like any other reversible reaction, the equilibrium position is affected by changes in temperature, pressure and concentration. Changing the equilibrium position changes the cell potential. To get around this, **standard conditions** are used to measure electrode potentials — using these conditions means you always get the same value for the electrode potential and you can compare values for different cells.

Tip: See pages 59-60 for more on how changes in concentration temperature and pressure affect the position of equilibrium.

Measuring standard electrode potentials

The standard electrode potential of a half-cell is the voltage measured under standard conditions when the half-cell is connected to a **standard hydrogen electrode**. The standard electrode potential of the hydrogen cell is given the value of 0.00 V. So, the voltage reading of the whole cell is equal to the standard electrode potential of whatever your hydrogen half-cell is attached to.

In the standard hydrogen electrode, hydrogen gas is bubbled into a solution of aqueous H^+ ions. A platinum foil electrode is used as a platform for the oxidation/reduction reactions — see Figure 1.

Tip: Electrode potentials can also be called 'redox potentials'. So, standard electrode potentials are also called standard redox potentials. Easy, huh?

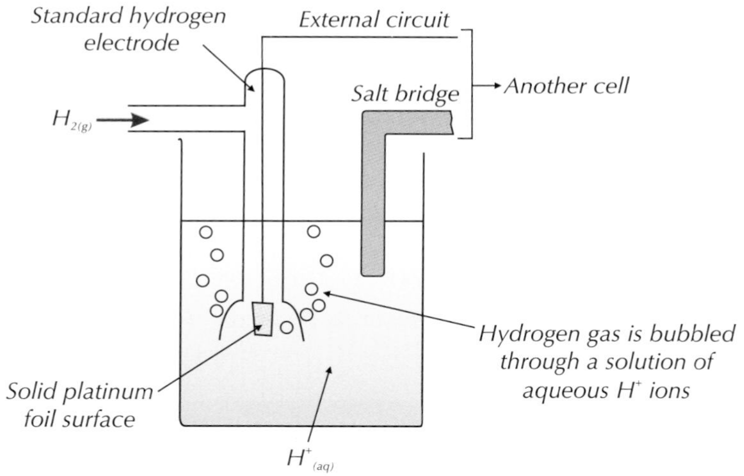

Figure 1: *The standard hydrogen electrode*

When measuring electrode potentials using the standard hydrogen electrode it is important that everything is done under standard conditions:

1. Any solutions of ions must have a concentration of 1.00 mol dm^{-3}.
2. The temperature must be 298 K (25 °C).
3. The pressure must be 100 kPa.

If standard conditions are maintained, the reading on the voltmeter when a half-cell is connected to the standard hydrogen electrode will be the standard electrode potential of that half-cell — see Figure 2.

Tip: The reading on the voltmeter could be positive or negative, depending on which way the electrons flow.

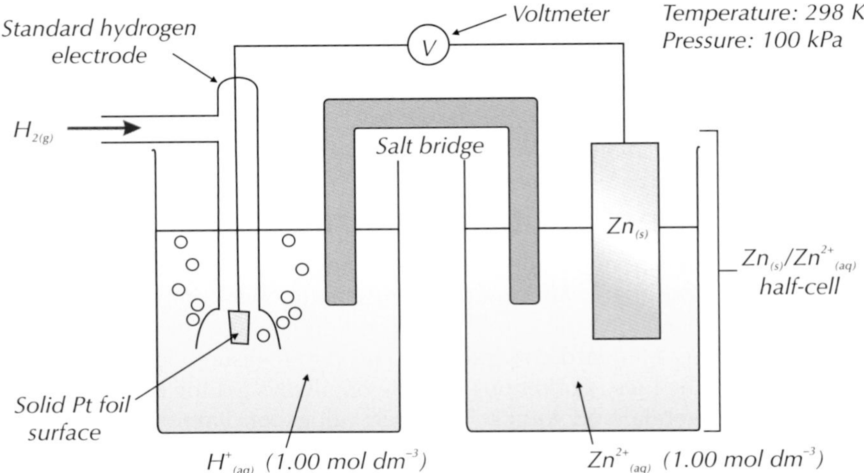

Figure 2: *Measuring the standard electrode potential of a $Zn_{(s)}/Zn^{2+}_{(aq)}$ half-cell.*

Tip: Notice how the pressure is 100 kPa, the temperature is 298 K and the H^+ and Zn^{2+} solutions both have concentrations of 1.00 mol dm^{-3}. These are the standard conditions.

Exam Tip
You could also be asked to draw a diagram of a set-up you could use to measure the standard cell potential of an electrochemical cell. Just follow all these rules, but swap the standard hydrogen electrode for a different half-cell.

In the exams, you could be asked to draw a diagram showing how the standard electrode potential of a particular half-cell could be measured. If you are, just remember these things:

- Always put the standard hydrogen electrode on the left.
- Make sure you draw a complete circuit — don't forget to include the salt bridge, the wire between the electrodes and the voltmeter.
- Label any solutions as being 1.00 mol dm^{-3}.
- If your half-cell contains aqueous ions of the same element in different oxidation numbers, don't forget to include a platinum electrode.

Practice Question — Application

Q1 When a $Pb^{2+}_{(aq)}/Pb_{(s)}$ half-cell under standard conditions was connected to a standard hydrogen electrode via a voltmeter, the reading on the voltmeter was –0.13 V.

a) What was the concentration of the Pb^{2+} solution in the $Pb^{2+}_{(aq)}/Pb_{(s)}$ half-cell

b) What is the standard electrode potential of the Pb^{2+}/Pb half-cell?

Practice Questions — Fact Recall

Q1 Give three factors that can influence electrode potentials.

Q2 Describe how a standard hydrogen electrode is set up and give the standard conditions used when measuring electrode potentials.

Q3 What is the electrode potential of the standard hydrogen electrode?

6. Electrochemical Series

The standard electrode potentials of different reactions are different (unsurprisingly). If you write a list of electrode potentials in order, you get an electrochemical series, which you can use to predict the outcome of a reaction.

Learning Objectives:

- Be able to calculate a standard cell potential by combining two standard electrode potentials.
- Be able to predict the feasibility of a reaction using standard cell potentials.
- Know the limitations of predictions about the feasibility of reactions, made using standard cell potentials, in terms of kinetics and concentration.

Specification Reference 5.2.3

What is an electrochemical series?

An **electrochemical series** is basically a big long list of electrode potentials for different electrochemical half-cells. They look something like this:

Half-reaction	E° / V
$Mg^{2+}_{(aq)} + 2e^- \rightleftharpoons Mg_{(s)}$	–2.37
$Al^{3+}_{(aq)} + 3e^- \rightleftharpoons Al_{(s)}$	–1.66
$Zn^{2+}_{(aq)} + 2e^- \rightleftharpoons Zn_{(s)}$	–0.76
$Ni^{2+}_{(aq)} + 2e^- \rightleftharpoons Ni_{(s)}$	–0.25
$2H^+_{(aq)} + 2e^- \rightleftharpoons H_{2\,(g)}$	0.00
$Sn^{4+}_{(aq)} + 2e^- \rightleftharpoons Sn^{2+}_{(aq)}$	+0.15
$Cu^{2+}_{(aq)} + 2e^- \rightleftharpoons Cu_{(s)}$	+0.34
$Fe^{3+}_{(aq)} + e^- \rightleftharpoons Fe^{2+}_{(aq)}$	+0.77
$Ag^+_{(aq)} + e^- \rightleftharpoons Ag_{(s)}$	+0.80
$Br_{2(l)} + 2e^- \rightleftharpoons 2Br^-_{(aq)}$	+1.09
$Cr_2O_7^{2-}{}_{(aq)} + 14H^+_{(aq)} + 6e^- \rightleftharpoons 2Cr^{3+}_{(aq)} + 7H_2O_{(l)}$	+1.33
$Cl_{2(g)} + 2e^- \rightleftharpoons 2Cl^-_{(aq)}$	+1.36
$MnO_4^-{}_{(aq)} + 8H^+_{(aq)} + 5e^- \rightleftharpoons Mn^{2+}_{(aq)} + 4H_2O_{(l)}$	+1.52

Figure 1: *A table showing an electrochemical series.*

Exam Tip
Don't panic — you don't have to memorise any of these values. You'll always be told them in the question if you need to use them.

The electrode potentials are written in order, starting from the most negative and going down to the most positive. The half-equations are always written as reduction reactions — but the reactions are reversible and can go the opposite way. When two half-equations are put together in an electrochemical cell, the one with the more negative electrode potential goes in the direction of oxidation (backwards) and the one with the more positive electrode potential goes in the direction of reduction (forwards).

Electrochemical series and reactivity

An electrochemical series shows you what's reactive and what's not. The more reactive a metal is, the more it wants to lose electrons to form a positive ion. More reactive metals have more negative standard electrode potentials.

Example

Magnesium is more reactive than zinc — so it's more eager to form 2+ ions than zinc is. The list of standard electrode potentials shows that Mg^{2+}/Mg has a more negative value than Zn^{2+}/Zn — its –2.37 V for Mg^{2+}/Mg and –0.76 V for Zn^{2+}/Zn. In terms of oxidation and reduction, magnesium would reduce Zn^{2+} (or Zn^{2+} would oxidise magnesium).

Exam Tip
If you're given the electrode potential of a half-cell and asked to say how reactive something is, make sure you identify whether it's a metal or a non-metal first — they're very different.

The more reactive a non-metal is, the more it wants to gain electrons to form a negative ion. More reactive non-metals have more positive standard electrode potentials.

Example

Chlorine is more reactive than bromine — so it's more eager to form a negative ion than bromine is. The list of standard electrode potentials shows that $Cl_2/2Cl^-$ is more positive than $Br_2/2Br^-$ — it's +1.36 V for $Cl_2/2Cl^-$ and +1.09 V for $Br_2/2Br^-$. In terms of oxidation and reduction, chlorine would oxidise Br^- (or Br^- would reduce chlorine).

Tip: You can use a standard hydrogen electrode to work out standard electrode potentials (see page 127 for more details).

Tip: Don't forget — cell potential is the voltage between two half-cells. See page 123 for more.

Tip: If $E^\ominus_{cell}$ is positive, the reaction is feasible (it could happen). There's more about this coming up on the next page.

Tip: If you can't remember which half-reaction in a cell goes backwards and which goes forwards, think NO P.R. — the more Negative electrode potential will go in the Oxidation direction and the more Positive electrode potential will go in the Reduction direction.

Tip: Once you know these steps, you can apply them to predict the outcome of any redox reaction.

Calculating cell potentials

You can use the information in an electrochemical series to calculate the **standard cell potential** ($E^\ominus_{cell}$) or **e.m.f.**, when two half-cells are connected together. All you have to do is work out which half-reaction is going in the direction of oxidation and which half-reaction is going in the direction of reduction. Then just substitute the $E^\ominus$ values into this equation:

$$E^\ominus_{cell} = E^\ominus_{reduced} - E^\ominus_{oxidised}$$

This is the standard electrode potential of the half-cell which goes in the direction of reduction (the one with the more positive electrode potential).

This is the standard electrode potential of the half-cell which goes in the direction of oxidation (the one with the more negative electrode potential).

Example Maths Skills

Calculate the standard cell potential of an Mg/Ag electrochemical cell using the two half-equations shown below:

$$Mg^{2+}_{(aq)} + 2e^- \rightleftharpoons Mg_{(s)} \qquad E^\ominus = -2.37$$

$$Ag^+_{(aq)} + e^- \rightleftharpoons Ag_{(s)} \qquad E^\ominus = +0.80$$

The Mg/Mg^{2+} half-cell has the more negative electrode potential, so this half reaction will go in the direction of oxidation. The Ag/Ag^+ half-cell has the more positive electrode potential and so will go in the direction of reduction.

$$E^\ominus_{cell} = E^\ominus_{reduced} - E^\ominus_{oxidised} = 0.80 - (-2.37) = \mathbf{+3.17\ V}$$

Predicting the direction of reactions

You can use electrode potentials to predict whether a redox reaction will happen and to show which direction it will go in. Just follow these steps:

1. Find the two half-equations for the redox reaction, and write them both out as reduction reactions.
2. Use an electrochemical series to work out which half-equation has the more negative electrode potential.
3. Write out the half-equation with the more negative electrode potential going in the backwards direction (oxidation) and the half-equation with the more positive electrode potential going in the forwards direction (reduction).
4. Combine the two half-equations and write out a full redox equation.

This is the feasible direction of the reaction and will give a positive overall $E^\ominus$ value. The reaction will not happen the other way round.

Example

Predict the direction of the reaction when a Zn/Zn^{2+} half-cell is connected to a Cu^{2+}/Cu half-cell.

1. Write down the two half-equations for the redox reaction as reduction reactions:

$$Zn^{2+}_{(aq)} + 2e^- \rightleftharpoons Zn_{(s)} \quad \text{and} \quad Cu^{2+}_{(aq)} + 2e^- \rightleftharpoons Cu_{(s)}$$

2. Look up the electrode potentials for the two half-equations:

$$Zn^{2+}_{(aq)} + 2e^- \rightleftharpoons Zn_{(s)} \qquad E^\ominus = -0.76\text{ V}$$
$$Cu^{2+}_{(aq)} + 2e^- \rightleftharpoons Cu_{(s)} \qquad E^\ominus = +0.34\text{ V}$$

3. The zinc half-reaction has the more negative electrode potential so write it out going backwards and the copper half-reaction going forwards.

$$Zn_{(s)} \rightarrow Zn^{2+}_{(aq)} + 2e^-$$
$$Cu^{2+}_{(aq)} + 2e^- \rightarrow Cu_{(s)}$$

4. Combine the half-equations to give the full redox equation:

$$Zn_{(s)} + Cu^{2+}_{(aq)} \rightarrow Zn^{2+}_{(aq)} + Cu_{(s)}$$

This full equation shows you the direction of the reaction — zinc metal will reduce copper(II) ions and copper(II) ions will oxidise zinc metal.

Just to back this up, if you calculate $E^\ominus_{cell}$ for this reaction...

$$E^\ominus_{cell} = E^\ominus_{reduced} - E^\ominus_{oxidised} = 0.34 - (-0.76) = +1.1\text{ V}$$

...you'll see that it's positive — so the reaction is feasible. By contrast, zinc(II) ions will not oxidise copper metal — this reaction would have a cell potential of –1.1 V.

Tip: These values for the electrode potentials came from the electrochemical series on page 129.

Tip: If you can't remember how to combine half-equations, have a look at pages 113-115.

You could also be given a reaction and asked whether or not it is feasible. If this is the case, you can follow the same method — just use the half-equations and the electrode potentials to work out the feasible direction of the reaction and see if it matches the direction given in the question.

Example

Predict whether copper will react with aqueous nickel ions.

First, find the two half-equations that would make up this reaction in an electrochemical series. Write them both out as reduction reactions:

$$Ni^{2+}_{(aq)} + 2e^- \rightleftharpoons Ni_{(s)} \qquad E^\ominus = -0.25\text{ V}$$
$$Cu^{2+}_{(aq)} + 2e^- \rightleftharpoons Cu_{(s)} \qquad E^\ominus = +0.34\text{ V}$$

The Ni/Ni^{2+} half-cell has the more negative electrode potential, so it will go in the direction of oxidation: $Ni_{(s)} \rightarrow Ni^{2+}_{(aq)} + 2e^-$

The Cu/Cu^{2+} half-cell has the more positive electrode potential, so it will go in the direction of reduction: $Cu^{2+}_{(aq)} + 2e^- \rightarrow Cu_{(s)}$

These two half-equations combine to give: $Ni_{(s)} + Cu^{2+}_{(aq)} \rightarrow Ni^{2+}_{(aq)} + Cu_{(s)}$

This shows the feasible direction of this reaction. It does not match the reaction described in the question, so copper will not react with nickel ions.

Problems with predicting reactions

A prediction using E° will only tell you if a reaction is possible under standard conditions. The prediction might be wrong if...

...the conditions are not standard

Changing the concentration (or temperature) of the solutions can cause the electrode potential to change. For example, the zinc/copper cell has these half equations in equilibrium:

$$Zn_{(s)} \rightleftharpoons Zn^{2+}_{(aq)} + 2e^-$$
$$Cu^{2+}_{(aq)} + 2e^- \rightleftharpoons Cu_{(s)}$$

If you increase the concentration of Zn^{2+}, that equilibrium will shift to the left, reducing the ease of electron loss. This will make the cell potential lower. If you increase the concentration of Cu^{2+}, that equilibrium will shift to the right, increasing the ease of electron gain. This will make the cell potential higher.

...the reaction kinetics are not favourable

The rate of a reaction may be so slow that the reaction might not appear to happen. Also, if a reaction has a high activation energy, this may stop it happening.

Tip: Remember — just because a reaction is feasible doesn't mean that it will actually happen.

Tip: You'll find the electrode potentials that you need to answer these questions in the electrochemical series on page 129.

Practice Questions — Application

Q1 For each of the combinations below state which species is more reactive and explain how you know, in terms of electrode potential.

a) Aluminium and nickel.

b) Bromine and chlorine.

c) Silver and copper.

Q2 Calculate E°_{cell} for the following reactions:

a) $Al_{(s)} + 3Ag^{+}_{(aq)} \rightarrow Al^{3+}_{(aq)} + 3Ag_{(s)}$

b) $Cu_{(s)} + Cl_{2(g)} \rightarrow Cu^{2+}_{(aq)} + 2Cl^{-}_{(aq)}$

c) $Sn^{2+}_{(aq)} + 2Fe^{3+}_{(aq)} \rightarrow Sn^{4+}_{(aq)} + 2Fe^{2+}_{(aq)}$

Q3 State whether or not these reactions are feasible:

a) $Mg_{(s)} + Ni^{2+}_{(aq)} \rightarrow Mg^{2+}_{(aq)} + Ni_{(s)}$

b) $2Br^{-}_{(aq)} + 2Fe^{3+}_{(aq)} \rightarrow 2Fe^{2+}_{(aq)} + Br_{2\,(l)}$

c) $Sn^{2+}_{(aq)} + Cu^{2+}_{(aq)} \rightarrow Sn^{4+}_{(aq)} + Cu_{(s)}$

Q4 Will Ag^{+} ions react with Sn^{2+} ions in solution? Explain your answer.

Practice Questions — Fact Recall

Q1 What is an electrochemical series?

Q2 In what direction are half-equations written in electrochemical series?

Q3 A half-reaction has a very positive electrode potential. Is it more likely to go in the direction of oxidation or reduction?

Q4 Give two reasons why a prediction made about the feasibility of a reaction using E°_{cell} might be wrong.

7. Energy Storage Cells

The last few topics told you all about electrochemical cells. This one's all about what electrochemical cells are actually used for — in particular, how electrochemical cells are used as energy storage cells (batteries).

Learning Objectives:

- Be able to apply principles of electrode potentials to modern storage cells.
- Know the benefits and risks of electrochemical cells.

Specification Reference 5.2.3

What are energy storage cells?

Energy storage cells (batteries) have been around for ages and modern ones work just like an electrochemical cell. For example the nickel-iron cell was developed way back at the start of the 1900s and is often used as a back-up power supply because it can be repeatedly charged and is very robust.

You can work out the voltage produced by these cells by using the electrode potentials of the substances used in the cell. There are lots of different cells and you won't be asked to remember the $E^\ominus$ for the reactions, but you might be asked to work out the cell potential (voltage) for a given cell... so here's an example I prepared earlier.

Tip: <u>Anode</u> and <u>cathode</u> are just names for the electrodes in an electrochemical cell.

Example

The nickel-iron cell has a nickel oxide hydroxide (NiOOH) cathode and an iron (Fe) anode with potassium hydroxide as the electrolyte. Using the half-equations given:

a) write out the full equation for the reaction.

b) calculate the voltage produced by the nickel-iron cell.

$Fe(OH)_2 + 2e^- \rightleftharpoons Fe + 2OH^-$ $\quad E^\ominus = -0.44\ V$

$NiOOH + H_2O + e^- \rightleftharpoons Ni(OH)_2 + OH^-$ $\quad E^\ominus = +0.76\ V$

a) First work out which half-equation will go in the forward (reduction) direction and which in the reverse (oxidation) direction. The iron half-equation has the more negative electrode potential, so it will go in the direction of oxidation: $Fe + 2OH^- \rightleftharpoons Fe(OH)_2 + 2e^-$
The other half-equation will go in the direction of reduction:
$NiOOH + H_2O + e^- \rightleftharpoons Ni(OH)_2 + OH^-$
Now to find the overall equation for the reaction, just balance the number of electrons and then combine the two half-equations.

$$2NiOOH + 2H_2O + Fe \rightleftharpoons 2Ni(OH)_2 + Fe(OH)_2$$

(The e^- and the OH^- are not shown because they cancel out.)

b) To calculate the voltage you use the same formula that you use to work out cell potential (see page 130). So the voltage is...

$$E^\ominus_{cell} = E^\ominus_{reduced} - E^\ominus_{oxidised}$$
$$= +0.76 - (-0.44) = \mathbf{1.2\ V}$$

Figure 1: An assortment of batteries — these are all electrochemical cells.

Tip: See pages 113-115 for more on combining half-equations into full equations.

Recharging energy storage cells

Some energy storage cells, like the nickel-iron cell, are rechargeable. Rechargeable energy storage cells can be recharged because the reactions that occur within them are reversible. To recharge these batteries, a current is supplied to force electrons to flow in the opposite direction around the circuit and reverse the reactions. This is possible because none of the substances in a rechargeable battery escape or are used up. In the exam you could be asked to write equations for the reaction that occurs when an energy storage cell is recharged. These are just the equations for the storage cell in reverse.

Figure 2: A lithium ion battery being recharged.

Tip: When an energy storage cell is being used, the cell is discharging — this is the opposite of recharging the cell.

Example

When the nickel-iron cell is recharged, the half-equations for the reaction are:

$$Fe(OH)_2 + 2e^- \rightleftharpoons Fe + 2OH^-$$

$$Ni(OH)_2 + OH^- \rightleftharpoons NiOOH + H_2O + e^-$$

So, the overall equation when a nickel-iron cell is recharged is:

$$2Ni(OH)_2 + Fe(OH)_2 \rightleftharpoons 2NiOOH + 2H_2O + Fe$$

Benefits and risks of electrochemical cells

Electrochemical cells have many advantages — they can be cheap to make and have relatively high power densities (a small cell can produce a lot of energy).

However, the production of the cells involves the use of toxic chemicals, which need to be disposed of once the cell has reached the end of its life span. The chemicals used to make the cells are also often very flammable. E.g. lithium (commonly used in rechargeable batteries) is highly reactive and will catch fire if a fault causes it to overheat.

Tip: Choosing energy supplies is often a case of weighing up the risks and benefits associated with the manufacture, use and disposal of the fuel and its casing.

Practice Questions — Application

Q1 Nickel/cadmium batteries are a common type of rechargeable battery. The redox equation for the reaction that happens when this type of battery is discharging is shown below:

$$Cd_{(s)} + 2NiOOH_{(s)} + 2H_2O_{(l)} \rightleftharpoons Cd(OH)_{2(s)} + 2Ni(OH)_{2(s)} \quad E^\circ = +1.4\text{ V}$$

Suggest an equation for the redox reaction that occurs when this type of battery is recharging.

Q2 Zinc-carbon dry cell batteries are commonly used in TV remote controls and torches. The half-equations for the reactions that occur when this type of battery is discharging are shown below:

$$Zn_{(s)} \rightarrow Zn^{2+}_{(aq)} + 2e^- \quad E^\circ = -0.76\text{ V}$$

$$2MnO_{2(s)} + 2NH_4^+{}_{(aq)} + 2e^- \rightarrow Mn_2O_{3(s)} + 2NH_{3(aq)} + H_2O_{(l)} \quad E^\circ = +0.75\text{ V}$$

a) Calculate E°_{cell} for this cell.

b) Write an equation for the overall reaction occurring in this cell.

Q3 Lead-acid cells are used in car batteries. The half-equations for the two half-cells used to make this type of battery are shown below:

$$PbSO_{4(s)} + 2e^- \rightleftharpoons Pb_{(s)} + SO_4^{2-}{}_{(aq)} \quad E^\circ = -0.36\text{ V}$$

$$PbO_{2(s)} + SO_4^{2-}{}_{(aq)} + 4H^+_{(aq)} + 2e^- \rightleftharpoons PbSO_{4(s)} + 2H_2O_{(l)} \quad E^\circ = +1.69\text{ V}$$

Write half-equations for the reactions that occur in this type of battery when it is being recharged.

Tip: Remember, for Q2 and Q3 the first thing you need to do is to work out which half-reaction is going forwards (reduction) and which is going backwards (oxidation).

Figure 3: Lead-acid car batteries being recharged.

Tip: When a rechargeable battery is being used, the forward reaction will be taking place and E°_{cell} will be positive. When the battery is being recharged, the reverse reaction will be taking place and E°_{cell} will be negative.

Practice Questions — Fact Recall

Q1 What is the common name for an energy storage cell?

Q2 Give the equation you would use to calculate the cell potential of an energy storage cell.

Q3 Why can some energy storage cells be recharged?

8. Fuel Cells

Fuel cells are really handy — they can generate electricity without producing too much pollution and they're more efficient than petrol engines.

Learning Objective:

- Be able to explain that a fuel cell uses the energy from the reaction of a fuel with oxygen to create a voltage.
- Be able to explain the changes that take place at each electrode in a fuel cell.

Specification Reference 5.2.3

What are fuel cells

A **fuel cell** produces electricity by reacting a fuel with oxygen. The fuel is oxidised at the anode and the oxidant is reduced at the cathode.

Hydrogen-oxygen fuel cells

In a hydrogen-oxygen fuel cell, the fuel used is hydrogen. Hydrogen-oxygen fuel cells can operate in acidic or alkaline conditions. Figure 1 shows how an acidic hydrogen-oxygen fuel cell works:

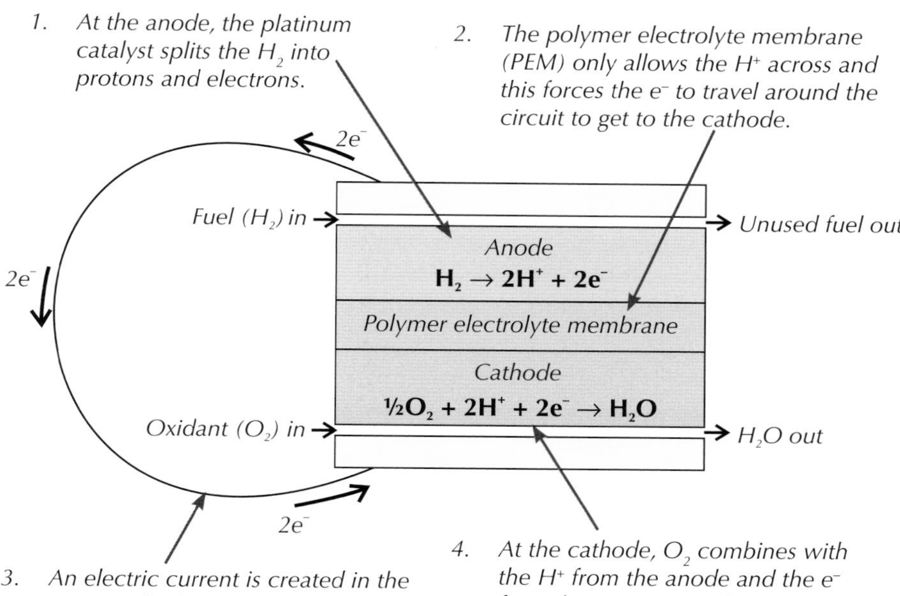

1. At the anode, the platinum catalyst splits the H_2 into protons and electrons.
2. The polymer electrolyte membrane (PEM) only allows the H^+ across and this forces the e^- to travel around the circuit to get to the cathode.
2e⁻
2e⁻
Fuel (H_2) in
Unused fuel out
Anode
$H_2 \rightarrow 2H^+ + 2e^-$
Polymer electrolyte membrane
Cathode
$\frac{1}{2}O_2 + 2H^+ + 2e^- \rightarrow H_2O$
Oxidant (O_2) in
H_2O out
2e⁻
3. An electric current is created in the circuit, which can be used to power something like a car or a bike.
4. At the cathode, O_2 combines with the H^+ from the anode and the e^- from the circuit to make H_2O. This is the only waste product.

Figure 1: *An acidic hydrogen-oxygen fuel cell*

The fuel cell shown in Figure 1 involves H^+ ions crossing the electrolyte in order to balance the half-reactions at each electrode. This makes it an acidic fuel cell. The overall redox reaction for this cell, found by combining the half-equations, is:

$$\frac{1}{2}O_2 + H_2 \rightarrow H_2O$$

You can also make alkaline hydrogen-oxygen fuel cells. The set-up is very similar to the cell in Figure 1, except that the electrolyte is alkaline and the polymer electrolyte membrane only allows OH^- ions across. In an alkaline hydrogen-oxygen fuel cell, the half-equations are:

$$\text{Anode: } H_2 + 2OH^- \rightarrow 2H_2O + 2e^-$$
$$\text{Cathode: } \frac{1}{2}O_2 + H_2O + 2e^- \rightarrow 2OH^-$$

But the overall redox reaction happening in the alkaline fuel cell is the same as the overall reaction for the acidic fuel cell:

$$\frac{1}{2}O_2 + H_2 \rightarrow H_2O$$

Tip: There are lots of advantages of using a fuel cell, rather than a standard petrol engine. For example, fuel cells are more efficient at producing energy because energy is wasted during combustion as heat. They also produce a lot less pollution (such as CO_2). For hydrogen fuel cells, the only waste product is water.

You can calculate the cell potential of a fuel cell just like you would for any other cell.

Example — Maths Skills

$H_2 \rightleftharpoons 2H^+ + 2e^-$ $E^\ominus = 0.00$ V $\quad$ $\frac{1}{2}O_2 + 2H^+ + 2e^- \rightleftharpoons H_2O$ $E^\ominus = +1.23$ V

The $H_2/2H^+$ half-cell has the more negative electrode potential, so this half reaction will go in the direction of oxidation. The O_2/O^{2-} half-cell has the more positive electrode potential and so will go in the direction of reduction.

$$E^\ominus_{cell} = E^\ominus_{reduced} - E^\ominus_{oxidised} = 1.23 - (0.00) = +1.23 \text{ V}$$

Tip: This question might look a bit scary, since it's a slightly different type of fuel cell to the one on the previous page, but just remember — the fuel will be oxidised at the anode and the oxidant will be reduced at the cathode.

Practice Question — Application

Q1 The following reactions take place in a methanol fuel cell:

$CH_3OH + H_2O \rightleftharpoons CO_2 + 6H^+ + 6e^-$ $\quad E^\ominus = +0.046$ V

$1\frac{1}{2}O_2 + 6H^+ + 6e^- \rightleftharpoons 3H_2O$ $\quad E^\ominus = +1.23$ V

a) Write an overall equation for the reaction in the methanol fuel cell.

b) Which reaction occurs at: i) the cathode? ii) the anode?

c) What is the cell potential of the methanol fuel cell?

Practice Questions — Fact Recall

Q1 How does a fuel cell produce electricity?

Q2 Describe how an acidic hydrogen-oxygen fuel cell works.

Section Summary

Make sure you know...

- The meaning of the terms redox reaction, half-reaction, oxidising agent and reducing agent.
- What half-equations are and how to use them to write full equations for redox reactions.
- That oxidation numbers change as part of a redox reaction.
- What oxidation numbers are and how to use them to write redox equations.
- How to carry out redox titrations involving the manganate(VII) ion (MnO_4^-).
- How to carry out iodine-sodium thiosulfate ($I_2/S_2O_3^{2-}$) redox titrations.
- How to perform calculations based on experimental redox titration results.
- What electrochemical cells are and how to draw diagrams of them.
- How to set up an electrochemical cell and use it to measure voltages.
- What factors affect the electrode potential of a half-cell.
- How to use a standard hydrogen electrode to measure the standard electrode potential of a half-cell.
- What an electrochemical series is.
- How to calculate a standard cell potential using two standard electrode potentials.
- How to use standard electrode potentials to predict the direction of reactions.
- Why these reaction predictions are sometimes wrong.
- What energy storage cells are.
- How to calculate the voltages that energy storage cells produce (their cell potentials).
- The risks and benefits associated with using electrochemical cells.
- What fuel cells are and how they work.

Exam-style Questions

1 The table below shows a short electrochemical series:

Half-reaction	$E^{\ominus}$ (V)
$Al^{3+}_{(aq)} + 3e^- \rightleftharpoons Al_{(s)}$	–1.66
$Zn^{2+}_{(aq)} + 2e^- \rightleftharpoons Zn_{(s)}$	–0.76
$Ni^{2+}_{(aq)} + 2e^- \rightleftharpoons Ni_{(s)}$	–0.25
$Cu^{2+}_{(aq)} + 2e^- \rightleftharpoons Cu_{(s)}$	+0.34
$Fe^{3+}_{(aq)} + e^- \rightleftharpoons Fe^{2+}_{(aq)}$	+0.77

Using the information in the table, determine which of the following reactions is not feasible.

A $Zn_{(s)} + 2Fe^{3+}_{(aq)} \rightarrow Zn^{2+}_{(aq)} + 2Fe^{2+}_{(aq)}$

B $2Al_{(s)} + 3Ni^{2+}_{(aq)} \rightarrow 2Al^{3+}_{(aq)} + 3Ni_{(s)}$

C $Ni_{(s)} + Cu^{2+}_{(aq)} \rightarrow Ni^{2+}_{(aq)} + Cu_{(s)}$

D $3Zn_{(s)} + 2Al^{3+}_{(aq)} \rightarrow 3Zn^{2+}_{(aq)} + 2Al_{(s)}$

(1 mark)

2 Magnesium metal will react with iron(II) sulfate to give magnesium sulfate and metallic iron:

$$Mg_{(s)} + FeSO_{4\,(aq)} \rightarrow MgSO_{4\,(aq)} + Fe_{(s)}$$

Which of the following elements is reduced during this reaction?

A Mg

B Fe

C S

D O

(1 mark)

3 As part of a redox titration, a solution of a colourless reducing agent containing Fe(II) ions was placed in a conical flask. It was titrated with a solution of manganate(VII) ions. What colour change would you expect to see at the endpoint of this titration?

A The solution in the conical flask changes from colourless to orange.

B The solution in the conical flask changes from colourless to purple.

C The solution in the conical flask changes from purple to colourless.

D The solution in the conical flask changes from brown to colourless.

(1 mark)

4 Nickel-zinc cells are a type of rechargeable battery used in digital cameras. The half-equations for the reactions that occur in a nickel-zinc cell are shown below:

$NiOOH_{(s)} + H_2O_{(l)} + e^- \rightleftharpoons Ni(OH)_{2(s)} + OH^-_{(aq)}$ $E^\circ = ?\,V$

$Zn(OH)_{2(s)} + 2e^- \rightleftharpoons Zn_{(s)} + 2OH^-_{(aq)}$ $E^\circ = -1.25\,V$

When the cell discharges, the $Zn/Zn(OH)_2$ half-reaction goes in the oxidation direction.

(a) Give the equation for the overall reaction occurring in this cell as it discharges.

(2 marks)

(b) The standard cell potential for this cell is +1.73 V. Calculate the standard electrode potential of the $NiOOH/Ni(OH)_2$ half-reaction.

(2 marks)

5 Lithium-thionyl chloride cells are a type of energy storage cell (battery) used in medical applications. The half-equations for the two half-cells that make up this type of cell are shown below:

$Li^+_{(aq)} + e^- \rightleftharpoons Li_{(s)}$ $E^\circ = -3.04\,V$

$2SOCl_{2(aq)} + 4Li^+_{(aq)} + 4e^- \rightarrow 4LiCl_{(s)} + S_{(s)} + SO_{2(g)}$ $E^\circ = +0.47\,V$

(a) Give the equation for the overall reaction occurring in this cell as it discharges.

(2 marks)

(b) Calculate the cell potential for the reaction as the cell discharges.

(1 mark)

(c) Give one advantage and one disadvantage of using energy storage cells.

(2 marks)

6 The table below shows a short electrochemical series:

Half-reaction	E° (V)
$Mg^{2+}_{(aq)} + 2e^- \rightleftharpoons Mg_{(s)}$	–2.38
$V^{2+}_{(aq)} + 2e^- \rightleftharpoons V_{(s)}$	–1.18
$V^{3+}_{(aq)} + e^- \rightleftharpoons V^{2+}_{(aq)}$	–0.26
$Sn^{4+}_{(aq)} + 2e^- \rightleftharpoons Sn^{2+}_{(aq)}$	+0.15
$VO^{2+}_{(aq)} + 2H^+_{(aq)} + e^- \rightleftharpoons V^{3+}_{(aq)} + H_2O_{(l)}$	+0.34
$Fe^{3+}_{(aq)} + e^- \rightleftharpoons Fe^{2+}_{(aq)}$	+0.77
$VO_2^{\ +}{}_{(aq)} + 2H^+_{(aq)} + e^- \rightleftharpoons VO^{2+}_{(aq)} + H_2O_{(l)}$	+1.00

(a) (i) Using the information in the table, predict what reactions, if any, will occur when aqueous Sn^{2+} ions are mixed with an acidified solution of $VO_2^{\ +}$ ions. Explain your answer.

(4 marks)

(ii) Suggest two reasons why your predictions may be incorrect.

(2 marks)

(b) An electrochemical cell can be made by connecting an Mg^{2+}/Mg half-cell to an Fe^{2+}/Fe^{3+} half-cell.

(i) Draw a diagram to show how this cell could be set up in a laboratory.

(3 marks)

(ii) Calculate the cell potential (e.m.f.) of this cell.

(1 mark)

(iii) Write an equation for the overall reaction occurring in this cell.

(2 marks)

(c) Standard electrode potentials are measured relative to the standard hydrogen electrode.

(i) Explain what is meant by 'standard conditions'.

(3 marks)

(ii) The electrode itself is made of platinum foil.
Suggest why platinum is a suitable metal to use for this purpose.

(1 mark)

(d) When a standard hydrogen electrode was connected to an Ag^+/Ag half-cell, the reading on the voltmeter was +0.80 V.

(i) What is the standard electrode potential for the reaction $Ag^+_{(aq)} + e^- \rightleftharpoons Ag_{(s)}$?

(1 mark)

(ii) What does this electrode potential tell you about the reactivity of silver compared to vanadium? Explain your answer.

(2 marks)

7 Lithium-ion batteries are a type of rechargeable battery commonly used in mobile phones. The half-equations for the reactions that occur in a lithium-ion battery as it discharges are shown below:

$$Li^{+}_{(aq)} + CoO_{2(s)} + e^{-} \rightleftharpoons Li^{+}[CoO_2]^{-}_{(s)}$$

$$Li_{(s)} \rightleftharpoons Li^{+}_{(aq)} + e^{-}$$

(a) Give the overall equation for the reaction occurring in this cell as it is being recharged.

(1 mark)

(b) Explain why rechargeable batteries can be recharged.

(1 mark)

8 Brass is an alloy of copper and zinc. The percentage composition of copper in brass can be determined using an iodine-sodium thiosulfate titration because the copper ion (Cu^{2+}) is an oxidising agent.

1.00 g of brass was dissolved in acid and added to an excess of acidified potassium iodide solution. The equation for the reaction that took place is shown below.

$$2Cu^{2+}_{(aq)} + 4I^{-}_{(aq)} \rightarrow 2CuI_{(aq)} + I_{2\,(aq)}$$

This solution was then titrated against sodium thiosulfate.
The equation for this reaction is shown below.

$$I_{2\,(aq)} + 2S_2O_3^{\,2-}{}_{(aq)} \rightarrow 2I^{-}_{(aq)} + S_4O_6^{\,2-}{}_{(aq)}$$

It took 23.6 cm^3 of 0.500 mol dm^{-3} sodium thiosulfate solution to reach the end point of the reaction.

(a) Describe how you would perform the titration part of the experiment.

(5 marks)

(b) Use the information given above to calculate the number of moles of Cu^{2+} ions present in the brass solution.

(3 marks)

(c) Work out the percentage composition by mass of copper in the 1 g sample of brass.

(2 marks)

1. Transition Elements

Some of the most precious materials in the world are transition elements. Transition elements are responsible for some pretty interesting and important chemistry, which is why there's a whole section of this book devoted to them.

Learning Objectives:

- Be able to describe the elements Ti–Cu as transition elements, i.e. d-block elements that have an ion with an incomplete d-subshell.
- Be able to deduce the electron configuration of atoms and ions of the d-block elements of Period 4 (Sc–Zn), given the atomic number and charge.

Specification Reference 5.3.1

The d-block

The **d-block** is the block of elements in the middle of the periodic table. Most of the elements in the d-block are **transition elements** (or transition metals). You only need to know about the ones in the first row of the d-block (Period 4). These are the elements from titanium to copper — see Figure 1.

Period	Group 1	Group 2											Group 3	Group 4	Group 5	Group 6	Group 7	Group 0
							1 H Hydrogen 1											4 He 2
2	7 Li 3	9 Be 4											11 B 5	12 C 6	14 N 7	16 O 8	19 F 9	20 Ne 10
3	23 Na 11	24 Mg 12											27 Al 13	28 Si 14	31 P 15	32 S 16	35.5 Cl 17	40 Ar 18
4	39 K 19	40 Ca 20	45 Sc 21	48 Ti 22	51 V 23	52 Cr 24	55 Mn 25	56 Fe 26	59 Co 27	59 Ni 28	64 Cu 29	65 Zn 30	70 Ga 31	73 Ge 32	75 As 33	79 Se 34	80 Br 35	84 Kr 36
5	86 Rb 37	88 Sr 38	89 Y 39	91 Zr 40	93 Nb 41	96 Mo 42	98 Tc 43	101 Ru 44	103 Rh 45	106 Pd 46	108 Ag 47	112 Cd 48	115 In 49	119 Sn 50	122 Sb 51	128 Te 52	127 I 53	131 Xe 54
6	133 Cs 55	137 Ba 56	57-71 Lanthanides	179 Hf 72	181 Ta 73	184 W 74	186 Re 75	190 Os 76	192 Ir 77	195 Pt 78	197 Au 79	201 Hg 80	204 Tl 81	207 Pb 82	209 Bi 83	210 Po 84	210 At 85	222 Rn 86
7	223 Fr 87	226 Ra 88	89-103 Actinides															

s-block — d-block — p-block

Figure 1: *The three main blocks of the periodic table. The transition elements are in the d-block.*

What is a transition element?

Here's the definition of a transition element:

> A transition element is a d-block element that can form at least one stable ion with a partially filled d-subshell.

A **d-subshell** can take ten electrons. So transition elements form at least one ion with between one and nine electrons in the d-subshell. All the Period 4 d-block elements are transition elements apart from scandium and zinc (see page 143).

Figure 2: *A variety of transition metals.*

Electron configurations

The electron configurations of elements can be figured out by following a few simple rules:

- Electrons fill up the lowest energy **subshells** first.
- Electrons fill **orbitals** singly before they start sharing.

The transition metals generally follow the same rules — see Figure 3. The 4s subshell usually fills up first because it has lower energy than the 3d subshell. Once the 4s subshell is full, the 3d subshell starts to fill up. The 3d orbitals are occupied singly at first. They only double up when they have to. But, there are a couple of exceptions...

Tip: Electron orbitals and electron configurations were covered in Year 1, so if you've forgotten what they are have a quick skim over your Year 1 notes.

Tip: Subshells are made up of orbitals — for example, s-subshells contain one orbital, p-subshells contain three orbitals and d-subshells contain five orbitals. Each orbital can hold two electrons.

Tip: The electron configurations of all the Period 4 transition metals start in the same way — $1s^2 2s^2 2p^6 3s^2 3p^6$. This is the same as the electron configuration of the element argon, so [Ar] is often used as a short way of writing it.

- Chromium prefers to have one electron in each orbital of the 3d subshell and just one in the 4s subshell — this gives it more stability.
- Copper prefers to have a full 3d subshell and just one electron in the 4s subshell — it's more stable that way.

		3d					*4s*	
Ti	[Ar]	↑	↑				↑↓	[Ar] $3d^2 4s^2$
V	[Ar]	↑	↑	↑			↑↓	[Ar] $3d^3 4s^2$
Cr	[Ar]	↑	↑	↑	↑	↑	↑	[Ar] $3d^5 4s^1$
Mn	[Ar]	↑	↑	↑	↑	↑	↑↓	[Ar] $3d^5 4s^2$
Fe	[Ar]	↑↓	↑	↑	↑	↑	↑↓	[Ar] $3d^6 4s^2$
Co	[Ar]	↑↓	↑↓	↑	↑	↑	↑↓	[Ar] $3d^7 4s^2$
Ni	[Ar]	↑↓	↑↓	↑↓	↑	↑	↑↓	[Ar] $3d^8 4s^2$
Cu	[Ar]	↑↓	↑↓	↑↓	↑↓	↑↓	↑	[Ar] $3d^{10} 4s^1$

Figure 3: *The electron configurations of the Period 4 d-block transition metals.*

Transition metal ions

Transition metal atoms form positive ions. When this happens, the s electrons are removed first, then the d electrons.

Example

Iron forms Fe^{2+} ions and Fe^{3+} ions.

When it forms 2+ ions, it loses both its 4s electrons:

$$Fe = [Ar]3d^6 4s^2 \rightarrow Fe^{2+} = [Ar]3d^6$$

Only once the 4s electrons are removed can a 3d electron be removed.

$$\text{E.g. } Fe^{2+} = [Ar]3d^6 \rightarrow Fe^{3+} = [Ar]3d^5$$

Exam Tip
The atomic number in the periodic table tells you how many electrons each atom has — you should be able to work the electron configuration out from there.

You might be asked to write the electron configuration of a transition metal ion in the exam. To do this, just follow these steps:

- Write down the electron configuration of the atom.
- Work out how many electrons have been removed to make the ion by looking at the charge on the ion.
- Remove that number of electrons from the electron configuration, taking them out of the s-orbital first and then the d-orbitals.

Example

Write out the electron configuration of Mn^{2+} ions.

- The electron configuration of Mn atoms is $[Ar]3d^5 4s^2$.
- Two electrons are removed to convert Mn atoms into Mn^{2+} ions.
- Removing the electrons starting from the s-orbitals gives $[Ar]3d^5 4s^0$.
- So the electron configuration of Mn^{2+} ions is $[Ar]3d^5$.

Scandium and zinc

Sc and Zn aren't transition elements as their stable ions don't have partially filled d-subshells.

Scandium only forms one ion, Sc^{3+}, which has an empty d-subshell. Scandium has the electron configuration $1s^2 2s^2 2p^6 3s^2 3p^6 3d^1 4s^2$, so when it loses three electrons to form Sc^{3+}, it ends up with the electron configuration $1s^2 2s^2 2p^6 3s^2 3p^6$.

Zinc only forms one ion, Zn^{2+}, which has a full d-subshell. Zinc has the electron configuration $1s^2 2s^2 2p^6 3s^2 3p^6 3d^{10} 4s^2$. When it forms Zn^{2+} it loses two electrons, both from the 4s subshell. This means it keeps its full 3d subshell and becomes $1s^2 2s^2 2p^6 3s^2 3p^6 3d^{10}$.

Figure 4: *A lump of zinc.*

Practice Questions — Application

Q1 Write out the electron configurations for the following transition metal elements:

a) V b) Co c) Mn d) Ni

Q2 Write out the electron configurations for the following transition metal ions:

a) V^{3+} b) Co^{2+} c) Mn^{2+} d) Ni^{2+}

e) Cr^{2+} f) Ti^{3+} g) Ti^{4+}

Q3 Using electron configurations, explain why zinc is not a transition element, despite being in the d-block of the periodic table.

Exam Tip

If you're asked for a <u>full</u> electron configuration you need to write it all out starting from $1s^2$ — don't use [Ar].

Practice Questions — Fact Recall

Q1 Where in the periodic table are transition elements found?

Q2 What is the definition of a transition element?

Q3 How many electrons can a d-subshell hold?

Q4 Give two rules that are usually followed when working out electron configurations.

Q5 a) Explain why chromium has the electron configuration $[Ar]3d^5 4s^1$ and not $[Ar]3d^4 4s^2$ as you would expect.

b) Explain why copper has the electron configuration $[Ar]3d^{10} 4s^1$ and not $[Ar]3d^9 4s^2$ as you would expect.

Exam Tip

Chromium and copper have slightly odd electron configurations (see previous page). I'm afraid there's no easy way to work them out in the exam — you'll just have to learn 'em...

2. Transition Element Properties

The chemical properties of transition metals make them great for things like indicators, colouring agents, catalysts and even drugs. But before you can learn about these fascinating applications you have to learn the basics...

Learning Objectives:

- Be able to illustrate the formation of coloured transition metal ions, using at least two examples.
- Be able to illustrate, using at least two examples, the catalytic behaviour of the transition elements and their compounds and their importance in the manufacture of chemicals by industry.
- Be able to illustrate the existence of more than one oxidation state for each transition element in its compounds, using at least two examples.

Specification Reference 5.3.1

Chemical properties

The transition metals have a few special chemical properties that you need to know about:

- They can form **complex ions** — see pages 146-148.
  E.g. iron forms a complex ion with water — $[Fe(H_2O)_6]^{2+}$.
- They form coloured ions — see below.
  E.g. $Fe^{2+}_{(aq)}$ ions are pale green and $Fe^{3+}_{(aq)}$ ions are yellow.
- They're good **catalysts** — see next page.
  E.g. nickel is the catalyst used to harden margarine.
- They can exist in variable **oxidation states** — see below.
  E.g. iron can exist in the +2 oxidation state as Fe^{2+} ions and in the +3 oxidation state as Fe^{3+} ions.

Oxidation states and coloured ions

Some common coloured ions and oxidation states are shown below. The colours refer to the aqueous ions.

Element	Ion	Oxidation state	Colour
Ti	Ti^{2+}	+2	violet
	Ti^{3+}	+3	purple
V	V^{2+}	+2	violet
	V^{3+}	+3	green
	VO^{2+}	+4	blue
	VO_2^{+}	+5	yellow
Cr	Cr^{3+}	+3	green
	$Cr_2O_7^{2-}$	+6	orange
Mn	Mn^{2+}	+2	very pale pink/ colourless
	MnO_4^{2-}	+6	green
	MnO_4^{-}	+7	purple
Fe	Fe^{2+}	+2	pale green
	Fe^{3+}	+3	yellow
Co	Co^{2+}	+2	pink
Ni	Ni^{2+}	+2	green
Cu	Cu^{2+}	+2	pale blue

Figure 1: *The different colours of the aqueous transition metal ions.*

Tip: See page 114 for more on oxidation states and how to find them.

These elements show variable oxidation states because the energy levels of the 4s and the 3d subshells are very close to one another. So different numbers of electrons can be gained or lost using fairly similar amounts of energy.

Transition metal catalysts

Transition elements and their compounds make good **catalysts** because they can change oxidation states by gaining or losing electrons within their d orbitals. This means they can transfer electrons to speed up reactions. Transition metals are also good at adsorbing substances onto their surfaces to lower the activation energy of reactions.

Examples

- Iron is the catalyst used in the Haber process to produce ammonia.

$$N_{2(g)} + 3H_{2(g)} \xrightarrow{Fe_{(s)}} 2NH_{3(g)}$$

- Copper(II) sulfate ($CuSO_4$) is the catalyst used in the reaction of zinc and acids.

$$Zn_{(s)} + H_2SO_{4(aq)} \xrightarrow{CuSO_{4(s)}} ZnSO_{4(aq)} + H_{2(g)}$$

- Manganese(IV) oxide (MnO_2) is the catalyst used in the decomposition of hydrogen peroxide.

$$2H_2O_{2(aq)} \xrightarrow{MnO_{2(s)}} 2H_2O_{(l)} + O_{2(g)}$$

Catalysts are good for industry and for the environment as they allow reactions to happen faster and at lower temperatures and pressures, reducing energy usage.

Tip: Using transition element catalysts can pose health risks as many of the metals and their compounds are toxic. For example, long term exposure to copper can damage the liver and kidneys, and exposure to manganese can cause psychiatric problems.

HOW SCIENCE WORKS

The partially filled d-subshell

It's the partially filled d-subshell that causes the special chemical properties of transition metals. d-block elements without a partially filled d-subshell don't have these properties.

Example

Scandium and zinc don't form ions with partially filled d-subshells. As a result they don't have the same chemical properties as transition metals.

For example, they can't form complex ions, they don't form coloured ions, they can't exist in variable oxidation states and they don't catalyse any reactions.

Tip: There's more on scandium and zinc on page 143.

Practice Questions — Fact Recall

Q1 Transition elements have variable oxidation states.
State two other chemical properties of transition elements.

Q2 Match the transition metal ions (**A**–**D**) with the colour they'd be in solution (**1**–**4**).

A Fe^{3+}	**1** pale blue
B Mn^{2+}	**2** purple
C MnO_4^-	**3** yellow
D Cu^{2+}	**4** very pale pink

Q3 Name the catalyst used in the Haber process.

Learning Objectives:

- Be able to use and explain the term ligand in terms of coordinate (dative covalent) bonding to a metal ion or metal.
- Be able use the terms complex ion and coordination number.
- Be able to explain and use the term bidentate ligand (e.g. $NH_2CH_2CH_2NH_2$, 'en').
- Be able to give examples of complexes with six-fold coordination with an octahedral shape.
- Be able to give examples of complexes with four-fold coordination with a planar or tetrahedral shape.

Specification Reference 5.3.1

Tip: Charged complex ions are always written in square brackets and the charge is put to the top right of the square brackets, e.g. $[Cu(H_2O)_6]^{2+}$. Uncharged complex ions can be written with or without the brackets.

Tip: Chloride ions and cyanide ions both have more than one lone pair of electrons, but they are only able to donate one lone pair to a central metal ion to form a coordinate bond — so they are both monodentate ligands.

Tip: EDTA stands for ethylenediaminetetra-acetic acid.

3. Complex Ions

The ability to form complex ions is an important property of transition metals. You probably haven't come across complex ions before, but the next few pages should tell you everything you need to know.

What are complex ions?

A **complex ion** is a metal ion surrounded by coordinately bonded **ligands**.
A **coordinate bond** (or dative covalent bond) is a covalent bond in which both electrons in the shared pair come from the same atom, ion or molecule.
In a complex ion, they come from the ligands. So, a ligand is an atom, ion or molecule that donates a pair of electrons to a central metal ion.

Example

$[Cu(H_2O)_6]^{2+}$

The central metal ion is a Cu^{2+} ion and water molecules are acting as ligands. There are six water molecules, each forming a coordinate bond with the Cu^{2+} ion:

Arrows represent a coordinate bond.

Water molecules act as ligands.

Central transition metal ion.

The different types of ligand

A ligand must have at least one lone pair of electrons, or it won't have anything to use to form a coordinate bond. But, different ligands can have different numbers of lone pairs and can form different numbers of coordinate bonds. Ligands that can only form one coordinate bond are called **monodentate**.

Examples

Here are some examples of monodentate ligands:

$H-\ddot{N}(H)-H$	$:Cl^-$	$:CN^-$	$H_2\ddot{O}$
ammonia	*chloride ions*	*cyanide ions*	*water*

Ammonia only has one lone pair of electrons to donate to form a coordinate bond. Water has two lone pairs of electrons but because they are so close together, it can only form one coordinate bond at a time. Chloride ions and cyanide ions can also only form one coordinate bond with a metal ion.

Ligands that can form more than one coordinate bond are called **multidentate**.

Example

$EDTA^{4-}$ is a multidentate ligand:

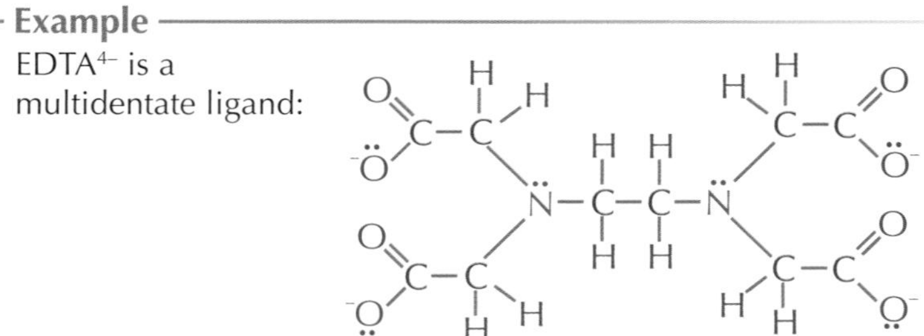

EDTA^{4-} has six lone pairs (two on nitrogen atoms and four on oxygen atoms) so it can form six coordinate bonds with a metal ion.

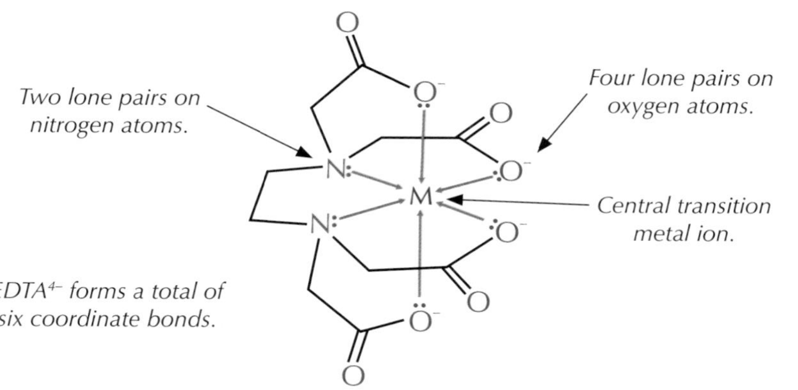

Two lone pairs on nitrogen atoms.
Four lone pairs on oxygen atoms.
Central transition metal ion.
EDTA⁴⁻ forms a total of six coordinate bonds.

Tip: EDTA^{4-} is hexadentate — hexa meaning six.

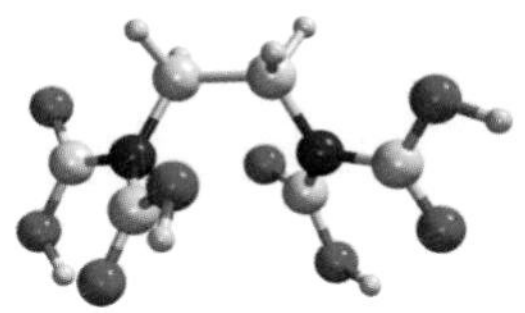

Figure 1: *Molecular model of EDTA.*

Tip: Don't worry — you won't be asked to draw out the structure of EDTA^{4-} in the exam.

Multidentate ligands that can form two coordinate bonds are called **bidentate**.

Example

Ethane-1,2-diamine ($\ddot{N}H_2CH_2CH_2\ddot{N}H_2$) is a bidentate ligand. It has two amine groups, each of which has a lone pair of electrons that it can donate to form a coordinate bond. In complex ions, each ethane-1,2-diamine molecule forms two coordinate bonds with the metal ion. In the complex ion below, there are three ethane-1,2-diamine molecules forming six coordinate bonds:

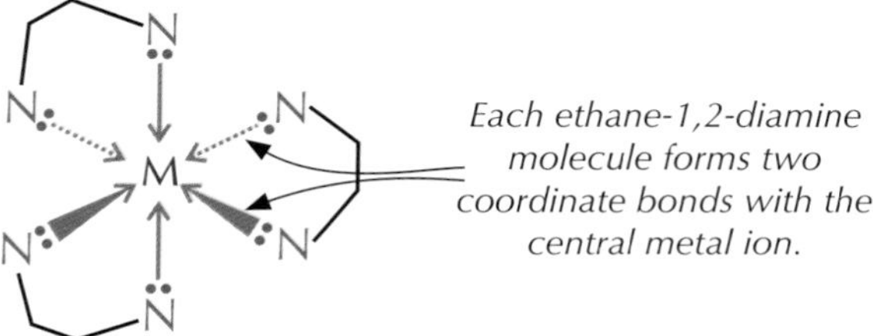

Each ethane-1,2-diamine molecule forms two coordinate bonds with the central metal ion.

Tip: Ethane-1,2-diamine ligands can be abbreviated to 'en'. For example, $[Cu(en)_3]^{2+}$.

Shapes of complex ions

The shape of a complex ion depends on its **coordination number**. This is the number of coordinate bonds that are formed with the central metal ion. The usual coordination numbers are 6 and 4. If the ligands are small, like H_2O, CN^- or NH_3, 6 can fit around the central metal ion. But if the ligands are larger, like Cl^-, only 4 can fit around the central metal ion.

Tip: A complex ion's coordination number depends on the <u>number of bonds</u> formed with the ligands — not the number of ligands. So, a complex ion that has 3 bidentate ligands will have a coordination number of 6 (3 ligands each forming 2 bonds).

Six coordinate bonds

Complex ions that contain six coordinate bonds have an octahedral shape. In an octahedral structure all of the bond angles are 90°.

Examples — Maths Skills

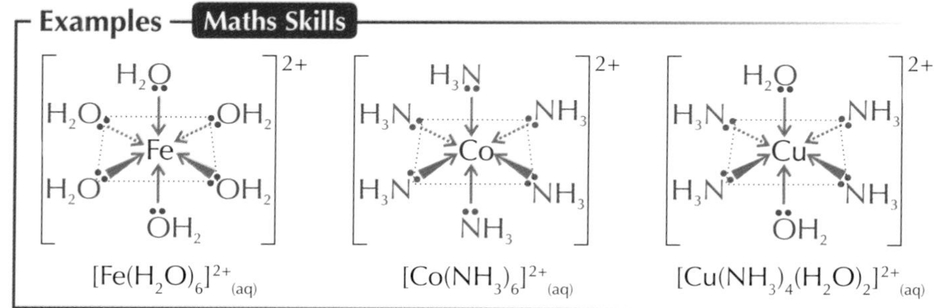

$[Fe(H_2O)_6]^{2+}_{(aq)}$
$[Co(NH_3)_6]^{2+}_{(aq)}$
$[Cu(NH_3)_4(H_2O)_2]^{2+}_{(aq)}$

Tip: In complex ions, the ligands don't all have to be the same — you can have mixtures of different ligands in the same complex.

Many octahedral complex ions are hexaaqua complexes. This means there are six water ligands around the central ion.

Figure 2: The flask on the left shows the pink colour of hexaaquacobalt(II) ions. The flask on the right shows the blue colour of cobalt(II) ions complexed as $[CoCl_4]^{2-}$.

The different types of bond arrow show that the complex is 3D. The wedge-shaped arrows represent bonds coming towards you and the dashed arrows represent bonds sticking out behind the molecule.

Four coordinate bonds

Complex ions with four coordinate bonds usually have a tetrahedral shape and 109.5° bond angles.

Examples — Maths Skills

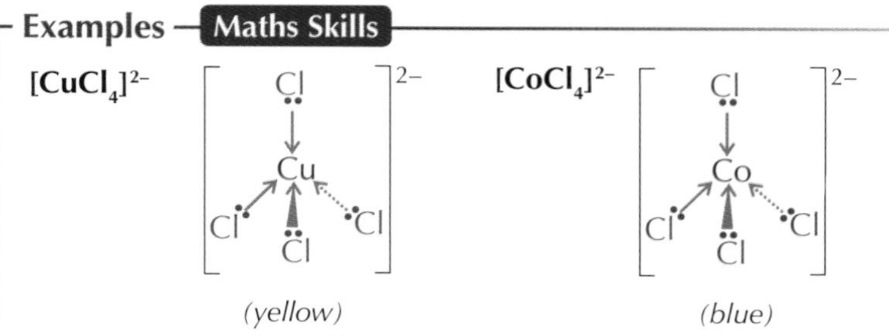

But in a few complexes, four coordinate bonds form a square planar shape. All of the bond angles in a square planar structure are 90°.

Tip: Cisplatin is used as an anti-cancer drug. See page 150 for more information on this.

Example — Maths Skills

Cisplatin ($Pt(NH_3)_2Cl_2$) (see page 149) has a square planar shape:

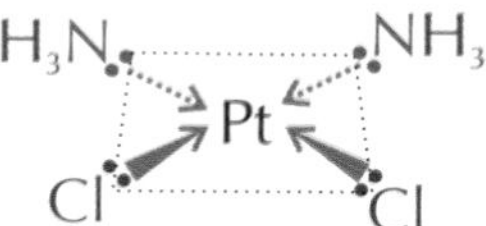

Practice Questions — Application

Tip: Remember, 'en' stands for one ethane-1,2-diamine ligand.

Q1 Give the shapes of the following complex ions and draw them:

a) $[CuF_6]^{4-}$ b) $[Fe(OH)_2(H_2O)_4]$ c) $[Fe(en)_3]^{3+}$

Q2 What is the coordination number of the transition metal in each of the complex ions in Q1?

Q3 $C_2O_4^{2-}$ is a bidentate ligand. Its structure is shown on the right.

a) Copy the diagram and circle the atoms that could form a coordinate bond with a metal ion.

b) $C_2O_4^{2-}$ forms an octahedral complex with Cr^{3+}. Give the formula of the complex ion formed.

Tip: To work out the overall charge on a complex ion you just add up all the charges of the ions in the complex.

Q4 $[Ni(CN)_4]^{2-}$ is a complex ion. In $[Ni(CN)_4]^{2-}$, the carbon from the CN^- ion donates one lone pair to the central Ni atom.

a) It does not have a tetrahedral shape. What shape could it have instead?

b) Draw the structure of $[Ni(CN)_4]^{2-}$.

Practice Questions — Fact Recall

Q1 Define the following terms:

a) Ligand b) Coordinate bond c) Complex ion

Q2 What is a bidentate ligand?

Q3 Give an example of an octahedral complex ion.

4. Isomerism in Complex Ions

Complex ions can show optical and cis-trans isomerism because the ligands can be arranged in various different ways around the central metal ion.

Learning Objectives:

- Be able to describe the types of stereoisomerism shown by complexes, including those associated with bidentate and multidentate ligands.
- Know that complexes can show optical isomerism, e.g. $[Ni(en)_3]^{2+}$.
- Know that complexes can show *cis-trans* isomerism, e.g. $Pt(NH_3)_2Cl_2$.
- Be able to describe the use of cisplatin as an anti-cancer drug and its action by binding to DNA in cancer cells, preventing division.

Specification Reference 5.3.1

Optical isomerism in complex ions

Optical isomerism is a type of stereoisomerism. Stereoisomers are molecules with the same structural formula but a different orientation of their bonds in space. For complex ions, optical isomers form when an ion can exist as two non-superimposable mirror images. This happens in octahedral complexes when three bidentate ligands are attached to the central ion. Optical isomers are also known as enantiomers.

Example — Maths Skills

When three ethane-1,2-diamine molecules ($H_2NCH_2CH_2NH_2$) use the lone pairs on both nitrogen atoms to coordinately bond with nickel, two optical isomers are formed.

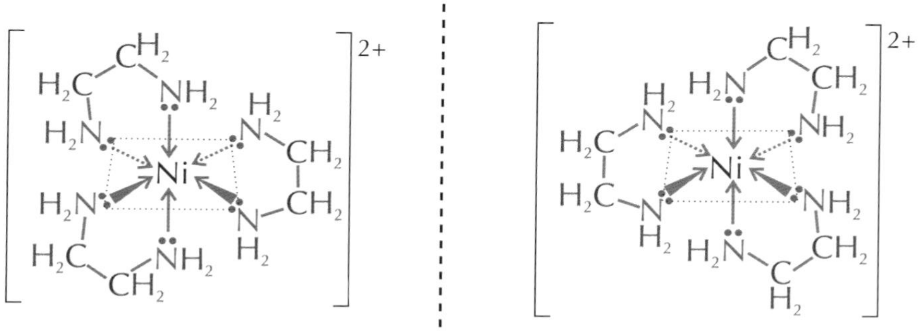

mirror line

Tip: If you're finding it difficult to see that the complexes in the example are mirror images of each other try building their 3D structures using a molecular model kit (or matchsticks and modelling clay).

Cis-trans isomerism in complex ions

Cis-trans isomerism is another type of stereoisomerism.

Cis-trans isomerism in square planar complex ions

Square planar complex ions that have two pairs of ligands show *cis-trans* isomerism. When two paired ligands are directly opposite each other it's the *trans* isomer and when they're next to each other it's the *cis* isomer.

Example — Maths Skills

$NiCl_2(NH_3)_2$ has *cis* and *trans* isomers.

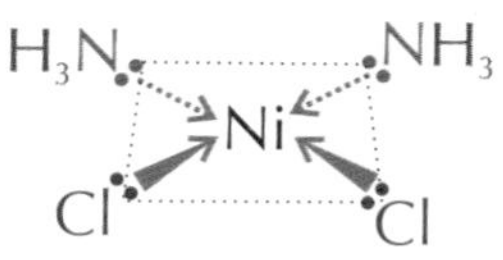

cis-$NiCl_2(NH_3)_2$

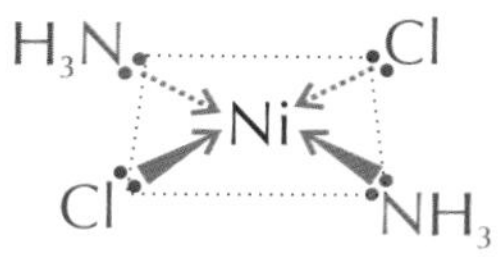

trans-$NiCl_2(NH_3)_2$

Exam Tip

If you're asked to draw a complex ion in the exam make sure you use dashed bonds and wedged bonds to show that the structure is 3D — you'll lose marks if you don't.

Cisplatin

Cisplatin is a complex of platinum(II) with two chloride ions and two ammonia molecules in a square planar shape (see Figure 1).

Tip: If the two chloride ligands were on opposite sides of the complex to each other the molecule would be transplatin. Transplatin has different biological effects to cisplatin.

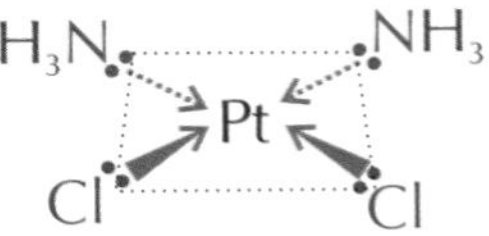

Figure 1: *The structure of cisplatin.*

Cisplatin can be used to treat some types of cancer. Cancer is caused by cells in the body dividing uncontrollably and forming tumours. Cisplatin is active against a variety of cancers, including lung and bladder cancer, because it prevents cancer cells from reproducing.

Before a cell can divide it has to replicate its DNA, which involves unwinding the two strands of the DNA double helix so that they can be copied. Cisplatin easily loses its chloride ligands through a displacement reaction and forms coordinate bonds with nitrogen atoms in the DNA molecule. This prevents the two strands from unwinding. So, the cell can no longer replicate its DNA and it can't divide.

Tip: The downside is that cisplatin also prevents normal cells from reproducing — including blood and hair cells. This can cause hair loss, and suppress the immune system, which increases the risk of infection. Cisplatin may also cause damage to the kidneys. Scientists always need to weigh up the benefits and risks of new inventions before releasing them for public use. See page 4 for more on decision-making in science.

HOW SCIENCE WORKS

Cis-trans isomerism in octahedral complex ions

Octahedral complexes with four ligands of one type and two ligands of another type can also exhibit *cis-trans* isomerism. If the two odd ligands are opposite each other you've got the *trans* isomer, if they're next to each other then you've got the *cis* isomer.

Example — Maths Skills

$NiCl_2(H_2O)_4$ has a *trans* and a *cis* isomer.

trans-$NiCl_2(H_2O)_4$ *cis*-$NiCl_2(H_2O)_4$

Practice Questions — Application

Q1 State what type of stereoisomerism the following complex ions will exhibit:

a) $PtCl_2(H_2O)_2$

b) $[Co(en)_3]^{2+}$

c) $Cu(OH)_2(H_2O)_4$

Q2 Draw the *cis* and *trans* isomers of $NiCl_2(H_2O)_2$.

Tip: If you're asked about the isomerism shown in a complex ion sometimes it helps to draw out the structure of the ion first — then you'll get a better idea of the possible isomers.

Practice Questions — Fact Recall

Q1 Name two types of stereoisomerism that complex ions can exhibit.

Q2 a) Draw the structure of cisplatin.

b) Cisplatin can be used to treat some types of cancer. Explain how cisplatin can work as an anti-cancer drug.

5. Ligand Substitution

Ligands around a central metal ion can switch places with other ligands in ligand substitution reactions.

Ligand substitution reactions

One ligand can be swapped for another ligand — this is **ligand substitution** (or ligand exchange). It pretty much always causes a colour change.

Substitution of similarly sized ligands

If the ligands are of similar size then the coordination number of the complex ion doesn't change, and neither does the shape.

Example

H_2O and NH_3 ligands are similarly sized and are both uncharged. This means that H_2O ligands can be exchanged with NH_3 ligands without any change in coordination number or shape. There will still be a colour change due to the change of ligand.

$$[Cr(H_2O)_6]^{3+}_{(aq)} + 6NH_{3(aq)} \rightarrow 6H_2O_{(l)} + [Cr(NH_3)_6]^{3+}_{(aq)}$$

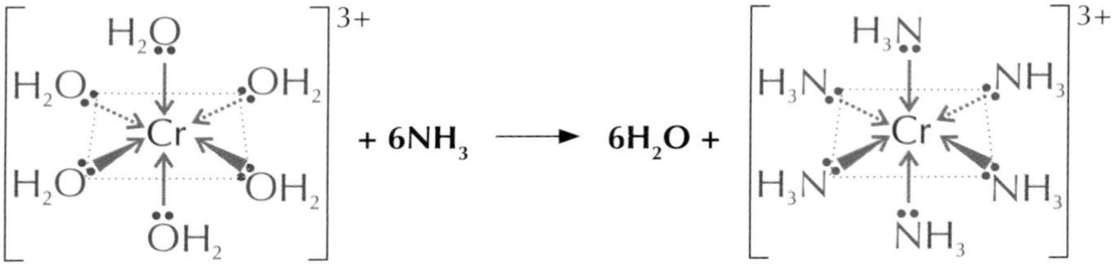

$$[Cr(H_2O)_6]^{3+} + 6NH_3 \longrightarrow 6H_2O + [Cr(NH_3)_6]^{3+}$$

Coordination number: 6
octahedral, dark green

Coordination number: 6
octahedral, purple

H_2O, NH_3, OH^- and CN^- are all similarly sized ligands.

Substitution of different sized ligands

If the ligands are different sizes there's a change of coordination number and a change of shape.

Example

In a copper-aqua complex, the H_2O ligands can be exchanged with Cl^- ligands. You can add Cl^- ions to a solution by adding hydrochloric acid. The shape of the complex changes from octahedral to tetrahedral because fewer of the larger Cl^- ligands can fit around the central metal ion. There is also a colour change during this reaction.

$$[Cu(H_2O)_6]^{2+}_{(aq)} + 4Cl^-_{(aq)} \rightleftharpoons 6H_2O_{(l)} + [CuCl_4]^{2-}_{(aq)}$$

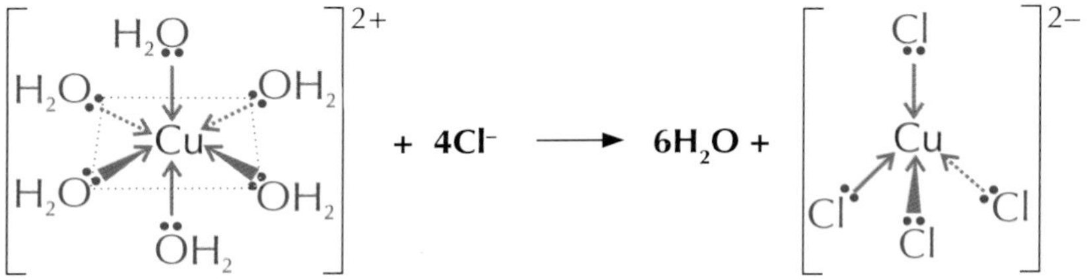

$$[Cu(H_2O)_6]^{2+} + 4Cl^- \longrightarrow 6H_2O + [CuCl_4]^{2-}$$

Coordination number: 6
octahedral, pale blue

Coordination number: 4
tetrahedral, yellow-green

Learning Objectives:

- Be able to describe the ligand substitution reaction and the accompanying colour change in the formation of $[Cr(NH_3)_6]^{3+}$ from $[Cr(H_2O)_6]^{3+}$.
- Be able to describe the ligand substitution reactions and the accompanying colour changes in the formation of $[Cu(NH_3)_4(H_2O)_2]^{2+}$ and $[CuCl_4]^{2-}$ from $[Cu(H_2O)_6]^{2+}$.
- Be able to interpret and predict the outcome of unfamiliar ligand substitution reactions.
- Be able to explain the biochemical importance of iron in haemoglobin, including ligand substitution involving O_2 and CO.

Specification Reference 5.3.1

Exam Tip
When you're writing ligand substitution reactions in the exam make sure your equations are balanced.

Tip: Remember — complex ions with a coordination number of four are usually tetrahedral. Complex ions with a coordination number of six are usually octahedral.

Tip: Have a look back at pages 147-148 for a reminder about the shapes of complex ions.

Tip: In the example on the right you only get *trans*-$[Cu(NH_3)_4(H_2O)_2]^{2+}$ when an excess of NH_3 is added. Otherwise you get $Cu(OH)_2(H_2O)_4$ (a blue precipitate) instead.

Exam Tip:
You could be asked to predict the outcome of unfamiliar reactions in the exam so try to remember that H_2O, NH_3, OH^-, and CN^- ligands are about the same size but Cl^- ions are a lot larger.

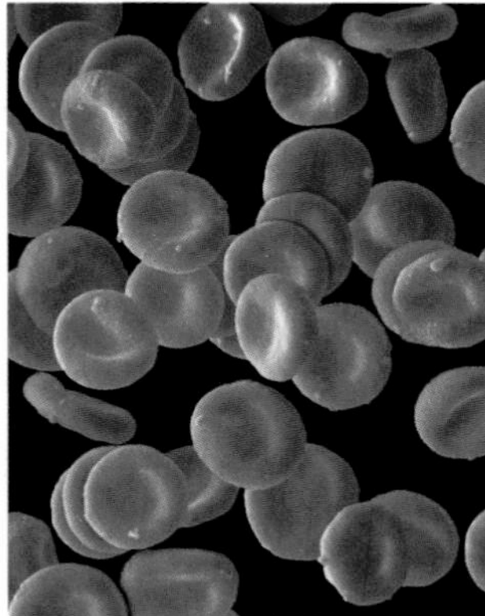

Figure 1: Red blood cells are packed full of haemoglobin.

Tip: When the Fe^{2+} ion is bound to water the complex is called deoxyhaemoglobin and when it's bound to oxygen it's called oxyhaemoglobin.

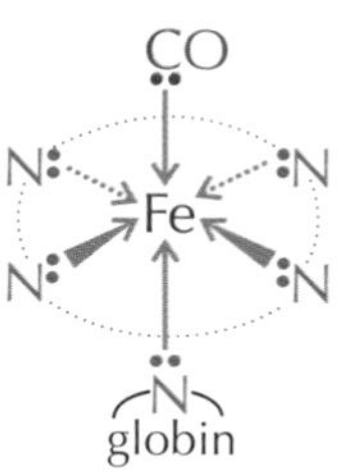

Figure 3: Carboxyhaemoglobin.

Partial substitution of ligands

Sometimes the substitution is only partial — not all of the six H_2O ligands are substituted.

Example

In a copper-aqua complex, some of the H_2O ligands can be exchanged with NH_3 ligands whilst some H_2O ligands remain where they are.

In this example, four of the H_2O ligands are substituted with NH_3 ligands. The shape of the complex changes from octahedral to elongated octahedral and there is also a colour change.

$$[Cu(H_2O)_6]^{2+}_{(aq)} + 4NH_{3(aq)} \rightarrow 4H_2O_{(l)} + [Cu(NH_3)_4(H_2O)_2]^{2+}_{(aq)}$$

octahedral *pale blue* — *elongated octahedral* *deep blue*

Haem and haemoglobin

Haemoglobin is a protein found in blood that helps to transport oxygen around the body. It contains Fe^{2+} ions, which are hexa-coordinated — six lone pairs are donated to them to form six coordinate bonds. Four of the lone pairs come from nitrogen atoms, which form a circle around the Fe^{2+}. This part of the molecule is called haem. The molecule that the four nitrogen atoms are part of is a multidentate ligand called a **porphyrin**. A protein called a globin and either an oxygen or a water molecule also bind to the Fe^{2+} ion to form an octahedral structure — see Figure 2.

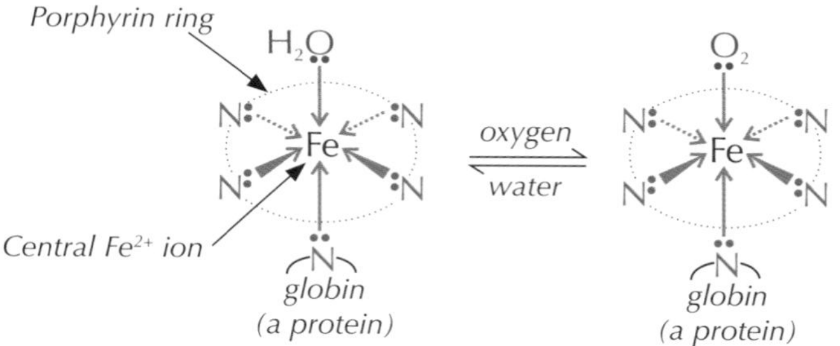

Figure 2: The structure of haemoglobin when it is bound to oxygen or water.

In the body, both water and oxygen will bind to the Fe^{2+} ions as ligands, so the complex can transport oxygen to where it's needed, and then swap it for a water molecule. In the lungs, where the oxygen concentration is high, water ligands are substituted for oxygen molecules to form oxyhaemoglobin, which is carried around the body in the blood. When the oxyhaemoglobin gets to a place where oxygen is needed, the oxygen molecules are exchanged for water molecules. The haemoglobin then returns to the lungs and the whole process starts again. The process of oxygen transport is summarised in Figure 4 (on the next page).

Carbon monoxide poisoning

When carbon monoxide is inhaled, the haemoglobin can substitute its water ligands for carbon monoxide ligands, forming carboxyhaemoglobin (Figure 3). This is bad news because carbon monoxide forms a very strong bond with the Fe^{2+} ion and doesn't readily exchange with oxygen or water ligands, meaning the haemoglobin can't transport oxygen any more. Carbon monoxide poisoning starves the organs of oxygen — it can cause headaches, dizziness, unconsciousness and even death if it's not treated.

Summary of the oxygen transport process

Here's an overview of how haemoglobin transports oxygen round the body:

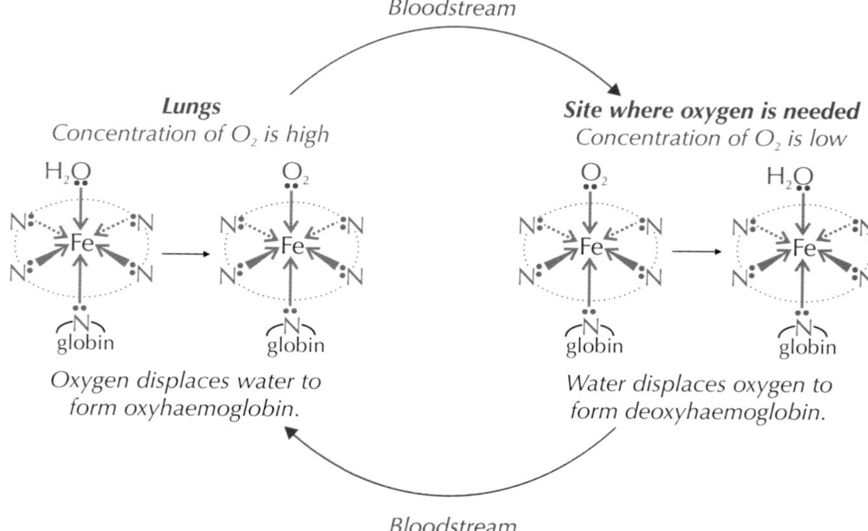

Figure 4: *The role of haemoglobin in the transport of oxygen around the body.*

Tip: It's the oxyhaemoglobin in red blood cells that makes them red.

Practice Questions — Application

Q1 The H_2O ligands in $[Fe(H_2O)_6]^{3+}$ can be exchanged for other ligands. Predict the shape of the complex ions formed after the following substitutions:

a) All the H_2O ligands exchanged for OH^- ligands.

b) The six H_2O ligands exchanged for four Cl^- ligands.

Q2 Write an equation for the formation of $[MnCl_4]^{2-}$ from a hexa-aqua manganese(II) ion and chloride ions.

Q3 The metal-aqua ion $[Cu(H_2O)_6]^{2+}$ will undergo a ligand substitution reaction with hydroxide ions to form $[Cu(OH)_4(H_2O)_2]^{2-}$.

a) Write an equation for this reaction.

b) State the shape of $[Cu(OH)_4(H_2O)_2]^{2-}$.

Practice Questions — Fact Recall

Q1 State whether the colour, coordination number and/or the shape of the complex ion changes in the following situations.

a) Ligand exchange of similarly sized ligands.

b) Ligand exchange of differently sized ligands.

Q2 a) What is the role of haemoglobin in the body?

b) Where do the six coordinate bonds come from in haemoglobin?

Q3 Haemoglobin is found in red blood cells.

a) Explain what happens to haemoglobin in the lungs.

b) Explain what happens to haemoglobin at sites where oxygen is needed.

Q4 Explain why carbon monoxide is toxic.

6. Precipitation Reactions

Many transition metals form coloured hydroxide precipitates. Which is pretty handy because it lets us test which transition metal might be in a solution.

Learning Objectives:

- Be able to describe the precipitation reactions, including ionic equations and the accompanying colour changes, of $Cu^{2+}_{(aq)}$, $Fe^{2+}_{(aq)}$, $Fe^{3+}_{(aq)}$, $Mn^{2+}_{(aq)}$ and $Cr^{3+}_{(aq)}$ with aqueous sodium hydroxide and aqueous ammonia (including with excess aqueous sodium hydroxide and aqueous ammonia).
- Be able to interpret and predict the outcome of unfamiliar precipitation reactions.

Specification Reference 5.3.1

Transition metal precipitates

When you mix an aqueous solution of transition metal ions with aqueous sodium hydroxide (NaOH) or aqueous ammonia (NH_3) you get a coloured hydroxide **precipitate**.

Notation for precipitation reactions

As you've seen over the last few pages, in aqueous solutions, transition elements take the form $[M(H_2O)_6]^{n+}$. When you're dealing with precipitation reactions they can also be written as $M^{n+}_{(aq)}$ — you can leave out the water ligands. For example, the aqueous copper(II) ion can be written as either $[Cu(H_2O)_6]^{2+}_{(aq)}$ or $Cu^{2+}_{(aq)}$. You can also leave water ligands out of the formula of the precipitate. So the formula of the copper hydroxide precipitate can be written as $Cu(OH)_2(H_2O)_4$ or $Cu(OH)_2$.

Reactions with NaOH and NH_3

In water, sodium hydroxide dissociates into Na^+ and OH^- ions. It's the OH^- ions which react with the transition metal complex.

Tip: The OH^- ions don't actually replace the water ligands. They just take one H^+ from a water ligand. So the OH^- ion becomes an H_2O molecule and an H_2O ligand becomes an OH^- ligand.

Example

$$[Fe(H_2O)_6]^{2+}_{(aq)} + 2OH^-_{(aq)} \rightarrow Fe(OH)_2(H_2O)_{4(s)} + 2H_2O_{(l)}$$

pale green — *green precipitate (darkens on standing)*

This can also be written as: $Fe^{2+}_{(aq)} + 2OH^-_{(aq)} \rightarrow Fe(OH)_{2(s)}$

Aqueous transition metal ions will react with ammonia to produce the same hydroxide precipitate as in their reaction with aqueous sodium hydroxide. The ammonia molecules remove H^+ ions from water ligands, creating OH^- ligands.

Tip: Remember that a precipitate is a solid formed in a solution.

Example

$$[Fe(H_2O)_6]^{2+}_{(aq)} + 2NH_{3(aq)} \rightarrow Fe(OH)_2(H_2O)_{4(s)} + 2NH_4^+{}_{(aq)}$$

pale green — *green precipitate (darkens on standing)*

Here are the other reactions that you need to know...

Copper(II)

$$[Cu(H_2O)_6]^{2+}_{(aq)} + 2OH^-_{(aq)} \rightarrow Cu(OH)_2(H_2O)_{4(s)} + 2H_2O_{(l)}$$

$$[Cu(H_2O)_6]^{2+}_{(aq)} + 2NH_{3(aq)} \rightarrow Cu(OH)_2(H_2O)_{4(s)} + 2NH_4^+{}_{(aq)}$$

pale blue — *blue precipitate*

In excess NH_3, $Cu(OH)_2(H_2O)_{4(s)}$ reacts further to form $[Cu(NH_3)_4(H_2O)_2]^{2+}_{(aq)}$ which is a dark blue colour.

Figure 1: *Iron(II) hydroxide (left) and copper(II) hydroxide (right).*

Manganese(II)

$$[Mn(H_2O)_6]^{2+}_{(aq)} + 2OH^-_{(aq)} \rightarrow Mn(OH)_2(H_2O)_{4(s)} + 2H_2O_{(l)}$$

$$[Mn(H_2O)_6]^{2+}_{(aq)} + 2NH_{3(aq)} \rightarrow Mn(OH)_2(H_2O)_{4(s)} + 2NH_4^+{}_{(aq)}$$

pale pink — *pink/buff precipitate (darkens on standing)*

Iron(III)

$$[Fe(H_2O)_6]^{3+}_{(aq)} + 3OH^-_{(aq)} \rightarrow Fe(OH)_3(H_2O)_{3(s)} + 3H_2O_{(l)}$$

$$[Fe(H_2O)_6]^{3+}_{(aq)} + 3NH_{3(aq)} \rightarrow Fe(OH)_3(H_2O)_{3(s)} + 3NH_4^+{}_{(aq)}$$

yellow — *orange precipitate (darkens on standing)*

Figure 2: *Manganese(II) hydroxide (left) and iron(III) hydroxide (right).*

Chromium(III)

$$[Cr(H_2O)_6]^{3+}_{(aq)} + 3OH^-_{(aq)} \rightarrow Cr(OH)_3(H_2O)_{3(s)} + 3H_2O_{(l)}$$

$$[Cr(H_2O)_6]^{3+}_{(aq)} + 3NH_{3(aq)} \rightarrow Cr(OH)_3(H_2O)_{3(s)} + 3NH_4^+{}_{(aq)}$$

green — *grey-green precipitate*

In excess NaOH, $Cr(OH)_3(H_2O)_{3(s)}$ reacts further to form $[Cr(OH)_6]^{3-}_{(s)}$ which is a dark green colour. In excess NH_3, $Cr(OH)_3(H_2O)_{3(s)}$ reacts further to form $[Cr(NH_3)_6]^{3+}_{(aq)}$ which is a purple colour.

Exam Tip

Notice that the metal ions with a 2+ charge form precipitates with two hydroxide ions and the metal ions with a 3+ charge form precipitates with three hydroxide ions — it makes it a bit easier to remember the equations.

Practice Questions — Application

Q1 A scientist has a solution of Fe ions. Describe a test the scientist could use to determine whether the ions are Fe^{2+} ions or Fe^{3+} ions.

Q2 A few drops of aqueous ammonia are added to a pink aqueous cobalt(II) solution. A blue precipitate is formed. Write an equation for the reaction that's likely to have taken place.

Practice Questions — Fact Recall

Q1 Write an equation for the reaction of copper(II) ions with sodium hydroxide solution.

Q2 What would you observe as sodium hydroxide solution is added to a solution of iron(III) ions?

7. Transition Metals and Redox

You learnt all about redox reactions on pages 113-114. In redox reactions, one species gains electrons and is reduced, another loses electrons and is oxidised. Here's a nice topic all about redox reactions involving transition elements.

Learning Objectives:

- Know the redox reactions and accompanying colour changes for the interconversion between Fe^{2+} and Fe^{3+}.
- Know the redox reactions and accompanying colour changes for the interconversion between Cr^{3+} and $Cr_2O_7^{2-}$.
- Know the redox reactions and accompanying colour changes for the reduction of Cu^{2+} to Cu^+ and disproportionation of Cu^+ to Cu^{2+} and Cu.
- Be able to interpret and predict the outcome of unfamiliar redox reactions.

Specification Reference 5.3.1

Transition metal redox reactions

Transition elements can exist in many different **oxidation states**. They can change oxidation state by gaining or losing electrons in redox reactions. This often brings about a colour change.

Interconversion between Fe^{3+} and Fe^{2+}

Iron ions can gain and lose electrons to switch between the Fe^{2+} and Fe^{3+} states when appropriate oxidising and reducing agents are added to their solutions.

The oxidation of Fe^{2+} to Fe^{3+} by Mn(VII) ions in acid solution

Acidified potassium manganate(VII) solution, $KMnO_{4(aq)}$, is used as an oxidising agent. It contains manganate(VII) ions (MnO_4^-), in which manganese has an oxidation state of +7. The manganese(VII) ions are reduced to Mn^{2+} ions and the Fe^{2+} ions are oxidised to Fe^{3+}.

Half equations: $MnO_4^- + 8H^+ + 5e^- \rightarrow Mn^{2+} + 4H_2O$ *and* $Fe^{2+} \rightarrow Fe^{3+} + e^-$

Five electrons are transferred in the first half-equation and only one is transferred in the second half-equation. So to get the full equation you need to multiply the second half-equation by five, then cancel out the electrons.

So the full equation is: $\mathbf{MnO_4^- + 8H^+ + 5Fe^{2+} \rightarrow Mn^{2+} + 4H_2O + 5Fe^{3+}}$

Tip: The H^+ ions are there because the $KMnO_4$ is acidified.

$Fe^{2+}_{(aq)}$ is pale green and $Fe^{3+}_{(aq)}$ is yellow, so you'll see a colour change from pale green to yellow during this reaction.

The reduction of Fe^{3+} to Fe^{2+} by iodide ions in solution

Iodide solution, $I^-_{(aq)}$, is a reducing agent. The iodide ions have an oxidation state of –1. They can be oxidised to neutral iodine molecules, $I_{2(aq)}$, during a redox reaction with Fe^{3+} ions. The Fe^{3+} ions are reduced.

Half-equations: $2I^- \rightarrow I_2 + 2e^-$ *and* $Fe^{3+} + e^- \rightarrow Fe^{2+}$

Full equation: $\mathbf{2I^- + 2Fe^{3+} \rightarrow 2Fe^{2+} + I_2}$

Exam Tip
Don't worry — you won't be expected to memorise and reproduce these full equations in the exams. You could be asked to construct and interpret redox equations from half-equations and oxidation numbers though — so make sure you understand how to do it.

Interconversion between Cr^{3+} and $Cr_2O_7^{2-}$

Chromium ions can gain and lose electrons easily to switch between Cr^{3+} (oxidation state = +3) and $Cr_2O_7^{2-}$ (Cr oxidation state = +6) when appropriate oxidising and reducing agents are added to solutions.

The oxidation of Cr^{3+} to dichromate(VI) $Cr_2O_7^{2-}$

There are a couple of steps in this reaction.

Firstly, Cr^{3+} ions in $Cr(OH)_6^{3-}$ are oxidised to CrO_4^{2-} where they have an oxidation state of +6. Hydrogen peroxide solution, $H_2O_{2(aq)}$, is used as the oxidising agent. The oxygen in H_2O_2 is reduced from an oxidation state of –1 to –2 in hydroxide ions, $OH^-_{(aq)}$.

Exam Tip
You will be expected to know the colour changes that take place during these reactions.

Half-equations: $H_2O_2 + 2e^- \rightarrow 2OH^-$

$2Cr(OH)_6^{3-} + 4OH^- \rightarrow 2CrO_4^{2-} + 8H_2O + 6e^-$

Full equation: $3H_2O_2 + 2Cr(OH)_6^{3-} \rightarrow 2OH^- + 2CrO_4^{2-} + 8H_2O$

dark green *yellow*

In the second step, dilute sulfuric acid is added to the chromate(VI) solution ($CrO_4^{2-}{}_{(aq)}$) to produce a dichromate(VI) solution ($Cr_2O_7^{2-}{}_{(aq)}$).

$$2CrO_4^{2-}{}_{(aq)} + 2H^+_{(aq)} \rightarrow Cr_2O_7^{2-}{}_{(aq)} + H_2O_{(l)}$$

yellow *orange*

Tip: There are a couple of colour changes in the oxidation of Cr^{3+} to $Cr_2O_7^{2-}$. You start with a dark green solution ($Cr(OH)_6^{3-}$) then a yellow one (CrO_4^{2-}) and finally an orange solution ($Cr_2O_7^{2-}$).

The reduction of $Cr_2O_7^{2-}$ to Cr^{3+} by acidified zinc

Acidified zinc, $Zn_{(aq)}$, is a reducing agent. The zinc atoms (oxidation state 0) are oxidised to Zn^{2+} ions (oxidation state +2) in a redox reaction with $Cr_2O_7^{2-}$ ions.

Half-equations: $Zn \rightarrow Zn^{2+} + 2e^-$

$Cr_2O_7^{2-} + 14H^+ + 6e^- \rightarrow 2Cr^{3+} + 7H_2O$

Full equation: $Cr_2O_7^{2-} + 14H^+ + 3Zn \rightarrow 2Cr^{3+} + 7H_2O + 3Zn^{2+}$

Figure 1: *Left — chromate (CrO_4^{2-}) solution. Right — dichromate ($Cr_2O_7^{2-}$) solution.*

Copper redox reactions

Cu^{2+} ions can be reduced to Cu^+, giving an oxidation state change of +2 to +1.

Example

$Cu^{2+}_{(aq)}$ (pale blue) is reduced to the off-white precipitate copper(I) iodide by iodide ions, $I^-_{(aq)}$. $2Cu^{2+}_{(aq)} + 4I^-_{(aq)} \rightarrow 2CuI_{(s)} + I_{2(aq)}$

Disproportionation of Cu^+ ions

$Cu^+_{(aq)}$ is unstable and spontaneously disproportionates — this means it is oxidised and reduced at the same time. So if you have two Cu^+ ions, one gains an electron (is reduced) to become Cu, the other loses an electron (is oxidised) to become Cu^{2+}.

$$2Cu^+_{(aq)} \rightarrow Cu_{(s)} + Cu^{2+}_{(aq)}$$

Practice Questions — Fact Recall

Q1 Give an example of an oxidising agent which could be used in the conversion of Fe^{2+} to Fe^{3+}.

Q2 Aqueous hydrogen peroxide is added to an aqueous chromium(III) solution. Aqueous chromate(VI) ions are produced.

a) What is the change in oxidation state when Cr^{3+} ions are oxidised to CrO_4^{2-} ions?

b) What colour change is observed during this reaction?

c) What would the product be if dilute sulfuric acid was added to the chromate(VI) solution?

d) What colour change would be observed if dilute sulfuric acid was added to the chromate(VI) solution?

Q3 What does disproportionation mean?

8. Tests for Ions

PRACTICAL ACTIVITY GROUP 4

Learning Objectives:

- Know how to carry out the qualitative analysis of ions on a test tube scale (PAG 4).
- Know the processes and techniques needed to identify the following anions in an unknown compound: CO_3^{2-}, Cl^-, Br^-, I^-, and SO_4^{2-}.
- Know the processes and techniques needed to identify the following cations in an unknown compound: NH_4^+, Cu^{2+}, Fe^{2+}, Fe^{3+}, Mn^{2+}, and Cr^{3+}.

Specification Reference 5.3.2

Tip: Think about any safety precautions you might need to consider before doing these tests.

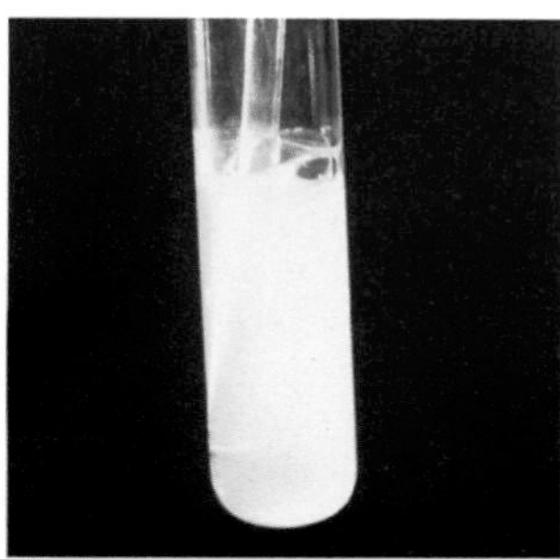

Figure 1: *Limewater turns cloudy when carbon dioxide is added to it.*

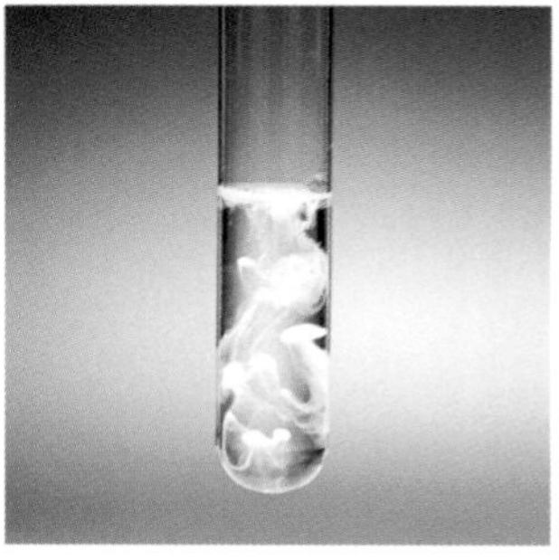

Figure 2: *Barium sulfate is a white precipitate.*

It's really important that you know how to identify certain ions. You need to know the simple tests for some transition metal ions, as well as some common ions. You'll have come across some of these tests before so with any luck, this shouldn't be too tricky...

Identifying transition metal ions

Many transition metal ions form coloured precipitates when aqueous sodium hydroxide is added (see page 154). This is a good way to identify which transition metal ions are in a solution. To carry out the tests, add $NaOH_{(aq)}$ solution, dropwise from a pipette, to a test tube containing the unknown solution and record the colour of any precipitate formed. The table below shows some of the ions that can be identified using this method.

Ion	Observation
Cu^{2+}	blue precipitate
Fe^{2+}	green precipitate
Fe^{3+}	orange precipitate
Mn^{2+}	pink / buff precipitate
Cr^{3+}	grey-green precipitate

Test for halides

To test for halide ions just add nitric acid, then silver nitrate solution. If chloride, bromide or iodide is present, a precipitate will form. The colour of the precipitate depends on the halide present — silver chloride (AgCl) is a white precipitate, silver bromide (AgBr) is a cream precipitate and silver iodide (AgI) is a yellow precipitate.

Test for carbonates

To test an unknown solution for carbonates (CO_3^{2-}), add a dilute strong acid (e.g. dilute nitric acid or dilute hydrochloric acid). If carbonates are present then carbon dioxide will be released. To see if carbon dioxide is produced, you need to bubble any gas created through limewater. If carbon dioxide is present, then it'll turn the limewater cloudy (see Figure 1).

Example

Calcium carbonate reacts with hydrochloric acid to produce carbon dioxide, water and calcium chloride. The equation for this reaction is:

$$CaCO_{3(s)} + 2HCl_{(aq)} \rightarrow CO_{2(g)} + H_2O_{(l)} + CaCl_{2(aq)}$$

Test for sulfates

To test for sulfate ions (SO_4^{2-}), add a dilute strong acid followed by few drops of barium nitrate solution, $Ba(NO_3)_{2(aq)}$, to a solution of the unknown substance. If you get a white precipitate it'll be barium sulfate, which tells you that there are sulfate ions in the solution (see Figure 2). You need to add the dilute acid to make sure you don't end up with a false positive due to carbonate or sulfite ions, which also produce a white precipitate when reacted with barium nitrate. Adding the acid removes any carbonates and sulfites present that might interfere with the test.

Example

Sodium sulfate reacts with $Ba(NO_3)_2$ solution to give barium sulfate and sodium nitrate:

$$Na_2SO_{4\,(aq)} + Ba(NO_3)_{2\,(aq)} \rightarrow BaSO_{4\,(s)} + 2NaNO_{3\,(aq)}$$

Tip: You could use barium chloride to test for sulfates instead of barium nitrate.

Test for ammonium ions

Ammonia gas (NH_3) is alkaline, so you can check for it using a damp piece of red litmus paper. If there's ammonia present, the paper will turn blue. You'll also be able to smell ammonia — it has a distinctive, pungent smell.

You can use this to test whether a substance contains ammonium ions (NH_4^+). Add a few drops of aqueous sodium hydroxide to your unknown substance in a test tube and warm the mixture. Hold a piece of damp litmus paper near the top of the test tube. If the paper turns blue it means ammonia is being given off and there are ammonium ions in your substance.

Tip: The litmus paper needs to be damp so the ammonia gas can dissolve and make the colour change.

Example

Ammonium chloride reacts with sodium hydroxide to give ammonia, water and sodium chloride.

$$NH_4Cl_{(aq)} + NaOH_{(aq)} \rightarrow NH_{3(g)} + H_2O_{(l)} + NaCl_{(aq)}$$

Practice Questions — Application

Q1 An unknown solution is put through a series of tests to determine which ions are present.
Firstly, $NaOH_{(aq)}$ is added. A blue precipitate is formed.
Secondly, dilute hydrochloric acid is added. The gas produced is delivered into limewater. The limewater goes cloudy.
Which ions are present in the unknown solution?

Q2 Two students add barium nitrate solution to an unknown solution to try and determine which ions are present. A white precipitate is formed. One student claims that this means sulfate ions are present in the solution. The other student claims that this means carbonate ions are present in the solution.
Comment on the conclusion of each student.

Exam Tip
If you're asked how to test for a particular ion in the exam, or you're asked to draw conclusions from a set of results, you need to think about what ions could be present that could give false positives. Have they been dealt with or could they interfere with the test? Also, remember to always consider the effect that adding substances during a test could have. Have ions been added that will affect the results?

Practice Questions — Fact Recall

Q1 Give the colour of the precipitate formed when $NaOH_{(aq)}$ is added to solutions of the following ions:
a) Mn^{2+}, b) Fe^{2+}, c) Cr^{3+}?

Q2 Name a dilute acid used in the test for:
a) carbonate ions b) halide ions

Q3 What colour will damp red litmus paper go in the presence of ammonium ions?

Section Summary

Make sure you know...

- That transition elements are d-block elements that have an ion with a partially filled d-subshell.
- That the elements Ti–Cu are transition elements.
- How to work out the electron configuration of atoms and ions of the d-block elements of Period 4 (Sc–Zn).
- Why scandium and zinc aren't transition elements.
- That transition elements can form complex ions.
- That transition elements can form coloured ions.
- That transition elements have variable oxidation states.
- That transition elements make great catalysts because of their variable oxidation states.
- The common colours of different transition metal ions and their oxidation states.
- That a complex ion is a metal ion surrounded by coordinately bonded ligands.
- That a ligand is an atom, ion or molecule that can form coordinate bonds with a central metal ion.
- That coordination number is the number of coordinate bonds formed with the central metal ion in a complex ion.
- What bidentate ligands are and that $NH_2CH_2CH_2NH_2$ (en) is a bidentate ligand.
- Examples of complexes with a coordination number of six and an octahedral shape.
- Examples of complexes with a coordination number of four and a tetrahedral or square planar shape.
- That complexes such as $[Ni(en)_3]^{2+}$ can show optical isomerism.
- That complexes such as $Pt(NH_3)_2Cl_2$ can show *cis-trans* isomerism.
- That cisplatin is used as an anti-cancer drug and how it works.
- That ligands can be substituted for one another in ligand substitution reactions.
- The ligand substitution reaction and the colour change for the formation of $[Cr(NH_3)_6]^{3+}$ from $[Cr(H_2O)_6]^{3+}$.
- The ligand substitution reactions and the colour changes for the formation of $[Cu(NH_3)_4(H_2O)_2]^{2+}$ and $[CuCl_4]^{2-}$ from $[Cu(H_2O)_6]^{2+}$.
- How the iron in haemoglobin allows oxygen to be transported around the body.
- Why the ligand substitution of oxygen or water for carbon monoxide in haemoglobin is so dangerous.
- The ionic equations for the precipitation reactions of $Cu^{2+}_{(aq)}$, $Mn^{2+}_{(aq)}$, $Fe^{2+}_{(aq)}$, $Fe^{3+}_{(aq)}$ and $Cr^{3+}_{(aq)}$ with aqueous sodium hydroxide or aqueous ammonia.
- The colour changes that happen when $Cu^{2+}_{(aq)}$, $Mn^{2+}_{(aq)}$, $Fe^{2+}_{(aq)}$, $Fe^{3+}_{(aq)}$ and $Cr^{3+}_{(aq)}$ react with aqueous sodium hydroxide or aqueous ammonia.
- The ionic equation and colour change when $Cu^{2+}_{(aq)}$ reacts with excess ammonia.
- The ionic equation and colour change when $Cr^{3+}_{(aq)}$ reacts with excess sodium hydroxide or excess ammonia.
- That transition elements can undergo redox reactions.
- The redox reactions in the interconversion between Fe^{2+} and Fe^{3+}.
- The redox reactions in the interconversion between Cr^{3+} and $Cr_2O_7^{2-}$.
- The redox reactions in the reduction of Cu^{2+} and the disproportionation of Cu^{+}.
- How to carry out tests to identify the following anions in unknown compounds: CO_3^{2-}, Cl^-, Br^-, I^-, and SO_4^{2-}.
- How to carry out tests to identify the following cations in unknown compounds: NH_4^+, Cu^{2+}, Fe^{2+}, Fe^{3+}, Mn^{2+}, and Cr^{3+}.

Exam-style Questions

1 Which of the following shows an incorrect electron configuration for the given transition element?

A vanadium: $1s^2\ 2s^2\ 2p^6\ 3s^2\ 3p^6\ 3d^3\ 4s^2$

B chromium: $1s^2\ 2s^2\ 2p^6\ 3s^2\ 3p^6\ 3d^5\ 4s^1$

C manganese: $1s^2\ 2s^2\ 2p^6\ 3s^2\ 3p^6\ 3d^6\ 4s^1$

D iron: $1s^2\ 2s^2\ 2p^6\ 3s^2\ 3p^6\ 3d^6\ 4s^2$

(1 mark)

2 Which of the following statements about the transition metal complex $[Cu(H_2O)_6]^{2+}{}_{(aq)}$ is untrue?

A When chloride ions are added, a yellow square planar complex is formed.

B When $NaOH_{(aq)}$ is added, a blue precipitate is formed.

C When excess $NH_{3(aq)}$ is added, a dark blue solution is formed.

D $[Cu(H_2O)_6]^{2+}{}_{(aq)}$ is octahedral and pale blue in solution.

(1 mark)

3 A student is given an unknown solution containing a transition metal complex and asked to identify the ions present. The student carries out three tests on three separate samples, the results of which are shown below.

Test 1: A few drops of $NaOH_{(aq)}$ are added to the unknown solution and a grey-green precipitate forms.

Test 2: Dilute nitric acid is added to the unknown solution. The gas produced was bubbled through limewater. No change was observed in the limewater.

Test 3: Nitric acid is added to the unknown solution, followed by silver nitrate. A white precipitate forms.

What is the formula of the unknown transition metal complex?

A $[FeCl_4]^{2-}$

B $Cr_2(CO_3)_3$

C $Fe_2(SO_4)_3$

D $[CrCl_4]^-$

(1 mark)

4 Brass is an alloy of mainly copper and zinc.

(a) Dissolving brass in acid produces a solution which contains aqueous copper ions.

(i) What colour is the aqueous Cu^{2+} ion?

(1 mark)

(ii) Write down the full electron configurations of the copper atom and the Cu^{2+} ion.

(2 marks)

(iii) Explain why the Cu^{2+} ion has the chemical properties associated with transition metal elements.

(1 mark)

(b) In the solution the $[Cu(H_2O)_6]^{2+}$ complex ion forms.

(i) In this complex ion, water acts as a ligand.
Explain the meaning of the term ligand.

(1 mark)

(ii) Draw the 3D structure of $[Cu(H_2O)_6]^{2+}$ and state its shape.

(2 marks)

(iii) What is the coordination number of this ion?

(1 mark)

5 Many complex ions exist as stereoisomers.

(a) $CoCl_2(NH_3)_2$ exists as two stereoisomers.

(i) Give the shape of the $CoCl_2(NH_3)_2$ ion.

(1 mark)

(ii) What type of stereoisomerism does $CoCl_2(NH_3)_2$ exhibit?

(1 mark)

(iii) Draw the two possible stereoisomers of $CoCl_2(NH_3)_2$.

(2 marks)

(b) The ethanedioate ion is a bidentate ligand. When it binds to chromium(III) ions it forms a complex ion with stereoisomers. The structure of the ethanedioate ion is shown below.

Ethanedioate ion

(i) What type of stereoisomerism does $[Cr(C_2O_4)_3]^{3-}$ exhibit?

(1 mark)

(ii) Describe how the ethanedioate ion bonds to the chromium ion.

(2 marks)

(iii) Draw two stereoisomers of $[Cr(C_2O_4)_3]^{3-}$.

(2 marks)

6 Fe^{2+} is a transition element ion that can undergo a wide variety of reactions.

(a) What is a transition element?

(1 mark)

(b) $Fe^{2+}_{(aq)}$ can react with sodium hydroxide to form a precipitate.

(i) Write down the ionic equation for this reaction.

(1 mark)

(ii) What colour is the precipitate?

(1 mark)

(c) Fe^{2+} can combine with ligands to form complex ions.

(i) Write an equation for the reaction between the hexaaqua iron(II) ion ($[Fe(H_2O)_6]^{2+}$) and $Cl^-_{(aq)}$ ions to form a tetrahedral complex.

(2 marks)

(ii) Draw the structure of the complex ion formed in part **(c) (i)**.

(1 mark)

(iii) The hexaaqua iron(II) ion will also react with six CN^- ions in a ligand substitution reaction. Write down the equation for this reaction.

(1 mark)

(iv) State whether you expect the coordination number, shape and/or colour of the complex ion to change during the reaction in **(c) (iii)**. Explain your answer.

(3 marks)

7 Hydrogen peroxide, $H_2O_{2(aq)}$, is used as an oxidising agent in the oxidation of $Cr(OH)_6{}^{3-}{}_{(aq)}$ to form $CrO_4{}^{2-}{}_{(aq)}$.

(a) $Cr(OH)_6{}^{3-}{}_{(aq)}$ is formed from $Cr^{3+}_{(aq)}$ ions.

(i) How can $Cr(OH)_6{}^{3-}{}_{(aq)}$ be formed from the hexaaqua chromium(III) ion?

(1 mark)

(ii) Write the balanced, full equation for the reaction in part **(a) (i)**.

(1 mark)

(b) The half-equations for the redox reaction between H_2O_2 and $Cr(OH)_6{}^{3-}$ are:

$$H_2O_2 + 2e^- \rightarrow 2OH^-$$

$$2Cr(OH)_6{}^{3-} + 4OH^- \rightarrow 2CrO_4{}^{2-} + 8H_2O + 6e^-$$

(i) Write the balanced, full equation for this redox reaction.

(1 mark)

(ii) How many moles of H_2O_2 are needed to fully oxidise 4 moles of $Cr(OH)_6{}^{3-}$?

(1 mark)

(iii) Describe the colour change that is observed during this reaction.

(1 mark)

(iv) Once chromate, $CrO_4{}^{2-}$, is formed, suggest a method to convert it to dichromate, $Cr_2O_7{}^{2-}$.

(1 mark)

Learning Objectives:

- Be able to compare the Kekulé and delocalised models of benzene in terms of p-orbital overlap forming a delocalised π-system.
- Understand the experimental evidence for a delocalised, rather than Kekulé, model for benzene in terms of bond lengths, enthalpy change of hydrogenation and resistance to reaction.
- Be able to use IUPAC rules of nomenclature for systematically naming substituted aromatic compounds.

Specification Reference 6.1.1

Tip: In skeletal structures like this one...

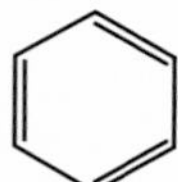

...there is a carbon atom at each corner and you work out the positions of the hydrogens by looking at the number of bonds coming from each carbon. There should be four — if there aren't, add one or more hydrogens.

Tip: pm stands for picometre. A picometre is 1×10^{-12} metres — that's very small indeed.

1. Benzene

Benzene is one of the most important molecules in organic chemistry. Loads of exciting organic molecules contain benzene rings, like aspirin, morphine, dopamine and styrene (to name just a few).

What is benzene?

Benzene has the formula C_6H_6. It has a cyclic structure, as its six carbon atoms are joined together in a ring. The ring itself is planar (flat) and the hydrogens all stick out in the same plane. There are two main models to explain the structure of the benzene ring — the Kekulé model and the delocalised model.

The Kekulé model

This was proposed by German chemist Friedrich August Kekulé in 1865. He came up with the idea of a ring of C atoms with alternating single and double bonds between them (see Figure 1).

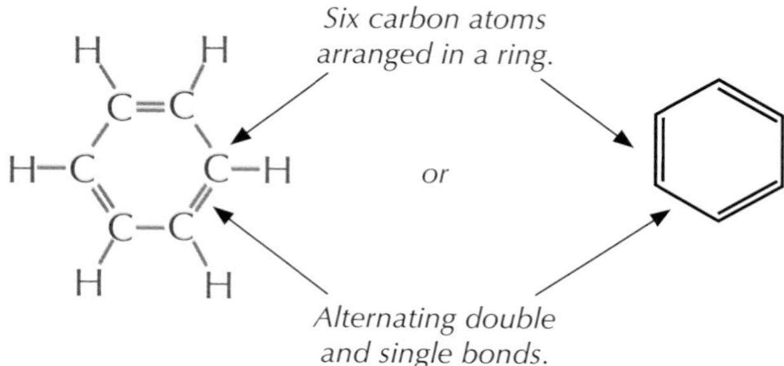

Figure 1: *The structure of benzene according to Kekulé.*

He later adapted the model to say that the benzene molecule was constantly flipping between two forms (isomers) by switching over the double and single bonds (see Figure 2).

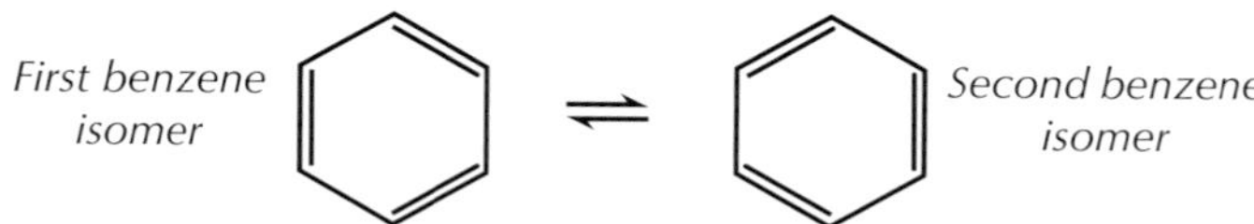

Figure 2: *Benzene flipping between two forms in the adapted Kekulé model.*

HOW SCIENCE WORKS

If the Kekulé model was correct, you'd expect there to always be three bonds with the length of a C–C bond (154 pm) and three bonds with the length of a C=C bond (134 pm). However X-ray diffraction studies have shown that all the carbon-carbon bonds in benzene have the same length (140 pm) — they're between the length of a single bond and a double bond. So the Kekulé structure can't be quite right, but it's still used today as it's useful for drawing reaction mechanisms.

The delocalised model

The bond-length observations are explained by the **delocalised** model. In this model, the p-orbitals of all six carbon atoms overlap to create a π-system. This π-system is made up of two ring-shaped clouds of electrons — one above and one below the plane of the six carbon atoms (see Figure 3).

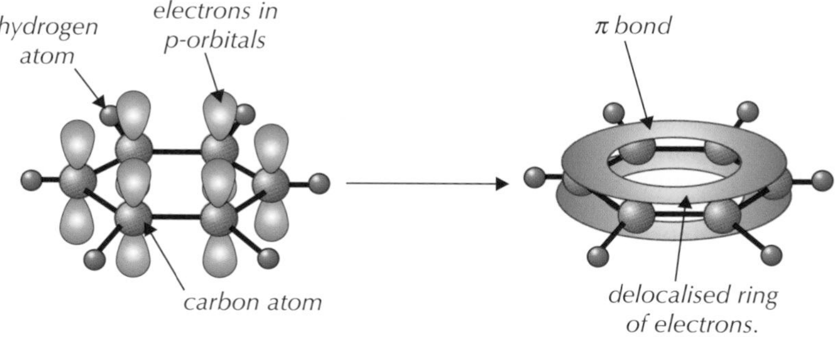

Figure 3: *The formation of π bonds in benzene.*

All the carbon-carbon bonds in the ring are the same length because all the bonds are the same. The electrons in the rings are said to be delocalised because they don't belong to a specific carbon atom. They are represented as a circle in the ring of carbons rather than as double or single bonds (see Figure 5).

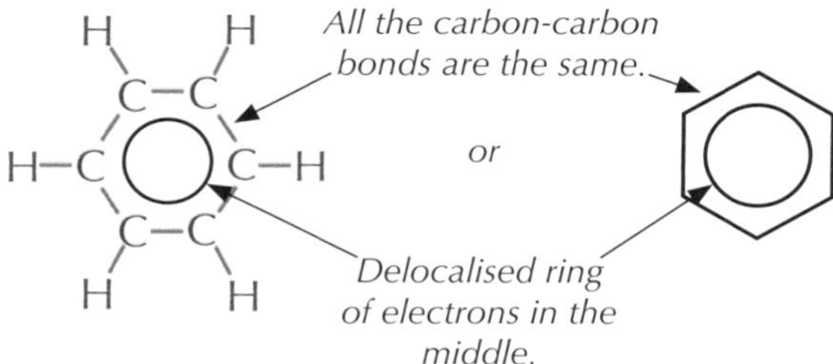

Figure 5: *The structure of benzene according to the delocalised model.*

Evidence for delocalisation

If you react an alkene with hydrogen gas, two atoms of hydrogen add across the double bond. This is called **hydrogenation**, and the enthalpy change of the reaction is the enthalpy change of hydrogenation.

Cyclohexene has one double bond. When it's hydrogenated, the enthalpy change is –120 kJ mol^{-1}. If benzene had three double bonds (as in the Kekulé structure), you'd expect it to have an enthalpy of hydrogenation of –360 kJ mol^{-1}. But the experimental enthalpy of hydrogenation of benzene is –208 kJ mol^{-1} — far less exothermic than expected (see Figure 6).

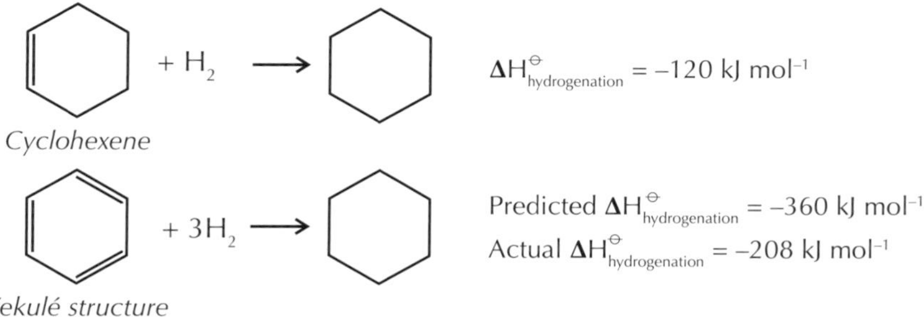

Figure 6: *Enthalpies of hydrogenation for cyclohexene and benzene.*

Tip: Check out your Year 1 notes if you're struggling to remember p-orbitals.

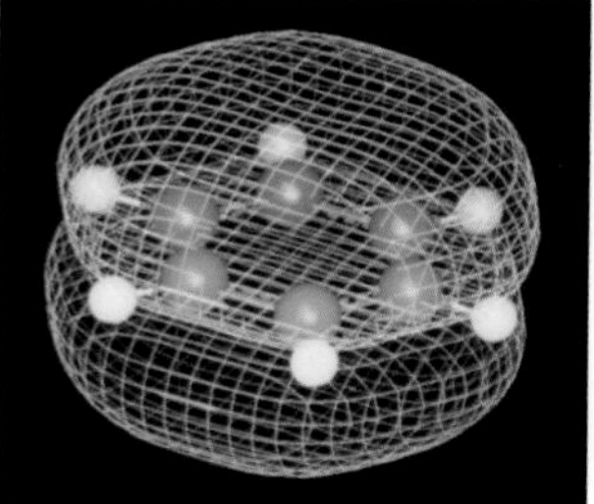

Figure 4: *A computer graphic showing the structure of benzene.*

Tip: There's lots more on models and theories in the How Science Works section (see pages 1-4).

Tip: If something's been hydrogenated it means that hydrogen has been added to it.

Tip: See page 91 for more on enthalpy.

Exam Tip
For the exam you need to know three pieces of evidence for the delocalised model of benzene — bond length data (page 164), enthalpy change data (page 165) and the fact that benzene is relatively unreactive (there's more about this coming up on page 168).

Tip: Non-aromatic molecules are called <u>aliphatic</u> molecules — don't get the terms aromatic and aliphatic mixed up.

Energy is put in to break bonds and released when bonds are made. So more energy must have been put in to break the bonds in benzene than would be needed to break the bonds in the Kekulé structure. This difference indicates that benzene is more stable than the Kekulé structure would be. This is thought to be due to the delocalised ring of electrons. In a delocalised ring the electron density is shared over more atoms, which means that the molecule is more stable.

Naming aromatic compounds

Compounds containing a benzene ring are called arenes or '**aromatic compounds**'. Aromatic compounds all contain a benzene ring. Naming them can be a bit tricky. They're named in two ways:

1. In some cases, the benzene ring is the main functional group and the molecule is named as a substituted benzene ring — the suffix is -benzene and there are prefixes to represent any other functional groups.

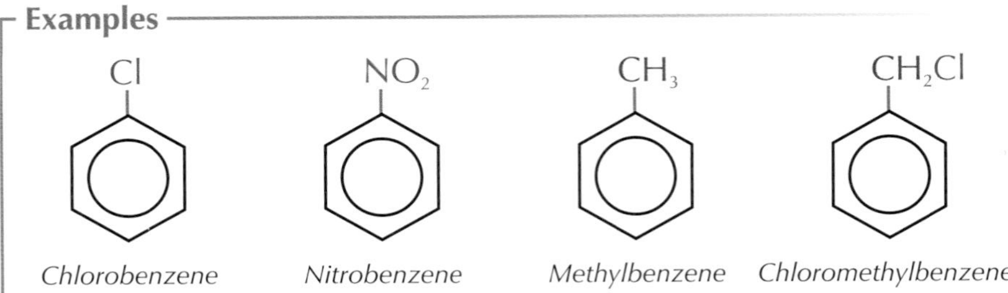

2. In other cases, the benzene ring is not the main functional group and the molecule is named as having a phenyl group (C_6H_5) attached. Phenyl- is used as a prefix to show the molecule has a benzene ring and the suffix comes from other functional groups on the molecule (e.g. -ol if it's an alcohol, -amine if it's an amine).

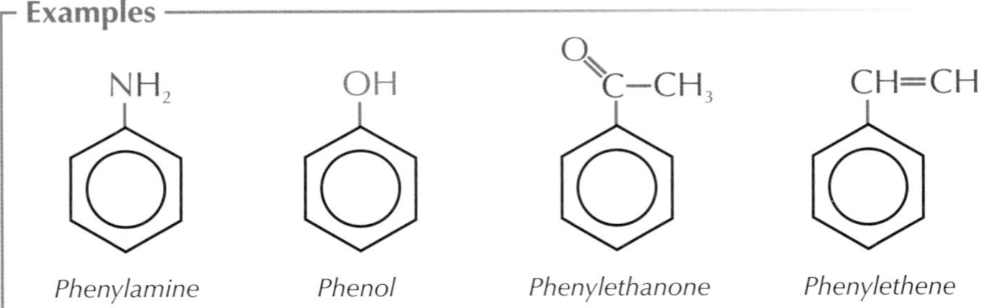

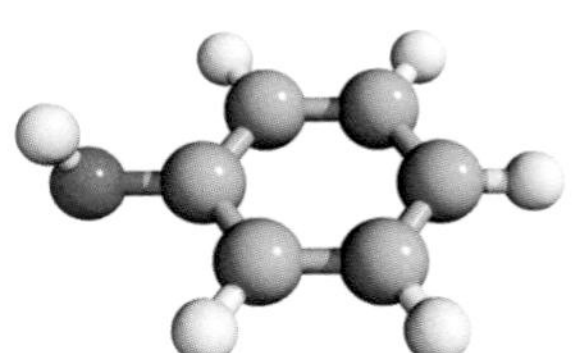

Figure 7: *A molecular model of phenol.*

Unfortunately there's no simple rule to help you remember which molecules should be something –benzene and which molecules should be phenyl–something. You just have to learn these examples.

Numbering the benzene ring

If there is more than one functional group attached to the benzene ring, you have to number the carbons to show where the groups are. If all the functional groups are the same, pick any group to start from and count round either clockwise or anticlockwise — whichever way gives the smallest numbers. If the functional groups are different, start from whichever functional group gives the molecule its suffix (e.g. the –OH group for a phenol) and continue counting round whichever way gives the smallest numbers.

Tip: If there is only one functional group you don't have to number the carbons because all the positions around the carbon ring are the same.

Examples

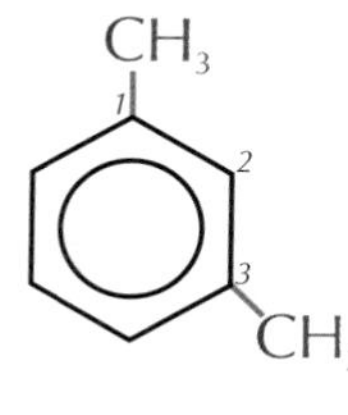

This benzene ring only has methyl groups attached so it will be named as a substituted benzene ring.

Starting from the methyl group at the top and counting clockwise there is another methyl group on carbon-3.

So this is 1,3-dimethylbenzene.

OH, Cl, 1, 2, 3, 4, Cl

This benzene ring has an OH group attached so the stem is phenol.

Starting from the OH group (the group which gives the molecule its name) and counting anticlockwise there are chlorines on carbon-2 and carbon-4.

So this is 2,4-dichlorophenol.

Exam Tip

You're unlikely to be asked to name anything too complicated in the exam. If you need to give the product of a reaction, don't try and name it unless they specifically ask for the name — giving the structure should be enough to get the marks.

Practice Questions — Application

Q1 Name these aromatic compounds:

a) NO_2, NO_2

b) OH, CH_3

c) NH_2, Cl, Cl, Cl

Q2 The graph below shows the enthalpies of hydrogenation of cyclohexene and benzene.

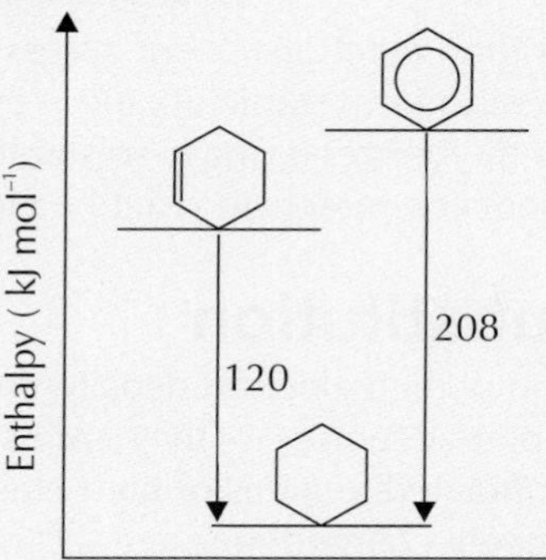

a) Describe Kekulé's model for the structure of benzene.

b) Use the information in the graph to explain why Kekulé's model for the structure of benzene was incorrect.

Practice Questions — Fact Recall

Q1 Describe the structure of benzene according to the delocalised model.

Q2 Explain how information on the bond lengths in benzene provides support for the delocalisation model.

Q3 What are aromatic compounds?

2. Reactions of Benzene

There are quite a few reactions that chemists can use to add different functional groups to benzene — that's what makes it so good as a starting point for making other compounds. Some reactions that you need to know are coming up...

Learning Objectives:

- Be able to explain the relative resistance to bromination of benzene, compared with alkenes, in terms of the delocalised electron density of the π-system in benzene compared with the localised electron density of the π-bond in alkenes.
- Be able to describe the mechanism of electrophilic substitution of aromatic compounds with a halogen in the presence of a halogen carrier.
- Be able to describe the mechanism of electrophilic substitution of aromatic compounds with concentrated nitric acid in the presence of concentrated sulfuric acid.
- Be able to interpret unfamiliar electrophilic substitution reactions of aromatic compounds, including prediction of mechanisms.

Specification Reference 6.1.1

Alkenes, benzene and addition reactions

Alkenes react easily with bromine water at room temperature. The reaction is the basis of the test for a double bond, as the orange colour of the bromine water is lost. It's an addition reaction — bromine atoms are added to the alkene.

Example

Ethene will react with bromine water in an electrophilic addition reaction.

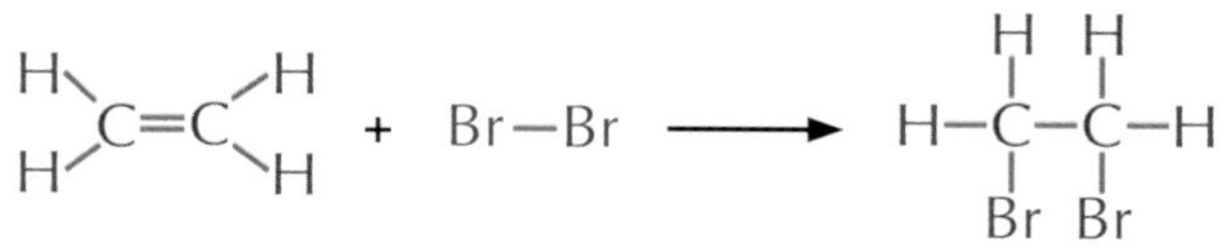

ethene *bromine* *1,2-dibromoethane*

This reaction occurs because the alkene C=C bond is a localised area of high electron density — it attracts an electrophile which adds to the double bond.

If the Kekulé structure (see page 164) was correct, you'd expect a similar reaction between benzene and bromine. In fact, to make it happen you need hot benzene and ultraviolet light — and it's still a real struggle.

This difference between benzene and other alkenes is explained by the π-system in benzene — the delocalised electron rings above and below the plane of carbon atoms (see page 165). They make the benzene ring very stable, and spread out the negative charge. So benzene is very unwilling to undergo addition reactions which would destroy the stable ring.

So, in alkenes, addition reactions occur across C=C bonds as electrophiles react with them to form stable alkanes. In benzene, this reaction isn't as favourable because the benzene ring is so stable and the negative charge is spread out. So benzene prefers to react by **electrophilic substitution**.

Electrophilic substitution

The benzene ring is a region of high electron density, so it attracts **electrophiles**. Electrophiles are electron pair acceptors — they are usually electron deficient (short of electrons) so are attracted to areas of high electron density. Common electrophiles include positively charged ions (e.g. H^+ or NO_2^+), and polar molecules (e.g. carbonyl compounds), which have a partial positive charge.

As the benzene ring's so stable, it tends to undergo electrophilic substitution reactions, which preserve the delocalised ring. The general mechanism for electrophilic substitution on a benzene ring is shown below:

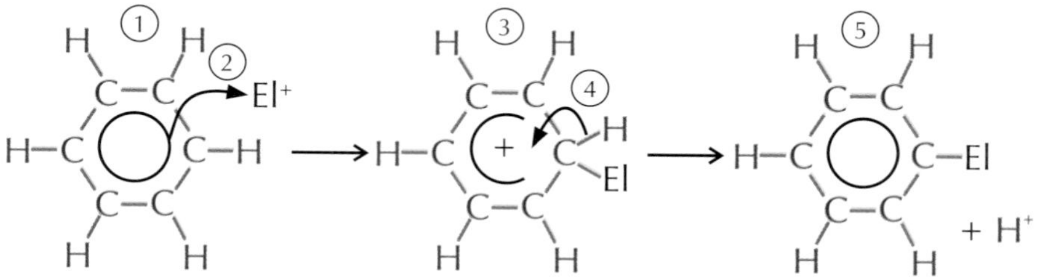

Tip: Benzene's stability and reluctance to undergo addition reactions is further evidence for the delocalised model (see page 165).

Tip: Remember, electrophiles are positively charged ions or polar molecules that are attracted to areas of negative charge.

1. The electron dense region at the centre of the benzene ring attracts an electrophile (El^+).
2. The electrophile steals a pair of electrons from the centre of the benzene ring and forms a bond with one of the carbons.
3. This partially breaks the delocalised electron ring and gives the molecule a positive charge.
4. To regain the stability of the benzene ring, the carbon which is now bound to the electrophile loses a hydrogen.
5. So you get the substitution of an H^+ with the electrophile.

You need to know two electrophilic substitution mechanisms for benzene — halogenation using a halogen carrier (below) and the nitration reaction (see page 170).

Halogenation using a halogen carrier

A **halogen carrier** can be used to add a halogen atom onto a benzene ring via an electrophilic substitution reaction. Without the halogen carrier, the electrophile doesn't have a strong enough positive charge to attack the stable benzene ring. Here's a bit about how halogen carriers work:

Halogen carriers make the electrophile stronger by accepting a lone pair of electrons from the electrophile. As the lone pair of electrons is pulled away, the polarisation in the electrophile increases and a permanent dipole forms. This makes it a much, much stronger electrophile, and gives it a strong enough charge to react with the benzene ring. Examples of halogen carriers include aluminium halides (e.g. $AlCl_3$), iron halides (e.g. $FeCl_3$) and iron.

Example

Aluminium chloride can combine with a bromine molecule to form a more reactive polarised species.

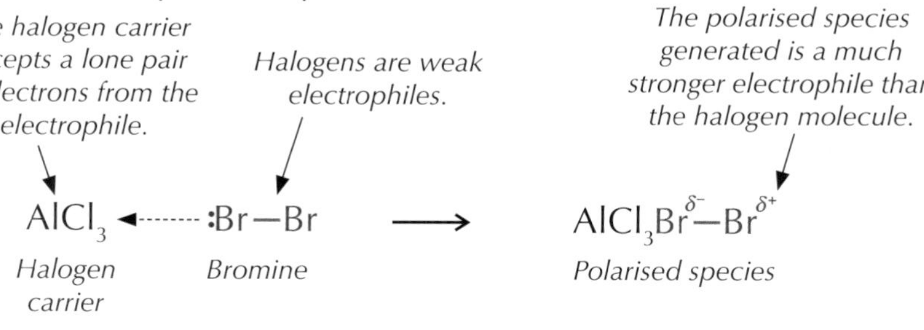
The halogen carrier accepts a lone pair of electrons from the electrophile.
Halogens are weak electrophiles.
The polarised species generated is a much stronger electrophile than the halogen molecule.
AlCl3
:Br—Br
AlCl3Br$^{\delta-}$—Br$^{\delta+}$
Halogen carrier
Bromine
Polarised species

Here's the overall equation for a halogenation reaction using a halogen carrier:

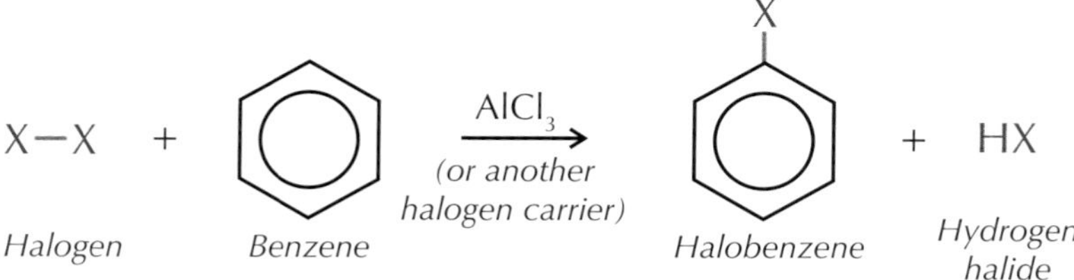
X—X
+
AlCl3
(or another halogen carrier)
X
+
HX
Halogen
Benzene
Halobenzene
Hydrogen halide

And here's an example of an electrophilic substitution reaction using a halogen carrier:

Example

Benzene will react with bromine, Br–Br, in the presence of aluminium chloride, $AlCl_3$. Br–Br is the electrophile. $AlCl_3$ acts as the halogen carrier. A Br atom is substituted in place of a H atom.

Tip: Don't get confused between electrophiles and nucleophiles. Just remember, electrophiles love electrons.

Tip: The horseshoe shape in the centre of the benzene ring in step three of the mechanism is just showing that the delocalisation of electrons around the ring has been partially broken.

Tip: It'll help if you remember the mechanism has two steps — addition of the electrophile to form a positively charged intermediate, followed by loss of H^+ from the carbon atom attached to the electrophile.

Tip: Chlorine will react with aluminium chloride in exactly the same way.

Tip: The halogen carrier acts as a catalyst — it speeds up the reaction without being used up.

Tip: The H in the hydrogen halide is the one that's been kicked off the benzene ring (and replaced with an X).

Electrons in the benzene ring are attracted to the partially positively charged bromine atom. Two electrons from the benzene bond with the bromine, the Br–Br bond is broken and a Br^- ion is formed. This partially breaks the delocalised ring and gives it a positive charge.

The negatively charged Br^- ion bonds with the hydrogen. This removes the hydrogen from the ring, forming HBr and bromobenzene.

$AlCl_3Br^{\delta-}$–$Br^{\delta+}$ + benzene → intermediate (H, Br, +) → bromobenzene + HBr + $AlCl_3$

The polarised Br–Br attacks the benzene ring. *An unstable intermediate forms.* *The H^+ ion is lost and the catalyst is reformed.*

Exam Tip

When drawing the intermediates of these reactions, make sure the horseshoe in the middle of the benzene ring comes over half way up:

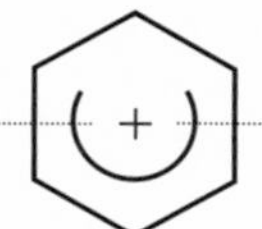

If you make it any smaller you'll lose marks.

Nitration

When you warm benzene with concentrated nitric acid and concentrated sulfuric acid, you get nitrobenzene. The overall equation for this reaction is:

$$HNO_3 + C_6H_6 \xrightarrow{H_2SO_4} C_6H_5NO_2 + H_2O$$

Nitric acid *Benzene* *Nitrobenzene*

Tip: This mechanism works for other arenes too, not just benzene. Take a look at the next page for an example.

Sulfuric acid acts as a catalyst — it helps to make the nitronium ion, NO_2^+, which is the electrophile. The formation of the nitronium ion is the first step of the reaction mechanism. The equation for this reaction is shown below:

$$\mathbf{HNO_3 + H_2SO_4 \rightarrow HSO_4^- + NO_2^+ + H_2O}$$

Exam Tip

In the exam, you might be asked to write out the equation for the formation of the nitronium ion before giving the rest of the mechanism for nitration — so make sure you learn it.

Once the nitronium ion has been formed, it can react with benzene to form nitrobenzene. This is the electrophilic substitution step in the reaction.

Here's the mechanism for the electrophilic substitution part of the reaction:

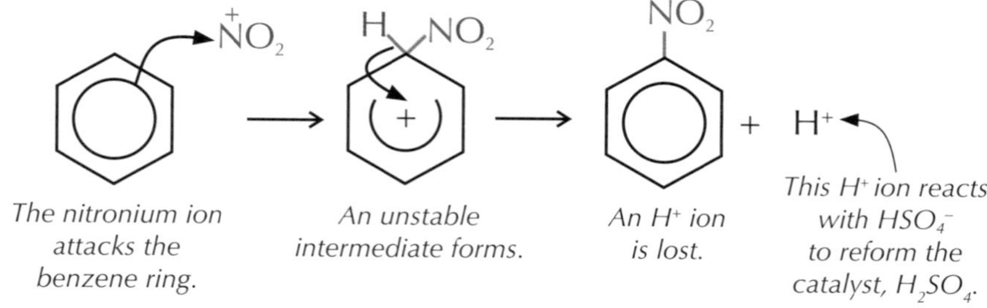
NO_2^+
H
NO_2
NO_2
+ H^+
The nitronium ion attacks the benzene ring.
An unstable intermediate forms.
An H^+ ion is lost.
This H^+ ion reacts with HSO_4^- to reform the catalyst, H_2SO_4.

Figure 1: Blocks of TNT explosives. Substitution of three hydrogen atoms for NO_2 groups on a methylbenzene molecule will produce TNT.

If you only want one NO_2 group added (mononitration), you need to keep the temperature below 55 °C. Above this temperature you'll get lots of substitutions.

Example

Warming methylbenzene with concentrated nitric acid and concentrated sulfuric acid at a temperature below 55 °C will produce 1-methyl-2-nitrobenzene.

$$C_6H_5CH_3 + NO_2^+ \rightarrow [\text{intermediate}] \rightarrow \text{1-methyl-2-nitrobenzene} + H^+$$

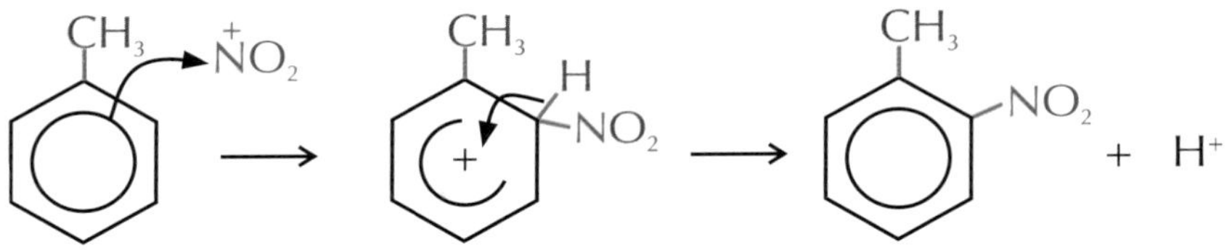

Tip: This reaction will produce some 1-methyl-2-nitrobenzene, some 1-methyl-3-nitrobenzene and some 1-methyl-4-nitrobenzene. But the majority of the product formed will be the 1-methyl-2-nitrobenzene. The reasons for this are quite complicated and you don't need to know them for A Level (but if you're interested ask your teacher...).

Practice Questions — Application

Q1 The structure of 1-chloro-2,4,6-trimethylbenzene is shown below.

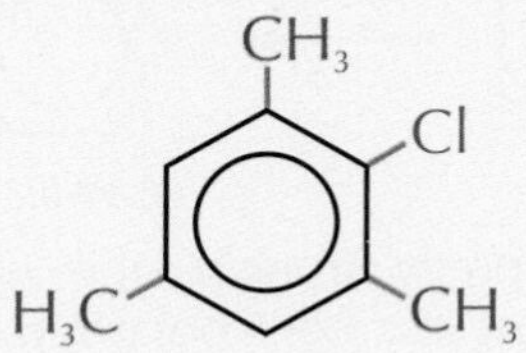

a) Write out the equation for the production of 1-chloro-2,4,6-trimethylbenzene from 1,3,5-trimethylbenzene and chlorine.

b) Suggest a suitable catalyst for this reaction.

c) Outline the mechanism for this reaction.

Q2 a) Draw the mechanism for the formation of nitrobenzene from benzene and concentrated nitric acid.

b) What two conditions are needed for this reaction to occur?

Q3 A scientist is trying to create the explosive TNT. The IUPAC name for TNT is 1-methyl-2,4,6-trinitrobenzene.

a) Draw the structure of TNT.

b) The scientist uses a nitration reaction to create TNT. What is important about the temperature that the reaction is carried out at? Explain your answer.

Exam Tip

Examiners can be tricksy and you might have to draw a mechanism for an odd looking molecule in the exam. Don't panic. All electrophilic substitution reaction mechanisms are the same — use the steps shown on the previous pages and make sure your equation is balanced and you'll be fine.

Practice Questions — Fact Recall

Q1 Explain why alkenes will react via addition reactions at room temperature but benzene won't.

Q2 Explain why electrophiles are attracted to aromatic compounds.

Q3 a) Give two examples of halogen carriers.

b) Explain why halogen carriers are needed for benzene to react with Br_2.

Q4 Write an equation to show the formation of a nitronium ion (NO_2^+) from chemical reagents.

Tip: A reagent is a chemical that can be used straight out of a bottle or container.

Learning Objective:

- Be able to describe the electrophilic substitution of aromatic compounds with a haloalkane or acyl chloride in the presence of a halogen carrier (Friedel-Crafts reaction) and its importance to synthesis by formation of a C–C bond to an aromatic ring.

Specification Reference 6.1.1

3. Friedel-Crafts

Because benzene is so stable, it's fairly unreactive. Friedel-Crafts is a useful process for overcoming this problem.

Acylation

Friedel-Crafts acylation is used to add an acyl group (–C(=O)–R) to the benzene ring. It results in the formation of a new C–C bond, which are difficult to make, and so this reaction is important in organic synthesis. Once an acyl group has been added, the side chains can be modified by further reactions to produce useful products, making this a very versatile reaction in organic synthesis. The products of the reaction are HCl and a phenylketone. The reactants need to be heated under reflux in a non-aqueous environment for the reaction to occur. Here's the equation for the reaction:

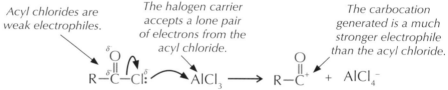

$$R{-}C({=}O){-}Cl \;+\; C_6H_6 \xrightarrow[\text{reflux}]{AlCl_3} C_6H_5{-}C({=}O){-}R \;+\; HCl$$

Acyl chloride *Benzene* *Phenylketone*

An electrophile has to have a pretty strong positive charge to be able to attack the stable benzene ring — most just aren't polarised enough. But some can be made into stronger electrophiles using a catalyst called a **halogen carrier**.

Friedel-Crafts acylation uses an acyl chloride to provide the electrophile and a halogen carrier such as $AlCl_3$. $AlCl_3$ accepts a lone pair of electrons from the acyl chloride. As the lone pair of electrons is pulled away, the polarisation in the acyl chloride increases and it forms a carbocation. This makes it a much, much stronger electrophile, and gives it a strong enough charge to react with the benzene ring. The formation of the carbocation is the first step in the reaction mechanism and is shown below:

Acyl chlorides are weak electrophiles. *The halogen carrier accepts a lone pair of electrons from the acyl chloride.* *The carbocation generated is a much stronger electrophile than the acyl chloride.*

$$R{-}\overset{\delta+}{C}({=}\overset{\delta-}{O}){-}\overset{\delta-}{Cl}{:} \;\; AlCl_3 \longrightarrow R{-}\overset{+}{C}{=}O \;+\; AlCl_4^-$$

And here's the second step in the reaction mechanism, the electrophilic substitution bit:

$$C_6H_6 + R{-}\overset{+}{C}{=}O \longrightarrow [C_6H_6{-}C({=}O)R]^+ \;\; (AlCl_4^-) \longrightarrow C_6H_5{-}C({=}O){-}R \;+\; HCl \;+\; AlCl_3$$

Electrons in the benzene ring are attracted to the positively charged carbocation. Two electrons from the benzene bond with the carbocation. This partially breaks the delocalised ring and gives it a positive charge.

The negatively charged $AlCl_4^-$ ion is attracted to the positively charged ring. One chloride ion breaks away from the aluminium chloride ion and bonds with the hydrogen. This removes the hydrogen from the ring, forming HCl. It also allows the catalyst to reform. Any acyl chloride can react with benzene in this way.

Figure 1: *Charles Friedel — co-developer of Friedel-Crafts acylation.*

Tip: A phenylketone is produced, unless R is just H, in which case an aldehyde called benzenecarbaldehyde, or benzaldehyde, is formed.

Exam Tip
You could draw out the full structure of benzene when writing out this equation — but these simplified diagrams are a lot quicker and could save you valuable time in your exam.

Example

Ethanoyl chloride reacts with benzene to produce phenyl ethanone:

$$CH_3COCl + AlCl_3 \rightarrow CH_3CO^+ + AlCl_4^-$$

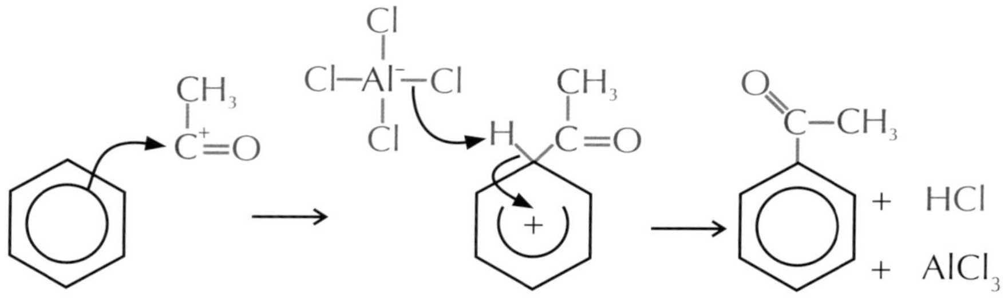

Alkylation

The Friedel-Crafts alkylation reaction works very much like the acylation reaction — except instead of putting an acyl group onto a benzene ring, it's an alkyl group. Here's the general equation for the reaction.

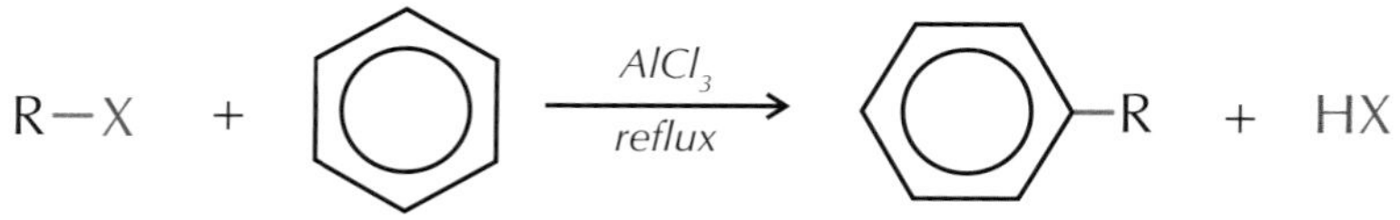

Haloalkane *Benzene* *Phenyl alkane*

And to show you just how similar alkylation is to acylation, here's an example showing the mechanism.

Example

1-chloropropane reacts with benzene to produce propylbenzene:

$$C_3H_7Cl + AlCl_3 \rightarrow C_3H_7^+ + AlCl_4^-$$

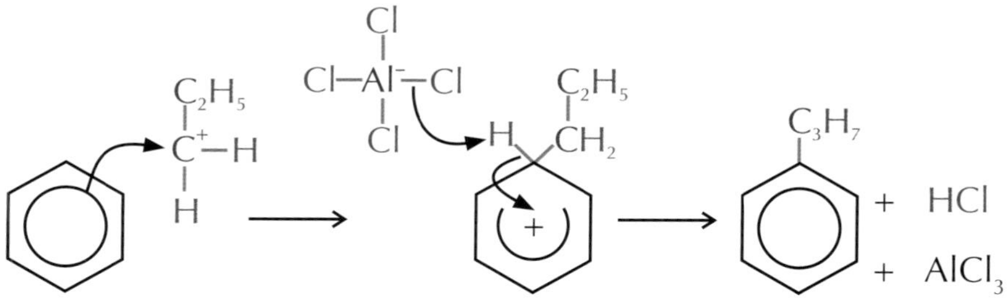

Exam Tip

When drawing these mechanisms in your exam, make sure your curly arrows clearly go from the delocalised ring of electrons to the carbocation and from the C-H bond back to the delocalised electron ring. Just drawing your curly arrows to/from the centre of benzene won't be enough to get you all the marks.

Practice Question — Application

Q1 Phenylmethanal can be produced using Friedel-Crafts acylation.

a) Write out an equation for this reaction.

b) Suggest a suitable catalyst for this reaction.

c) Name and outline the mechanism for this reaction.

Practice Questions — Fact Recall

Q1 Why are Friedel-Crafts reactions important to synthesis?

Q2 Explain the role of $AlCl_3$ in Friedel-Crafts acylation.

Learning Objectives:

- Be able to use IUPAC rules of nomenclature for systematically naming phenols.
- Understand the weak acidity of phenols shown by the neutralisation reaction with NaOH but absence of reaction with carbonates.
- Understand the relative ease of electrophilic substitution of phenol compared with benzene, in terms of electron pair donation to the π-system from an oxygen p-orbital in phenol.
- Be able to describe the electrophilic substitution reactions of phenol with bromine to form 2,4,6-tribromophenol, and with dilute nitric acid to form 2-nitrophenol.
- Understand the 2- and 4-directing effect of electron-donating groups (OH, NH_2) and the 3-directing effect of electron-withdrawing groups (NO_2) in electrophilic substitution of aromatic compounds.
- Be able to predict the substitution products of aromatic compounds by directing effects and the importance to organic synthesis.

Specification Reference 6.1.1

4. Substituted Benzene Rings

Substituted benzene rings are just benzene rings with one or more hydrogens replaced by something else. For example, phenols have an –OH group attached to a benzene ring. This gives them different properties to benzene.

Phenols

Phenol has the formula C_6H_5OH. Other phenols have various groups attached to the benzene ring.

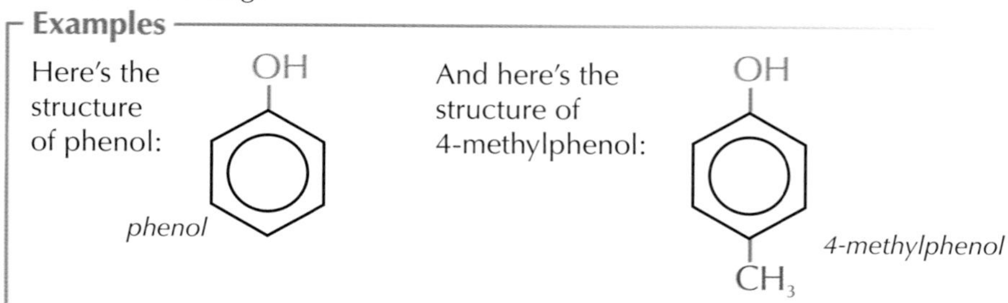

Examples
Here's the structure of phenol:
OH
phenol
And here's the structure of 4-methylphenol:
OH
CH_3
4-methylphenol

Phenols are named in a very similar way to alcohols except you add the suffix -phenol instead of -ol. You have to number the carbon atoms too — the carbon with the –OH group attached is always carbon-1.

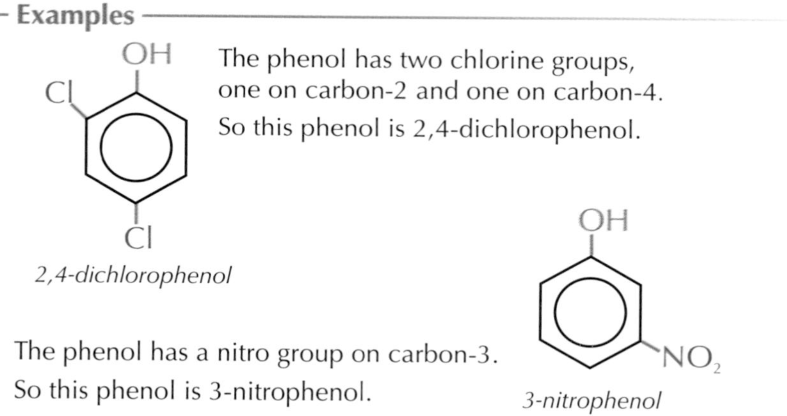

Examples
OH
Cl
Cl
2,4-dichlorophenol
The phenol has two chlorine groups, one on carbon-2 and one on carbon-4.
So this phenol is 2,4-dichlorophenol.
OH
NO_2
3-nitrophenol
The phenol has a nitro group on carbon-3.
So this phenol is 3-nitrophenol.

Phenol reactions

Phenol is weakly acidic, so will undergo typical acid-base reactions.

$$\text{acid} + \text{base} \rightarrow \text{salt} + \text{water}$$

Phenol reacts with sodium hydroxide solution at room temperature to form sodium phenoxide and water.

$$C_6H_5OH + NaOH \longrightarrow C_6H_5O^-Na^+ + H_2O$$

phenol *sodium phenoxide*

Phenol doesn't react with sodium carbonate solution though. Sodium carbonate is not a strong enough base and so can't remove the hydrogen ion from the oxygen atom.

Electrophilic substitution

If you shake phenol with orange bromine water, it will undergo an electrophilic substitution reaction — bromine atoms will be added to the phenol ring. Benzene doesn't react with bromine water (see page 168), so phenol's reaction must be to do with the OH group.

During the reaction, one of the lone pairs of electrons in a p-orbital of the oxygen atom overlaps with the delocalised ring of electrons in the benzene ring (see Figure 1) — this pair of electrons is partially delocalised into the π-system. This increases the electron density of the ring, making it more likely than benzene to be attacked by electrophiles.

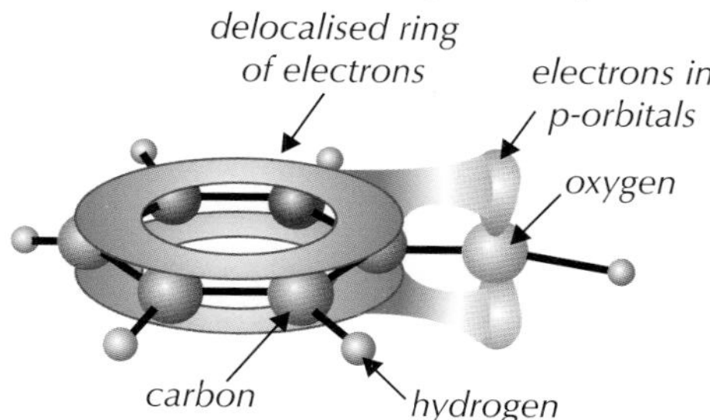

***Figure 1:** The orbital overlap during the reaction of phenol with bromine.*

Tip: EDG is an electron donating group, such as $-OH$ or $-NH_2$.

Electron-donating groups

In an unsubstituted benzene ring, all the carbon atoms are the same so electrophiles can react with any of them. If you have a substituted benzene ring, such as phenol, the functional group can change the electron density at certain carbon atoms, making them more or less likely to be react.

Electron-donating groups include $-OH$ and $-NH_2$ — they have electrons in orbitals that overlap with the delocalised ring and increase its electron density. In particular, they increase the electron density at carbons 2-, 4- and 6-, so electrophiles are most likely to react at these positions (see Figure 2).

***Figure 2:** The expected positions of electrophiles added onto a benzene with an electron-donating group.*

***Figure 3:** Bromination of phenol. The reaction of phenol with bromine produces 2,4,6-tribromophenol, a white precipitate.*

Example

The hydrogen atoms at 2, 4 and 6 are substituted by bromine atoms. The product is called 2,4,6-tribromophenol — it's insoluble in water and precipitates out of the mixture to form a white solid (see Figure 3). It smells of antiseptic.

phenol (OH; positions 2, 3, 4, 5, 6) + $3Br_2$ ⟶ 2,4,6-tribromophenol (OH; Br, Br, Br) + 3HBr

Exam Tip
Don't forget to mention electron density when you're answering exam questions on the reactivity of phenol — it's the increased electron density in the ring that allows the bromine to react with phenol.

Example

Phenol reacts with dilute nitric acid to give two isomers of nitrophenol, and water. Nitrating phenol is much easier than nitrating benzene — that requires concentrated nitric acid and a concentrated sulfuric acid catalyst. The difference is due to the activating effect of the OH group again — and that's also why you're most likely to get NO_2 groups at positions 2 and 4 on the carbon ring.

$$\text{phenol} + 2HNO_3 \xrightarrow{H_2SO_4} \text{2-nitrophenol} + \text{4-nitrophenol} + 2H_2O$$

phenol *2-nitrophenol* *4-nitrophenol*

Electron-withdrawing groups

$-NO_2$ is an electron-withdrawing group. It doesn't have any orbitals that can overlap with the delocalised ring and it's electronegative, so it withdraws electron density from the ring.

In particular, it withdraws electron density at carbons 2-,4- and 6-, so electrophiles are unlikely to react at these positions. This has the effect of directing electrophilic substitution to the 3- and 5- positions (see Figure 4).

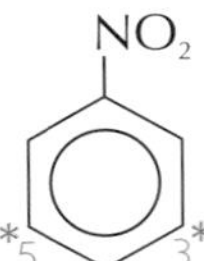

Figure 4: *The expected positions of electrophiles added onto a benzene with an electron withdrawing group.*

Knowing about electron-donating and electron-withdrawing groups means you can predict the properties of electrophilic substituted reactions.

Example

Predict the product of the following reaction:

$$C_6H_5NO_2 + AlCl_3 + CH_3CH_2Cl \longrightarrow ?$$

$-NO_2$ is electron-withdrawing, so directs electrophilic substitution to carbon 3. The product is 3-ethylnitrobenzene:

$$C_6H_4(NO_2)(CH_2CH_3) + AlCl_3 + HCl$$

The benzene ring's only substituted once, so it doesn't matter whether you number the carbons clockwise or anticlockwise. This means the 3- and the 5- positions are the same.

Tip: The $AlCl_3$ here is just a halogen carrier — see p.169.

Practice Questions — Application

Q1 Name the following phenols:

a)

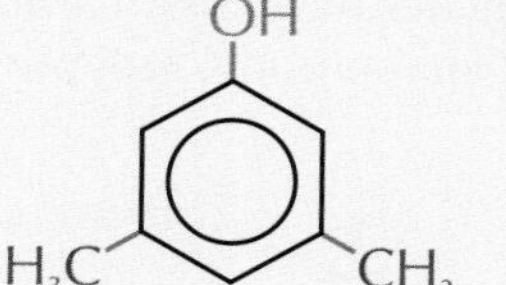

b)

OH

H_3C NO_2

c)

OH

H_3C CH_3

d)

OH

H_3C CH_3

Cl

Q2 Write equations for the reaction of each of the phenols in Q1 with $NaOH_{(aq)}$ at room temperature.

Q3 Describe what would happen if you reacted 2-methylphenol with sodium carbonate.

Q4 Trifluoromethylbenzene reacts with an excess of fluorine. The trifluoromethyl group is an electron withdrawing group. Draw the organic product of the reaction.

Tip: Remember that when you name molecules you write the prefixes in alphabetical order — for example, ethyl comes before methyl. (You ignore any di- or tri- bits though — for example, ethyl comes before dimethyl.)

Practice Questions — Fact Recall

Q1 Explain why phenol will react with bromine water but benzene won't.

Q2 Draw the structure of the organic product that forms when phenol reacts with bromine water.

Q3 a) Give an example of an electron-withdrawing group.

b) Give two examples of electron-donating groups.

5. Aldehydes and Ketones

Learning Objective:

- Be able to describe the oxidation of aldehydes using $Cr_2O_7^{2-}/H^+$ (i.e. $K_2Cr_2O_7/H_2SO_4$) to form carboxylic acids (PAG 7).

Specification Reference 6.1.2

Aldehydes and ketones are compounds that are made by oxidising alcohols. You've met aldehydes and ketones before, but just in case you can't remember, here's a quick review...

What are aldehydes and ketones?

Aldehydes and **ketones** are both **carbonyl compounds** as they both contain the carbonyl functional group, C=O. The difference is, they've got their carbonyl groups in different positions. Aldehydes have their carbonyl group at the end of the carbon chain. Ketones have their carbonyl group in the middle of the carbon chain, see Figure 1.

Carbonyl group at the end of the carbon chain. — R–C(=O)–H (Aldehyde)

Carbonyl group in the middle of the carbon chain. — R–C(=O)–R (Ketone)

Figure 1: *The difference between an aldehyde and a ketone. 'R' represents a carbon chain of any length.*

Nomenclature

Aldehydes have the suffix -al. You don't have to say which carbon the functional group is on — it's always on carbon-1. Naming aldehydes follows very similar rules to the naming of alcohols.

Tip: This is all a recap of stuff you learnt at Year 1, so if it doesn't seem familiar, have a look at your Year 1 notes.

Example

2-ethylpentanal ($CH_3CH_2CH_2CH(CH_2CH_3)CHO$)

The longest carbon chain containing the aldehyde functional group is 5 carbon atoms, so the stem is pentane.

There's an ethyl- group attached to the second carbon atom so there's a 2-ethyl- prefix.

So, the aldehyde is called 2-ethylpentanal.

The suffix for ketones is -one. For ketones with five or more carbons, you always have to say which carbon the functional group is on. (If there are other groups attached, such as methyl groups, you have to say it for four-carbon ketones too.)

Tip: When naming ketones, the carbonyl group has the highest priority. So you always number the carbons from the end that means the carbonyl group carbon has the <u>lowest number</u> possible.

Example

3-methylbutan-2-one ($CH_3CH(CH_3)COCH_3$)

The longest continuous carbon chain is 4 carbon atoms, so the stem is butane.

The carbonyl is found on the second carbon atom and there is a methyl group on the third carbon.

So, the ketone is called 3-methylbutan-2-one.

Oxidising aldehydes

Aldehydes can be easily oxidised to carboxylic acids because there's a hydrogen attached to the carbonyl group:

$$R-\overset{O}{\overset{\|}{C}}-H + [O] \longrightarrow R-\overset{O}{\overset{\|}{C}}-OH$$

You can oxidise aldehydes using the same conditions as for oxidising alcohols — you need to reflux them with an oxidising agent such as acidified potassium dichromate(VI) ($K_2Cr_2O_7/H_2SO_4$).

PRACTICAL ACTIVITY GROUP 7

The only way to oxidise a ketone would be to break a carbon-carbon bond so ketones are not easily oxidised:

```
     O
     ||
R—C—R  +  [O]  ⟶  Nothing
                    happens
```

Tip: You learnt about oxidising alcohols in Year 1 — check back if you need a reminder.

Practice Questions — Application

Q1 Name these molecules:

a)
```
   H  H  O  H
   |  |  ||  |
H—C—C—C—C—H
   |  |      |
   H  H      H
```

b)
```
  H3C  H  O
    |   |  ||
H—C—C—C—H
    |   |
  H3C  CH2
        |
       CH3
```

Q2 One of the molecules in Q1 can be oxidised with acidified potassium dichromate(VI). Which molecule can be oxidised, and what is the product of this oxidation?

Q3 Which of the carbonyls (**A**-**D**) below can be oxidised to carboxylic acids?

A
```
   H  H     H
   |  |     |
H—C—C—C—C—H
   |  |  ||  |
   H  H  O  H
```

B
```
   H  O  H
   |  ||  |
H—C—C—C—H
   |      |
   H      H
```

C
```
     H  H
     |  |
O=C—C—H
        |
        H
```

D
```
       O
       ||
    H—C
       |
H3C—C—CH3
       |
      CH3
```

Q4 Write an equation for the oxidation of ethanal to ethanoic acid.

Tip: Remember, when you're naming molecules, the carbon attached to the group that gives the molecule its name (e.g. the –OH group in an alcohol) must be included in the chain used to find the stem of the name. Even if it's not the longest carbon chain in the molecule.

Tip: You can use [O] to stand for the oxidising agent in questions 4 (phew...).

Practice Questions — Fact Recall

Q1 What is the difference between an aldehyde and a ketone?

Q2 Give the molecular formula of the negative ion that is found in potassium dichromate(VI).

Q3 What type of compound is produced when an aldehyde is oxidised?

6. Reducing Carbonyls

Learning Objectives:

- Be able to describe nucleophilic addition reactions of carbonyl compounds with $NaBH_4$ to form alcohols.
- Be able to outline the mechanism for nucleophilic addition reactions of aldehydes and ketones with $NaBH_4$.

Specification Reference 6.1.2

Reduction is the opposite of oxidation. So you can reduce aldehydes, ketones and carboxylic acids to alcohols. Read on for a bit more detail...

Reducing aldehydes and ketones

In Year 1, you saw how primary alcohols can be oxidised to produce aldehydes and carboxylic acids, and how secondary alcohols can be oxidised to make ketones. Using a reducing agent you can reverse these reactions. $NaBH_4$ (sodium tetrahydridoborate(III) or sodium borohydride) is usually the reducing agent used. But in equations, [H] is often used to indicate a hydrogen from a reducing agent. The equation below shows the reduction of an aldehyde to a primary alcohol:

$$R-C(=O)-H + 2[H] \longrightarrow R-CH(OH)-H$$

Exam Tip
When you're writing equations like this in an exam make sure you balance the [H]s as well as the molecules.

And here's the reduction of a ketone to a secondary alcohol:

$$R-C(=O)-R + 2[H] \longrightarrow R-CH(OH)-R$$

Nucleophilic addition reactions

You need to understand the reaction mechanisms for the reduction of aldehydes and ketones back to alcohols. These are **nucleophilic addition** reactions — an H^- ion from the reducing agent acts as a nucleophile and adds on to the δ^+ carbon atom of a carbonyl group. You haven't covered nucleophilic addition reactions before so here's the mechanism...

Tip: Remember that a nucleophile is an electron pair donor. They react with atoms with a positive, or partial positive, charge.

$$R-\overset{\delta+}{C}(=\overset{\delta-}{O})-H \; + \; :H^- \longrightarrow R-CH(O^-)-H \xrightarrow{\;H^{\delta+}-O^{\delta-}-H^{\delta+}\;} R-CH(OH)-H + {}^-\ddot{O}H$$

1. The C=O bond is polar so the $C^{\delta+}$ attracts the negatively charged lone pair of electrons on the H^- ion.
2. The H^- ion attacks the slightly positive carbon atom and donates its lone pair of electrons, forming a dative covalent bond with the carbon.
3. As carbon can only have 4 bonds, the addition of the H^- ion causes one of the carbon-oxygen bonds to break. This forces a lone pair of electrons from the C=O double bond onto the oxygen.
4. The negatively charged oxygen donates its lone pair of electrons to a $H^{\delta+}$ atom on a water molecule and...
5. ...the electrons from the O–H bond are donated to the $O^{\delta-}$ atom.
6. A primary alcohol and an ^-OH ion are produced.

Exam Tip
You need to be able to draw the mechanism for the reduction of any aldehyde or ketone — so make sure you understand all the steps of these nucleophilic addition reactions.

The mechanism for the reduction of a ketone is the same as for an aldehyde — you just get a secondary alcohol at the end instead of a primary alcohol:

This reaction mechanism can be applied to any aldehyde or ketone.

Example

Propanal can be reduced to propan-1-ol:

Exam Tip

You must draw the curly arrows coming from the lone pair of electrons, or from a covalent bond. If you don't — you won't get the marks for the mechanism in the exam.

Practice Questions — Application

Q1 For each molecule below, draw the mechanism for its reduction to an alcohol.

a) $CH_3CH_2CH_2CHO$

b) $CH_3COCH_2CH_2CH_2CH_3$

c) $CH_3CH_2COCH_2CH_3$

d) $(CH_3)_2C(H)-CH(CH_2CH_3)-CHO$

Q2 Write an equation for the reduction of pentan-2-one to pentan-2-ol. Use [H] to represent a reducing agent.

Q3 Write an equation for the reduction of 2-methylhexanal to an alcohol. Use [H] to represent a reducing agent.

Q4 Write an equation for the reduction of pentan-2,4-dione to an alcohol. Use [H] to represent a reducing agent.

Q5 The product of reducing molecule **X** is 2-methylbutan-1,3-diol. Write down the structural formula of molecule **X**.

Tip: Don't forget — aldehydes are reduced to primary alcohols and ketones are reduced to secondary alcohols.

Tip: Remember that all the carbonyl groups in a molecule will be reduced if you add a reducing agent.

Practice Questions — Fact Recall

Q1 Name a reducing agent which could be used to reduce an aldehyde to a primary alcohol.

Q2 Is a secondary alcohol formed by reducing an aldehyde or a ketone?

Q3 Name the reaction mechanism that takes place when ketones are reduced to alcohols.

Learning Objectives:

- Be able to describe nucleophilic addition reactions of carbonyl compounds with HCN to form hydroxynitriles.
- Be able to outline the mechanism for nucleophilic addition reactions of aldehydes and ketones with HCN.
- Be able to describe the use of 2,4-dinitrophenyl hydrazine to detect the presence of a carbonyl group in an organic compound, and identify a carbonyl compound from the melting point of the derivative (PAG 7).
- Be able to describe the use of Tollens' reagent to detect the presence of an aldehyde group, and distinguish between aldehydes and ketones, explained in terms of the oxidation of aldehydes to carboxylic acids with reduction of silver ions to silver (PAG 7).

Specification Reference 6.1.2

7. Reactions with Carbonyls

Using tests to identify unknown compounds is an important skill if you want to be a CSI agent. But it's also pretty useful in the lab when you want to know what you've made — a few tests you've got to know are covered below.

Hydrogen cyanide

Hydrogen cyanide reacts with carbonyl compounds to produce hydroxynitriles (molecules with a CN and OH group). This is another example of a nucleophilic addition reaction — a nucleophile attacks the molecule, causing an extra group to be added. Here's the mechanism for the reaction:

$R_2C^{\delta+}=O^{\delta-}$ + $:CN^-$ (1) (2) (3) ⟶ $R_2C(CN)-\ddot{O}^-$ + H^+ (4) ⟶ $R_2C(CN)OH$

1. Hydrogen cyanide's a weak acid — it partially dissociates in water to form H^+ ions and CN^- ions: $HCN \rightleftharpoons H^+ + CN^-$.
2. The CN^- ion from the HCN attacks the partially positive carbon atom and donates a pair of electrons forming a bond with the carbon.
3. A pair of electrons from the C=O double bond is pushed onto the oxygen.
4. The oxygen bonds to a H^+ ion (from either hydrogen cyanide or water) to form the hydroxyl group (OH) and a hydroxynitrile is produced.

Hydrogen cyanide is very toxic, so this reaction is normally done with acidified sodium cyanide ($NaCN/H^+$), which is less dangerous but still provides the CN^- and H^+ ions required for the reaction (see below).

Example

Propanone and acidified sodium cyanide react to form 2-hydroxy-2-methylpropanenitrile. The mechanism for this reaction is shown below:

$CH_3C^{\delta+}(=O^{\delta-})CH_3$ + $:CN^-$ ⟶ $CH_3C(CN)(\ddot{O}^-)CH_3$ + H^+ ⟶ $CH_3C(OH)(CN)CH_3$

Risk assessments

A **risk assessment** involves reviewing the hazards of the reacting chemicals, the products and any conditions needed, such as heat. You don't have to wrap yourself in cotton wool, but you do have to take all reasonable precautions to reduce the risk of an accident.

Example

Here's a bit of a risk assessment for reacting hydrogen cyanide with a carbonyl compound:

Hydrogen cyanide (HCN) is an extremely toxic gas. So to reduce the risk, acidified sodium cyanide is used instead. This is also toxic but it can be stored more safely. Acidified sodium cyanide is used for the reaction to supply both the CN^- ions and the H^+ ions needed. However, the reaction should still be done in a fume cupboard as there is still a risk of some HCN gas being released from the solution.

Figure 1: *Warning labels on the bottles of chemicals warn you if a chemical is dangerous.*

Brady's reagent

Brady's reagent is 2,4-dinitrophenylhydrazine (2,4-DNPH) (see Figure 2) dissolved in methanol and concentrated sulfuric acid.

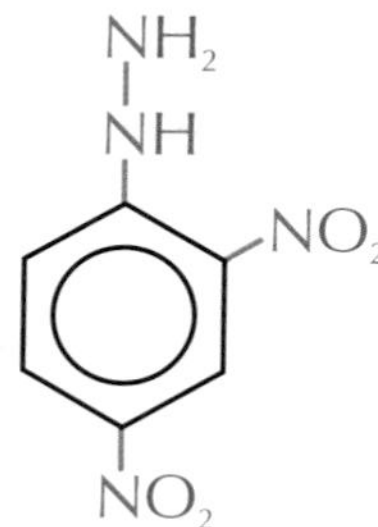

Figure 2: *Brady's reagent (2,4-dinitrophenylhydrazine).*

The 2,4-dinitrophenylhydrazine forms a bright orange precipitate if a carbonyl group is present (see Figure 3). This only happens with C=O groups, not with ones like COOH, so it only tests for aldehydes and ketones.

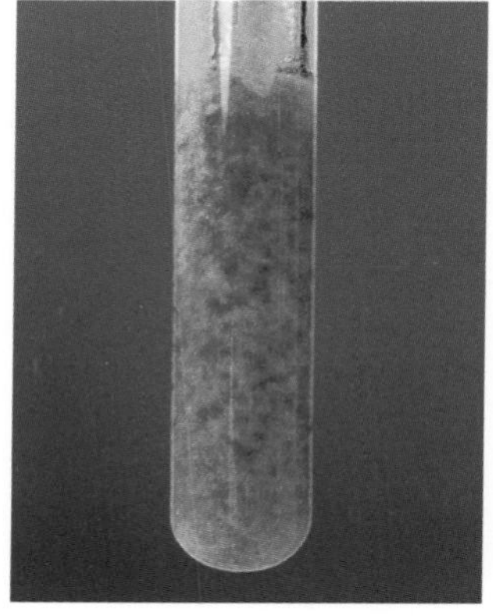

Figure 3: *Brady's reagent reacting with propanone.*

Tip: A derivative of a compound is a similar compound to the original or one that has been made from it.

Using melting points to identify unknown carbonyls

The orange precipitate is a derivative of the carbonyl compound. Each different carbonyl compound produces a crystalline derivative with a different melting point. So if you measure the melting point of the crystals and compare it against the known melting points of the derivatives, you can identify the carbonyl compound.

Example

An unknown carbonyl compound, molecule **J**, is reacted with Brady's reagent and an orange precipitate is formed. The melting point of the product was found to be 115.3 °C. Use the table below to identify molecule **J**.

Carbonyl compound	Melting point of 2,4-DNPH derivative (°C)
Propanal	156
Methylpropanal	182
Butan-2-one	115
3-methylbutan-2-one	124

Butan-2-one has a 2,4-DNPH derivative with a melting point of 115 °C. So molecule **J** must be butan-2-one.

Tip: There's more about how to find the melting point of a substance on page 228.

Tollens' reagent

PRACTICAL ACTIVITY GROUP 7

This test lets you distinguish between an aldehyde and a ketone. It uses the fact that an aldehyde can be easily oxidised to a carboxylic acid, but a ketone can't.

Remember, the only way to oxidise a ketone would be to break a carbon-carbon bond so ketones are not easily oxidised (see pages 178-179).

$$R-\overset{\overset{\displaystyle O}{\|}}{C}-R + [O] \longrightarrow \text{Nothing happens}$$

Tip: In these equations [O] is used to represent an oxidising agent.

But aldehydes can be easily oxidised to carboxylic acids because they have a hydrogen attached to the carbonyl group:

$$R-\overset{\overset{\displaystyle O}{\|}}{C}-H + [O] \longrightarrow R-\overset{\overset{\displaystyle O}{\|}}{C}-OH$$

As the aldehyde is oxidised, the oxidising agent is reduced — so a reagent is used that changes colour as it's reduced.

Tip: Silver nitrate dissolved in aqueous ammonia is sometimes called ammoniacal silver nitrate.

Tollens' reagent is a colourless solution of silver nitrate ($AgNO_3$) dissolved in aqueous ammonia. If it's heated in a test tube with an aldehyde, a silver mirror forms after a few minutes (see Figure 4). As the aldehyde is oxidised the silver ions in the Tollens' reagent are reduced, producing a silver mirror:

Colourless *Silver*

$$Ag^+_{(aq)} + e^- \rightarrow Ag_{(s)}$$

Silver ions in the Tollens' reagent are reduced.

Electrons come from the oxidation of the aldehyde.

The silver produced forms a silver mirror.

Tip: Aldehydes and ketones are flammable, so they must be heated in, e.g. a water bath, rather than over a flame. See pages 11 and 12 for more on methods of heating substances without using a naked flame.

As ketones aren't easily oxidised, they won't react with Tollens' reagent — so there'll be no colour change.

Figure 4: *Tollens' reagent. The test tube on the left shows the unreacted Tollens' reagent. The test tube on the right shows the result of a reaction with an aldehyde.*

Practice Questions — Application

Q1 a) Draw the structure of the hydroxynitrile that would be produced if 2-methylpropanal was reacted with HCN. The structure of 2-methylpropanal is shown below:

$$H-\underset{\underset{\displaystyle H}{|}}{\overset{\overset{\displaystyle H}{|}}{C}}-\underset{\underset{\displaystyle CH_3}{|}}{\overset{\overset{\displaystyle H}{|}}{C}}-\overset{\overset{\displaystyle O}{\|}}{C}-H$$

b) Draw the mechanism for this reaction.

Q2 Describe what you would observe if you reacted each of the compounds below with: a) Brady's reagent, b) Tollens' reagent.

i)
$$H-\underset{\underset{\displaystyle H}{|}}{\overset{\overset{\displaystyle H}{|}}{C}}-\underset{\underset{\displaystyle CH_3}{|}}{\overset{\overset{\displaystyle H}{|}}{C}}-\overset{\overset{\displaystyle O}{\|}}{C}-H$$

ii)
$$H-\underset{\underset{\displaystyle H}{|}}{\overset{\overset{\displaystyle H}{|}}{C}}-\underset{\underset{\displaystyle CH_3}{|}}{\overset{\overset{\displaystyle H}{|}}{C}}-\overset{\overset{\displaystyle O}{\|}}{C}-OH$$

Practice Questions — Fact Recall

Q1 What does Brady's reagent test for?

Q2 Describe how you could use Brady's reagent and melting point data to determine the identity of an unknown compound.

Q3 What is Tollens' reagent?

Q4 Give the formula of the positive ion present in Tollens' reagent.

8. Carboxylic Acids

You've met these crazy compounds before, but here's a bit more detail about them and their reactions.

Learning Objectives:

- Be able to explain the water solubility of carboxylic acids in terms of hydrogen bonding.
- Understand the reactions in aqueous conditions of carboxylic acids with metals and bases (including carbonates, metal oxides and alkalis). (PAG 7)

Specification Reference 6.1.3

What are carboxylic acids?

Carboxylic acids contain the carboxyl functional group –COOH.

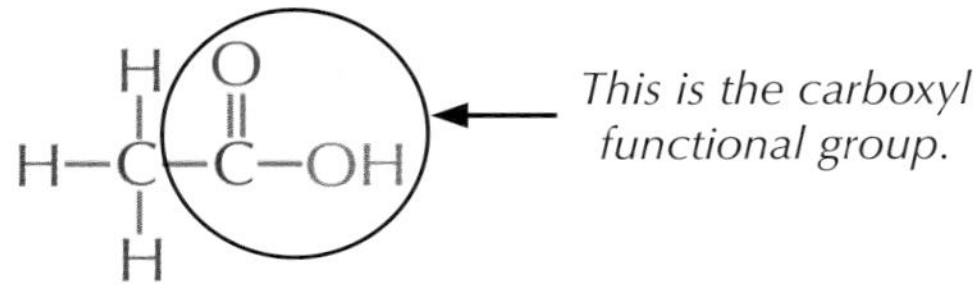

This is the carboxyl functional group.

To name them, you find and name the longest alkane chain, take off the 'e' and add '–oic acid'. The carboxyl group is always at the end of the molecule and when naming it's more important than other functional groups — so all the other functional groups in the molecule are numbered starting from this carbon.

Tip: A carboxyl group contains a carbonyl group and a hydroxyl group on the same carbon atom.

Example

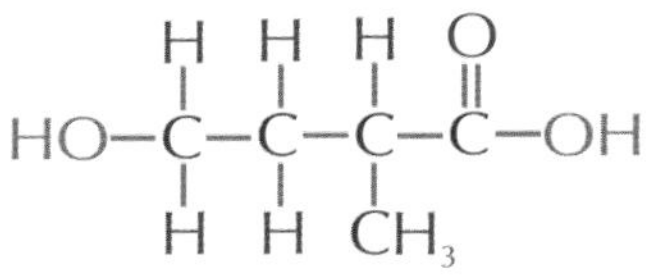

The longest continuous carbon chain is 4 carbon atoms, so the stem is butane.

Numbering of the carbons starts at the COOH group so there's a COOH group on carbon-1, a methyl group on carbon-2 and a hydroxyl group on carbon-4.

So, this is 4-hydroxy-2-methylbutanoic acid.

Tip: You've already covered how to name carboxylic acids in Year 1 so this should just be a recap.

Solubility of carboxylic acids

Carboxylic acids are **polar** molecules, since electrons are drawn from the carbon atoms in the carbonyl groups towards the more **electronegative** oxygen atoms. This makes small carboxylic acids very soluble in water, as they form hydrogen bonds with the water molecules (see Figure 1).

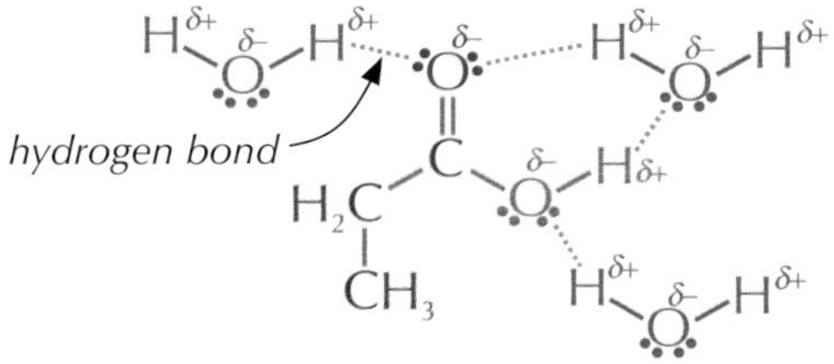

hydrogen bond

Figure 1: *Hydrogen bonds between propanoic acid and water molecules.*

Exam Tip
If you're asked to draw hydrogen bonding in an exam don't forget to mark on the lone pairs of electrons and label the hydrogen bond and all the δ+ and δ– atoms.

Dissociation of carboxylic acids

Carboxylic acids are weak acids — in water they partially dissociate into a carboxylate ion and an H^+ ion.

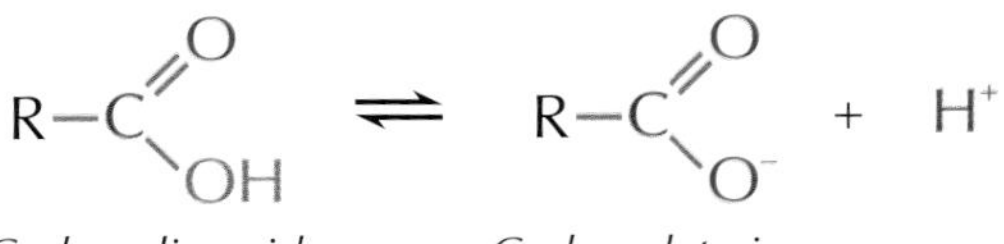

$$RCOOH \rightleftharpoons RCOO^- + H^+$$

Carboxylic acid *Carboxylate ion*

This reaction is reversible but the equilibrium lies to the left because most of the molecules don't dissociate.

Tip: See page 64 for more on the dissociation of weak acids.

Reaction with metals, carbonates and bases

Tip: Salts of carboxylic acids are called carboxylates and their names end with –oate.

PRACTICAL ACTIVITY GROUP 7

Carboxylic acids react with the more reactive metals in a redox reaction to form a salt and hydrogen gas.

Example

$$2CH_3COOH_{(aq)} + Mg_{(s)} \rightarrow (CH_3COO)_2Mg_{(aq)} + H_{2(g)}$$

Ethanoic acid — *Magnesium ethanoate*

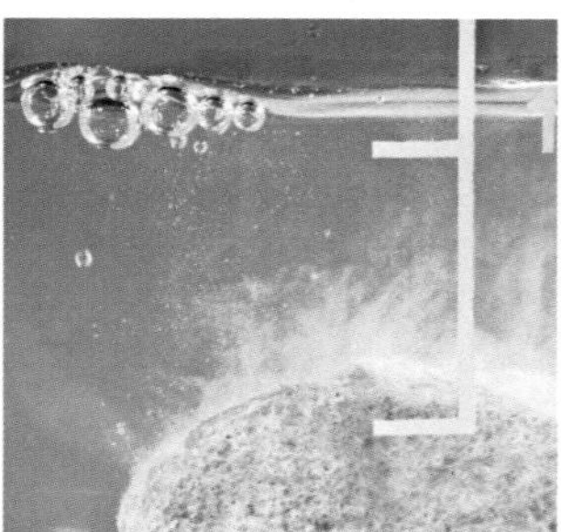

Figure 2: *Calcium carbonate reacting with ethanoic acid. The reaction gives off bubbles of carbon dioxide.*

Carboxylic acids react with carbonates (CO_3^{2-}) to form a salt, carbon dioxide and water.

Example

$$2CH_3COOH_{(aq)} + Na_2CO_{3(s)} \rightarrow 2CH_3COONa_{(aq)} + H_2O_{(l)} + CO_{2(g)}$$

Ethanoic acid — *Sodium carbonate* — *Sodium ethanoate*

In reactions between carboxylic acids and metals, and carboxylic acids and carbonates, the gas evolved during the reaction fizzes out of the solution.

Carboxylic acids are neutralised by bases (like metal oxides and hydroxides) to form a salt and water.

Example

$$2CH_3COOH_{(aq)} + MgO_{(s)} \rightarrow (CH_3COO)_2Mg_{(aq)} + H_2O_{(l)}$$

Ethanoic acid — *Magnesium ethanoate*

Tip: Simple carboxylic acids form 1– ions (e.g. CH_3COO^-). So you need one molecule to react with a 1+ ion (like sodium), but two to react with a 2+ ion (like magnesium).

Practice Questions — Application

Q1 Below are two carboxylic acids:

(i)

```
   O
   ||
H—C—OH
```

(ii)

```
   H   H   H   H   O
   |   |   |   |   ||
H—C—C—C—C—C—OH
   |   |   |   |
   H  OH   H  C2H5
```

a) Name these carboxylic acids.

b) Write a balanced equation for the reaction of carboxylic acid (i) with magnesium metal.

c) Write a balanced equation for the reaction of carboxylic acid (ii) with sodium carbonate (Na_2CO_3).

Q2 Write a balanced equation for the reaction between 2-methylbutanoic acid and $NaOH_{(aq)}$.

Exam Tip
When you're naming molecules in the exam, check your spelling. You'll lose marks even if there's only one letter out of place.

Practice Questions — Fact Recall

Q1 Write down the functional group of carboxylic acids.

Q2 Explain why small carboxylic acids, like ethanoic acid, are highly soluble in water. Draw a diagram to help you explain your answer.

Q3 Describe what you would observe if a carboxylic acid reacted with magnesium metal.

Tip: Remember to double check that your equations balance when you've finished.

9. Acyl Chlorides

Acyl chlorides are a particularly useful type of carbonyl compound because they are good starting points for making lots of different types of molecule.

Learning Objectives:

- Be able to explain the formation of acyl chlorides from carboxylic acids using $SOCl_2$.
- Understand the use of acyl chlorides in synthesis in formation of esters, carboxylic acids and primary and secondary amides.

Specification Reference 6.1.3

What are acyl chlorides?

Acyl (or acid) chlorides have the functional group COCl — their general formula is $C_nH_{2n-1}OCl$. Naming acyl chlorides is similar to naming carboxylic acids. All their names end in –oyl chloride and the carbon atoms are numbered from the end with the acyl functional group.

Example

```
   H  H  CH3 H  O
   |  |  |   |  ||
H—C—C—C—C—C—Cl
   |  |  |   |
   H  H  H   CH3
```

2,3-dimethylpentanoyl chloride

The longest continuous carbon chain is 5 carbon atoms, so the stem is pentane.

There are methyl groups on carbon-2 and carbon-3.

So, it's 2,3-dimethylpentanoyl chloride.

They're made by reacting carboxylic acids with $SOCl_2$ (thionyl chloride) — the –OH group in the acid is replaced by –Cl.

Example

$CH_3CH_2COOH + SOCl_2 \longrightarrow CH_3CH_2COCl + SO_2 + HCl$

propanoic acid → *propanoyl chloride*

Reactions of acyl chlorides

Acyl chlorides can react with a wide range of different molecules. In each of these reactions, Cl is substituted by an oxygen or nitrogen group — they're nucleophilic substitution reactions:

Reaction with water

Acyl chlorides react vigorously with cold water, producing a carboxylic acid.

```
   H  O                         H  O
   |  ||                        |  ||
H—C—C—Cl  +  H2O  ———→  H—C—C—OH  +  HCl
   |                            |
   H                            H
```

Ethanoyl chloride → *Ethanoic acid*

Figure 1: *The reaction of an acyl chloride with water. You can see the misty fumes of HCl that are being given off.*

Reaction with alcohols

Acyl chlorides react vigorously with alcohols at room temperature, producing an ester.

```
                              H     O
   H  O                       |    //        H
   |  ||                   H—C—C            |
H—C—C—Cl  +  CH3OH  ———→     |    \        |
   |                          H     O—C—H  +  HCl
   H                                   |
                                       H
```

Ethanoyl chloride + *Methanol* → *Methyl ethanoate*

This irreversible reaction is a much easier, faster way to produce an ester than esterification (see page 190).

Reaction with ammonia

Acyl chlorides react violently with ammonia at room temperature, producing a **primary amide**.

$$CH_3COCl + NH_3 \longrightarrow CH_3CONH_2 + HCl$$

Ethanoyl chloride — *Ethanamide*

Reaction with amines

Acyl chlorides react violently with **amines** at room temperature, producing a **secondary amide**.

$$CH_3COCl + CH_3NH_2 \longrightarrow CH_3CONHCH_3 + HCl$$

Ethanoyl chloride — *Methylamine* — *N-methylethanamide*

Tip: See pages 197-200 for more on amines and amides.

Reaction with phenol

Acyl chlorides react slowly with phenol at room temperature, producing an ester.

$$CH_3COCl + HO{-}C_6H_5 \rightleftharpoons CH_3COO{-}C_6H_5 + HCl$$

Ethanoyl chloride — *Phenol* — *Phenyl ethanoate*

You can normally make esters by reacting an alcohol with a carboxylic acid. Phenols react very slowly with carboxylic acids, so it's faster to use an acyl chloride.

Practice Questions — Application

Q1 Name the acyl chlorides that are shown below:

(a) $HCOCl$ (b) CH_3CH_2COCl (c) $CH_3CH(CH_3)COCl$

Q2 Write out the equations for the following reactions of the compounds in question 1:

a) The acyl chloride in Q1a with methanol.

b) The acyl chloride in Q1b with water.

c) The acyl chloride in Q1c with ammonia.

Practice Questions — Fact Recall

Q1 What is the general formula for an acyl chloride?

Q2 Write out a reaction for making ethanoyl chloride from ethanoic acid.

Q3 What are the products when an acyl chloride is reacted with:

a) water? b) an alcohol? c) ammonia? d) an amine?

10. Esters

You met esters and esterification before in Year 1, but there are a few more reactions and properties you're going to have to learn for your exams.

Naming esters

An **ester** is formed by reacting an alcohol with a carboxylic acid or a carboxylic acid derivative (see next page). So the name of an ester is made up of two parts — the first bit comes from the alcohol, and the second bit from the carboxylic acid (or its derivative).

To name an ester, just follow these steps:

1. Look at the alkyl group that came from the alcohol. This is the first bit of the ester's name.
2. Now look at the part that came from the carboxylic acid. Swap its '-oic acid' ending for 'oate' to get the second bit of the name.
3. Put the two parts together.

Example

Methanoic acid reacts with ethanol to produce the ester shown below:

1. This part of the ester came from the alcohol. It's an ethyl group, so the first part of the ester's name is ethyl-.
2. This part of the ester came from the carboxylic acid. It was methanoic acid, so the second part of the ester's name is -methanoate.
3. So this ester is ethyl methanoate.

The same rules apply even if the carbon chains are branched or if the molecule has a benzene ring attached. Always number the carbons starting from the carbon atoms in the C–O–C bond.

Examples

This ester has a methyl group that came from the alcohol so the name begins with methyl-.

There is a benzene ring that came from benzoic acid so the name ends in -benzoate.

So this is methyl benzoate.

This ester has an ethyl group that came from the alcohol and the carboxylic acid part was 2-methylbutanoic acid, so it is called ethyl 2-methylbutanoate.

Sometimes you may be asked to predict which alcohol and which carboxylic acid are needed to form a particular ester.

Example

There are 3 carbons in the part of the molecule that came from the acid so the stem is propane. This part came from propanoic acid.

There is one carbon in the section that came from the alcohol so the stem is methane. This part of the molecule came from methanol.

Learning Objectives:

- Be able to describe the esterification of carboxylic acids with alcohols in the presence of an acid catalyst.
- Be able to describe the esterification of acid anhydrides with alcohols.
- Be able to describe the hydrolysis of esters in hot aqueous acid to form carboxylic acids and alcohols.
- Be able to describe the hydrolysis of esters in hot aqueous alkali to form carboxylate salts and alcohols.

Specification Reference 6.1.3

Tip: A carboxylic acid derivative is just something that can be made from a carboxylic acid — like an acyl chloride.

Tip: Be careful — the name of the ester is written the opposite way round to the formula.

Tip: Here's how you'd number the carbons in ethyl 2-methylbutanoate:

It doesn't matter that there are two C_1s (and C_2s) because one's in the bit that came from the alcohol and the other's in the bit from the acid.

Practice Question — Application

Q1 Two esters are shown on the right:

(i) H–C(=O)–O–CH₃ (ii) C₆H₅–C(=O)–O–CH₂–CH₃

a) Name these esters

b) State a carboxylic acid and an alcohol that could have reacted to form each of these esters.

Producing esters

Producing esters using alcohols and carboxylic acids

If you heat a carboxylic acid with an alcohol in the presence of a strong acid catalyst, you get an ester. It's called an **esterification** reaction.

The H^+ ion catalyst comes from the strong acid.

$$R{-}COOH + R{-}OH \underset{\text{reflux}}{\overset{H^+}{\rightleftharpoons}} R{-}COO{-}R + H_2O$$

Carboxylic acid *Alcohol* *Ester* *Water*

Tip: This reaction is also a condensation reaction — molecules are combining by releasing a small molecule (e.g. water).

Concentrated sulfuric acid (H_2SO_4) is usually used as the acid catalyst but other strong acids such as HCl or H_3PO_4 can also be used.

Example

Ethanoic acid reacts with ethanol to produce ethyl ethanoate and water.

$$CH_3COOH + CH_3CH_2OH \overset{H^+}{\rightleftharpoons} CH_3COOCH_2CH_3 + H_2O$$

Ethanoic acid *Ethanol* *Ethyl ethanoate* *Water*

Exam Tip
These reactions are reversible, so don't forget the forwards-backwards arrows (⇌) when you're writing these equations in the exam.

The reaction is reversible, so you need to separate out the product as it forms. Small esters are very volatile, so for them you can just warm the mixture and distil off the ester. Large esters are harder to form so it's best to heat them under reflux and use distillation to separate the ester from the other compounds.

Tip: If you can't remember what distillation or refluxing apparatus look like have a look at page 226.

Producing esters from alcohols and acid anhydrides

An **acid anhydride** is made from two identical carboxylic acid molecules. The two carboxylic acid molecules are joined together via an oxygen with the carbonyl groups on either side. Acid anhydride formation is shown below.

$$2\,R{-}COOH \longrightarrow (R{-}CO)_2O + H_2O$$

An OH group and a H are removed as H_2O. *Two carboxylic acids joined via an oxygen.*

2 × Carboxylic acid *Acid anhydride*

Tip: At first glance acid anhydrides can seem a bit daunting, but when you realise that they're just two carboxylic acids stuck together they don't look quite so bad.

If you know the name of the carboxylic acid, acid anhydrides are easy to name — just take away 'acid' and add 'anhydride'. So methanoic acid gives methanoic anhydride, ethanoic acid gives ethanoic anhydride, etc.

Example

$$2\,CH_3COOH \longrightarrow (CH_3CO)_2O + H_2O$$

2 × Ethanoic acid — Ethanoic anhydride

> **Tip:** You can also produce esters from alcohols and acyl chlorides — see page 187 for this reaction.

Acid anhydrides can react with alcohols to make esters too. The acid anhydride is warmed with the alcohol. No catalyst is needed. The products are an ester and a carboxylic acid which can then be separated by distillation.

$$R^1COOCOR^2 + R^3OH \longrightarrow R^1COOR^3 + R^2COOH$$

Acid anhydride — Alcohol — Ester — Carboxylic acid

The acid anhydride is split up. *The hydrogen is lost from the alcohol.* *The pieces join up to form an ester and a carboxylic acid.*

> **Tip:** This way of making esters is simpler as the reaction isn't reversible — so you can just collect and separate the products at the end of the reaction. However, esters aren't generally produced on an industrial scale in this way as acid anhydrides are expensive.

Example

Ethanoic anhydride reacts with methanol to form methyl ethanoate and ethanoic acid.

$$(CH_3CO)_2O + CH_3OH \longrightarrow CH_3COOCH_3 + CH_3COOH$$

Ethanoic anhydride — Methanol — Methyl ethanoate — Ethanoic acid

Practice Questions — Application

Q1 Write an equation to show the formation of propyl pentanoate from an acid and an alcohol.

Q2 Write an equation to show the formation of butyl methanoate and methanoic acid from an acid anhydride and an alcohol.

> **Tip:** Yes, I know... Learning the reactions of acid anhydrides is hard. The only thing to do is practise, practise, practise until you can do them standing on your head. Hard work never killed anyone (apart from my aunt Sally — but that's another story).

Hydrolysis of esters

Hydrolysis is when a substance is split up by water — but using just water can be very slow, so an acid or an alkali is often added to speed it up. There are two types of hydrolysis of esters — acid hydrolysis and base hydrolysis. With both types you get an alcohol, but the second product in each case is different.

> **Tip:** Hydrolysis comes from two Greek words — 'hydro' meaning water and 'lysis' meaning to separate. So hydrolysis means separation using water. Simple.

Acid hydrolysis

Acid hydrolysis splits the ester into an acid and an alcohol — it's the reverse of the reaction on page 190. You have to heat the ester under reflux with a dilute acid, such as hydrochloric or sulfuric. The ester will then split back into the carboxylic acid and alcohol it was originally made from.

$$RCOOR + H_2O \underset{\text{reflux}}{\overset{H^+}{\rightleftharpoons}} RCOOH + R{-}OH$$

Ester — Water — Carboxylic acid — Alcohol

Figure 1: *A molecular model of methanol.*

Example

Acid hydrolysis of methyl ethanoate produces ethanoic acid and methanol:

$$\underset{\textit{Methyl ethanoate}}{CH_3COOCH_3} + \underset{\textit{Water}}{H_2O} \underset{\text{reflux}}{\overset{H^+}{\rightleftharpoons}} \underset{\textit{Ethanoic acid}}{CH_3COOH} + \underset{\textit{Methanol}}{CH_3OH}$$

As these acid hydrolysis reactions are reversible you need to use lots of water to push the equilibrium over to the right so you get lots of product. See pages 49-61 for more on reversible reactions and equilibria.

Base hydrolysis

For a base hydrolysis reaction you have to reflux the ester with a dilute alkali, such as sodium hydroxide. When heated, OH^- ions from the base react with the ester and you get a carboxylate salt and an alcohol.

$$\underset{\textit{Ester}}{RCOOR} + OH^- \xrightarrow{\text{reflux}} \underset{\textit{Carboxylate ion}}{RCOO^-} + \underset{\textit{Alcohol}}{R{-}OH}$$

Tip: The carboxylate ion will form a salt with the positive ion from the alkali. For example, in this reaction sodium ethanoate would be formed if the alkali used was sodium hydroxide:

$$CH_3COO^-Na^+$$

Example

Base hydrolysis of methyl ethanoate produces ethanoate ions and methanol:

$$\underset{\textit{Methyl ethanoate}}{CH_3COOCH_3} + OH^- \xrightarrow{\text{reflux}} \underset{\textit{Ethanoate ion}}{CH_3COO^-} + \underset{\textit{Methanol}}{CH_3OH}$$

Practice Question — Application

Q1 To the right is the ester methyl propanoate:

$$CH_3CH_2COOCH_3$$

Write an equation to show:

a) the acid hydrolysis of this ester,

b) the base hydrolysis of this ester.

Practice Question — Fact Recall

Q1 What two products are produced when an ester is broken down by:

a) acid hydrolysis?

b) base hydrolysis?

Section Summary

Make sure you know...

- The Kekulé and delocalised models of benzene.
- The evidence that supports the delocalised model of benzene, including its bond lengths, its enthalpy change of hydrogenation and its stability (resistance to reaction).
- How to name aromatic compounds.
- Why it's difficult to get benzene to react with bromine, compared to other alkenes.
- The mechanism for the electrophilic substitution of arenes with a halogen.
- The mechanism for the electrophilic substitution of arenes with nitric acid.
- That Friedel-Crafts reactions add acyl or alkyl groups onto benzene rings.
- What phenols are and how to name them.
- That phenol will react with bases (but not carbonates) to form salts.
- Why phenol reacts more easily with bromine than benzene does.
- How phenol reacts with bromine to form 2,4,6-tribromophenol.
- How phenol reacts with dilute nitric acid to form 2-nitrophenol.
- That an electron-donating group on a benzene ring makes electrophiles more likely to react with carbons 2, 4 and 6.
- That an electron-withdrawing group on a benzene ring makes electrophiles more likely to react with carbons 3 and 5.
- How to predict the substitution products of aromatic compounds by directing effects
- That you can oxidise alcohols using acidified potassium dichromate(VI) ($K_2Cr_2O_7/H_2SO_4$).
- That you can reduce aldehydes and ketones to alcohols using $NaBH_4$.
- The mechanism for the nucleophilic addition reaction of an aldehyde or a ketone with $NaBH_4$.
- How hydroxynitriles can be formed by nucleophilic addition reactions of carbonyl compounds with HCN.
- The mechanism for nucleophilic addition reactions of aldehydes and ketones with HCN.
- That you can use Brady's reagent (2,4-dinitrophenylhydrazine) to test for a carbonyl group.
- How to use Brady's reagent to identify a carbonyl compound from the melting point of the derivative.
- That you can use Tollens' reagent to distinguish between aldehydes and ketones.
- What carboxylic acids are and how to name them.
- That carboxylic acids are soluble in water because they form hydrogen bonds with water molecules.
- The reactions of carboxylic acids with metals, carbonates and bases.
- How acyl chlorides are formed from carboxylic acids using $SOCl_2$.
- How acyl chlorides are used in the synthesis of esters, carboxylic acids and primary and secondary amides.
- What esters are and how to name them.
- How to make esters using carboxylic acids and alcohols or acid anhydrides and alcohols.
- The reactions for the acid and base hydrolysis of esters.

Exam-style Questions

1 The longest carbon chain in a carboxylic acid is 4 carbons long. What is the maximum number of carbons that it could have?

A 4

B 6

C 8

D 10

(1 mark)

2 Which of the following could not have been the result of a Friedel-Crafts reaction?

A C_6H_5-CHO

B $C_6H_5-CH_3$

C C_6H_5-Cl

D $C_6H_5-C(=O)-CH_2CH_3$

(1 mark)

3 Esterification is the formation of an ester by reacting a carboxylic acid and an alcohol in the presence of a catalyst. Which of the following would be a suitable catalyst for this reaction?

A Dilute H_2SO_4

B Concentrated NaOH

C Dilute NH_3

D Concentrated H_3PO_4

(1 mark)

4 Phenol is reacted with iodine. Which of the following is the most likely product as a result of this reaction?

A 2-iodophenol

B 3-iodophenol

C 5-iodophenol

D 6-iodophenol

(1 mark)

5 A scientist is trying to synthesise the explosive picryl chloride (1-chloro-2,4,6-trinitrobenzene) from benzene. The synthesis route used by the scientist is shown below.

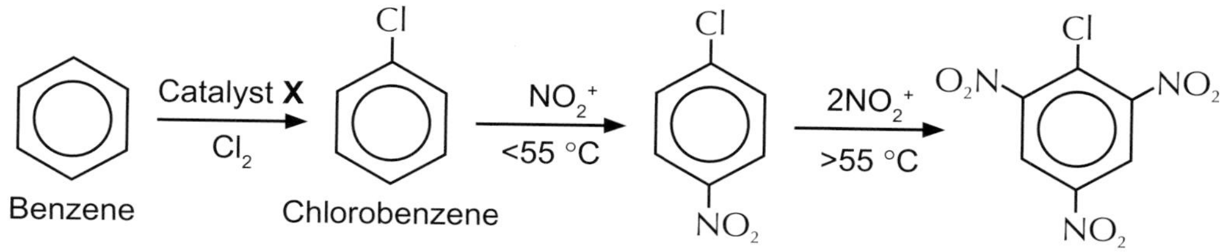

Molecule **A** Picryl chloride

(a) (i) Give the catalyst (Catalyst **X**) required to produce chlorobenzene from benzene.

(1 mark)

(ii) Describe the role of Catalyst **X** in the reaction between benzene and Cl_2.

(3 marks)

(b) (i) Write an equation for the production of the NO_2^+ ion in the second step of this synthesis.

(1 mark)

(ii) Draw the mechanism for the reaction of NO_2^+ with chlorobenzene to produce Molecule **A**.

(4 marks)

(iii) Name Molecule **A**.

(1 mark)

6 The following molecules are all derived from propane.

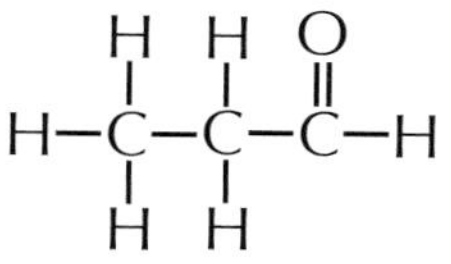

Molecule **X**

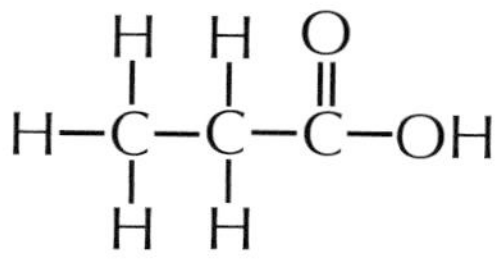

Molecule **Y**

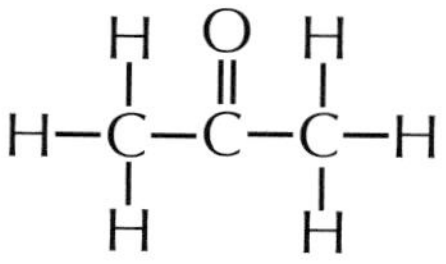

Molecule **Z**

(a) Name molecules **X**, **Y** and **Z**.

(3 marks)

(b) Molecule **Z** can be reduced to an alcohol using a hydride ion.

(i) Give a reducing agent that you could use for this reaction.

(1 mark)

(ii) Draw the mechanism for the reaction of Molecule **Z** with H^-.

(4 marks)

(iii) Write the equation for this reaction using [H] to represent the reducing agent.

(2 marks)

(c) Molecule **Y** is a carboxylic acid.

(i) Explain why Molecule **Y** is soluble in water.

(2 marks)

(ii) Write an equation for the reaction of molecule **Y** with sodium carbonate (Na_2CO_3).

(2 marks)

(d) State the reagents needed to produce molecule **X** from propan-1-ol.

(1 mark)

(e) Compounds **X**, **Y** and **Z** are treated with Brady's reagent and Tollens' reagent.

Explain how you could distinguish between molecules **X**, **Y** and **Z** using the results of these reactions.

(3 marks)

7 2-methylpropanoic acid is a carboxylic acid.

(a) Draw the structure of this carboxylic acid.

(1 mark)

(b) Carboxylic acids react with alcohols to form esters.

(i) Draw the structure of the ester that would be formed if 2-methylpropanoic acid reacted with methanol.

(1 mark)

(ii) Give the IUPAC name for this ester.

(1 mark)

(iii) Suggest a suitable catalyst for this reaction.

(1 mark)

(iv) Write an equation for the hydrolysis of this ester with dilute alkali. Show the structure of the reactants and products in your answer.

(2 marks)

1. Amines and Amides

Well, two new functional groups — I bet you're dizzy with excitement. Amines and amides are organic compounds that contain nitrogen atoms. This topic will tell you all about them...

What are amines?

If one or more of the hydrogens in ammonia (NH_3) is replaced with an organic group, you get an **amine**. If one hydrogen is replaced with an organic group, you get a primary amine — if two are replaced, it's a secondary amine, three means it's a tertiary amine and if a fourth organic group is added, it's called a quaternary ammonium ion (see Figure 1).

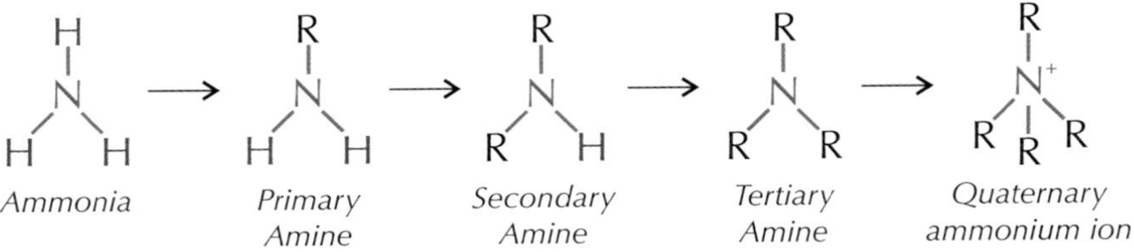

Figure 1: *Diagram showing the different types of amine.*

Naming amines

Naming amines is similar to naming other organic compounds. The suffix is -amine (or -amine ion if it's a quaternary ammonium ion). The prefix depends on what organic groups are attached. If the organic groups are all the same you also need to add di- for secondary amines, tri- for tertiary amines and tetra- for quaternary ammonium ions.

Examples

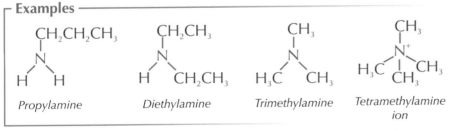

$CH_2CH_2CH_3$ on N, with H, H	CH_2CH_3 on N, with H, CH_2CH_3	CH_3 on N, with H_3C, CH_3	CH_3 on N^+, with H_3C, CH_3, CH_3
Propylamine	*Diethylamine*	*Trimethylamine*	*Tetramethylamine ion*

If the amine has more than one type of organic group attached, you list the different groups in alphabetical order.

Example

CH_3 on N, with H, $CH_2CH_2CH_3$

This is a secondary amine. It has a methyl group and a propyl group attached.

So this is methylpropylamine.

The basicity of amines

In amines, the lone pair of electrons on the nitrogen atom can form a dative (coordinate) bond with an H^+ ion — the amine donates its lone pair of electrons and 'accepts' the proton (see Figure 2).

Learning Objectives:

- Be able to explain the basicity of amines in terms of proton acceptance by the nitrogen lone pair.
- Know that amines react with dilute acids, e.g. $HCl_{(aq)}$, to form salts.
- Be able to describe the preparation of aliphatic amines by substitution of haloalkanes with excess ethanolic ammonia and amines.
- Be able to describe the preparation of aromatic amines by reduction of nitroarenes using tin and concentrated hydrochloric acid.
- Be able to recognise structures of primary and secondary amides.

Specification Reference 6.2.1, 6.2.2

Tip: If you need a reminder on the basic rules of how to name organic compounds, have a look back at your Year 1 notes.

Tip: Amines can also be named using the prefix 'amino-'. So aminopropane is the same molecule as propylamine.

Tip: Basicity is a measure of how good a base a compound is.

Exam Tip
If you're asked to draw a species that has a charge, don't forget to put the species in brackets and add the charge.

Dative bonds are covalent bonds where both electrons have come from the same atom.

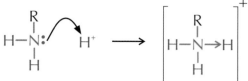

$$H{-}\overset{\overset{R}{|}}{\underset{\underset{H}{|}}{N}}{:}\ \ H^+ \longrightarrow \left[H{-}\overset{\overset{R}{|}}{\underset{\underset{H}{|}}{N}}{\rightarrow}H \right]^+$$

Figure 2: *Formation of a dative bond between a primary amine and an H⁺ ion.*

Bases can be defined as proton acceptors or electron donors. An amine can accept a proton (H^+ ion) by donating its lone pair of electrons — so amines are bases.

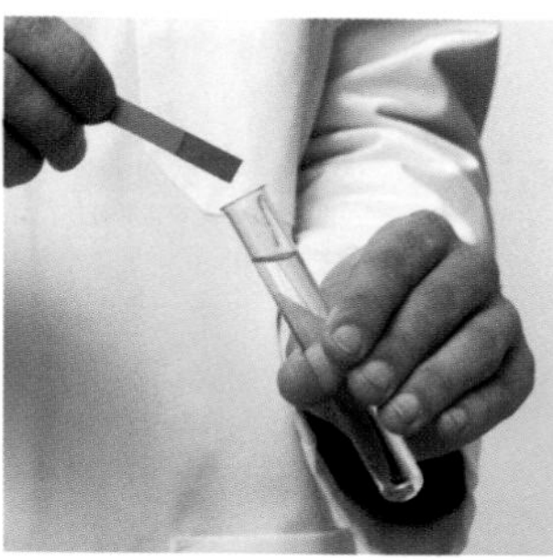

Figure 3: *A student testing an amine solution using litmus paper. The paper has turned blue, showing that the solution is alkaline.*

Amine salts

Amines are neutralised by acids to make ammonium salts.

Examples

Methylamine reacts with hydrochloric acid to form methylammonium chloride:

$$\mathbf{CH_3NH_2 + HCl \rightarrow CH_3NH_3^+Cl^-}$$

Ethylamine reacts with sulfuric acid to form diethylammonium sulfate:

$$\mathbf{2CH_3CH_2NH_2 + H_2SO_4 \rightarrow (CH_3CH_2NH_3^+)_2SO_4^{2-}}$$

Tip: Aliphatic amines are amines without a benzene ring. Amines with a benzene ring are called aromatic amines.

Producing amines

Producing aliphatic amines from haloalkanes

Amines can be made by heating a haloalkane with an excess of ethanolic ammonia (that's just ammonia dissolved in ethanol).

Tip: Producing an amine from a haloalkane and ammonia is an example of a nucleophilic substitution reaction.

Example

Ethylamine can be produced by heating bromoethane with ammonia:

$$2\,NH_3 + CH_3CH_2Br \longrightarrow H{-}\overset{\overset{H}{|}}{\underset{\underset{H}{|}}{C}}{-}\overset{\overset{H}{|}}{\underset{\underset{H}{|}}{C}}{-}\overset{\overset{H}{|}}{N}{-}H + NH_4^+Br^-$$

ammonia *bromoethane* *ethylamine*

But things aren't that simple. You'll actually get a mixture of primary, secondary and tertiary amines, and quaternary ammonium salts, as more than one hydrogen is likely to be substituted.

Tip: If you use an excess of ammonia, the bromoethane molecules are more likely to bump into ammonia molecules than secondary or tertiary amines, so you'll increase the yield of the primary amine. If you use an excess of bromoethane, the reverse is true and you'll increase the yield of the quaternary ammonium ions.

Example

When producing ethylamine you'll actually get a mixture of ethylamine, diethylamine, triethylamine and tetraethylamine ions:

$$NH_3 + CH_3CH_2Br \rightarrow \begin{cases} NH_2CH_3CH_2 \\ NH(CH_3CH_2)_2 \\ N(CH_3CH_2)_3 \\ N(CH_3CH_2)_4^+ \end{cases} + NH_4^+Br^-$$

This is because bromoethane can react with ethylamine to form diethylamine:

$$2\ H_3CH_2C{-}\overset{\displaystyle H}{\overset{|}{N}}{-}H + CH_3CH_2Br$$

ethylamine *bromoethane*

$$\downarrow$$

$$H_3CH_2C{-}\overset{\displaystyle H}{\overset{|}{N}}{-}CH_2CH_3 + CH_3CH_2NH_3^+Br^-$$

diethylamine

Diethylamine can also react with bromoethane to form triethylamine, and so on...

Tip: As long as the nitrogen atom has a lone pair of electrons, it can go on to react again.

You can separate the products using distillation if you're trying to make one particular amine.

Producing aromatic amines by reducing a nitro compound

Aromatic amines are produced by reducing an aromatic nitro compound, such as nitrobenzene. There are two steps to the method:

- First you need to heat a mixture of a nitro compound, tin metal and concentrated hydrochloric acid under reflux — this makes an aromatic ammonium salt.
- Then to turn the salt into an aromatic amine, you need to add an alkali, such as sodium hydroxide solution.

Tip: You saw how to make nitrobenzene from benzene on page 170.

Example

Phenylamine can be made by reducing nitrobenzene:

- Mixing nitrobenzene with tin (Sn) and concentrated HCl and heating under reflux produces the salt $C_6H_5NH_3^+\ Cl^-$.
- Adding NaOH to this salt then releases phenylamine.

Here's the overall equation for the reaction:

$$C_6H_5NO_2 + 6[H] \xrightarrow[\text{2. } NaOH_{(aq)}]{\text{1. Sn, conc. HCl, reflux}} C_6H_5NH_2 + 2H_2O$$

Nitrobenzene *Phenylamine*

Tip: The [H] in the equation represents the reducing agent (which is the Sn/HCl mixture here).

Amides

Amides are carboxylic acid derivatives. They contain the functional group $-CONH_2$. The carbonyl group pulls electrons away from the rest of the $-CONH_2$ group, so amides behave differently from amines. You get primary and secondary amides depending on how many carbon atoms the nitrogen is bonded to.

$$R{-}\overset{\displaystyle O}{\overset{\|}{C}}{-}\overset{\displaystyle H}{\overset{|}{N}}{-}H \qquad R_1{-}\overset{\displaystyle O}{\overset{\|}{C}}{-}\overset{\displaystyle H}{\overset{|}{N}}{-}R_2$$

primary amide *secondary amide*

Tip: In the secondary amide, one of the hydrogens attached to the nitrogen is replaced by an alkyl group.

Naming amides

Amides all have the suffix -amide. If the molecule is a primary amide, then the name is simply the stem of the carbon chain, followed by -amide.

> **Tip:** When numbering the main carbon chain in amides, the -CON- carbon is always carbon-1.

Example

```
    H   H   O
    |   |   ||
H — C — C — C — NH2
    |   |
    H   H
```

The molecule is a primary amide so the suffix is -amide. The main carbon chain (the longest chain that contains the carbonyl carbon) is three carbon atoms long, so the molecule is propanamide.

Secondary amides also have a prefix to describe the alkyl chain that is attached directly to the nitrogen atom. The prefix has the general form N-alkyl-.

> **Tip:** The N- at the start of the names of secondary amides tells you that the alkyl group is attached to the nitrogen atom.

Example

```
    H   H   O   H   H   H
    |   |   ||  |   |   |
H — C — C — C — N — C — C — H
    |   |           |   |
    H   H           H   H
```

The molecule is a secondary amide so the suffix is -amide. The main carbon chain is three carbon atoms long, so the name of the molecule is based on propanamide. The alkyl group attached to the nitrogen atom is two carbon atoms long, so it's N-ethylpropanamide.

> **Tip:** Don't forget that you list alkyl groups in alphabetical order when you're naming molecules. (You can ignore the effect of any di's or tri's at the front though.)

Practice Questions — Application

Q1 Name these amines:

a) N bonded to CH_2CH_3, H and H

b) N bonded to $CH_2CH_2CH_3$, H and $CH_2CH_2CH_3$

c) N bonded to CH_3, H_3C and CH_2CH_3

Q2 Write an equation for the reaction between trimethylamine ($N(CH_3)_3$) and hydrochloric acid.

Q3 Write an equation to show the formation of methylamine from chloromethane.

Q4 Write an equation to show the formation of 3-methylphenylamine from 3-methylnitrobenzene. The structure of 3-methylphenylamine is shown on the right.

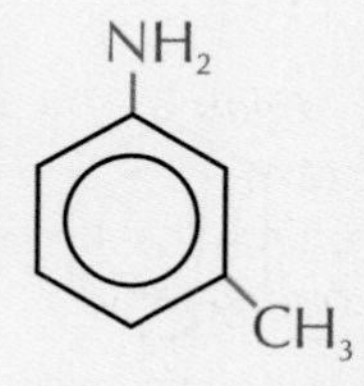

Practice Questions — Fact Recall

Q1 What is a tertiary amine?

Q2 Explain why amines can act as bases.

Q3 a) How can an amine be produced from a haloalkane?

b) Explain why a mixture of primary, secondary, tertiary and quaternary amines are produced in these reactions.

Q4 Describe how aromatic amines can be produced.

Q5 What is the functional group of a primary amide?

2. Amino Acids

Amino acids contain both an amine group and a carboxylic acid group. This leads to them having some interesting properties and reactions, as they can act as both acids and bases.

Learning Objectives:

- Know that the general formula for an α-amino acid is $RCH(NH_2)COOH$.
- Be able to describe the reactions of the carboxylic acid group in amino acids with alkalis and in the formation of esters.
- Be able to describe the reaction of the amine group in amino acids with acids.

Specification Reference 6.2.2

What are amino acids?

An **amino acid** has two functional groups — an amine group (NH_2) and a carboxyl group (COOH). There are a few different types of amino acid, but at A-level you only need to know about **α-amino acids**. α-amino acids have both groups attached to the same carbon atom — the 'α carbon'. The general formula of an α-amino acid is $RCH(NH_2)COOH$, where R is an alkyl side-chain which varies from one α-amino acid to the next. The general structure of an α-amino acid is given in Figure 1.

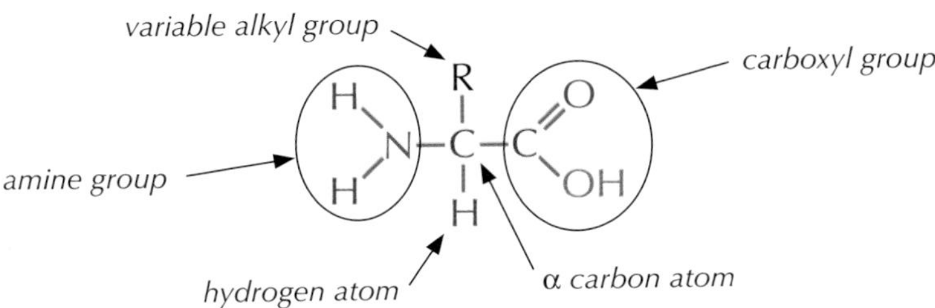

Figure 1: *The general structure of an amino acid.*

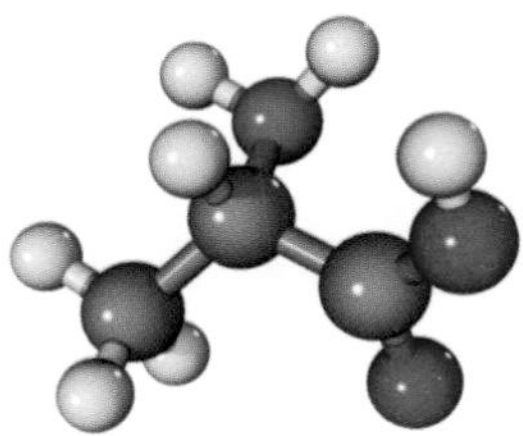

Figure 2: *Model of the amino acid alanine which has CH_3 as the R group.*

Reactions with acids and alkalis

Amino acids contain both an acidic carboxylic acid and a basic amine group. This means they can react with both acids and alkalis to form salts.

- The carboxylic acid group in an amino acid can react with an alkali to form a conjugate base — $RCH(NH_2)COO^-$. This can combine with a positive ion to form a salt. The general equation for this reaction using NaOH is:

$$H_2N{-}CH(R){-}COOH + NaOH \longrightarrow H_2N{-}CH(R){-}COO^-Na^+ + H_2O$$

Figure 3: *The reaction of an amino acid with NaOH to form its conjugate base.*

Example

Aminoethanoic acid will react with sodium hydroxide to form the salt of its conjugate base:

$$H_2N{-}CH_2{-}COOH + NaOH \longrightarrow H_2N{-}CH_2{-}COO^-Na^+ + H_2O$$

Tip: Amino acids are really important for life — they join together to form proteins in our bodies.

- Meanwhile, the amine group can react with an acid to form a salt of the conjugate acid. The general equation for this reaction using HCl is:

$$H_2N{-}CH(R){-}COOH + HCl \longrightarrow Cl^-\ H_3N^+{-}CH(R){-}COOH$$

Figure 4: *The reaction of an amino acid with HCl to form its conjugate acid.*

Tip: A conjugate base is just the deprotonated form of an acid. A conjugate acid is the protonated form of a base.

Example

Aminoethanoic acid will react with hydrochloric acid to form the salt of its conjugate acid:

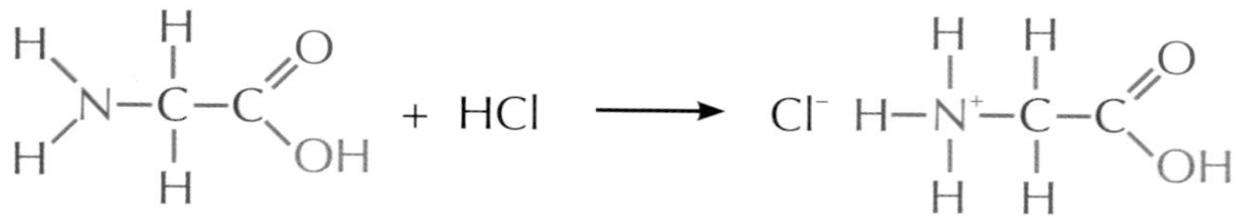

$$H_2N{-}CH_2{-}COOH + HCl \longrightarrow Cl^- \; H_3N^+{-}CH_2{-}COOH$$

Formation of esters

Tip: See page 186 for more on the reactions of carboxylic acids.

Just like other carboxylic acids, the carboxylic acid group in an amino acid can react with an alcohol in the presence of a strong acid catalyst (normally sulfuric acid) to form an ester.

Tip: Just like in the esterification of carboxylic acids, the whole of the -OR group in the new ester product comes from the alcohol.

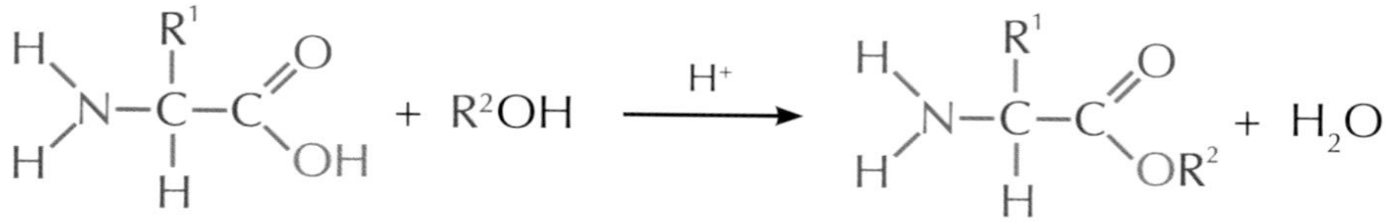

$$H_2N{-}CH(R^1){-}COOH + R^2OH \xrightarrow{H^+} H_2N{-}CH(R^1){-}COOR^2 + H_2O$$

Figure 5: *The reaction of an amino acid with an alcohol in acid to form an ester.*

Example

2-aminopropanoic acid will react with methanol in the presence of sulfuric acid to form methyl-2-aminopropanoate.

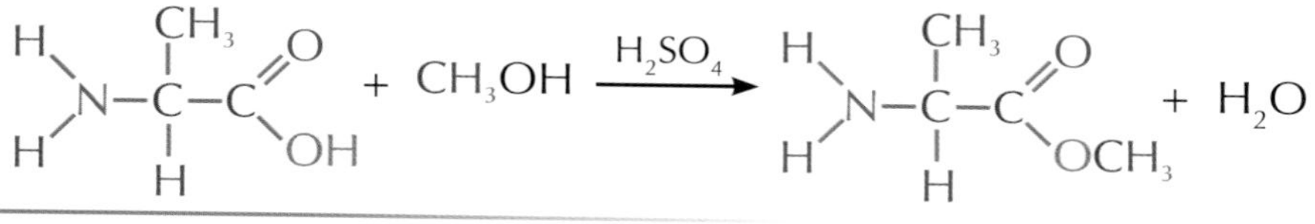

$$H_2N{-}CH(CH_3){-}COOH + CH_3OH \xrightarrow{H_2SO_4} H_2N{-}CH(CH_3){-}COOCH_3 + H_2O$$

Practice Question — Application

Q1 The amino acid valine is shown below:

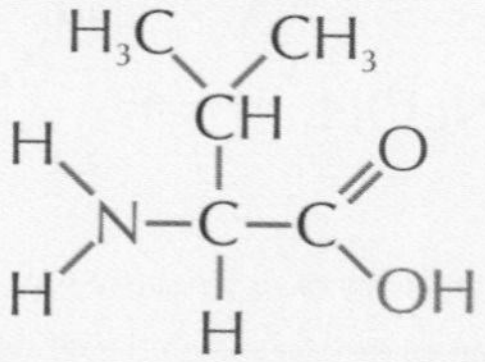

$$H_2N{-}CH(CH(CH_3)_2){-}COOH$$

a) Write an equation for the reaction between valine and sodium hydroxide.

b) Write an equation for the reaction between valine and hydrogen bromide

c) Write an equation for the reaction between valine and 2-methylpropan-1-ol in the presence of sulfuric acid.

Practice Questions — Fact Recall

Q1 What is the general formula of an α-amino acid?

Q2 What two key functional groups are found in amino acids?

Q3 Draw the general structure of an α-amino acid, using R to represent the variable group.

3. Chirality

When a carbon atom is attached to four different groups, the groups can be arranged in two different ways around the carbon atom. This leads to two stereoisomers, called optical isomers, being formed.

Learning Objectives:

- Know that optical isomerism is an example of stereoisomerism.
- Be able to describe optical isomers as non-superimposable mirror images about a chiral centre.
- Be able to identify chiral centres in a molecule of any organic compound.

Specification Reference 6.2.2

Optical isomerism

Stereoisomerism is when two molecules have the same structural formula, but a different arrangement of atoms in space. *E*/*Z* isomerism, which you met in Module 4 is one example of stereoisomerism, where atoms are arranged differently around a C=C double bond. **Optical isomerism** is another type of stereoisomerism. Optical isomers have a **chiral** carbon atom. A chiral (or asymmetric) carbon atom is one that has four different groups attached to it.

Example

The molecule below, 1-aminoethanol, has a chiral carbon atom.

H, C, H_2N, CH_3, OH

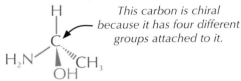

This carbon is chiral because it has four different groups attached to it.

It's possible to arrange the groups in two different ways around chiral carbon atoms so that two different molecules are made — these molecules are called **enantiomers** or optical isomers. The enantiomers are mirror images and no matter which way you turn them, they can't be superimposed.

Example — Maths Skills

Here are the two enantiomers of 1-aminoethanol. It doesn't matter how many times you turn and twist them, they can't be superimposed.

H, C, H_2N, CH_3, OH | H, C, H_3C, NH_2, OH

mirror

One enantiomer is usually labelled D and the other L — luckily you don't have to worry about which is which. Chiral compounds are very common in nature, but you usually only find one of the enantiomers — for example, all naturally occurring amino acids are L-amino acids (except glycine which isn't chiral) and most sugars are D-isomers.

Optical isomers are optically active — they rotate plane-polarised light. The two enantiomers of an optically active molecule will rotate the plane-polarised light in opposite directions. One enantiomer rotates it in a clockwise direction, and the other rotates it in an anticlockwise direction.

Drawing optical isomers

You have to be able to draw optical isomers. Just follow these steps each time:

1. Locate the chiral centre — look for the carbon atom with four different groups attached.
2. Draw one enantiomer in a tetrahedral shape — put the chiral carbon atom at the centre and the four different groups in a tetrahedral shape around it. Don't try to draw the full structure of each group — it gets confusing.

Tip: The best way to get your head around optical isomerism is to get a molecular modelling kit and have a go at making the isomers yourself. Give it a go — you know you want to.

Tip: If molecules can be superimposed, they're achiral — and there's no optical isomerism.

Figure 1: *Left-handed and right-handed scissors. These pairs of scissors are mirror images of each other — look closely and you'll see that they can't be superimposed on each other.*

3. Draw the mirror image of the enantiomer — put in a mirror line next to the enantiomer and then draw the mirror image of the enantiomer on the other side of it.

Don't panic. There are some examples below to help you get to grips with this.

Example — Maths Skills

Draw the two enantiomers of 2-hydroxypropanoic acid. The structure of 2-hydroxypropanoic acid is shown below.

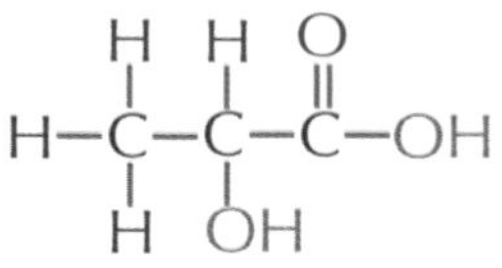

```
   H  H  O
   |  |  ||
H—C—C—C—OH
   |  |
   H  OH
```

1. Locate the chiral centre — the chiral carbon in this molecule is the carbon with the groups H, OH, COOH and CH_3 attached.

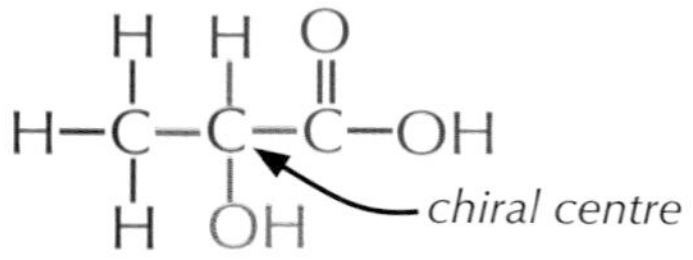

```
   H  H  O
   |  |  ||
H—C—C—C—OH
   |  |
   H  OH      ← chiral centre
```

2. Draw one enantiomer in a tetrahedral shape — put the chiral carbon atom at the centre and the groups H, OH, COOH and CH_3 in a tetrahedral shape around it.

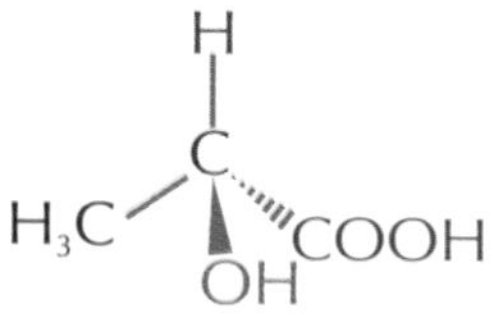

```
      H
      |
      C
 H3C /  \ COOH
     OH
```

3. Then draw its mirror image beside it.

```
      H          :          H
      |          :          |
      C          :          C
 H3C /  \ COOH   :  HOOC /  \ CH3
     OH          :       OH
```

Tip: The chiral centre and the chiral carbon atom are the same thing.

Tip: Remember, those dashed lines mean the bond is pointing into the page and the solid wedged lines mean the bond is pointing out of the page towards you.

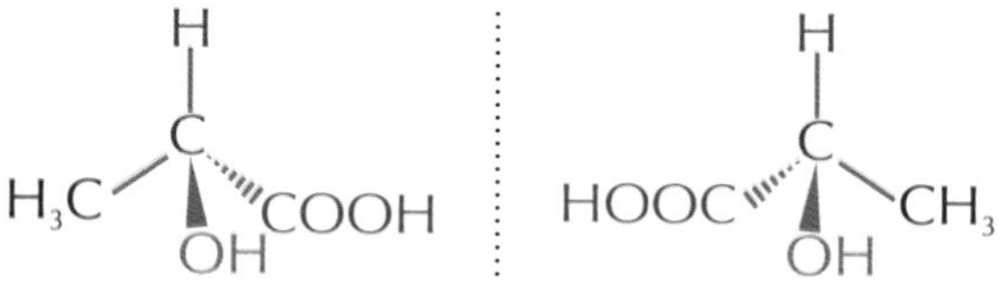

If you're just given the structural formula of a molecule in the exam, the easiest way to spot any chiral centres is to draw out the displayed formula first.

Example — Maths Skills

Draw the two enantiomers of butan-2-ol ($CH_3CH_2CHOHCH_3$).

Draw out the displayed formula and locate the chiral centre.

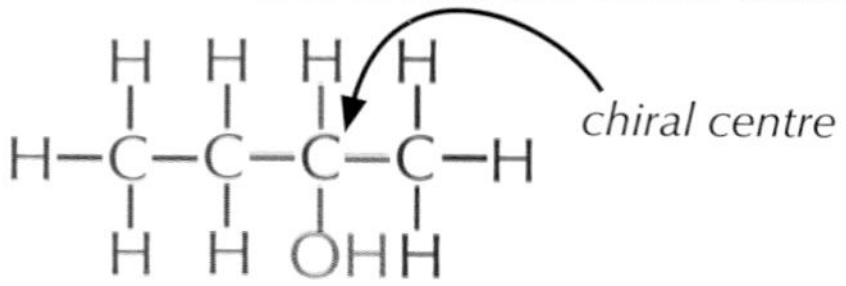

```
   H  H  H  H
   |  |  |  |        chiral centre
H—C—C—C—C—H
   |  |  |  |
   H  H  OH H
```

Draw one enantiomer in a tetrahedral shape, then draw its mirror image beside it.

```
        H            :          H
        |            :          |
        C            :          C
 H3CH2C /  \ CH3     :   H3C /  \ CH2CH3
        OH           :       OH
```

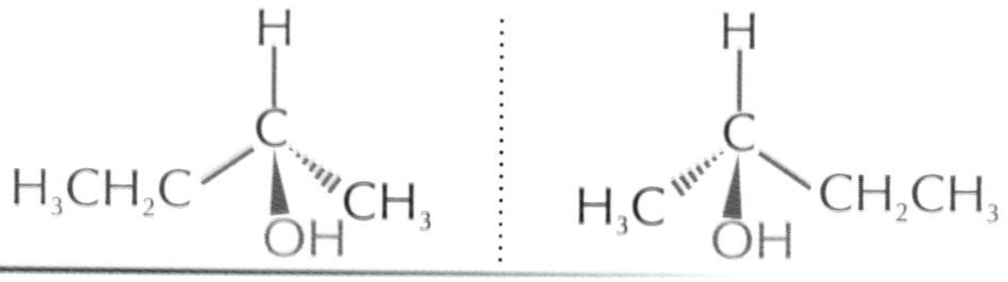

Tip: Don't forget, the chiral carbon is the one with four <u>different</u> groups attached to it.

Molecules with more than one chiral carbon

Some molecules contain more than one chiral carbon, and you need to be able to spot them all.

Example — Maths Skills

Circle all the chiral centres in the following organic molecule:

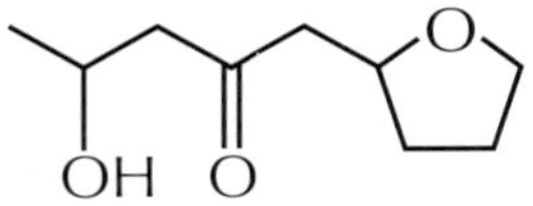

The structure shown is a skeletal formula — to find the carbon atoms that have four different groups attached, it can be helpful to show all the hydrogen atoms as well.

Although this carbon is attached to the same ring twice, it's chiral because the order of the atoms in the ring is different depending on which way round you go. Going clockwise round the ring from the chiral carbon you get -O-CH_2-CH_2-CH_2-, whilst going anticlockwise you get -CH_2-CH_2-CH_2-O-. So they count as two different groups.

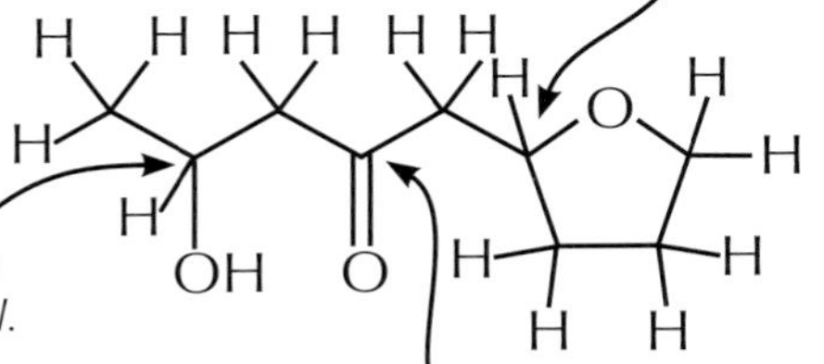

This carbon has four different groups attached, so it's chiral.

A carbon needs to have four different groups attached to be chiral, so this carbon is achiral, even though the three groups it's attached to are different.

The chiral centres are:

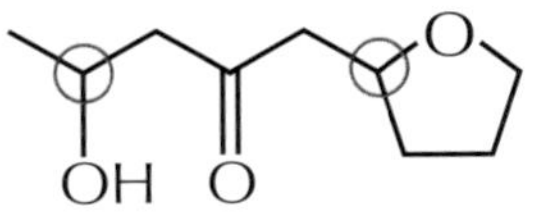

Tip: In skeletal formulas, the carbon atoms are located on the corners of the chain, and at the ends of bonds that don't have any other atoms attached. The C–H hydrogen atoms aren't shown at all.

If a molecule has more than one chiral centre, it will have more than two optical isomers.

Example — Maths Skills

The molecule on the right is 3-methylpentan-2-ol. It contains two chiral carbons, marked with asterisks.

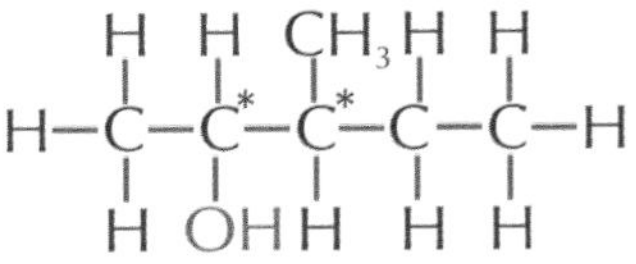

As a result, there are four different optical isomers of this molecule:

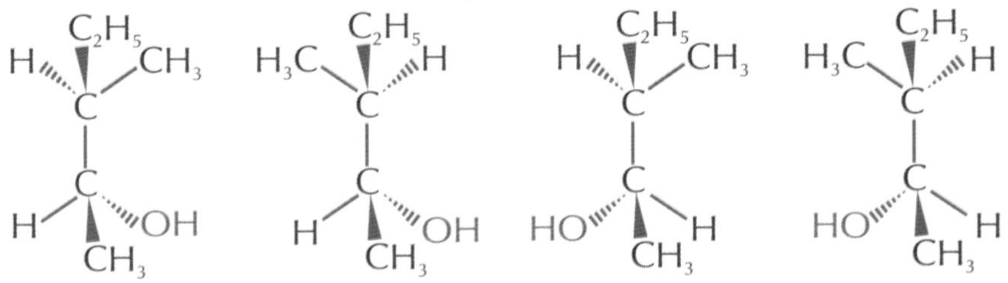

Initial drawing of molecule.

Just top carbon mirror imaged.

Just bottom carbon mirror imaged.

Both carbons mirror imaged.

Tip: To make sure you get all the enantiomers of a molecule with more than one chiral carbon, first draw out the molecule with both chiral centres shown in 3D. Then draw it again, with the mirror image of one of the chiral carbons. Then draw it with the mirror image of the other chiral carbon. Then draw it with both chiral carbons mirror imaged. If you do this every time, you'll get all the enantiomers and won't accidentally draw one twice.

Practice Questions — Application

Q1 Circle the chiral carbon(s) in each of these molecules.

a)
```
   H  H  H
   |  |  |
H—C—C—N—H
   |  |
   H  Br
```

b)
```
   H  Cl CH3 H
   |  |  |   |
H—C—C—C—C—H
   |  |  |   |
   H  H  CH3 H
```

c)
```
    H3C H  H
     |  |  |
H3C—C—C—C—H
     |  |  |
     H  Br H
```

d)
```
   H  H  H  H  Cl
   |  |  |  |  |      H
H—C—C—C—C—C=C<
   |  |  |  |         H
   H  F  H  CH3
```

Q2 Draw the two enantiomers of the following molecules.

a)
```
   H  H  H  CH3 H
   |  |  |  |   |
H—C—C—C—C—C—H
   |  |  |  |   |
   H  H  H  H   OH
```

b)
```
    Cl H
    |  |
Cl—C—C—Br
    |  |
    H  CH3
```

c)
```
     H  H
     |  |
HO—C—C—OH
     |  |
     H  F
```

d)
```
   H  H  H
   |  |  |
H—C—C—N—H
   |  |
   H  C2H5
```

Q3 Circle all the chiral centres in the following molecule:

```
        O
      /   \
     |     |
      \   /
        |
   \   /  \   /\
    \ /    \ /
     |      |\
            OH
```

Q4 Draw all the enantiomers of the following molecule:

```
   OH H  OH H  H
   |  |  |  |  |
H—C—C—C—C—C—H
   |  |  |  |  |
   CH3 H H  H  H
```

Q5 Here is an equation for the reaction between butanone and HCN.

```
   H  H  O  H                          H  H  OH
   |  |  ‖  |                          |  |  |
H—C—C—C—C—H   +   HCN   →   H—C—C—C—CH3
   |  |     |                          |  |  |
   H  H     H                          H  H  C≡N
```

butanone → *2-hydroxy-2-methylbutanenitrile*

Draw the two optical isomers that can be formed via this reaction.

Tip: When you're drawing out the enantiomers for molecules just write out the structural formula of each group — don't try and draw the displayed formula for each one or your diagram will become too confusing.

Practice Questions — Fact Recall

Q1 What is a stereoisomer?

Q2 What is optical isomerism?

Q3 What is a chiral carbon?

4. Addition Polymers

Lots of small molecules (called monomers) can join together to form really long molecules (called polymers). Polymers that are formed from alkenes are called addition polymers. You met these in Year 1 but here's a recap...

What are addition polymers?

The double bonds in alkenes or substituted alkenes can break and then join together to make long chains called **addition polymers**. It's like they're holding hands in a big line. The individual, small molecules are called **monomers** and the process of making an addition polymer is called addition polymerisation.

Example

Polyphenylethene is made by the addition polymerisation of phenylethene:

Double bond breaks — *Lots of monomers join together*

phenylethene (monomer) → *section of polyphenylethene (polymer)*

Repeat units

Addition polymers are made up of **repeat units** (a bit of molecule that repeats over and over again). The repeat unit looks very similar to the monomer but the double bond has opened out. You can spot that a polymer is an addition polymer because the main chain of the repeat unit will only contain carbon-carbon bonds. You need to be able to draw repeat units from the structure of a monomer and vice versa.

Example

Polychloroethene is made from chloroethene. To draw the repeating unit of polychloroethene, first draw the two C=C carbons, replace the double bond with a single bond and add a bond to each of the carbons. This forms the polymer backbone. Then just fill in the rest of the groups in the same way they surrounded the double bond.

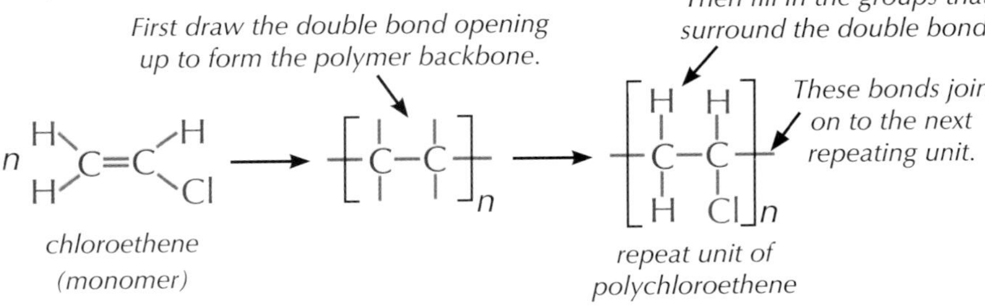
Then fill in the groups that surround the double bond.
First draw the double bond opening up to form the polymer backbone.
These bonds join on to the next repeating unit.
chloroethene (monomer)
repeat unit of polychloroethene

The polymer chain is made up of repeat units joined together, so this is what a section of the chain would look like:

Learning Objectives:

- Be able to predict whether a polymer has formed by addition polymerisation.
- Be able to predict the repeat unit of an addition polymer from a given monomer.
- Be able to predict the monomer required for a given section of an addition polymer molecule.

Specification Reference 6.2.3

Tip: Polyphenylethene is more commonly known as polystyrene.

Figure 1: *Two different forms of polyphenylethene. Expanded polyphenylethene is used in packaging and high density polyphenylethene is used to make plastic models.*

Tip: The '*n*' after the brackets is the number of repeat units in the polymer.

Exam Tip
Make sure you draw the bonds that join onto the next repeat unit, or you may lose marks in the exam.

Finding the monomer of a polymer chain

To draw the monomer from a polymer chain, you first need to find the repeat unit. For an addition polymer, the backbone of the repeat unit will always be two carbons long. Then, to find the monomer, you need to remove the empty bonds (which join on to the next repeat unit) and replace the central carbon-carbon bond with a double bond.

Example

A section of the polymer chain of polypropene is shown on the right:

```
  H  H   H  H   H  H
  |  |   |  |   |  |
--C--C---C--C---C--C--
  |  |   |  |   |  |
  H  CH3 H  CH3 H  CH3
```

The main chain of the polymer only contains carbon atoms, so it's an addition polymer. This means the repeat unit will contain a two-carbon section from the main polymer chain:

```
 [ H  H   ]             H       H
 [ |  |   ]              \     /
--C--C--      ------>     C = C
 [ |  |   ]              /     \
 [ H  CH3 ]n            H       CH3
```

repeat unit of polypropene — *propene (monomer)*

Tip: The names of polymers can be written with or without the brackets — e.g. poly(propene) or polypropene.

Practice Questions — Application

Q1 Draw the monomers that formed these repeat units:

```
a) [ Br  H  ]      b) [ H3C  H  ]      c) [ H  H       ]
   [ |   |  ]         [ |    |  ]         [ |  |       ]
  --C----C--         --C-----C--         --C--C--       
   [ |   |  ]         [ |    |  ]         [ |  |       ]
   [ H   Br ]n        [ H    OH ]n        [ H  C6H5    ]n
```

Q2 Draw the repeat units of the polymers that would be formed from these monomers:

```
a)    H     H  H        b) F       H        c)        H  OH
      |     |  |            \     /          H         |  |
   H--C--C=C--C--H           C = C            \ C=C----C--H
      |  |     |            /     \          H /       |
      H  H     H           H       Br                  H
```

Tip: There isn't too much to learn about addition polymers but you're going to need to know about condensation polymers too — they're covered in the next topic.

Q3 Teflon® is a polymer commonly used to coat non-stick pans. The structure of a short stretch of Teflon® is shown below.

```
     F  F  F  F  F  F  F  F
     |  |  |  |  |  |  |  |
-----C--C--C--C--C--C--C--C-----
     |  |  |  |  |  |  |  |
     F  F  F  F  F  F  F  F
```

Draw the structure of the monomer that's used to make Teflon®.

Figure 2: A Teflon® coated frying pan.

Practice Questions — Fact Recall

Q1 What types of monomers form addition polymers?

Q2 What name is given to the process of forming an addition polymer?

Q3 What is a repeat unit?

5. Condensation Polymers

Addition polymers aren't the only type of polymers you need to know about. You also need to know about condensation polymers — they're a bit different. Read on to find out more...

Learning Objectives:

- Be able to describe how polyesters are formed by condensation polymerisation.
- Be able to describe how polyamides are formed by condensation polymerisation.
- Be able to describe the acid and base hydrolysis of the ester groups in polyesters and the amide groups in polyamides.
- Be able to predict the repeat unit of a condensation polymer from a given monomer(s).
- Be able to predict the monomer(s) required for a given section of a condensation polymer molecule.
- Be able to predict whether a given polymer has formed by condensation polymerisation.

Specification Reference 6.2.3

What are condensation polymers?

Condensation polymerisation usually involves two different types of monomer. Each monomer has at least two functional groups. The functional groups react to form a link, creating polymer chains. Each time a link is formed, a small molecule is lost (often water) — that's why it's called condensation polymerisation.

Examples of **condensation polymers** include polyamides and polyesters. In polyesters, an ester link (–COO–) is formed between the monomers. In polyamides, amide links (–CONH–) are formed between the monomers.

Polyamides

Reactions between dicarboxylic acids and diamines make **polyamides**. The carboxyl groups of dicarboxylic acids react with the amino groups of diamines to form **amide links**. A water molecule is lost each time an amide link is formed — it's a condensation reaction (see Figure 1).

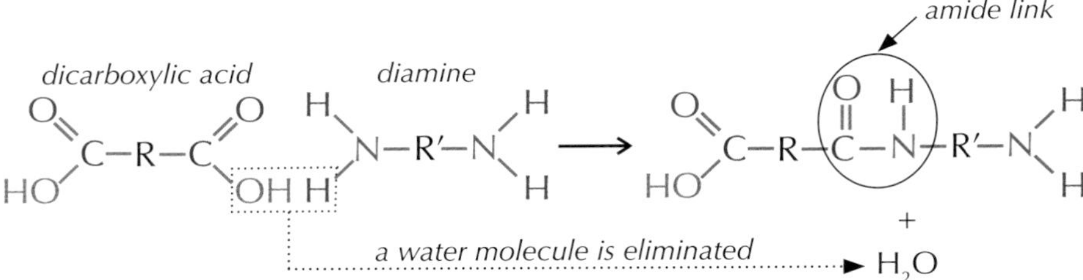

***Figure 1:** The formation of an amide link.*

Dicarboxylic acids and diamines have functional groups at both ends, which means that they can each form two amide links and long chains can form.

Examples

Nylon 6,6 is made from hexane-1,6-dicarboxylic acid and 1,6-diaminohexane:

$$n\ HOOC-(CH_2)_4-COOH + n\ H_2N-(CH_2)_6-NH_2 \rightarrow \left[-CO-(CH_2)_4-CO-NH-(CH_2)_6-NH-\right]_n + 2nH_2O$$

hexane-1,6-dicarboxylic acid — *1,6-diaminohexane* — *nylon 6,6*

Nylon fibre is very strong, elastic and quite abrasion-resistant (it won't wear away easily).

Tip: The formation of polyamides is very similar to the formation of polyesters (next page).

Figure 2: *A bulletproof vest made out of Kevlar®.*

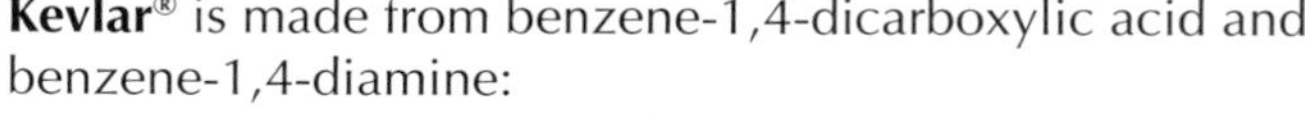

Kevlar® is made from benzene-1,4-dicarboxylic acid and benzene-1,4-diamine:

$$n\ \mathrm{HOOC{-}C_6H_4{-}COOH} + n\ \mathrm{H_2N{-}C_6H_4{-}NH_2} \longrightarrow \left[\mathrm{{-}CO{-}C_6H_4{-}CO{-}NH{-}C_6H_4{-}NH{-}}\right]_n + 2n\mathrm{H_2O}$$

benzene-1,4-dicarboxylic acid *benzene-1,4-diamine* *Kevlar®*

Kevlar® is really strong and light — five times stronger than steel. It's not stretchy, and is quite stiff. It's most famous for its use in bulletproof vests.

Polyesters

The carboxyl groups of dicarboxylic acids can react with the hydroxyl groups of diols to form **ester links** — it's another condensation reaction (see Figure 3).

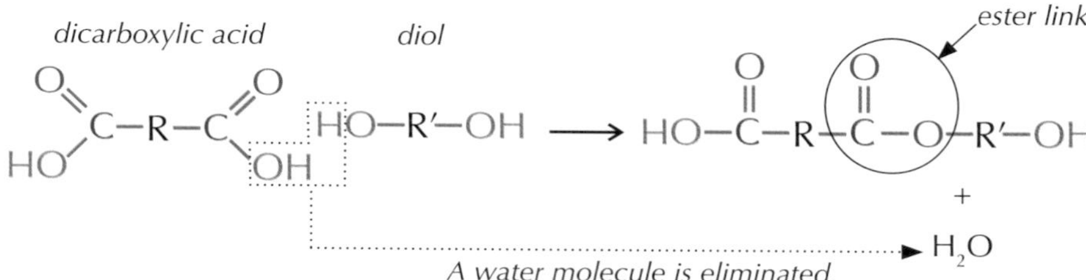

Figure 3: *The formation of an ester link.*

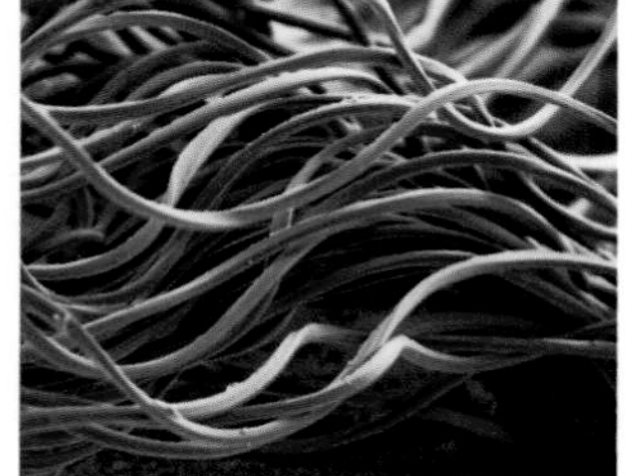

Figure 4: *Scanning electron microscopy of synthetic polyester fibres.*

Polymers that are joined by ester links are called **polyesters**. Polyester fibres are used in clothing — they are strong (but not as strong as nylon), flexible and abrasion-resistant.

Examples

Terylene™ (PET) is formed from benzene-1,4-dicarboxylic acid and ethane-1,2-diol.

$$n\ \mathrm{HOOC{-}C_6H_4{-}COOH} + n\ \mathrm{HO{-}CH_2{-}CH_2{-}OH} \longrightarrow \left[\mathrm{{-}CO{-}C_6H_4{-}CO{-}O{-}CH_2{-}CH_2{-}O{-}}\right]_n + 2n\mathrm{H_2O}$$

benzene-1,4-dicarboxylic acid *ethane-1,2-diol* *Terylene™*

Figure 5: *The containers that microwave meals come in are made of Terylene™.*

Terylene™ is used in clothes to keep them crease-free and make them last longer.

Poly(lactic acid) (PLA) is made from lactic acid (2-hydroxypropanoic acid). Lactic acid monomers can form polymers on their own because they contain both a hydroxy group and a carboxylic acid group.

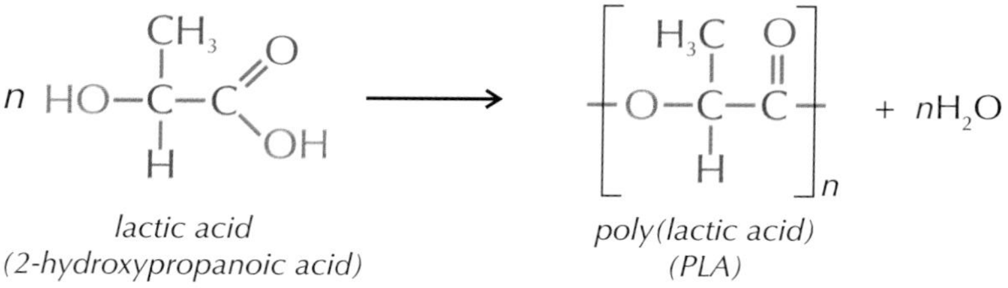

$$n\ \mathrm{HO{-}C(CH_3)(H){-}COOH} \longrightarrow \left[\mathrm{{-}O{-}C(H_3C)(H){-}C(=O){-}}\right]_n + n\mathrm{H_2O}$$

lactic acid (2-hydroxypropanoic acid) → *poly(lactic acid) (PLA)*

Poly(lactic acid) is a biodegradable and renewable polymer.

Figure 6: *A cup made out of poly(lactic acid) or PLA. This cup is made from renewable materials and is biodegradable.*

Hydrolysis of polyesters and polyamides

The ester or amide link in polyesters and polyamides can be broken down by **hydrolysis** — water molecules are added back in and the links are broken. The products of the hydrolysis are the monomers that were used to make the polymer — you're basically reversing the condensation reaction that was used to make them:

$$n\text{(monomers)} \underset{\text{hydrolysis}}{\overset{\text{condensation}}{\rightleftharpoons}} \text{polymer} + \text{water}$$

In practice, hydrolysis with just water is far too slow, so the reaction is done with an acid or a base. Polyamides will hydrolyse more easily with an acid than a base. The general equation for the acid hydrolysis of a polyamide is shown below:

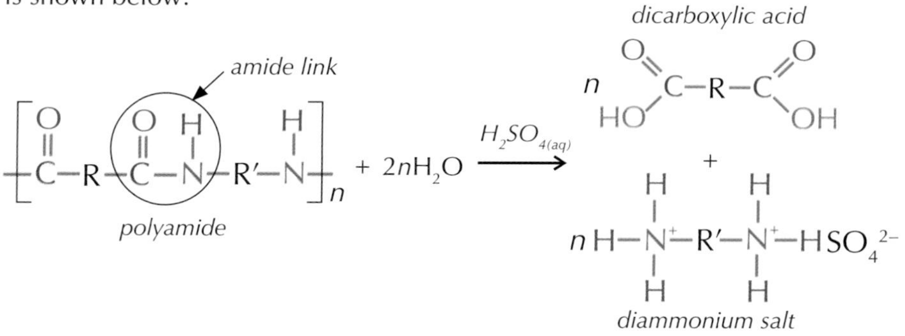

$$\left[\mathrm{{-}C(=O){-}R{-}C(=O){-}N(H){-}R'{-}N(H){-}}\right]_n + 2n\mathrm{H_2O} \xrightarrow{\mathrm{H_2SO_{4(aq)}}} n\ \mathrm{HOOC{-}R{-}COOH} + n\ \mathrm{H{-}N^+H_2{-}R'{-}N^+H_2{-}H\ SO_4^{2-}}$$

(amide link; polyamide; dicarboxylic acid; diammonium salt)

Figure 7: *The acid catalysed hydrolysis of a polyamide.*

Tip: If you were to acid hydrolyse a polyester you would get a diol instead of a diamine, but other than that the equation would be exactly the same.

Polyesters will hydrolyse more easily with a base. A metal salt of the dicarboxylic acid is formed.

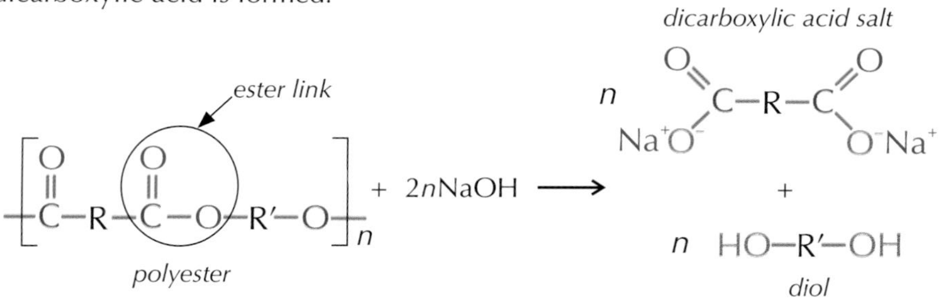

$$\left[\mathrm{{-}C(=O){-}R{-}C(=O){-}O{-}R'{-}O{-}}\right]_n + 2n\mathrm{NaOH} \longrightarrow n\ \mathrm{Na^+\,{}^-O(O=)C{-}R{-}C(=O)O^-\,Na^+} + n\ \mathrm{HO{-}R'{-}OH}$$

(ester link; polyester; dicarboxylic acid salt; diol)

Figure 8: *The base catalysed hydrolysis of a polyester.*

Tip: If you were to hydrolyse a polyamide with a base you would get a diamine instead of a diol.

Identifying monomers

In your exam, you might be asked to identify the monomers that formed a particular condensation polymer. To do this just follow these steps:

- Remove the bond in the middle of the amide or ester links — that's the bond between the C=O group and the NH group in polyamides or the bond between the C=O group and the oxygen in polyesters.
- Add OH groups on to the C=O groups to make carboxyl groups.
- For polyamides, add hydrogens on to the NH groups to make NH_2 groups
- For polyesters, add hydrogens on to the oxygens to make OH groups and add OH groups on to any terminal carbon atoms.

Example

Draw the monomers that formed this condensation polymer:

```
  [ O  H  H  O  H CH3 H ]
  [ ‖  |  |  ‖  |  |  | ]
 -[-C--C--C--C--N--C--N-]-
  [    |  |        |    ]
  [    H  H        H    ]n
```

This is a polyamide so if you remove the bond in the middle of the amide link you get:

```
O  H  H  O                  H CH3 H
‖  |  |  ‖                  |  |  |
C--C--C--C        and       N--C--N
   |  |                        |
   H  H                        H
```

Adding an OH group on to the C=O groups gives you:

```
         H  H
 O       |  |       O
  \\     |  |     //
    C----C--C----C
  /      |  |      \
HO       H  H       OH
```

And adding a hydrogen on to each of the NH groups gives you:

```
         CH3
H        |        H
  \      |      /
    N----C----N
  /      |      \
H        H        H
```

So these must be the monomers that joined to form the polymer.

Tip: This example is a polyamide. You do exactly the same for a polyester but you end up with a dicarboxylic acid and a diol.

Exam Tip
Don't be caught out — there won't necessarily be two different monomers. There could be one monomer with a COOH <u>and</u> an NH_2 group on it.

Finding repeat units from monomers

If you know the formulas of a pair of monomers that react together in a condensation polymerisation reaction, you can work out the repeat unit of the condensation polymer that they would form. Here are the steps you should take:

- Draw out the two monomer molecules next to each other.
- Remove an OH from the dicarboxylic acid, and an H from the nitrogen atom in the diamine — that gives you a water molecule.
- Join the C and the N together to make an amide link.
- Take another H and OH off the ends of your molecule.
- Draw brackets around your structure, with the bonds at the ends of the structure extending through the brackets. There's your repeat unit.

Example

Draw the repeat unit of the condensation polymer that is made from 1,4-diaminobutane, $H_2N(CH_2)_4NH_2$, and decanedioic acid, $HOOC(CH_2)_8COOH$.

If you draw out the monomers next to each other, this makes it easier to see which groups will be lost to form the water molecule:

$$H_2N-(CH_2)_4-NH_2 \quad + \quad HO-C(=O)-(CH_2)_8-C(=O)-OH$$

Draw a bond between the C and the N that have lost groups to the water molecule:

$$H-N(H)-(CH_2)_4-\underbrace{N(H)-C(=O)}_{\text{amide link}}-(CH_2)_8-C(=O)-OH$$

To get the repeat unit, all that needs to be done now is to remove another -OH and -H from the groups at the ends of the molecule and add brackets. Add an '*n*' after the brackets, too.

$$\left[N(H)-(CH_2)_4-N(H)-C(=O)-(CH_2)_8-C(=O) \right]_n$$

If you start by drawing the monomers the other way round, your repeat unit may end up looking slightly different:

$$HO-C(=O)-(CH_2)_8-C(=O)-OH \quad + \quad H-N(H)-(CH_2)_4-N(H)-H$$

$$\downarrow$$

$$\left[C(=O)-(CH_2)_8-C(=O)-N(H)-(CH_2)_4-N(H) \right]_n$$

Tip: Even if you've got a dicarboxylic acid and a diol, the -OH group is always lost from the carboxylic acid.

Tip: You could have a monomer that contains an acyl chloride group rather than a carboxylic acid group. To draw the polymer, the steps are exactly the same except rather than removing an -OH group from the C=O carbon, you'll remove a chlorine atom. This means a molecule of HCl (rather than water) is lost.

Tip: If you've got a diol rather than a diamine, the process is exactly the same except you end up with a polyester rather than a polyamide.

Tip: It doesn't matter which way round you draw the repeat unit — both ways are correct.

More complex condensation polymers

Not all condensation polymers are made up from a dicarboxylic acid and a diamine or diol. For example, molecules that contain both an amine and an alcohol group can react with dicarboxylic acids in a condensation polymerisation reaction. The polymers they form contain both amide and ester links.

Example

4-aminobutan-1-ol contains an amine and an alcohol group. It can react with dicarboxylic acids, such as butanedioic acid, in a condensation polymerisation reaction:

$$n\,HO{-}(CH_2)_4{-}NH_2 \;+\; n\,HOOC{-}(CH_2)_2{-}COOH$$

4-aminobutan-1-ol *butanedioic acid*

$$\downarrow$$

$$\left[O{-}(CH_2)_4{-}\underbrace{NH{-}C({=}O)}_{\text{Amide link.}}{-}(CH_2)_2{-}C({=}O) \right]_n \;+\; 2nH_2O$$

Amide link.

The ester link goes between the repeat units.

Tip: You could also draw the repeat unit so that the ester link is in the middle and the amide link is split between the repeat units — both ways are correct.

If a molecule contains a carboxylic acid group and either an alcohol or an amine group, it can polymerise with itself to from a condensation polymer with only one monomer.

Example

3-aminopropanoic acid contains both an amine and a carboxylic acid group. It can react with itself to form a condensation polymer:

$$n\,H_2N{-}(CH_2)_2{-}C({=}O){-}OH \longrightarrow \left[NH{-}(CH_2)_2{-}C({=}O) \right]_n + nH_2O$$

3-aminopropanoic acid

Tip: When a molecule can form a condensation polymer with itself, it's called 'self polymerisation'.

Practice Questions — Application

Q1 Identify whether the following are formulas of polyesters or polyamides and draw the monomer(s) they were formed from.

a) $\left[C({=}O){-}CH(CH_3){-}C({=}O){-}NH{-}C_6H_4{-}NH \right]_n$

b) $\left[O{-}CH(C_6H_5){-}C({=}O) \right]_n$

c) $\left[C({=}O){-}CH(C_6H_5){-}NH \right]_n$

d) $\left[C({=}O){-}CH_2{-}C({=}O){-}NH{-}C(CH_3)H{-}C(CH_3)H{-}NH \right]_n$

e) $\left[C({=}O){-}CH(OH){-}CHCl{-}C({=}O){-}O{-}CH(CH_3){-}O \right]_n$

Tip: If you think that a polymer was made from only one monomer, you'll need to look at both ends of the repeating unit to work out what type of polymer (polyester or polyamide) it is.

Q2 Write equations for the acid hydrolysis of the following polymers:

a) 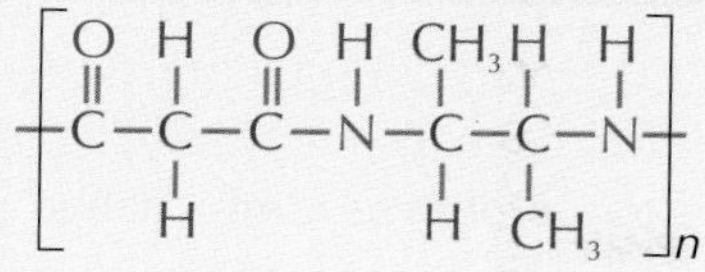
```
 ┌ O  H  O  H  CH3 H  H  ┐
   ‖  |  ‖  |  |   |  |
 ─┼C──C──C──N──C───C──N─┼─
      |        |   |
 └    H        H   CH3   ┘n
```

b) 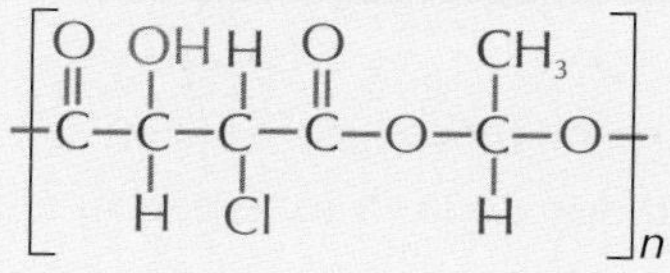
```
 ┌ O  OH H  O        CH3   ┐
   ‖  |  |  ‖        |
 ─┼C──C──C──C──O──C──O─┼─
      |  |           |
 └    H  Cl          H     ┘n
```

Q3 Write equations for the hydrolysis of the following polymers in the presence of NaOH.

a) 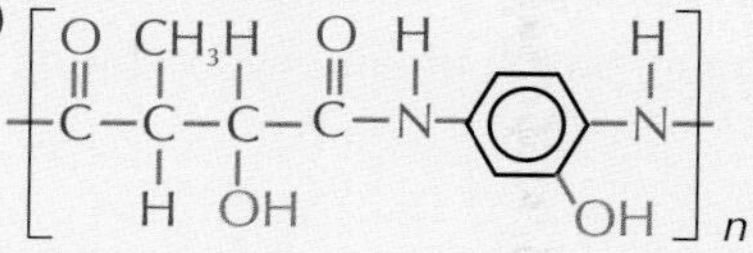
```
 ┌ O  CH3 H  O  H                H ┐
   ‖  |   |  ‖  |                |
 ─┼C──C───C──C──N──(benzene ring)──N─┼─
      |   |                  |
 └    H   OH                 OH     ┘n
```

b) 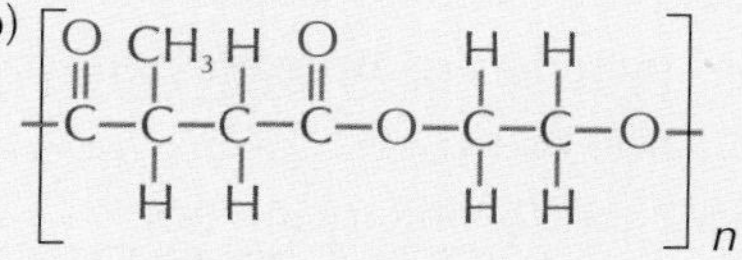
```
 ┌ O  CH3 H  O        H  H     ┐
   ‖  |   |  ‖        |  |
 ─┼C──C───C──C──O──C──C──O─┼─
      |   |           |  |
 └    H   H           H  H     ┘n
```

Q4 Draw the repeat units of the polymers that would be formed from these monomers:

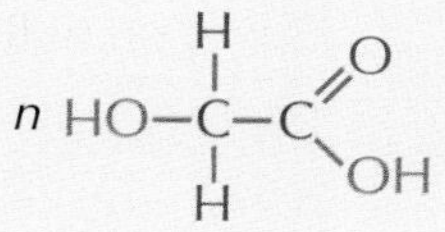

a) 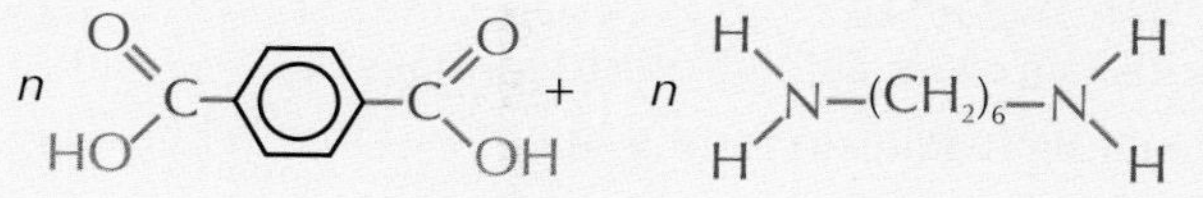
```
      O              O                H            H
       ╲\           //                 ╲          ╱
 n      C─(benzene ring)─C      +   n   N─(CH2)6─N
       ╱             ╲                 ╱          ╲
     HO               OH              H            H
```

b)
```
        H
        |     O
 n HO─C──C//
        |    ╲
        H     OH
```

c)
```
    H    H
     ╲   |    O
 n    N──C──C//
     ╱   |    ╲
    H    H     OH
```

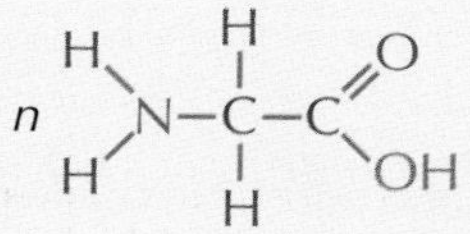

d) 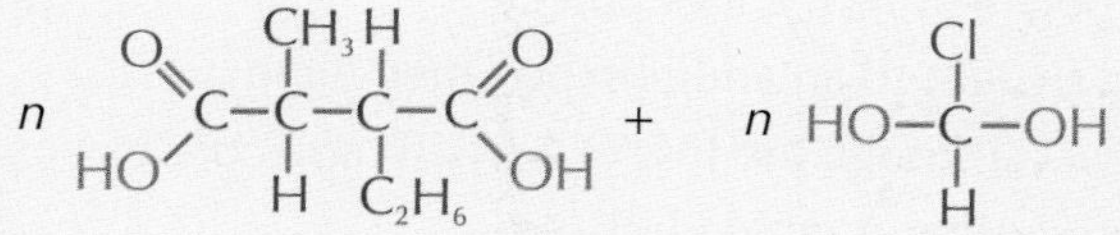
```
      O     CH3 H     O                     Cl
       ╲\   |   |    //                     |
 n      C───C───C───C      +     n  HO──C──OH
       ╱    |   |    ╲                      |
     HO     H   C2H6  OH                    H
```

Practice Questions — Fact Recall

Q1 What small molecule is released when a condensation polymer forms from a dicarboxylic acid and a diamine?

Q2 Name the types of molecules that can join together to form:

a) polyamides b) polyesters

Q3 Name the type of link that joins the monomers together in:

a) polyamides b) polyesters

Q4 Why is hydrolysis performed in the presence of an acid or a base, as opposed to just using water?

Q5 What are the products when polyesters are hydrolysed in the presence of an alkali?

Exam Tip

In the exam, you could also be asked to compare condensation polymers with addition polymers (which were covered on pages 207-208). So you need to know the details of both types of polymerisation.

Section Summary

Make sure you know...

- What amines are and how to name them.
- That amines are bases and can donate their lone pair of electrons to a proton to form a dative (coordinate) bond.
- The reactions of amines with acids to form ammonium salts.
- That you can make aliphatic amines from haloalkanes and excess ethanolic ammonia.
- How to make aromatic amines by reducing aromatic nitro compounds with tin and hydrochloric acid.
- What amides are and how to name them.
- The difference between primary and secondary amides.
- That amino acids are molecules that contain an amino group and a carboxylic acid group.
- That α-amino acids have the amino and carboxylic acid groups on the same carbon.
- That the general formula of an α-amino acid is $RCH(NH_2)COOH$.
- That the carboxylic acid group in amino acids can react with alkalis to form a salt.
- That the amine group in amino acids can react with acids to form a salt.
- That the carboxylic acid group in amino acids can react with alcohols in the presence of an acid catalyst to form esters.
- That optical isomerism is a type of stereoisomerism.
- That optical isomers are non-superimposable mirror images.
- That chiral molecules can form optical isomers.
- How to identify chiral centres.
- How to draw optical isomers.
- That addition polymers are formed through the polymerisation of alkenes and substituted alkenes.
- How to predict the repeat unit of an addition polymer from a monomer.
- How to identify the monomer that makes up a section of an addition polymer chain.
- That condensation polymerisation forms polymers through the loss of a small molecule.
- That condensation polymers are held together by ester or amide linkages.
- That polyamides are formed through the condensation polymerisation of dicarboxylic acids and diamines.
- That polyesters are formed through condensation polymerisation when carboxylic acid and alcohol functional groups react.
- That condensation polymers can be broken down by hydrolysis.
- How polyesters and polyamides can be hydrolysed in the presence of acids and bases.
- How to predict the repeat unit of a condensation polymer from (a) given monomer(s).
- How to identify the monomer(s) that a given condensation polymer was formed from.
- How to identify whether addition or condensation polymerisation will/has taken place from given monomers or a section of polymer.

Exam-style Questions

1 Which of the following molecules contains two chiral carbons?

A

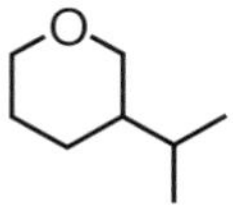

B

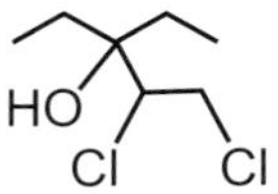

C

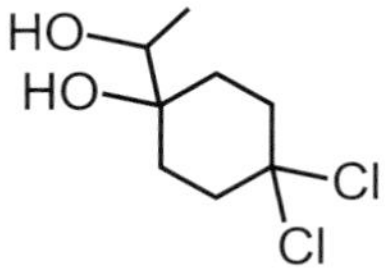

D

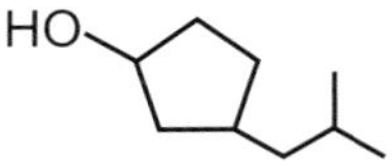

(1 mark)

2 Which of the options below shows the correct repeat unit and type of polymerisation that occurs when the following molecule is polymerised?

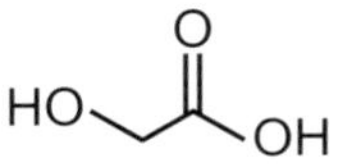

	Repeat Unit	Type of Polymerisation
A	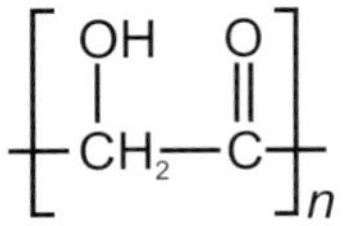 $\left[-CH(OH)-C(=O)- \right]_n$	Condensation
B	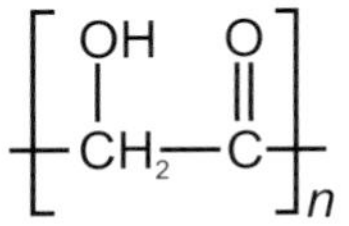 $\left[-CH(OH)-C(=O)- \right]_n$	Addition
C	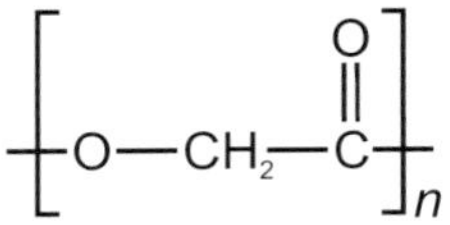 $\left[-O-CH_2-C(=O)- \right]_n$	Condensation
D	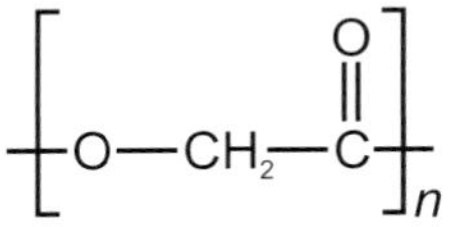 $\left[-O-CH_2-C(=O)- \right]_n$	Addition

(1 mark)

3 Which of the following molecules would you not expect to find in the product mixture when 2-chlorobutane is reacted with an excess of ethanolic ammonia?

A $NH_4^+Cl^-$

B $CH_3CH_2CH_2CH_2NH_2$

C $N(CH(CH_3)CH_2CH_3)_4^+$

D $NH(CH(CH_3)CH_2CH_3)_2$

(1 mark)

4 This question is about amino acids and their properties.

The structures of three different amino acids are shown below:

A **B** 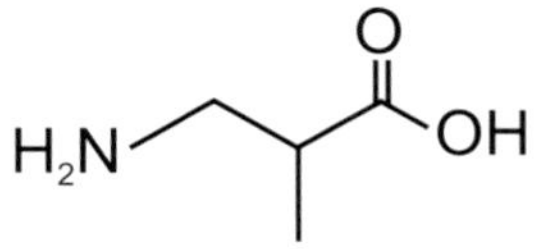 **C**

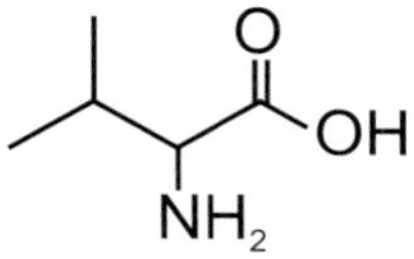

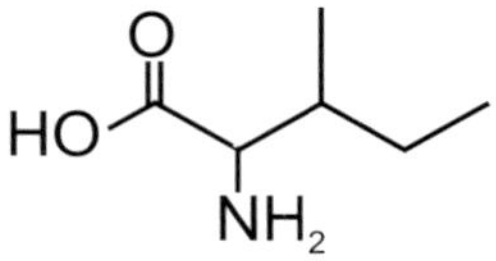

NH_2 OH H_2N OH HO NH_2

(a) (i) Which of the amino acids (**A**, **B** and **C**) are α-amino acids? Explain your answer.

(2 marks)

(ii) Write down the general formula of an α-amino acid.

(1 mark)

(b) The common name for amino acid **A** is valine. Like many other amino acids, valine shows optical isomerism.

(i) Draw the two optical isomers of valine.

(2 marks)

(ii) Draw the skeletal structure of the molecule that would be formed if valine was heated under reflux with ethanol in the presence of an acid catalyst.

(1 mark)

(c) Amino acids can be involved in polymerisation reactions.

(i) Predict the type of polymerisation that amino acids will undergo.

(1 mark)

(ii) Draw a section of the polymer chain that would be formed from two molecules of amino acid **C**.

(1 mark)

(iii) Give the reagents and conditions needed to break down the polymer chain formed by amino acid **C** into its constituent monomers.

(1 mark)

5 A research chemist is investigating the reactions of 2-methyl-2-penten-4-ol, the structure of which is shown below:

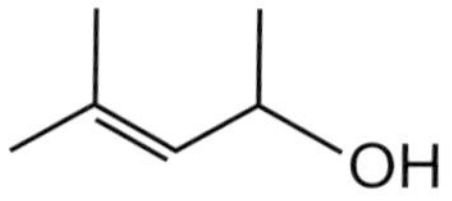

2-methyl-2-penten-4-ol

(a) 2-methyl-2-penten-4-ol exhibits stereoisomerism.

(i) Explain what is meant by the term stereoisomer and state the type of stereoisomerism shown by 2-methyl-2-penten-4-ol.

(2 marks)

(ii) What feature of 2-methyl-2-penten-4-ol enables it to show stereoisomerism?

(1 mark)

(iii) Draw two stereoisomers of 2-methyl-2-penten-4-ol.

(2 marks)

(b) Under certain conditions, 2-methyl-2-penten-4-ol will polymerise to form an addition polymer. Draw the repeat unit of the polymer formed when 2-methyl-2-penten-4-ol polymerises.

(1 mark)

(c) 2-methyl-2-penten-4-ol can be converted into 2-methylpentan-2,4-diol. The structure of 2-methylpentan-2,4-diol is shown below.

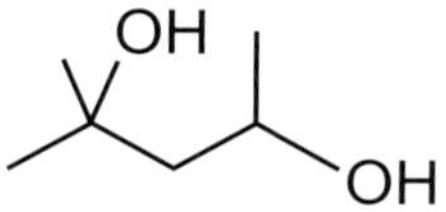

2-methylpentan-2,4-diol

Does 2-methylpentan-2,4-diol exhibit stereoisomerism? Explain your answer.

(2 marks)

(d) 2-methylpentan-2,4-diol can be used in a second synthesis reaction to form the condensation polymer shown below:

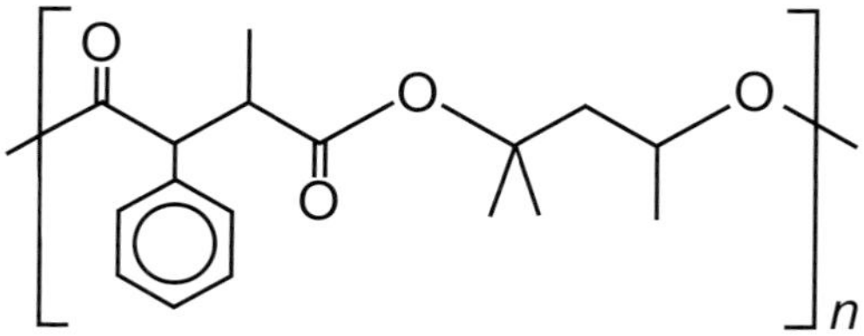

(i) Draw the structure of the molecule which would react with 2-methylpentan-2,4-diol to form this polymer.

(1 mark)

(ii) State what type of condensation polymer this is.

(1 mark)

1. Making Carbon-Carbon Bonds

Learning Objectives:

- Understand that C–C bond formation is used in synthesis to increase the length of a carbon chain
- Be able to describe the formation of C–C≡N by reaction of haloalkanes with CN^- and ethanol, including the nucleophilic substitution mechanism.
- Be able to describe the formation of C–C≡N by reaction of carbonyl compounds with HCN, including the nucleophilic addition mechanism.
- Be able to describe the reactions of nitriles by reduction (e.g. with H_2/Ni) to form amines and by acid hydrolysis to form carboxylic acids.
- Be able to describe the formation of a substituted aromatic C–C by alkylation (using a haloalkane) and acylation (using an acyl chloride) in the presence of a halogen carrier (Friedel-Crafts reaction).

Specification Reference 6.2.4

Organic Chemistry is all about carbon compounds and how they react. But getting one carbon to react with another and form a new carbon-carbon bond is surprisingly hard. Here are some reactions that let you do it.

Extending the carbon chain

In organic synthesis, it's useful to have ways of making a carbon chain longer. You can't just put two carbon chains together and expect them to react though. Instead, you have to use reactants and reagents that have a nucleophilic or electrophilic carbon atom.

Reactions of cyanide to form C–C bonds

Cyanide (CN^-) is an ion containing a negatively charged carbon atom, so it's a nucleophile (an electron pair donor). It'll react with carbon centres that have a slight positive charge to create a new carbon-carbon bond.

Reaction with a haloalkane to form a nitrile:

$$-C^{\delta+}-X^{\delta-} + {}^{-}C{\equiv}N \longrightarrow -C-C{\equiv}N$$

Reaction with a carbonyl to form a hydroxynitrile:

$$>C^{\delta+}{=}O + {}^{-}C{\equiv}N \longrightarrow -C(OH)-C{\equiv}N$$

Figure 1: *Reactions of cyanide ions with partially positive carbon centres to form new carbon-carbon bonds.*

So you can increase the length of a carbon chain by reacting an organic compound that contains a slightly positive carbon centre with a cyanide reagent such as potassium cyanide (KCN), sodium cyanide (NaCN) or hydrogen cyanide (HCN).

Reactions of cyanide with haloalkanes

Haloalkanes usually contain a polar carbon-halogen bond. The halogen is generally more electronegative than carbon, making the carbon electron deficient. You saw in Module 4 that nucleophiles, such as hydroxide ions and water, will react with the positive carbon centre in haloalkanes to replace the halogen atom. This is a nucleophilic substitution reaction. If you reflux a haloalkane with potassium (or sodium) cyanide in ethanol, then the cyanide ions can react with the haloalkane by nucleophilic substitution. This forms an organic compound that contains a -C≡N functional group where the halogen used to be — this is called a **nitrile**. The general equation for the reaction is:

$$R{-}X + CN^- \xrightarrow[\text{reflux}]{\text{ethanol}} R{-}C{\equiv}N + X^-$$

Example

When 1-bromo-2-methylpropane is heated under reflux with hydrogen cyanide in ethanol, it reacts to form 3-methylbutanenitrile:

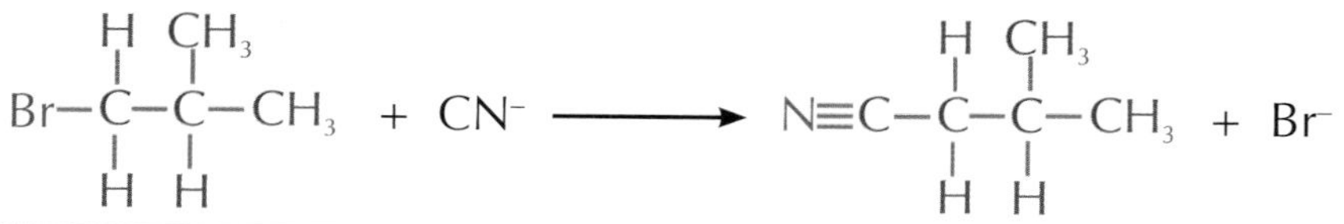

$$\mathrm{BrCH_2CH(CH_3)CH_3} + \mathrm{CN^-} \longrightarrow \mathrm{N{\equiv}C{-}CH_2CH(CH_3)CH_3} + \mathrm{Br^-}$$

This is the mechanism for the nucleophilic substitution reaction between cyanide and a haloalkane, using bromoethane as an example:

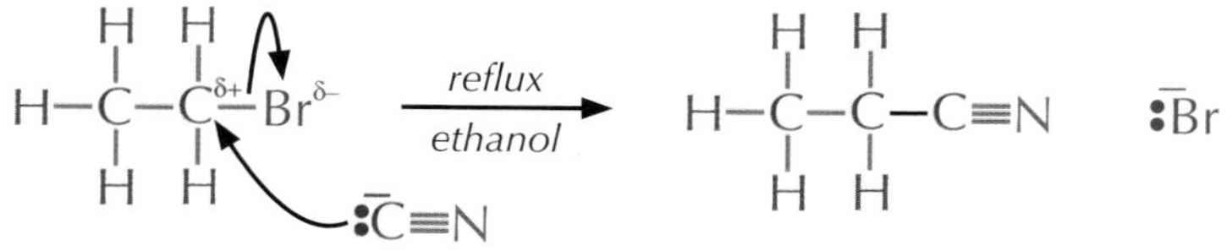

$$\mathrm{CH_3CH_2^{\delta+}{-}Br^{\delta-}} + {:}\mathrm{\bar{C}{\equiv}N} \xrightarrow[\text{ethanol}]{\text{reflux}} \mathrm{CH_3CH_2C{\equiv}N} + {:}\mathrm{\bar{B}r}$$

Figure 2: *The mechanism of the nucleophilic substitution reaction between a haloalkane and cyanide.*

Tip: You have to use ethanol as a solvent instead of water. If you used water, the water molecules could act as a competing nucleophile and you'd get some alcohol product.

Reactions of cyanide with carbonyls

Aldehydes and ketones are both carbonyl compounds — they contain a polar C=O bond. If you mix them with hydrogen cyanide, the cyanide ion will react with the positive carbon centre to form -C(OH)C≡N group — this is called a **hydroxynitrile**.

Tip: There's more about the reactions of carbonyl compounds on pages 182-184.

Example

Butanone reacts with hydrogen cyanide in a nucleophilic addition reaction to form 2-hydroxy-2-methylbutanenitrile:

$$\mathrm{CH_3CH_2COCH_3} + \mathrm{HCN} \longrightarrow \mathrm{CH_3CH_2C(OH)(C{\equiv}N)CH_3}$$

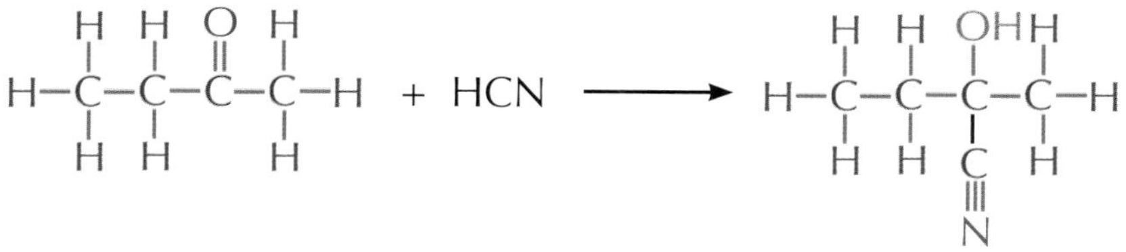

butanone *2-hydroxy-2-methylbutanenitrile*

The reaction is an example of a nucleophilic addition reaction. The general mechanism for the reaction is:

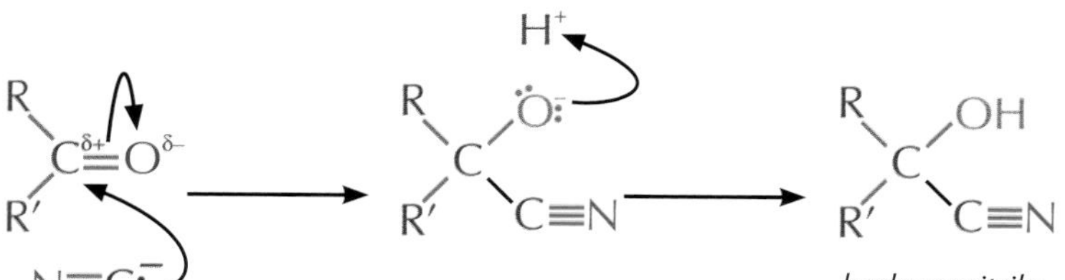

$$\mathrm{RR'C^{\delta+}{=}O^{\delta-}} + \mathrm{N{\equiv}C{:}^-} \longrightarrow \mathrm{RR'C(O^-)C{\equiv}N} \xrightarrow{\mathrm{H^+}} \mathrm{RR'C(OH)C{\equiv}N}$$

hydroxynitrile

Figure 3: *The mechanism of the nucleophilic addition reaction between a carbonyl and cyanide.*

Tip: Hydrogen cyanide could also be called methane nitrile. Hydrogen cyanide is the molecule's old name and methane nitrile is its name assigned by the IUPAC naming conventions. Hydrogen cyanide is more common, so this is the name you should use.

Reactions of nitrile groups

Once you've added another carbon atom onto the carbon chain and formed a nitrile (or a hydroxynitrile), it's easy to convert the nitrile into a new functional group. This is because nitrile groups are very reactive. This is really useful in synthesis — you can make a number of different compounds from a nitrile.

Reduction of nitriles

You can reduce a nitrile to a primary amine by a number of different methods.

1. You can use lithium aluminium hydride ($LiAlH_4$ — a strong reducing agent), followed by some dilute acid.
   The general equation for the reaction with a nitrile is:

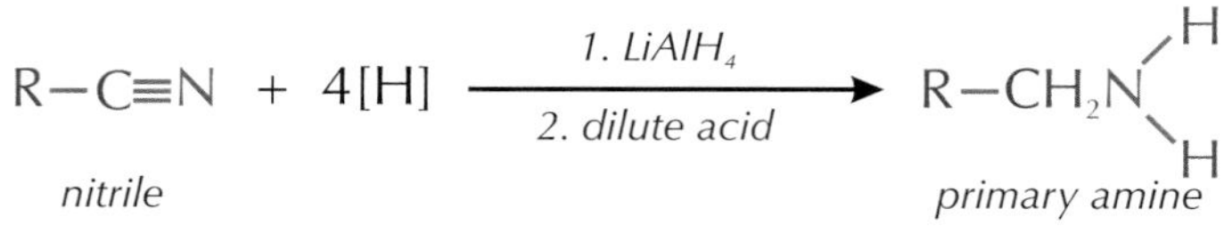

$$R{-}C{\equiv}N + 4[H] \xrightarrow[\text{2. dilute acid}]{\text{1. } LiAlH_4} R{-}CH_2NH_2$$

nitrile → primary amine

Figure 4: *The general reaction for the reduction of a nitrile with $LiAlH_4$.*

   You can also reduce hydroxynitriles using this method.
   The general equation for the reaction is:

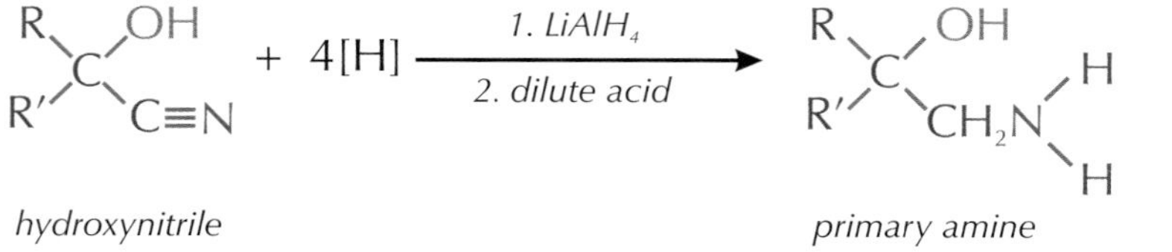

$$RR'C(OH)C{\equiv}N + 4[H] \xrightarrow[\text{2. dilute acid}]{\text{1. } LiAlH_4} RR'C(OH)CH_2NH_2$$

hydroxynitrile → primary amine

Figure 5: *The general reaction for the reduction of a hydroxynitrile with $LiAlH_4$.*

Examples

Here's the equation for the formation of ethylamine from ethanenitrile:

$$CH_3C{\equiv}N + 4[H] \xrightarrow[\text{2. dilute acid}]{\text{1. } LiAlH_4} CH_3CH_2NH_2$$

Ethanenitrile → *Ethylamine*

Here's the equation for the formation of 1-aminobutan-2-ol from 2-hydroxybutanenitrile:

$$CH_3CH_2CH(OH)C{\equiv}N + 4[H] \xrightarrow[\text{2. dilute acid}]{\text{1. } LiAlH_4} CH_3CH_2CH(OH)CH_2{-}NH_2$$

2-hydroxybutanenitrile → *1-aminobutan-2-ol*

Tip: Forming amines by reducing nitriles is useful if you just want the primary amine because you can't get further substitutions — the primary amine is the only product, unlike for nucleophilic substitution of a haloalkane with ammonia (see page 198).

Tip: The prefix amino- tells you there's an amine group, just like the suffix -amine.

2. The method above is great in the lab, but $LiAlH_4$ is too expensive for industrial use. In industry, nitriles are reduced using hydrogen gas with a metal catalyst, such as platinum or nickel, at a high temperature and pressure — this is called catalytic hydrogenation. The general equations for the reduction of a nitrile or a hydroxynitrile are:

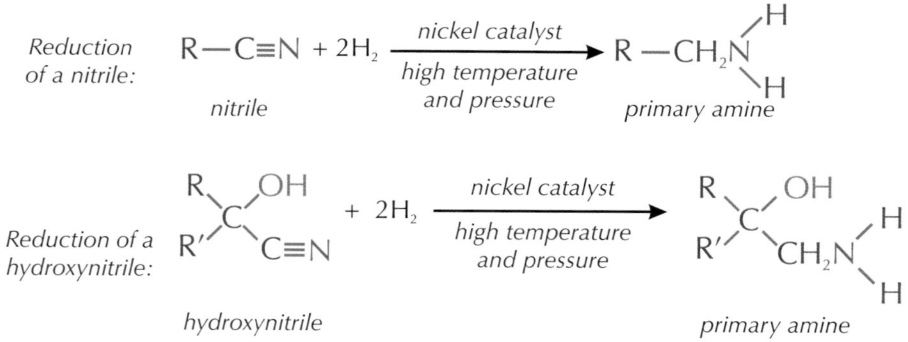

Reduction of a nitrile:

$$R{-}C{\equiv}N + 2H_2 \xrightarrow[\text{high temperature and pressure}]{\text{nickel catalyst}} R{-}CH_2NH_2$$

nitrile → primary amine

Reduction of a hydroxynitrile:

$$RR'C(OH)C{\equiv}N + 2H_2 \xrightarrow[\text{high temperature and pressure}]{\text{nickel catalyst}} RR'C(OH)CH_2NH_2$$

hydroxynitrile → primary amine

Figure 6: *The general reactions for the reduction of nitriles and hydroxynitriles with H_2 and a nickel catalyst.*

Hydrolysis of nitriles

If you reflux a nitrile in dilute hydrochloric acid, then the nitrile group will be hydrolysed to form a carboxylic acid. The carbon of the nitrile starting material becomes the carbon of the carboxyl group in the product.

$$R-C\equiv N + 2H_2O + HCl \xrightarrow{reflux} R-C(=O)OH + NH_4Cl$$

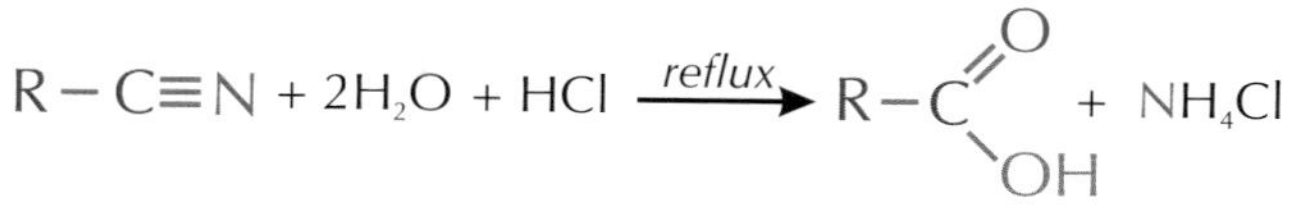

nitrile *carboxylic acid*

Figure 7: *The general reaction for the hydrolysis of a nitrile.*

You can do the same with a hydroxynitrile:

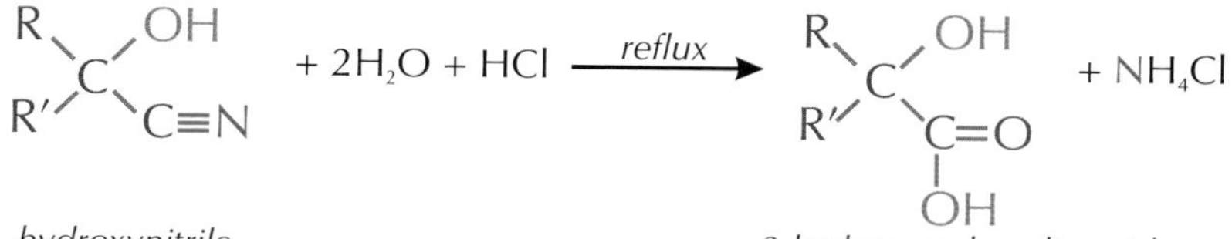

$$RR'C(OH)C\equiv N + 2H_2O + HCl \xrightarrow{reflux} RR'C(OH)C(=O)OH + NH_4Cl$$

hydroxynitrile *2-hydroxycarboxylic acid*

Figure 8: *The general reaction for the hydrolysis of a hydroxynitrile.*

Examples

If you reflux propanenitrile with dilute hydrochloric acid, you form propanoic acid:

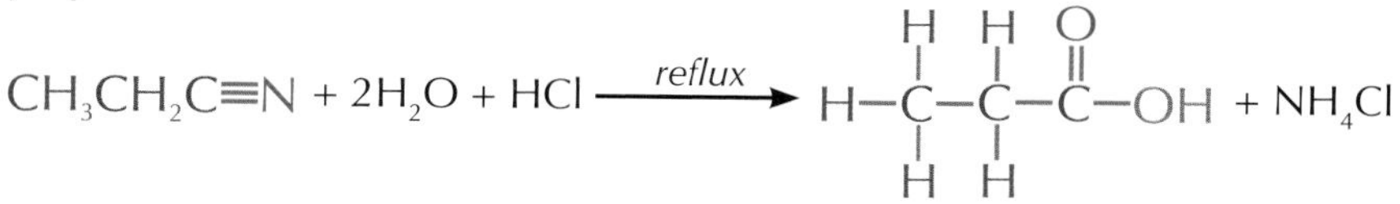

$$CH_3CH_2C\equiv N + 2H_2O + HCl \xrightarrow{reflux} CH_3CH_2COOH + NH_4Cl$$

If you reflux 2-hydroxybutanenitrile with dilute hydrochloric acid, you form 2-hydroxybutanoic acid:

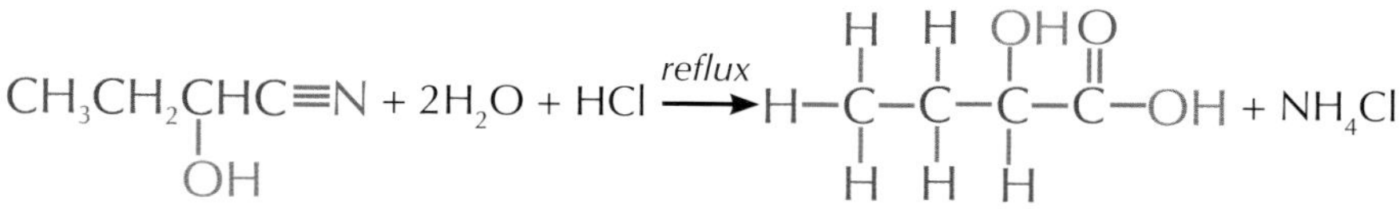

$$CH_3CH_2CH(OH)C\equiv N + 2H_2O + HCl \xrightarrow{reflux} CH_3CH_2CH(OH)COOH + NH_4Cl$$

Tip: Hydrolysis means using water to break up a compound. Here, the -C≡N bond reacts with water to break up and form $-COO^-$ and NH_4^+.

Tip: The hydrochloric acid is diluted in water, so there are lots of water molecules in the mixture that can take part in these hydrolysis reactions.

Using nitriles in synthetic routes

If the product of a synthesis reaction contains one more carbon in the chain than the starting compound had, then it's likely that the synthetic route will include formation of a nitrile or hydroxynitrile. It's possible the synthetic route will have two steps — the first to make the nitrile in order to extend the carbon chain, and the second to react the nitrile group and form a different functional group.

Example

Plan a two-step synthetic route to synthesise 3-methylbutamine from 1-chloro-2-methylpropane. You should include all reagents and conditions, as well as showing any intermediate products.

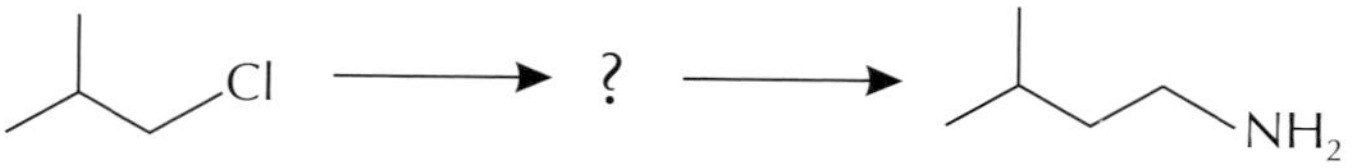

$$(CH_3)_2CHCH_2Cl \longrightarrow \; ? \longrightarrow (CH_3)_2CHCH_2CH_2NH_2$$

The product has one more carbon than the starting compound, so the synthetic route must include formation of a new carbon-carbon bond. The starting compound is a chloroalkane so one way to form the new carbon-carbon bond is to react it with a cyanide ion in a nucleophilic substitution reaction to form a nitrile.

Tip: Nitriles can react to make lots of different functional groups, which makes them useful in synthesis.

Tip: You could also use other cyanide compounds, such as NaCN or HCN, in the first step of this synthetic route.

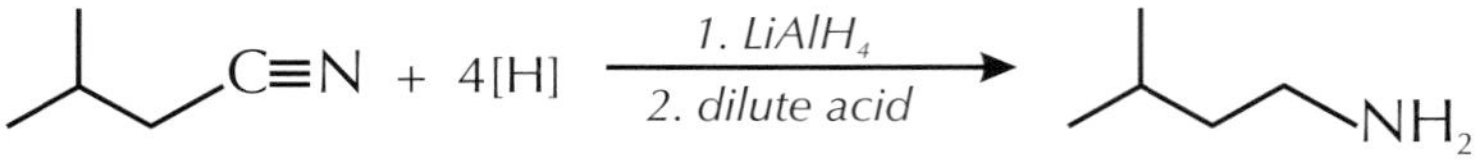

Tip: There are other ways to reduce nitriles on page 222.

The first step of the synthetic route is:

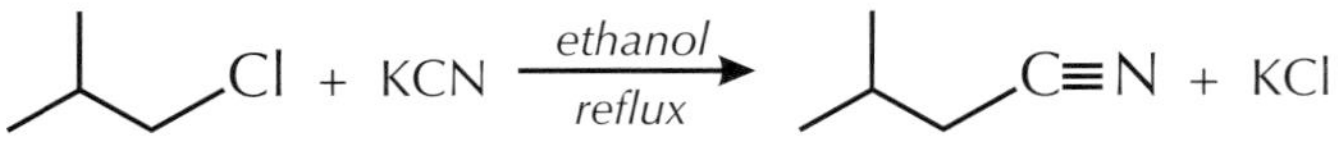

$$(CH_3)_2CHCH_2Cl + KCN \xrightarrow[\text{reflux}]{\text{ethanol}} (CH_3)_2CHCH_2C{\equiv}N + KCl$$

The nitrile can then be reduced to form a primary amine — and there's your product. So the second step could be:

$$(CH_3)_2CHCH_2C{\equiv}N + 4[H] \xrightarrow[\text{2. dilute acid}]{\text{1. } LiAlH_4} (CH_3)_2CHCH_2CH_2NH_2$$

Overall the synthetic route is:

$$(CH_3)_2CHCH_2Cl \xrightarrow[\text{ethanol, reflux}]{KCN} (CH_3)_2CHCH_2C{\equiv}N \xrightarrow[\text{2. dilute acid}]{\text{1. } LiAlH_4} (CH_3)_2CHCH_2CH_2NH_2$$

Forming new C–C bonds to benzene rings

You can form new carbon-carbon bonds to benzene rings using Friedel-Crafts reactions. To do this, you reflux benzene with a halogen carrier (e.g. $AlCl_3$) and either a haloalkane or an acyl chloride. A new carbon-carbon bond is formed between the benzene ring and the halogenated carbon in the organic reactant. This is an electrophilic substitution reaction.

Tip: See pages 172 for more on Friedel-Crafts reactions.

If you use a haloalkane, you get Friedel-Crafts alkylation:

$$C_6H_6 + R{-}Cl \xrightarrow[\text{reflux}]{AlCl_3} C_6H_5R + HCl$$

Figure 9: *Friedel-Crafts alkylation reaction.*

Tip: 'Alkylation' means adding an alkyl group. 'Acylation' means adding an acyl (-COR) group.

If you use an acyl chloride, you get Friedel-Crafts acylation:

$$C_6H_6 + RCOCl \xrightarrow[\text{reflux}]{AlCl_3} C_6H_5COR + HCl$$

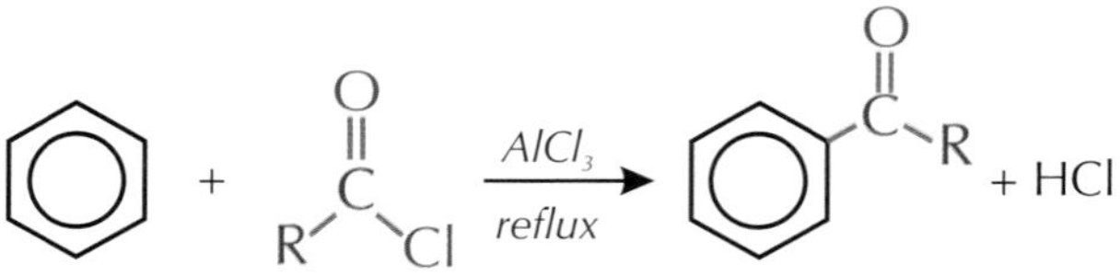

Figure 10: *Friedel-Crafts acylation reaction.*

You may have to design a synthetic route that includes using a Friedel-Crafts reaction.

Example

Consider the following reaction scheme:

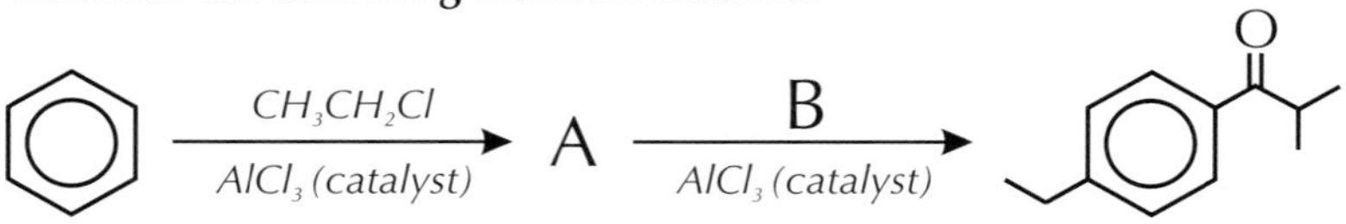

$$C_6H_6 \xrightarrow[AlCl_3\text{ (catalyst)}]{CH_3CH_2Cl} A \xrightarrow[AlCl_3\text{ (catalyst)}]{B} CH_3CH_2C_6H_4COCH(CH_3)_2$$

What is A, the organic product of the first step?

In the first step, benzene is reacted with chloroethane and a halogen carrier. It's a Friedel-Crafts alkylation reaction, so the product is ethylbenzene:

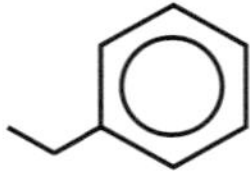

What is the reagent, B, in the second step?

Ethylbenzene (the product from the first step) is acylated in the second step, so the reaction will be a Friedel-Crafts acylation.

The reagent is 2-methylpropanoylchloride:

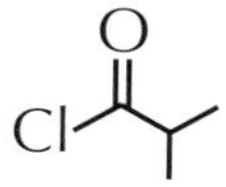

Cl O

Tip: This reaction would give you a mixture of the desired product: O, along with some of this side product: O.

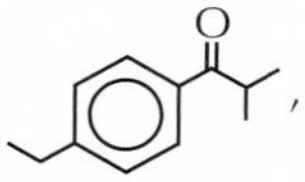

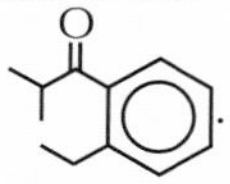

You'd have to purify the reaction mixture after the reaction was finished in order to get a sample containing only the desired product.

Practice Questions — Application

Q1 The following reaction scheme shows a route for synthesising 2-hydroxy-3-methylpentanoic acid from 2-methylbutanal.

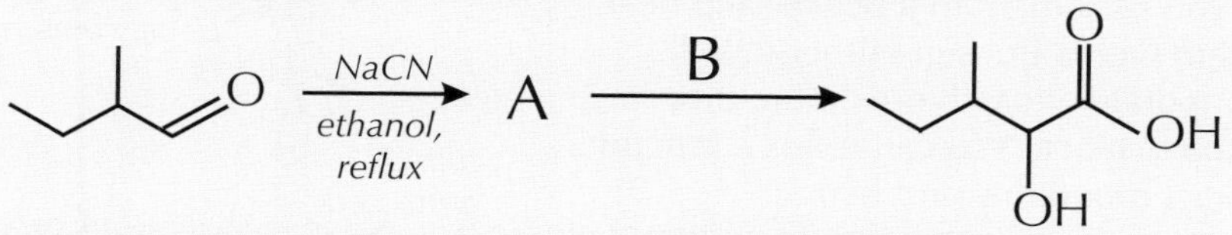

O —NaCN / ethanol, reflux→ A —B→ O OH OH

a) Draw the skeletal formula of the organic compound, A, formed when 2-methylbutanal is heated under reflux with sodium cyanide in ethanol.

b) Give the reagents and conditions, B, that could be used to convert the organic product, A, into 2-hydroxy-3-methylpentanoic acid.

Q2 The reaction scheme below shows some reactions of 2-chlorobutane.

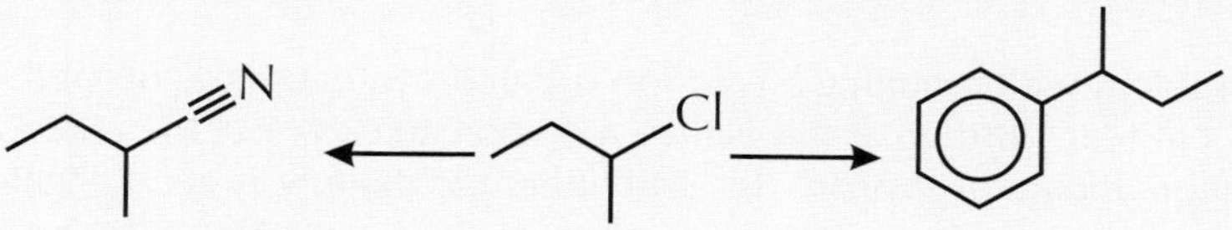

N ← Cl →

2-methylbutanenitrile *2-chlorobutane* *(1-methylpropyl)benzene*

a) Give the reagents and conditions needed in the reaction that converts 2-chlorobutane to 2-methylbutanenitrile.

b) 2-methylbutanenitrile can be reduced using hydrogen and a nickel catalyst at high temperature and pressure. Draw the skeletal formula of the product of this reaction.

c) Give the reagents and conditions needed in the reaction to convert 2-chlorobutane to (1-methylpropyl)benzene.

Exam Tip
Make sure you give the right type of formula if you're asked for one in the exam (e.g. skeletal or displayed) — otherwise you might lose marks.

Practice Questions — Fact Recall

Q1 What type of reaction takes place when a haloalkane is heated under reflux with sodium cyanide in ethanol?

Q2 What type of compound is formed when a carbonyl compound reacts with hydrogen cyanide?

Q3 Name two reactions that could be used to form new carbon-carbon bonds with a benzene ring.

Learning Objective:

- Be able to describe and carry out the techniques and procedures used for the preparation and purification of organic solids involving use of a range of techniques including:
  (i) Organic preparation by distillation and heating under reflux using Quickfit apparatus.
  (ii) Purification of an organic solid using filtration under reduced pressure, recrystallisation and measurement of melting points (PAG 6).

Specification Reference 6.2.5

Tip: Have a look back at your Year 1 notes if all this distillation and reflux business seems a bit hazy — it's all there in Module 4.

Tip: The glassware you use in organic synthesis is normally a type of Quickfit® apparatus. These are pieces of apparatus with ground glass joints that can be fitted together easily in a variety of different ways to form the set-up for a number of different techniques.

Tip: See page 14 for more details on how to carry out a filtration under reduced pressure.

2. Practical Techniques in Organic Synthesis

PRACTICAL ACTIVITY GROUP 6

There was a whole host of techniques in Year 1 for making and purifying organic liquids. Now it's time for organic solids. Making them is quite similar, but you can purify them in slightly different ways.

Preparation of organic substances

Organic reactions are slow and the substances are usually flammable and volatile (they've got low boiling points). If you stick them in a beaker and heat them with a Bunsen burner they'll evaporate or catch fire before they have time to react. You can reflux a reaction to get round this problem.
The mixture's heated in a flask fitted with a vertical Liebig condenser (see Figure 1) — so when the mixture boils, the vapours are condensed and recycled back into the flask. This stops reagents being lost from the flask, and gives them time to react.

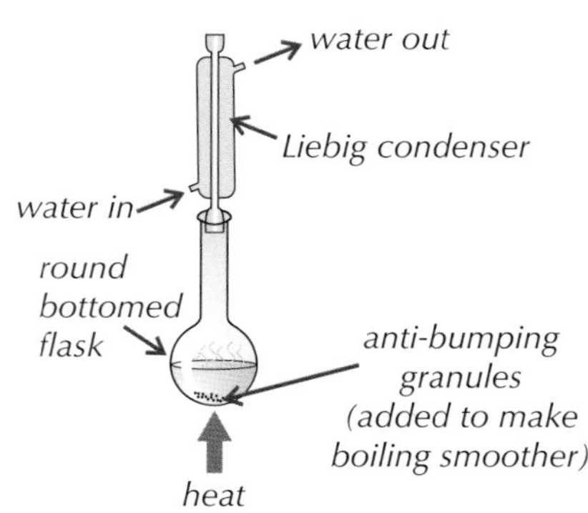

Figure 1: *Reflux apparatus.*

One problem with refluxing a reaction is that it can cause the desired product to react further. If this is the case you can carry out the reaction in a distillation apparatus instead. In distillation, the mixture is gently heated and substances evaporate out of the mixture in order of increasing boiling point. If you know the boiling point of your pure product, you can use the thermometer to tell you when it's evaporating, and therefore when it's condensing. If the product of a reaction has a lower boiling point than the starting materials then the reaction mixture can be heated so that the product evaporates from the reaction mixture as it forms. The starting materials will stay in the reaction mixture as long as the temperature is controlled.

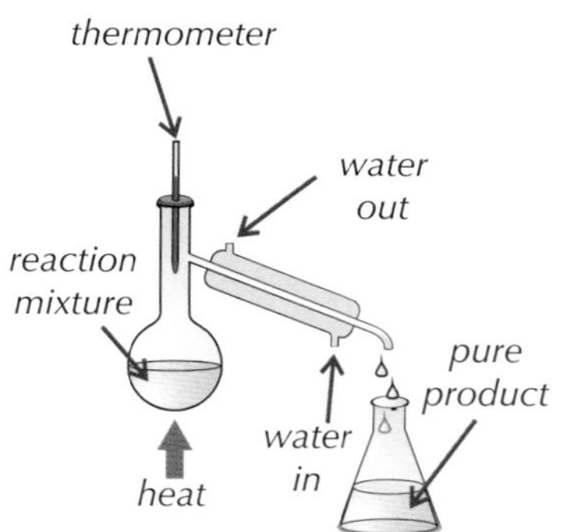

Figure 2: *Distillation apparatus.*

Filtration under reduced pressure

If your product is a solid, you can separate it from any liquid impurities by filtering it under reduced pressure. The reaction mixture is poured into a Büchner funnel with a piece of filter paper in it. The Büchner funnel is on top of a sealed sidearm flask which is connected to a vacuum line, causing it to be under reduced pressure. The reduced pressure causes suction through the funnel which causes the liquid to pass quickly into the flask, leaving behind dry crystals of your product.

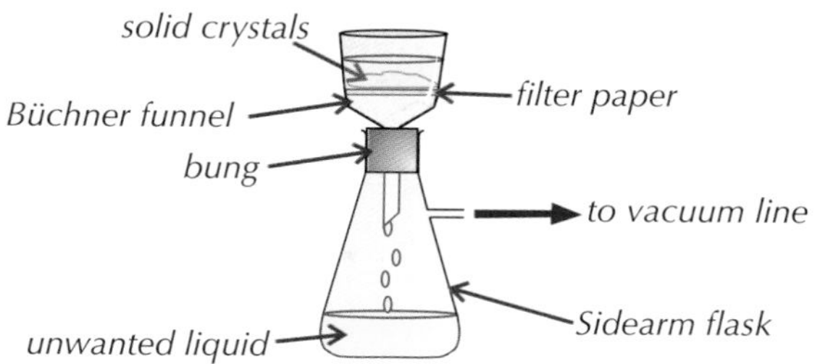

Figure 3: *Filtration apparatus.*

Figure 4: *The apparatus used to carry out a filtration under reduced pressure.*

Recrystallisation

If the product of an organic reaction is a solid, then the simplest way of purifying it is a process called **recrystallisation**. Here's how it's done:

- Heat a suitable solvent on a hot plate or in a water bath. Slowly add the hot solvent to a flask containing the impure solid until the solid just dissolves and you have a saturated solution of the impure product. It's important not to add too much solvent, so add it a bit at a time, keep the flask you're adding it to warm (e.g. on a hot plate) and swirl it regularly.
- Once the solid has dissolved, you should filter the saturated solution to remove any solid impurities. You can do this by carrying out a filtration using fluted filter paper (see page 15 for how to do this). The filter funnel you use and the flask that the filtrate runs into should be warm to stop the saturated solution from cooling down too quickly.
- Once any solid impurities have been filtered out, you need to slowly cool the solution. Leave it to cool at room temperature first and then use an ice bath to cool it further. Crystals of the product will form as it cools. The impurities will stay in solution, as they are present in much smaller amounts than the product, so take much longer to crystallise out.
- If no crystals form when you cool your solution, it could be because you added too much solvent. You can evaporate off some of the excess solvent by putting the flask back on a hot plate or in a water bath. It could also be because there's nothing for the crystals to form on — they need a point to start from. A scratch on the glass container is usually enough, so try gently scratching the inside of the flask with a glass rod.
- Once the crystals have formed, you can separate them from the solution by filtration under reduced pressure. Wash the crystals left in the Büchner funnel with ice-cold solvent to rinse through any remaining solvent that may contain impurities, then leave the crystals to dry. You should have crystals of your product that are much purer than the original solid.

Tip: Always carry out a risk assessment before you carry out any of the techniques on these pages.

Tip: In a saturated solution, the maximum possible amount of solid is dissolved in the solvent.

Tip: The more slowly the solution is cooled the larger the crystals will be. If you cool it too quickly the crystals could be so small that they'll pass through the filter paper and you'll struggle to separate them from the solution. Cooling too quickly can also cause the impurities to crystallise.

Choosing the solvent for recrystallisation

When you recrystallise a product, you must use an appropriate solvent for that particular substance. It will only work if the solid is very soluble in the hot solvent, but nearly insoluble when the solvent is cold. If your product isn't soluble enough in the hot solvent, you won't be able to dissolve it at all. If your product is too soluble in the cold solvent, most of it will stay in the solution even after cooling. When you filter it, you'll lose most of your product, giving you a very low yield. The impurities you want to remove from your product also need to be very soluble in the solvent when it is both hot and cold. This way, they'll stay in the solution as the product recrystallises, and be washed away when you carry out the filtration.

Tip: It's possible that not all of a product will recrystallise out of solution, so its yield will be reduced. But the crystals that do form will be really pure, which is often very important in things like drug synthesis.

Testing the purity of an organic solid

Tip: Some capillary tubes are already sealed at one end, but some are open at both ends. If that's the case you'll need to seal it yourself. Just place the end of the capillary tube in a Bunsen flame at an angle of 45° and rotate it. You won't need to leave it in the flame for very long before it seals.

Most pure substances have a specific melting and boiling point. If they contain impurities, the melting point's lowered and the boiling point is raised. If they're very impure, melting and boiling will occur across a wide range of temperatures. To accurately measure the melting point of an organic solid, you need to put a small amount of the solid in a capillary tube that's sealed at one end. To do this, put the solid in a watch glass and press the open end of the capillary tube into the substance. You should get a small 'plug' of the solid at the end of the tube. Turn the tube the other way up and tap it gently on a solid surface to knock the solid down to the bottom of the tube. Once you've done this, there are a couple of ways you can measure the melting point:

Examples

- Suspend the capillary tube in a beaker of oil with a very sensitive thermometer. Slowly heat the oil, with constant stirring, until the solid just begins to melt, and read the temperature on the thermometer. Wait until the solid has completely melted, and record the temperature on the thermometer again. This gives you the range of the melting point.
- You can also measure the melting point of a solid using a piece of equipment called a melting point apparatus (see Figure 5). The capillary tube and the thermometer are slotted into the machine which contains a metal block that is slowly warmed. There's a magnifying glass in front of the slot where the capillary tube is held, so you can spot exactly when the crystals start and finish melting.

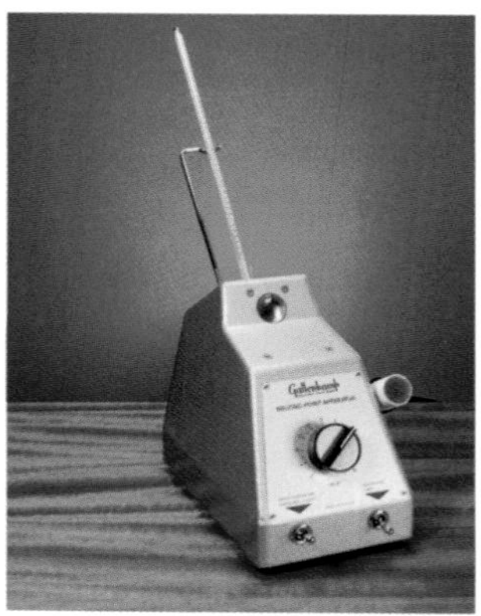

Figure 5: A melting point apparatus.

Once you've measured the melting point of your sample, you can compare it to the known melting point of the substance to determine its purity. If the melting points are similar then your sample is quite pure, but if your value is much lower than the standard value, your sample contains impurities.

Tip: You could also use a piece of equipment called a Thiele tube to measure the melting point of a solid.

Practice Questions — Application

Q1 Use the table below to choose an appropriate solvent for the recrystallisation of benzoic acid. Explain your answer.

Solvent	Solubility of benzoic acid when solvent is hot	Solubility of benzoic acid when solvent is cold
Ethanol	Soluble	Soluble
Water	Soluble	Insoluble
Cyclohexane	Insoluble	Insoluble

Q2 A student measures the melting points of three different samples of aspirin. In its pure form, aspirin has a melting point of 138-140 °C. Use the data in Figure 6 to put the samples A, B and C in order of increasing purity. Explain your answer.

Sample	Melting point range (°C)
A	134-137
B	121-129
C	127-132

Figure 6: Melting points of three solids.

Practice Questions — Fact Recall

Q1 What technique is used to heat an organic reaction mixture without losing any volatile substances?

Q2 What is filtration under reduced pressure used for when purifying an organic solid?

Q3 How could you test the purity of an organic solid?

3. Functional Groups and their Typical Reactions

Organic Chemistry is all about spotting functional groups and predicting how they'll react and what they'll form when they do react. Here's a summary of the reactions and functional groups in A Level Chemistry.

Learning Objectives:
- Be able to identify the individual functional groups in an organic molecule containing several functional groups.
- Be able to predict the properties and reactions of an organic molecule containing several functional groups.

Specification Reference 6.2.5

Types of reaction

In Organic Chemistry you can classify all the different reactions based on what happens to the molecules involved. All of the reactions you've met will fit into one of these seven types.

Reaction Type	Description	Examples of functional groups that undergo this type of reaction
Addition	Two molecules join together to form a single product. Involves breaking a double bond.	>C=C< –C(=O)– –C(=O)–H
Elimination / Dehydration	Involves removing a functional group which is released as part of a small molecule. Often, a double bond is formed. In dehydration, water is lost.	–X *(X is a halogen. HX eliminated)* –OH *(H_2O eliminated)*
Substitution	A functional group is swapped for a new one.	–OH –X benzene ring C–H *(H replaced)*
Condensation	Two molecules are joined together with the loss of a small molecule, e.g. water or HCl.	–C(=O)–OH –C(=O)–X –C(=O)–NH_2 –OH –NH_2
Hydrolysis	Water is used to split apart a molecule, creating two smaller ones.	–C(=O)–O– –C(=O)–O–C(=O)– –C(=O)–N–
Oxidation	Oxidation is the loss of electrons. In Organic Chemistry, it usually means gaining an oxygen atom or losing a hydrogen atom.	–CH₂–OH → –C(=O)–H → –C(=O)–OH –CH(–)–OH → –C(=O)–
Reduction	Reduction is the gain of electrons. In Organic Chemistry, it usually means gaining a hydrogen atom or losing an oxygen atom.	–C(=O)–OH → –C(=O)–H → –CH₂–OH –C(=O)– → –CH(–)–OH

Tip: Hydrolysis is the opposite reaction to condensation.

Tip: Polyesters and polyamides can be hydrolysed to their constituent monomers.

Tip: Reduction is the opposite reaction to oxidation.

Functional groups

Functional groups are the parts of a molecule that are responsible for the way the molecule reacts. Substances are grouped into families called **homologous series** based on what functional groups they contain. Here's a round-up of all the ones you've studied:

> **Exam Tip**
> You need to learn all of these functional groups off by heart — they won't be given to you in the exam.

> **Tip:** Aromatic compounds can also be called 'arenes'.

> **Tip:** Amines are classed as primary, secondary, tertiary or quaternary ammonium ions depending on whether the nitrogen is bonded to one, two, three or four carbon atoms.

> **Tip:** Amides can be classed as primary or secondary depending on whether the nitrogen is bonded to one or two carbon atoms.

Homologous series	Functional group	Properties	Typical reactions
Alkane	only C–C and C–H	Non-polar, unreactive.	Radical substitution
Alkene	C=C	Non-polar, electron-rich double bond.	Electrophilic addition
Aromatic compounds	H H C–C –C ◯ C–H C–C H H	Stable delocalised ring of electrons.	Electrophilic substitution
Alcohol	–OH	Polar C–OH bond.	Nucleophilic substitution, dehydration/elimination
		Lone pair on oxygen can act as a nucleophile.	Esterification, nucleophilic substitution
Haloalkane	–X (X is a halogen)	Polar C–X bond.	Nucleophilic substitution, elimination
Amine	–N(–)–	Lone pair on nitrogen can act as a base or a nucleophile.	Neutralisation, nucleophilic substitution
Amide	–C(=O)–NH_2	–	–
Nitrile	–C≡N	Electron deficient carbon centre.	Reduction, hydrolysis
Aldehyde	–C(=O)–H	Polar C=O bond.	Nucleophilic addition, reduction, oxidation
Ketone	–C(=O)–	Polar C=O bond.	Nucleophilic addition, reduction
Carboxylic acid	–C(=O)–OH	Electron deficient carbon centre.	Neutralisation, esterification
Ester	–C(=O)–O–	Electron deficient carbon centre.	Hydrolysis
Acyl chloride	–C(=O)–Cl	Electron deficient carbon centre.	Nucleophilic substitution, condensation (lose HCl), Friedel-Crafts acylation
Acid anhydride	–C(=O)–O–C(=O)–	Electron deficient carbon centre.	Esterification

The functional groups in a molecule give you clues about its properties and reactions. For example, a -COOH group will (usually) make the molecule acidic and mean it will form esters with alcohols.

In the exam, you may be asked to identify all the functional groups in a molecule. There may be more than one, and you need to be able to recognise them all.

Examples

The molecule on the right has three functional groups: a carboxylic acid group, an amine group and an amide group.

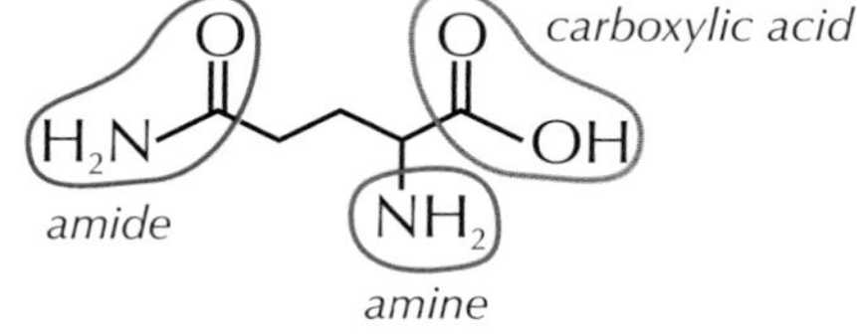

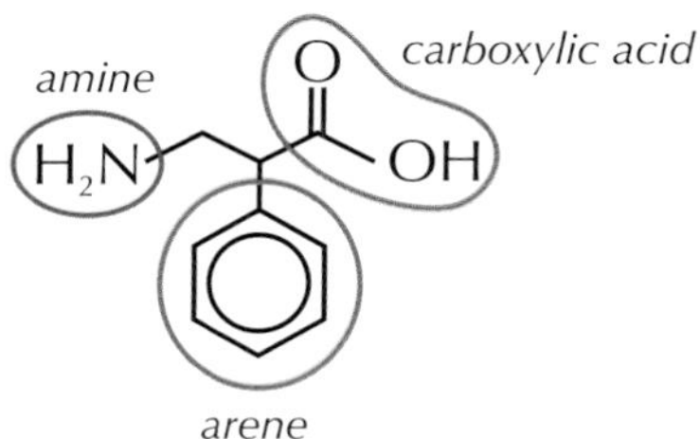

The molecule on the left has three functional groups: a carboxylic acid group, an arene group and an amine group.

The molecule on the right has three functional groups: an ester group and two alkene groups.

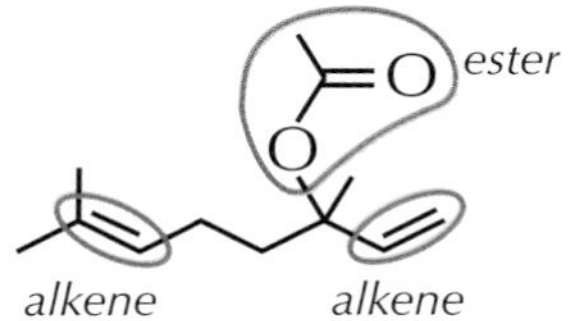

Tip: A carboxylic acid group can also be called a 'carboxyl group'.

Practice Questions — Application

Q1 For the molecule on the right:

a) Name the functional groups.

b) Explain why you might expect this molecule to undergo an oxidation reaction. What different functional group would the product of oxidation contain?

Q2 The molecules below all contain a variety of functional groups:

A: 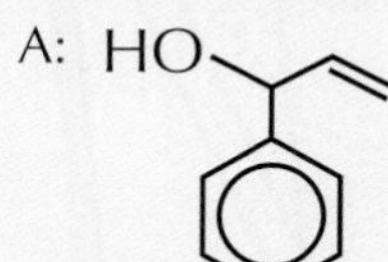 B: 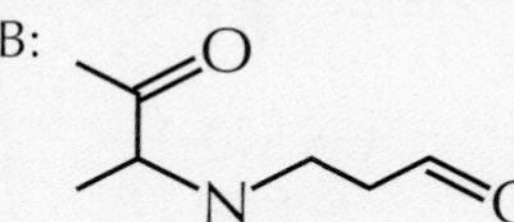 C: 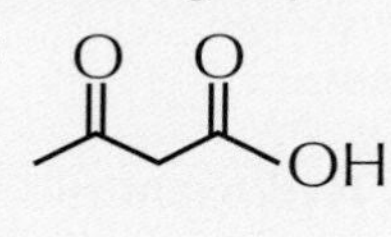

a) Which of the molecules contain an alcohol group?

b) Which of the molecules would you expect to take part in condensation reactions?

c) Which of the molecules could take part in reduction reactions to form secondary alcohols?

Practice Questions — Fact Recall

Q1 Draw the displayed formula of each of these functional groups:

a) arene b) primary amine c) ester

Q2 Name these functional groups:

a) -C≡N b) $-CONH_2$ c) -CHO

Learning Objective:

- Be able to devise multi-stage synthetic routes for preparing organic compounds.

Specification Reference 6.2.5

4. Synthetic Routes

In your exam, you may be asked to suggest a pathway for the synthesis of a particular molecule. The pathway may contain more than one step. These pages contain a summary of some of the reactions you should know.

Devising synthetic routes

HOW SCIENCE WORKS

Chemists have got to be able to make one compound from another. It's vital for things like designing medicines. Chemists use **synthetic** routes to show the reagents, conditions and any special procedures needed to get from one compound to another. The reaction schemes on the next two pages show some of the synthetic routes you've come across in the A Level Chemistry course. These reactions are covered elsewhere in the book, or in your Year 1 notes, so check back for extra details.

Synthesis routes for aliphatic compounds

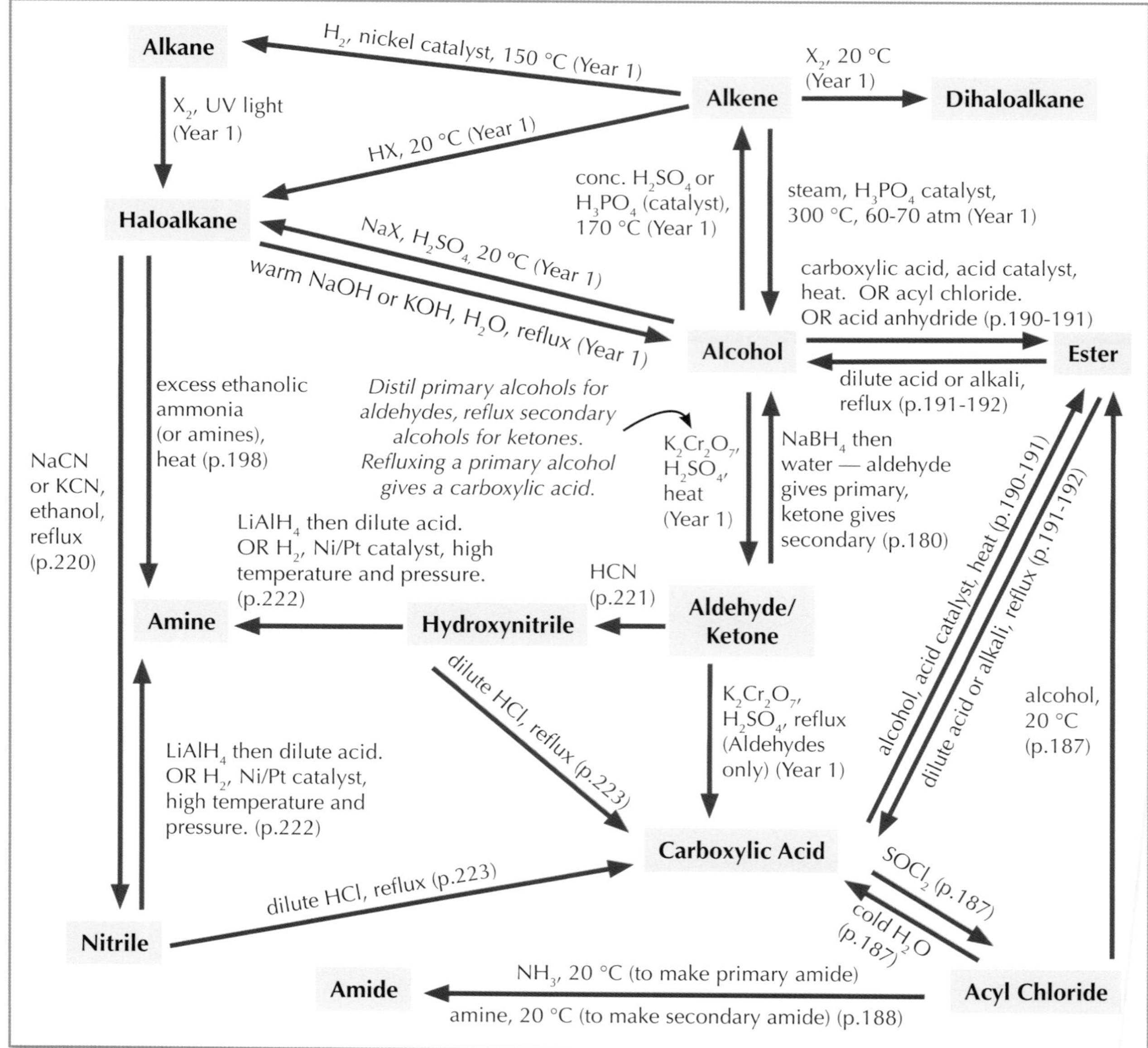

Synthetic routes for aromatic compounds

There aren't so many of these reactions to learn — so make sure you know all the itty-bitty details. If you can't remember any of the reactions, look back to the relevant pages and take a quick peek over them.

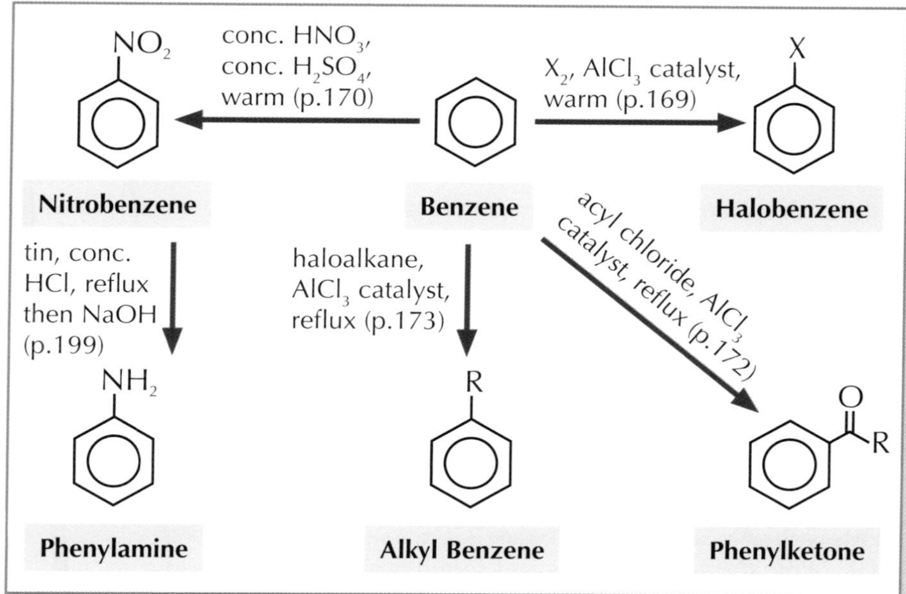

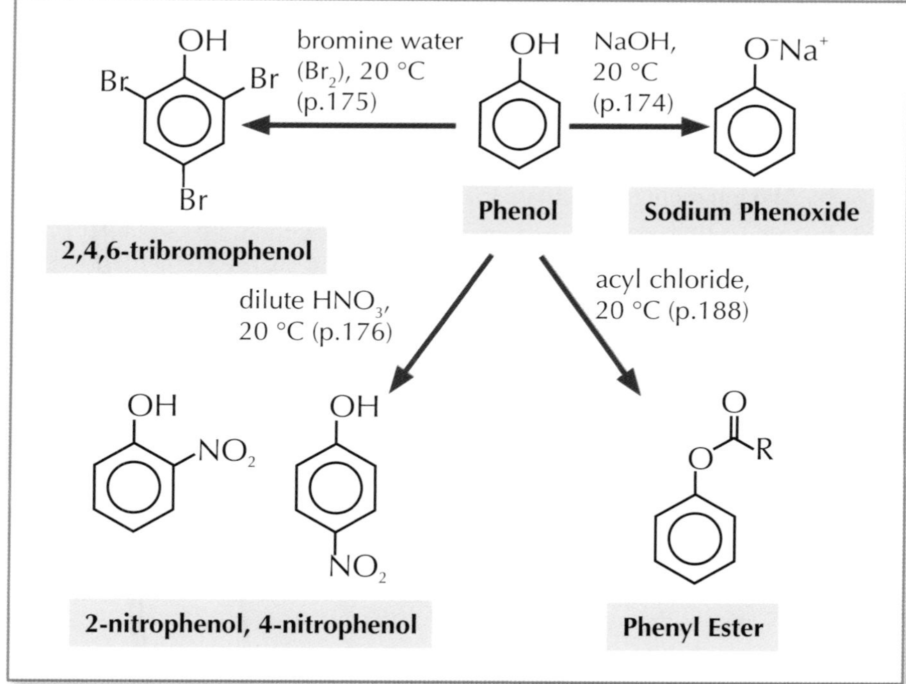

Tip: If you do any of these synthesis reactions in class, remember to carry out a risk assessment first.

Exam Tip
When you're writing down step-wise syntheses in the exam don't forget to put the conditions as well as the reagents. You might lose marks if you don't.

Tip: Functional groups on side-chains attached to a benzene ring will normally react in the same way as they would if they were in an aliphatic compound (see the reactions on the previous page).

Exam Tip
There may be fewer reactions involving aromatic compounds but they're just as likely to come up in the exam as the reactions on the previous page — so make sure you learn both sets of synthetic routes.

Organic synthesis in the exam

In your exams, you could be asked to provide a step-wise synthesis for the production of one chemical from another. You might have to use any of the reactions mentioned on the previous two pages so it's really important that you learn them all really well.

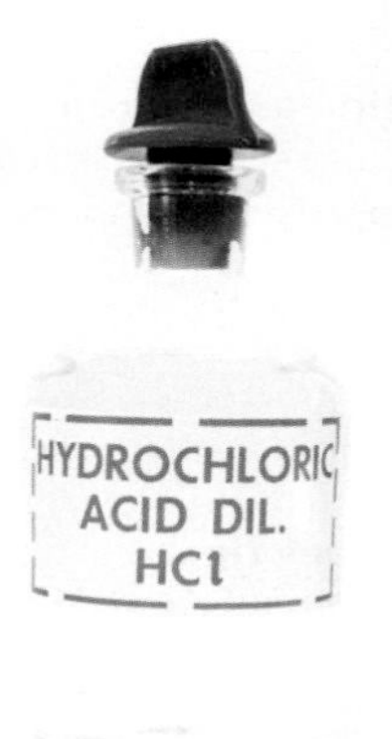

Figure 1: *Reagents are chemicals that can be taken from bottles or containers.*

If you're asked how to make one compound from another in the exam, include:

- The names and quantities of all the reagents needed.
- Any special procedures, such as refluxing.
- The conditions needed, e.g. high temperature or pressure, or the presence of a catalyst.
- Any safety precautions, e.g. if there are things like hydrogen chloride around, you really don't want to go breathing them in, so do the reaction in a fume cupboard.

Exam technique

In the exam you may be asked to 'identify' the name of a reagent used in a synthesis step. A reagent is just a chemical that can be used straight out of a bottle or container, for example, hydrochloric acid (HCl) or sodium hydroxide (NaOH). You must be really careful about this...

Example

Identify the reagent used to transform a bromoalkane into an alcohol.

Giving the reagent as OH^- in this case would be incorrect as you can't just take it out of a bottle. A correct answer would be, e.g. $NaOH_{(aq)}$.

Exam Tip

For questions like these you don't have to give the mechanisms or equations for the reactions.

Practice Questions — Application

Q1 Write down the reagents and conditions you would use to carry out the following organic syntheses.

a) Making ethanol from ethene using steam hydration.

b) Forming bromomethane from methane.

Q2 The following syntheses require two-steps. Write down the reagents and conditions you would use to carry out each step.

a) Creating propanal from 1-bromopropane.

b) Making methyl butanoate from butanal.

Q3 In an organic synthesis, benzene was heated with H_2SO_4 and HNO_3 to make an intermediate, X. A tin catalyst and HCl were then added and the mixture was refluxed before adding NaOH to make the overall product, Y. Identify X and Y.

Q4 Give a three-step synthesis of dibromoethane starting from ethanal. In your second synthesis step you should form ethene. For each step, give the reagents and conditions you would use to carry out the reaction.

Q5 Give a three-step synthesis of propanone starting from propene. In your first synthesis step you should form 2-bromopropane. For each step, give the reagents and conditions you would use to carry out the reaction.

Exam Tip

You need to be specific when you're talking about reagents in the exam. Make sure you write down exactly what you need to use — writing 'an alcohol' when you really mean 'ethanol' just won't get you all of the marks.

Practice Questions — Fact Recall

Q1 Name three types of organic compound that can react in one step to form a haloalkane.

Q2 Name three types of organic compound that you could synthesise from an aldehyde in one step.

Q3 Give the reagent and conditions you need in order to make a phenyl ester from phenol.

Section Summary

Make sure you know...

- That carbon-carbon bond formation is used in synthesis to increase the length of a carbon chain.
- That haloalkanes react with cyanide ions in ethanol in a nucleophilic substitution reaction to form nitriles, which results in the formation of a new C–C bond.
- The mechanism for the nucleophilic substitution reaction between haloalkanes and cyanide ions.
- That carbonyls, such as aldehydes and ketones, will react with hydrogen cyanide (HCN) in a nucleophilic addition reaction to form hydroxynitriles, which results in the formation of a new C–C bond.
- The mechanism for the electrophilic addition reaction between carbonyl compounds and hydrogen cyanide.
- How nitriles and hydroxynitriles can be reduced to form amines.
- How nitriles and hydroxynitriles can be hydrolysed with acid to form carboxylic acids.
- That Friedel-Crafts alkylation, using a haloalkane and a halogen carrier, can be used to form new C–C bonds to an aromatic ring.
- That Friedel-Crafts acylation, using an acyl chloride and a halogen carrier, can be used to form new C–C bonds to an aromatic ring.
- The techniques and procedures involved in preparing an organic compound, including using Quickfit apparatus, and the procedures for distillation and heating under reflux.
- How to purify an organic solid by filtration under reduced pressure.
- How to purify an organic solid by recrystallisation.
- How to check the purity of an organic solid by measuring its melting point.
- How to identify the functional groups in a molecule containing more than one functional group.
- How to predict the properties and reactions of an organic molecule based on its functional groups.
- How to devise multi-stage synthetic routes for preparing different organic compounds.

Exam-style Questions

1 Which of the molecules, **A**-**D**, would not be a valid starting compound for synthesising the molecule shown on the right in two steps or fewer?

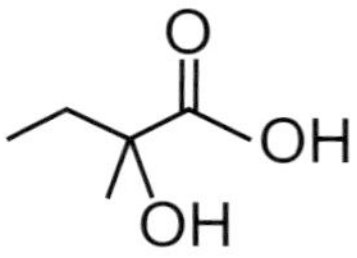

A

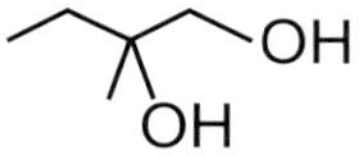

B

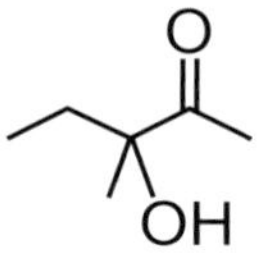

C

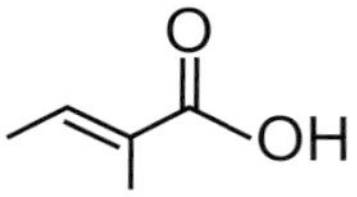

D

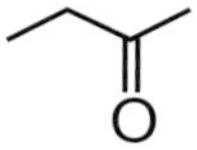

(1 mark)

2 A student is carrying out a recrystallisation to purify an organic solid. Which of the following actions could result in the student getting a very low yield of the solid after recrystallisation?

Action 1: The student dissolved the solid in the smallest possible amount of hot solvent.

Action 2: The organic solid was soluble in the solvent when warm, but only partially soluble when cold.

Action 3: The student washed the crystals with some ice-cold solvent after filtering the recrystallised solid under reduced pressure.

A Actions 1, 2 and 3

B Only action 2

C Actions 2 & 3

D Only action 3

(1 mark)

3 Which of the following is not a valid two-step synthetic route?

A nitrile → amine → alcohol

B hydroxynitrile → carboxylic acid → acyl chloride

C benzene → phenyl ketone → phenyl alcohol

D benzene → nitrobenzene → phenylamine

(1 mark)

4 The drug procaine, shown below, is commonly used as a local anaesthetic.

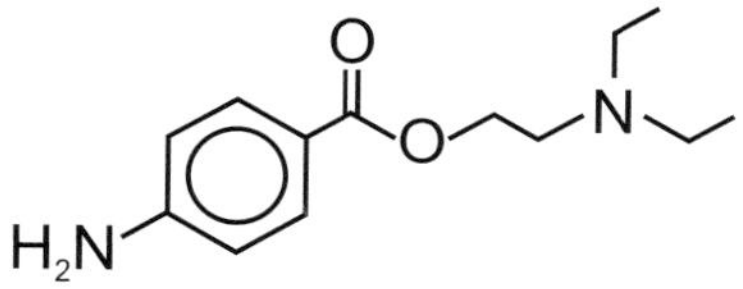

(a) Redraw the structure of procaine, and circle and name all of the functional groups.

(2 marks)

(b) Procaine can be synthesised in two steps from 4-aminobenzoic acid. The reaction scheme is shown below, with some of the details missing.

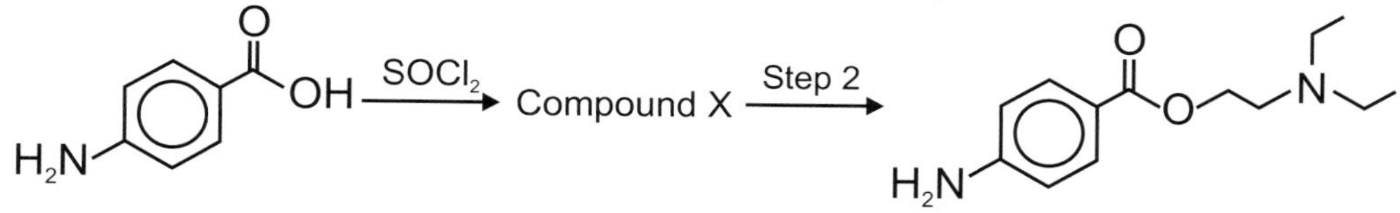

$\xrightarrow{SOCl_2}$ Compound X $\xrightarrow{\text{Step 2}}$

(i) Draw the structure of Compound X, the organic product formed when 4-aminobenzoic acid is reacted with $SOCl_2$.

(1 mark)

(ii) Draw the reagent needed in Step 2 of the synthesis, and give the conditions needed for the reaction.

(2 marks)

(c) A chemist synthesises procaine in a laboratory. He measures the melting point of his final product, and finds it to be in the range of 48-53 °C. The recorded melting point of procaine is 61 °C.

(i) What does the chemist's measured melting point for procaine tell you about his sample?

(1 mark)

(ii) Suggest one procedure the chemist could carry out that could improve the concordance between the melting point of his sample and the recorded value.

(1 mark)

5 The organic compound, Y, can be synthesised from benzene via the following three-stage reaction scheme:

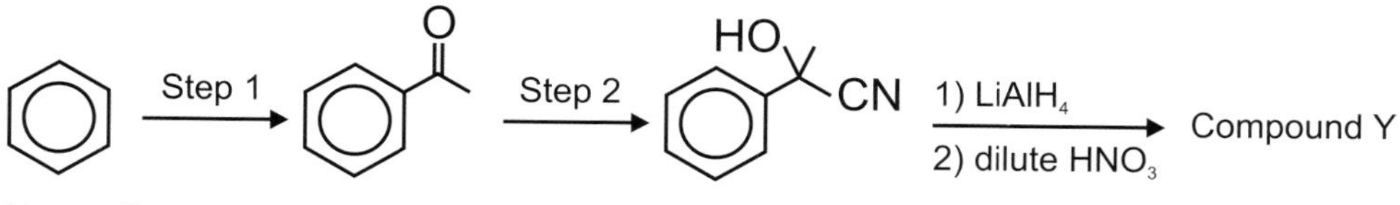

Step 1 → Step 2 → 1) $LiAlH_4$ 2) dilute HNO_3 → Compound Y

(a) Name the reagents and conditions needed in Step 1 of the reaction scheme.

(1 mark)

(b) (i) Name the reagent(s) needed in Step 2 of the reaction scheme.

(1 mark)

(ii) Draw and name the mechanism for the reaction that occurs in Step 2.

(4 marks)

(c) Draw the structure of Compound Y.

(1 mark)

1. Tests for Organic Functional Groups

PRACTICAL ACTIVITY GROUP 7

Learning Objectives:
- Be able to qualitatively analyse organic functional groups on a test tube scale, and know the processes and techniques needed to identify specific organic functional groups in an unknown compound (PAG 7).
- Know how to identify alkenes by reaction with bromine (PAG 7).
- Know how to identify haloalkanes by reaction with aqueous silver nitrate in ethanol (PAG 7).
- Know how to identify phenols by weak acidity but no reaction with CO_3^{2-} (PAG 7).
- Know how to identify carboxylic acids by reaction with CO_3^{2-}.
- Know how to identify carbonyl compounds by reaction with 2,4-DNP (PAG 7).
- Know how to identify aldehydes by reaction with Tollens' reagent.
- Know how to identify primary and secondary alcohols and aldehydes by reaction with acidified dichromate (PAG 7).

Specification Reference 6.3.1

If you're given an unknown organic compound, there are several tests you can carry out to work out what it is. It's very important for each test to know what you're testing for, and how you will know if the result is positive. You've come across all of these tests already, but they're nicely summarised for you on the next few pages.

Testing for alkenes

To test whether an unknown compound is an alkene, you have to add bromine water. What you're actually testing for is unsaturation — the presence of double bonds (see page 168). Here's what you do:

1. Add 2 cm^3 of the substance that you want to test to a test tube.
2. Add 2 cm^3 of orange bromine water to the test tube.
3. Shake the test tube (see Figure 1) and watch what happens.

If the substance contains an alkene functional group, the solution will decolourise (go from orange, the colour of bromine water, to colourless). If there isn't an alkene present, nothing will happen.

Figure 1: *Shaking a test tube containing an alkene and bromine water turns the solution from orange to colourless.*

Testing for haloalkanes

To test whether an unknown compound is a haloalkane, or contains a halogen, you have to add aqueous silver nitrate in ethanol. Here's how:

1. Add five drops of the unknown substance to a test tube.
2. Add 1 cm^3 of ethanol and 1 cm^3 of aqueous silver nitrate.
3. Place the test tube in a water bath to warm it.
4. Watch for a precipitate and observe the colour (see Figure 2).

Haloakane	Colour of precipitate
fluoroalkane	no precipitate forms
chloroalkane	white
bromoalkane	pale cream
iodoalkane	pale yellow

Figure 2: *Results of adding ethanol and aqueous silver nitrate to haloakanes.*

Tip: You may see aqueous silver nitrate called silver nitrate solution. Don't worry — they're the same thing.

Testing for phenols

Testing for phenols is a bit trickier, as you have to carry out a couple of reactions. What you're actually testing is the weak acidic nature of phenols (see page 174). First, you use the following method to test for a reaction with sodium hydroxide — sodium hydroxide is a strong base and so will react with any acid.

1. Add 2 cm^3 of the unknown substance to a test tube.
2. Add 1 small spatula of solid sodium hydroxide (or 2 cm^3 of sodium hydroxide solution).

If the substance contains an acid, such as a phenol, the solution will fizz and a colourless solution of a sodium salt will form. If the substance is not acidic, nothing will happen.

Next, you need to use the following test to see if the unknown substance will react with a carbonate — a much weaker base than sodium hydroxide. Carbonates will only react with strong acids, not weak acids such as a phenol.

1. Add 2 cm^3 of the unknown substance to a test tube.
2. Add 1 small spatula of a solid carbonate or 2 cm^3 of a carbonate solution (sodium carbonate will work nicely).

If the substance contains a phenol, nothing will happen. If the substance contains a strong acid, the solution will fizz as carbon dioxide gas is released.

Tip: Before carrying out any of the tests on these pages, you need to think about any safety issues that might be involved.

Tip: To confirm the presence of a phenol, you need it to react with NaOH, but not Na_2CO_3.

Tip: This second test forms the basis for the test to identify carboxylic acids (see below).

Testing for carboxylic acids

Unlike phenols, carboxylic acids do react with carbonates to form a salt, carbon dioxide and water (see page 186). The general equation for this reaction, using solid sodium carbonate, is:

$$2RCOOH_{(aq)} + Na_2CO_{3\ (s)} \rightarrow 2RCOO^-Na^+_{(aq)} + CO_{2\ (g)} + H_2O_{(l)}$$

You can use this reaction to test whether a substance is a carboxylic acid. Here's what to do:

1. Add 2 cm^3 of the substance that you want to test to a test tube.
2. Add 1 small spatula of a solid carbonate (or 2 cm^3 of a carbonate solution) e.g. sodium carbonate.
3. If the solution begins to fizz, bubble the gas that it produces through some limewater in a second test tube (see Figure 4).

If the unknown compound contains a carboxylic acid, the solution will fizz as carbon dioxide gas is produced. When you bubble carbon dioxide through limewater, the limewater turns cloudy.
If there isn't a carboxylic acid present, the limewater will stay colourless — you may not get a reaction at all.

LIME WATER
Figure 3: A set-up used to test for carboxylic acids with carbonate ions and limewater.

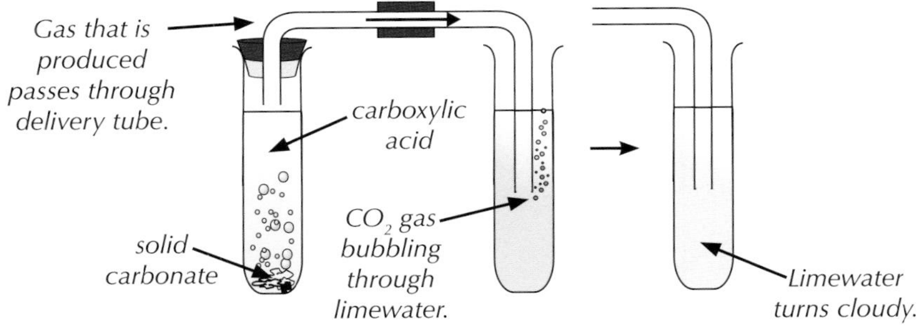
Gas that is produced passes through delivery tube.
carboxylic acid
solid carbonate
CO_2 gas bubbling through limewater.
Limewater turns cloudy.
Figure 4: *The test for identifying carboxylic acids.*

Tip: In this test, you need to make sure the reaction vessel is airtight, and the only place the gas can escape is through the tube that leads to the test tube containing limewater.

Tip: You may sometimes see 2,4-DNPH called 2,4-DNP.

Tip: The solution you've made at the end of step 1 is known as Brady's reagent.

Exam Tip
You won't need to remember specific quantities and concentrations for the exams — just make sure you know the reagents, the method and the expected observations.

Testing for aldehydes and ketones

With this test, you need to use the reagent 2,4-dinitrophenylhydrazine (2,4-DNPH). It may be a bit of a mouthful to say, but it's great for testing for aldehydes and ketones (see page 183).

1. Dissolve 0.2 g of 2,4-DNPH in 1 cm^3 of sulfuric acid, 2 cm^3 of water and 5 cm^3 of methanol.
2. In a different test tube, add 5 drops of the unknown substance to 2 cm^3 of your solution from step 1.
3. Shake the test tube and watch for a precipitate.

If the unknown compound is an aldehyde or a ketone, the 2,4-DNPH will react with the carbonyl group and a bright orange precipitate will form.
If there isn't an aldehyde or ketone group present, nothing will happen.

Testing for aldehydes

This is another test for carbonyls (see above) but this time, it allows you to tell aldehydes and ketones apart. Unfortunately you have to prepare the reagent yourself. Mean.

1. Put 2 cm^3 of 0.10 mol dm^{-3} silver nitrate solution in a test tube.
2. Add 5 drops of 0.80 mol dm^{-3} sodium hydroxide solution. A light brown precipitate should form.
3. Add drops of dilute ammonia solution until the brown precipitate dissolves completely. You have now prepared the reagent known as Tollens' reagent (see Figure 6).
4. Add 10 drops of aldehyde or ketone and place the test tube in a warm water bath. Wait for a few minutes (see Figure 7).

If the substance contains an aldehyde, a silver mirror (a thin coating of silver) forms on the walls of the test tube (see Figures 5 and 7).
There's no reaction with other carbonyls, such as ketones.

Figure 5: *The colourless solution in the test tube on the left shows the unreacted Tollens' reagent. The test tube on the right shows the result of a reaction with an aldehyde.*

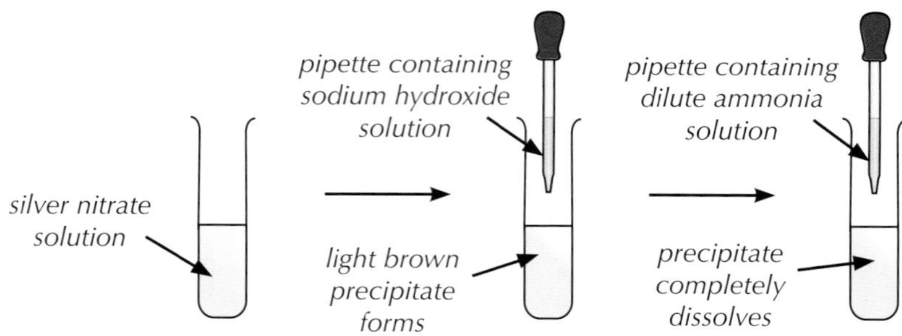

Figure 6: *Preparing Tollens' reagent.*

Tip: Aldehydes and ketones are flammable, so the test tube should be heated in a water bath, rather than over a flame. See pages 11-12 for more on heating methods that don't involve naked flames.

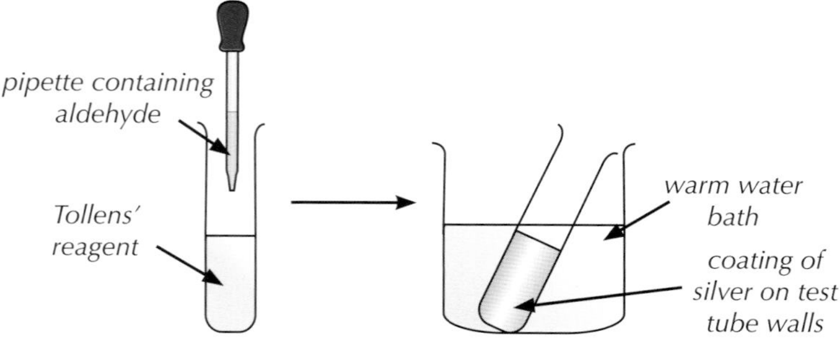

Figure 7: *Using Tollens' reagent to identify the presence of an aldehyde.*

Testing for primary and secondary alcohols

This test allows you to test for the presence of primary or secondary alcohols, but doesn't distinguish between them. Here's how:

1. Add 10 drops of the unknown substance to 2 cm^3 of acidified potassium dichromate(VI) solution in a test tube.
2. Warm the mixture gently in a water bath and watch for a colour change.

If a primary or secondary alcohol is present, the orange solution slowly turns green (see Figures 8 and 9). If a tertiary alcohol is present, nothing will happen.

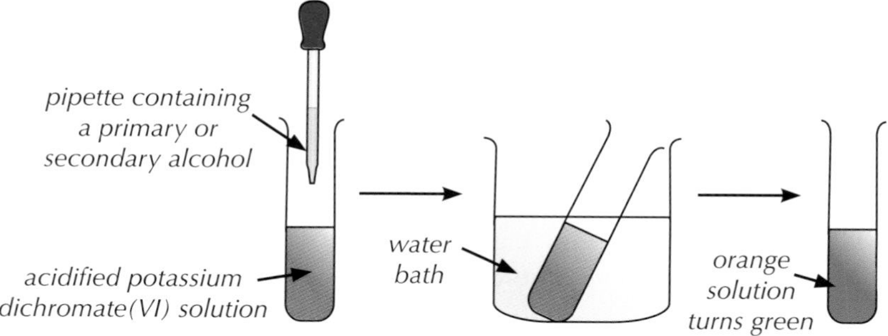

Figure 9: *Testing for primary and secondary alcohols.*

Tip: Primary alcohols are oxidised to aldehydes and then to carboxylic acids. Secondary alcohols are oxidised to ketones.

Figure 8: *The orange solution in the test tube on the left shows the unreacted acidified potassium dichromate. The test tube on the right shows the result of a reaction with a primary or secondary alcohol.*

Tip: The colour change is the orange dichromate(VI) ion ($Cr_2O_7^{2-}$) being reduced to the green chromium(III) ion (Cr^{3+}).

Practice Questions — Application

Q1 A student has an unknown organic compound. They add it to a test tube containing a solution of ethanol and aqueous silver nitrate. They warm the test tube for a while, and a pale cream precipitate forms. What functional group does the unknown compound contain?

Q2 A student has three test tubes. Each test tube contains one of three organic compounds: propanal, propanoic acid and propanone. Outline a series of tests the student could carry out to identify which test tube contains which compound. You should include details of any reagents, conditions and expected observations.

Q3 A student is investigating the behaviour of primary alcohols.

a) She firstly adds a primary alcohol to a solution containing acidified potassium dichromate(VI) ions. What colour change would you expect her to see?

b) She then adds a spatula of calcium carbonate to the resulting solution. The solution starts to fizz. The student bubbles the resulting gas through a test tube containing limewater. What would you expect the student to observe?

Practice Questions — Fact Recall

Q1 What reagent would you add to an unknown substance to test whether it contained an alkene?

Q2 What colour precipitate would you expect to form if you added aqueous silver nitrate to a test tube containing iodopropane?

Q3 Describe how you would test a sample of a compound to find out if it contained a phenol.

Q4 Describe what you would see if you added 2,4-dinitrophenylhydrazine to a solution containing a substance with a carbonyl group.

Tip: Qualitative analysis is a vital part of organic chemistry. It involves using tests, such as the ones outlined on these pages, to work out what functional groups are present in a compound. These tests are used by research scientists for identifying unknown compounds or confirming the identity of a product in organic synthesis.

HOW SCIENCE WORKS

Learning Objective:

- Be able to interpret one-way TLC chromatograms in terms of R_f values (PAG 6).

Specification Reference 6.3.1

Tip: Before carrying out any chromatography experiment, you need to do a risk assessment.

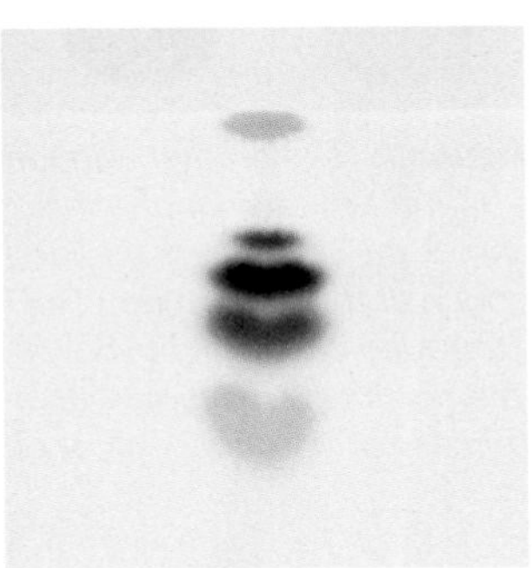

Figure 1: *A TLC chromatogram.*

Tip: If the chemicals in your mixture are colourless, you'll have to treat the dried plate with a chemical like iodine or ninhydrin to make the spots visible.

Tip: R_f stands for 'retardation factor'.

Tip: The distance travelled by the solvent is the distance between the base line and the solvent front.

2. Chromatography

Chromatography is used to separate and identify chemicals in mixtures.

The basics

Chromatography is used to separate different substances in a mixture — once the mixture's separated out, you can often identify the components, for example, different organic compounds. There are quite a few different types of chromatography (you might have tried paper chromatography already) but the ones you need to know about are thin-layer chromatography (TLC) and gas chromatography (GC) — there's more about GC in the next topic.

Thin-layer chromatography

PRACTICAL ACTIVITY GROUP 6

In **thin-layer chromatography** (**TLC**) a solvent, such as ethanol, moves over a glass or plastic plate which is covered in a thin layer (0.1-0.3 mm thick) of solid, e.g. silica gel or aluminium powder.

Here's how you separate a mixture using TLC:

1. Draw a pencil line near the bottom of the plate — this is called the base line. Put a spot of the mixture to be separated on the line.
2. Put the plate in a beaker containing a small amount of solvent — the level of solvent should cover the bottom of the plate, but not the spot.
3. Put a watch glass over the top of the beaker (this stops the solvent from evaporating). As the solvent spreads up the plate, the different substances in the mixture move with it, but different distances — so they separate out.

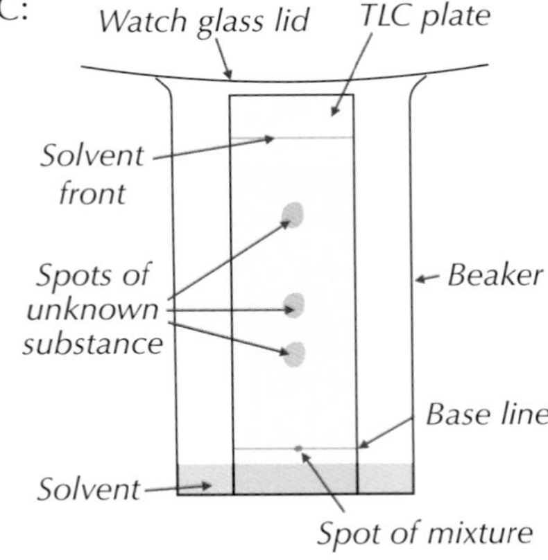

Figure 2: *A thin-layer chromatography plate.*

4. When the solvent's nearly reached the top, take the plate out of the beaker and mark the distance that the solvent has moved (the **solvent front**) in pencil.

Then you can leave the plate in a safe place to dry out before you analyse it. The plate, with its pattern of spots, is called a **chromatogram** (see Figure 1).

R_f values

An R_f **value** is the ratio of the distance travelled by a spot to the distance travelled by the solvent. You can calculate them using this formula:

$$R_f \text{ value} = \frac{\text{distance travelled by spot}}{\text{distance travelled by solvent}}$$

When you're measuring how far a spot has travelled, you just measure from the base line (point of origin) to the vertical centre of the spot.

You can work out what was in a mixture by calculating an R_f value for each spot on the TLC plate and comparing your experimental values to the R_f values of known substances in a data book. This isn't always accurate as R_f values are affected by external conditions and changes in the set-up of the plate (see the next page) so it's good to run a pure sample of what you think your unknown is, alongside your unknown, to double-check.

Example — Maths Skills

A sugar solution containing a mixture of three sugars is separated using TLC. The chromatogram is shown on the right.

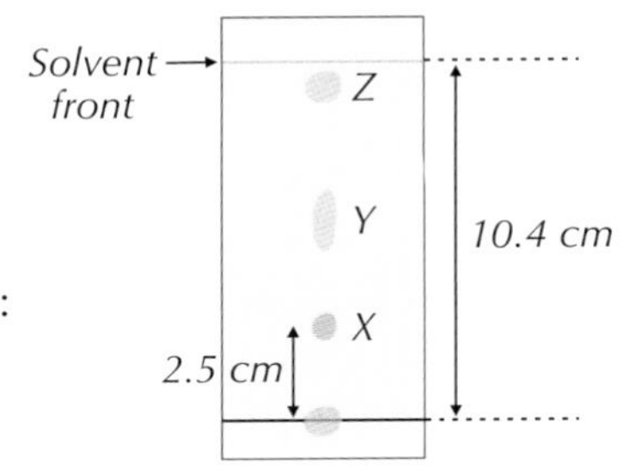

a) Calculate the R_f value of spot X.

To find the R_f value of spot X all you have to do is stick the numbers into the formula:

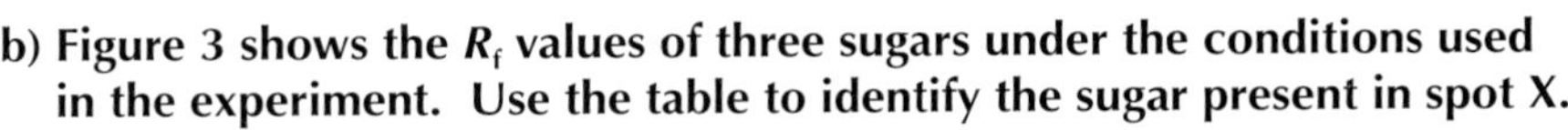

$$R_f \text{ value} = \frac{\text{distance travelled by spot}}{\text{distance travelled by solvent}}$$

$= 2.5 \text{ cm} \div 10.4 \text{ cm} = 0.24$

b) Figure 3 shows the R_f values of three sugars under the conditions used in the experiment. Use the table to identify the sugar present in spot X.

Spot X has an R_f value of 0.24. Fructose also has an R_f value of 0.24. So fructose is the sugar present in spot X.

Sugar	R_f value
Glucose	0.20
Fructose	0.24
Xylose	0.30

Figure 3: *R_f values of sugars.*

Factors affecting R_f values

How far an organic molecule travels up the plate depends on how strongly it's attracted to the layer of solid on the surface of the plate. The attraction between a substance and the solid surface of the plate is called **adsorption**. A substance that is strongly adsorbed will move slowly, so it won't travel as far as one that's only weakly adsorbed. This means it will have a smaller R_f value. Chemical properties, such as polarity, affect how strongly adsorbed a particular substances is to the plate.

The distance a particular substance moves up the plate also depends on the solid coating on the plate, the solvent used, and other external variables such as temperature. This means small changes in the TLC set-up, or the room you carry out your experiment in, can cause changes in the R_f value. So, once you've identified what you think an unknown compound is, it's best to check you're right by running a pure sample of the known substance alongside your unknown compound on a TLC plate. Identical substances should travel the same distance up the plate, i.e. have the same R_f value, as long as all other variables are controlled.

Exam Tip
Being able to use thin-layer chromatography to analyse organic compounds is a great example of How Science Works.

Tip: If you're given a drawing of a TLC plate that's to scale, you can use a ruler to measure the distances between the base line, the solvent front and the spots.

Practice Question — Application

Q1 A student used thin-layer chromatography to separate out a mixture of three amino acids. The chromatogram that she produced is shown on the right.

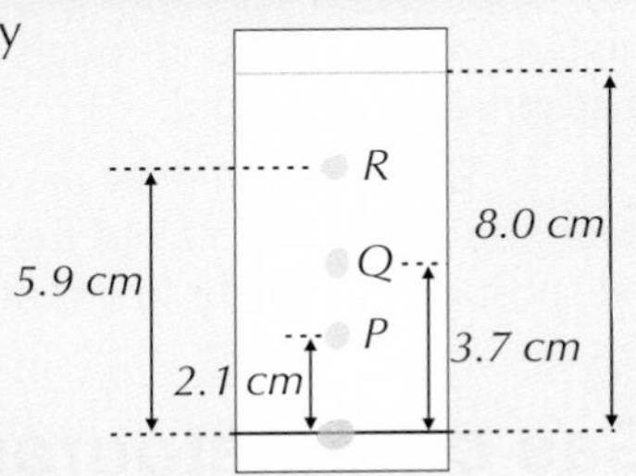

a) Calculate the R_f values of the three spots, P, Q and R.

b) Use the table in Figure 4 to identify the amino acid present in each spot.

c) Apart from using Figure 4, how could the student confirm that each amino acid has been identified correctly?

Tip: R_f values are always between 0 and 1.

Amino acid	R_f value
Glycine	0.26
Alanine	0.39
Tyrosine	0.46
Valine	0.61
Leucine	0.74

Figure 4: *R_f values of amino acids.*

Practice Questions — Fact Recall

Q1 Explain why mixtures separate during thin-layer chromatography.

Q2 Give the formula for calculating R_f values.

Q3 Name two things that can affect the R_f value of a certain compound.

Learning Objective:

- Be able to interpret gas chromatograms in terms of retention times, and the amounts and proportions of the components in a mixture.

Specification Reference 6.3.1

3. Gas Chromatography

The second type of chromatography you need to know about is gas chromatography. It's more high-tech than thin-layer chromatography, but the idea's just the same — things separating so you can identify them.

What is gas chromatography?

If you've got a mixture of volatile liquids (ones that turn into gases easily), then **gas chromatography** (GC) is the way to separate them out so that you can identify them. In gas chromatography, the sample to be analysed is injected into the machine, where it is vaporised (turned into a gas). A stream of carrier gas carries the sample through a coiled tube coated with a viscous liquid (such as an oil) or a solid.

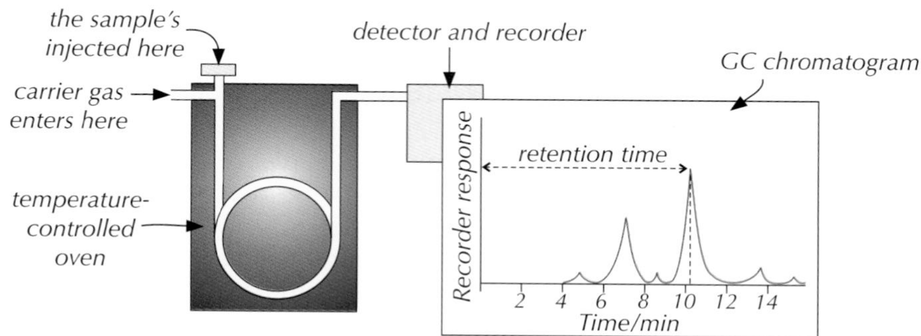

Figure 1: *Gas chromatography equipment and a chromatogram.*

Exam Tip
If you're writing about gas chromatography where the tube is coated in a liquid, then solubility is the word you need to use. If the tube is coated in a solid, you need to use adsorption — just like in TLC (see page 243-244).

If the tube is coated in liquid, the components of the mixture will constantly dissolve in it, evaporate into the gas, and then redissolve as they travel through the tube. The solubility of each component of the mixture determines how long it spends dissolved in the liquid and how long it spends moving along the tube in the gas. A substance with a high solubility will spend more time dissolved, so will take longer to travel through the tube to the detector than one with a lower solubility.

If the tube is coated in a solid, then the separation works in the same way as thin-layer chromatography (see page 243). How long each part of the mixture takes to travel through the tube will depend on how strongly it is adsorbed to the solid.

The time taken for the substances to pass through the coiled tube and reach the detector is called the **retention time**. It can be used to help identify the substances present in the mixture (see below).

Tip: Changes in the environment and in the set-up of your gas chromatography equipment affect retention times. This means reference values may not always match experimental ones you collect (see next page).

Gas chromatograms

A gas **chromatogram** is a graph showing a series of peaks at the times when the detector senses something other than the carrier gas leaving the tube. They can be used to identify the substances within a sample and their relative proportions.

Each peak on a chromatogram corresponds to a substance with a particular **retention time**. Retention times are measured from zero to the centre of each peak, and can be looked up in a reference table, to identify the substances present.

The area under each peak is proportional to the relative amount of each component that's present in the mixture (see Figure 2). For example, if a peak has three times the area of another peak, it tells you that there is three times as much of the first substance in the mixture (compared to the second substance).

retention time

This peak corresponds to the most abundant component in the mixture as it has the largest peak area.

This peak has the shortest retention time so it will have spent the least time dissolved in the liquid.

Recorder response

2 4 6 8 10 12 14

Time/min

Figure 2: *A gas chromatogram showing the separation of three components in a mixture.*

You can calculate the proportion of a component in a mixture by comparing the area under its peak on a gas chromatogram, to the total area under all the peaks on the chromatogram. You can use this formula to do this:

$$\text{Percentage in original mixture} = \frac{\text{area of peak}}{\text{total area of all peaks}}$$

Tip: If you're looking at the amount of each compound present, it's the area of the peaks (not the height) that's important — the tallest peak won't always represent the most abundant substance.

Retention times

You can use retention times to identify the components of a mixture. By comparing experimental retention times to retention times from reference tables and data books, you can work out the likely identity of an unknown compound. If you wanted to know if a mixture contained octane, you could run a sample of the mixture through the system, then look up the retention time for octane run under those conditions and see if it's the same as the retention time for a peak in your GC spectrum.

If you're looking up retention times in a reference table, you must make sure that the conditions under which you did your experiment were the same as the conditions used when the data in the reference table was collected (e.g. at the same temperature).

There are several factors that affect retention times:

- Solubility or adsorption — this determines how long each component of the mixture spends in the stationary phase, and how long they spend moving along the tube in the gas. If the stationary phase is a liquid, then the more soluble a substance is, the more time it will spend dissolved. If the stationary phase is a solid, then the more strongly a substance is attracted to the solid, the more time it will spend adsorbed on the surface. It will therefore take longer to travel through the tube to the detector than one that is less soluble or less strongly adsorbed.
- Boiling point — a substance with a high boiling point will spend more time condensed as a liquid in the tube than as a gas. This means it will take longer to travel through the tube than one with a lower boiling point.
- Temperature of the gas chromatography instrument — a high temperature means the substance will spend more time evaporated in the gas and so will move along the tube quickly. It shortens the retention time for all the substances in the tube.

Tip: You could also run gas chromatography on a pure sample of what you think the unknown substance is and then compare the retention times.

Tip: Adsorption is to do with how well a substance is attracted to the surface of a solid. Solubility is to do with how well something dissolves in a liquid. Make sure you use the right term depending on whether the stationary phase is a solid or a liquid.

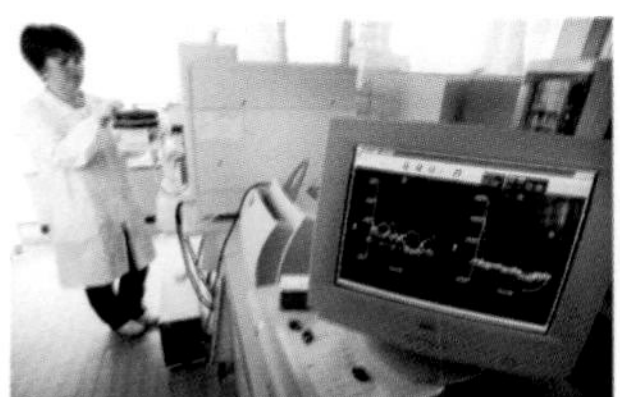

Figure 3: *A researcher using a gas chromatograph to separate and identify the chemicals in a sample.*

External calibration curves

The area under the peak of a GC chromatogram gives you the relative amount of a substance, but finding the exact concentration is a bit trickier. To work out the concentration of a particular substance in a sample, you need create an **external calibration curve**. Fortunately it's not too hard — just follow these steps.

1. First, create a series of standard solutions of different concentrations of analyte — this is the substance you've chosen to detect for your calibration.
2. One by one, inject your standard solutions into a gas chromatography instrument and record the result.
3. For the chromatogram of each standard solution, calculate the area under the peak that corresponds to the analyte.
4. Plot these area values on a graph of area against concentration and then draw a line of best fit to create an external calibration curve.

It's a good idea to run a blank when you're making a calibration curve. A blank is just a solution containing all the solvents and reagents used when making the standard solutions, but no analyte. By subtracting the chromatogram of the blank from each of the chromatograms of your standard solutions, you can find a corrected peak value — one that takes into account the effect of reagents and solvents on the peak areas.

Your calibration curve is now ready to use — by reading along to the line of best fit, you can work out the concentration that corresponds to the area of a peak.

Exam Tip
Don't worry if the points you plot make a curve instead of a line. Just draw a curve that fits most of the points (a line of best fit) and read off the values in the same way.

Tip: Your calibration curve can be a straight line or a curve.

Tip: If you need the integration values for the areas of gas chromatography peaks in the exams, you'll be given them — you don't need to know how to work them out.

Tip: You can't just use one calibration curve for every gas chromatography experiment you ever do. As with retention times, calibration curves vary depending on external conditions and the set-up of your gas chromatography equipment.

Example — Maths Skills

On a chromatogram, the area under the peak for substance X is 360 units. Estimate the concentration of substance X in the sample by drawing an external calibration curve, using the data in the table below. The areas have been corrected using a blank.

Concentration (mol dm^{-3})	0.00	0.25	0.50	0.60
Area (units)	0	190	410	500

First, plot the points from the table on a graph. Concentration is always plotted on the *x*-axis and area on the *y*-axis. Then draw a line (or curve) of best fit through your data set.

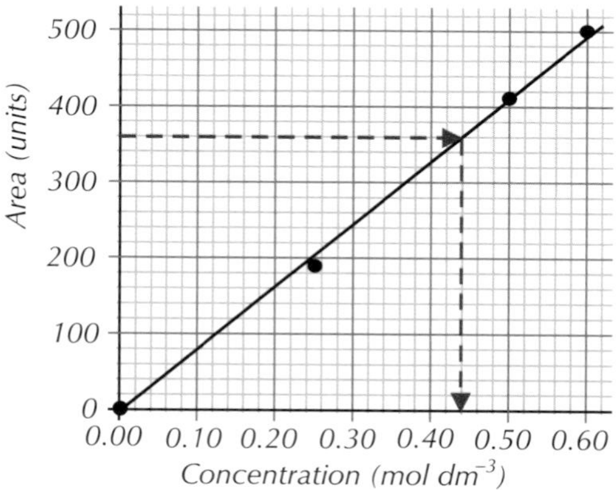

Now work out what concentration corresponds to an area of 360 units by drawing a line from 360 on the *y*-axis to where it meets the curve, and then drawing a line from this point down to the *x*-axis.
Read off the result on the *x*-axis.
So the concentration of substance X is **0.44 mol dm^{-3}**.

Practice Questions — Application

Q1 A scientist is using gas chromatography to purify an organic product. She knows that the pure product is more soluble in the oil than the impurities. Will the pure product reach the detector before or after the impurities? Explain your answer.

Q2 Below is a gas chromatogram for a mixture of three components.

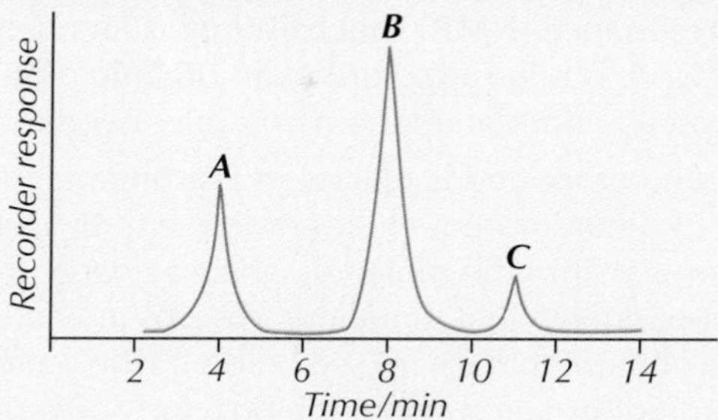

a) State which peak, A, B or C, corresponds to the component that spends the highest proportion of its time in the tube evaporated in the carrier gas.

b) One component of the mixture is hexene. Run under the same conditions, pure hexene has a retention time of 8 minutes. Which of the components, A, B or C, is hexene?

c) The smallest proportion of the mixture is made up of decene. Which of the components, A, B or C, is decene?

Q3 A gas chromatogram has two peaks.
Peak 1 has an area of 32 cm², and Peak 2 has an area of 16 cm².

a) Given that the only responses on the chromatogram were Peak 1 and Peak 2, what percentage of the original mixture was made up of the chemical that caused Peak 2?

b) Below is an external calibration curve for a chemical, X, that caused Peak 2. Estimate the concentration of X in the sample.

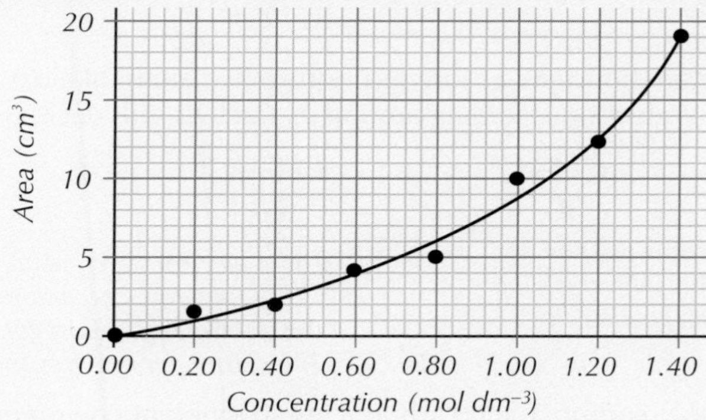

Tip: Gas chromatography is a really popular method amongst scientists for working what unknown substances a mixture might contain.

HOW SCIENCE WORKS

Exam Tip
Remember, in your exam answers it's 'retention time' that you need to talk about for gas chromatography and 'R_f value' for thin-layer chromatography — don't get them mixed up.

Exam Tip
In the exam, you may have to create your own calibration curve by plotting a graph.

Practice Questions — Fact Recall

Q1 Briefly explain why the components in a mixture separate out during gas chromatography when oil is used to coat the coiled tube.

Q2 What is retention time a measure of?

Q3 What does the area under each peak on a gas chromatogram tell you?

Q4 Describe how you could create an external calibration curve to work out the concentration of a substance.

4. NMR Spectroscopy

NMR (nuclear magnetic resonance) spectroscopy provides information on the different environments of atoms in molecules.

Learning Objectives:

- Be able to describe the use of tetramethylsilane, TMS, as the standard for chemical shift measurements.
- Be able to analyse a carbon-13 NMR spectrum of an organic molecule to make predictions about the number of carbon environments in an organic molecule, the different types of carbon environment present, from chemical shift values, and the possible structures for the molecule.
- Be able to predict a carbon-13 NMR spectrum for a given molecule.

Specification Reference 6.3.2

NMR spectroscopy and radio waves

Nuclear magnetic resonance (**NMR**) **spectroscopy** is an analytical technique that you can use to work out the structure of an organic molecule. The way that NMR works is pretty complicated, but you only need to know the basics.

A sample of a compound is placed in a strong magnetic field and exposed to a range of different frequencies of low-energy radio waves. The nuclei of certain atoms within the molecule absorb energy from the radio waves. The amount of energy that a nucleus absorbs at each frequency will depend on the environment that it's in (see below). The pattern of these absorptions gives you information about the positions of certain atoms within the molecule, and about how many atoms of that type the molecule contains. You can piece these bits of information together to work out the structure of the molecule.

The two types of NMR spectroscopy you need to know about are **carbon-13 NMR** (or **^{13}C NMR**) and high resolution proton NMR (or ^{1}H NMR). Carbon-13 NMR gives you information about the number and type of carbon environments that are in a molecule. High resolution proton NMR gives you information about the number of hydrogen atoms that are in a molecule, and the environments that they're in.

Exam Tip
You won't be asked how an NMR spectrometer works, but it'll help you to understand the spectra if you know the basics.

Nuclear environments

A nucleus is partly shielded from the effects of an external magnetic field by its surrounding electrons. Any other atoms and groups of atoms that are around a nucleus will also affect the amount of electron shielding. So the nuclei in a molecule feel different magnetic fields depending on their environments.

Example

If a carbon atom bonds to a more electronegative atom (like oxygen) the amount of electron shielding around its nucleus will decrease.

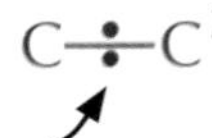

These electrons provide the carbon atoms with shielding from a magnetic field.

These electrons are pulled further away from the carbon atom by the electronegative oxygen atom. The carbon atom is less shielded.

This means that carbon 1 and carbon 2 are in different environments.

Nuclei in different environments will absorb different amounts of energy at different frequencies. It's these differences in absorption of energy between environments that you're looking for in NMR spectroscopy.

An atom's environment depends on all the groups that it's connected to, going right along the molecule — not just the atoms it's directly bonded to. To be in the same environment, two atoms must be joined to exactly the same things.

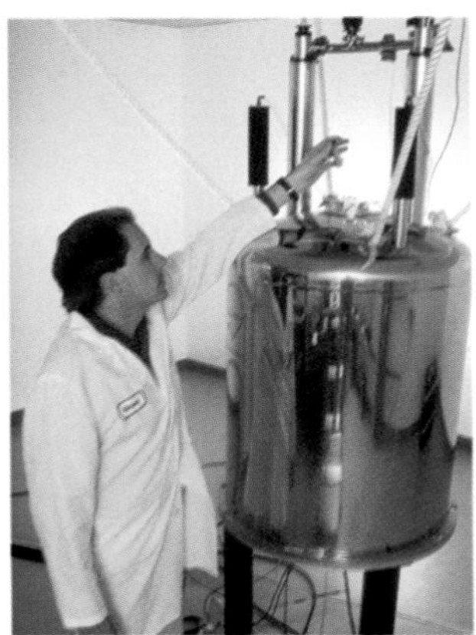

***Figure 1:** An NMR spectrometer.*

Examples

Chloroethane has 2 carbon environments — its carbons are bonded to different atoms.

```
   H  H
   |  |
H—C—C—Cl
   |  |
   H  H
```

```
   H  H  H  H
   |  |  |  |
H—C—C—C—C—Cl
   |  |  |  |
   H  H  H  H
```

1-chlorobutane has 4 carbon environments — the carbons are different distances from the Cl atom, so their environments are different.

2-chloropropane has 2 carbon environments — it's symmetrical, so the carbons on each end are in the same environment.

```
   H  H  H
   |  |  |
H—C—C—C—H
   |  |  |
   H  Cl H
```

Chemical shift

NMR spectroscopy measures differences in the energy absorbed by nuclei in different environments relative to a standard substance — the difference is called the **chemical shift** (δ). The standard substance is tetramethylsilane (TMS).

```
       CH3
       |
  H3C—Si—CH3
       |
       CH3
```

tetramethylsilane (TMS)

This molecule has 12 hydrogen atoms in identical environments and 4 carbon atoms in identical environments. This means that, in both proton NMR and ^{13}C NMR, it will produce a single absorption peak. Chemical shift is measured in parts per million (ppm) relative to TMS. So the single peak produced by TMS is given a chemical shift value of 0. You'll often see a peak at δ = 0 on a spectrum. This is because TMS is added to the test compound for calibration purposes.

Tip: Here's the ^{13}C NMR spectrum for TMS:

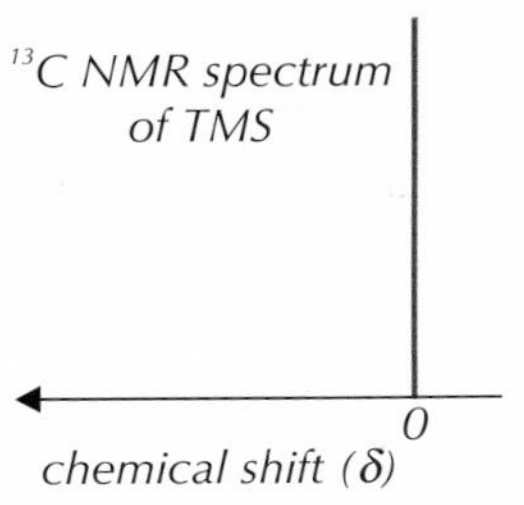

Tip: TMS is chosen as a standard because the absorption peak is at a lower frequency than just about everything else.

Interpreting ^{13}C NMR spectra

If you have a sample of a chemical that contains carbon atoms you can use a ^{13}C NMR spectrum of the molecule to help work out what it is. The spectrum gives you information about the number of carbon environments in the molecule.

Example — Maths Skills

Ethanol has two carbon environments...

```
   H  H
   |2 |1
H—C—C—OH
   |  |
   H  H
```

...and its ^{13}C NMR spectrum has two peaks.

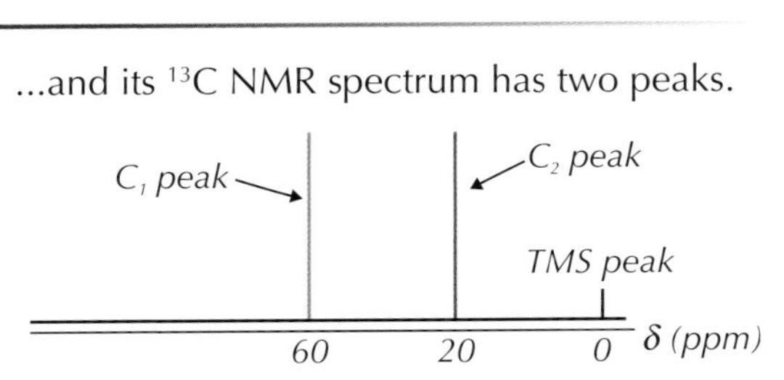

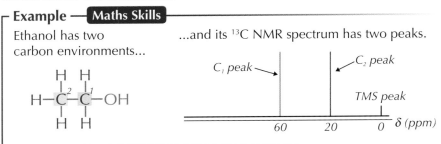

Tip: The number of peaks of a ^{13}C spectrum doesn't necessarily equal the number of carbons in the molecule, as the molecule could have more than one carbon atom in the same environment.

Here are the three steps to follow to interpret a ^{13}C NMR spectrum:

1. Count the number of peaks in the spectrum (excluding the TMS peak) — this number is equal to the number of carbon environments in the molecule.
2. Use a diagram of chemical shift data to work out what kind of carbon environment is causing each peak. A diagram of typical chemical shift data for carbon-13 NMR is shown in Figure 2 on the next page.
3. Use this information to figure out the structure of the molecule.

Exam Tip
You'll get a diagram like this in the exam, so you don't need to learn it (phew). Just read up from any chemical shift value to find what groups could be causing a peak there.

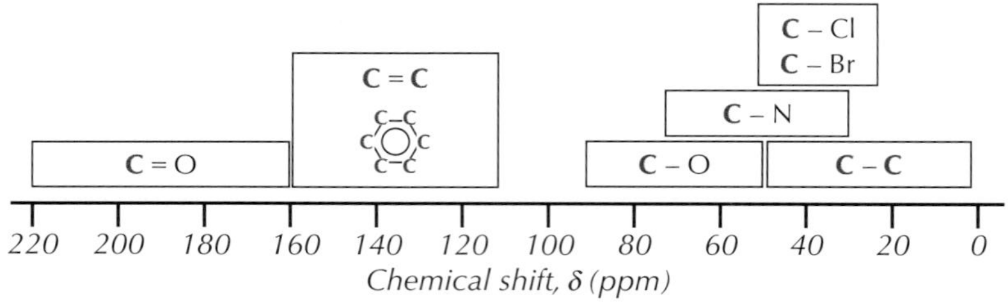

Figure 2: *Chemical shift data for carbon-13 NMR relative to TMS.*

Example — Maths Skills

The carbon-13 NMR spectrum of a ketone with the molecular formula $C_5H_{10}O$ is shown below. Use the spectrum to identify the molecule.

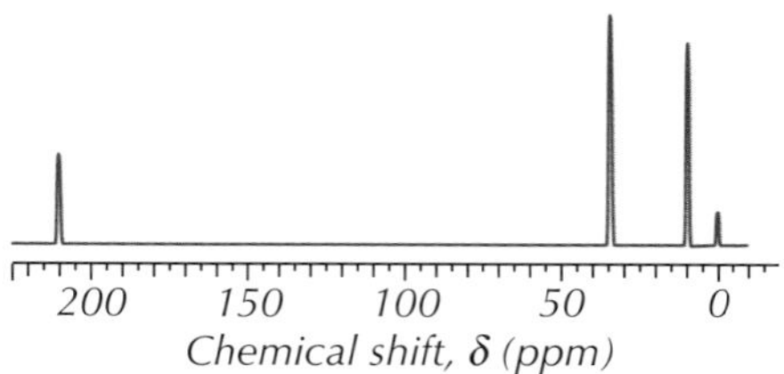

1. The spectrum has three peaks, so the molecule must have three carbon environments.
2. The peak at δ = 10 ppm represents carbon atoms in alkyl groups. We're told that the molecule is a ketone so the peak at δ = 35 ppm must also be due to carbons in C–C bonds (rather than C–N, C–Cl or C–Br bonds), as ketones only contain C, H, and O atoms. The carbons causing this peak have a different chemical shift to those causing the first peak, so they must be in a slightly different environment. The peak at δ = 210 ppm is due to the carbon atom in the C=O group in the ketone.
3. You know you're looking for a ketone with the formula $C_5H_{10}O$ that has three different carbon environments. The only one that fits the bill is pentan-3-one:

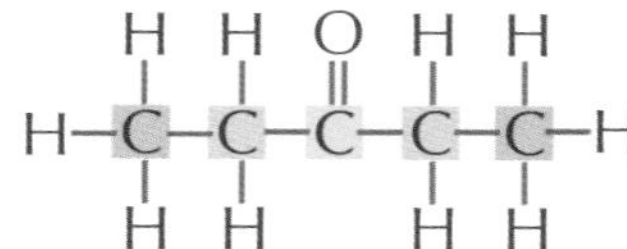

Tip: The best way to figure out the structure of a molecule is often to sketch out some possibilities. Then you can rule out any that don't have the right number of carbon environments or chemical shift values.

Tip: Don't forget that if there's a peak at δ = 0 it's a TMS peak, so you can ignore it.

Tip: There are actually three ketones that have the formula $C_5H_{10}O$ (you could try sketching them all out) but pentan-3-one is the only one that has three carbon environments.

^{13}C NMR spectra of cyclic molecules

The number of peaks on the ^{13}C spectrum of a cyclic compound depends on the symmetry of the molecule. Here's an example to show how it works:

Example — Maths Skills

The ^{13}C NMR spectrum of an aromatic molecule with the formula $C_6H_4Cl_2$ is shown below. Identify the molecule that produced this spectrum.

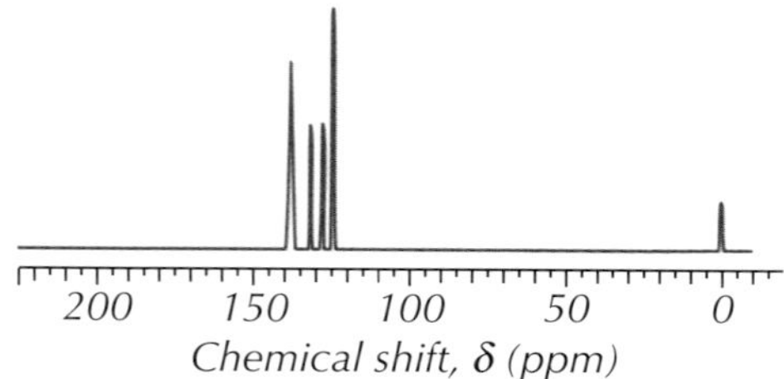

Exam Tip
Watch out for the scale on ^{13}C spectra in the exam — the chemical shift <u>increases</u> from <u>right to left</u>.

1. The spectrum has four peaks, so it must have four carbon environments.
2. All four peaks are between δ = 120 ppm and δ = 140 ppm. Looking at the chemical shift table these can only be due to alkene groups or carbons in a benzene ring. Since the question tells you that the molecule is aromatic, these carbons must be in a benzene ring.
3. There are only three aromatic molecules with the formula $C_6H_4Cl_2$ — they're all isomers of dichlorobenzene.

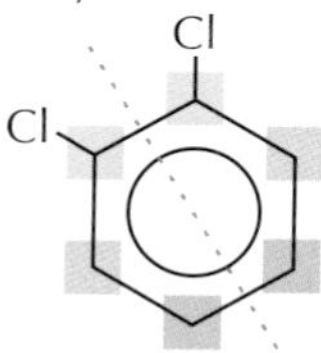

1,2-dichlorobenzene

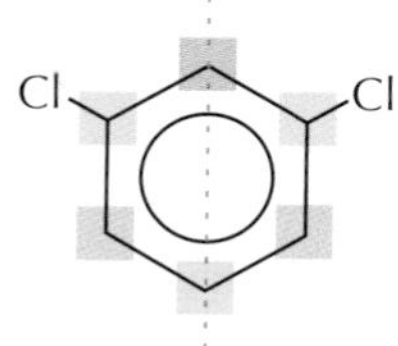

1,3-dichlorobenzene

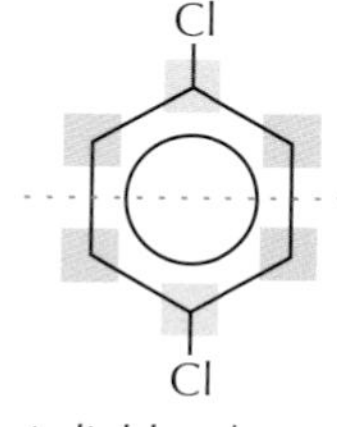

1,4-dichlorobenzene

If you look at the symmetry of the molecules you can see that 1,2-dichlorobenzene has three carbon environments, while 1,3-dichlorobenzene has four and 1,4-dichlorobenzene only has two. So the spectrum must have been produced by 1,3-dichlorobenzene.

Tip: Benzene (C_6H_6) is completely symmetrical. It only has one peak on its ^{13}C NMR spectrum as all of its carbon atoms are in the same environment.

Tip: If a cyclic molecule is symmetrical, you can draw a mirror line (like the dashed lines on the molecules on the left) across it. Atoms or groups that are in the same place on opposite sides of the line will be in the same environment.

Predicting ^{13}C NMR spectra

If you know the structure of a molecule, it's easy to predict what its ^{13}C NMR spectrum will look like.

Here are the steps to follow to predict a ^{13}C NMR spectrum:

1. Identify all the different carbon environments present in the molecule.
2. Look up the chemical shift values of the different environments in a chemical shift diagram.

Tip: Drawing the spectrum of a molecule is really tricky — you don't know exactly where each peak will appear, or how tall each peak will be. But, you can predict how many peaks there will be, and roughly where they will appear on the spectrum.

Example — Maths Skills

The molecular structure of ethyl ethanoate is shown below. Predict the number of peaks, and their corresponding shifts, on the carbon-13 NMR spectrum of ethyl ethanoate.

```
  H  O      H  H
  |  ||     |  |
H-C--C--O---C--C-H
  |         |  |
  H         H  H
```

1. There are four carbon environments — two different C–C environments, one C=O environment and one C–O environment, so there will be four peaks on the spectrum.
2. The two peaks for the C–C environments will have a shift between δ = 0 ppm and δ = 50 ppm. The peak for the C=O environment will have a shift between δ = 160 ppm and δ = 180 ppm. The peak for the C–O environment will have a shift between δ = 50 ppm and δ = 90 ppm.
3. This is what the spectrum actually looks like:

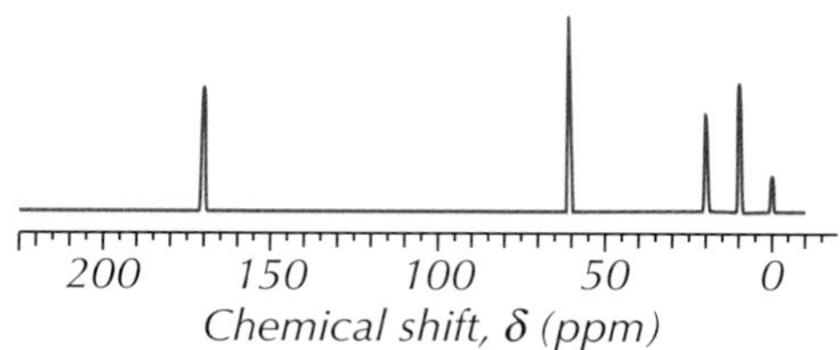

Exam Tip
It's unlikely you'll be asked to draw your prediction of a spectrum — just make sure you can work out the number of peaks and the range of shifts for each one and you'll get the marks.

Practice Questions — Application

Tip: This is the structure of 4-chlorocyclohexanone:

Q1 How many peaks would you see on a ^{13}C NMR spectrum of:

a) butanal? b) pentane?

c) 2-methylpropane? d) 4-chlorocyclohexanone?

Tip: Use the chemical shift data diagram from page 250 to help you with these questions.

Q2 The carbon-13 NMR spectrum of a compound with the molecular formula C_5H_{12} is shown below.

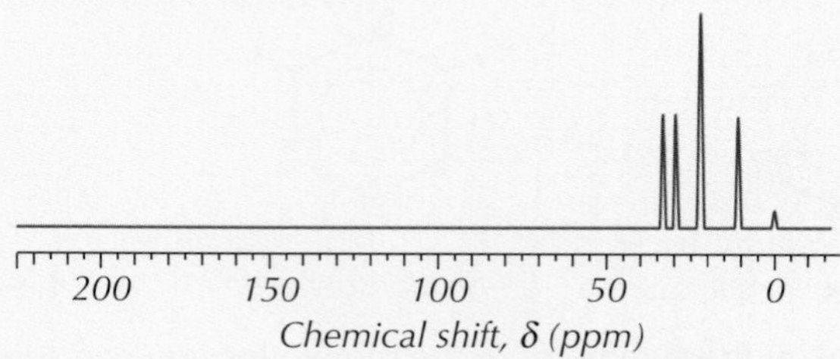

Use the spectrum to identify the molecule. Explain your reasoning.

Tip: Matching peaks to groups isn't always easy, because some of the chemical shift ranges overlap (e.g. a peak at δ = 25 could be caused by C–C, C–Cl or C–Br). You might have to use other information that you're given — for instance if you're told that the molecule's a hydrocarbon, then it couldn't have C–Cl or C–Br in it.

Q3 The carbon-13 NMR spectrum of a molecule with the formula $C_4H_{10}O$ is shown below.

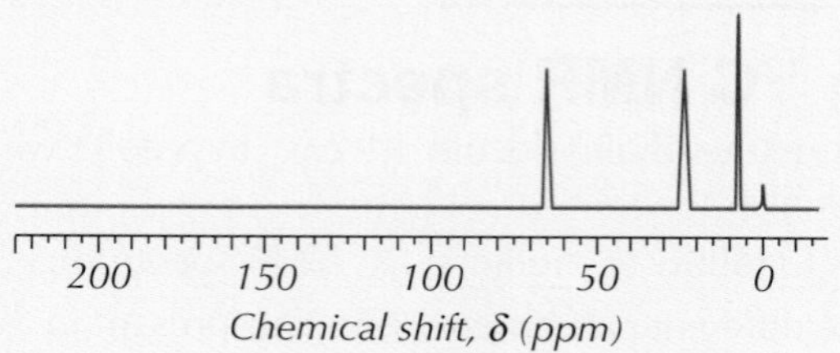

a) What type of carbon is causing the peak at δ = 65?

b) Use the spectrum to identify the molecule. Explain your reasoning.

Tip: The structure of 3-buten-2-one is:

```
H     H  O  H
 \    |  ‖  |
  C=C-C-C-H
 /          |
H           H
```

Q4 Identify which of the spectra below, A, B, C or D, is the carbon-13 NMR spectrum for 3-buten-2-one.

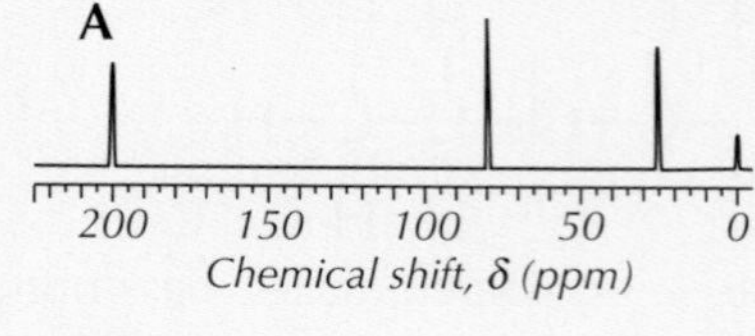

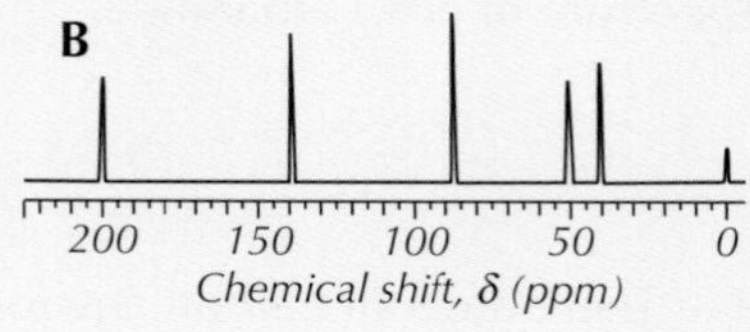

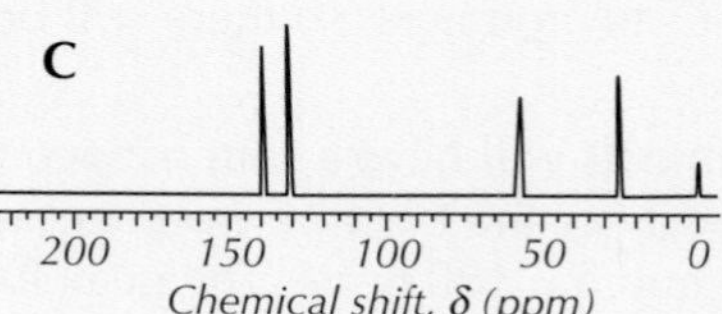

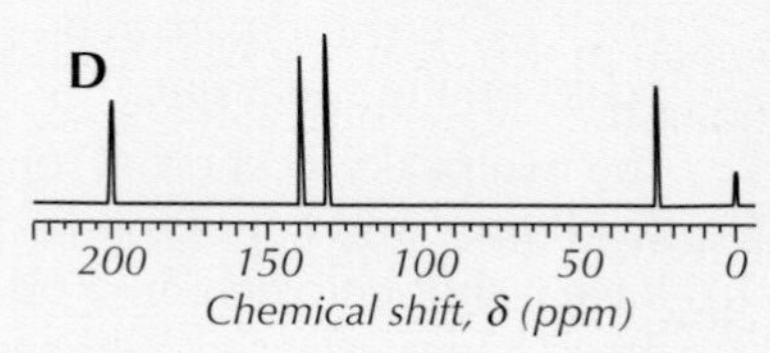

Tip: Scientists use NMR spectroscopy to provide evidence that a certain compound has been synthesised. HOW SCIENCE WORKS

Practice Questions — Fact Recall

Q1 What is the standard substance used in NMR?

Q2 What does the number of peaks on the carbon-13 NMR spectrum of a compound correspond to?

5. Proton NMR Spectroscopy

This topic is all about proton NMR, also known as ¹H NMR. It works in pretty much the same way as ¹³C NMR except this time the spectra tell you about the different hydrogen environments in a molecule.

Learning Objective:

- Be able to analyse a high resolution proton NMR spectrum of an organic molecule to make predictions about the number of proton environments in the molecule, the different types of proton environment present (from chemical shift values) and the relative numbers of each type of proton present from relative peak areas, using integration traces or ratio numbers, when required.

Specification Reference 6.3.2

Hydrogen environments

Each peak on a proton NMR spectrum is due to one or more hydrogen nuclei (protons) in a particular environment. The relative area under each peak tells you the relative number of H atoms in each environment.

Example — Maths Skills

The spectrum below is the proton NMR spectrum of ethanoic acid (CH_3COOH).

ethanoic acid

There are two peaks so there are H atoms in two different environments.

ratio of areas under peaks = 1:3

Peak due to TMS — set at 0 ppm.

12 10 8 6 4 2 0

Chemical shift, δ (ppm)

There are two peaks — so there are two environments. The area ratio is 1 : 3 — so there's 1 H atom in the environment at δ = 11.5 ppm to every 3 H atoms in the other environment. If you look at the structure of ethanoic acid, this makes sense:

3 H atoms attached to CH_2COOH.

1 H atom attached to $COOCH_3$.

Tip: A relative area (or area ratio) of 1 : 3 means that the area under the second peak is three times bigger than the area under the first peak — so it must have been created by three times as many hydrogens.

You can predict the number of peaks on a proton NMR spectrum, and the ratio of the areas under each peak, by looking at the structure of a molecule.

Example — Maths Skills

How many peaks will be present on the proton NMR spectrum of 1-chloropropanone? Predict the ratio of the areas of these peaks.

By looking at the structure of 1-chloropropanone, we can see that there are two different hydrogen environments, which means there will be 2 peaks on the proton NMR spectrum.

There are 2 hydrogens in one environment and 3 hydrogens in the other so the ratio of the peak areas will be 2 : 3.

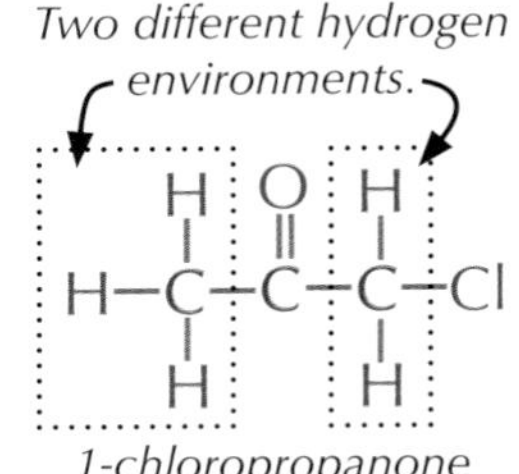

1-chloropropanone

Exam Tip
Highlight all the hydrogens that are in the same environment the same colour — then you can go back and count up how many environments there are.

Integration traces

Proton NMR spectra can get quite cramped. Sometimes it's not easy to see the ratio of the areas — so an **integration trace** is often shown. The height increases shown on the integration trace are proportional to the areas of the peaks.

Example — Maths Skills

Here's the spectrum for ethanoic acid again:

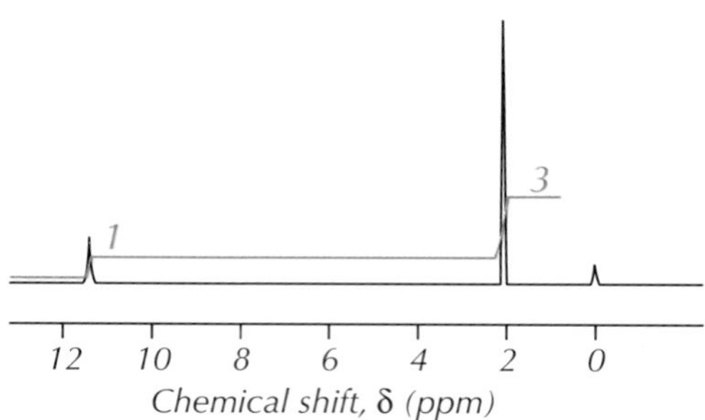

The integration trace (shown in green on the diagram) has a peak around 11.5 ppm and one around 2 ppm.

The heights of the vertical lines are in the ratio 1 : 3 — this means that for every one hydrogen in the first environment there are three in the second environment.

Tip: If the ratio of areas isn't given to you, you can use a ruler to measure the ratios off the integration trace. Measure the heights of the trace peaks and divide the measurements by the smallest peak height, et voilá — you've got your area ratio.

Exam Tip
Have a look at a copy of the data sheet that you'll get in the exam before the day (you can download one from OCR's website). Then you'll know exactly what's on it.

Chemical shift

You can use a diagram like the one shown in Figure 1 to identify which functional group each peak in a proton NMR spectrum is due to. Don't worry — you don't need to learn it. You'll be given one in your exam, so use it. The copy you get in your exam may look a little different, and have different values — they depend on the solvent, temperature and concentration.

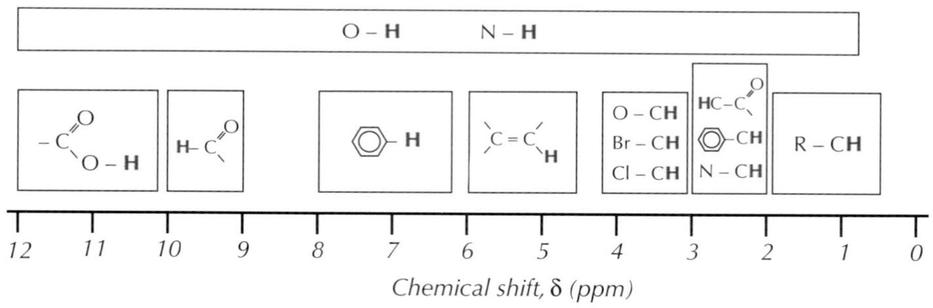

Figure 1: *Chemical shift data for proton NMR relative to TMS*

You can also use the diagram in Figure 1 to work out the different peaks on a proton NMR spectrum, from the structure of a molecule.

Example — Maths Skills

According to the shift diagram, ethanoic acid (CH_3COOH) should have a peak at 10 – 12 ppm due to an H atom in a -COOH group, and a peak at 2 – 3 ppm due to H atoms in a CH_3CO– group.

You can see these peaks on the proton NMR spectrum of ethanoic acid, on the next page.

Tip: This is the structure of ethanoic acid:

```
   H  O
   |  ||
H–C–C–OH
   |
   H
```

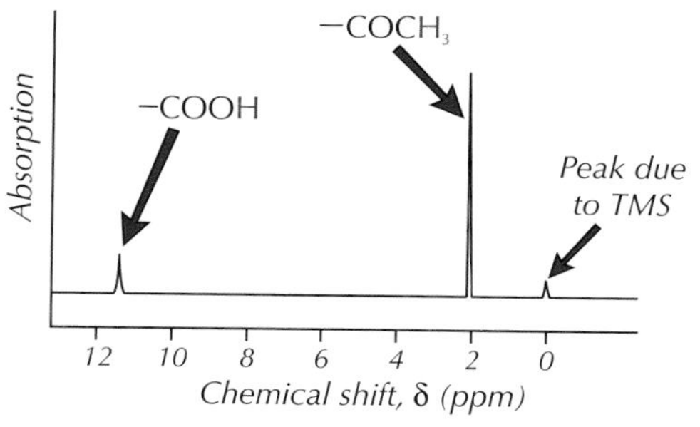

Tip: Remember, if there's a peak at 0, it's just TMS and you can ignore it.

Practice Questions — Application

Q1 a) How many hydrogen environments are there in the molecule 1,2,2-tribromopropane?

b) How many peaks will the proton NMR spectrum of 1,2,2-tribromopropane have?

Q2 Draw an alkane molecule that has two hydrogen environments.

Q3 The proton NMR spectrum of a haloalkane molecule is shown on the right.

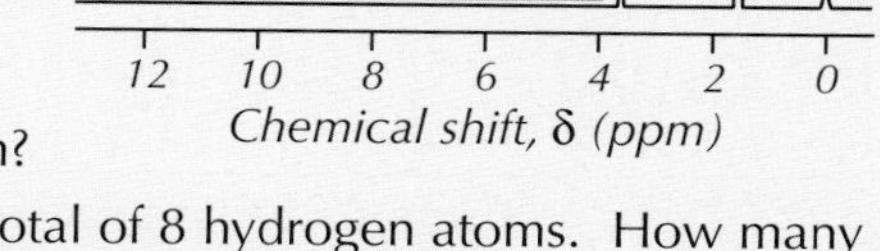

a) How many hydrogen environments are there in this molecule?

b) What is the area ratio of the peaks on this spectrum?

c) This molecule contains a total of 8 hydrogen atoms. How many hydrogen atoms are there in each environment?

Q4 A scientist produces a proton NMR spectrum of a hydrocarbon. It has two peaks, one at δ = 1.7 ppm and one at δ = 4.8 ppm.

a) What is causing the peak at δ = 1.7 ppm?

b) What is causing the peak at δ = 4.8 ppm?

Q5 The ester methyl ethanoate is shown on the right.

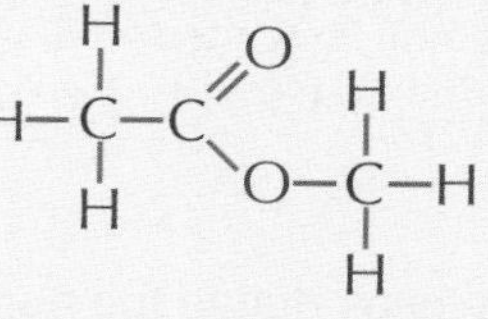

a) How many peaks will there be on the proton NMR spectrum of methyl ethanoate?

b) What will the area ratio of the peaks on this spectrum be?

c) Predict the approximate δ values of all the peaks in this spectrum.

Tip: Use the chemical shift data diagram from page 254 to help you with these questions.

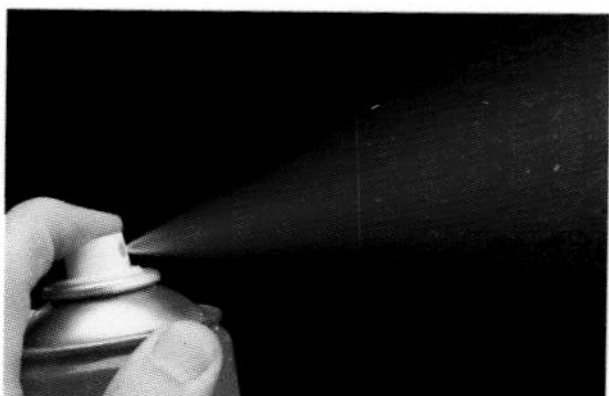

Figure 2: *Methyl ethanoate is used as a solvent in many fast-drying spray paints and spray glues.*

Practice Questions — Fact Recall

Q1 What does the number of peaks on a proton NMR spectrum tell you?

Q2 What does the area under the peaks on a proton NMR spectrum tell you?

Q3 What information would the height increases of the integration trace on a proton NMR spectrum give you?

6. More Proton NMR Spectroscopy

Learning Objectives:

- Know how to use a high resolution proton NMR spectrum to make predictions about the number of non-equivalent protons adjacent to a given proton from the spin-spin splitting pattern, using the $n + 1$ rule.
- Understand the need for deuterated solvents, e.g. $CDCl_3$, when running an NMR spectrum.
- Know how to identify O–H and N–H protons by proton exchange using D_2O.
- Know how to use the high resolution proton NMR spectrum of a molecule to predict possible structures for the molecule.
- Be able to predict the proton NMR spectrum for a given molecule.

Specification Reference 6.3.2

Tip: You don't need to know why proton NMR peaks split. It's all down to how the tiny magnetic fields of the hydrogen nuclei interact — it's pretty tricky stuff...

Tip: Multiplets don't stop at quartets — you can go even higher. Here are some of the names for other peak splitting patterns:

5 peaks = quintet
6 peaks = sextet
7 peaks = heptet
8 peaks = octet

Time for some more about proton NMR spectra, including how NMR spectra can help you to identify molecules — plus a bit about how they're made.

Splitting patterns

The peaks on a proton NMR spectrum may be split into smaller peaks (this is called spin-spin splitting). These split peaks are called **multiplets**. The splitting is caused by the influence of non-equivalent hydrogen atoms that are bonded to neighbouring carbons — these are carbons one along in the carbon chain from the carbon the hydrogen's attached to. Peaks always split into the number of non-equivalent hydrogens on the neighbouring carbons, plus one. It's called the ***n* + 1 rule**. Some of the different **splitting patterns** you'll find in proton NMR spectra are shown in Figure 1.

Type of peak	Structure of peak	Number of hydrogens on adjacent carbons
Singlet		0
Doublet		1
Triplet		2
Quartet		3

Figure 1: *Splitting patterns in proton NMR.*

Example — Maths Skills

Here's the proton NMR spectrum for 1,1,2-trichloroethane:

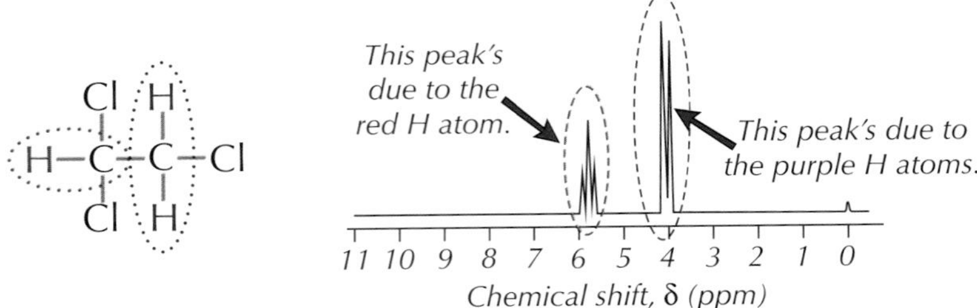

The peak due to the purple hydrogens is split into two because there's one hydrogen on the adjacent carbon atom. The peak due to the red hydrogen is split into three because there are two hydrogens on the adjacent carbon atom.

These splitting rules work just the same for cyclic (ring) compounds too. For example, look at the molecule oxetane (shown below). It has two hydrogen environments, so it has two peaks on its proton NMR spectrum:

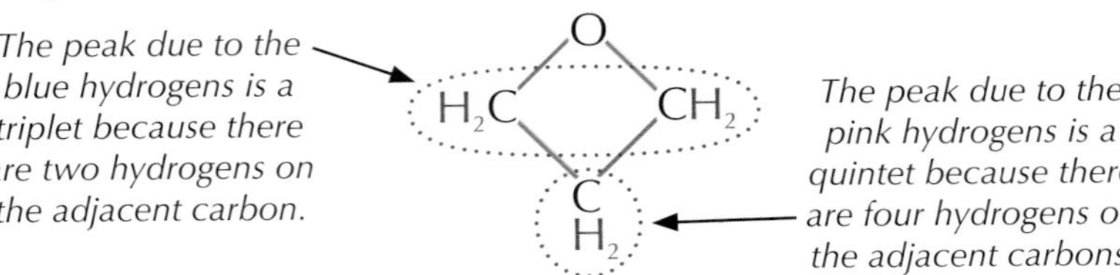

The peak due to the blue hydrogens is a triplet because there are two hydrogens on the adjacent carbon.
The peak due to the pink hydrogens is a quintet because there are four hydrogens on the adjacent carbons.

Practice Questions — Application

Q1 A proton attached to carbon-1 causes a triplet on a proton NMR spectrum. How many hydrogens are on the carbon adjacent to carbon-1?

Q2 The structure of 2-chlorobut-2-ene has been drawn on the right with its hydrogen environments numbered. For each environment, say how its peak would be split on a proton NMR spectrum of the molecule.

```
1  H  Cl  H   H  3
   |  |   |   |
H—C—C═C—C—H
   |       2  |
   H          H
```

Tip: If you want to work out the number of hydrogens on an adjacent carbon from a peak you have to take 1 away from the number of peaks that it's split in to.

Deuterated solvents

NMR spectra are recorded with the molecule that is being analysed in solution. But if you used a ordinary solvent, like water or ethanol, the hydrogen nuclei in the solvent would add peaks to the proton NMR spectrum and confuse things.

To overcome this, the hydrogen nuclei in the solvent are replaced with deuterium (D) — an isotope of hydrogen with one proton and one neutron (see Figure 2). Deuterium nuclei don't absorb the radio wave energy, so they don't add peaks to the spectrum. A commonly used example of a '**deuterated solvent**' is deuterated chloroform, $CDCl_3$ (see Figure 3).

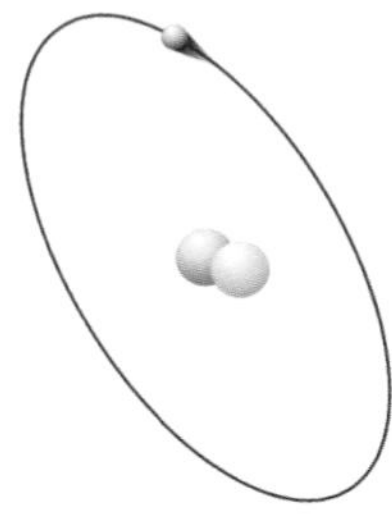

Figure 2: *Atomic model of deuterium. Deuterium has one neutron and one proton in its nucleus, whereas hydrogen has no neutrons.*

```
    Cl
    |
Cl—C—Cl
    |
    D
```

Figure 3: *Deuterated chloroform.*

Identifying OH and NH protons

The chemical shift due to protons (H atoms) attached to oxygen (OH) or nitrogen (NH) is very variable — check out the huge ranges given in the diagram on page 254. They make a broad peak that isn't usually split (it's a singlet).

There's a clever little trick that chemists can use to identify OH and NH protons. You just run two spectra of the molecule — one with a little deuterium oxide, D_2O, added. If an OH or NH proton is present it'll swap with deuterium (to become an OD or ND group) and, hey presto, the peak that was caused by that group will disappear. (This is because deuterium doesn't absorb the radio wave energy).

Example — Maths Skills

This is the structure of ethanol:

```
   H  H
   |  |
H—C—C—OH
   |  |
   H  H
```

Here's the proton NMR spectrum of ethanol:

2Hs in CH_2 (a quartet because it's next to CH_3)

1H in OH (singlet)

3Hs in CH_3 (a triplet because it's next to CH_2)

TMS peak

10 9 8 7 6 5 4 3 2 1 0

Chemical shift, δ (ppm)

Tip: If a proton NMR spectrum has a triplet and a quartet (like the one on the left) it's very likely that the molecule that produced the spectrum will contain a CH_2CH_3 group.

Tip: Peaks caused by H atoms bonded to an O or an N (e.g. OH in alcohols or NH_2 in amines) always appear as singlets.

Tip: Remember — splitting is caused by non-equivalent protons. Take the proton NMR spectrum of ethane as an example. All the protons in ethane are equivalent, so you would get a singlet (there would be no splitting).

And here's the spectrum produced with a little D_2O added to the ethanol:

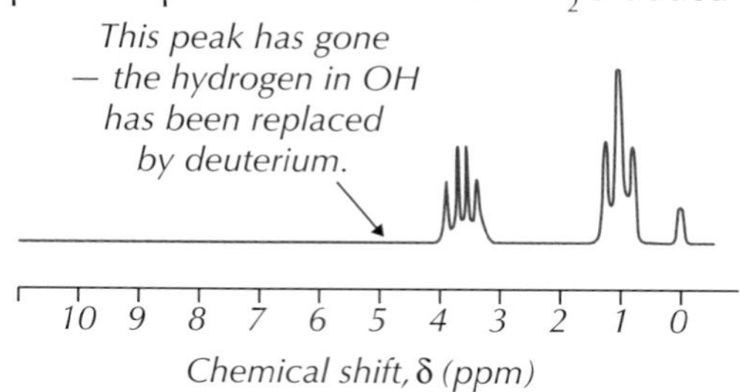

Predicting structures from proton NMR spectra

Proton NMR spectra provide you with an awful lot of information to analyse. Here's a run down of the things to look out for:

- The number of peaks tells you how many different hydrogen environments there are in your compound.
- You can use the chemical shift of each peak to work out what type of environment the hydrogen is in.
- The ratio of the peak areas tells you about the relative number of hydrogens in each environment.
- The splitting pattern of each peak tells you the number of hydrogens on the adjacent carbon. You can use the $n + 1$ rule to work this out.

And here's an example to help you on your way...

Tip: Remember, you might be given the ratio of the peak areas, or you might have to work it out from integration traces.

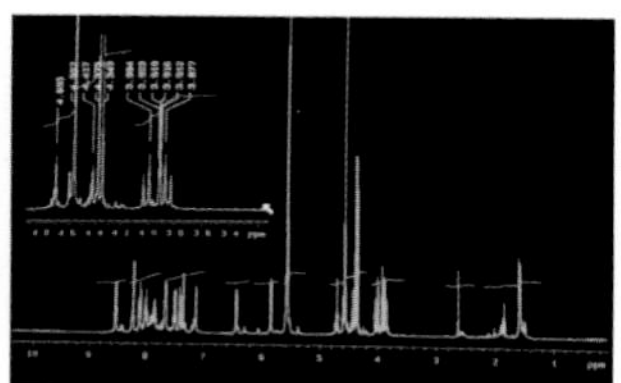

Figure 4: Proton NMR spectrum. Splitting patterns on the spectra of large organic molecules can be very complicated. Thankfully you'll never have to deal with one like this in the exam.

Exam Tip
When you're analysing a spectrum in an exam, write down all the information you're given and can work out first. Then try and work out the structure — that way you're less likely to miss out an important detail.

Example — Maths Skills

The proton NMR spectrum of a carboxylic acid is shown below. Use the spectrum and the chemical shift data on page 254 to predict its structure.

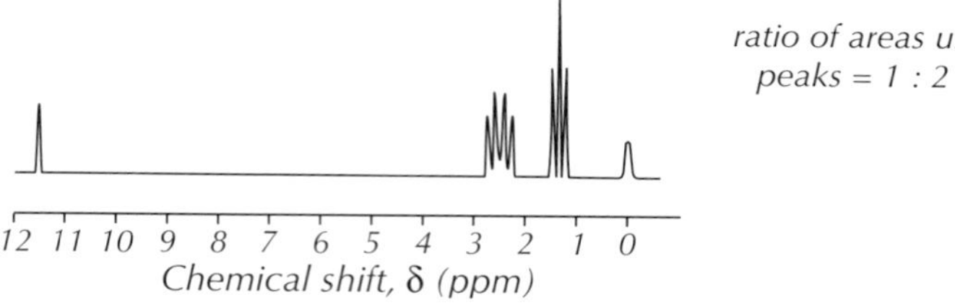

- There are three peaks so there are three different hydrogen environments.
- Using the chemical shift data, the peak at δ = 1.2 ppm should represent hydrogens in an R–CH group, the peak at δ = 2.4 ppm should represent hydrogens in a –CHCO– group, and the peak at δ = 11.5 ppm should represent a hydrogen in a –COOH group.
- From the area ratios, there's one proton in the environment at δ = 11.7 ppm for every two in the environment at δ = 2.4 ppm and every three in the environment at δ = 1.2 ppm. To fit this data the groups must be –COOH, $–CH_2CO–$ and $–CH_3$.

Now you know the molecule must contain these groups: –C(=O)–OH, –CH(H)–C(=O)–, H–C(H)(H)–

- The peak at δ = 1.2 ppm is a triplet, so these protons must have two neighbouring hydrogens. The peak at δ = 2.4 ppm is a quartet, so these protons have three neighbouring hydrogens. The peak at δ = 11.5 ppm is a singlet, so these protons have no neighbouring hydrogens.

Now all you have to do is fit the groups together in a way that matches the splitting pattern:

```
   H  H  O
   |  |  ||
H—C—C—C—OH
   |  |
   H  H
```

So this is the proton NMR spectrum of propanoic acid.

Exam Tip
Always go back and check to see if your structure matches the spectrum — you need to make sure you haven't overlooked an important piece of information.

Predicting proton NMR spectra

As well as predicting the structure of a molecule from a proton NMR spectrum, you can also predict the proton NMR spectrum from the structure of a molecule. You have to think about the same things:

- How many different hydrogen environments there are in the compound tells you the number of peaks.
- The type of environment each hydrogen is in allows you to work out the chemical shift of each peak.
- The relative number of hydrogens in each environment tells you the ratio of the peak areas.
- The number of hydrogens on the adjacent carbon tells you splitting pattern of each peak.

Example — Maths Skills

The molecular structure of ethyl ethanoate is shown below. Predict the peaks of the proton NMR spectrum of ethyl ethanoate, including the chemical shifts, area ratios and splitting patterns.

```
   H  O     H  H
   |  ||    |  |
H—C—C—O—C—C—H
   |        |  |
   H        H  H
```

There are three different hydrogen environments, so there will be three peaks.

```
   H  O           H            H
   |  ||          |            |
H—C—C—       —O—C—        R—C—H
   |              |            |
   H              H            H
```

Hydrogen environment	$CH_3CO–$	$–OCH_2–$	$–CH_3$
Chemical shift	δ = 2-3 ppm	δ = 3-4 ppm	δ = 0.5-2 ppm
Area ratio	3	2	3
Splitting pattern	singlet as no hydrogens on neighbouring carbon	quartet due to the three hydrogens on neighbouring carbon	triplet due to the two hydrogens on neighbouring carbon

This is what the proton NMR spectrum of ethyl ethanoate actually looks like:

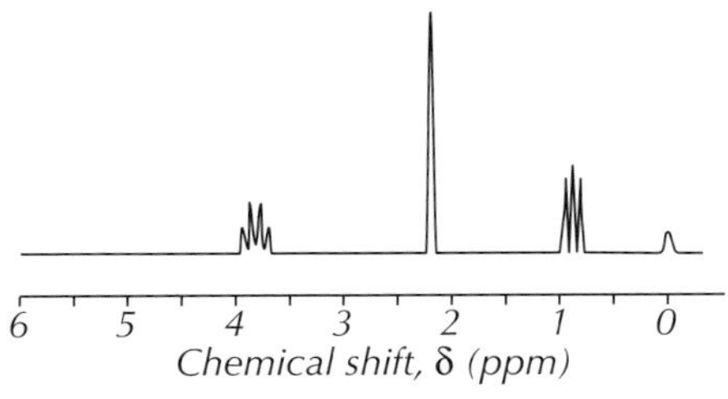

Tip: If you're asked to predict the spectrum of a particular molecule, and you're not shown its displayed structure, draw it out. This will make it so much easier to identify and work out what environment all the hydrogens are in.

Tip: Unless you're asked to specifically, don't worry about trying to draw out your prediction of a spectrum — just make sure you know how to work out how many peaks there will be, what each peak will look like and what range of shifts it will appear between.

Practice Questions — Application

Q1 Use the proton NMR spectrum of compound **X** below, along with the chemical shift data on page 254, to work out the structure of compound **X**. HINT: Compound **X** has the molecular formula C_4H_8O.

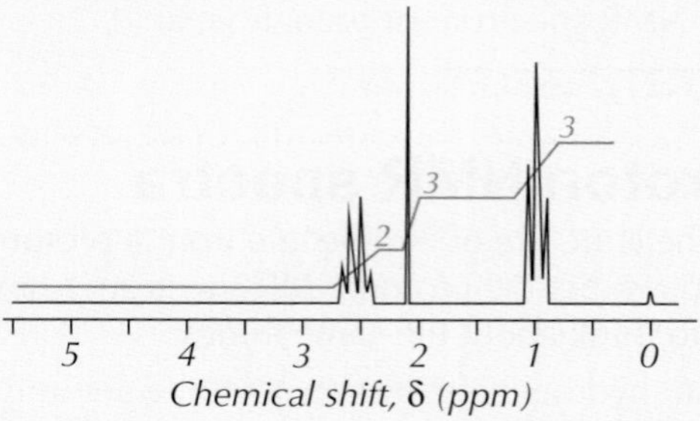

> **Tip:** Remember to use all the different types of information that the spectrum gives you...

Q2 A high resolution proton NMR spectrum of an ester is shown below. Use the spectrum along with the chemical shift data on page 254, to work out the structure of the compound.

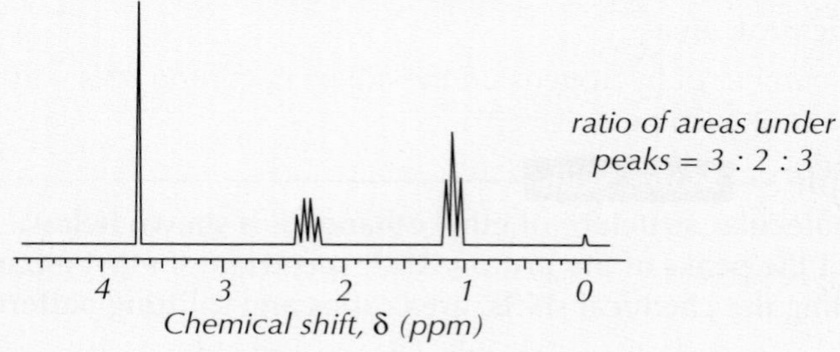

> **Tip:** Remember esters have the functional group –COO– and are made from an alcohol and a carboxylic acid (see pages 189-190).

Q3 The diagram below shows the structure of pentan-3-one. Predict what pentan-3-one's proton NMR spectrum will look like in terms of the number of peaks, their position and their splitting patterns.

```
    H  H  O  H  H
    |  |  ‖  |  |
 H—C—C—C—C—C—H
    |  |     |  |
    H  H     H  H
```

> **Exam Tip**
> It's really important that you use the right terms in your exam answers. Talk about peaks as doublets, triplets etc.

Practice Questions — Fact Recall

Q1 What is the $n + 1$ rule?

Q2 What's the technical name for a peak on an NMR spectrum that's been split into four smaller peaks?

Q3 Suggest one solvent that could be used to dissolve a sample for analysis by proton NMR.

Q4 You have a sample of a chemical that you think contains an OH group. Explain how you can use NMR spectroscopy to confirm that it does.

7. More on Spectra

Finally the end of the analysis section is in sight... This last topic's about how you can put together information from lots of different techniques to work out a molecule's structure.

Learning Objective:

- Be able to deduce the structures of organic compounds from different analytical data, including elemental analysis, mass spectra, IR spectra and NMR spectra.

Specification Reference 6.3.2

Using elemental analysis

In elemental analysis, experiments determine the masses or percentage compositions of different elements in a compound. This data can help you to work out the empirical and molecular formulae of a compound. Look back at your Year 1 notes to remind yourself how to do this. Knowing the molecular formula is useful when working out the structure of the compound from different spectra.

Predicting structures from spectra

All the spectroscopy techniques you've met so far will give clues to the identity of a mystery molecule, but you can be more certain about a structure (and avoid jumping to wrong conclusions) if you look at data from several different types of spectrum.

Tip: Read over your Year 1 notes for more on mass spectra and IR spectra.

Example — Maths Skills

The following spectra were all obtained from the same molecule. Deduce the structure of the molecule.

Mass spectrum

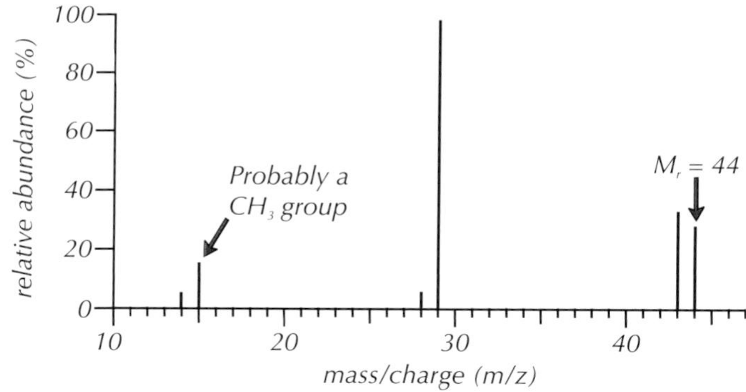

This tells you that the molecule has a molecular mass of 44 and is likely to contain a CH_3 group.

Exam Tip
Don't forget that in the exam you'll have NMR data diagrams and infrared absorption data tables to use. There are versions of these on pages 250, 254 and 320.

Infrared spectrum

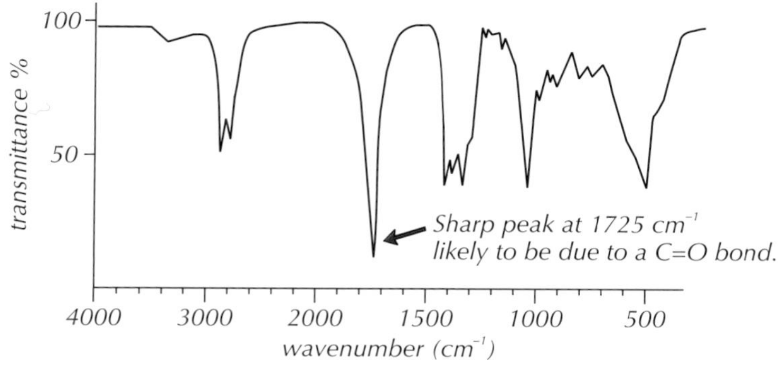

Figure 1: Researchers using different types of spectra to identify a molecule.

This IR spectrum strongly suggests a C=O bond in an aldehyde, ketone, ester, carboxylic acid, amide, acyl chloride or acid anhydride.

Since it doesn't also have a broad absorption between 2500 cm^{-1} and 3300 cm^{-1}, this molecule does not contain an O–H bond, so it can't be a carboxylic acid. Also, as there is no absorption between 3300 cm^{-1} and 3500 cm^{-1} there is no N–H bond either, so the molecule can't be an amide.

Proton NMR

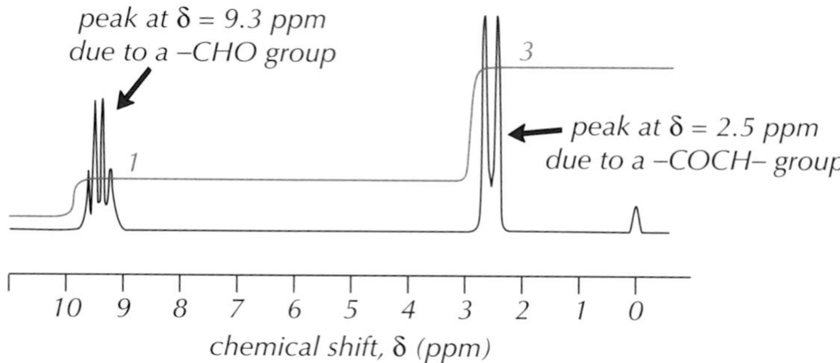

The proton NMR spectrum suggests a molecule with two hydrogen environments. The peak at δ = 9.3 ppm is due to a hydrogen in a –CHO group. (It can't be an amide group because the IR spectrum ruled that out, and it can't be a phenol group because that would give a molecule with an M_r higher than 44.) The peak at δ = 2.5 ppm is due to the hydrogen atoms in a –COCH– group. (It can't be R–NH, R–OH or HC–N because there aren't peaks matching these groups on the IR spectrum and it can't be a methylbenzene group because that would give a molecule with an M_r higher than 44.)

The area under the peaks is in the ratio 1 : 3, which means they must be –CHO and $–COCH_3$ groups. The splitting pattern shows that the protons must be on adjacent carbon atoms because they are splitting each other.

Tip: When you're solving a problem like this one, try starting off by quickly jotting down everything you can learn from each of the spectra. That way you shouldn't miss any information.

^{13}C NMR

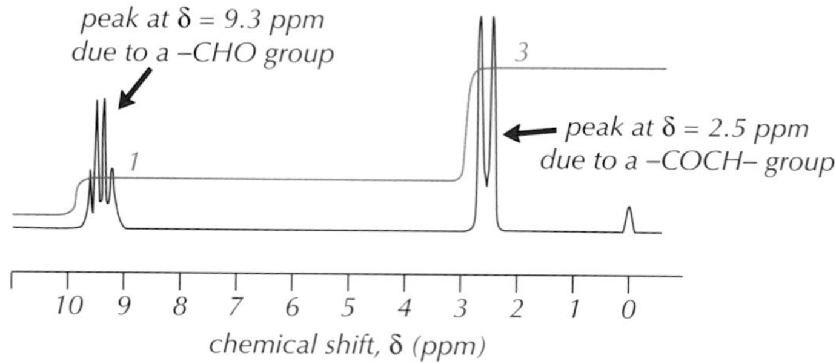

The ^{13}C NMR spectrum shows that the molecule has two carbon environments. The peak at δ = 200 ppm corresponds to a carbon in a carbonyl group and the peak at δ = 40 ppm is due to an alkyl carbon. (It can't be caused by a C–N carbon because there isn't a peak matching that on the IR spectrum, and it can't be a C–Cl or C–Br carbon because that would give a molecule with an M_r higher than 44.)

Tip: The four different types of spectra are most useful for different things. A mass spectrum gives you the M_r of the molecule. IR spectra are really handy for identifying functional groups. NMR spectra are best for working out the fine structure of the molecule once you know its formula.

Putting all this together we have a molecule with a molecular mass of 44, which contains a $–CH_3$ group next to an aldehyde group.

So the structure of the molecule must be:

```
   H  O
   |  ||
H—C—C—H
   |
   H
```

...which is the aldehyde ethanal.

Tip: When you've come up with your final answer it's a good idea to check it against all the spectra — just to make doubly sure that it fits.

You won't always get all four different kinds of spectra — sometimes you'll have to work out a structure from two or three different types of data.

Example — Maths Skills

An alkene with a molar mass of 56 g mol^{-1} is burnt in excess oxygen to produce 8.8 g of carbon dioxide and 3.6 g of water. The proton NMR spectrum of the alkene is shown below.
Use this data to identify the alkene.

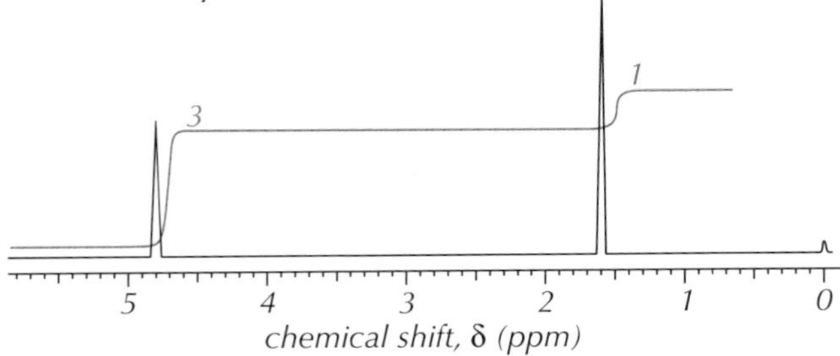

Elemental analysis

- The moles of CO_2 and H_2O produced are:

$$\text{moles } CO_2 = \frac{\text{mass}}{M_r} = \frac{8.8}{12 + (16 \times 2)} = \frac{8.8}{44} = 0.20 \text{ moles}$$

$$\text{moles } H_2O = \frac{\text{mass}}{M_r} = \frac{3.6}{(2 \times 1) + 16} = \frac{3.6}{18} = 0.20 \text{ moles}$$

- 1 mole of CO_2 contains 1 mole of carbon atoms, so you must have started with 0.20 moles of carbon atoms. 1 mole of H_2O contains 2 moles of hydrogen atoms, so you must have started with 0.40 moles (0.20 × 2) of hydrogen atoms.
- So the C : H ratio is 0.20 : 0.40, which gives a whole number C : H ratio of 1 : 2. So the empirical formula of this hydrocarbon is CH_2.
- The mass of the empirical formula is (12 × 1) + (2 × 1) = 14 g.
- Divide the molar mass of the alkene by this and you get 56 ÷ 14 = 4, so you need to scale the empirical formula up by 4 to get the molecular formula. So the molecular formula of the alkene is C_4H_8.

There are three alkene isomers with this molecular formula:

```
      H  H  H          H  H  H  H         H  CH3  H
H     |  |  |          |  |  |  |         |  |   /
  >C=C—C—C—H       H—C—C=C—C—H       H—C—C=C
H        |  |          |        |         |      \
         H  H          H        H         H       H
```

but-1-ene   *but-2-ene*   *2-methylpropene*

Tip: When you get to the stage where you're sure what the formula of the mystery compound is, it's a really good idea to sketch out all the isomers it could possibly be. It's usually easier to narrow down a list of options than to try drawing a molecule that fits from scratch.

Exam Tip
There's usually just one mark for identifying the molecule in a question like this. The rest come from explaining all the info you can get from the spectra — so don't worry if you can't work out exactly what it is.

Now you can use the proton NMR spectrum to work out which isomer it is.

Proton NMR

- The alkene molecule has two hydrogen environments.
- The area under the peaks is in the ratio 1 : 3.
- The peak at δ = 1.6 ppm must be due to an R–CH group (it's probably the CH_3 group). It's a singlet, so it can't be next door to any other hydrogens.
- The peak at δ = 4.8 ppm must be the H–C=C group (the alkene group). It's also a singlet, so it can't be next door to any other hydrogens either.

But-1-ene has four hydrogen environments, so it can't be that. But-2-ene and 2-methylpropene both have two hydrogen environments in a ratio of 1 : 3. But only 2-methylpropene has two singlets on its proton NMR spectrum. So the unknown alkene must be 2-methylpropene.

Practice Questions — Application

Tip: Use the tables and diagrams on pages 250, 254 and 320 to help you answer these questions.

Q1 All four spectra shown below are for the same molecule. Use them to identify the molecule.

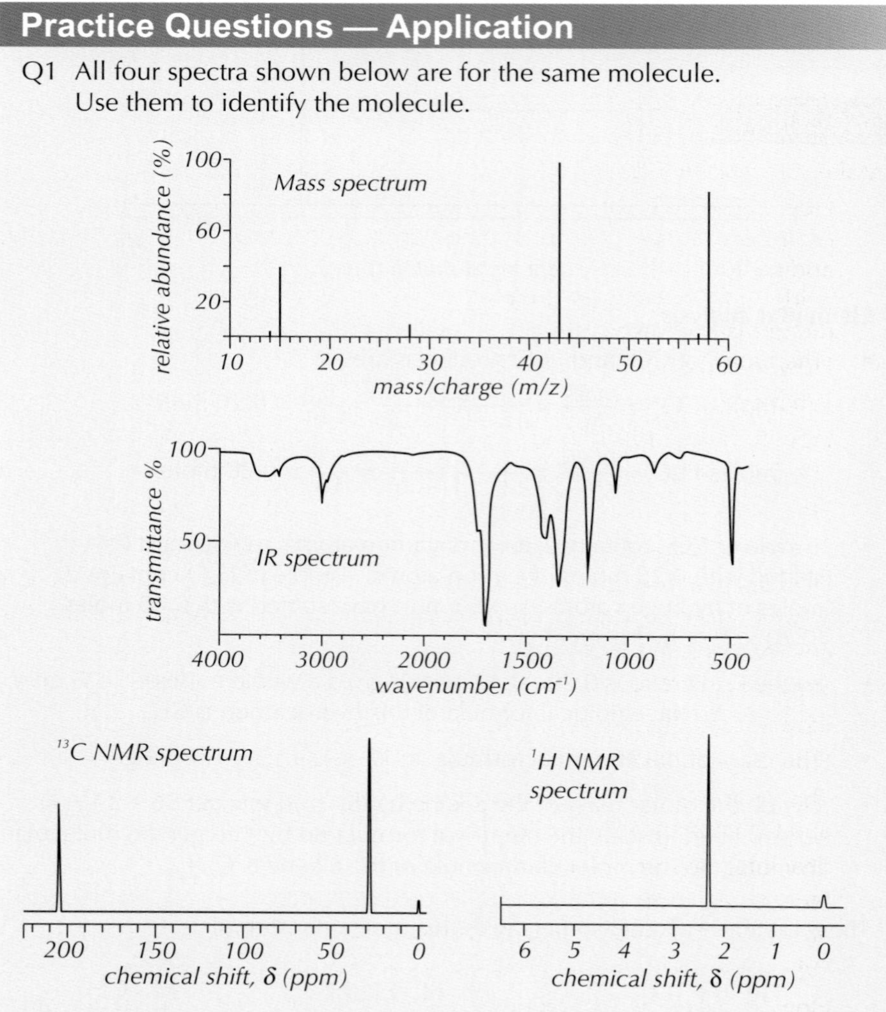

Q2 A molecule with molar mass 88 g mol^{-1} is found to have percentage composition of 55.0% carbon, 9.0% hydrogen and 36.0% oxygen by mass. The IR spectrum and the ^{13}C NMR spectrum of the molecule are shown on the next page. Use this data to identify the molecule.

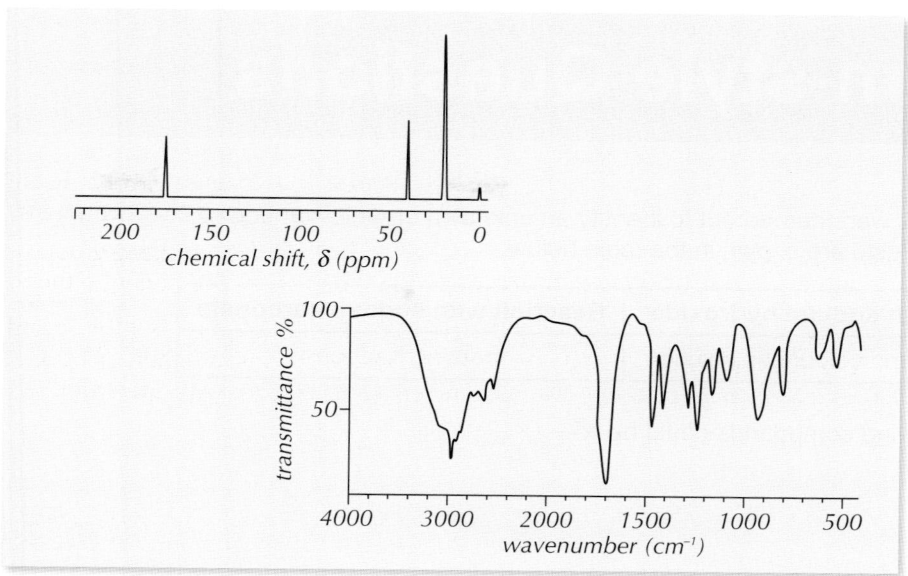

Section Summary

Make sure you know...

- How to use different tests to identify organic functional groups in an unknown compound, including: bromine water as a test for alkenes, aqueous silver nitrate as a test for haloalkanes, sodium hydroxide and sodium carbonate as a test for phenols, sodium carbonate and limewater as a test for carboxylic acids, 2,4-DNP as a test for carbonyls, Tollens' reagent as a test for aldehydes and acidified potassium dichromate(VI) as a test for primary and secondary alcohols.
- How to carry out thin-layer chromatography.
- What an R_f value is and how to calculate one using a TLC chromatogram.
- How R_f values from TLC chromatograms can be used to analyse organic compounds.
- The factors that can affect the R_f values.
- How to interpret a gas chromatogram (including retention times and relative peak areas).
- The factors that affect retention times in gas chromatography.
- How to draw and use external calibration curves to estimate concentrations of components in mixtures.
- That ^{13}C NMR (carbon-13 NMR) gives you information about the number and type of carbon environments in a molecule.
- Why tetramethylsilane (TMS) is used as a standard in NMR spectroscopy.
- How to use a ^{13}C NMR spectrum to work out the structure of a molecule.
- How to predict what a ^{13}C NMR spectrum will look like for a specific molecule.
- That proton NMR (^{1}H NMR) gives you information about the number of hydrogen atoms in a molecule and the environments they're in.
- That integration traces/area ratios tell you the relative number of hydrogen atoms in different environments.
- How to use peak splitting patterns on a proton NMR spectrum to work out how many hydrogens there are on the neighbouring carbons (using the $n + 1$ rule).
- Why samples for proton NMR spectroscopy have to be dissolved in deuterated solvents, like $CDCl_3$.
- How to use deuterium oxide (D_2O) to confirm that a molecule contains a hydrogen atom in an OH or NH group using proton NMR spectroscopy.
- How to use a proton NMR spectrum to work out the structure of a molecule.
- How to predict the proton NMR spectrum for a molecule.
- How to combine data from different analytical methods to find the structure of an unknown molecule.

Exam-style Questions

1 Two chemical tests were carried out to identify an unknown organic compound, X. The results of the tests are shown in the table below.

Reaction with sodium hydroxide	Reaction with sodium carbonate
fizzes and forms colourless solution	nothing happens

Which of the following compounds could be X?

A CH_3NH_2

B $CH_3CH_2NH_2$

C CCl_3COOH

D C_6H_5OH

(1 mark)

2 A chemist is carrying out gas chromatography on a mixture of volatile liquids. How will increasing the temperature of the equipment affect the retention times of the components in the mixture?

A The retention times will stay the same.

B The retention times of all of the components in the mixture will decrease.

C The retention times of all of the components in the mixture will increase

D The retention times of only the most soluble components in the mixture will decrease.

(1 mark)

3 Look at the structure of the molecule below:

```
    H  O  H  H
    |  ‖  |  |
H—C—C—C—C—H
    |  |  |  |
    H  H  H  H
```

Which of the following statements is **not** correct?
You can use the diagrams on pages 250 and 254 to help you with this question.

A A bright orange precipitate forms when it is reacted with 2,4–DNP.

B The proton NMR spectrum has a singlet peak at δ = 2 – 3 ppm.

C A silver mirror forms when it is warmed with Tollens' reagent.

D The 13C NMR spectrum has a peak at δ = 160 – 220 ppm.

(1 mark)

4 The proton NMR spectrum of an alcohol is shown below.

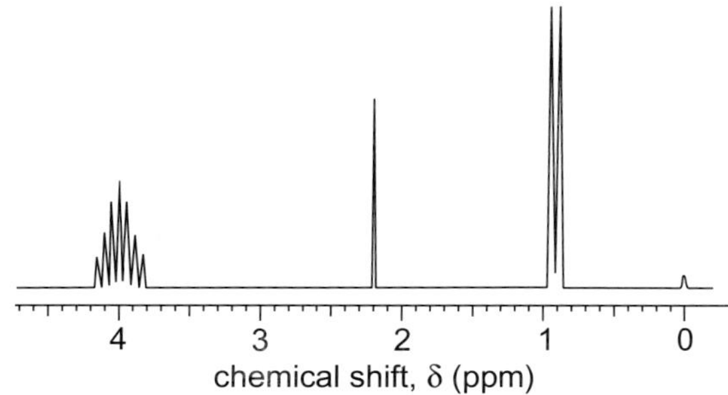

(a) Suggest a solvent that you could use to dissolve the sample for this spectrum.

(1 mark)

(b) Use the chemical shift values and splitting patterns to identify the chemical. Explain your reasoning. You may use the diagram on page 254 to help with this question.

(6 marks)

(c) A second proton NMR spectrum was produced for the same molecule, but this time a little D_2O was added to the sample. Explain how this spectrum would look different to the first one.

(1 mark)

5 A scientist has a sample which contains a mixture of three different chemicals. He uses thin-layer chromatography to separate out the components of the mixture. The thin-layer chromatogram that he produces is shown below.

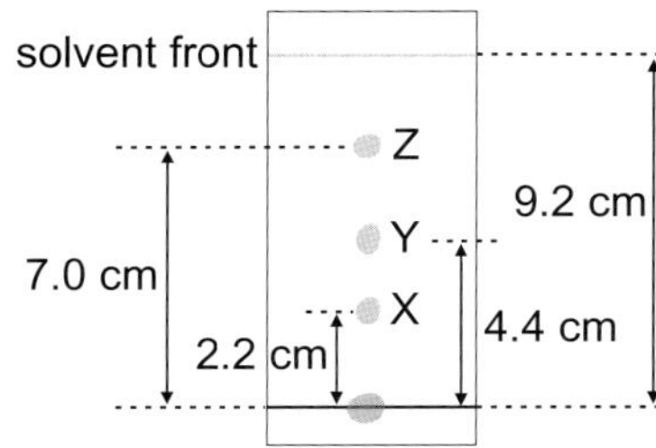

(a) Explain why the components of the mixture separate as they travel up the plate.

(2 marks)

(b) Calculate the R_f value of spot X.

(1 mark)

(c) The chemical responsible for spot Y is made up of a carbonyl with the formula C_3H_6O. Outline a test that the scientist could carry out, on a pure sample of this chemical, to identify the structure of the carbonyl.

(3 marks)

(d) The scientist reacts a pure sample of the chemical responsible for spot Z with bromine water. The solution turns from orange to colourless. What functional group is present in the chemical responsible for spot Z?

(1 mark)

6 A student is given samples of two unknown chemicals. She is asked to use analysis techniques to identify the chemicals.

(a) The student is told that the first chemical has the molecular formula $C_3H_6Cl_2$. She produces a proton NMR spectrum of this chemical, which is shown below.

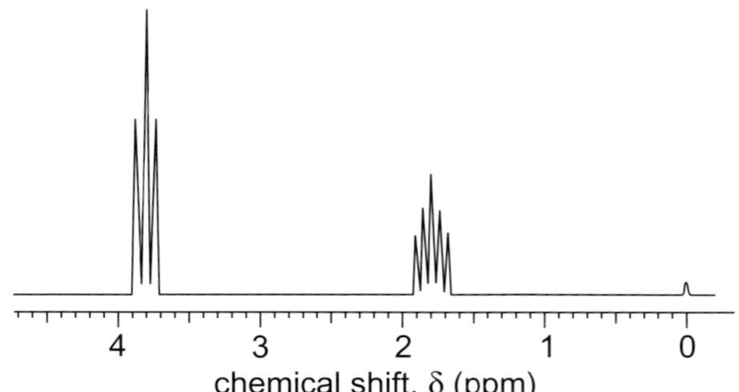

Use the chemical shift values and splitting patterns to identify the chemical. Explain your reasoning.
You may use the diagram on page 254 to help with this question.

(6 marks)

(b) The chemical in the second sample contains only carbon, hydrogen and oxygen. The mass spectrum and the ^{13}C NMR spectrum of this compound are shown below.

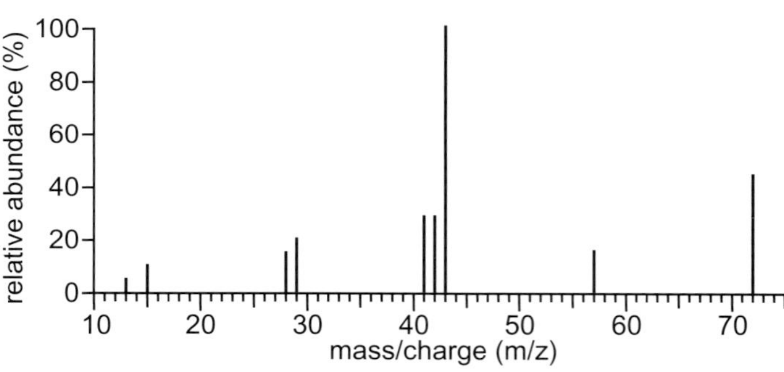

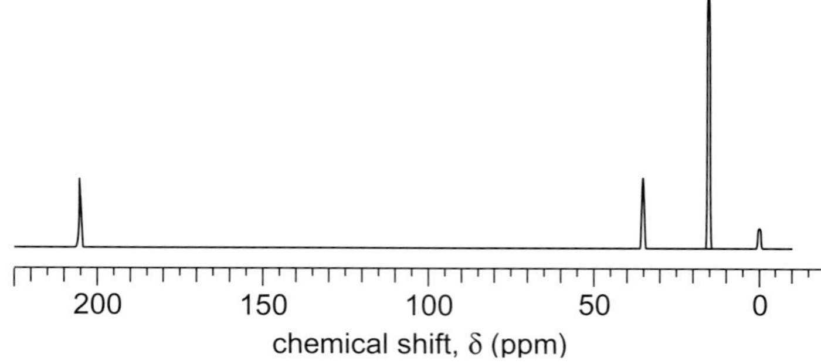

Use these spectra to identify the molecule. Explain your reasoning.
You may use the diagram on page 250 to help with this question.

(5 marks)

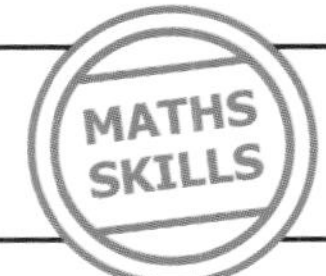

Maths Skills

Maths skills for A Level Chemistry

Maths crops up quite a lot in A Level Chemistry so it's really important that you've mastered all the maths skills you'll need before sitting your exams. Maths skills are covered throughout this book but here's an extra little section, just on maths, to help you out.

Exam Tip
Around 20% of the marks in the exams will depend on your maths skills. That's a lot of marks so it's definitely worth making sure you're up to speed.

1. Exam Technique

The way you answer calculation questions in the exams is important — you should always show your working, and remember all those pesky things like units and significant figures when giving your final answer.

Tip: All the examples in this book that include the kind of maths you're expected to know for your exams are clearly marked. You can spot them by the big label that says...

Maths Skills

Showing your working

When you're doing calculations the most important thing to remember is to show your working. You've probably heard it a million times before but it makes perfect sense. You won't get a mark for a wrong answer but you could get marks for the method you used to work out the answer.

Units

Make sure you always give the correct units for your answer.

Example — Maths Skills

Here's an example of a question where you need to change the units so they match the answer the examiner wants.

1 Calculate the free energy change for the following reaction at 298 K, giving your answer in kJ mol^{-1}:

$MgCO_3 \rightarrow MgO + CO_2$ $\Delta H^{\circ} = 1.17 \times 10^5$ J mol^{-1}
$\Delta S^{\circ} = 175$ J K^{-1} mol^{-1}

(2 marks)

Here you use the equation: $\Delta G = \Delta H - T\Delta S$. Plugging the numbers in gives you an answer of +64 900 J mol^{-1} to three significant figures. But the question asks for the answer in kJ mol^{-1}, so you have to divide by 1000, giving an answer of 64.9 kJ mol^{-1}. If you left your answer as +64 900 J mol^{-1} you'd lose a mark.

Exam Tip
You'll need to know what units your figures need to be in for different formulas — see pages 271-273 for the units used in different formulas and pages 274-275 for how to convert between units.

Standard form

You might need to use numbers written in standard form in calculations. Standard form is used for writing very big or very small numbers in a more convenient way. Standard form must always look like this:

This number must always be between 1 and 10. → $A \times 10^n$ ← *This number is an integer and tells you the number of places and the direction in which the decimal point moves.*

Tip: '*A*' can be 1 or any number up to 10 but it can't be 10 — there can only be a single digit before the decimal point, and this digit can't be 0.

You need to be able to convert between numbers written in ordinary form and standard form.

Exam Tip
If you're asked specifically to give a number in ordinary or standard form then you'll need to make sure you've written it in the correct way. If you're not told how to write a number then give it in the form that the numbers in the question are in.

Examples — Maths Skills

Here's how to write 3 500 000 in standard form.

- First write all the digits up to the last non-zero digit. Put a decimal point after the first digit and a '× 10' at the end:

$$3.5 \times 10$$

- Then count how many places the decimal point has moved to the left. This number sits to the top right of the 10, as a superscript.

$$3\,500\,000 = 3.5 \times 10^{6}$$

- Et voilà... that's 3 500 000 written in standard form.

Here are some more examples.

- You can write 450 000 as 4.5×10^{5}.
- The number 0.000056 is 5.6×10^{-5} in standard form — the *n* is negative because the decimal point has moved to the right instead of the left.
- You can write 0.003456 as 3.456×10^{-3}.

Tip: It's important to remember which way to move the decimal point. If *n* is positive then it means the number you're converting is a large number, and you'll need to move the decimal point to the right — you need more digits in front of the decimal point. If *n* is negative then you're dealing with a very small number and the decimal point needs to move to the left.

Significant figures

Use the number of significant figures given in the question as a guide for how many to give in the answer. You should always give your answer to the lowest number of significant figures (s.f.) given in the question — if you're really unsure, write down the full answer and then round it to 3 s.f. It always helps to write down the number of significant figures you've rounded to after your answer — it shows the examiner you haven't just made a mistake in your calculation.

Exam Tip
You might get told in the question how many significant figures or decimal places to give your answer to. If you are, make sure that you follow the instructions — you'll lose marks if you don't.

Examples — Maths Skills

In this question the data given to you is a good indication of how many significant figures you should give your answer to.

1 (b) Calculate the free energy change of a reaction carried out at 298 K, given that $\Delta H = -2.43$ kJ mol^{-1} and $\Delta S = 94.5$ J mol^{-1} K^{-1}.
(2 marks)

All the data values in the question are given to 3 s.f. so it makes sense to give your answer to 3 s.f. too. But sometimes it isn't as clear as that.

3 (b) 18.5 cm^3 of a 0.65 mol dm^{-3} solution of potassium hydroxide reacts with 1.5 mol dm^{-3} sulfuric acid. Calculate the volume of sulfuric acid needed to neutralise the potassium hydroxide.
(2 marks)

There are two types of data in this question, volume data and concentration data. The volume data is given to 3 s.f. and the concentration data is given to 2 s.f. You should always give your answer to the lowest number of significant figures given — in this case that's to 2 s.f. The answer in full is 4.00833... cm^3 so the answer rounded correctly would be 4.0 cm^3 (2 s.f.).

Tip: Even if the last significant figure is a zero, you still need to include it in your answer.

2. Formulas and Equations

A big part of the maths you need to do in chemistry involves using formulas and equations. So here's a nice page with them all neatly summarised for you.

Amounts of substances

First up are perhaps a couple of the most useful equations of all...

$$\text{Number of moles} = \frac{\text{Number of particles you have}}{\text{Number of particles in a mole } (N_A = 6.02 \times 10^{23})}$$

$$\text{Number of moles} = \frac{\text{Mass of substance}}{\text{Molar mass}} \quad \text{also written as...} \quad n = \frac{m}{M_r}$$

Tip: M_r is relative molecular mass (or relative formula mass). You work it out by adding up the A_r (atomic mass) of each atom in the compound.

You'll need these ones when you're dealing with solutions...

$$\text{Number of moles} = \frac{\text{Concentration (in mol dm}^{-3}\text{)} \times \text{Volume (in cm}^3\text{)}}{1000}$$

$$\text{Number of moles} = \text{Concentration (in mol dm}^{-3}\text{)} \times \text{Volume (in dm}^3\text{)}$$

Tip: In the formula for working out the number of moles of a gas, the "24" comes from the fact that at room temperature and pressure one mole of any gas occupies 24 dm^3. See your Year 1 notes for more on this.

...and these when you've got gases at room temperature and pressure.

$$\text{Number of moles} = \frac{\text{Volume (in dm}^3\text{)}}{24} \qquad \text{Number of moles} = \frac{\text{Volume (in cm}^3\text{)}}{24\,000}$$

These two are handy when you're working out how much stuff you've made...

$$\%\text{ atom economy} = \frac{\text{Molecular mass of desired product}}{\text{Sum of molecular masses of reactants}} \times 100$$

$$\%\text{ yield} = \frac{\text{Actual yield}}{\text{Theoretical yield}} \times 100$$

Tip: The sum of the molecular masses of the reactants is the same as the sum of the molecular masses of the products.

Here's the ideal gas equation, which allows you to convert between the volume, pressure and number of moles of a gas at a given temperature:

$$pV = nRT$$

volume (m^3) → V; *pressure (Pa)* → p; *the gas constant (= 8.314 J K^{-1} mol^{-1})* → R; *temperature (K)* → T; *number of moles* → n

Exam Tip
All these formulas are really important — you have to learn them because they won't be given to you in the exam.

Reaction rates

The rate equation links the rate of a reaction to the concentration of the reactants, the orders of these reactants, and the rate constant:

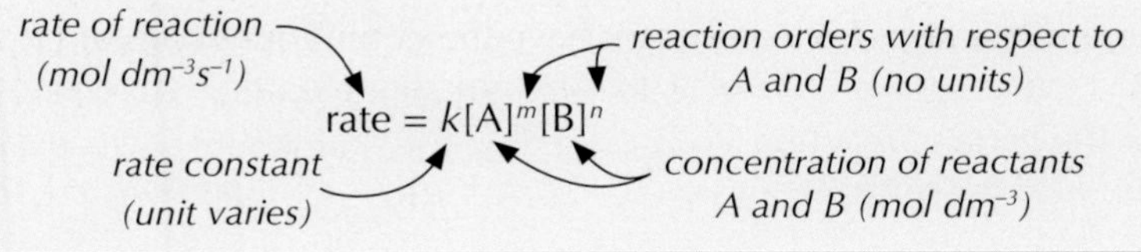

Tip: In this equation there are only two reactants (A and B), but you can have more. Here's the equation if you have three reactants: rate = $k[A]^m[B]^n[C]^x$

Tip: The Arrhenius equation looks a bit beastly, but luckily you don't have to learn it — both its forms will be given to you on the data sheet.

You can calculate the rate constant, k, for a reaction using the Arrhenius equation:

$$k = Ae^{\frac{-E_a}{RT}}$$

pre-exponential factor (units vary) → A; *activation energy (J mol^{-1})* → E_a; *temperature (K)* → T; *8.31 (J K^{-1} mol^{-1})* → R; *rate constant (units vary)* → k

This rearranges into a logarithmic form:

$$\ln k = \frac{-E_a}{RT} + \ln A$$

If a reaction is first order, then the rate constant can be calculated from the half-life of the reaction, using the equation:

$$k = \frac{\ln 2}{t_{½}}$$

rate constant (s^{-1} for a first order reaction.) → k; *half life (s)* → $t_{½}$

pH

Tip: Make sure you know how to use the log button on your calculator.

You need to be able to convert between pH and the concentration of H^+ ions in a solution, and vice versa:

$$pH = -\log_{10}[H^+] \qquad [H^+] = 10^{-pH}$$

Tip: You may also see '$\log_{10} x$' written as '$\log x$'.

You need to be able to convert between pK_a and K_a:

$$pK_a = -\log_{10} K_a \qquad K_a = 10^{-pK_a}$$

Equilibria

Tip: The lower-case letters a, b, d and e are the number of moles of each substance in the equation. The square brackets, [ ], mean concentration in mol dm^{-3}.

You need to be able to work out equilibrium constants for reactions.

Here's the equation for the equilibrium constant (K_c).

For the general reaction $aA + bB \rightleftharpoons dD + eE$:

$$K_c = \frac{[D]^d[E]^e}{[A]^a[B]^b}$$

where [X] is the concentration of X (mol dm^{-3})

For a weak acid, the acid dissociation constant, K_a, has units of mol dm^{-3}, and is found using the formula:

$$K_a = \frac{[H^+]^2}{[HA]}$$

Tip: In pure water, $[H^+] = [OH^-]$ so $K_w = [H^+]^2$.

Water has a special dissociation constant, called the ionic product of water, K_w. The units of K_w are mol^2 dm^{-6}, and it's found using the formula:

$$K_w = [H^+][OH^-]$$

Equilibrium reactions between gases have the equilibrium constant K_p.

For the general reaction $aA + bB \rightleftharpoons dD + eE$:

$$K_p = \frac{p(D)^d p(E)^e}{p(A)^a p(B)^b}$$

where p(X) is the partial pressure of X (Pa)

You can work out the mole fractions and partial pressures of the gases in a mixture using the following equations:.

$$\text{mole fraction of a gas in a mixture} = \frac{\text{number of moles of substance}}{\text{total number of moles of all substances in the mixture}}$$

$$\text{partial pressure of a gas in a mixture (Pa)} = \text{mole fraction} \times \text{total pressure of the mixture (Pa)}$$

Tip: The mole fraction of a substance doesn't have any units.

Energy changes

Energy changes include enthalpy changes, entropy changes and free energy changes for reaction, as well as electrode potentials of electrochemical cells.

There are two formulas you need to calculate enthalpy changes of a reaction. Here's one:

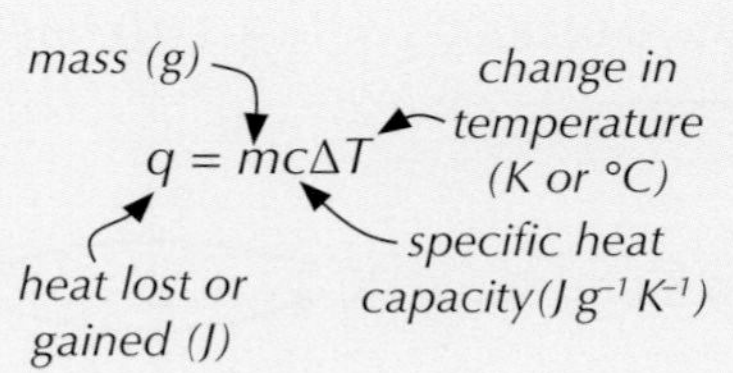

It doesn't matter whether the temperature is in K or °C — it's the change in temperature that goes into the formula, and that will be the same no matter what the units are.

Exam Tip
Make sure you can rearrange all these formulas and give the units of each quantity as well.

And the slightly easier:

Enthalpy change of reaction = Total energy absorbed – Total energy released

To calculate the entropy of a system, you use:

$\Delta S = S_{\text{products}} - S_{\text{reactants}}$ where ΔS is the entropy change in J K^{-1} mol^{-1}

If you know the enthalpy change, the entropy change and temperature of a reaction, you can calculate the free energy change (ΔG) using:

$$\Delta G = \Delta H - T\Delta S$$

Free energy change (J mol^{-1})
Temperature (K)
Enthalpy change (J mol^{-1})
Entropy change (J K^{-1} mol^{-1})

Finally, here's the equation to calculate the electrode potential of an electrochemical cell:

$$E^\ominus_{\text{cell}} = E^\ominus_{\text{reduced}} - E^\ominus_{\text{oxidised}}$$

Tip: Electrode potentials are always measured in volts (V).

3. Units

Units aren't the most exciting bit of chemistry but you need to be able to use them. Here's how to convert between units and work them out from scratch.

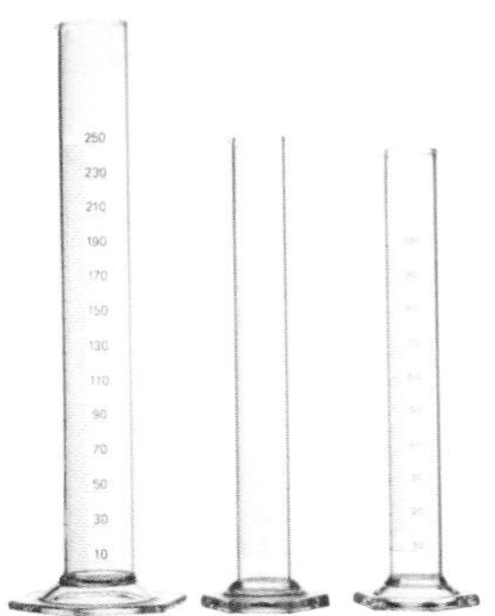

***Figure 1:** Measuring cylinders like these measure volumes in cm^3.*

Converting between units

Volume

Volume can be measured in m^3, dm^3 and cm^3.

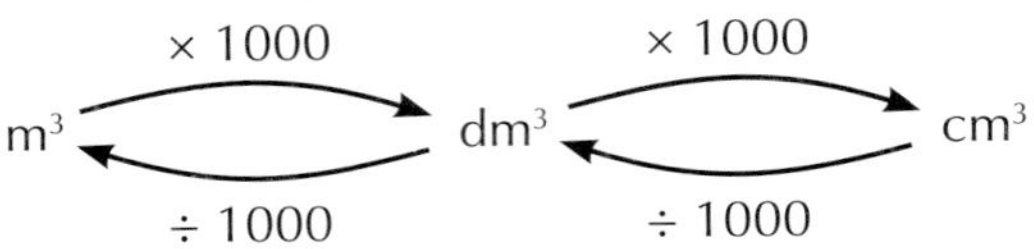

Example — Maths Skills

Write 0.3 cm^3 in dm^3 and m^3.

First, to convert 0.3 cm^3 into dm^3 you need to divide by 1000.

$$0.3 \div 1000 = 0.0003\ dm^3 = 3 \times 10^{-4}\ dm^3$$

Then, to convert 0.0003 dm^3 into m^3 you need to divide by 1000.

$$0.0003 \div 1000 = 0.0000003\ m^3 = 3 \times 10^{-7}\ m^3$$

Tip: Standard form (that's showing numbers as, for example, 3×10^{-7}) is covered on pages 269-270.

Temperature

Temperature can be measured in K and °C.

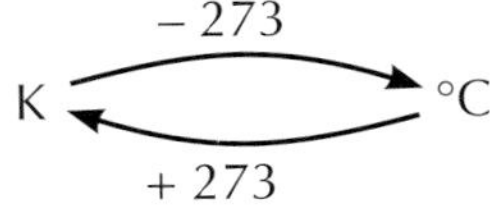

Example — Maths Skills

Write 25 °C in kelvins.

To convert 25 °C into K you need to add 273: $25 + 273 = 298$ K

Exam Tip
Make sure you practise these conversions. It could save you valuable time in the exam if you can change between units confidently.

Pressure

Pressure can be measured in Pa and kPa.

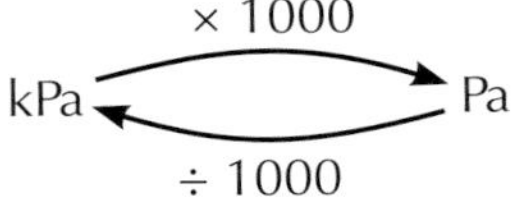

Tip: A kPa is bigger than a Pa, so you'd expect the number to get smaller when you convert from Pa to kPa — each unit is worth more so you'll have fewer of them.

Example — Maths Skills

Write 3200 Pa in kPa.

To convert 3200 Pa into kPa you need to divide by 1000.

$$3200 \div 1000 = 3.2\ kPa$$

Mass

Mass can be measured in kg and g.

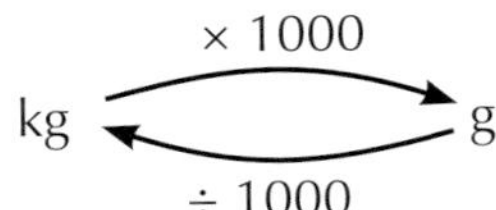

Example — Maths Skills

Write 5.2 kg in g.

To convert 5.2 kg into g you need to multiply by 1000.

$$5.2 \times 1000 = 5200\ g$$

***Figure 2:** This balance measures mass in g.*

Energy

Energy can be measured in kJ and J.

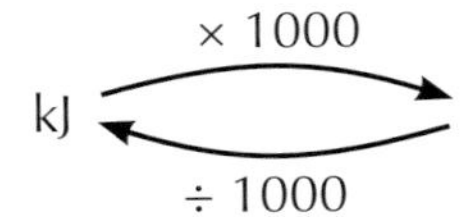

Example — Maths Skills

Write 78 kJ in J.

To convert 78 kJ into J you need to multiply by 1000.

$$78 \times 1000 = 78\,000 \text{ J} = 7.8 \times 10^4 \text{ J}$$

> **Tip:** If you get a bit confused converting between units, thinking about a conversion you are confident with might help. For example, if you know that 1 kJ is 1000 J, you know that to get from kJ to J you must have to multiply by 1000 — simple.

Concentration

Concentration can be measured in mol dm^{-3} and mol cm^{-3}.

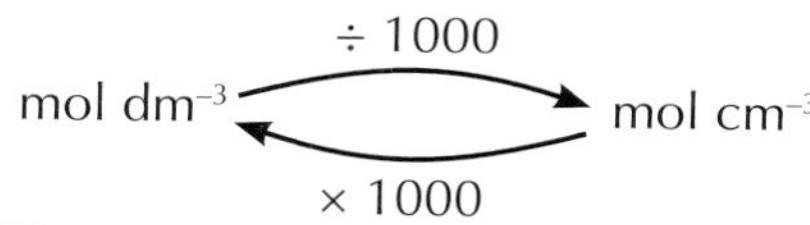

Example — Maths Skills

Write 0.5 mol dm^{-3} in mol cm^{-3}.

To convert 0.5 mol dm^{-3} into mol cm^{-3} you need to divide by 1000.

$$0.5 \div 1000 = 0.0005 \text{ mol cm}^{-3}$$

Life gets a bit confusing if you have to do lots of calculations one after the other — sometimes it can be difficult to keep track of your units. To avoid this, write down the units you're using with each line of the calculation. Then when you get to the end you know what units to give with your answer.

Figure 3: When you're under pressure in an exam it's really easy to make mistakes. So don't be afraid to use your calculator, even for really simple calculations.

Calculating units

Some things, like the equilibrium constant (K_c) and the rate constant (k), have variable units. This means you'll need to work the units out — you can't just learn them. To work out the units, you just follow these steps:

- Substitute the units that you know into the equation you're using.
- Cancel out units wherever possible — if the same unit is present on the top and the bottom of a fraction, you can cancel them out.
- Get rid of any fractions by using the index law $\frac{1}{a^n} = a^{-n}$ — any positive powers on the bottom of the fraction become negative and any negative powers become positive.

> **Exam Tip**
> Always, always, always give units with your answers. It's really important that the examiner knows what units you're working in — 10 g is very different from 10 kg.

Example — Maths Skills

The rate equation for the reaction $CH_3COCH_3 + I_2 \rightarrow CH_3COCH_2I + H^+ + I^-$ is Rate = $k[CH_3COCH_3][H^+]$. The rate of reaction is in mol dm^{-3} s^{-1} and the concentrations are in mol dm^{-3}. Find the units of k.

$$\text{Rate} = k[CH_3COCH_3][H^+] \qquad \text{so} \qquad k = \frac{\text{Rate}}{[CH_3COCH_3]\,[H^+]}$$

First substitute in the units you know:

$$\text{units of } k = \frac{\text{mol dm}^{-3}\text{s}^{-1}}{(\text{mol dm}^{-3})(\text{mol dm}^{-3})}$$

Cancel out units where you can. In this case you can cancel a mol dm^{-3} from the top and the bottom of the fraction:

$$\text{units of } k = \frac{\cancel{\text{mol dm}^{-3}}\text{s}^{-1}}{(\cancel{\text{mol dm}^{-3}})(\text{mol dm}^{-3})} = \frac{\text{s}^{-1}}{\text{mol dm}^{-3}}$$

Then get rid of the fraction by using the index law $\frac{1}{a^n} = a^{-n}$:

$$\text{units of } k = \text{s}^{-1}\,\text{mol}^{-1}\,\text{dm}^3$$

> **Tip:** If you have more than one of a particular unit multiplied together, you add the powers together (see p.276), e.g. (mol dm^{-3})(mol dm^{-3}) is (mol^2 dm^{-6}).

> **Tip:** Just writing mol is the same as writing mol^1, so 1/mol = mol^{-1}.

4. Indices and Logarithms

Indices and logarithms have opposite roles in maths. Indices raise a number to a power, whilst logarithms find out what a number has been raised to.

Indices

Indices are the little numbers that you raise things to the power of:

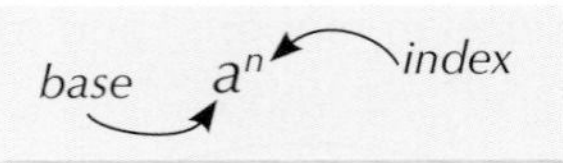

Indices can be positive or negative numbers. A positive index tells you how many times to multiply number by itself.

Examples — Maths Skills

$2^5 = 2 \times 2 \times 2 \times 2 \times 2 = \mathbf{32}$ $10^3 = 10 \times 10 \times 10 = \mathbf{1000}$

Tip: Indices are used a lot in rate equations. Have a look at page 31 to see them in action.

This is how to calculate a negative index: $a^{-n} = \frac{1}{a^n}$

Examples — Maths Skills

$4^{-2} = \frac{1}{4 \times 4} = \mathbf{0.0625}$ $5^{-3} = \frac{1}{5 \times 5 \times 5} = \mathbf{0.008}$

There are some rules for using indices in calculations that are useful to know:

- If you raise a number to the power 1, the answer is that number:

$$\mathbf{a^1 = a}$$

- If you raise a number to the power 0, the answer is 1:

$$\mathbf{a^0 = 1}$$

- If you multiply a number raised to a power by the same number raised to a different power, the answer is the same as the number raised to the sum of the two powers:

$$\mathbf{a^n \times a^m = a^{(n+m)}}$$

- If you divide a number raised to a power by the same number raised to a different power, the answer is the same as the number raised to the value of the first power minus the value of the second power:

$$\mathbf{a^n \div a^m = a^{(n-m)}}$$

- A number raised to a power on the bottom of a fractions is the same as that number raised to the negative of the power:

$$\mathbf{\frac{1}{a^n} = a^{-n}}$$

Tip: These rules all apply to indices you find in units as well as in numerical equations.

Examples — Maths Skills

$7^1 = \mathbf{7}$ $11^0 = \mathbf{1}$ $3^2 \times 3^4 = 3^6 = \mathbf{729}$

$4^7 \div 4^5 = 4^2 = \mathbf{16}$ $\frac{1}{\text{mol dm}^{-3}} = \mathbf{mol^{-1}\ dm^3}$

The number 'e'

The number 'e' crops up occasionally in chemistry. Like 'π', it is a fixed, irrational number with an infinite number of decimal places.

$$e = 2.718281828459045235360...$$

In most of the calculations involving e that you will come across, it is raised to a power. To stop you having to type in a long string of numbers every time you do these calculations, there should be a button on your calculator that looks a bit like this: [e■].

Tip: The indices rules on the previous page all apply to calculations involving e raised to a power.

Examples — Maths Skills

$e^9 = \mathbf{8103.1}$ $e^{-4} = \mathbf{0.01832}$ $e^0 = \mathbf{1}$

Logarithms

Logarithms tell you how many times a number (the **base**) has been multiplied by itself to get to another number. They are the opposite of indices.

$$\text{If } a^n = x \quad \text{then} \quad \log_a x = n$$

It's important to specify the base of your logarithm, but some numbers are so common they have they're own symbols:

- You often want to know how many times the number 10 has been multiplied by itself. Sometimes $\log_{10} x$ is just written as $\log x$.
- The **natural logarithm** is the logarithm with a base of e. You write $\log_e x$ as $\ln x$.

These two functions are used so often that you'll probably have a button for each of them on your calculator — handy.

Tip: Your calculator may well have buttons that look like: [log■□], [log] and [ln]. The first button lets you specify your base. The second is $\log_{10}$ and the third is $\log_e$.

Tip: Logarithms tell you the order of magnitude a number is in, so they're really useful for comparing numbers that fall across a very large range.

Examples — Maths Skills

$\log_2 16 = \mathbf{4}$ $\log 100 = \mathbf{2}$ $\ln 14 = \mathbf{2.6}$

Just like for indices, there are some rules for working with logarithms in calculations that are useful to know:

- The logarithm of two things multiplied together is the same as the sum of their individual logarithms:

$$\boldsymbol{\log_a (xy) = \log_a x + \log_a y}$$

- The logarithm of the value of the base raised to a power is the value of the power:

$$\boldsymbol{\log_a a^x = x}$$

Tip: The pH scale is a logarithmic scale in base 10. Have a look at page 69 to see more about it.

Example — Maths Skills

You can use these rules to rearrange the Arrhenius equation into its logarithmic form:

$$k = Ae^{\frac{-E_a}{RT}}$$

Taking the natural logarithm of both sides gives you:

$$\ln (k) = \ln (Ae^{\frac{-E_a}{RT}})$$

Using the first rule, you know that $\ln (xy) = \ln x + \ln y$, so:

$$\ln k = \ln (A) + \ln(e^{\frac{-E_a}{RT}})$$

Using the second rule, you know that $\ln e^x = x$, so:

$$\ln k = \frac{-E_a}{RT} + \ln A$$

This is the logarithmic form of the Arrhenius equation.

Tip: To make your calculations clear, always put brackets around the thing you're taking the log of. For example, $\log (a + b)$ and $\log(a) + b$ both clearly show what you're doing in a calculation. If you just write log a + b, it's not obvious what's being done.

Tip: See pages 41-44 for lots more about the Arrhenius equation.

5. Graphs

You should have had lots of practice drawing and interpreting graphs in Year 1. Being able to interpret graphs can be really important in chemistry, so here's a recap of some of the trickier bits.

Straight line graphs

All straight line graphs have the general equation:

$$y = mx + c$$

(*y* = dependent variable, *x* = independent variable, *m* = gradient, *c* = y-intercept)

Tip: Straight line graphs you're likely to come across include rate-concentration graphs for first order reactions (page 29) and Arrhenius plots (page 43).

If you have an equation in this form and you plot a graph of the dependent variable against the independent variable, then the gradient of the graph will be equal to *m*, and the *y*-intercept will be equal to *c*.

Example — Maths Skills

The logarithmic form of the Arrhenius equation is: $\ln k = \frac{-E_a}{RT} + \ln A$

This is an equation in the form $y = mx + c$ where:

$\ln k = y$, $\frac{-E_a}{R} = m$, $\frac{1}{T} = x$, $\ln A = c$

So if you plot a graph of $\ln k$ against $\frac{1}{T}$, it will have a gradient equal to $\frac{-E_a}{R}$ and a *y*-intercept of $\ln A$.

Finding the gradient of a straight line graph

The gradient of a graph tells you how much the *y* value changes as you change the *x* value — it's a measure of the steepness of your graph.

gradient = change in *y* ÷ change in *x*

Tip: The change in *y* can be written as Δy, and the change in *x* can be written as Δx.

To measure the gradient of a straight line, start by picking two points on the line that are easy to read. Draw a vertical line down from one point and a horizontal line across from the other to make a triangle. The length of the vertical side of the triangle is the change in *y* and the length of the horizontal side is the change in *x*.

Tip: A line that slopes downwards from left to right has a negative gradient, because *y* decreases as *x* increases.

Example — Maths Skills

First order reactions have the rate equation: Rate = *k*[A].

This is in the form $y = mx + c$, where Rate = *y*, *k* = *m*, [A] = *x* and 0 = *c*.

So a graph of rate against [A] will have a gradient equal to *k*.

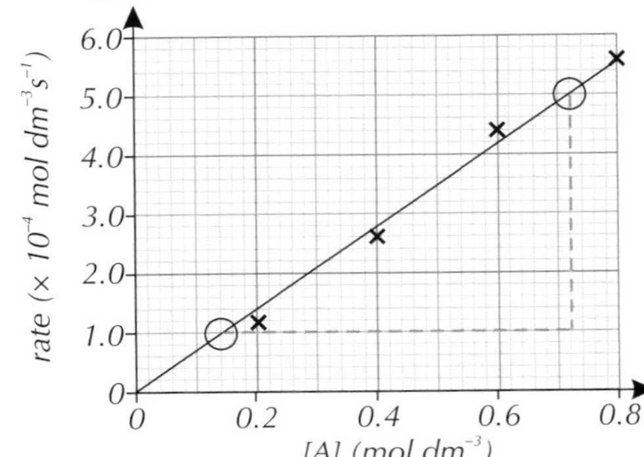

$\Delta x = 0.72 - 0.14 = 0.58$

$\Delta y = (5.0 \times 10^{-4}) - (1.0 \times 10^{-4}) = 4.0 \times 10^{-4}$

Gradient $= (4.0 \times 10^{-4}) \div 0.58 = 6.9 \times 10^{-4}$

$k = \mathbf{6.9 \times 10^{-4}\ s^{-1}}$

Exam Tip
Always check the labels of the axes. Here, the *y* axis units are 10^{-4} mol dm^{-3} s^{-1} so each of the values on the *y* axis is multiplied by 10^{-4} to find its true value.

Finding the intercept of a graph

The *y*-intercept of a graph is the point at which the line of best fit crosses the *y* axis. You may have to extrapolate your line of best fit beyond your data points to find the *y*-intercept.

> **Tip:** Finding a value by extending your line of best fit beyond your data points is called extrapolation. Finding a value between two of your data points using a line of best fit is called interpolation.

Example — Maths Skills

From the logarithmic form of the Arrhenius equation, $\ln k = \frac{-E_a}{RT} + \ln A$, you know that the y-intercept of a graph of ln *k* against $\frac{1}{T}$ is equal to ln *A*.

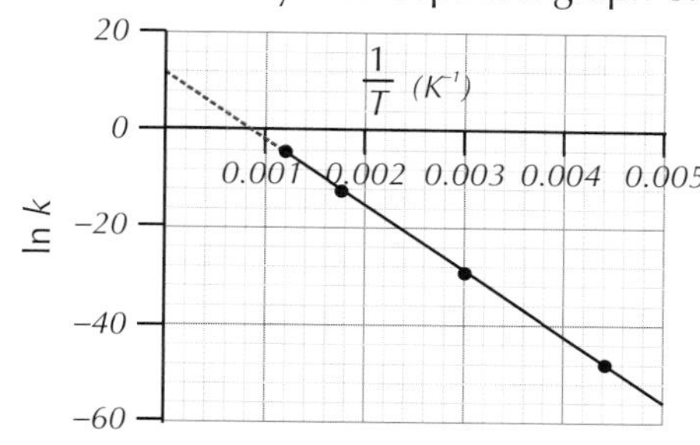

By extrapolating the line of best fit for this graph to the point where $x = 0$, you can see that $y = 12$.

So ln A = **12**

> **Tip:** You can't find the *y*-intercept from a graph if the axes have been contracted. Both axes need to run continuously from zero for it to work.

Finding the gradient of a curve

The gradient is different at different points along a graph. To find the gradient at a particular point, you first have to draw a tangent to the curve at that point, and then find the gradient of that. To draw a tangent:

Example — Maths Skills

The gradient of a graph of concentration against time at any point is equal to the rate of the reaction at that time.

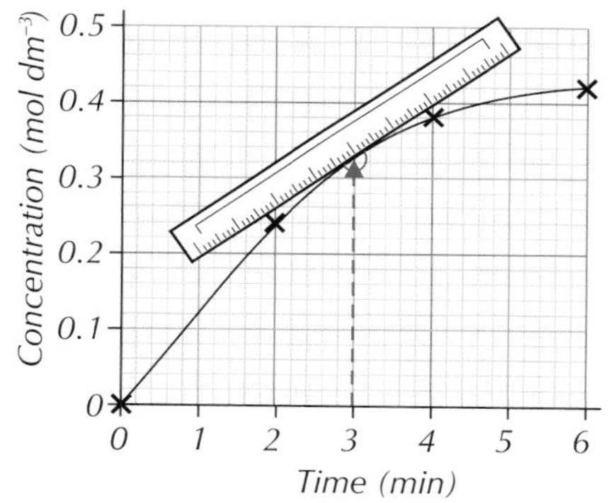

1. To find the rate after three minutes, place a ruler at the point on the curve at 3 minutes so that it's just touching the curve. Position the ruler so that you can see the whole curve.
2. Adjust the ruler until the space between the ruler and the curve is equal on both sides of the point.

> **Tip:** There's more about finding gradients on page 21, and also in your Year 1 notes.

3. Draw a line along the ruler to make the tangent. Extend the line right across the graph — it'll help to make your gradient calculation easier as you'll have more points to choose from.

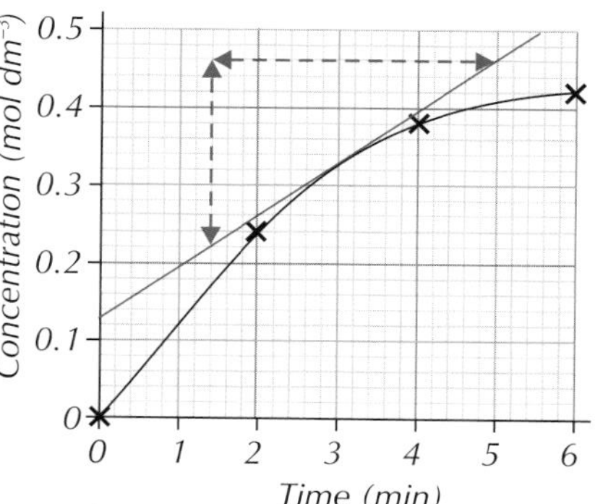

4. Calculate the gradient of the tangent to find the rate:
   - gradient = change in *y* ÷ change in *x*
     $= (0.46 - 0.22) \div (5.0 - 1.4) = 0.067 \text{ mol dm}^{-3}\text{ min}^{-1}$
   - So, the rate of reaction at 3 mins was $0.067 \text{ mol dm}^{-3}\text{ min}^{-1}$.

1. Exam Structure and Technique

Passing exams isn't all about revision — it really helps if you know how the exam is structured and have got your exam technique nailed so that you pick up every mark you can.

***Figure 1:** The Room of Doom awaits you. But don't panic — prepare properly and there's no reason you can't ace the exam.*

Course structure

OCR A A-Level Chemistry is split into six modules:

Module 1 — Development of practical skills in chemistry

Module 2 — Foundations in chemistry

Module 3 — Periodic table and energy

Module 4 — Core organic chemistry

Module 5 — Physical chemistry and transition elements

Module 6 — Organic chemistry and analysis

The first four Modules were covered in the Year 1 book. The final two are covered in this book.

Exam Tip
Make sure you have a good read through this exam structure. It might not seem important now but you don't want to get any nasty surprises just before an exam.

Exam structure

For OCR A A-Level Chemistry you're gonna have to sit through three exams:

- Paper 1 — Periodic table, elements and physical chemistry
- Paper 2 — Synthesis and analytical techniques
- Paper 3 — Unified chemistry

Papers 1 and 2 are both 2 hours and 15 minutes long. Paper 3 is 1 hour and 30 minutes long. The exams will cover material from both years of your A-Level course, so you need to learn everything from Year 1 as well as Year 2. Papers 1 and 2 are worth 100 marks each, and Paper 3 is worth 70 marks.

- Paper 1 covers material from Modules 1, 2, 3 and 5. It's split up into two sections. Section A has 15 marks' worth of multiple choice questions. Section B has 85 marks' worth of short and extended answer questions.
- Paper 2 covers material from Modules 1, 2, 4 and 6. It's split up into two sections. Section A has 15 marks' worth of multiple choice questions. Section B has 85 marks' worth of short and extended answer questions.
- Paper 3 covers content from all six modules. It has 70 marks' worth of short and extended answer questions.

Exam Tip
All of the exams will have a mixture of short answer and long answer questions. Short answer questions are broken down into lots of parts but they can still be worth loads of marks overall.

Level of Response questions

The exam papers include some extended response questions, where you'll usually be asked to explain or describe something at a bit more length. Some of these questions may be marked using a Level of Response mark scheme. All this means is that you'll receive marks based on the quality of your response — not just its scientific content. So the more fully explained, better structured and more coherent your answer is, the more marks you'll get.

These questions will be clearly marked on your paper, so make sure you know which ones they are and write full and well thought-out answers.

Exam Tip
Don't worry too much about Level of Response questions. Really, you should be looking to give full and coherent explanations for every extended response question.

Synoptic assessment

All the exam papers will contain some synoptic assessment. This sounds complicated but don't worry, all it means is that you could be asked to draw together and apply different bits of chemistry knowledge in the same question.

Examples

Bringing together knowledge from different parts of the course.

You might be asked how you could synthesise and purify an organic acid, and then be asked to calculate its K_a. This draws together knowledge from Modules 4, 5 and 6.

Applying knowledge from different areas to a new context.

You might be asked to draw on your knowledge of chirality to identify the stereoisomers of an organic drug molecule you've not seen before.

Exam Tip

Don't stress out about synoptic assessment. You need to learn material from lots of modules for all the exams anyway, so as long as you've learnt it all thoroughly it shouldn't be a problem.

Time management

This is one of the most important exam skills to have. How long you spend on each question is really important in an exam — it could make all the difference to your grade. Some questions will require lots of work for only a few marks but other questions will be much quicker. Don't spend ages struggling with questions that are only worth a couple of marks — move on. You can come back to them later when you've bagged loads of other marks elsewhere.

Example

The questions below are both worth the same number of marks but require different amounts of work.

1 (a) Define the term 'lattice enthalpy'.

(2 marks)

2 (a) Use the Arrhenius plot to calculate the pre-exponential factor, *A*, of the reaction.

(2 marks)

Question 1 (a) only requires you to write down a definition — if you can remember it this shouldn't take you too long.

Question 2 (a) requires you to find the *y* intercept of a graph and then put this equal to ln *A* to calculate the pre-exponential factor — this may take you longer than writing down a definition.

So, if you're running out of time it makes sense to do questions like 1 (a) first and come back to 2 (a) if you've got time at the end.

Exam Tip

Everyone has their own method of getting through the exams. Some people find it easier to go through the paper question by question and some people like to do the questions they find easiest first. The most important thing is to find out the way that suits you best <u>before</u> the exams — that means doing all the practice exams you can before the big day.

Exam Tip

Don't forget to go back and do any questions that you left the first time round — you don't want to miss out on marks because you forgot to do the question.

It's worth keeping in mind that the multiple choice questions are all only worth 1 mark, even though some of them could be quite tricky and time-consuming. Don't make the mistake of spending too much time on these. If you're struggling with some of them, move on to the written answer questions where there are more marks available and then go back to the harder multiple choice questions later.

Exam Tip

<u>Never</u> leave a multiple choice question unanswered at the end of the exam. Even if it's a complete guess, you'll have a 25% chance of getting the mark. And if you can eliminate one or two of the options quickly, then your chances are even better.

Command words

Command words are just the bit of the question that tell you what to do. You'll find answering exam questions much easier if you understand exactly what they mean, so here's a brief summary table of the most common command words:

Command word:	What to do:
Give / Name / State	Give a brief one or two word answer, or a short sentence.
Identify	Say what something is.
Describe (an observation)	Write about what you would expect to happen in a reaction, e.g. colour change or the formation of a precipitate.
Outline / Describe (an experiment)	Write about each step in an experiment — including any equipment you would use, the reagents required and any reaction conditions (e.g. temperature, presence of a catalyst). If you are identifying a substance, you should also include any physical changes you would expect to see, such as a precipitate being formed.
Explain	Give reasons for something.
Suggest / Predict	Use your scientific knowledge to work out what the answer might be.
Calculate	Work out the solution to a mathematical problem.
Deduce / Determine	Use the information given in the question to work something out.
Compare	Give the similarities and differences between two things.
Contrast	Give the differences between two things.

Exam Tip
Some questions might contain more than one command word. For example, a question could start 'state and explain'. In this case, you should treat the question a little bit like two questions rolled into one. Make sure you clearly state what the question asks for and then go on to the explanation.

Some questions will also ask you to answer 'using the information / data provided' (e.g. a graph, table, equation, etc.). When that's the case, you must use the information given and you may need to refer to it in your answer to get all the marks. Some questions may also ask you to answer 'using your calculation' — it's the same here, you need to use your answer to a particular calculation, otherwise you won't get the marks. Not all of the questions will have command words — instead they may just ask a which / what / how type of question.

Exam data sheet

When you sit your exams, you'll be given a data sheet as an insert within the exam paper. On it you'll find some useful information to help you with your exam, including...

- the molar gas volume at room temperature and pressure
- the Avogadro constant
- the specific heat capacity and the ionic product of water
- the relationship between tonnes and grams
- the gas constant
- the exponential and logarithmic forms of the Arrhenius equation
- the characteristic infrared absorptions, ^{13}C NMR shifts and ^{1}H NMR shifts of some common functional groups.

The data sheet will also contain a copy of the periodic table. You might have seen a few slightly different versions of the periodic table — for example, some tables include the lanthanides and actinides, and others don't. In the exam, make sure you use the information from the periodic table on the data sheet, even if you think it's slightly different to something you've seen elsewhere. The information on the data sheet will be what the examiners use to mark the exam papers.

Exam Tip
It's a good idea to have a look at an exam data sheet before going in to the exam — you should be able to find it on the OCR website.

2. Diagrams

When you're asked to draw diagrams or mechanisms in an exam it's important that you draw everything correctly and include all the details that are needed.

Organic reaction mechanisms

Organic reaction mechanisms are used to show what happens during a chemical reaction. One of the most common mistakes with these is to get the curly arrows wrong.

Example

When you're drawing organic reaction mechanisms the curly arrows must come from either a lone pair of electrons or from a bond, like this:

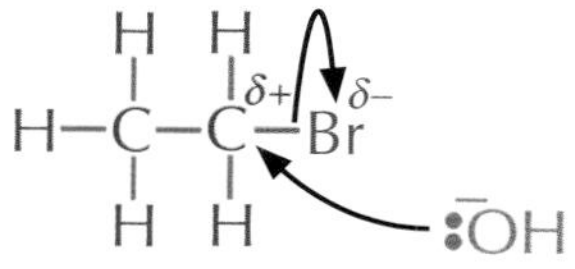

```
    H  H
    |  |δ+  δ–
H—C—C—Br
    |  |
    H  H      :OH⁻
```

The mechanisms below are incorrect — you wouldn't get marks for them:

You won't get marks if the curly arrows come from atoms, like this...

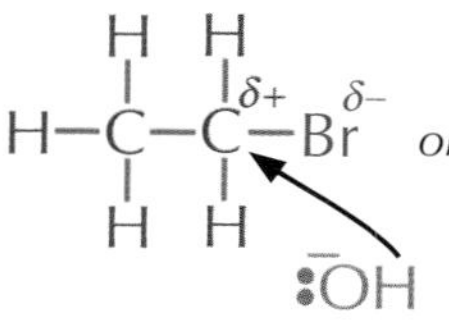

```
    H  H
    |  |δ+  δ–
H—C—C—Br
    |  |
    H  H
           :OH⁻
```

or this...

```
    H  H
    |  |δ+  δ–
H—C—C—Br
    |  |
    H  H
           :OH⁻
```

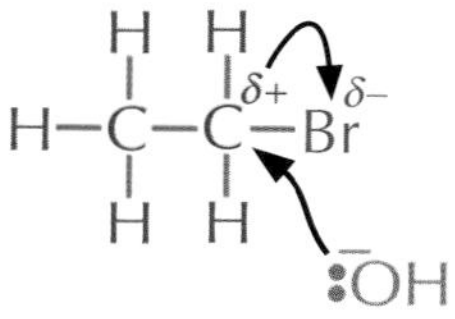

Tip: It's important that the curly arrows come from a lone pair or a bond because that's where the electrons are found. Remember, curly arrows are supposed to show the movement of electrons.

Exam Tip
Make sure that you draw carbocations with a full positive charge (+) and dipoles clearly as dipoles (δ+) — you will lose marks in the exams if it's not clear which you mean.

Displayed and skeletal formulas

Displayed formulas show how all the atoms are connected in a molecule. It's surprisingly easy to make mistakes when drawing them.

Examples

If a question asks you for a displayed formula you have to show all of the bonds and all of the atoms in the molecule. That means you have to draw displayed formulas like this:

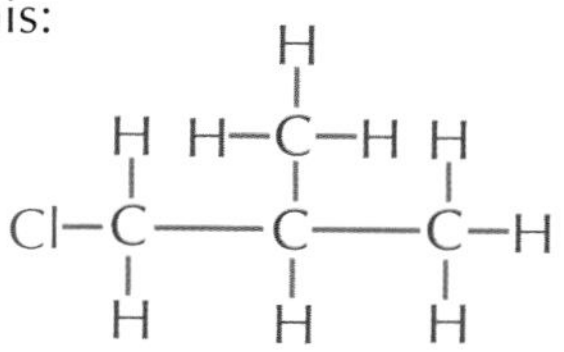

```
          H
          |
   H   H—C—H   H
   |      |      |
Cl—C——–C——–C—H
   |      |      |
   H      H      H
```

And not like this:

```
   H  CH₃
   |   |
Cl—C—C—CH₃
   |   |
   H   H
```

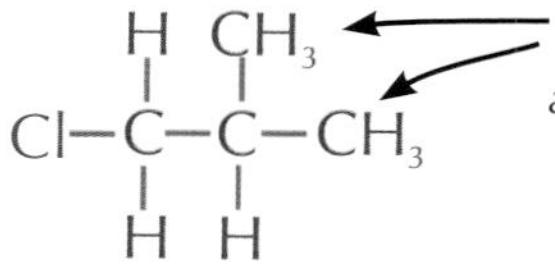

Some of the bonds between the carbon atoms and the hydrogen atoms haven't been shown, so it's not a displayed formula and you wouldn't get the marks.

If you're not asked specifically for a displayed formula then either of the diagrams above will do. Just make sure that the bonds are always drawn between the right atoms. For example, ethanol should be drawn like this:

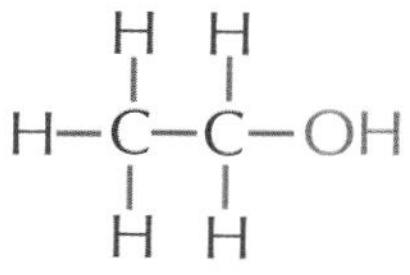

```
   H  H
   |  |
H—C—C—OH
   |  |
   H  H
```

And not like this:

```
   H  H
   |  |
H—C—C—HO
   |  |
   H  H
```

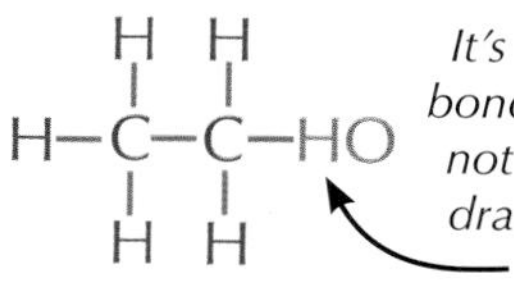

It's the oxygen that's bonded to the carbon, not the hydrogen, so drawing it like this is just wrong.

Tip: A displayed formula shows how all the atoms are arranged and all the bonds between them.

Skeletal formulas are handy when you're drawing larger organic molecules. There's a pretty good chance that you'll have to draw skeletal formulas in your exams, so you need to be able to draw them properly. Remember — bonds between carbon atoms are shown by a line and carbon atoms are found at each end. Atoms that aren't carbon or hydrogen have to be drawn on:

Exam Tip
If you're not totally comfortable drawing skeletal formulas draw out the displayed formula first and that'll help you to see what atoms need to be drawn in the skeletal formula.

Example

1,5-difluoropentane ($FCH_2CH_2CH_2CH_2CH_2F$)

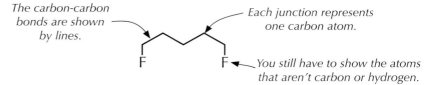

The carbon-carbon bonds are shown by lines.

Each junction represents one carbon atom.

F F

You still have to show the atoms that aren't carbon or hydrogen.

You don't draw any carbon or hydrogen atoms from the main carbon chain when you're drawing skeletal formulas, so the diagrams below are both wrong.

C C C F F

You don't show the carbon atoms or the hydrogen atoms.

H F F

Exam Tip
Make sure you've got everything the question asks for in your answer. For example, if the question asks you to include lone pairs and dipoles in a diagram, don't forget to include them.

Hydrogen bonds

Drawing hydrogen bonds is a common exam question. You need to know how to draw them properly to pick up all the marks you can.

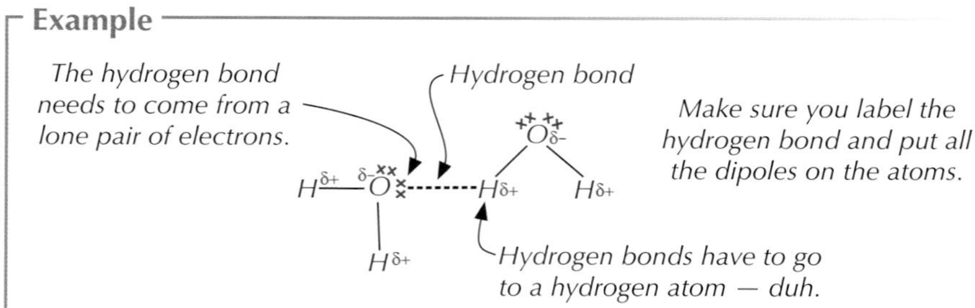
Example
The hydrogen bond needs to come from a lone pair of electrons.
Hydrogen bond
Make sure you label the hydrogen bond and put all the dipoles on the atoms.
Hydrogen bonds have to go to a hydrogen atom — duh.

General advice on diagrams

These pages cover some of the types of diagram that are likely to come up in your exams. But you could be asked to draw other diagrams. Whatever diagram you're drawing, make sure it's really clear. A small scribble in the bottom corner of a page isn't going to show enough detail to get you the marks. Draw the diagrams nice and big, but make sure that you stay within the space given for that answer. It may also help to add clear, concise labels to your diagram, particularly for things like drawings of the apparatus needed for an experiment. If you've drawn a diagram incorrectly, don't scribble part of it out and try to fix it — it'll look messy and be really hard for the examiner to figure out what you're trying to show. Cross the whole thing out and start again. And always double check that you've included all the things that you should have done.

3. The Periodic Table — Facts and Trends

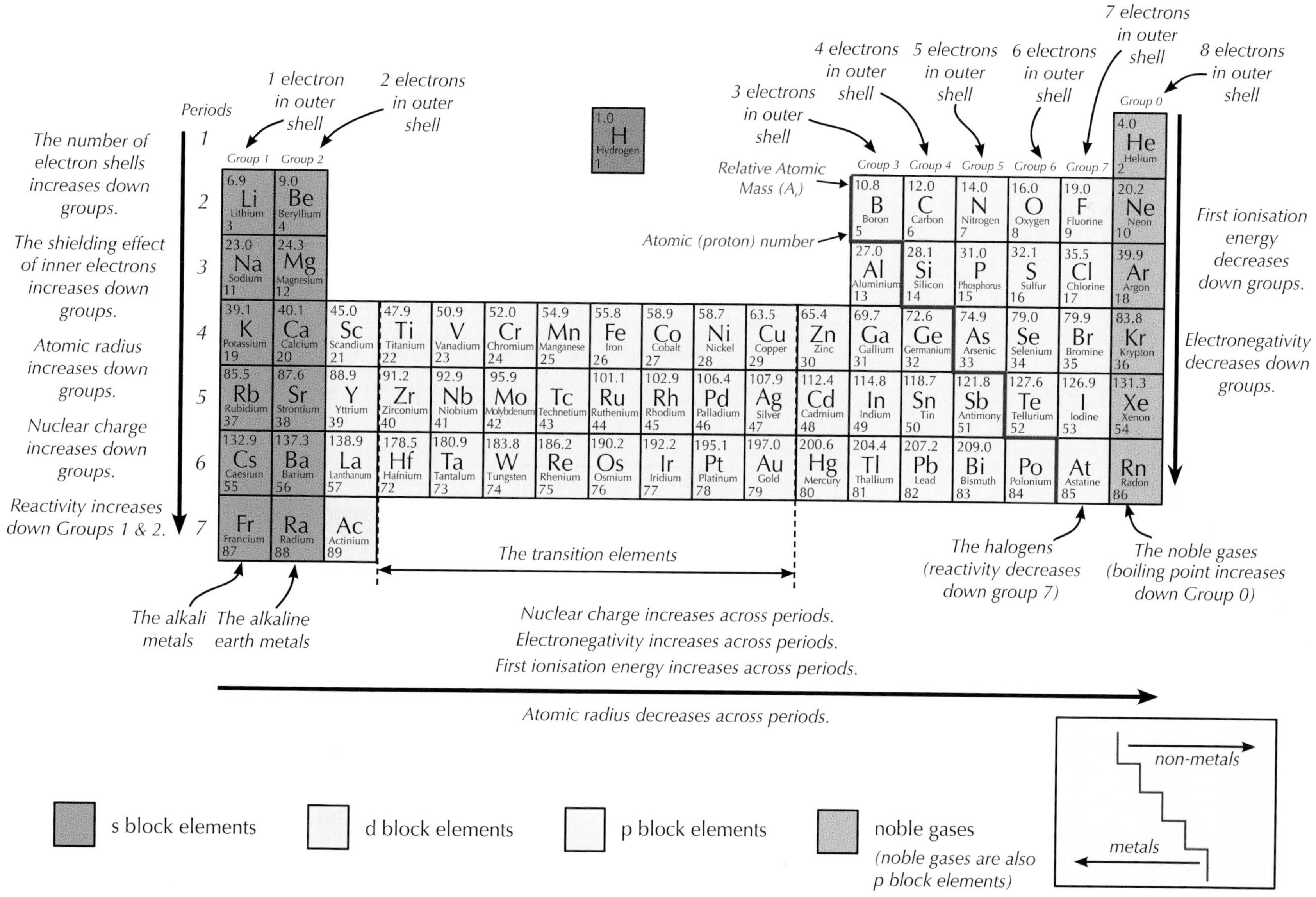

1.0 H Hydrogen 1

Periods	Group 1	Group 2											Group 3	Group 4	Group 5	Group 6	Group 7	Group 0
1																		4.0 He Helium 2
2	6.9 Li Lithium 3	9.0 Be Beryllium 4											10.8 B Boron 5	12.0 C Carbon 6	14.0 N Nitrogen 7	16.0 O Oxygen 8	19.0 F Fluorine 9	20.2 Ne Neon 10
3	23.0 Na Sodium 11	24.3 Mg Magnesium 12											27.0 Al Aluminium 13	28.1 Si Silicon 14	31.0 P Phosphorus 15	32.1 S Sulfur 16	35.5 Cl Chlorine 17	39.9 Ar Argon 18
4	39.1 K Potassium 19	40.1 Ca Calcium 20	45.0 Sc Scandium 21	47.9 Ti Titanium 22	50.9 V Vanadium 23	52.0 Cr Chromium 24	54.9 Mn Manganese 25	55.8 Fe Iron 26	58.9 Co Cobalt 27	58.7 Ni Nickel 28	63.5 Cu Copper 29	65.4 Zn Zinc 30	69.7 Ga Gallium 31	72.6 Ge Germanium 32	74.9 As Arsenic 33	79.0 Se Selenium 34	79.9 Br Bromine 35	83.8 Kr Krypton 36
5	85.5 Rb Rubidium 37	87.6 Sr Strontium 38	88.9 Y Yttrium 39	91.2 Zr Zirconium 40	92.9 Nb Niobium 41	95.9 Mo Molybdenum 42	Tc Technetium 43	101.1 Ru Ruthenium 44	102.9 Rh Rhodium 45	106.4 Pd Palladium 46	107.9 Ag Silver 47	112.4 Cd Cadmium 48	114.8 In Indium 49	118.7 Sn Tin 50	121.8 Sb Antimony 51	127.6 Te Tellurium 52	126.9 I Iodine 53	131.3 Xe Xenon 54
6	132.9 Cs Caesium 55	137.3 Ba Barium 56	138.9 La Lanthanum 57	178.5 Hf Hafnium 72	180.9 Ta Tantalum 73	183.8 W Tungsten 74	186.2 Re Rhenium 75	190.2 Os Osmium 76	192.2 Ir Iridium 77	195.1 Pt Platinum 78	197.0 Au Gold 79	200.6 Hg Mercury 80	204.4 Tl Thallium 81	207.2 Pb Lead 82	209.0 Bi Bismuth 83	Po Polonium 84	At Astatine 85	Rn Radon 86
7	Fr Francium 87	Ra Radium 88	Ac Actinium 89															

1 electron in outer shell (Group 1). 2 electrons in outer shell (Group 2). 3 electrons in outer shell (Group 3). 4 electrons in outer shell (Group 4). 5 electrons in outer shell (Group 5). 6 electrons in outer shell (Group 6). 7 electrons in outer shell (Group 7). 8 electrons in outer shell (Group 0).

Relative Atomic Mass (A_r)

Atomic (proton) number

The number of electron shells increases down groups.

The shielding effect of inner electrons increases down groups.

Atomic radius increases down groups.

Nuclear charge increases down groups.

Reactivity increases down Groups 1 & 2.

First ionisation energy decreases down groups.

Electronegativity decreases down groups.

The alkali metals — *The alkaline earth metals*

The transition elements

The halogens (reactivity decreases down group 7)

The noble gases (boiling point increases down Group 0)

Nuclear charge increases across periods.
Electronegativity increases across periods.
First ionisation energy increases across periods.

Atomic radius decreases across periods.

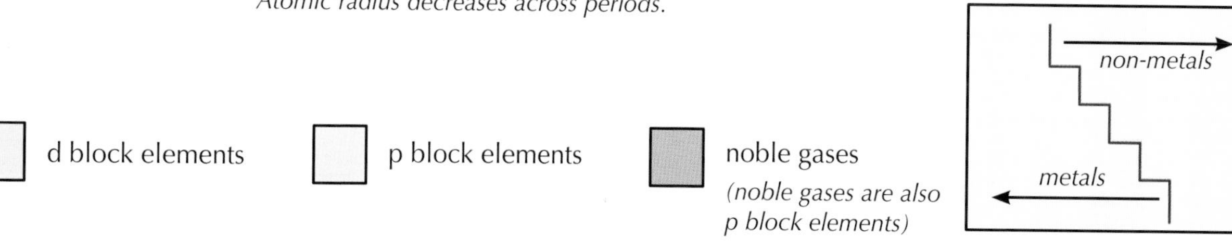

s block elements

d block elements

p block elements

noble gases
(noble gases are also p block elements)

Answers

Module 5

Section 1 — Reaction Rates

1. Monitoring Reactions

Page 20 — Application Questions

Q1 a) E.g. measure the change in pH using a pH meter.
b) E.g. measure the loss of mass using a mass balance, measure the volume of gas produced using a gas syringe, measure the change in pH using a pH meter.
c) E.g. use colorimetry to measure the change in absorbance, measure the loss of mass using a mass balance, measure the volume of gas produced using a gas syringe.

Q2 The calculated rate would be less than the true rate. Not all of the gas produced would be collected, as some would escape from the system. This means that the reaction would appear to have produced less gas than it really had, and so the rate would appear lower.

Q3 Initial number of moles HCl = conc × vol
= 1.50 × (250 ÷ 1000)
= 0.375

Time / seconds	Mass lost / g	Concentration of HCl / mol dm^{-3}
0	0.00	**1.50**
10	0.600	**1.36**
20	1.18	**1.22**
30	1.77	**1.08**
40	2.37	**0.942**
50	2.94	**0.808**
60	3.51	**0.674**

Q4 $Na_2CO_3 + H_2SO_4 \rightarrow Na_2SO_4 + H_2O + CO_2$
Initial number of moles H_2SO_4 = conc × vol
= 1.00 × (100 ÷ 1000)
= 0.100

Time / seconds	Concentration of H_2SO_4 / mol dm^{-3}
0	**1.00**
15	**0.999**
30	**0.997**
45	**0.996**
60	**0.995**
75	**0.984**

See page 19 for a full method for this type of question.

Page 20 — Fact Recall Questions

Q1 Continuous monitoring is a method for following the progress of a reaction. It involves taking measurements at regular intervals, over the course of a reaction, to measure the loss of a reactant or the formation of a product.

Q2

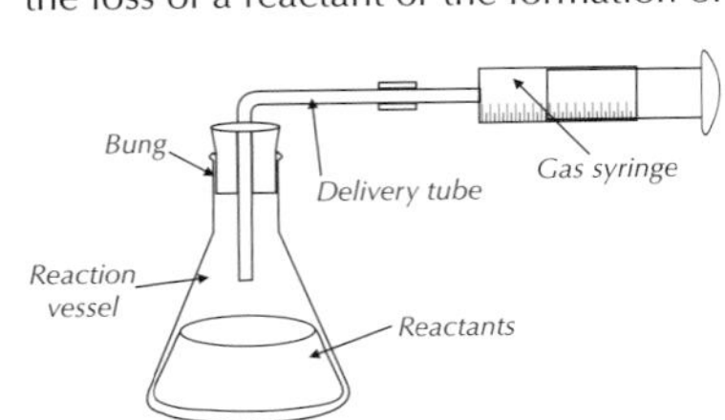

Q3 Colorimeters measure the absorbance of a particular wavelength of light by a solution.

Q4 E.g. you could measure the loss of mass, at regular intervals, as a gaseous product forms and escapes. By carrying out the reaction on a balance, you can follow how the mass changes throughout the experiment. / You could collect the gas in a gas syringe and record the volume of gas produced, at regular intervals, over the course of the reaction.

2. Concentration-Time Graphs

Page 22 — Application Questions

Q1 a)

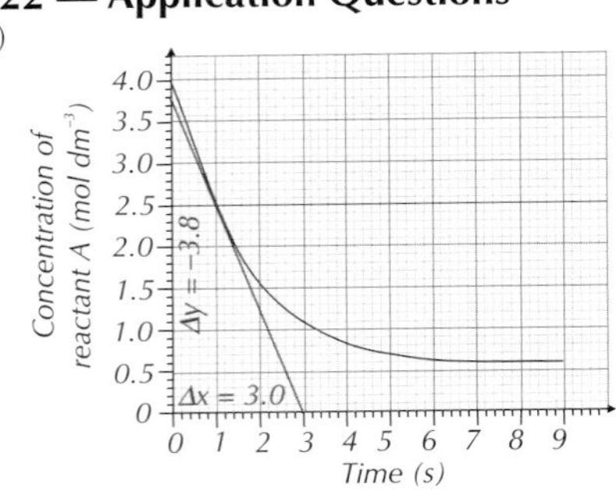

$$\text{Rate} = \frac{\Delta y}{\Delta x} = \frac{-3.8}{3.0} = \mathbf{-1.3\ mol\ dm^{-3}\ s^{-1}}$$

Drawing tangents accurately is tricky so there may be some variation between the answer you got and the 'official' answer. Don't worry though — in the exam, you'll usually be allowed a range of answers if you're asked to calculate a gradient. So for part a) allow yourself anything from −0.9 to −1.7.

b)

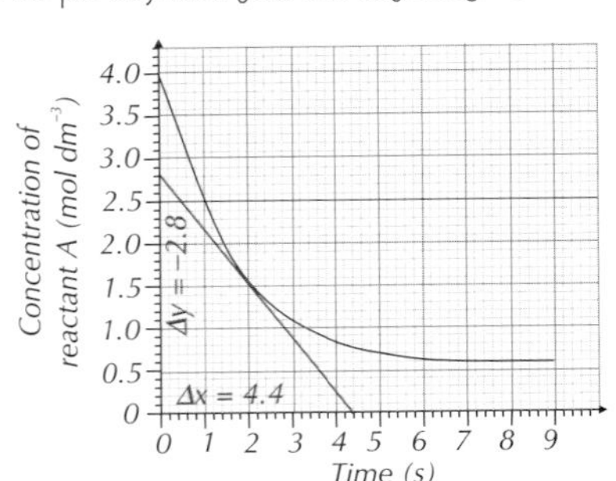

$$\text{Rate} = \frac{\Delta y}{\Delta x} = \frac{-2.8}{4.4} = \mathbf{-0.64\ mol\ dm^{-3}\ s^{-1}}$$

For part b) anything from −0.44 to −0.84 is OK.

c)

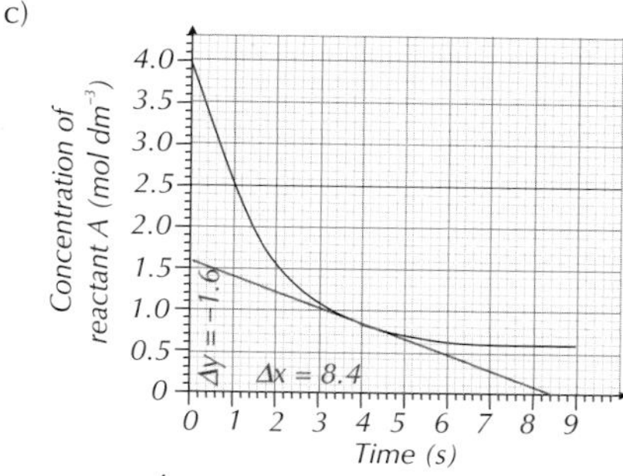

$$\text{Rate} = \frac{\Delta y}{\Delta x} = \frac{-1.6}{8.4} = \mathbf{-0.19\ mol\ dm^{-3}\ s^{-1}}$$

For part c) anything from −0.13 to −0.25 will do.

Q2 a)

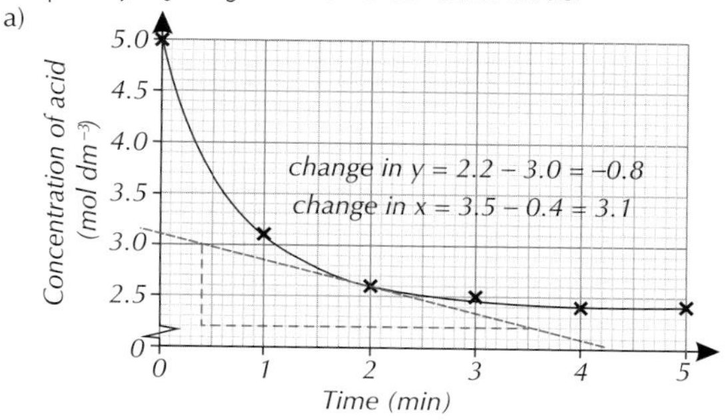

b) see above

c) E.g. gradient = change in y ÷ change in x
= −0.8 ÷ 3.1 = −0.258...
So the rate is **0.26 mol dm^{-3} min^{-1} (2 s.f.)**

Page 22 — Fact Recall Question

Q1 Measure the gradient of the graph / the gradient of a tangent to the graph at that particular time. The gradient is equal to the rate of reaction.

3. Initial Rates

Page 26 — Application Questions

Q1 E.g.

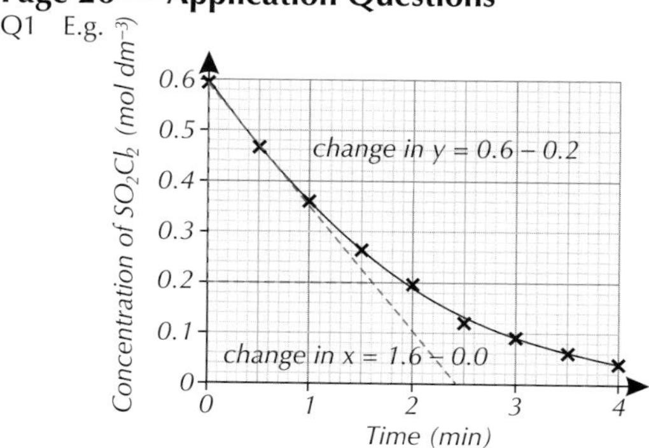

Gradient = change in y ÷ change in x
= (0.20 − 0.60) ÷ (1.6 − 0.0)
= −0.4 ÷ 1.6 = −0.25
So the rate is **0.25 mol dm^{-3} min^{-1} (2 s.f.)**

Q2 The rate of each reaction = $\frac{20\ cm^3}{\text{time taken}}$

Trial number	[HCl] / mol dm^{-3}	Time to produce 20 cm^3 $H_{2(g)}$ / s	Initial rate / cm^3 s^{-1}
1	1.25	5.1	3.9
2	0.800	15.3	1.3
3	0.500	31.5	0.63

Page 26 — Fact Recall Questions

Q1 Measure the gradient of a concentration-time graph at time = 0 s

Q2 E.g. The concentration of each reactant doesn't change significantly over the time period of your clock reaction / the temperature stays constant / when the endpoint is seen, the reaction has not proceeded too far.

4. Reaction Orders

Page 30 — Application Questions

Q1 a) Looking at experiments 1 and 2: doubling [O_3] doubles the rate so the reaction is order 1 with respect to O_3. Looking at experiments 2 and 3: tripling [C_2H_4] triples the rate so the reaction is order 1 with respect to C_2H_4.

b) Overall order = order with respect to [O_3] + order with respect to [C_2H_4] = 0 + 1 = **1**

The overall order is the sum of the orders with respect to each reactant.

Q2 a) A = first order
B = zero order
C = second order

b) (i) If [A] was halved the rate of reaction would also halve.
(ii) If [B] was tripled the rate of reaction would stay the same.
(iii) If [C] was doubled, the reaction rate would increase by a factor of four (quadruple).

Q3

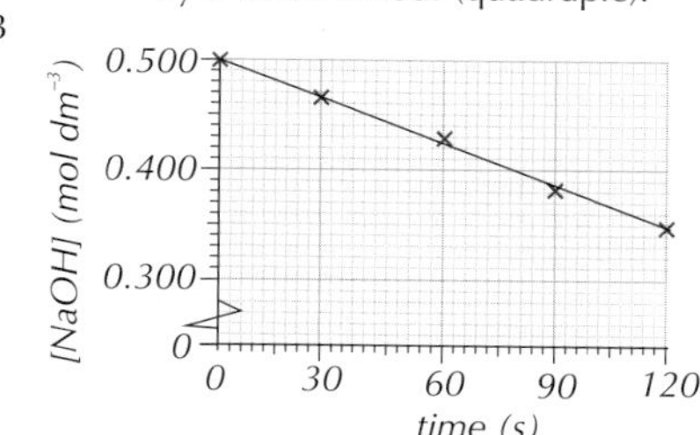

The concentration-time graph is a straight line, so the reaction is zero order with respect to NaOH.

Q4 Looking at experiments 1 and 2: doubling [B] quadruples the rate so the reaction is order 2 with respect to B. Looking at experiments 2 and 3: tripling [C] triples the rate so the reaction is order 1 with respect to C. Look at experiments 2 and 4: the reaction is first order with respect to C so, doubling [C] will double the rate of reaction to 2.00 mol dm^{-3} s^{-1}. So halving [A] must have halved the reaction rate back down to 1.00 mol dm^{-3} s^{-1}. This means that the reaction is first order with respect to A.

You could also work out the order with respect to A from experiments 3 and 4. Decreasing [C] by a third decreases the rate from 3.00 mol dm^{-3} s^{-1} to 2.00 mol dm^{-3} s^{-1}. Halving [A] decreases the rate from 2.00 mol dm^{-3} s^{-1} to 1.00 mol dm^{-3} s^{-1}, so the reaction must be first order with respect to A.

Page 30 — Fact Recall Questions

Q1 The reaction order with respect to a particular reactant tells you how the reactant's concentration affects the rate of reaction.

Q2 a) E.g. find the gradient at various points along a concentration-time graph. Plot rate of reaction against concentration to produce a rate-concentration graph / Find the initial rate of the reaction at varying initial concentrations of one of the reactants, and plot the initial rate of the reaction against the initial reactant concentration to produce a rate-concentration graph.

b) The shape of the rate-concentration graph indicates the order of reaction (horizontal line = zero order, straight line through the origin = first order, curve = second order).

5. Rate Equations

Page 32 — Application Question

Q1 a) Rate = $k[Na_2S_2O_3]$

b) Rate = $4.67 \times 10^{-1} \times 0.45$ = **0.21 mol dm^{-3} s^{-1}**

Even though you're given the concentration of HCl in the question, you don't need to use it in your calculation, as [HCl] isn't in the rate equation.

Page 32 — Fact Recall Questions

Q1 The rate equation tells you how the rate of a reaction is affected by the concentration of the reactants.

Q2 a) The rate constant.

b) The concentration of reactant A.

c) The order of the reaction with respect to A.

Q3 rate = $k[A]^m[B]^n[C]^x$

6. The Rate Constant

Page 36 — Application Questions

Q1 a) Rate = $k[NO]^2[Cl_2]$

b) $5.85 \times 10^{-6} = k(0.400)^2(0.400)$ so

$$k = \frac{5.85 \times 10^{-6}}{[0.400]^2[0.400]} = 9.14 \times 10^{-5}$$

Now find the units for k:

$$k = \frac{\text{mol dm}^{-3}\text{ s}^{-1}}{(\text{mol dm}^{-3})^2(\text{mol dm}^{-3})} = \text{mol}^{-2}\text{ dm}^6\text{ s}^{-1}$$

$k = 9.14 \times 10^{-5}$ mol^{-2} dm^6 s^{-1}

c) Rate = $k[NO]^2[Cl_2]$

Rate = $(9.14 \times 10^{-5}) \times (0.500)^2 \times 0.200$

= **4.57×10^{-6} mol dm^{-3} s^{-1}**

Q2 *For a first order reaction, the rate constant is equal to the gradient of its rate-concentration graph:*

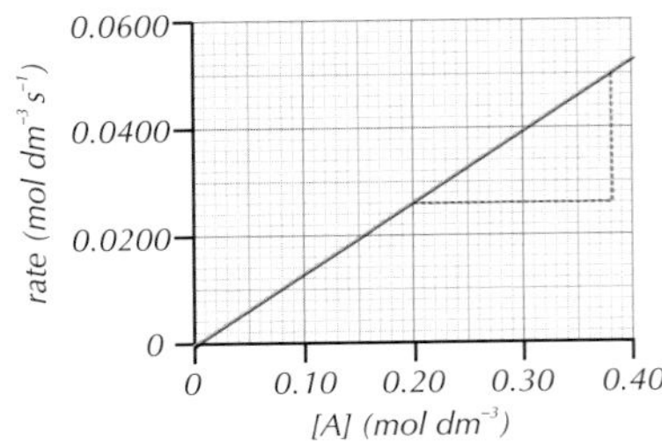

E.g. gradient = change in y ÷ change in x

= $(0.0500 - 0.0260) \div (0.38 - 0.20)$

= $0.024 \div 0.18 = 0.13$

Now find the units for k: $k = \frac{\text{mol dm}^{-3}\text{ s}^{-1}}{(\text{mol dm}^{-3})} = \text{s}^{-1}$

$k = 0.13$ s^{-1}

Q3 a)

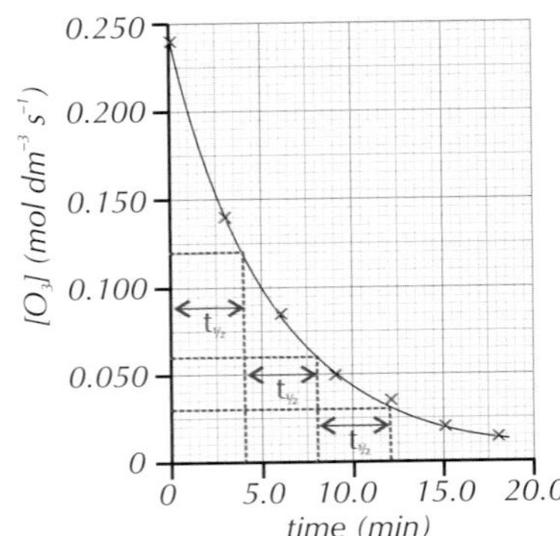

$[O_3]$ from 0.240 to 0.120 mol dm^{-3} = **4.0 minutes**

$[O_3]$ from 0.120 to 0.060 mol dm^{-3} = **4.0 minutes**

$[O_3]$ from 0.060 to 0.030 mol dm^{-3} = **4.0 minutes**

b) The half-life is always 4.0 minutes, so the reaction is first order with respect to $[O_3]$.

$$k = \frac{\ln 2}{t_{1/2}}$$

You first have to convert the half-life from minutes into seconds:

$t_{1/2} = 4.0 \times 60 = 240$ s

$k = \frac{\ln 2}{240}$ = **2.9×10^{-3} s^{-1}**

Page 36 — Fact Recall Questions

Q1 Measure the gradient of the line of best fit (a straight line), which is equal to the rate constant of the reaction.

Q2 The half-life of a reaction is the amount of time it takes for half of the reactant to be used up.

Q3 $k = \frac{\ln 2}{t_{1/2}}$

7. The Rate-Determining Step

Page 40 — Application Questions

Q1 Rate = $k[A]^2[B]$

Don't forget to include the rate constant in your answer. If you've just written rate = $[A]^2[B]$, your answer's not right, even though you've done all the hard work working out the reaction orders.

Q2 Rate = $k[Br_2][NO]$

Q3 a) Step 1. The rate equation shows that the rate-determining step involves two molecules of NO_2, and there are two NO_2 molecules in step 1.

Don't forget — if it's in the rate equation it must be involved in the rate-determining step.

b) If the reaction had a one-step mechanism, that step would have to involve CO. CO is not in the rate equation so can't be involved in the rate-determining step. So a one-step mechanism isn't possible.

Q4 E.g. $O_{3(g)} \rightarrow O_{2(g)} + O\bullet_{(g)}$

$O\bullet_{(g)} + O_{3(g)} \rightarrow 2O_{2(g)}$

If you didn't get this answer don't worry. As long at the equations add up to the overall equation, the first step (the rate-determining step) only involves one molecule of O_3 and your equations are balanced you can have the mark.

Q5 E.g. $H_2O_{2(aq)} + I^-_{(aq)} \rightarrow H_2O_{(l)} + IO^-_{(aq)}$

$H_2O_{2(aq)} + IO^-_{(aq)} \rightarrow H_2O_{(l)} + O_{2(g)} + I^-_{(aq)}$

Don't forget — if you're given a reaction involving a catalyst, make sure the catalyst is regenerated at the end. If the catalyst hasn't been regenerated then you must have gone wrong somewhere.

Page 40 — Fact Recall Questions

Q1 The rate-determining step is the slowest step in a reaction mechanism, so it's the step which determines the overall rate of the reaction.

Q2 2

Q3 1

8. The Arrhenius Equation

Page 44 — Application Questions

Q1 a) Reaction B will have a larger rate constant, as the activation energy is lower than Reaction A. This means that the $\frac{-E_a}{RT}$ term will be smaller and less negative, so the rate constant, k, will be greater since $k = Ae^{\frac{-E_a}{RT}}$.

b) The reaction at 45 °C will be faster than the reaction at 30 °C. This is because a larger value of T causes the $\frac{-E_a}{RT}$ term in the Arrhenius equation to be smaller and less negative, so $k = Ae^{\frac{-E_a}{RT}}$ will be greater. A larger value of k means a faster rate of reaction.

Q2 a) *To draw the Arrhenius plot, you first have to calculate ln k and 1/T.*

Temperature (K)	k ($dm^3\ mol^{-1}\ s^{-1}$)	$1/T$ (K^{-1})	ln k
280	1.25×10^{-21}	0.00357	–48.131
300	1.79×10^{-19}	0.00333	–43.167
320	1.38×10^{-17}	0.00313	–38.822
340	6.34×10^{-16}	0.00294	–34.994
360	1.91×10^{-14}	0.00278	–31.589
380	4.02×10^{-13}	0.00263	–28.542

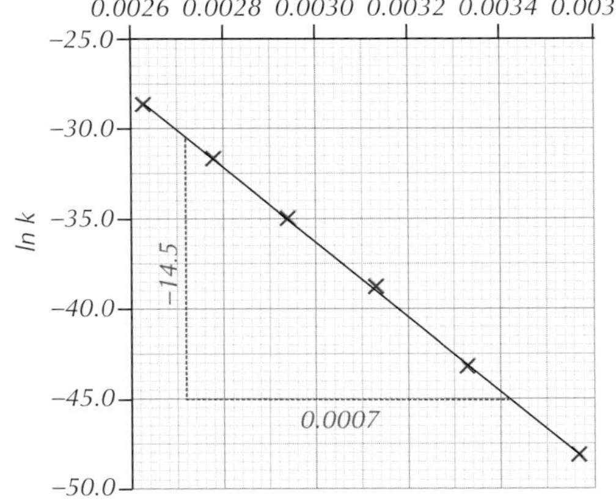

b) Gradient $= \frac{-E_a}{R} = \frac{\text{change in } y}{\text{change in } x} = \frac{-14.5}{0.0007} = -20\ 714...$

$-E_a = -20\ 714... \times 8.31 = -172\ 135...\ J\ mol^{-1}$

E_a = **172 kJ mol⁻¹**

If you've drawn this graph with a sensible scale, it probably won't show the y-intercept, so the best way to find A is by substituting your value for E_a back into the Arrhenius equation.

c) $\ln k = \frac{-E_a}{RT} + \ln A$

When $\ln k = -34.994$, $1/T = 0.00294$

So $-34.994 = -(0.00294 \times \frac{172\,135...}{8.31}) + \ln A$

$\ln A = -34.994 + 60.9$

$\ln A = 25.9...$

$A = e^{25.9...} = \mathbf{1.78 \times 10^{11}\ mol\ dm^{-3}\ s^{-1}}$

If you calculated A using the y intercept, you should have found that ln A = 26.3, so $A = e^{26.3} = 2.6 \times 10^{11}\ mol\ dm^{-3}\ s^{-1}$.

Page 44 — Fact Recall Questions

Q1 a) The rate constant, units vary.

b) The activation energy, in $J\ mol^{-1}$.

c) The temperature, in K.

d) The pre-exponential factor, units vary but are the same as the rate constant.

Q2 $\ln k = \frac{-E_a}{RT} + \ln A$

Q3 The gradient is equal to the value of $\frac{-E_a}{R}$, so can be used to find the activation energy of the reaction.

Exam-style Questions — Pages 46-48

1 C ***(1 mark)***

2 A ***(1 mark)***

rate = $k[A][B]^2$, so k = rate ÷ ($[A][B]^2$)
= 0.00238 ÷ (0.426 × 0.775²) = 0.00930 $mol^{-2}\ dm^6\ s^{-1}$

3 D ***(1 mark)***

4 B ***(1 mark)***

5 a) The reaction is first order with respect to H_2 ***(1 mark)*** and second order with respect to NO ***(1 mark)***.

Finding the reaction order with respect to NO is tricky. You know the reaction is first order with respect to H_2 from experiments 1 and 2, so if only $[H_2]$ changed from experiment 2 to 3 you would expect the rate of reaction to halve. But the rate of reaction is four times greater than this, so the reaction must be second order with respect to NO.

b) rate = $k[H_2][NO]^2$ ***(1 mark)***

c) rate = $k[H_2][NO]^2$ so k = rate ÷ $[H_2][NO]^2$

E.g. Using experiment 1:

$k = (4.5 \times 10^{-3}) \div (6 \times 10^{-3})(3 \times 10^{-3})^2 = 8.3 \times 10^4$

$k = mol\ dm^{-3}\ s^{-1} \div (mol\ dm^{-3})(mol\ dm^{-3})^2 = mol^{-2}\ dm^6\ s^{-1}$

$k = \mathbf{8.3 \times 10^4\ mol^{-2}\ dm^6\ s^{-1}}$

(3 marks for correct answer, otherwise 1 mark for correct method and 1 mark for correct units.)

d) rate = $k[H_2][NO]^2$

$= (8.3 \times 10^4) \times (2.5 \times 10^{-3}) \times (4.5 \times 10^{-3})^2$

$= \mathbf{4.2 \times 10^{-3}\ mol\ dm^{-3}\ s^{-1}}$

(1 mark for correct value, 1 mark for correct units — full marks if the method is correct but error carried forward from (c).)

If you used 6.5×10^5 as your value for k, an answer of rate = 0.0329 $mol\ dm^{-3}\ s^{-1}$ will get you full marks.

e) (i) The rate equation shows that the rate-determining step involves 2 molecules of NO and 1 molecule of H_2 ***(1 mark)***. There are 2 molecules of H_2 in the overall equation so there must be another step involving another molecule of H_2 ***(1 mark)***.

(ii) A possible mechanism for this reaction would be:

Step 1: $2NO + H_2 \rightarrow N_2O + H_2O$

Step 2: $N_2O + H_2 \rightarrow H_2O + N_2$

(1 mark for the left hand side of step 1, 1 mark for rest of step 1 and step 2.)

Other mechanisms are possible and will gain credit as long as:

- *The reactants in the first equation are 2NO and H_2.*
- *The steps add together to give the overall reaction.*
- *Both equations are balanced.*

6 a)

T / °C	k / $mol^{-1}\ dm^3\ s^{-1}$	T / K	$1/T$ / K^{-1}	ln k
50	1.96×10^{-31}	323	0.00310	–70.7
100	1.36×10^{-28}	373	0.00268	–64.2
150	2.01×10^{-26}	423	0.00236	–59.2
250	2.50×10^{-23}	523	0.00191	–52.0
300	3.47×10^{-22}	573	0.00175	–49.4

(2 marks — 1 mark for correctly converting T (°C) values into 1/T (K^{-1}), 1 mark for correctly converting k ($mol^{-1}\ dm^3\ s^{-1}$) values into ln k.)

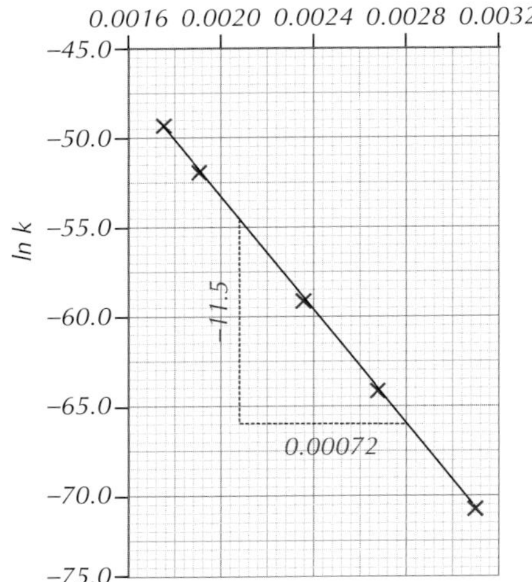

(3 marks — 1 mark for correct axes with reasonable scale, 1 mark for correctly plotted points, 1 mark for line of best fit.)

b) (i) Gradient = $\frac{-E_a}{R} = \frac{-11.5}{0.00072} = -15\ 972$ ***(1 mark)***

$E_a = 15\ 972 \times 8.31 = 132\ 729...$ J mol^{-1}

= **133 kJ mol^{-1}** ***(1 mark — allow between 120 and 146 kJ mol^{-1})***

(ii) $\ln k = \frac{-E_a}{RT} + \ln A$

When $\ln k = -66.0$, $1/T = 0.0028$ K^{-1}

$-66.0 = -(0.0028 \times \frac{132\,729...}{8.31}) + \ln A$

$\ln A = -66.0 + 44.7... = -21.2...$ ***(1 mark)***

$A = e^{-21.2...} =$ **5.7×10^{-10} $mol^{-1}\ dm^3\ s^{-1}$** ***(1 mark – allow between 7.62×10^{-12} and 5.06×10^{-8})***

If you plotted a graph that showed the y-intercept through the y-axis at $x = 0$, then you could have calculated A by finding the y-intercept. The y-intercept you found should have been −21.9, so $A = e^{-21.9} = 3.1 \times 10^{-10}$.

7 a) (i) First order ***(1 mark)***.

(ii)

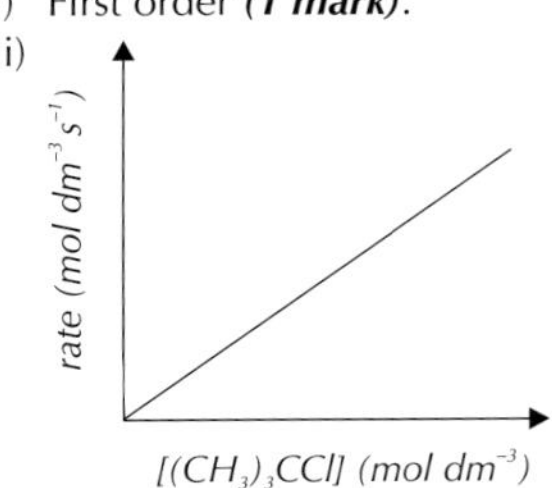

(1 mark)

b) rate = $k[(CH_3)_3CCl]$ ***(1 mark)***

c) (i)

Rate = $\frac{\Delta y}{\Delta x} = \frac{-0.70}{55} = 0.013$ mol $dm^{-3}\ s^{-1}$

(1 mark — allow between 0.008 and 0.017)

(ii)

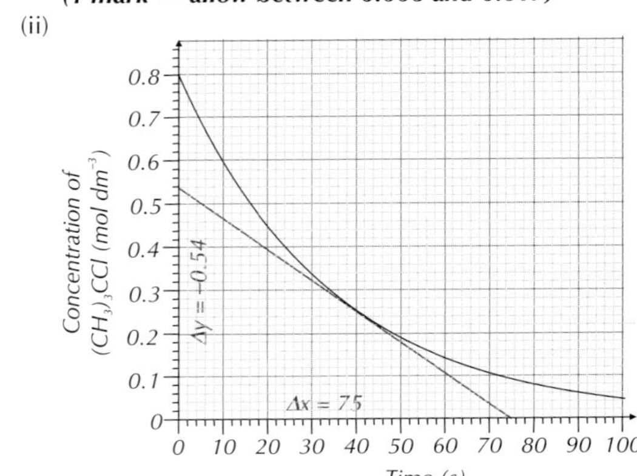

Rate = $\frac{\Delta y}{\Delta x} = \frac{-0.54}{75} = 0.0072$ mol $dm^{-3}\ s^{-1}$

(1 mark — allow between 0.0048 and 0.0096)

d)

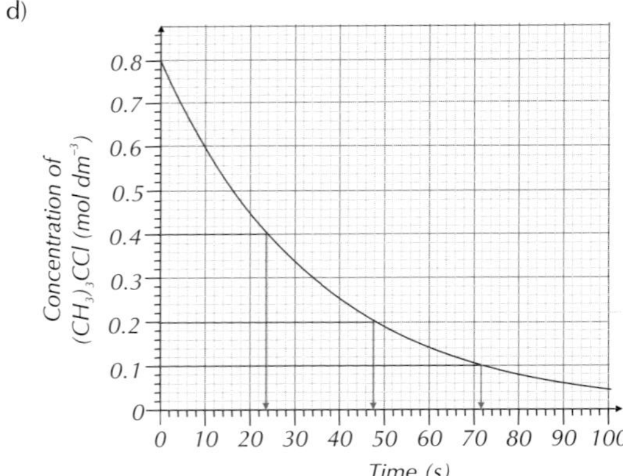

The half-life is **24 seconds** ***(1 mark)***.

e) The reaction is first order, so $k = \frac{\ln 2}{t_{1/2}} = \frac{\ln 2}{24} =$ **0.029 s^{-1}** ***(1 mark)***

f) rate = $k[(CH_3)_3CCl] = 0.029 \times 1.35$
= **0.0392 mol $dm^{-3}\ s^{-1}$** ***(1 mark)***

g) E.g. First step: $(CH_3)_3CCl \rightarrow (CH_3)_3C^+ + Cl^-$ ***(1 mark)***
Second step: $(CH_3)_3C^+ + OH^- \rightarrow (CH_3)_3COH$ ***(1 mark)***

Other mechanisms are possible and will gain credit as long as:

- The only reactant in the first equation is $(CH_3)_3CCl$.
- The steps add together to give the overall reaction.
- Both equations are balanced.

Section 2 — Equilibrium

1. The Equilibrium Constant

Pages 53-54 — Application Questions

Q1 a) $K_c = \frac{[C_2H_5OH]}{[C_2H_4][H_2O]}$

b) The equation tells you that if 1 mole of C_2H_5OH decomposes, 1 mole of C_2H_4 and 1 mole of H_2O are formed. So if 1.85 moles of C_2H_4 are produced at equilibrium, there will also be **1.85** moles of H_2O. 1.85 moles of C_2H_5OH has decomposed so there must be 5 – 1.85 = **3.15** moles of C_2H_5OH remaining.

c) The volume of the reaction is 15.0 dm³. So the molar concentrations are:
$[H_2O] = [C_2H_4] = 1.85 \div 15.0 =$ **0.123 mol dm⁻³**.
$[C_2H_5OH] = 3.15 \div 15.0 =$ **0.210 mol dm⁻³**.

d) $K_c = \frac{[C_2H_5OH]}{[C_2H_4][H_2O]} = \frac{0.210}{(0.123)(0.123)} = 13.9$

units of $K_c = \frac{(\text{mol dm}^{-3})}{(\text{mol dm}^{-3})(\text{mol dm}^{-3})} = \frac{1}{(\text{mol dm}^{-3})}$

K_c = **13.9 mol⁻¹ dm³**

Setting your answer out like this makes it clear to the examiner what you've done and means you're more likely to pick up some method marks.

e) $K_c = \frac{[C_2H_5OH]}{[C_2H_4][H_2O]}$ so $3.8 = \frac{0.80}{[C_2H_4][H_2O]}$

$[C_2H_4][H_2O] = 0.80 \div 3.8 = 0.21$
$[C_2H_4] = [H_2O] = \sqrt{0.21} =$ **0.46 mol dm⁻³**

Q2 a) $K_c = \frac{[SO_3]^2}{[SO_2]^2[O_2]}$

b) $K_c = \frac{[SO_3]^2}{[SO_2]^2[O_2]} = \frac{0.360^2}{(0.250)^2(0.180)} = 11.5$

units of $K_c = \frac{(\text{mol dm}^{-3})^2}{(\text{mol dm}^{-3})^2(\text{mol dm}^{-3})} = \frac{1}{(\text{mol dm}^{-3})}$

K_c = **11.5 mol⁻¹ dm³**

c) $[SO_2]^2 = \frac{[SO_3]^2}{K_c \times [O_2]} = \frac{0.360^2}{15 \times 0.180} = 0.048$

$[SO_2] = \sqrt{0.048} =$ **0.22 mol dm⁻³**

Q3 Initial moles of $Fe^{2+} = \frac{0.500 \times 250}{1000} = 0.125$ mol

No. of moles of Fe^{2+} at equilibrium
$= \frac{0.0844 \times 500}{1000} = 0.0422$ mol

No. of moles of Fe^{3+} at equilibrium
= No. of moles of Fe^{2+} lost = 0.125 – 0.0422 = 0.0828 mol
So at equilibrium,
$[Ag^+] = [Fe^{2+}] = 0.0844$ mol dm⁻³
$[Fe^{3+}] = \frac{0.0828 \times 1000}{500} = 0.1656$ mol dm⁻³

You don't need to work out the number of moles of $Ag_{(s)}$ at equilibrium as solid products are not included in K_c.

So $K_c = \frac{[Fe^{3+}]}{[Fe^{2+}][Ag^+]} = \frac{0.1656}{0.0844 \times 0.0844} = 23.2$

units of $K_c = \frac{(\text{mol dm}^{-3})}{(\text{mol dm}^{-3})^2} = \frac{1}{(\text{mol dm}^{-3})} = \text{mol}^{-1}\text{ dm}^3$

K_c = **23.2 mol⁻¹ dm³**

Page 54 — Fact Recall Questions

Q1 A dynamic equilibrium occurs when a reversible reaction is still happening but the forward and backward reaction are going at exactly the same rate so there is no overall change in the concentrations of the reagents.

Q2 For a dynamic equilibrium to be established it must be a closed system and the temperature must be constant.

Q3 $K_c = \frac{[D]^d[E]^e}{[A]^a[B]^b}$

Q4 The units of K_c change depending on the concentration terms in the reaction.

2. Gas Equilibria

Page 58 — Application Questions

Q1 a) $2NH_{3(g)} + 1\frac{1}{2}O_{2(g)} \rightleftharpoons N_{2(g)} + 3H_2O_{(g)}$

b) total pressure = $p(NH_3) + p(O_2) + p(N_2) + p(H_2O)$

c) total pressure = 42 + 85 + 21 + 12 = **160 kPa**

d) mole fraction of gas in a mixture = number of moles of gas ÷ total number of moles of gas in a mixture
So mole fraction of H_2O = 12 ÷ 160 = **0.075**

Q2 No. moles of He = 4.00 ÷ 4 = 1.00
No. moles of O_2 = 2.81 ÷ (16 × 2) = 0.0878...
Total moles of gas = 1.00 + 0.0878... = 1.0878...
Mole fraction of O_2 = 0.0878... ÷ 1.0878... = 0.0807...
So partial pressure of O_2 = 0.0807... × 8.12
= **0.655 kPa (3 s.f.)**

Q3 a) $K_p = \frac{p(C_6H_{12})}{p(C_6H_6) \times p(H_2)^3}$

b) Since the partial pressures of all three gases are equal,
$p(C_6H_{12}) = p(C_6H_6) = p(H_2) = x$

$4.80 \times 10^{-13} = \frac{x}{x \times (x)^3} = \frac{1}{x^3}$

$x^3 = \frac{1}{4.80 \times 10^{-13}} = 2.083... \times 10^{12}$

$x = \sqrt[3]{2.083... \times 10^{12}}$
x = **12 800 kPa**

Q4 a) $2HF \rightleftharpoons H_2 + F_2$
Equal amounts of H_2 and F_2 are produced, so if there are 9.340 moles of F_2 present at equilibrium, there are also 9.340 moles of H_2.
Since 2 moles of HF produce 2 moles of product gases, the total number of moles of gas at equilibrium will be 24.32.
Mole fraction of H_2 = 9.340 ÷ 24.32 = 0.384...
Partial pressure of H_2 = 0.384... × 2313 = **888.3 kPa**

b) partial pressure of H_2 = partial pressure of F_2, so partial pressure of F_2 = 888.3 kPa.
$p(HF)$ = 2313 – 888.3 – 888.3 = 536.4 kPa

$K_p = \frac{p(H_2) \times p(F_2)}{p(HF)^2} = 888.3 \times 888.3 \div (536.4)^2 = 2.742$

units of $K_p = \frac{(\text{kPa})^2}{(\text{kPa})^2}$ = no units

So K_p = **2.742**

Page 58 — Fact Recall Questions

Q1 The partial pressure of a gas is the individual pressure that it exerts on a system.

Q2 mole fraction of a gas = number of moles of that gas ÷ total number of moles of gas in the mixture

Q3 The equilibrium constant for a reversible reaction where some, or all, of the reactants and products are gases.

Q4 $K_p = \frac{p(D)^d p(E)^e}{p(A)^a p(B)^b}$

3. Changing the Equilibrium

Page 61 — Application Questions

Q1 a) No effect — if the concentration of C_2F_4 increases the equilibrium will shift to counteract the change and K_c will stay the same.

b) The reaction is endothermic in the forward direction so increasing the temperature will shift the equilibrium to the right. As a result more product will be produced, so K_c will increase.

c) No effect — catalysts only affect the time taken to reach equilibrium and not the position of the equilibrium itself.

It's only changing temperature that changes the value of K_c.

Q2 a) Exothermic. If decreasing the temperature increases K_c then it must increase the amount of product formed. The equilibrium must have shifted to the right, so the forward reaction must be exothermic.

b) (i) The equilibrium would shift to the left.

(ii) The value of K_p would not change.

Q3 a) Increase the temperature.

b) E.g. decrease the pressure / increase the concentration of the reactants.

Page 62 — Fact Recall Questions

Q1 If there's a change in concentration, pressure or temperature then an equilibrium will move to help counteract the change.

Q2 a) It will increase K_c.

b) It will decrease K_c.

Q3 If the concentration of a reagent is changed the equilibrium will shift and the concentrations of other reagents will also change. So K_c will stay the same.

Q4 Increasing the pressure has no affect on the value of K_p.

Q5 Adding a catalyst doesn't change the position of the equilibrium or K_c, but it decreases the time taken to reach equilibrium.

Exam-style Questions — page 63

1 D ***(1 mark)***

2 a) (i) $K_c = \frac{[CO_2]\,[H_2]^4}{[CH_4]\,[H_2O]^2}$ ***(1 mark).***

(ii) $K_c = (0.200 \times (0.280)^4) \div (0.0800 \times (0.320)^2) = 0.150$

K_c = (mol dm^{-3} × (mol dm^{-3})^4) ÷ (mol dm^{-3} × (mol dm^{-3})^2) = mol^2 dm^{-6} so K_c = **0.150 mol² dm⁻⁶**

(2 marks for correct answer, otherwise 1 mark for correct substitution of values into the expression from part (i).)

b) (i) $[CH_4] = \frac{[CO_2]\,[H_2]^4}{K_c \times [H_2O]^2}$

$= (0.420 \times 0.480^4) \div (0.0800 \times 0.560^2)$

= **0.889 mol dm⁻³**

(2 marks for correct answer, otherwise 1 mark for correct equation.)

(ii) Lower ***(1 mark)***. K_c is lower at temperature Z than at temperature Y. This means temperature Z has caused the equilibrium to shift to the left ***(1 mark)***. As the reaction is endothermic in the forward direction, the temperature must be lowered to make it shift in the exothermic direction ***(1 mark)***.

c) The value of K_c would not change ***(1 mark)***. Catalysts do not affect the position of the equilibrium, only the time taken to reach equilibrium ***(1 mark)***.

Section 3 — Acids, Bases and pH

1. Acids and Bases

Page 68 — Application Questions

Q1 a) Full: $2HCl_{(aq)} + 2Na_{(s)} \rightarrow 2NaCl_{(aq)} + H_{2(g)}$

Ionic: $2H^+_{(aq)} + 2Na_{(s)} \rightarrow 2Na^+_{(aq)} + H_{2(g)}$

Make sure you always include the H⁺ ions in your ionic equations.

b) Full: $H_2SO_{4(aq)} + CaCO_{3(s)} \rightarrow CaSO_{4(aq)} + H_2O_{(l)} + CO_{2(g)}$

Ionic: $2H^+_{(aq)} + CO_3{}^{2-}{}_{(s)} \rightarrow H_2O_{(l)} + CO_{2(g)}$

c) Full: $HNO_{3(aq)} + KOH_{(aq)} \rightarrow KNO_{3(aq)} + H_2O_{(l)}$

Ionic: $H^+_{(aq)} + OH^-_{(aq)} \rightarrow H_2O_{(l)}$

d) Full: $2HCN_{(aq)} + Na_2O_{(s)} \rightarrow 2NaCN_{(aq)} + H_2O_{(l)}$

Ionic: $2H^+_{(aq)} + Na_2O_{(s)} \rightarrow H_2O_{(l)} + 2Na^+_{(aq)}$

Q2 a) $H_2CO_{3(aq)} + H_2O_{(l)} \rightleftharpoons H_3O^+_{(aq)} + HCO_3{}^-{}_{(aq)}$

acid 1 base 2 acid 2 base 1

b) $CH_3NH_{2(aq)} + H_2O_{(l)} \rightleftharpoons CH_3NH_3{}^+ + OH^-$

base 1 acid 2 acid 1 base 2

c) $CH_3COO^-_{(aq)} + NH_4{}^+{}_{(aq)} \rightleftharpoons CH_3COOH_{(aq)} + NH_{3(aq)}$

base 1 acid 2 acid 1 base 2

d) $HCl_{(aq)} + OH^-_{(aq)} \rightleftharpoons Cl^-_{(aq)} + H_2O_{(l)}$

acid 1 base 2 base 1 acid 2

Page 68 — Fact Recall Questions

Q1 a) A Brønsted-Lowry acid is a proton donor.

b) A Brønsted-Lowry base is a proton acceptor.

Q2 a) An acid that can only release one proton per molecule into solution, for example, HCl.

Other monobasic acids you could have mentioned include HNO_3, HBr and CH_3COOH.

b) An acid that can release two protons per molecule into solution, for example, H_2SO_4.

Other dibasic acids you could have mentioned include H_2CO_3 and H_2SO_3.

c) An acid that can release three protons per molecule into solution, for example, H_3PO_4.

Another tribasic acid you could have mentioned is citric acid ($C_6H_8O_7$).

Q3 a) A strong acid.

b) A weak base.

Q4 A conjugate pair is a set of two species that can be transformed into each other by gaining or losing a proton.

Q5 a) hydrogen gas and a salt

b) carbon dioxide, water and a salt

c) water and a salt

2. pH Calculations

Page 69 — Application Questions

Q1 $pH = -\log_{10}[H^+] = -\log_{10}[0.05] = \mathbf{1.3}$

Q2 $[H^+] = 10^{-pH} = 10^{-2.86} = \mathbf{1.4 \times 10^{-3}\ mol\ dm^{-3}}$

Q3 $pH = -\log_{10}[H^+] = -\log_{10}[0.02] = \mathbf{1.7}$

Page 70 — Application Questions

Q1 HCl is monobasic so [H⁺] = [HCl] = 0.08 mol dm⁻³

$pH = -\log_{10}[H^+] = -\log_{10}[0.08] = \mathbf{1.1}$

Q2 HNO_3 is monobasic so $[H^+] = [HNO_3]$ = 0.12 mol dm⁻³

$pH = -\log_{10}[H^+] = -\log_{10}[0.12] = \mathbf{0.92}$

Q3 $[H^+] = 10^{-pH} = 10^{-0.96} = 0.11$ mol dm⁻³

HCl is monobasic so [HCl] = [H⁺] = **0.11 mol dm⁻³**

Q4 $[H^+] = 10^{-pH} = 10^{-1.28} = 0.052$ mol dm⁻³

HNO_3 is monobasic so $[HNO_3]$ = [H⁺] = **0.052 mol dm⁻³**

Page 70 — Fact Recall Questions

Q1 $pH = -\log_{10}[H^+]$

Q2 $[H^+] = 10^{-pH}$

Q3 Monobasic means that each molecule of acid releases one proton.

Q4 For strong monobasic acids the concentration of H^+ ions is the same as the concentration of the acid.

3. The Ionic Product of Water

Page 72 — Application Questions

Q1 For pure water $[H^+] = [OH^-]$ so $K_w = [H^+]^2$.
$[H^+] = \sqrt{K_w} = \sqrt{1.47 \times 10^{-14}} = 1.21... \times 10^{-7}$
$pH = -\log_{10} [H^+] = -\log_{10} (1.21... \times 10^{-7}) = \mathbf{6.916}$

Q2 For pure water $[H^+] = [OH^-]$ so $K_w = [H^+]^2$.
$[H^+] = \sqrt{K_w} = \sqrt{2.92 \times 10^{-14}} = 1.70... \times 10^{-7}$
$pH = -\log_{10} [H^+] = -\log_{10} (1.70... \times 10^{-7}) = \mathbf{6.767}$

Page 73 — Application Questions

Q1 KOH is a strong base so $[OH^-] = [KOH] = 0.200$ mol dm^{-3}
$K_w = [H^+][OH^-]$ so $[H^+] = K_w \div [OH^-]$
$= (5.48 \times 10^{-14}) \div 0.200 = 2.74 \times 10^{-13}$
$pH = -\log_{10} [H^+] = -\log(2.74 \times 10^{-13}) = \mathbf{12.562}$

Q2 NaOH is a strong base so $[OH^-] = [KOH] = 0.155$ mol dm^{-3}
$K_w = [H^+][OH^-]$ so $[H^+] = K_w \div [OH^-]$
$= (6.81 \times 10^{-15}) \div 0.155 = 4.39... \times 10^{-14}$
$pH = -\log_{10} [H^+] = -\log_{10} (4.39... \times 10^{-14}) = \mathbf{13.357}$

Q3 KOH is a strong base so $[OH^-] = [KOH] = 0.0840$ mol dm^{-3}
$K_w = [H^+][OH^-]$ so $[H^+] = K_w \div [OH^-]$
$= (2.93 \times 10^{-15}) \div 0.0840 = 3.48... \times 10^{-14}$
$pH = -\log_{10} [H^+] = -\log_{10} (3.48... \times 10^{-14}) = \mathbf{13.457}$

Q4 $[H^+] = 10^{-pH} = 10^{-12.40} = 3.981... \times 10^{-13}$ mol dm^{-3}
$K_w = [H^+][OH^-]$ so $[OH^-] = K_w \div [H^+]$
$= (6.8 \times 10^{-15}) \div (3.981... \times 10^{-13}) = 0.017$ mol dm^{-3}
KOH is a strong base so $[KOH] = [OH^-] = \mathbf{0.017\ mol\ dm^{-3}}$

Q5 $[H^+] = 10^{-pH} = 10^{-13.98} = 1.047... \times 10^{-14}$ mol dm^{-3}
$K_w = [H^+][OH^-]$ so $[OH^-] = K_w \div [H^+]$
$= (2.92 \times 10^{-14}) \div (1.047... \times 10^{-14}) = 2.79...$ mol dm^{-3}
NaOH is a strong base so $[NaOH] = [OH^-] = \mathbf{2.8\ mol\ dm^{-3}}$

Q6 $[H^+] = 10^{-pH} = 10^{-13.25} = 5.623... \times 10^{-14}$ mol dm^{-3}
$K_w = [H^+][OH^-]$ so $[OH^-] = K_w \div [H^+]$
$= (1.47 \times 10^{-14}) \div (5.623... \times 10^{-14}) = 0.261...$ mol dm^{-3}
KOH is a strong base so $[KOH] = [OH^-] = \mathbf{0.26\ mol\ dm^{-3}}$

Page 73 — Fact Recall Questions

Q1 $K_w = [H^+][OH^-]$
For this question you can't put $K_w = [H^+]^2$ because this only applies to pure water.

Q2 mol^2 dm^{-6}

Q3 In pure water, $[H^+] = [OH^-]$ so $K_w = [H^+]^2$.

4. The Acid Dissociation Constant

Page 77 — Application Questions

Q1 a) $K_a = [H^+][CN^-] \div [HCN]$ or $K_a = [H^+]^2 \div [HCN]$
b) $K_a = [H^+]^2 \div [HCN]$ so $[H^+]^2 = K_a \times [HCN]$
$= (4.9 \times 10^{-10}) \times 2.0 = 9.8 \times 10^{-10}$
$[H^+] = \sqrt{9.8 \times 10^{-10}} = 3.1... \times 10^{-5}$ mol dm^{-3}
$pH = -\log_{10} [H^+] = -\log_{10} [3.1... \times 10^{-5}] = \mathbf{4.50}$

Q2 $[H^+] = 10^{-pH} = 10^{-3.80} = 1.5... \times 10^{-4}$ mol dm^{-3}
$K_a = [H^+]^2 \div [HNO_2]$ so $[HNO_2] = [H^+]^2 \div K_a$
$= (1.5... \times 10^{-4})^2 \div 4.0 \times 10^{-4} = \mathbf{6.3 \times 10^{-5}\ mol\ dm^{-3}}$

Q3 $[H^+] = 10^{-pH} = 10^{-4.11} = 7.7... \times 10^{-5}$ mol dm^{-3}
$K_a = [H^+]^2 \div [HA] = (7.7... \times 10^{-5})^2 \div 0.280$
$= \mathbf{2.2 \times 10^{-8}\ mol\ dm^{-3}}$

Q4 $[H^+] = 10^{-pH} = 10^{-3.67} = 2.1... \times 10^{-4}$ mol dm^{-3}
$K_a = [H^+]^2 \div [HCOOH]$ so $[HCOOH] = [H^+]^2 \div K_a$
$= (2.1... \times 10^{-4})^2 \div (1.8 \times 10^{-4}) = \mathbf{2.5 \times 10^{-4}\ mol\ dm^{-3}}$

Q5 $K_a = 10^{-pKa} = 10^{-4.78} = \mathbf{1.6 \times 10^{-5}\ mol\ dm^{-3}}$

Q6 $[H^+] = 10^{-pH} = 10^{-4.50} = 3.1... \times 10^{-5}$ mol dm^{-3}
$K_a = [H^+]^2 \div [HA] = (3.1... \times 10^{-5})^2 \div 0.154$
$= 6.4... \times 10^{-9}$ mol dm^{-3}
$pK_a = -\log_{10} (K_a) = -\log_{10} (6.4... \times 10^{-9}) = \mathbf{8.19}$

Q7 $K_a = 10^{-pKa} = 10^{-3.14} = 7.24 \times 10^{-4}$ mol dm^{-3}
$[H^+] = 10^{-pH} = 10^{-3.20} = 6.31 \times 10^{-4}$ mol dm^{-3}
$K_a = [H^+]^2 \div [HF]$ so $[HF] = [H^+]^2 \div K_a$
$= (6.31 \times 10^{-4})^2 \div 7.24 \times 10^{-4} = \mathbf{5.5 \times 10^{-4}\ mol\ dm^{-3}}$

Q8 $K_a = 10^{-pKa} = 10^{-4.50} = 3.1... \times 10^{-5}$ mol dm^{-3}
$K_a = [H^+]^2 \div [HX]$ so $[H^+]^2 = K_a \times [HX]$
$= (3.1... \times 10^{-5}) \times 0.60 = 1.8... \times 10^{-5}$ mol^2 dm^{-6}
so $[H^+] = \sqrt{1.8 \times 10^{-5}} = 4.3... \times 10^{-3}$ mol dm^{-3}
$pH = -\log_{10} [H^+] = -\log_{10} [4.3... \times 10^{-3}] = \mathbf{2.36}$

Page 77 — Fact Recall Questions

Q1 mol dm^{-3}

Q2 a) $K_a = [H^+][A^-] \div [HA]$ or $K_a = [H^+]^2 \div [HA]$
b) $[HA] = [H^+][A^-] \div K_a$ or $[HA] = [H^+]^2 \div K_a$

Q3 a) $pK_a = -\log_{10}(K_a)$
b) $K_a = 10^{-pKa}$

5. Buffer Action

Page 80 — Fact Recall Questions

Q1 A buffer is a solution that minimises changes in pH when small amounts of acid or alkali are added.

Q2 By mixing a weak acid with a salt of its conjugate base, or by reacting an excess of a weak acid with a strong alkali.
When describing how to prepare a buffer from an acid and a base, make sure you say that the acid is in excess — you might lose a mark if you don't.

Q3 a) When acid is added $[H^+]$ increases. Most of the extra H^+ ions combine with A^- ions to form HA. This shifts the equilibrium to the left so $[H^+]$ is reduced to almost its original value and so the pH doesn't change much.
b) When a base is added $[OH^-]$ increases. Most of the extra OH^- ions react with H^+ ions to form water. This removes H^+ ions from the solution so the equilibrium shifts to the right and the HA dissociates to compensate. More H^+ ions are formed and so the pH doesn't change much.

Q4 A carbonic acid-hydrogencarbonate buffer system is used to buffer the pH of blood and keep it at 7.35 and 7.45.

6. Calculating the pH of Buffers

Page 83 — Application Questions

Q1 a) $CH_3CH_2COOH \rightleftharpoons H^+ + CH_3CH_2COO^-$ so
$$K_a = \frac{[H^+][CH_3CH_2COO^-]}{[CH_3CH_2COOH]}$$
b) $K_a = [H^+][CH_3CH_2COO^-] \div [CH_3CH_2COOH]$ so
$[H^+] = (K_a \times [CH_3CH_2COOH]) \div [CH_3CH_2COO^-]$
$= ((1.35 \times 10^{-5}) \times 0.200) \div 0.350 = \mathbf{7.71 \times 10^{-6}\ mol\ dm^{-3}}$
c) $pH = -\log_{10} [H^+] = -\log_{10} (7.71 \times 10^{-6}) = \mathbf{5.113}$

Q2 $CH_3COOH \rightleftharpoons H^+ + CH_3COO^-$ so
$K_a = [H^+][CH_3COO^-] \div [CH_3COOH]$ so
$[H^+] = (K_a \times [CH_3COOH]) \div [CH_3COO^-]$
$= ((1.74 \times 10^{-5}) \times 0.150) \div 0.250 = 1.04... \times 10^{-5}$ mol dm^{-3}
$pH = -\log_{10} [H^+] = -\log_{10} (1.04... \times 10^{-5}) = \mathbf{4.981}$

Q3 a) $CH_3CH_2COOH + KOH \rightarrow CH_3CH_2COO^-K^+ + H_2O$
b) initial moles CH_3CH_2COOH = (conc. × vol.) ÷ 1000
= (0.500 × 30.0) ÷ 1000 = **0.0150 moles**.
initial moles KOH = (conc. × vol.) ÷ 1000
= (0.250 × 20.0) ÷ 1000 = **5.00 × 10^{-3} moles**.

c) From the equation: moles of salt = moles of base $= 5.00 \times 10^{-3}$ moles. Also, 1 mole of base neutralises 1 mole of acid so 5.00×10^{-3} moles of base neutralises 5.00×10^{-3} moles of acid.
So $0.0150 - (5.00 \times 10^{-3}) = 0.0100$ moles of acid remain.
Total volume = 30.0 + 20.0 = 50.0 cm^3
conc. acid in buffer = (moles × 1000) ÷ vol.
= (0.0100 × 1000) ÷ 50.0 = **0.200 mol dm^{-3}**
conc. salt in buffer = (moles × 1000) ÷ vol.
$= ((5.00 \times 10^{-3}) \times 1000) \div 50.0 =$ **0.100 mol dm^{-3}**

d) $K_a = [H^+][CH_3CH_2COO^-] \div [CH_3CH_2COOH]$ so
$[H^+] = (K_a \times [CH_3CH_2COOH]) \div [CH_3CH_2COO^-]$
$= ((1.35 \times 10^{-5}) \times 0.200) \div 0.100$
$= 2.70 \times 10^{-5}$ mol dm^{-3}

e) $pH = -\log_{10} [H^+] = -\log_{10} (2.70 \times 10^{-5}) =$ **4.569**

Q4 initial moles HCOOH = (conc. × vol.) ÷ 1000
$= (0.200 \times 25.0) \div 1000 = 5.00 \times 10^{-3}$ moles.
initial moles NaOH = (conc. × vol.) ÷ 1000
$= (0.100 \times 15.0) \div 1000 = 1.50 \times 10^{-3}$ moles.
$HCOOH + NaOH \rightarrow HCOO^-Na^+ + H_2O$ so
moles of salt = moles of base $= 1.50 \times 10^{-3}$ moles. Also, 1 mole of base neutralises 1 mole of acid so 1.50×10^{-3} moles of base neutralises 1.50×10^{-3} moles of acid.
So $(5.00 \times 10^{-3}) - (1.50 \times 10^{-3}) = 3.50 \times 10^{-3}$ moles of acid remain.
Total volume = 15.0 + 25.0 = 40.0 cm^3
final conc. acid = (moles × 1000) ÷ vol.
$= ((3.50 \times 10^{-3}) \times 1000) \div 40.0 = 0.0875$ mol dm^{-3}
final conc. salt = (moles × 1000) ÷ vol.
$= ((1.50 \times 10^{-3}) \times 1000) \div 40.0 = 0.0375$ mol dm^{-3}
$K_a = [H^+][HCOO^-] \div [HCOOH]$ so
$[H^+] = (K_a \times [HCOOH]) \div [HCOO^-]$
$= ((1.60 \times 10^{-4}) \times 0.0875) \div 0.0375$
$= 3.73... \times 10^{-4}$ mol dm^{-3}
$pH = -\log_{10} [H^+] = -\log_{10} (3.73 \times 10^{-4}) =$ **3.428**

7. pH Curves and Titrations

Page 87 — Application Questions

Q1 a) Strong base/weak acid, phenolphthalein/cresol purple
b) Strong acid/weak base, methyl orange
c) Strong acid/strong base, phenolphthalein/cresol purple/ litmus
d) Weak base/strong acid, methyl orange

Q2 Any curve where the vertical section covers pH 6.8 to pH 8.0. E.g.

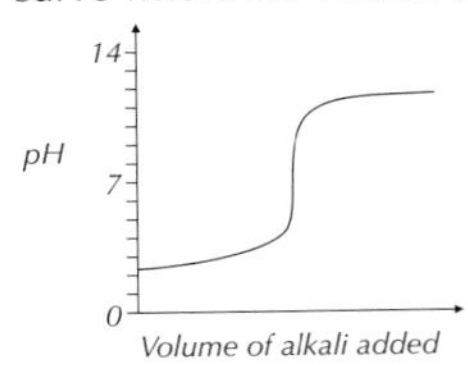

You could also have drawn a curve showing an acid being added to an alkali.

Page 88 — Fact Recall Questions

Q1 a)

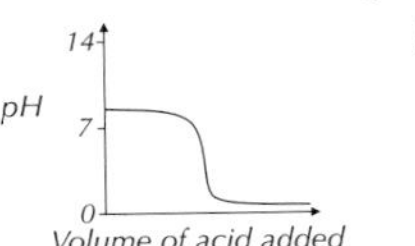

b)

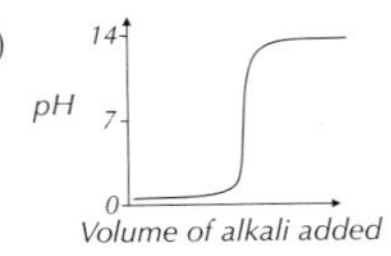

c)

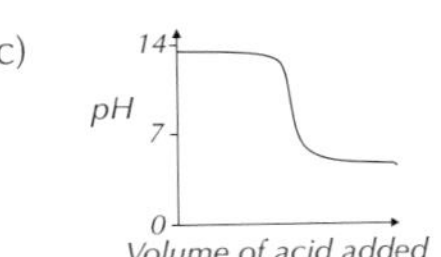

If the question says that a strong acid neutralises a strong base, the base is being neutralised so it's the acid that's added.

Q2 a) At the end point of a titration a tiny amount of acid/base causes a sudden big change in pH and the base/acid is just neutralised.
b) The pH indicator changes colour/the pH meter shows a sudden big change.
c) The pH curve becomes close to vertical.

Q3 For an indicator to be suitable it must change colour over a narrow pH range that lies entirely within the vertical part of the pH curve for the titration.

Exam-style Questions — pages 89-90

1 B ***(1 mark)***

2 D ***(1 mark)***

3 a) (i) $HCOOH \rightleftharpoons H^+ + HCOO^-$ ***(1 mark)***
(ii) $K_a = [H^+][HCOO^-] \div [HCOOH]$ or
$K_a = [H^+]^2 \div [HCOOH]$ ***(1 mark)***
(iii) $[H^+] = 10^{-pH} = 10^{-2.18} = 6.6... \times 10^{-3}$
$K_a = [H^+]^2 \div [HCOOH] = (6.6... \times 10^{-3})^2 \div 0.240$
$= 1.8... \times 10^{-4}$ mol dm^{-3}
$pK_a = -\log_{10} (K_a) = -\log_{10} (1.8... \times 10^{-4}) =$ **3.74**
(3 marks for correct answer, otherwise 1 mark for $[H^+] = 6.6... \times 10^{-3}$ and 1 mark for $K_a = 1.8... \times 10^{-4}$.)

b) (i) $K_a = [H^+][HCOO^-] \div [HCOOH]$ so
$[H^+] = (K_a \times [HCOOH]) \div [HCOO^-]$
$= ((1.8 \times 10^{-4}) \times 0.084) \div (0.060)$
$= 2.5... \times 10^{-4}$ mol dm^{-3} ***(1 mark)***
$pH = -\log_{10} [H^+] = -\log_{10} (2.5... \times 10^{-4}) =$ **3.60** ***(1 mark)***.

You calculated K_a for this acid in a previous part of the question. If you got it wrong then, you could still get full marks for this part of the question if everything else you did was right.

(ii) $HCOOH + NH_3 \rightarrow HCOO^- + NH_4^+$ ***(1 mark)***.
acid 1 base 2 base 1 acid 2
(1 mark for correctly identifying acids and bases, 1 mark for correct pairings).

(iii) $HCOOH \rightleftharpoons H^+ + HCOO^-$. Adding an acid increases $[H^+]$ ***(1 mark)***. The excess H^+ combines with $HCOO^-$ to form HCOOH ***(1 mark)***, so the equilibrium shifts to the left reducing the H^+ concentration to close to its original value and maintaining the pH ***(1 mark)***.

4 a) (i) $K_w = [H^+][OH^-]$ ***(1 mark)***
(ii) $pH = -\log_{10} [H^+]$ ***(1 mark)***

b) NaOH is a strong base so
$[OH^-] = [NaOH] = 0.150$ mol dm^{-3}
$K_w = [H^+][OH^-]$ so $[H^+] = K_w \div [OH^-]$
$= (1.00 \times 10^{-14}) \div 0.150 = 6.66... \times 10^{-14}$ mol dm^{-3}
$pH = -\log_{10} [H^+] = -\log_{10} [6.66... \times 10^{-14}] =$ **13.176**
(3 marks for correct answer, otherwise 1 mark for $[OH^-] = 0.150$ and 1 mark for $[H^+] = 6.66... \times 10^{-4}$.)

c) (i) B ***(1 mark)***

This titration was a strong acid against a strong base so the curve should start at around pH 14 and fall to around pH 1.

(ii) HCl is a strong acid and fully dissociates so
$[H^+] = [HCl] = 0.203$ mol dm^{-3}
$pH = -\log_{10} [H^+] = -\log_{10} (0.203) =$ **0.693**
(2 marks for correct answer, otherwise 1 mark for $[H^+] = 0.203$ mol dm^{-3}.)

d) (i) Any weak acid (e.g. methanoic acid/ethanoic acid/ hydrogen cyanide) ***(1 mark)***. Any strong base (e.g. potassium hydroxide/sodium hydroxide) ***(1 mark)***.
(ii) Phenolphthalein ***(1 mark)***

Section 4 — Enthalpy, Entropy and Free Energy

1. Enthalpy Changes

Page 92 — Fact Recall Questions

Q1 Enthalpy change is the heat energy transferred in a reaction at constant pressure.
Q2 ΔH
Q3 a) Enthalpy change of formation is the enthalpy change when 1 mole of a compound is formed from its elements.
b) Second electron affinity is the energy needed to change 1 mole of gaseous 1– ions into 1 mole of gaseous 2– ions.
c) The enthalpy change of hydration is the enthalpy change when 1 mole of gaseous ions is dissolved in water.
Q4 a) Enthalpy change of atomisation of an element.
b) The first ionisation energy.
Q5 a) $\Delta_{hyd}H$
b) $\Delta_{sol}H$

2. Lattice Enthalpy

Page 94 — Application Questions

Q1 a) Larger ions attract less strongly because their charge density is lower. So the larger the ionic radii of the ions involved, the less exothermic the lattice enthalpy. The ionic radii increase from Cl^- to I^-, so the lattice enthalpy becomes less exothermic from NaCl to NaI.
b) NaCl contains the strongest ionic bonds.
Q2 The standard lattice enthalpy of CaO would be more negative than the standard lattice enthalpy of K_2O. This is because CaO only contains 2+ ions while K_2O contains 1+ ions. The higher the charge on the ions, the more energy is released when the ionic lattice forms and the more negative the lattice enthalpy will be.

Page 94 — Fact Recall Questions

Q1 a) The lattice enthalpy is the enthalpy change when 1 mole of a solid ionic compound is formed from its gaseous ions.
b) $\Delta_{LE}H$
Q2 The more negative the lattice enthalpy, the stronger the ionic bonding in the lattice.
Q3 Ionic charge and ionic radius.

3. Born-Haber Cycles

Page 98 — Application Questions

Q1 E.g.

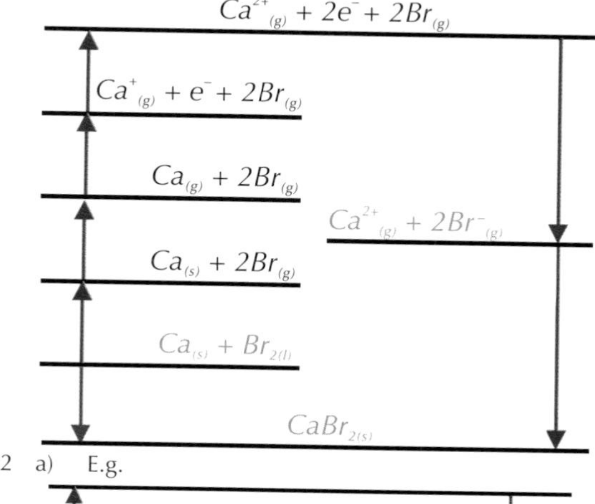

Q2 a) E.g.

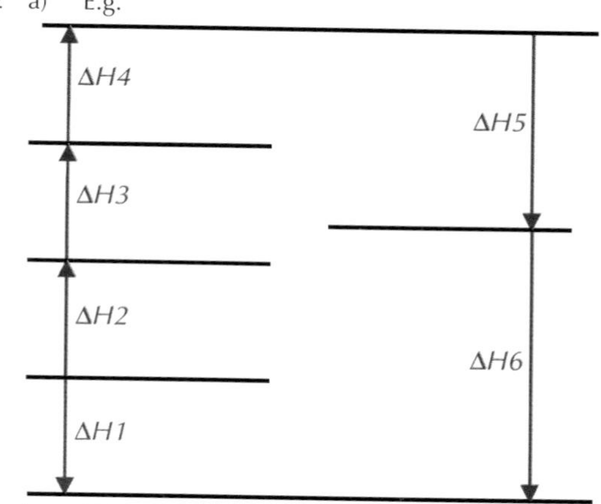

b) $\Delta H1 = \Delta H2 + \Delta H3 + \Delta H4 + \Delta H5 + \Delta H6$
$= (+122) + (+159) + (+520) + (-349) + (-861)$
$= \mathbf{-409\ kJ\ mol^{-1}}$

Q3 a) E.g.

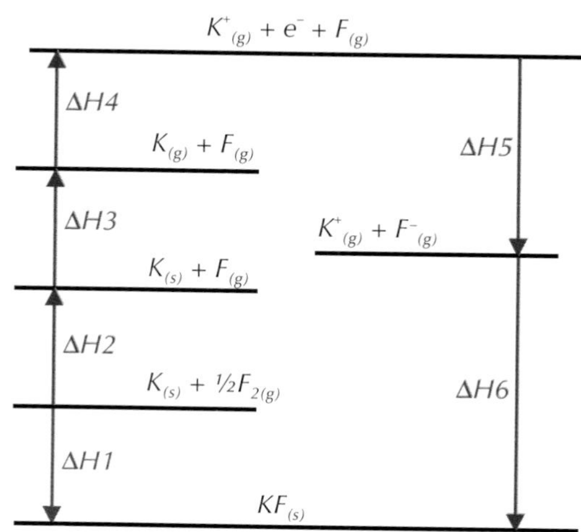

b) $\Delta H6 = -\Delta H5 - \Delta H4 - \Delta H3 - \Delta H2 + \Delta H1$
$= -(-328) - (+419) - (+89) - (+79) + (-563)$
$= \mathbf{-822\ kJ\ mol^{-1}}$

4. Enthalpies of Solution

Page 102 — Application Questions

Q1 $\Delta H3 = \Delta H1 + \Delta H2 = -(-861) + (-520 + -364) = \mathbf{-23\ kJ\ mol^{-1}}$

Q2 a)

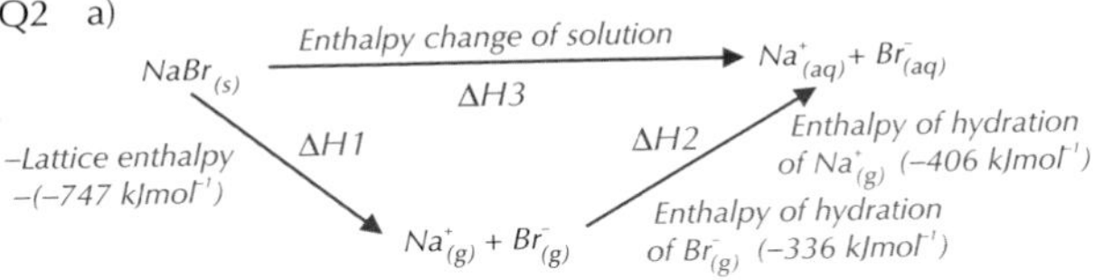

b) $\Delta H3 = \Delta H1 + \Delta H2 = -(-747) + (-406 + -336)$
$= \mathbf{+5\ kJ\ mol^{-1}}$

Q3 a) $\Delta H3 = \Delta H1 + \Delta H2 = -(-807) + (-520 + -336)$
$= \mathbf{-49\ kJ\ mol^{-1}}$

b) $\Delta H3 = \Delta H1 + \Delta H2 = -(-701) + (-322 + -364)$
$= \mathbf{+15\ kJ\ mol^{-1}}$

c) $\Delta H3 = \Delta H1 + \Delta H2 = -(-2440) + (-1921 + (-336 \times 2))$
$= \mathbf{-153\ kJ\ mol^{-1}}$

Q4 Magnesium ions (Mg^{2+}) are smaller and have a higher charge than potassium ions (K^+). The higher charge and smaller size create a higher charge density. This creates a stronger attraction for the water molecules and gives magnesium ions a much more negative enthalpy of hydration than potassium ions.

Page 102 — Fact Recall Questions

Q1 a) The bonds between the ions break, and bonds between the ions and water are made.

b) Bonds breaking is endothermic and bonds being made is exothermic.

Q2 The lattice enthalpy and enthalpy change of hydration.

Q3 Ionic charge and ionic radius.

5. Entropy

Page 105 — Application Questions

Q1 The entropy will increase when the solid sodium hydroxide dissolves in the aqueous hydrogen chloride. The entropy of the water will increase when it turns to a gas and the entropy of the sodium chloride will decrease when it turns to a solid.

Q2 $\Delta S = S_{products} - S_{reactants}$
$= (214 + (2 \times 69.9)) - (186 + (2 \times 205))$
$= \mathbf{-242\ J\ K^{-1}\ mol^{-1}}$

Q3 $\Delta S = S_{products} - S_{reactants}$
$= ((3 \times 31.6) + (2 \times 69.9)) - (248 + (2 \times 206))$
$= \mathbf{-425\ J\ K^{-1}\ mol^{-1}}$

Page 105 — Fact Recall Questions

Q1 a) It is a measure of the amount of disorder in a system (e.g. the number of ways that particles can be arranged and the number of ways that the energy can be shared out between particles).

b) ΔS

Q2 a) The entropy increases because particles move around more in gases than in liquids and their arrangement is more disordered.

b) The entropy increases because particles move around more in solution than in solids and their arrangement is more disordered.

c) The entropy increases because the more gaseous particles you've got, the more ways they and their energy can be arranged.

6. Free Energy Change

Page 108 — Application Questions

Q1 a) $\Delta S = S_{products} - S_{reactants}$
$= ((2 \times 28.3) + (3 \times 27.0)) - (51.0 + (3 \times 32.5))$
$= \mathbf{-10.9\ J\ K^{-1}\ mol^{-1}}$

b) $\Delta H^\circ = -130\ kJ\ mol^{-1} = -130 \times 10^3\ J\ mol^{-1}$
$\Delta G = \Delta H - T\Delta S$
$= -130 \times 10^3 - (298 \times -10.9)$
$= \mathbf{-127\ 000\ J\ mol^{-1}}$ (3 s.f.)

c) The reaction is feasible at 298 K because ΔG is negative.

Q2 a) (i) $\Delta H^\circ = 71.0\ kJ\ mol^{-1} = 71.0 \times 10^3\ J\ mol^{-1}$
$\Delta G = \Delta H - T\Delta S$
$= 71.0 \times 10^3 - (298 \times 176)$
$= \mathbf{18\ 600\ J\ mol^{-1}}$ (3 s.f.)
The reaction is not feasible at 298 K because ΔG is positive.

(ii) $\Delta H^\circ = 71.0\ kJ\ mol^{-1} = 71.0 \times 10^3\ J\ mol^{-1}$
$\Delta G = \Delta H - T\Delta S$
$= (71.0 \times 10^3) - (600 \times 176)$
$= \mathbf{-34\ 600\ J\ mol^{-1}}$ (3 s.f.)
The reaction is feasible at 600 K because ΔG is negative.

b) $\Delta H^\circ = 71.0\ kJ\ mol^{-1} = (71.0 \times 10^3)\ J\ mol^{-1}$
$T = \Delta H \div \Delta S = (71.0 \times 10^3) \div 176 = \mathbf{403\ K}$ (3 s.f.)

Q3 $\Delta H^\circ = 178\ kJ\ mol^{-1} = 178 \times 10^3\ J\ mol^{-1}$
$T = \Delta H \div \Delta S = (178 \times 10^3) \div 165 = \mathbf{1080\ K}$ (3 s.f.)

Page 108 — Fact Recall Questions

Q1 a) Free energy change is a measure used to predict whether a reaction is feasible.

b) ΔG

Q2 $\Delta G = \Delta H - T\Delta S$

Q3 E.g. The reaction could have a very high activation energy / the rate of reaction might be so slow that you don't notice it happening.

Q4 no

Q5 $T = \Delta H \div \Delta S$

Exam-style Questions — pages 110-112

1 A ***(1 mark)***.

Higher ionic charges result in more negative standard lattice enthalpies and smaller ionic radii result in more negative standard lattice enthalpies. B and C can be ruled out because Na, Cl, K and Br are all singly charged ions. D can be ruled out because Mg and S are larger ions than Be and O.

2 C ***(1 mark)***.

According to the equation $\Delta G = \Delta H - T\Delta S$ for a reaction to be feasible at any temperature, ΔH must be negative and ΔS must be positive.

3 a)

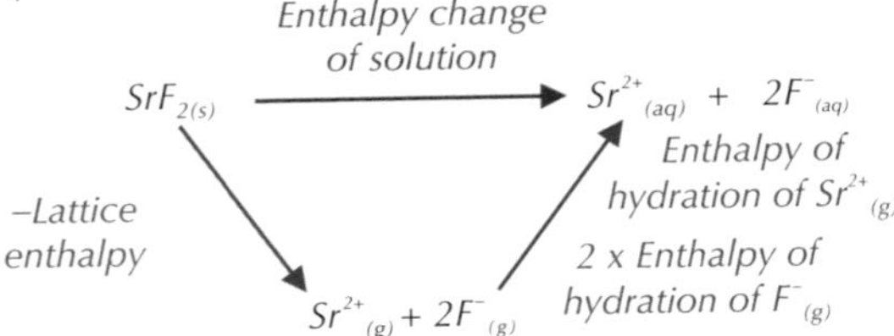

(1 mark for a complete correct cycle, 1 mark for correctly labelled arrows)

b) Enthalpy change of solution ($SrF_{2(s)}$)
= –lattice enthalpy ($SrF_{2(s)}$)
+ enthalpy of hydration ($Sr_2{}^{+}{}_{(g)}$)
+ [2 × enthalpy of hydration ($F^{-}_{(g)}$)] ***(1 mark)***
= –(–2492) + (–1480) + (2 × –506) = **0 kJ mol^{-1}** ***(1 mark)***

You have to double the enthalpy of hydration for F^- because there are two in SrF_2.

4 a) Increase. 2 moles of solid reactant produce 1 mole of solid product and 1 mole of gaseous product. Gases have higher entropy than solids ***(1 mark)***.

b) $\Delta S = S_{products} - S_{reactants}$
= (32.0 + 214) – (53.0 + 5.70)
= +187.3 J K^{-1} mol^{-1} ***(1 mark)***.
ΔH° = +127 kJ mol^{-1} = +127 × 10^3 J mol^{-1}
$\Delta G = \Delta H - T\Delta S$ ***(1 mark)***.
= (+127 × 10^3) – (1473 × +187.3) ***(1 mark)***.
= **–149000 J mol^{-1}** or **–149 kJ mol^{-1}** (3 s.f.) ***(1 mark)***.

c) If the free energy change is negative or equal to zero the reaction is feasible ***(1 mark)***.

d) $T = \Delta H \div \Delta S$ ***(1 mark)***.

e) T = (+127 × 10^3) ÷ 187.3
= 678 K
(1 mark for correct substitution, 1 mark for correct answer).

Don't forget, reactions become feasible when ΔG is 0 J mol^{-1}.

f) The enthalpy change of formation is the enthalpy change when 1 mole of a compound is formed from its elements ***(1 mark)***.

g) The formation of manganese(IV) oxide would be exothermic ***(1 mark)***.

It's an exothermic reaction because ΔH is negative.

5 a) It is the enthalpy change when 1 mole of a solid ionic lattice is formed from its gaseous ions ***(1 mark)***.

b)

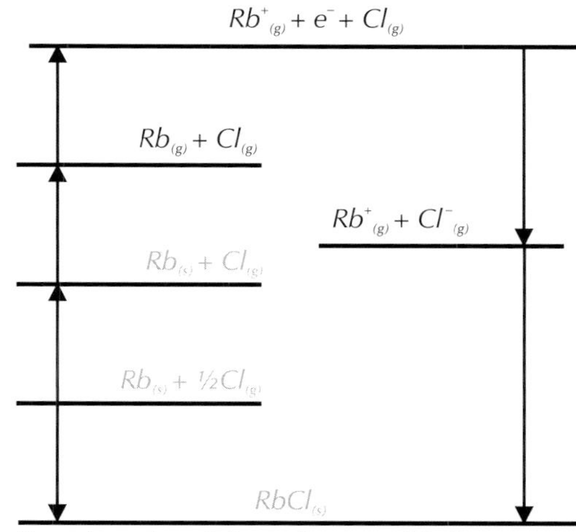

(3 marks — 1 mark for each correct label).

c) $\Delta H6 = -\Delta H5 - \Delta H4 - \Delta H3 - \Delta H2 + \Delta H1$
= –(–349) – (+403) – (+81) – (+122) + (–435)
= **–692 kJ mol^{-1}**
(3 marks for correct answer, otherwise 1 mark for correct equation, 1 mark for correct substitution)

d) Sodium has a smaller ionic radius than rubidium ***(1 mark)***. Smaller ions have a higher charge density and attract more strongly ***(1 mark)***. So more energy is released when sodium chloride forms than when rubidium chloride forms ***(1 mark)***.

e)

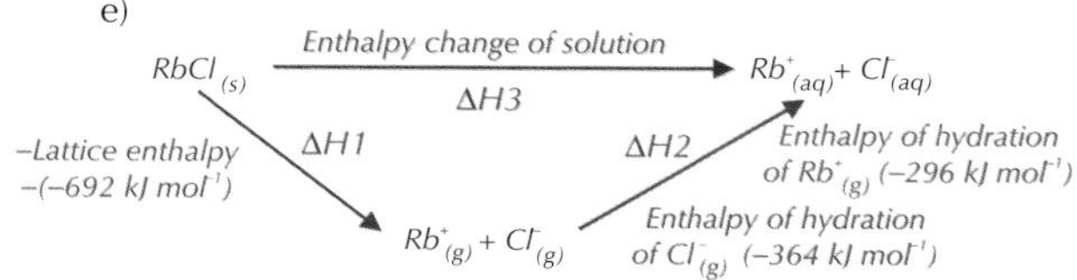

$\Delta H3 = \Delta H1 + \Delta H2$ = –(–692) + (–296 + –364) ***(1 mark)***
= **+32 kJ mol^{-1}** ***(1 mark)***

If you used the value of –300 kJ mol^{-1} for the standard lattice enthalpy of rubidium chloride you'll get an answer of –360 kJ mol^{-1}. If you got this answer, give yourself full marks.

Section 5 — Redox and Electrode Potentials

1. Redox Reactions

Page 115 — Application Questions

Q1 $2Fe_{(s)} + 3Cu^{2+}_{(aq)} \rightarrow 2Fe^{3+}_{(aq)} + 3Cu_{(s)}$

Q2 $Cl_{2(g)} + 2e^- \rightarrow 2Cl^-_{(aq)}$

Q3 a) $Zn \rightarrow Zn^{2+} + 2e^-$
$Cr_2O_7^{2-} + 14H^+ + 6e^- \rightarrow 2Cr^{3+} + 7H_2O$
b) $Cr_2O_7^{2-} + 14H^+ + 3Zn \rightarrow 2Cr^{3+} + 3Zn^{2+} + 7H_2O$
Don't forget to finish off by double-checking that the charges on each side of the equation balance.

Q4 a) +6
b) $CH_3CH_2OH + H_2O \rightarrow CH_3COOH + 4H^+ + 4e^-$
$Cr_2O_7^{2-} + 14H^+ + 6e^- \rightarrow 2Cr^{3+} + 7H_2O$
c) $3CH_3CH_2OH + 2Cr_2O_7^{2-} + 16H^+$
$\rightarrow 3CH_3COOH + 4Cr^{3+} + 11H_2O$

Page 115 — Fact Recall Questions

Q1 a) Something that accepts electrons and gets reduced.
b) Something that donates electrons and gets oxidised.

Q2 It decreases.

2. Redox Titrations

Page 119 — Application Questions

Q1 a) $MnO_4^-{}_{(aq)} + 8H^+_{(aq)} + 5Fe^{2+}_{(aq)} \rightarrow Mn^{2+}_{(aq)} + 4H_2O_{(l)} + 5Fe^{3+}_{(aq)}$
b) Moles Fe^{2+} = (conc. × volume) ÷ 1000
= (0.0500 × 28.2) ÷ 1000 = **1.41 × 10^{-3} moles**
c) From the balanced equation, 5 moles of Fe^{2+} reacts with 1 mole of MnO_4^- and so 1.41 × 10^{-3} moles of Fe^{2+} must react with (1.41 × 10^{-3}) ÷ 5
= 2.82 × 10^{-4} moles of MnO_4^-.
Conc. MnO_4^- = (moles × 1000) ÷ volume
= ((2.82 × 10^{-4}) × 1000) ÷ 30.0 = **9.40 × 10^{-3} mol dm^{-3}**

Q2 $MnO_4^-{}_{(aq)} + 8H^+_{(aq)} + 5Fe^{2+}_{(aq)} \rightarrow Mn^{2+}_{(aq)} + 4H_2O_{(l)} + 5Fe^{3+}_{(aq)}$
Moles Fe^{2+} = (conc. × volume) ÷ 1000
= (0.600 × 28.0) ÷ 1000 = 0.0168 moles.
5 moles of Fe^{2+} reacts with 1 mole of MnO_4^- and so 0.0168 moles of Fe^{2+} must react with (0.0168) ÷ 5
= 3.36 × 10^{-3} moles of MnO_4^-.
Volume MnO_4^- = (moles × 1000) ÷ conc.
= ((3.36 × 10^{-3}) × 1000) ÷ 0.0750 = **44.8 cm^3**

Q3 a) $Cr_2O_7^{2-}{}_{(aq)} + 14H^+_{(aq)} + 6Fe^{2+}_{(aq)} \rightarrow 2Cr^{3+}_{(aq)} + 7H_2O_{(l)} + 6Fe^{3+}_{(aq)}$
b) Moles $Cr_2O_7^{2-}$ = (conc. × volume) ÷ 1000
= (0.150 × 22.2) ÷ 1000 = **3.33 ×10^{-3} moles**

c) From the balanced equation, 1 mole of $Cr_2O_7^{2-}$ reacts with 6 moles of Fe^{2+}, so 3.33×10^{-3} moles of $Cr_2O_7^{2-}$ must react with $(3.33 \times 10^{-3}) \times 6$ $= 0.01998$ moles of Fe^{2+}.
Conc. Fe^{2+} = (moles × 1000) ÷ volume
= (0.01998 × 1000) ÷ 20.0 = **0.999 mol dm⁻³**

Q4 $Cr_2O_7^{2-}{}_{(aq)} + 14H^+{}_{(aq)} + 6Fe^{2+}{}_{(aq)} \rightarrow 2Cr^{3+}{}_{(aq)} + 7H_2O_{(l)} + 6Fe^{3+}{}_{(aq)}$
Moles $Cr_2O_7^{2-}$ = (conc. × volume) ÷ 1000
= (0.0550 × 24.0) ÷ 1000 = 1.32×10^{-3} moles.
1 mole of $Cr_2O_7^{2-}$ reacts with 6 moles of Fe^{2+}, so 1.32×10^{-3} moles of $Cr_2O_7^{2-}$ must react with $(1.32 \times 10^{-3}) \times 6 = 7.92 \times 10^{-3}$ moles of Fe^{2+}.
Volume Fe^{2+} = (moles × 1000) ÷ conc.
= $((7.92 \times 10^{-3}) \times 1000) \div 0.450$ = **17.6 cm³**

Q5 a) $Cr_2O_7^{2-}{}_{(aq)} + 14H^+{}_{(aq)} + 3Zn_{(s)} \rightarrow 2Cr^{3+}{}_{(aq)} + 7H_2O_{(l)} + 3Zn^{2+}{}_{(aq)}$
b) Moles $Cr_2O_7^{2-}$ = (conc. × volume) ÷ 1000
= (0.230 × 30.0) ÷ 1000 = **6.90×10^{-3} moles**
c) Using the balanced equation, 1 mole of $Cr_2O_7^{2-}$ reacts with 3 moles of Zn, so 6.90×10^{-3} moles of $Cr_2O_7^{2-}$ must react with $(6.90 \times 10^{-3}$ moles$) \times 3 = 0.0207$ moles of Zn.
mass Zn = moles × M_r
= 0.0207 × 65.4 = **1.35 g**

Page 119 — Fact Recall Questions

Q1 E.g. Acidified potassium manganate(VII) solution/$KMnO_{4(aq)}$ / Acidified potassium dichromate(VI) solution/$K_2Cr_2O_{7(aq)}$.
Q2 Acid is added to make sure there are enough H^+ ions to allow all the oxidising agent to be reduced.
Q3 E.g. the end point is when the mixture in the flask just becomes tainted with the colour of the oxidising agent.

3. More on Titrations

Page 122 — Application Questions

Q1 a) Moles $Na_2S_2O_3$ = (conc. × volume) ÷ 1000
= (0.200 × 41.1) ÷ 1000 = **0.00822 moles**.
b) Using the balanced equation given in the question, 1 mole of I_2 reacts with 2 moles of $Na_2S_2O_3$ and so 0.00822 moles of $Na_2S_2O_3$ must react with 0.00822 ÷ 2 = **0.00411 moles** of I_2.
c) Using the balanced equation:
$IO_3^-{}_{(aq)} + 5I^-{}_{(aq)} + 6H^+{}_{(aq)} \rightarrow 3I_{2\,(aq)} + 3H_2O_{(l)}$,
1 mole of IO_3^- will react to give 3 moles of I_2. So, 0.00411 moles of I_2 will be produced from 0.00411 ÷ 3 = **0.00137 moles** of IO_3^-.
d) Concentration of IO_3^- = (moles × 1000) ÷ volume
= (0.00137 × 1000) ÷ 13.2 = **0.104 mol dm⁻³**

Q2 a) Moles $Na_2S_2O_3$ = (conc. × volume) ÷ 1000
= (0.750 × 4.00) ÷ 1000 = **0.00300 moles**.
b) Using the balanced equation given in the question, 2 moles of $Na_2S_2O_3$ react with 1 mole of I_2, and so 0.00300 moles of $Na_2S_2O_3$ must react with 0.00300 ÷ 2 = 0.00150 moles of I_2.
The total volume of the solution formed by adding the potassium manganate(VII) solution to the acidified potassium iodide solution was (39 + 61) = 100 cm³.
But only 25.0 cm³ of the solution was used in the titration, so the total number of moles of I_2 formed in the oxidation reaction was 0.00150 × (100 ÷ 25)
= **0.00600 moles**.
c) Using the balanced equation given in the question, 5 moles of I_2 will be produced from 2 moles of MnO_4^-.
So, 0.00600 moles of I_2 will be produced from (0.00600 ÷ 5) × 2 = 0.00240 moles of MnO_4^-.
Concentration of MnO_4^- = (moles × 1000) ÷ volume
= (0.00240 × 1000) ÷ 39.0 = **0.0615 mol dm⁻³**

Q3 Moles $Na_2S_2O_3$ = (conc. × volume) ÷ 1000
= (0.0600 × 22.3) ÷ 1000 = (1.338×10^{-3}) moles.
Using the balanced equation given in the question, 1 mole of I_2 reacts with 2 moles of $Na_2S_2O_3$ and so 1.338×10^{-3} moles of $Na_2S_2O_3$ must react with $1.338 \times 10^{-3} \div 2$
$= 6.69 \times 10^{-4}$ moles of I_2.
Using the balanced equation given in the question, 1 mole of $Cr_2O_7^{2-}$ will produce 3 moles of I_2. So, 6.69×10^{-4} moles of I_2 will be produced from $(6.69 \times 10^{-4}) \div 3 = 2.23 \times 10^{-4}$ moles of $Cr_2O_7^{2-}$.
Concentration of $Cr_2O_7^{2-}$ = (moles × 1000) ÷ volume
= $((2.23 \times 10^{-4}) \times 1000) \div 15.0$ = **1.49×10^{-2} mol dm⁻³**

Page 122 — Fact Recall Questions

Q1 $IO_3^-{}_{(aq)} + 5I^-{}_{(aq)} + 6H^+{}_{(aq)} \rightarrow 3I_{2(aq)} + 3H_2O_{(l)}$
Q2 $I_{2\,(aq)} + 2S_2O_3^{2-}{}_{(aq)} \rightarrow 2I^-{}_{(aq)} + S_4O_6^{2-}{}_{(aq)}$
Q3 Put the flask containing the iodine solution under a burette. From the burette, add sodium thiosulfate solution to the flask drop by drop. When the iodine colour fades to a pale yellow, add 2 cm³ of starch solution (to detect the presence of iodine). The solution in the conical flask will go dark blue, showing there's still some iodine there. Add sodium thiosulfate one drop at a time until the blue colour disappears. Record the volume of sodium thiosulfate added to the solution.

4. Electrochemical Cells

Pages 125-126 — Application Questions

Q1 a)

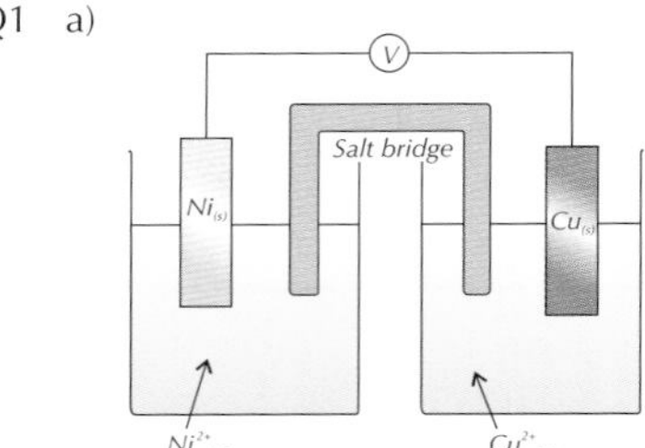

b) The Ni/Ni^{2+} reaction goes in the direction of oxidation (Ni is oxidised and Cu^{2+} is reduced).
You know that Ni is oxidised because the Ni/Ni^{2+} half-reaction has the more negative electrode potential.

Q2 a) $Ag^+{}_{(aq)} + e^- \rightarrow Ag_{(s)}$
b) $Ca_{(s)} \rightarrow Ca^{2+}{}_{(aq)} + 2e^-$
Q3 The Mg^{2+}/Mg half-cell.

Page 126 — Fact Recall Questions

Q1 a) platinum / graphite
b) Platinum/graphite is a solid that conducts electricity (so it will complete the circuit). It is also inert, so it won't react with the solutions in the half-cell.
Q2 a) It allows ions to flow between the half-cells and balance out the charges, completing the circuit.
b) The cell potential / the voltage between the two half-cells.
Q3 reduction
Q4 The metal that is very easy to oxidise.

5. Standard Electrode Potentials

Page 128 — Application Question

Q1 a) 1.00 mol dm⁻³
All solutions being at 1.00 mol dm⁻³ is part of the definition of standard conditions..
b) –0.13 V

Page 128 — Fact Recall Questions

Q1 E.g. temperature, pressure and concentrations of reactants.

Q2 Hydrogen gas is bubbled into a solution of aqueous H^+ ions. The electrode is made of platinum foil. The standard conditions used are a temperature of 298 K (25 °C), a pressure of 100 kPa and all solutions of ions have a concentration of 1.00 mol dm^{-3}.

Q3 0.00 V

6. Electrochemical Series

Page 132 — Application Questions

Q1 a) Aluminium — they are both metals and aluminium has the more negative standard electrode potential.

b) Chlorine — they are both non-metals and chlorine has the more positive standard electrode potential.

c) Copper — they are both metals and copper has the more negative (less positive) standard electrode potential.

Although the electrode potential for copper is positive, it is still more negative than that for silver, so copper is more reactive.

Q2 a) $Al^{3+}_{(aq)} + 3e^- \rightleftharpoons Al_{(s)}$ $E^\circ = -1.66$ V

$Ag^+_{(aq)} + e^- \rightleftharpoons Ag_{(s)}$ $E^\circ = +0.80$ V

$E^\circ_{cell} = E^\circ_{reduced} - E^\circ_{oxidised} = 0.80 - (-1.66)$

$= 2.46 =$ **+2.5 V (2 s.f.)**

b) $Cu^{2+}_{(aq)} + 2e^- \rightleftharpoons Cu_{(s)}$ $E^\circ = +0.34$ V

$Cl_{2\,(g)} + 2e^- \rightleftharpoons 2Cl^-_{(aq)}$ $E^\circ = +1.36$

$E^\circ_{cell} = E^\circ_{reduced} - E^\circ_{oxidised} = 1.36 - 0.34$

$= 1.02 =$ **+1.0 V (2 s.f.)**

c) $Sn^{4+}_{(aq)} + 2e^- \rightleftharpoons Sn^{2+}_{(aq)}$ $E^\circ = +0.15$ V

$Fe^{3+}_{(aq)} + e^- \rightleftharpoons Fe^{2+}_{(aq)}$ $E^\circ = +0.77$ V

$E^\circ_{cell} = E^\circ_{reduced} - E^\circ_{oxidised} = 0.77 - 0.15 =$ **+0.62 V (2 s.f.)**

Q3 a) $Mg^{2+}_{(aq)} + 2e^- \rightleftharpoons Mg_{(s)}$ $E^\circ = -2.37$ V

$Ni^{2+}_{(aq)} + 2e^- \rightleftharpoons Ni_{(s)}$ $E^\circ = -0.25$ V

Oxidation reaction: $Mg_{(s)} \rightarrow Mg^{2+}_{(aq)} + 2e^-$

Reduction reaction: $Ni^{2+}_{(aq)} + 2e^- \rightarrow Ni_{(s)}$

Redox reaction: $Mg_{(s)} + Ni^{2+}_{(aq)} \rightarrow Mg^{2+}_{(aq)} + Ni_{(s)}$

This matches the direction of the reaction given in the question, so this reaction is feasible.

b) $Fe^{3+}_{(aq)} + e^- \rightleftharpoons Fe^{2+}_{(aq)}$ $E^\circ = +0.77$ V

$Br_{2(aq)} + 2e^- \rightleftharpoons 2Br^-_{(aq)}$ $E^\circ = +1.09$ V

Oxidation reaction: $Fe^{2+}_{(aq)} \rightarrow Fe^{3+}_{(aq)} + e^-$

Reduction reaction: $Br_{2(l)} + 2e^- \rightarrow 2Br^-_{(aq)}$

Redox reaction: $2Fe^{2+}_{(aq)} + Br_{2\,(l)} \rightarrow 2Fe^{3+}_{(aq)} + 2Br^-_{(aq)}$

This does not match the direction of the reaction given in the question, so this reaction is not feasible.

c) $Sn^{4+}_{(aq)} + 2e^- \rightleftharpoons Sn^{2+}_{(aq)}$ $E^\circ = +0.15$ V

$Cu^{2+}_{(aq)} + 2e^- \rightleftharpoons Cu_{(s)}$ $E^\circ = +0.34$ V

Oxidation reaction: $Sn^{2+}_{(aq)} \rightarrow Sn^{4+}_{(aq)} + 2e^-$

Reduction reaction: $Cu^{2+}_{(aq)} + 2e^- \rightarrow Cu_{(s)}$

Redox reaction: $Sn^{2+}_{(aq)} + Cu^{2+}_{(aq)} \rightarrow Sn^{4+}_{(aq)} + Cu_{(s)}$

This matches the direction of the reaction given in the question, so this reaction is feasible.

Q4 $Sn^{4+}_{(aq)} + 2e^- \rightleftharpoons Sn^{2+}_{(aq)}$ $E^\circ = +0.15$

$Ag^+_{(aq)} + e^- \rightleftharpoons Ag_{(s)}$ $E^\circ = +0.80$

Oxidation reaction: $Sn^{2+}_{(aq)} \rightarrow Sn^{4+}_{(aq)} + 2e^-$

Reduction reaction: $Ag^+_{(aq)} + e^- \rightarrow Ag_{(s)}$

Redox reaction: $Sn^{2+}_{(aq)} + 2Ag^+_{(aq)} \rightarrow Sn^{4+}_{(aq)} + 2Ag_{(s)}$

This matches the direction of the reaction described in the question, so this reaction is feasible.

Page 132 — Fact Recall Questions

Q1 A list of electrode potentials for different electrochemical half-cells, written in order from the most negative to the most positive.

Q2 In the direction of reduction.

Q3 Reduction.

Q4 Any two from, e.g. the conditions are not standard / the reaction kinetics are not favourable / the activation energy may be too high / the rate of reaction may be too slow.

7. Energy Storage Cells

Page 134 — Application Questions

Q1 $2Ni(OH)_{2(s)} + Cd(OH)_{2(s)} \rightarrow 2NiOOH_{(s)} + Cd_{(s)} + 2H_2O_{(l)}$

Q2 a) $E^\circ_{cell} = E^\circ_{reduced} - E^\circ_{oxidised} = 0.75 - (-0.76)$

$= 1.51 =$ **+1.5 V (2 s.f.)**

b) $2MnO_{2(s)} + 2NH_4{}^+_{(aq)} + Zn_{(s)}$

$\rightarrow Mn_2O_{3(s)} + 2NH_{3(aq)} + H_2O_{(l)} + Zn^{2+}_{(aq)}$

Q3 $PbSO_{4(s)} + 2e^- \rightleftharpoons Pb_{(s)} + SO_4{}^{2-}_{(aq)}$

$PbSO_{4(s)} + 2H_2O_{(l)} \rightleftharpoons PbO_{2(s)} + SO_4{}^{2-}_{(aq)} + 4H^+_{(aq)} + 2e^-$

Look at the half-cell half-equations given in the question. The top reaction has the more negative electrode potential. When the battery is discharging that one will go in the direction of oxidation and the bottom one will go in the direction of reduction. So when the battery is being recharged, the half-equations will go in the opposite directions.

Page 134 — Fact Recall Questions

Q1 battery

Q2 $E^\circ_{cell} = E^\circ_{reduced} - E^\circ_{oxidised}$

Q3 Some energy storage cells can be recharged because the reactions that occur within them can be reversed if a current is supplied to force the electrons to flow in the opposite direction around the circuit.

8. Fuel Cells

Page 136 — Application Question

Q1 a) $CH_3OH + 1\frac{1}{2}O_2 \rightleftharpoons CO_2 + 2H_2O$

b) (i) $1\frac{1}{2}O_2 + 6H^+ + 6e^- \rightleftharpoons 3H_2O$

(ii) $CH_3OH + H_2O \rightleftharpoons CO_2 + 6H^+ + 6e^-$

c) $E^\circ_{cell} = E^\circ_{reduced} - E^\circ_{oxidised}$

$= +1.23 - (+0.046) = 1.184 =$ **+1.2 V (2 s.f.)**

Page 136 — Fact Recall Questions

Q1 Fuel cells produce electricity by reacting a fuel with an oxidant.

Q2 At the anode, the platinum catalyst splits the H_2 into protons and electrons. The polymer electrolyte membrane (PEM) only allows the H^+ across. This forces the electrons to travel around the circuit to get to the cathode. At the cathode, O_2 combines with the H^+ from the anode and the electrons from the circuit to make H_2O. So an electric current is created in the circuit.

Exam-style Questions — pages 137-140

1 D *(1 mark)*

If you use the electrochemical series to work out the feasible direction for these four reactions, you'll find that the only one where the direction doesn't match the question is D.

2 B *(1 mark)*

The oxidation number of iron drops from +2 to 0.

3 B *(1 mark)*

4 a) $2NiOOH_{(s)} + Zn_{(s)} + 2H_2O_{(l)} \rightarrow 2Ni(OH)_{2(s)} + Zn(OH)_{2(s)}$

(1 mark for correct reactants and products, 1 mark for balancing).

b) $E^\ominus_{cell} = E^\ominus_{reduced} - E^\ominus_{oxidised}$ so
$E^\ominus_{reduced} = E^\ominus_{cell} + E^\ominus_{oxidised} = 1.73 + (-1.25) = $ **+0.480 V**
(2 marks for correct answer, otherwise 1 mark for correct substitution).

You know you're looking for $E_{reduced}$ because $Zn_{(s)}$ is being oxidised, so $NiOOH_{(s)}$ must be being reduced.

5 a) $4Li_{(s)} + 2SOCl_{2(aq)} \rightarrow 4LiCl_{(s)} + S_{(s)} + SO_{2(g)}$
(1 mark for correct reactants and products, 1 mark for balancing)

First you need to work out which half-equation will go in the oxidation direction and which in the reduction direction. Then write out the half-equation for the oxidation reaction the right way round. Finally, you can balance and combine them. What a lot of work for a measly two marks...

b) $E^\ominus_{cell} = E^\ominus_{reduced} - E^\ominus_{oxidised} = 0.47 - (-3.04)$
$= 3.51 =$ **3.5 V (2 s.f.)** ***(1 mark)***

c) Advantages: any one from, e.g. they are cheap to make / they have relatively high power densities / some types are rechargeable ***(1 mark)***.
Disadvantages: any one from, e.g. producing them involves using toxic chemicals which need to be disposed of safely / the chemical used to make the cells are often very flammable ***(1 mark)***.

6 a) (i) $E^\ominus$ for Sn^{4+}/Sn^{2+} is more negative than $E^\ominus$ for VO_2^+/VO^{2+}, so Sn^{2+} ions will react with VO_2^+ ions ***(1 mark)***.
$2VO_2^+{}_{(aq)} + Sn^{2+}{}_{(aq)} + 4H^+{}_{(aq)}$
$\rightarrow 2VO^{2+}{}_{(aq)} + Sn^{4+}{}_{(aq)} + 2H_2O_{(l)}$ ***(1 mark)***.
$E^\ominus$ for Sn^{4+}/Sn^{2+} is more negative than $E^\ominus$ for VO^{2+}/V^{3+}, so Sn^{2+} ions will react with VO^{2+} ions created in the previous reaction ***(1 mark)***.
$2VO^{2+}{}_{(aq)} + Sn^{2+}{}_{(aq)} + 4H^+{}_{(aq)} \rightarrow 2V^{3+} + Sn^{4+} + 2H_2O$
(1 mark).

The V^{3+} ions made in this reaction don't react with the Sn^{2+} ions because the electrode potential for V^{3+}/V^{2+} is more negative than that for Sn^{4+}/Sn^{2+}.

(ii) Any two from: e.g. the conditions may not be standard / the reaction kinetics may not be favourable/the rate of reaction may be too slow / the activation energy may be too high
(1 mark for each, maximum 2 marks).

b) (i)

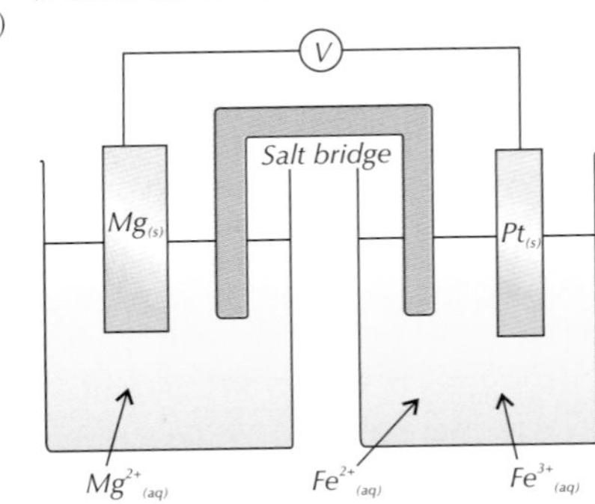

(1 mark for complete circuit with voltmeter and salt bridge, 1 mark for Mg/Mg^{2+} half-cell correct, 1 mark for Fe^{2+}/Fe^{3+} half-cell correct).

Don't forget to include the platinum electrode for the Fe^{2+}/Fe^{3+} half-cell.

(ii) $E_{cell} = E_{reduced} - E_{oxidised} = 0.77 - (-2.38)$
$= 3.15 =$ **3.2 V (2 s.f.)** ***(1 mark)***

(iii) $Mg_{(s)} + 2Fe^{3+} \rightarrow Mg^{2+}{}_{(aq)} + 2Fe^{2+}$ ***(1 mark for correct reactants and products, 1 mark for balancing)***

c) (i) A temperature of 298 K ***(1 mark)***. A pressure of 100 kPa ***(1 mark)***. Any solutions of ions have a concentration of 1.00 mol dm^{-3} ***(1 mark)***.
(ii) E.g. platinum is inert / platinum is a solid that conducts electricity ***(1 mark)***.

d) (i) +0.80 V ***(1 mark)***.
(ii) Silver is less reactive than vanadium ***(1 mark)*** because the Ag^+/Ag half-cell has a less negative electrode potential than the V^{2+}/V half-cell ***(1 mark)***.

7 a) $Li^+[CoO_2]^-{}_{(s)} \rightleftharpoons CoO_{2(s)} + Li_{(s)}$ ***(1 mark)***
b) The reactions that occur within them can be reversed if a current is supplied to force the electrons to flow in the opposite direction around the circuit ***(1 mark)***.

8 a) Place the flask containing the iodine solution produced by the reaction underneath a burette ***(1 mark)***. From the burette, add sodium thiosulfate solution to the flask drop by drop ***(1 mark)***. When the iodine colour fades to a pale yellow, add starch solution ***(1 mark)***. The solution in the conical flask will go dark blue, showing there's still some iodine there ***(1 mark)***. Add sodium thiosulfate one drop at a time until the blue colour disappears — this is the end point of the reaction ***(1 mark)***.

b) Moles $Na_2S_2O_3$ = (conc. × volume) ÷ 1000
= (0.500 × 23.6) ÷ 1000 = 0.0118 moles ***(1 mark)***.
Using the balanced equation given in the question, 1 mole of I_2 reacts with 2 moles of $Na_2S_2O_3$ and so 0.0118 moles of $Na_2S_2O_3$ must react with 0.0118 ÷ 2
= 0.0059 moles of I_2 ***(1 mark)***.
Using the balanced equation given in the question, 2 moles of Cu^{2+} will react to give 1 mole of I_2. So, 0.0059 moles of I_2 will be formed from 0.0059 × 2 = **0.0118 moles** of Cu^{2+} ***(1 mark)***.

c) mass = number of moles × M_r = 0.0118 × 63.5
= 0.7493 g of copper present in the brass ***(1 mark)***.
So, (0.7493 ÷ 1) × 100 = 74.93%. The brass is **74.9%** copper (to 3 s.f.) ***(1 mark)***.

Section 6 — Transition Elements

1. Transition Elements

Page 143 — Application Questions

Q1 a) [Ar]3d^{3}4s^2
b) [Ar]3d^{7}4s^2
c) [Ar]3d^{5}4s^2
d) [Ar]3d^{8}4s^2

For these questions you don't have to write [Ar]. Writing out the whole electron configuration starting from 1s^2 is fine too.

Q2 a) [Ar]3d^2
b) [Ar]3d^7
c) [Ar]3d^5
d) [Ar]3d^8

Don't forget, the s electrons are always removed first, then the d electrons.

e) [Ar]3d^4
f) [Ar]3d^1
g) [Ar]

Q3 Zinc has the electron configuration 1s^{2}2s^{2}2p^{6}3s^{2}3p^{6}3d^{10}4s^2. It can only form Zn^{2+} ions which have an electron configuration of 1s^{2}2s^{2}2p^{6}3s^{2}3p^{6}3d^{10}. This ion has a full d-subshell, so zinc cannot form a stable ion with a partially filled d-subshell and it therefore can't be a transition metal.

Page 143 — Fact Recall Questions

Q1 In the d-block.
Q2 A transition element is a d-block element that can form one or more stable ions with an incomplete d-subshell.

Q3 10

Q4 Electrons fill up the lowest energy subshells first and electrons fill orbitals singly before they start sharing.

Q5 a) Chromium prefers to have one electron in each orbital of the 3d subshell and just one in the 4s subshell because this gives it more stability.

b) Copper prefers to have a full 3d subshell and one electron in the 4s subshell because it's more stable that way.

2. Transition Element Properties

Page 145 — Fact Recall Questions

Q1 Any two from: e.g. they can form complex ions / they form coloured ions / they make good catalysts.

Q2 A — 3 B — 4 C — 2 D — 1

Q3 Iron

3. Complex Ions

Page 148 — Application Questions

Q1 a) Octahedral:

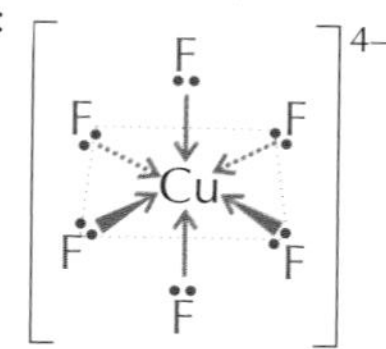

When you're drawing the shapes of ions and molecules make sure you include the dashed arrows and the wedged arrows to show that it's 3D.

b) Octahedral:

You could also draw this structure with the two ^-OH ligands next to each other. See page 150 for more on this.

c) Octahedral:

Q2 a) 6

b) 6

c) 6

Q3 a)

b) $[Cr(C_2O_4)_3]^{3-}$

Oxygen atoms are small so six of them will fit around a central metal ion and form coordinate bonds with it. This means that three molecules of $C_2O_4^{2-}$ will each form two coordinate bonds with the ion.

Q4 a) Square planar

b) or

Page 148 — Fact Recall Questions

Q1 a) An atom, ion or molecule that donates a pair of electrons to a central metal ion.

b) A covalent bond where both of the electrons in the shared pair come from the same atom, ion or molecule.

c) A metal ion surrounded by coordinately bonded ligands.

Q2 A ligand that can donate two lone pairs of electrons to a central metal ion to form two coordinate bonds.

Q3 E.g. $[Fe(H_2O)_6]^{2+}$ / $[Co(NH_3)_6]^{2+}$ / $[Cu(NH_3)_4(H_2O)_2]^{2+}$.

4. Isomerism in Complex Ions

Page 150 — Application Questions

Q1 a) *cis-trans* isomerism

b) optical isomerism

c) *cis-trans* isomerism

Q2 E.g. *cis*: *trans*:

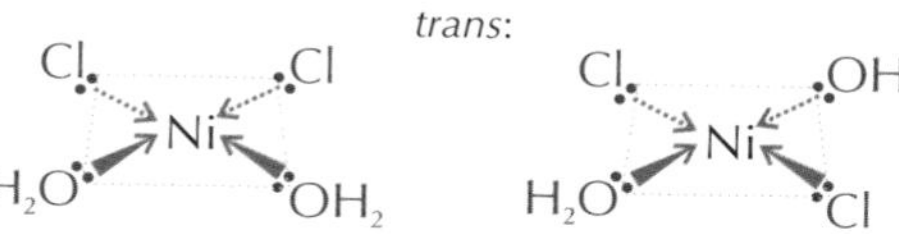

Page 150 — Fact Recall Questions

Q1 optical isomerism and *cis-trans* isomerism

Q2 a)

b) Cisplatin can bind to the DNA molecules in cancer cells and prevent them from dividing.

5. Ligand Substitution

Page 153 — Application Questions

Q1 a) octahedral

b) tetrahedral

Q2 $[Mn(H_2O)_6]^{2+}_{(aq)} + 4Cl^-_{(aq)} \rightleftharpoons [MnCl_4]^{2-}_{(aq)} + 6H_2O_{(l)}$

Q3 a) $[Cu(H_2O)_6]^{2+}_{(aq)} + 4OH^-_{(aq)} \rightarrow [Cu(OH)_4(H_2O)_2]^{2-}_{(aq)} + 4H_2O_{(l)}$

b) (elongated) octahedral

Page 153 — Fact Recall Questions

Q1 a) There will be no change in coordination number or shape but the colour may change.

b) There will be a change in coordination number and shape and the colour may change.

Q2 a) It helps transport oxygen around the body.

b) Four come from nitrogen atoms in the porphyrin ring, one comes from a nitrogen atom in a globin protein and one comes from either water or oxygen.

Q3 a) In the lungs, the concentration of oxygen is high. So water ligands that were bound to the haemoglobin are substituted for oxygen ligands, forming oxyhaemoglobin.

b) At sites where oxygen is needed the concentration of oxygen is low. So oxygen ligands that were bound to haemoglobin are substituted for water ligands, forming deoxyhaemoglobin.

Q4 Carbon monoxide is a very strong ligand for haemoglobin. When it is inhaled, it binds to the central Fe^{2+} ion and prevents it from binding to oxygen. As a result, oxygen can no longer be transported around the body.

6. Precipitation Reactions

Page 155 — Application Questions

Q1 E.g. the scientist could add aqueous sodium hydroxide / ammonia to the solution. If a green precipitate forms iron(II) ions are present. If an orange precipitate forms iron(III) ions are present.

Q2 $[Co(H_2O)_6]^{2+}_{(aq)} + 2NH_{3(aq)} \rightarrow Co(OH)_2(H_2O)_{4(s)} + 2NH_4{}^{+}{}_{(aq)}$

Page 155 — Fact Recall Questions

Q1 $[Cu(H_2O)_6]^{2+}_{(aq)} + 2OH^-_{(aq)} \rightarrow Cu(OH)_2(H_2O)_{4(s)} + 2H_2O_{(l)}$
OR $Cu^{2+}_{(aq)} + 2OH^-_{(aq)} \rightarrow Cu(OH)_{2(aq)}$

Q2 An orange precipitate would form in the yellow solution. The precipitate would darken on standing.

7. Transition Metals and Redox

Page 157 — Fact Recall Questions

Q1 E.g. acidified potassium manganate(VII) / $KMnO_4$

Q2 a) +3 to +6
b) dark green to yellow
c) dichromate(VI), $Cr_2O_7{}^{2-}$
d) yellow to orange

Q3 Disproportionation means something is oxidised and reduced at the same time. E.g. two Cu^+ ions can disproportionate to produce Cu and Cu^{2+}.

8. Tests for Ions

Page 159 — Application Questions

Q1 Cu^{2+} and $CO_3{}^{2-}$.
$Cu^{2+}_{(aq)}$ ions produce a blue precipitate when $NaOH_{(aq)}$ is added. $CO_3{}^{2-}$ ions produce carbon dioxide when dilute hydrochloric acid is added, which turns limewater cloudy.

Q2 Both students could be correct but neither has enough evidence to be sure of their conclusion — both sulfate and carbonate ions could produce a white precipitate when barium nitrate solution is added.

Page 159 — Fact Recall Questions

Q1 a) Mn^{2+} — pink / buff
b) Fe^{2+} — green
c) Cr^{3+} — grey-green

Q2 a) E.g. nitric acid or hydrochloric acid.
b) Nitric acid.

Q3 Blue.

Exam-style Questions — pages 161-163

1 C ***(1 mark)***.
The electron configuration of manganese is $1s^2\,2s^2\,2p^6\,3s^2\,3p^6\,3d^5\,4s^2$.

2 A ***(1 mark)***.
When chloride ions are added to $[Cu(H_2O)_6]^{2+}_{(aq)}$, $[CuCl_4]^{2-}$ is formed, which is yellow and tetrahedral.

3 D ***(1 mark)***.
Test 1 confirms that $Cr^{3+}_{(aq)}$ ions are present. Test 2 confirms that carbonate ions are not present. Test 3 confirms that chloride ions are present.

4 a) (i) pale blue ***(1 mark)***
(ii) Cu: $1s^22s^22p^63s^23p^63d^{10}4s^1$ ***(1 mark)***
Cu^{2+}: $1s^22s^22p^63s^23p^63d^9$ ***(1 mark)***
(iii) Cu^{2+} has the characteristic chemical properties of transition element ions because it has a partially filled d-subshell ***(1 mark)***.

b) (i) A ligand is a species that donates an electron pair to form a coordinate bond with a central metal ion ***(1 mark)***.

(ii)

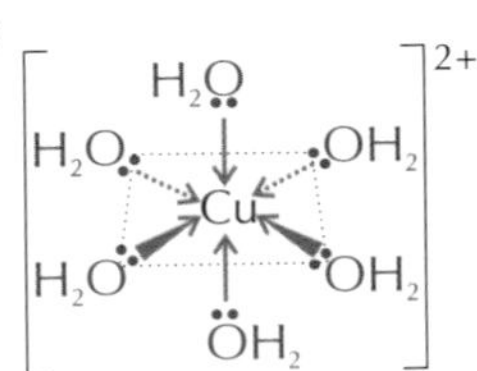

(1 mark)

Don't forget to include the charge on the complex ion when you're drawing its structure.

The shape of $[Cu(H_2O)_6]^{2+}$ is octahedral ***(1 mark)***.

(iii) 6 ***(1 mark)***

5 a) (i) square planar ***(1 mark)***
(ii) *cis-trans* isomerism ***(1 mark)***
(iii)

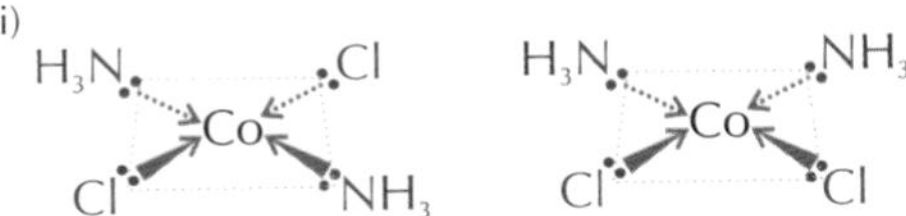

(1 mark for each correctly drawn isomer)

b) (i) optical isomerism ***(1 mark)***
(ii) The oxygen atoms have lone pairs of electrons ***(1 mark)*** which they can donate to the chromium(III) ion to form coordinate bonds ***(1 mark)***.
(iii)

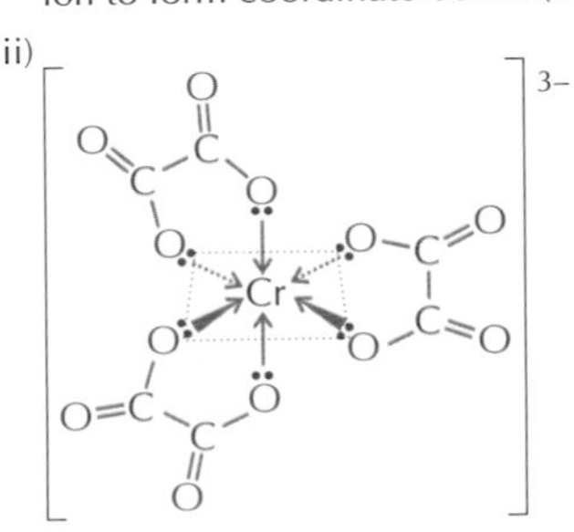

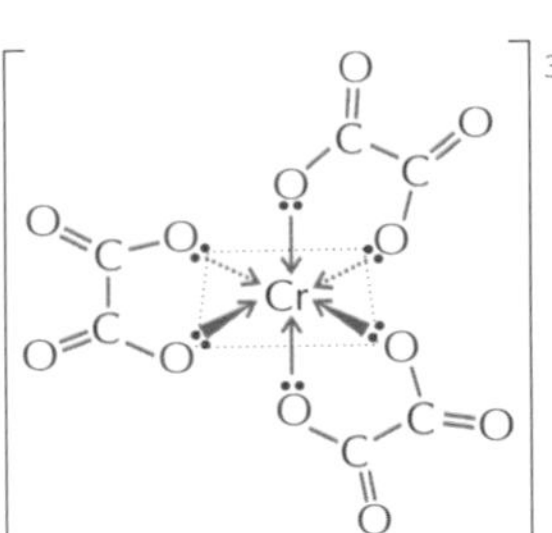

(1 mark for each correctly drawn isomer. The structures must be shown as 3D, i.e. with wedged and dotted bonds)

These are fiendishly difficult isomers to draw so don't worry if you've messed up your first few attempts. Make sure you get lots of practice drawing them before the exam and you'll be fine.

6 a) A transition element is an element that can form one or more stable ions with a partially filled d-subshell ***(1 mark)***.

b) (i) $[Fe(H_2O)_6]^{2+}_{(aq)} + 2OH^-_{(aq)} \rightarrow Fe(OH)_2(H_2O)_{4(s)}$
OR $Fe^{2+}_{(aq)} + 2OH^-_{(aq)} \rightarrow Fe(OH)_{2\,(s)}$ ***(1 mark)***
(ii) green ***(1 mark)***

c) (i) $[Fe(H_2O)_6]^{2+}_{(aq)} + 4Cl^-_{(aq)} \rightarrow [FeCl_4]^{2-}_{(aq)} + 6H_2O_{(l)}$
(1 mark for correct products, 1 mark for correctly balanced equation)

(ii)

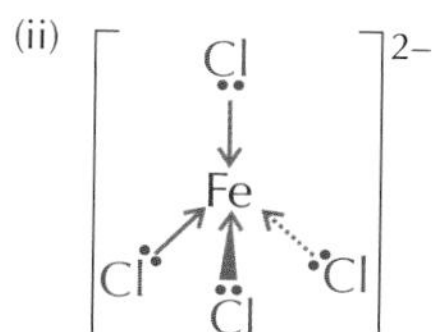

(1 mark)

You need to draw the structure in 3D, with wedged and dashed bonds to get the mark here.

(iii) $[Fe(H_2O)_6]^{2+}_{(aq)} + 6CN^-_{(aq)} \rightarrow [Fe(CN)_6]^{4-}_{(aq)} + 6H_2O_{(l)}$ ***(1 mark)***

(iv) The coordination number doesn't change because there are 6 ligands bonded to the Fe^{2+} before the reaction and 6 ligands bonded afterwards ***(1 mark)***. The shape of the complex ion doesn't change because the CN^- and H_2O ligands are similar sizes ***(1 mark)***. The colour of the complex ion may change as there has been a change in the type of ligand bonded to the Fe^{2+} ***(1 mark)***.

7 a) (i) By adding excess aqueous sodium hydroxide ***(1 mark)***.

(ii) $[Cr(H_2O)_6]^{3+} + 6OH^- \rightarrow [Cr(OH)_6]^{3-} + 6H_2O$ OR $Cr^{3+}_{(aq)} + 6OH^- \rightarrow [Cr(OH)_6]^{3-} + 6H_2O$ ***(1 mark)***

b) (i) $3H_2O_2 + 2Cr(OH)_6^{3-} \rightarrow 2OH^- + 2CrO_4^{2-} + 8H_2O$ ***(1 mark)***

(ii) 6 ***(1 mark)***

(iii) dark green → yellow ***(1 mark)***

(iv) Add dilute sulfuric acid ***(1 mark)***.

Module 6

Section 1 — Aromatic Compounds and Carbonyls

1. Benzene

Page 167 — Application Questions

Q1 a) 1,2-dinitrobenzene

b) 4-methylphenol

c) 2,4,6-trichlorophenylamine

Q2 a) Kekulé proposed that the structure of benzene was a ring of six carbons joined by alternating double and single bonds. He later adapted his model to say that the benzene molecule was constantly flipping between two isomers.

b) The $\Delta H^{\circ}_{hydrogenation}$ for cyclohexene is –120 kJ mol^{-1}. So if benzene had three double bonds you would expect it to have a $\Delta H^{\circ}_{hydrogenation}$ of –360 kJ mol^{-1}. But, $\Delta H^{\circ}_{hydrogenation}$ for benzene is only –208 kJ mol^{-1}. This is far less exothermic than expected, so benzene must be more stable than the proposed Kekulé structure and the Kekulé model cannot be correct.

Page 167 — Fact Recall Questions

Q1 According to the delocalised model, the p-orbitals of all six carbon atoms overlap to create a π-system. This is made up of two ring-shaped clouds of electrons — one above and one below the plane of the six carbon atoms. All the bonds in the ring are the same and so are the same length.

Q2 If the Kekulé model were correct, half of the bonds in benzene would be the length of C=C double bonds (134 pm) and the other half would be the length of C–C single bonds (154 pm). But X-ray diffraction studies have shown that all the bonds in benzene are the same length (140 pm — between that of single and double bonds). So this is evidence for the delocalised model.

Q3 Compounds that contain a benzene ring.

2. Reactions of Benzene

Page 171 — Application Questions

Q1 a) Cl–Cl + [1,3-dimethylbenzene] → [2-chloro-1,3-dimethylbenzene] + HCl

b) E.g. $AlCl_3$ / $FeCl_3$ / Fe.

c) E.g. $AlCl_3Cl^{\delta-}$–$Cl^{\delta+}$ + [1,3-dimethylbenzene] → [intermediate: Cl–, H, +] → HCl + $AlCl_3$ + [2-chloro-1,3-dimethylbenzene]

You could use another halogen carrier here (like Fe or $FeCl_3$) instead of $AlCl_3$.

Q2 a) [benzene] + NO_2^+ → [intermediate: H, NO_2, +] → [nitrobenzene] + H^+

b) An H_2SO_4 catalyst and a temperature below 55 °C.

Q3 a) [CH_3, O_2N, NO_2, NO_2 — 2,4,6-trinitromethylbenzene]

b) The scientist needs to carry out the reaction at a temperature above 55 °C. Below this temperature he will only achieve mononitration.

Page 171 — Fact Recall Questions

Q1 In alkenes, the C=C bond is a localised area of high electron density. It attracts an electrophile, which adds to the C=C double bond, forming a stable alkane. The delocalised electrons in benzene make the benzene ring very stable, and spread out the negative charge. So benzene is very unwilling to undergo addition reactions which would destroy the stable ring.

Q2 Aromatic compounds contain a benzene ring, which is a region of high electron density. Electrophiles are electron deficient so are attracted to the regions of high electron density found in aromatic compounds.

Q3 a) Any two from, e.g. $AlCl_3$ / Fe / $FeCl_3$.

b) Br_2 isn't a strong enough electrophile to react with the benzene ring on its own.

A halogen carrier will accept a lone pair of electrons from one of the bromine atoms, forming a polarised molecule, which is a much stronger electrophile than the original. This species is strong enough to react with the benzene ring.

Q4 $HNO_3 + H_2SO_4 \rightarrow HSO_4^- + NO_2^+ + H_2O$

3. Friedel-Crafts

Page 173 — Application Question

Q1 a) H–C(=O)–Cl + benzene → benzene–CHO + HCl

b) $AlCl_3$

c) Electrophilic substitution.

$CHOCl + AlCl_3 \rightarrow CHO^+ + AlCl_4^-$

You could draw the mechanism out with arrows or just show the equation (like above) for the first part of the mechanism.

$$\text{benzene} + H\text{–}\overset{+}{C}\text{=O} \rightarrow [\text{intermediate}] + AlCl_4^- \rightarrow C_6H_5CHO + HCl + AlCl_3$$

Page 173 — Fact Recall Questions

Q1 Friedel-Crafts reactions are important to synthesis because they allow the formation of C-C bonds to an aromatic ring to happen.

Q2 $AlCl_3$ acts as a halogen carrier. It catalyses the reaction by accepting a lone pair from the acyl chloride. This increases the polarisation of the acyl chloride, and makes it a stronger electrophile so it can react with the benzene ring.

4. Substituted Benzene Rings

Page 177 — Application Questions

Q1 a) 4-bromophenol

b) 3-methyl-5-nitrophenol

This isn't called 3-nitro-5-methylphenol because methyl comes before nitro alphabetically.

c) 3,5-dimethylphenol

d) 4-chloro-3,5-dimethylphenol

This isn't called 3,5-dimethyl-4-chlorophenol because chloro comes before methyl alphabetically.

Q2 a) 4-bromophenol (OH, Br) + NaOH → (O^-Na^+, Br) + H_2O

b) 3-methyl-5-nitrophenol (OH, H_3C, NO_2) + NaOH → (O^-Na^+, H_3C, NO_2) + H_2O

c) 3,5-dimethylphenol (OH, H_3C, CH_3) + NaOH → (O^-Na^+, H_3C, CH_3) + H_2O

d) 4-chloro-3,5-dimethylphenol (OH, H_3C, CH_3, Cl) + NaOH → (O^-Na^+, H_3C, CH_3, Cl) + H_2O

Q3 Nothing would happen.

Sodium carbonate isn't a strong enough base to react with 2-methylphenol.

Q4 benzene ring with CF_3, F, F (1-CF_3, 3-F, 5-F)

Page 177 — Fact Recall Questions

Q1 In benzene the p-orbital electrons are delocalised. This makes the benzene ring very stable so it is unwilling to undergo addition reactions with halogens. In phenol, one of the lone pairs of electrons in a p-orbital of the oxygen atom overlaps with the delocalised ring of electrons and is partially delocalised into the ring. This increases the electron density of the ring. This higher electron density means that phenol can polarise Br_2 and cause a reaction. (Benzene can't polarise Br_2 so no reaction occurs).

Q2 phenol ring with OH, Br, Br, Br (2,4,6-tribromophenol)

Q3 a) E.g. $-NO_2$

b) E.g. $-OH$, $-NH_2$

5. Aldehydes and Ketones

Page 179 — Application Questions

Q1 a) butan-2-one / butanone

You don't really need to say which carbon the functional group is on here, because it has to be carbon-2 — but in exams it's best to use the full systematic name (butan-2-one) to make sure you get the marks.

b) 2-ethyl-3-methylbutanal

Q2 2-ethyl-3-methylbutanal can be oxidised to 2-ethyl-3-methylbutanoic acid.

Q3 **C** and **D**

Q4 $CH_3CHO + [O] \rightarrow CH_3COOH$

Page 179 — Fact Recall Questions

Q1 Aldehydes have the carbonyl group at the end of the carbon chain, ketones have the carbonyl group in the middle of the carbon chain.

Q2 $Cr_2O_7^{2-}$

Q3 A carboxylic acid.

6. Reducing Carbonyls

Page 181 — Application Questions

Q1 a)

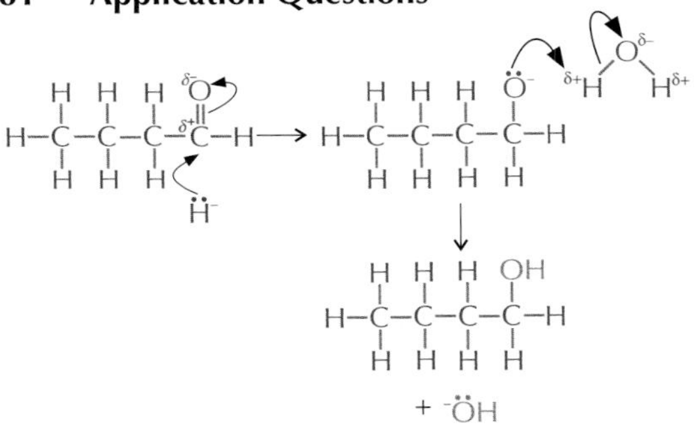

```
H  H  H  δ-O                 H  H  H  Ö-   δ+H  O δ-  Hδ+
|  |  |    ||                |  |  |  |
H-C--C--C--δ+C-H  ──>  H-C--C--C--C-H
|  |  |                      |  |  |  |
H  H  H   :H-                H  H  H  H
                                  ↓
                             H  H  H  OH
                             |  |  |  |
                           H-C--C--C--C-H
                             |  |  |  |
                             H  H  H  H
                               + -:ÖH
```

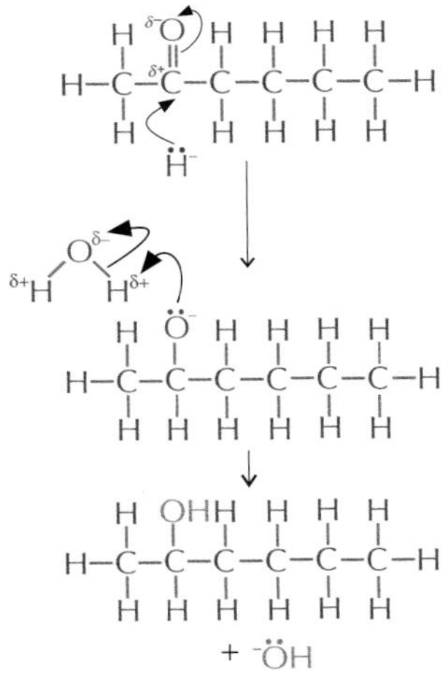

b)

```
H  δ-O  H  H  H  H
|   ||  |  |  |  |
H-C--δ+C--C--C--C--C-H
|       |  |  |  |
H  :H-  H  H  H  H
         ↓
δ+H  O δ-  Hδ+
H  Ö-  H  H  H  H
|  |   |  |  |  |
H-C--C--C--C--C--C-H
|  |   |  |  |  |
H  H   H  H  H  H
         ↓
H  OH  H  H  H  H
|  |   |  |  |  |
H-C--C--C--C--C--C-H
|  |   |  |  |  |
H  H   H  H  H  H
     + -:ÖH
```

c)

```
H  H  δ-O  H  H                  H  H  Ö-  H  H    δ+H  O δ-  Hδ+
|  |   ||  |  |                  |  |  |   |  |
H-C--C--δ+C--C--C-H  ──>  H-C--C--C--C--C-H
|  |       |  |                  |  |  |   |  |
H  H  :H-  H  H                  H  H  H   H  H
                                        ↓
                                 H  H  OH  H  H
                                 |  |  |   |  |
                               H-C--C--C--C--C-H
                                 |  |  |   |  |
                                 H  H  H   H  H
                                     + -:ÖH
```

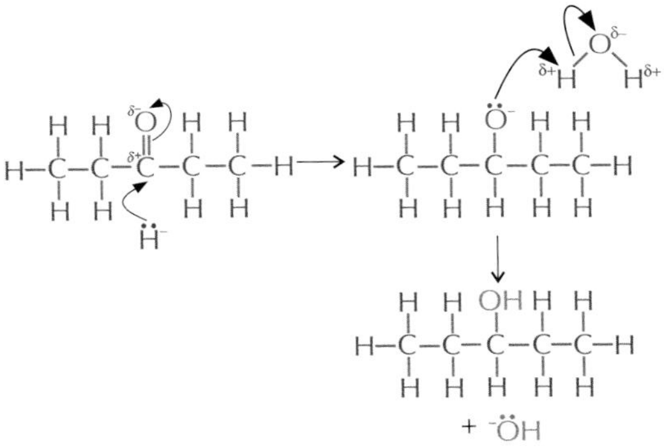

d)

```
                              δ+H  O δ-  Hδ+
H3C  H  δ-O                   H3C  H  Ö-
|    |   ||                   |    |  |
H-C--C--δ+C-H  ──>  H-C--C--C-H
|    |                        |    |  |
H3C  CH2   :H-                H3C  CH2 H
     |                             |
     CH3                           CH3
                                    ↓
                              H3C  H  OH
                              |    |  |
                            H-C--C--C-H
                              |    |  |
                              H3C  CH2 H        + -:ÖH
                                   |
                                   CH3
```

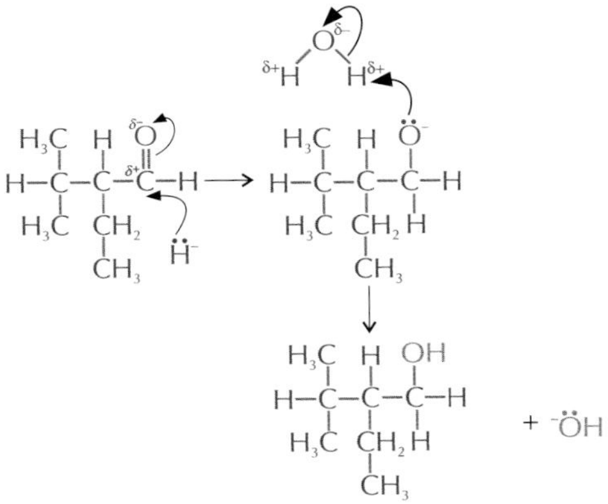

Q2 $CH_3COCH_2CH_2CH_3 + 2[H] \rightarrow CH_3CHOHCH_2CH_2CH_3$

Q3 $CHOCH(CH_3)CH_2CH_2CH_2CH_3 + 2[H] \rightarrow$
$CH_2OHCH(CH_3)CH_2CH_2CH_2CH_3$

Q4 $CH_3COCH_2COCH_3 + 4[H] \rightarrow CH_3CHOHCH_2CHOHCH_3$
This molecule started off with two ketone groups — so when it's reduced it will end up with two alcohol groups.

Q5 $CH_3COCH(CH_3)CHO$
This is tricky — it's all about working out that molecule X must have both a ketone group and an aldehyde group if it's going to produce the molecule given in the question.

Page 181 — Fact Recall Questions

Q1 E.g. $NaBH_4$

Q2 a ketone

Q3 nucleophilic addition

7. Reactions with Carbonyls

Page 184 — Application Questions

Q1 a)

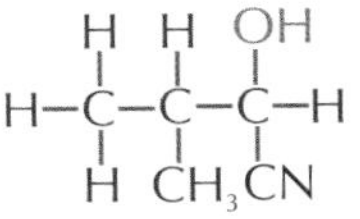

```
  H  H  OH
  |  |  |
H-C--C--C-H
  |  |  |
  H  CH3 CN
```

b)

```
  H  H  δ-O                    H  H  Ö-      H+
  |  |   ||                    |  |  |
H-C--C--δ+C-H  ──>  H-C--C--C-H
  |  |                         |  |  |
  H  CH3   :CN-                H  CH3 CN
                                  ↓
                               H  H  OH
                               |  |  |
                             H-C--C--C-H
                               |  |  |
                               H  CH3 CN
```

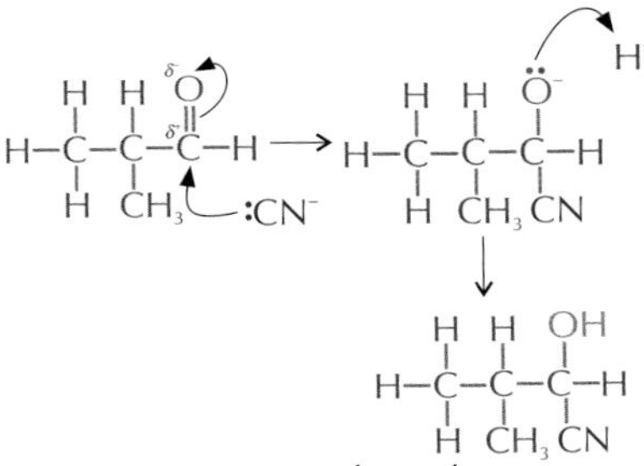

Q2 a) (i) orange precipitate formed
(ii) nothing happens
b) (i) silver mirror formed
(ii) nothing happens

Page 184 — Fact Recall Questions

Q1 carbonyl groups in aldehydes and ketones

Q2 When reacted with Brady's reagent, carbonyl compounds form derivatives of 2,4-DNPH. Each different carbonyl compound produces a crystalline derivative with a different melting point. So if you measure the melting point of the crystals and compare it against the known melting points of the derivatives, you can identify the carbonyl compound.

Q3 A solution of silver nitrate ($AgNO_3$) dissolved in aqueous ammonia.

Q4 Ag^+

8. Carboxylic Acids

Page 186 — Application Questions

Q1 a) (i) methanoic acid
(ii) 2-ethyl-4-hydroxypentanoic acid
b) $2HCOOH_{(aq)} + Mg_{(s)} \rightarrow (HCOO)_2Mg_{(aq)} + H_{2(g)}$
c) $2CH_3CHOHCH_2CH(C_2H_5)COOH_{(aq)} + Na_2CO_{3(s)} \rightarrow$
$2CH_3CHOHCH_2CH(C_2H_5)COONa_{(aq)} + H_2O_{(l)} + CO_{2(g)}$

Q2 $CH_3CH_2CH(CH_3)COOH_{(aq)} + NaOH_{(aq)} \rightarrow$
$CH_3CH_2CH(CH_3)COONa_{(aq)} + H_2O_{(l)}$

Page 186 — Fact Recall Questions

Q1 –COOH

Q2 Ethanoic acid is a polar molecule so it can form hydrogen bonds with water molecules. This means that it will easily dissolve in water.

Q3 A gas (hydrogen) would bubble out of the solution.

9. Acyl Chlorides

Page 188 — Application Questions

Q1 a) methanoyl chloride
b) propanoyl chloride
c) 2-methylpropanoyl chloride

Q2 a) $CHOCl + CH_3OH \rightarrow HCOOCH_3 + HCl$
b) $C_3H_5OCl + H_2O \rightarrow C_2H_5COOH + HCl$
c) $C_4H_7OCl + NH_3 \rightarrow C_3H_7CONH_2 + HCl$

Page 188 — Fact Recall Questions

Q1 $C_nH_{2n-1}OCl$

Q2 $CH_3COOH + SOCl_2 \rightarrow CH_3COCl + SO_2 + HCl$

Q3 a) A carboxylic acid and HCl.
b) An ester and HCl.
c) A primary amide and HCl.
d) A secondary amide and HCl.

10. Esters

Page 190 — Application Question

Q1 a) (i) methyl methanoate
(ii) ethyl benzoate
b) (i) methanol and methanoic acid
(ii) ethanol and benzoic acid

Page 191 — Application Questions

Q1 $CH_3CH_2CH_2OH + CH_3CH_2CH_2CH_2COOH \overset{H^+}{\rightleftharpoons} CH_3CH_2CH_2CH_2COOCH_2CH_2CH_3 + H_2O$

Q2 $HCOOCHO + CH_3CH_2CH_2CH_2OH \rightarrow CH_3CH_2CH_2CH_2OOCH_3 + HCOOH$

Page 192 — Application Question

Q1 a) $CH_3CH_2COOCH_3 + H_2O \overset{H^+}{\rightarrow} CH_3CH_2COOH + CH_3OH$
b) $CH_3CH_2COOCH_3 + OH^- \rightarrow CH_3CH_2COO^- + CH_3OH$
If you'd written an equation including the sodium from the sodium hydroxide that would have been fine here too ($CH_3CH_2COOCH_3 + NaOH \rightarrow CH_3CH_2COONa + CH_3OH$).

Page 192 — Fact Recall Question

Q1 a) A carboxylic acid and an alcohol.
b) A carboxylate salt and an alcohol.

Exam-style Questions — pages 194-196

Q1 C ***(1 mark)***

Q2 C ***(1 mark)***

Q3 D ***(1 mark)***

Q4 A ***(1 mark)***

Q5 a) (i) E.g. $AlCl_3$ / $FeCl_3$ / Fe ***(1 mark)***.
You could write down any correct halogen carrier here and get the mark.
(ii) The Cl_2 isn't a strong enough electrophile to react with the benzene ring by itself ***(1 mark)***. The halogen carrier (Catalyst X) pulls electrons away from the chlorine and forms a permanent dipole ***(1 mark)***. This makes the chlorine a much stronger electrophile and gives it a strong enough charge to react with the benzene ring ***(1 mark)***.
b) (i) $HNO_3 + H_2SO_4 \rightarrow HSO_4^- + NO_2^+ + H_2O$ ***(1 mark)***
(ii)

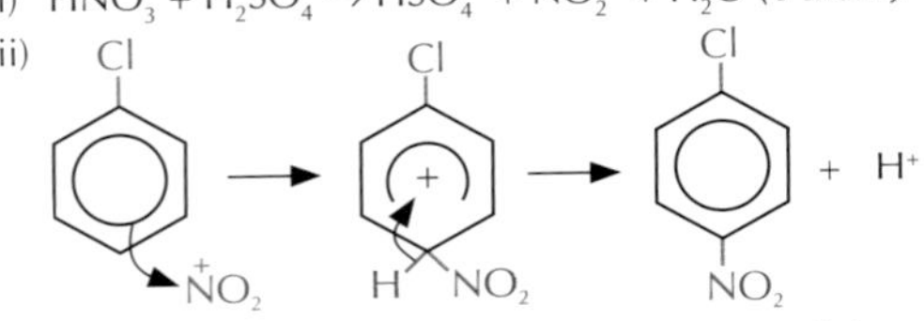

(1 mark for each correct curly arrow, 1 mark for correct intermediate, 1 mark for correct products)
(iii) 1-chloro-4-nitrobenzene ***(1 mark)***

Q6 a) molecule X — propanal ***(1 mark)***
molecule Y — propanoic acid ***(1 mark)***
molecule Z — propanone ***(1 mark)***
b) (i) E.g. $NaBH_4$ / sodium tetrahydridoborate(III) / sodium borohydride ***(1 mark)***.
(ii)

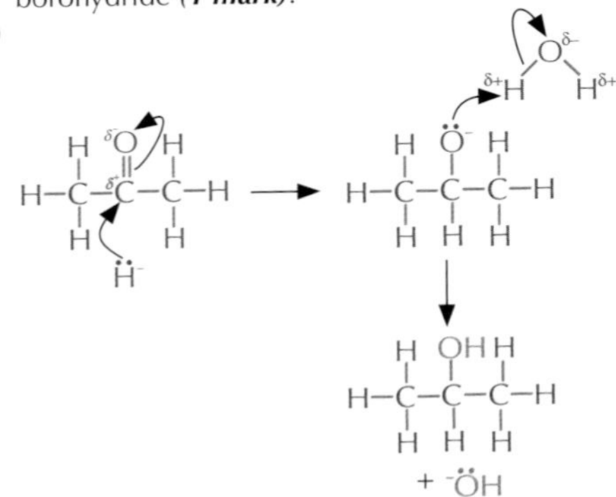

(1 mark for each correct curly arrow)
(iii) $CH_3COCH_3 + 2[H] \rightarrow CH_3CHOHCH_3$
(1 mark for correct products, 1 mark for correctly balanced equation)
c) (i) Molecule Y is polar because electrons are drawn from the carbon to the more electronegative oxygen atom ***(1 mark)***. This means that molecule Y can form hydrogen bonds with water molecules and so will be soluble ***(1 mark)***.
(ii) $2CH_3CH_2COOH_{(aq)} + Na_2CO_{3(s)} \rightarrow 2CH_3CH_2COONa_{(aq)} + H_2O_{(l)} + CO_{2(g)}$
(1 mark for correct products, 1 mark for correctly balanced equation)
d) E.g. acidified potassium dichromate(VI)/$K_2Cr_2O_7$ / H_2SO_4 ***(1 mark)***.
e) Molecule X (an aldehyde) will form a silver mirror with Tollens' reagent and an orange precipitate with Brady's reagent ***(1 mark)***. Molecule Y (a carboxylic acid) will not react with either reagent ***(1 mark)***. Molecule Z (a ketone) will form an orange precipitate with Brady's reagent but will not react with Tollens' reagent ***(1 mark)***.

7 a)

```
  H  H  O
  |  |  ||
H–C––C––C–OH
  |  |
  H  CH3
```

(1 mark)

b) (i)

```
  H  H   O      H
  |  |  //      |
H–C––C––C       |
  |  |   \      |
  H  CH3  O––C––H
                |
                H
```

(1 mark)

(ii) methyl 2-methylpropanoate (*1 mark)*
(iii) Any strong acid (e.g. $HCl/H_2SO_4/H_3PO_4$) (*1 mark).*
(iv)

$$CH_3CH(CH_3)COOCH_3 + OH^- \xrightarrow{\text{reflux}} CH_3CH(CH_3)COO^- + CH_3OH$$

(1 mark for correct equation, 1 mark for correct structure of products).

Section 2 — Nitrogen Compounds and Polymers

1. Amines and Amides

Page 200 — Application Questions

Q1 a) ethylamine
b) dipropylamine
c) ethyldimethylamine

Q2 $N(CH_3)_3 + HCl \rightarrow HN(CH_3)_3{}^+Cl^-$

Q3 $CH_3Cl + 2NH_3 \rightarrow CH_3NH_2 + NH_4{}^+Cl^-$

Q4 (methylnitrobenzene) + 6[H] $\xrightarrow[\text{2. NaOH}_{(aq)}]{\text{1. Sn, conc. HCl, reflux}}$ (methylphenylamine) + $2H_2O$

Page 200 — Fact Recall Questions

Q1 A tertiary amine is an organic molecule that consists of a nitrogen atom with three organic groups attached.

Q2 E.g. amines can act as proton acceptors by forming a dative bond with an H^+ ion. / Amines can donate their lone pair of electrons to an H^+ ion forming a dative covalent bond.

Q3 a) Heat the haloalkane with an excess of ethanolic ammonia.
b) More than one hydrogen on the nitrogen atom from ammonia can be substituted, so a mixture of primary, secondary and tertiary amines and quaternary ammonium ions is produced.

Q4 Take an aromatic nitro compound (e.g. nitrobenzene). Heat the nitro compound with tin metal and concentrated HCl under reflux to form a salt. Mix the salt with an alkali (e.g. NaOH) to produce an aromatic amine.

Q5 $-CONH_2$

2. Amino Acids

Page 202 — Application Question

Q1 a) $H_2N{-}CH(CH(CH_3)_2){-}COOH + NaOH \rightarrow H_2N{-}CH(CH(CH_3)_2){-}COO^-Na^+ + H_2O$

b) $H_2N{-}CH(CH(CH_3)_2){-}COOH + HBr \rightarrow Br^-\ H_3N^+{-}CH(CH(CH_3)_2){-}COOH$

c) $H_2N{-}CH(CH(CH_3)_2){-}COOH + CH_3CH(CH_3)CH_2OH \xrightarrow{H_2SO_4} H_2N{-}CH(CH(CH_3)_2){-}COOCH_2CH(CH_3)CH_3 + H_2O$

Page 202 — Fact Recall Questions

Q1 $RCH(NH_2)COOH$

Q2 Carboxyl groups (COOH) and amine groups (NH_2).

Q3 $H_2N{-}CH(R){-}COOH$

3. Chirality

Page 206 — Application Questions

Q1 a) 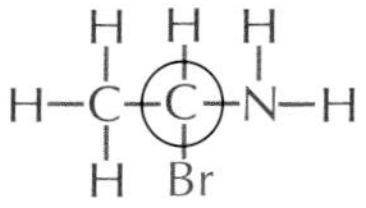 b) 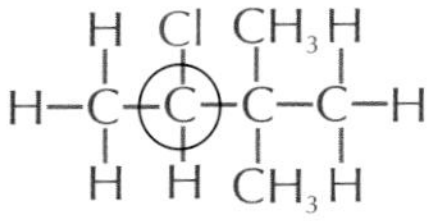 c) 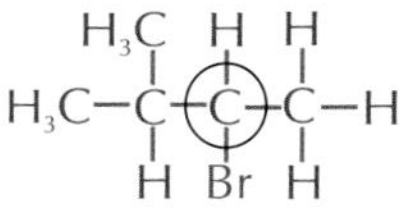 d)

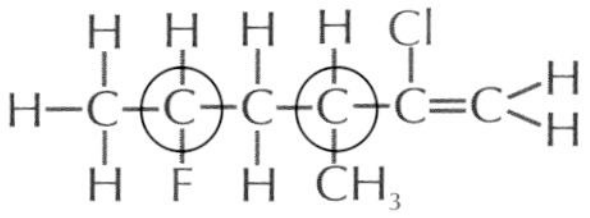

Q2 a) 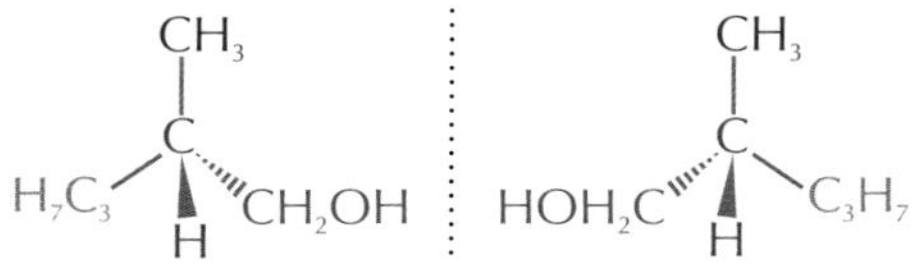 b) 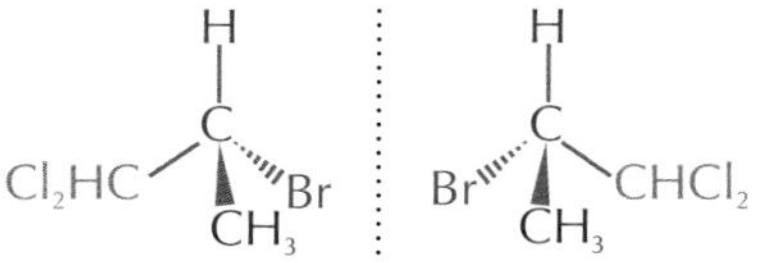 c) 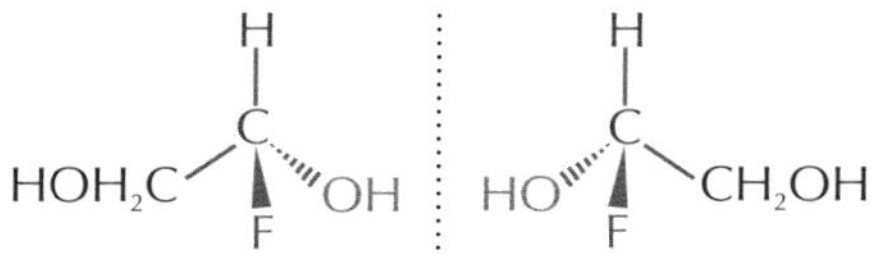 d)

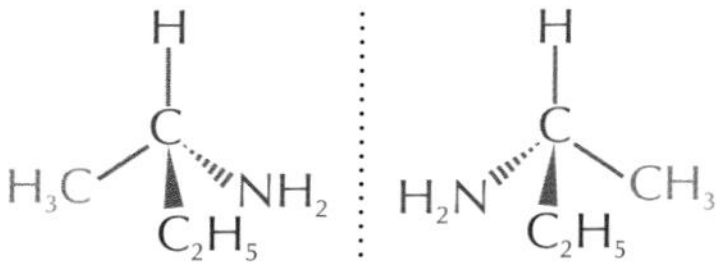

Q3

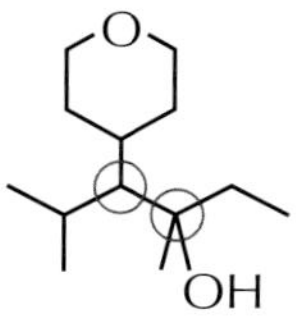

Q4

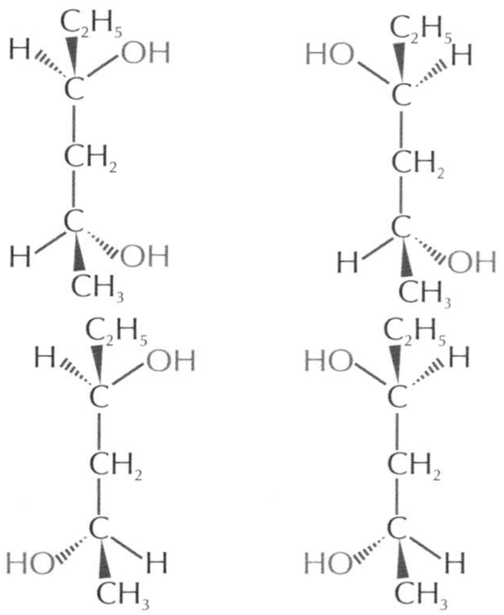

Q5

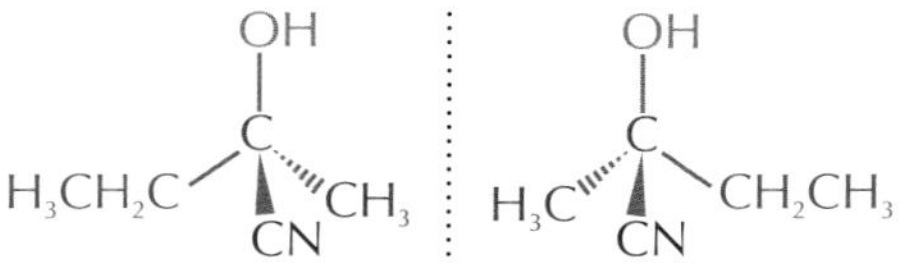

Page 206 — Fact Recall Questions

Q1 A molecule that has the same structural formula as another molecule but its atoms are arranged differently in space.

Q2 Optical isomerism is a type of stereoisomerism.
In optical isomers four groups are arranged in two different ways around a central carbon atom so that two different molecules are made — these molecules are non-superimposable mirror images of each other and are called enantiomers or optical isomers.

Q3 A chiral carbon atom is one that has four different groups attached to it.

4. Addition Polymers

Page 208 — Application Questions

Q1 a) 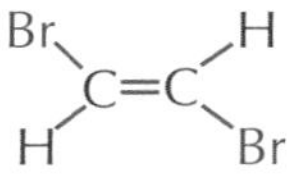 b) 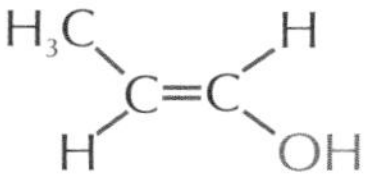 c)

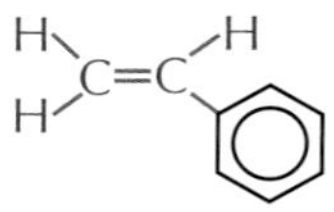

Q2 a) 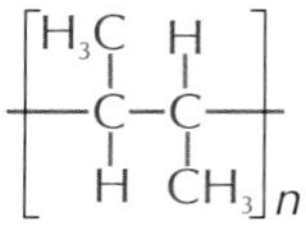 b) 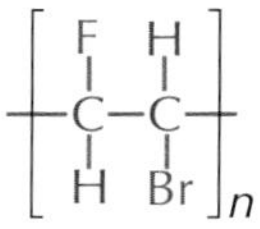 c)

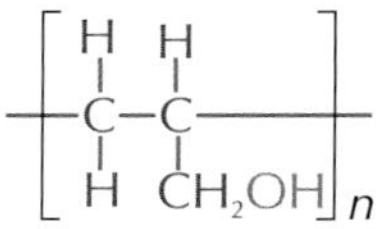

Q3

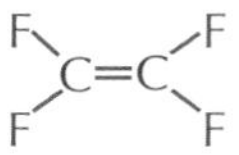

Page 208 — Fact Recall Questions

Q1 alkenes or substituted alkenes

Q2 addition polymerisation

Q3 A bit of molecule that repeats over and over again.

5. Condensation Polymers

Pages 214-215 — Application Questions

Q1 a) polyamide

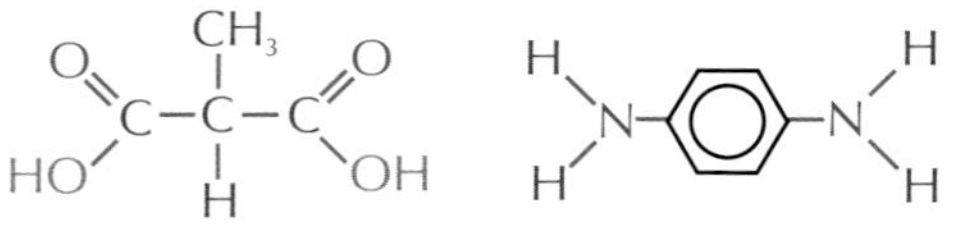

b) polyester

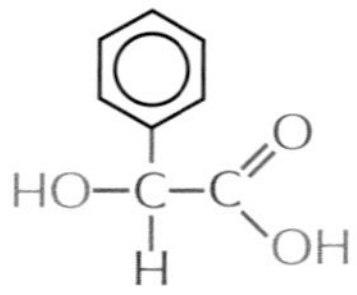

c) polyamide

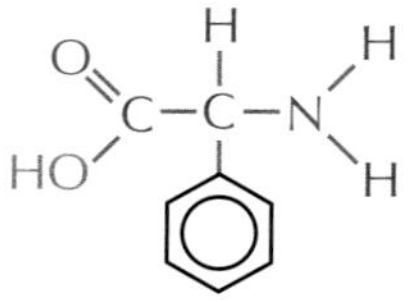

d) polyamide

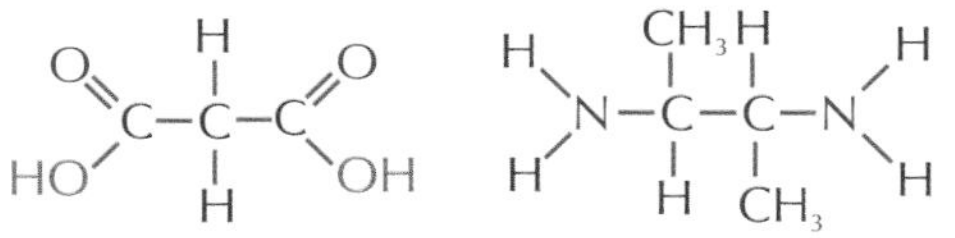

e) polyester

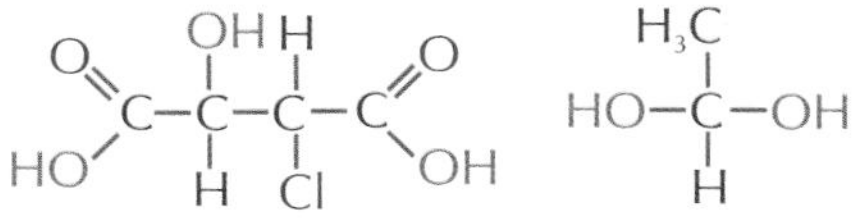

Q2 a) $+ 2nH_2O$

$H_2SO_{4(aq)}$

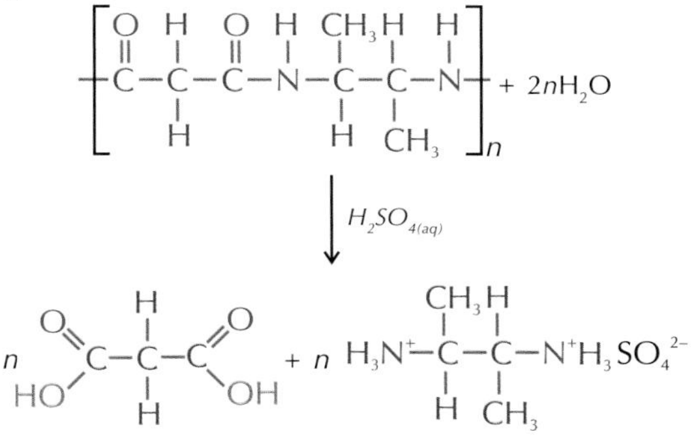

b) $+ 2nH_2O$

H_2SO_4

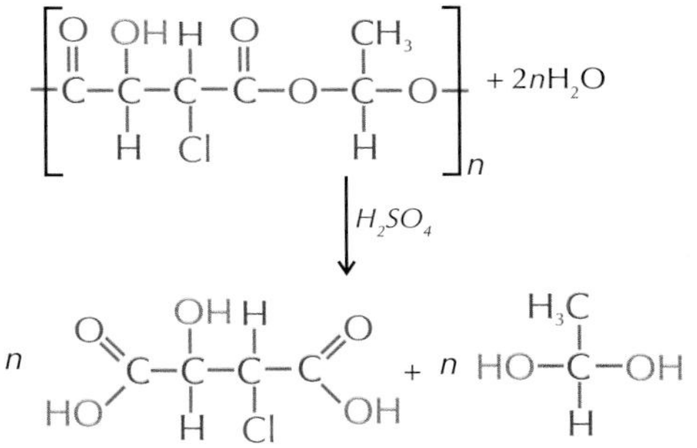

Q3 a) $+ 2nNaOH$

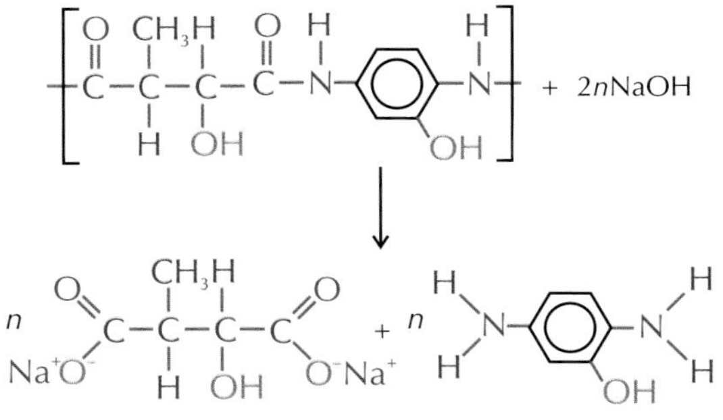

b) $+ 2nNaOH$

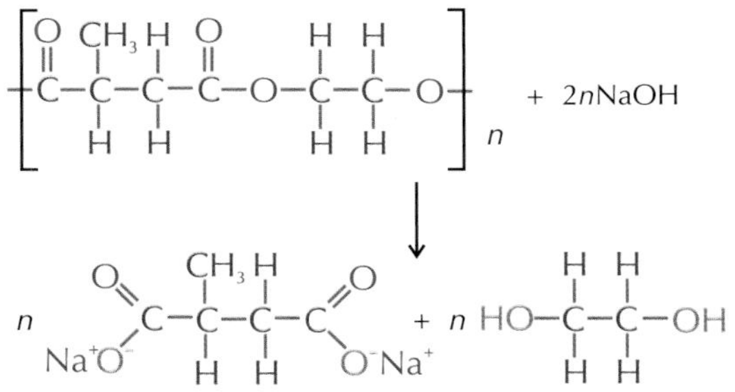

Q4 a)

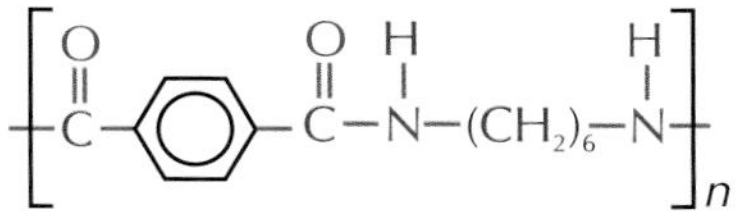

b)

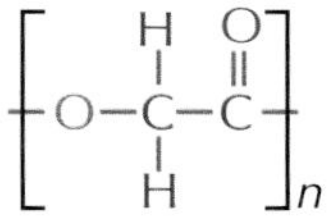

c)

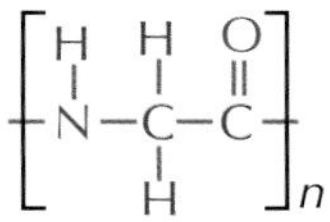

d)

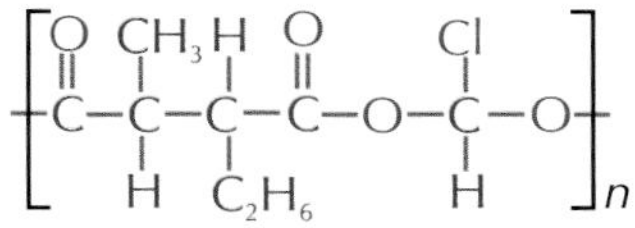

Page 215 — Fact Recall Questions

Q1 water

Q2 a) E.g. dicarboxylic acids and diamines.
b) E.g. dicarboxylic acids and diols.

Q3 a) amide links
b) ester links

Q4 Hydrolysis with just water is slow so an acid or an alkali is added to speed up the reaction.

Q5 E.g. a diol and a dicarboxylic acid salt.

Exam Style Questions — Pages 217-219

1 D ***(1 mark)***

2 C ***(1 mark)***

3 B ***(1 mark)***

4 a) (i) A and C are α-amino acids ***(1 mark)***, because they have their carboxyl group and amino group attached to the same carbon ***(1 mark)***.
(ii) $RCH(NH_2)COOH$ ***(1 mark)***

b) (i)

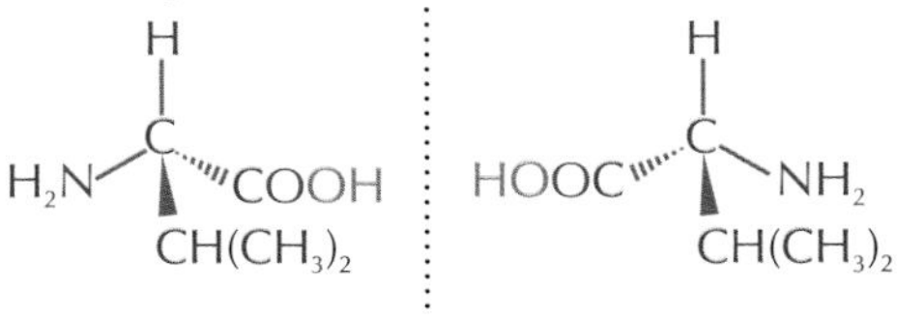

(1 mark for each correctly drawn isomer)

(ii)

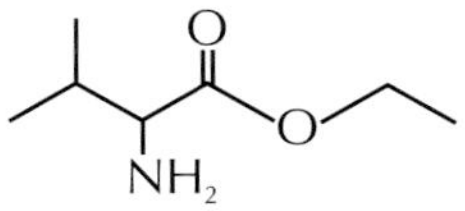

(1 mark)

c) (i) condensation polymerisation ***(1 mark)***
(ii)

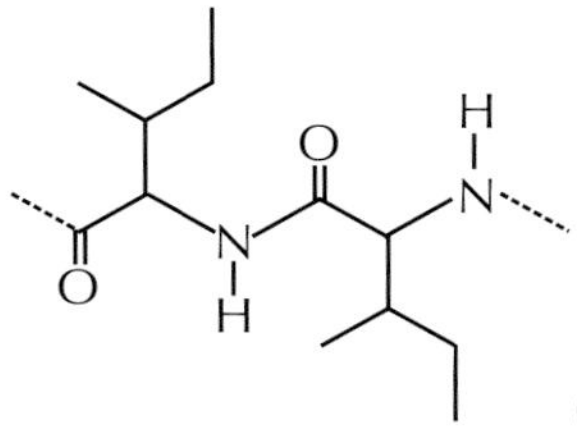

(1 mark)

The dotted lines show that the section is part of a longer polymer. You could also have drawn a displayed formula here. As long as you show the structure correctly, any type of drawing will do.

(iii) E.g. water and an alkali catalyst ***(1 mark)***.

5 a) (i) Stereoisomers are molecules with the same structural formula, but different arrangements of atoms in space ***(1 mark)***. 2-methyl-2-penten-4-ol shows optical isomerism ***(1 mark)***.

(ii) It has a chiral centre ***(1 mark)***.

(iii)

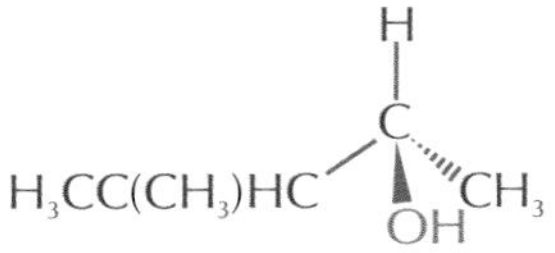

(1 mark)

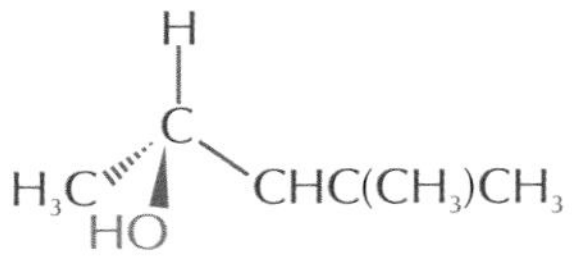

(1 mark)

b)

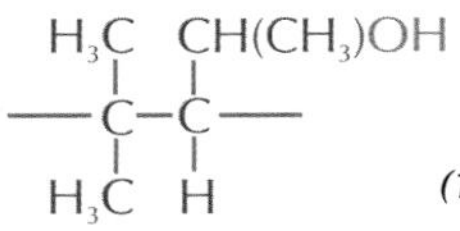

(1 mark)

c) Yes because it has a chiral carbon atom ***(1 mark)***.

d) (i)

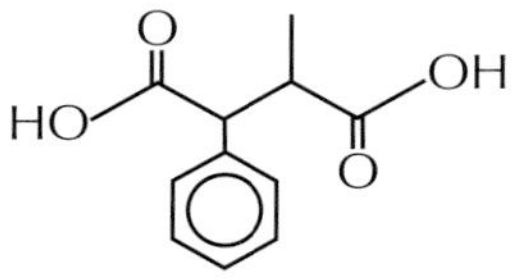

(1 mark)

It doesn't matter how you draw the molecule — whether you use a skeletal formula like this, or a displayed formula. As long as it's correct, you'll get the mark.

(ii) polyester ***(1 mark)***

Section 3 — Organic Synthesis and Practical Techniques

1. Making Carbon-Carbon Bonds

Page 225 — Application Questions

Q1 a)

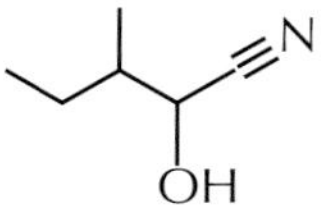

b) E.g. reflux, dilute hydrochloric acid

Q2 a) E.g. reflux, ethanol and NaCN / HCN / KCN

b)

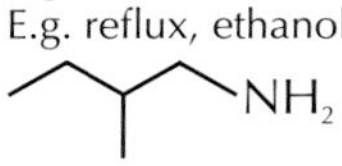

c) E.g. reflux, benzene, $AlCl_3$ (catalyst)

Page 225 — Fact Recall Questions

Q1 A nucleophilic substitution reaction.

Q2 A hydroxynitrile.

Q3 E.g Friedel-Crafts acylation and Friedel-Crafts alkylation.

2. Practical Techniques in Organic Synthesis

Page 228 — Application Questions

Q1 For recrystallisation to work, benzoic acid needs to be soluble in the hot solvent, but insoluble in the cold solvent. This means water is an appropriate choice of solvent for recrystallising benzoic acid.

Q2 Sample B is the least pure, followed by Sample C and then Sample A. Purity can be determined by how close the sample's melting point is to the standard value. The lower the melting point compared to the standard value, the less pure the sample will be. Also, the greater the range in melting point, the less pure the sample will be. Sample B has the lowest melting point compared to the standard value (138-140 °C), and the greatest range in its melting point, so it is the least pure sample. Sample A has a melting point very close to the standard value, and the range is also the smallest of the three samples, so it will be the most pure.

Page 228 — Fact Recall Questions

Q1 Reflux

Q2 To remove any liquid impurities from the solid.

Q3 E.g. Determine the melting point of the solid compared to the standard value of the pure solid.

3. Functional Groups and their Typical Reactions

Page 231 — Application Questions

Q1 a) alkenyl/alkene, haloalkane/bromoalkane, aldehyde

b) The molecule contains an aldehyde functional group which can be oxidised to form a carboxylic acid group.

Q2 a) A b) A and C c) B and C

Page 231 — Fact Recall Questions

Q1 a)

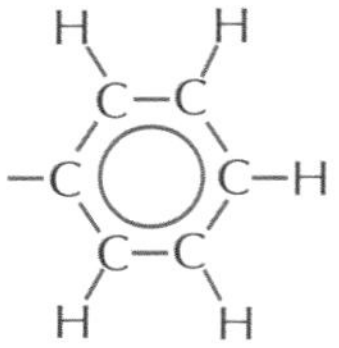

b)

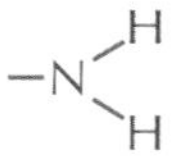

c)

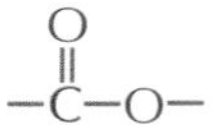

Q2 a) nitrile

b) (primary) amide

c) aldehyde

4. Synthetic Routes

Page 234 — Application Questions

Q1 a) H_3PO_4 catalyst, steam, 300 °C, 60-70 atm

b) Br_2, U.V. light

Q2 a) E.g. step 1: NaOH/KOH, H_2O, reflux
step 2: $K_2Cr_2O_7$, H_2SO_4, heat in distillation apparatus

You have to do this reaction in distillation apparatus so that you don't form the carboxylic acid.

b) E.g. step 1: $K_2Cr_2O_7$, H_2SO_4, reflux
step 2: methanol, conc. H_2SO_4, heat under reflux

You can't reduce the butanal to butan-1-ol and then react it with methanoic acid to get the ester — you'd end up with butyl methanoate, rather than methyl butanoate.

Q3 X is nitrobenzene. Y is phenylamine.

Q4 E.g. step 1: $NaBH_4$, then water
step 2: concentrated H_2SO_4/H_3PO_4 catalyst, 170 °C
step 3: Br_2, 20 °C

Q5 E.g. step 1: HBr, 20 °C
step 2: warm NaOH/KOH, H_2O, reflux
step 3: $K_2Cr_2O_7$, H_2SO_4, reflux

Page 234 — Fact Recall Questions

Q1 alkane, alcohol, alkene
Q2 alcohol, carboxylic acid, hydroxynitrile
Q3 acyl chloride, 20 °C

Exam-style Questions — Pages 236-237

1 B *(1 mark)*
2 B *(1 mark)*
3 A *(1 mark)*
4 a)

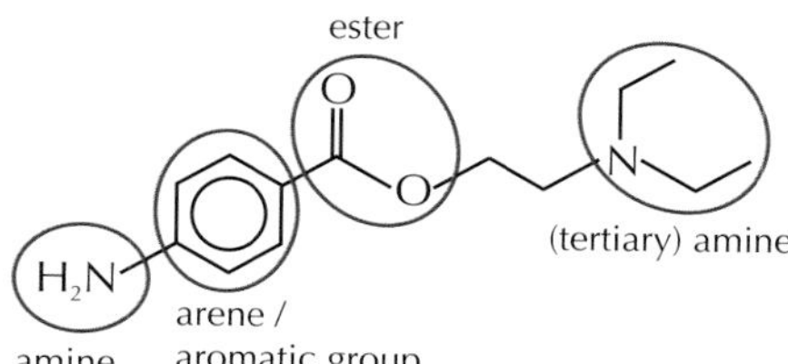

(2 marks — 1 mark for correctly circling all the functional groups, 1 mark for correct names.)

b) (i)

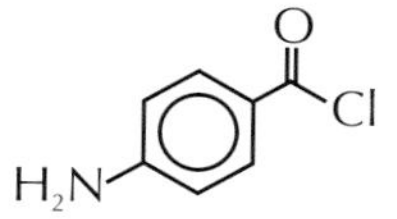

O
H_2N Cl

(1 mark)

(ii) The reagent is: HO N *(1 mark)*.

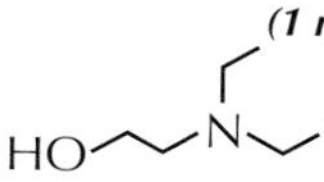

The conditions are 20 °C / room temperature *(1 mark)*.

c) (i) The sample is impure *(1 mark)*.
(ii) e.g. recrystallisation *(1 mark)*

5 a) e.g. ethanoyl chloride, $AlCl_3$ (catalyst), reflux *(1 mark)*
b) (i) HCN *(1 mark)*
(ii) The reaction occurs via a nucleophilic addition mechanism *(1 mark)*:

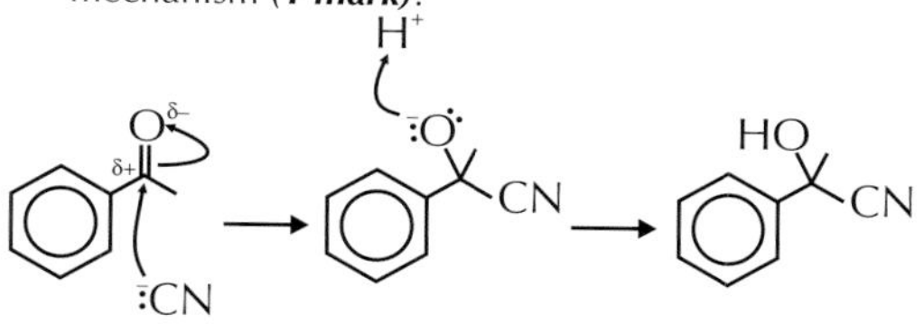

H^+
$O^{\delta-}$ $\delta+$:O: HO
CN CN
:CN

(3 marks — 1 mark for each correct curly arrow)

c) HO NH_2

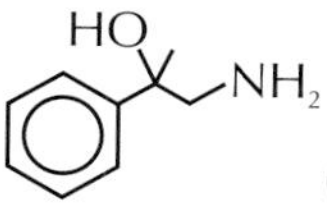

(1 mark)

Section 4 — Analysis

1. Tests for Organic Functional Groups

Page 241 — Application Questions

Q1 a bromoalkane
Q2 E.g. You could identify which test tube contained propanal using Tollens' reagent. Tollens' reagent is prepared by adding silver nitrate solution to a test tube and adding sodium hydroxide, so that a light brown precipitate forms. Dilute ammonia solution is then added until the precipitate dissolves. This solution is Tollens' reagent. It reacts with propanal, an aldehyde, when warmed, to produce a silver mirror. No reaction would be seen with propanone or propanoic acid. To identify which of the remaining test tubes contains propanoic acid, add 1 small spatula of solid calcium carbonate to a sample of each substance. The carboxylic acid will react with the calcium carbonate (seen as fizzing) to produce carbon dioxide gas which, when bubbled through limewater, will turn limewater cloudy. The remaining test tube will contain propanone as it does not react with calcium carbonate.
Q3 a) The acidified potassium dichromate(VI) solution would change from orange to green.
b) The limewater would turn cloudy.

Page 241 — Fact Recall Questions

Q1 bromine water
Q2 pale yellow
Q3 Add a sample of the unknown compound to a test tube and add 1 small spatula of solid sodium hydroxide/2 cm^3 of sodium hydroxide solution. If the solution fizzes and a colourless solution forms, then add another sample of the unknown compound to a separate test tube. Add 1 small spatula of solid sodium carbonate/2 cm^3 of sodium carbonate solution. If nothing happens, the unknown compound must be a weak acid, and so must be a phenol.
Q4 A bright orange precipitate would form.

2. Chromatography

Page 243 — Application Question

Q1 a) $R_f \text{ value} = \dfrac{\text{distance travelled by spot}}{\text{distance travelled by solvent}}$
Spot P: R_f value = 2.1 ÷ 8.0 = **0.26**
Spot Q: R_f value = 3.7 ÷ 8.0 = **0.46**
Spot R: R_f value = 5.9 ÷ 8.0 = **0.74**
b) Spot P contains glycine, spot Q contains tyrosine and spot R contains leucine.
c) The student could check each amino acid has been identified correctly by running a pure sample of each amino acid, alongside the mixture of amino acids, on the same TLC plate. The pure amino acids should travel the same distance up the plate/have the same R_f values as the corresponding amino acids in the mixture.

Page 243 — Fact Recall Questions

Q1 How far each part of the mixture travels up the plate depends on how strongly it's adsorbed to the surface of the plate. A substance that's strongly adsorbed spends more time stuck to the plate and less time dissolved in the solvent, so it moves slowly and doesn't travel as far as a weakly adsorbed substance. So the mixture separates out.
Remember, adsorption is the important idea here — as long as you're talking about differences in the strength of adsorption of the different components, you're on the right track.
Q2 $R_f \text{ value} = \dfrac{\text{distance travelled by spot}}{\text{distance travelled by solvent}}$
Q3 E.g. the solid coating on the TLC plate, the solvent, the temperature.

3. Gas Chromatography

Page 247 — Application Questions

Q1 Components that are more soluble in the oil take longer to travel through the tube, so the pure product will reach the detector after the impurities.
Q2 a) peak A
b) component B
c) component C

Q3 a) Total peak area = 32 + 16 = 48 cm^2
% of mixture that is Chemical 2 = (16 ÷ 48) × 100
= **33%**

This question is all about applying your maths and chemistry knowledge to a situation you've not met before. Don't panic if you get questions like these, that you may not have practised, in the exam. Just stay calm, think about exactly what the question asks and tells you, and you should be fine.

b) 1.32 mol dm^{-3}

Page 247 — Fact Recall Questions

Q1 Some of the components in a mixture will be more soluble in the liquid than others. This means that the components will spend different amounts of time dissolved in the liquid and travelling along the tube in the gas. So they will take different amounts of time to pass through the tube and will be separated out.

Q2 The time taken from the injection of a sample to the detection of a substance.

Q3 The area under each peak tells you the relative amount of each component that's present in the mixture.

Q4 E.g. first you need to create a series of standard solutions of different concentrations of analyte. One by one, inject the standard solutions into a gas chromatography instrument and record the result. Calculate the area under the peak corresponding to each standard solution. Correct the area of the peak for each concentration, using the chromatogram of a blank solution. Plot these values on a graph of area vs concentration. Then draw a line of best fit to create an external calibration curve.

4. NMR Spectroscopy

Page 252 — Application Questions

Q1 a) 4

The number of peaks on the ^{13}C NMR spectrum is the same as the number of carbon environments in the molecule...

b) 3

c) 2

This one's a bit tricky. If you draw the molecule, you should see that three of the carbons are CH_3 groups joined to the central carbon atom. These carbons are all in the same environment.

d) 4

Q2 There are four peaks on the spectrum, so the molecule must have four carbon environments. All the peaks lie between δ = 10 ppm and δ = 40 ppm. Since the molecule only contains carbon and hydrogen, these must all represent carbon atoms in alkyl groups. The formula of the molecule is C_5H_{12}, so it must be an isomer of pentane with four carbon environments.

The only molecule that fits this description is **2-methylbutane**:

```
  H CH3H  H
  |  |  |  |
H-C--C--C--C-H
  |  |  |  |
  H  H  H  H
```

Carbon 1 and the methyl group carbon are in the same environment. Carbons 2, 3 and 4 are all in different environments.

Q3 a) A carbon in a C–O environment.

b) There are three peaks on the spectrum, so the molecule must have three carbon environments. The peaks at δ = 8 ppm and δ = 25 ppm must represent carbons in alkyl groups. The peak at δ = 65 ppm must represent a carbon in a C–O bond. The formula of the molecule is $C_4H_{10}O$ and it must have three carbon environments.

The only molecule that fits this description is **2-methylpropan-1-ol**:

```
  H CH3H
  |  |  |
H-C--C--C-OH
  |  |  |
  H  H  H
```

Q4 D

There are four different carbon environments so there should be four peaks. There is one C=O environment which will have a peak between δ = 160 ppm and δ = 220 ppm. There are two different C=C environments which will have peaks between δ = 115 ppm and δ = 160 ppm. There is one C–C environment which will have a peak between δ = 0 ppm and δ = 50 ppm. This matches the information shown on spectrum D.

Page 252 — Fact Recall Questions

Q1 tetramethylsilane/TMS

Q2 The number of carbon environments in the molecule.

5. Proton NMR Spectroscopy

Page 255 — Application Questions

Q1 a) 2

That's one environment for the two hydrogens on carbon 1, and one environment for the three hydrogens on carbon 3.

b) 2

Q2 E.g.

```
  H  H  H
  |  |  |
H-C--C--C-H
  |  |  |
  H  H  H
```

This is propane. You could also have had other things like butane or 2-methylpropane, but not ethane — that's only got one hydrogen environment.

Q3 a) 2

b) 1 : 3

c) 2 in environment A and 6 in environment B.

You need to divide up the eight hydrogens between the two environments so that they end up in the ratio 1 : 3.

Q4 a) hydrogen atoms in an R–CH group

b) hydrogen atoms in an HC=C– group

You'd get the mark here for anything that showed clearly that you were talking about the right group (e.g. 'an H attached to a C=C group' or 'an H in an alkene group' would do for part b).

Q5 a) 2

b) 1 : 1

c) There will be one peak at δ = 2-3 ppm and another at δ = 3-4 ppm.

Page 255 — Fact Recall Questions

Q1 The number of hydrogen environments in the molecule.

Q2 The relative number of H atoms in each environment.

Q3 The relative areas under the peaks (and so the relative number of H atoms in each environment in the molecule).

6. More Proton NMR Spectroscopy

Page 257 — Application Questions

Q1 2

Think about the $n + 1$ rule — if the carbon next door has two hydrogens on it the peak will split into 2 + 1 = 3.

Q2 Environment 1: peak is a singlet / not split.
Environment 2: peak split into four / quartet.
Environment 3: peak split into two / doublet.

Page 260 — Application Questions

Q1 There are three peaks, so there must be three hydrogen environments in compound **X**.
The peak at δ = 2.5 ppm is likely to be formed by hydrogens in a –COCH– environment.
It can't be an R–NH, an HC–N or a methylbenzene environment because none of those would fit with the molecular formula. And it can't be an R–OH group because the peak isn't a singlet.
The peak at δ = 2.1 ppm is also likely to be formed by hydrogens in a –COCH– environment.
This isn't likely to be an R–OH group because the area ratio tells you that the environment contains more than one hydrogen.
The peak at δ = 1 ppm is likely to be formed by hydrogens in an R–CH environment.
It can't be an R–NH group because that wouldn't fit with the formula, and it isn't an R–OH group because it isn't a singlet.
From the area ratios, there are two protons in the environment at δ = 2.5 ppm for every three protons in the environment at δ = 2.1 ppm and for every three protons in the environment at δ = 1 ppm. To fit this data, the groups contained in compound **X** must be $–COCH_2–$, $–COCH_3$ and $–CH_3$.
We know that the molecular formula is C_4H_8O and that the $–CH_3$ group must be next to the $–COCH_2–$ (because their peaks are split into a triplet and a quartet).
So, the molecule must be **butan-2-one**:

```
    H  H  O  H
    |  |  ‖  |
 H—C—C—C—C—H
    |  |     |
    H  H     H
```

Q2 There are three peaks, so there must be three hydrogen environments.
The peak at δ = 1.1 ppm is likely to be formed by hydrogens in an R–CH environment.
It can't be an R–OH group or an R–NH group because you don't find either of those groups in esters.
The peak at δ = 2.3 ppm is likely to be formed by hydrogens in a –COCH– environment.
Again, it can't be any of the other groups that cause peaks at that chemical shift, because none of them appear in an ester.
The peak at δ = 3.7 ppm is likely to be formed by hydrogens in a HC–O– environment.
And again — an ester doesn't contain any of the other groups that could be causing a peak at this chemical shift.
From the area ratios, there are three protons in the environment at δ = 1.1 ppm for every two protons at δ = 2.3 ppm and for every three protons at δ = 3.7 ppm. To fit this data, the groups must be $–CH_3$, $–COCH_2–$ and $–O–CH_3$.
The peak at δ = 1.1 ppm is a triplet, suggesting that it is adjacent to a carbon with two hydrogens. The peak at δ = 2.3 ppm is a quartet, suggesting that it is adjacent to a carbon with three hydrogens. So these two groups must be next door to each other, giving $CH_3–CH_2C(O)–$. The peak at δ = 3.7 ppm is a singlet, so the $–O–CH_3$ group is not adjacent to any other hydrogens. So the molecule is an ester containing the groups $CH_3–CH_2C(O)–$ and $–O–CH_3$.
It must be **methyl propanoate**:

```
    H  H
    |  |   //O      H
 H—C—C—C           |
    |  |   \O—C—H
    H  H            |
                    H
```

Q3 There are two different hydrogen environments so there will be two peaks. The $–H_2CC(O)–$ environment will have a peak between δ = 2 ppm and δ = 3 ppm and the peak will be a quartet, because there are three hydrogens on the adjacent carbon. The $–CH_3$ environment will have a peak between δ = 0.5 ppm and δ = 2 ppm and the peak will be a triplet, because there are two hydrogens on the adjacent carbon.

Page 260 — Fact Recall Questions

Q1 The rule that states that, in proton NMR spectroscopy, peaks always split into the number of non-equivalent hydrogens on the neighbouring carbons, plus one.

Q2 a quartet

Q3 e.g. $CDCl_3$
Remember — the important thing here is that solvents for proton NMR can't contain any H atoms.

Q4 Run a proton NMR spectrum for the sample molecule just as normal. Then run another one with a little deuterium oxide/D_2O, added. If an OH proton is present, it'll swap with deuterium (to become an OD group). So the peak that was caused by the OH group on the first spectrum will be absent from the second spectrum.

7. More on Spectra

Pages 264-265 — Application Questions

Q1 The mass spectrum shows that the M_r of the molecule is 58. It has a peak at m/z = 15, so it may contain a CH_3 group. It has a peak at 43, so it may contain a CH_3CO group or a $CH_3CH_2CH_2$ group.
The IR spectrum has a peak at 1700 cm^{-1}, so the molecule contains a carbonyl (C=O) group. As there are no peaks between 2500 cm^{-1} and 3300 cm^{-1} it can't contain any O–H or N–H bonds. So it isn't a carboxylic acid or an amide.
The ^{13}C NMR spectrum has two peaks, so the molecule has two carbon environments. The peak at δ = 205 ppm is a carbon in a ketone or aldehyde group. The peak at δ = 29 ppm is a carbon in a C–C group.
The proton NMR spectrum has one singlet peak, so the molecule has one hydrogen environment and there are no hydrogen atoms on adjacent carbons. This singlet peak at δ = 2.3 ppm must be caused by hydrogens in a –CHCO– environment.
All the other groups that cause peaks at this chemical shift have been ruled out by the mass spectrum and IR spectrum.
The molecule must be a ketone or aldehyde with an M_r of 58 — so it must be propanone (CH_3COCH_3) or propanal (CH_3CH_2CHO). Propanone has two carbon environments and one hydrogen environment. Propanal has three carbon environments and three hydrogen environments. So the molecule must be **propanone**:

```
    H  O  H
    |  ‖  |
 H—C—C—C—H
    |     |
    H     H
```

It doesn't matter if you haven't answered this in exactly the same way as long as you've got most of the info down...

Q2 Mass of each element in 100 g:
C = 55.0 g H = 9.0 g O = 36.0 g
Moles of each element:
C= (55 ÷ 12) = 4.6 moles
H = (9.0 ÷ 1) = 9.0 moles
O = (36 ÷ 16) = 2.3 moles
Divide each by 2.3:
C = (4.6 ÷ 2.3) ≈ 2 H = (9.0 ÷ 2.3) ≈ 4
O = (2.3 ÷ 2.3) = 1
The ratio of C : H : O is 2 : 4 : 1.
So the empirical formula is C_2H_4O and empirical mass is (2 × 12) + (4 × 1) + 16 = 44 g
88 ÷ 44 = 2, so molecular formula is 2 times the empirical formula. The molecular formula is $C_4H_8O_2$.
The IR spectrum has a strong peak at 1700 cm^{-1} and a broad peak at 3000 cm^{-1}, so it must contain a C=O bond and an O–H bond in a carboxylic acid group. Therefore, the molecule must be a carboxylic acid.
The ^{13}C NMR spectrum has three peaks, so the molecule must have three carbon environments.
There are only two carboxylic acids with the formula $C_4H_8O_2$ — butanoic acid ($CH_3CH_2CH_2COOH$) and 2-methylpropanoic acid ($(CH_3)_2CHCOOH$). Butanoic acid has four carbon environments, but 2-methylpropanoic acid has three. So the molecule must be 2-methylpropanoic acid:

```
   H  H  O
   |  |  ||
H—C—C—C—OH
   |  |
   H  CH3
```

Exam-style Questions — pages 266-268

1 D *(1 mark)*
Only weak acids, such as phenol, will react with sodium hydroxide but not sodium carbonate. A and B are weak bases so would not react with sodium hydroxide or sodium carbonate, and C is a strong acid so would react with sodium hydroxide and sodium carbonate.

2 B ***(1 mark)***

3 C ***(1 mark)***
Only aldehydes will react with Tollens' reagent to form a silver mirror. The molecule in the question is a ketone, so nothing will happen.

4 a) E.g. $CDCl_3$ ***(1 mark)***.
Any deuterated solvent would get the mark here.

b) The molecule is propan-2-ol:

```
   H  H  H
   |  |  |
H—C—C—C—H
   |  |  |
   H  OH H
```

(1 mark for correctly identifying the molecule)
Plus any five from: There are three peaks, so the molecule must have three hydrogen environments ***(1 mark)***. The peak at δ = 0.9 ppm must be due to hydrogens in an R–CH environment ***(1 mark)***. This peak is a doublet, so there must be one hydrogen on adjacent carbons ***(1 mark)***. The singlet peak at δ = 2.2 ppm must be due to a hydrogen in the alcohol group / an R–OH environment ***(1 mark)***. The peak at δ = 4.0 ppm must be due to a hydrogen in an HC–O environment ***(1 mark)***. It is a heptet, so there must be six hydrogens on adjacent carbons ***(1 mark)***.

c) The (singlet) peak at δ = 2.2 ppm would be missing ***(1 mark)***.

5 a) Some components of the mixture will be more strongly adsorbed to the stationary phase than others ***(1 mark)***. So the components will spend different amounts of time adsorbed to the stationary phase and will travel different distances up the plate ***(1 mark)***.

b) R_f value = $\frac{\text{distance travelled by spot}}{\text{distance travelled by solvent}}$
= 2.2 cm ÷ 9.2 cm = **0.24** ***(1 mark)***

c) The unknown carbonyl is either propanone or propanal. To identify it, the scientist could react the unknown carbonyl with Tollens' reagent ***(1 mark)***. If the compound is propanone, nothing will happen ***(1 mark)***. If the unknown carbonyl is propanal, a silver mirror will form on the walls of the test tube ***(1 mark)***.

d) An alkene ***(1 mark)***.

6 a) The compound has two hydrogen environments ***(1 mark)***. The peak at δ = 1.8 ppm must represent hydrogens in R–CH environments ***(1 mark)***. The peak at δ = 3.8 ppm must come from hydrogens in an HC–Cl environment ***(1 mark)***. The peak at δ = 1.8 ppm is a quintet, so there must be four hydrogens on adjacent carbons ***(1 mark)***. The peak at δ = 1.8 ppm is a triplet, so there must be two hydrogens on adjacent carbons ***(1 mark)***. The only molecule with the formula $C_3H_6Cl_2$ that would fit this pattern of environments is 1,3-dichloropropane:

```
    H  H  H
    |  |  |
Cl—C—C—C—Cl
    |  |  |
    H  H  H
```

(1 mark)

b) The molecule is methylpropanal:

```
   H  CH3 O
   |  |   ||
H—C—C—C—H
   |  |
   H  H
```

(1 mark for correctly identifying the molecule)
Plus any four from: the molecular ion peak on the mass spectrum is at m/z = 72, so the molecular mass of the molecule must be 72 ***(1 mark)***. The mass spectrum has a peak at m/z = 15, so the molecule probably contains a CH_3 group ***(1 mark for any peak on the mass spectrum matched to a correct fragment of the molecule)***. The ^{13}C NMR spectrum has three peaks, so the molecule must have three carbon environments ***(1 mark)***. There is a peak at δ = 15 ppm and another at δ = 35 ppm, so the molecule must contain at least two carbons in C–C environments ***(1 mark)***. There is a peak at δ = 205 ppm, so the molecule must contain at least one carbon in an aldehyde or ketone C=O environment ***(1 mark)***. There are only three isomers that are aldehydes or ketones with an M_r of 72 — butanone, butanal and methylpropanal. ***(1 mark for any representation of the three possible isomers)***. Methylpropanal is the only possible isomer that has three carbon environments ***(1 mark)***.
There are usually more things to say than there are marks for this type of question, so you don't need to say all of this to get full marks. Just make sure you've made it clear to the examiner how you got to your answer.

Glossary

A

α-amino acid
An amino acid with the amino group and the carboxylic acid group attached to the same carbon.

Acid dissociation constant, K_a
An equilibrium constant specific to weak acids that relates the acid concentration to the concentration of $[H^+]$ ions. $K_a = [H^+][A^-] \div [HA]$.

Acidic buffer
A buffer with a pH of less than 7 made by mixing a weak acid with a salt of its conjugate base or by adding a small amount of strong alkali to an excess of weak acid.

Acyl chloride
An organic compound with the functional group –COCl.

Acylation
When an acyl group (–COR) is added to a molecule.

Addition polymer
A type of polymer formed by joining small alkenes (monomers) together.

Addition reaction
A reaction where two molecules join together to form a single product.

Adsorption
The attraction between a substance and the surface of a solid.

Alcohol
A substance with the general formula $C_nH_{2n+1}OH$.

Aldehyde
A substance with the general formula $C_nH_{2n}O$ which has a hydrogen and one alkyl group attached to the carbonyl carbon atom.

Alkylation
When an alkyl group is added to a molecule.

Amide
A carboxylic acid derivative containing the functional group $-CONH_2$.

Amide link
The -CONH- group which is found between monomers in a polyamide.

Amine
A molecule where one or more of the hydrogen atoms in ammonia have been replaced with an alkyl group.

Amino acid
A molecule with an amino group (NH_2) and a carboxyl group (COOH)

Aromatic compound
A compound that contains a benzene ring.

Arrhenius equation
An equation linking the rate constant of a reaction to the activation energy and temperature.

Arrhenius plot
A graph where 1/temperature is plotted against ln k, where k is the rate constant.

B

Benzene
An organic compound with the formula C_6H_6. Its six carbon atoms are joined together in a ring. The ring is planar (flat) and the hydrogens all stick out in the same plane.

Bidentate ligand
A ligand that can form two coordinate bonds.

Born-Haber cycle
An enthalpy cycle that allows you to calculate the lattice enthalpy for a system.

Brady's reagent
2,4-dinitrophenylhydrazine (2,4-DNPH) dissolved in methanol and concentrated sulfuric acid. Used to test for carbonyl compounds (aldehydes and ketones).

Brønsted-Lowry acid
A proton donor.

Brønsted-Lowry base
A proton acceptor.

Buffer
A solution that minimises changes in pH when small amounts of acid or alkali are added.

C

Carbonyl compound
A compound that contains a carbon-oxygen double bond.

Carboxylic acid
A substance which has a COOH group attached to the end of a carbon chain.

Catalyst
A substance that increases the rate of a reaction by providing an alternative reaction pathway with a lower activation energy. The catalyst is chemically unchanged at the end of the reaction.

Cell potential (E_{cell})
The voltage between two half-cells in an electrochemical cell.

Chemical shift
Nuclei in different environments absorb energy of different frequencies. NMR spectroscopy measures these differences relative to a standard substance — the difference is called the chemical shift (δ).

Chiral molecule
A molecule that contains a carbon atom with four different groups attached to it.

Chromatogram
A visual record (such as a pattern of spots or a graph) of the results of a chromatography experiment.

Chromatography
An analytical technique which is used to separate out mixtures.

Citation
Details about where to find the source of a piece of information.

Clock reaction
A method used to find the initial rate of a reaction. In clock reactions you measure the time it takes for a given amount of product to form.

Closed system
A system where nothing can get in or out.

Complex ion
A metal ion surrounded by coordinately bonded ligands.

Condensation polymer
A type of polymer formed through a series of condensation reactions.

Condensation reaction
A reaction in which two molecules join together with the loss of a small molecule, such as water or hydrogen chloride. The opposite of a hydrolysis reaction.

Conjugate pair
A set of two species that can be transformed into each other by gaining or losing a proton.

Continuous monitoring
A method used to monitor the progress of a reaction. The formation or loss of one of the substances in the reaction is measured at regular intervals over the entire course of the reaction, and the data is used to construct a concentration-time graph.

Coordinate bond
A covalent bond in which both electrons in the shared pair come from the same atom (also called a dative covalent bond).

Coordination number
The number of coordinate bonds that are formed with the central metal ion in a complex ion.

Corrosive substance
Something that may cause chemical burns.

D

d-block
The block of elements in the middle of the periodic table.

d-subshell
A type of subshell. Each can hold ten electrons.

Data logger
A piece of software on a tablet or computer that can record data readings as they are made and store them to be looked at later.

Dative covalent bond
A covalent bond in which both electrons in the shared pair come from the same atom (also called a coordinate bond).

Dependent variable
The variable that you measure during an experiment.

Deuterated solvent
A solvent which has had all of its hydrogen atoms exchanged for deuterium atoms.

Deuterium
An isotope of hydrogen. It contains one neutron, one proton and one electron.

Dibasic acid
An acid that can release two H^+ ions per molecule.

Distillation
An organic technique used to heat a reaction mixture. Any products that have a boiling point lower than the temperature of the reaction mixture will condense out of the reaction mixture as soon as they form. They can then be collected in a separate vessel.

Dynamic equilibrium
When the forward and backward reactions of a reversible reaction are happening at exactly the same rate, so the concentration of reactants and products doesn't change.

E

Electric heater
A piece of equipment used to heat a chemical mixture, using a plate of metal that is heated to a set temperature.

Electrochemical cell
An electrical circuit made from two metal electrodes (which are connected by a wire) dipped in salt solutions (which are connected by a salt bridge).

Electrochemical series
A list of electrode potentials written in order from most negative to most positive.

Electrode potential
The voltage measured when a half-cell is connected to a standard hydrogen electrode.

Electromotive force (e.m.f.)
Another name for cell potential.

Electrophile
An electron deficient (and usually positively charged) species which is attracted to regions of high electron density.

Electrophilic substitution
A reaction mechanism where an electrophile substitutes for another atom (usually a hydrogen) in a molecule.

Elimination reaction
A reaction where a functional group is lost from a molecule and released as a small molecule, such as a hydrogen halide or water.

Enantiomer
A molecule that has the same structural formula as another molecule but is a non-superimposable mirror image of the other molecule.

End point
The point in a titration at which all the acid is just neutralised and the pH curve becomes vertical.

Endothermic reaction
A reaction that absorbs heat energy (ΔH is positive).

Enthalpy change of atomisation of a compound ($\Delta_{at}H$)
The enthalpy change when 1 mole of a compound is converted to gaseous atoms.

Enthalpy change of atomisation of an element ($\Delta_{at}H$)
The enthalpy change when 1 mole of gaseous atoms is formed from an element.

Enthalpy change of formation ($\Delta_f H$)
The enthalpy change when 1 mole of a compound is formed from its elements.

Enthalpy change of hydration ($\Delta_{hyd}H$)
The enthalpy change when 1 mole of gaseous ions is dissolved in water.

Enthalpy change of solution ($\Delta_{sol}H$)
The enthalpy change when 1 mole of solute is dissolved in a solvent.

Entropy (S)
A measure of the dispersal of energy in a system (e.g. the number of ways that particles can be arranged and the number of ways that the energy can be shared out between the particles).

Equilibrium constant (K_c)
A ratio worked out from the concentration of the products and reactants once a reversible reaction has reached equilibrium.

Ester
A molecule that contains the functional group RCOOR.

Ester link
The -COO- group which is found between monomers in a polyester.

Esterification
Forming an ester by heating a carboxylic acid and an alcohol in the presence of a strong acid catalyst (or by reacting an acid anhydride with an alcohol).

Exothermic reaction
A reaction that gives out heat energy (ΔH is negative).

Feasible reaction
A reaction which has a free energy change that is less than or equal to zero and can happen by itself without energy being supplied.

Filtration
A technique used to separate solids from liquids.

Filtration under reduced pressure
A technique for removing liquid impurities from an organic solid.

First electron affinity
The energy needed to change 1 mole of gaseous atoms into 1 mole of gaseous 1– ions.

First ionisation energy
The energy needed to change 1 mole of gaseous atoms into 1 mole of gaseous 1+ ions.

Flammable
A substance that will easily catch fire.

Free energy change (ΔG)
A measure which links enthalpy and entropy changes to predict whether a reaction is feasible. $\Delta G = \Delta H - T\Delta S$

Fuel cell
A device that converts the energy of a fuel into electricity through an oxidation reaction.

Functional group
A group of atoms within a molecule that is responsible for its characteristic reactions (e.g. COOH for carboxylic acids, C=C for alkenes).

Gas chromatography (GC)
A type of chromatography where the sample is carried in a stream of gas through a coiled tube, coated with a viscous liquid (such as an oil) or a solid.

Gas equilibrium constant (K_p)
A ratio worked out from the partial pressures of the gaseous products and reactants once a reversible reaction has reached equilibrium.

Haemoglobin
A protein found in blood that helps to transport oxygen around the body.

Half-cell
One half of an electrochemical cell.

Half-equation
An equation that shows oxidation or reduction — one half of a full redox equation.

Half-life
The time it takes for half of the reactant to be used up during a reaction.

Halogen carrier
A molecule which can accept a halogen atom (e.g. $AlCl_3$). Used as a catalyst in the halogenation of benzene, and also in Friedel-Crafts acylation and alkylation.

Hess's law
The total enthalpy change of a reaction is always the same, no matter which route is taken.

Heterogeneous equilibrium
An equilibrium mixture where the reactants and products are in different states.

Homogeneous equilibrium
An equilibrium mixture where the reactants and products are in the same state.

Hydrolysis reaction
A reaction in which water is used to split apart a molecule, creating two smaller ones. The opposite of a condensation reaction.

Hydroxynitrile
An organic compound containing a -C≡N and an -OH functional group.

Independent variable
The variable that you change during an experiment.

Indicator
A substance that changes colour over a particular pH range.

Initial rates method
An experimental technique used to work out the initial rate of a reaction by timing how long it takes for a set amount of product to form or reactant to be used. This data can be used to work out the order of reaction with respect to each reactant.

Integration trace
A line on a proton NMR spectrum that has a change in height that is proportional to the area of the peak it's next to.

Ionic product of water
An equilibrium constant specific to water that describes the dissociation of water at a constant temperature. $K_w = [H^+][OH^-]$

Irritant
A substance that may cause inflammation or discomfort.

Ketone
A substance with the general formula $C_nH_{2n}O$ which has two alkyl groups attached to the carbonyl carbon atom.

Lattice enthalpy ($\Delta_{LE}H$)
The enthalpy change when 1 mole of a solid ionic compound is formed from its gaseous ions.

Le Chatelier's Principle
If there's a change in concentration, pressure or temperature, an equilibrium will move to help counteract the change.

Ligand
An atom, ion or molecule that donates a pair of electrons to a central metal ion in a complex ion.

Ligand substitution reaction
A reaction where one or more ligands are changed for one or more other ligands in a complex ion. (Also called a ligand exchange reaction.)

Logarithmic constant (pK_a)
The logarithmic form of the acid dissociation constant, K_a.
$pK_a = -\log_{10} K_a$

Melting point determination
A technique for determining the purity of an organic solid. The melting point of the sample solid is compared to the standard melting point of the pure solid. The closer the agreement between the two values, the more pure the sample is.

Methyl orange
A pH indicator that changes colour between pH 3.1 and 4.4.

Mole fraction
The proportion of a gas mixture that is a made up of a particular gas.

Monobasic acid
An acid that releases one H^+ ion per molecule. (Also known as a monoprotic acid.)

Monodentate ligand
A ligand that can only form one coordinate bond. (Also known as a unidentate ligand.)

Monomer
A small molecule which can join together with other monomers to form a polymer.

Multidentate ligand
A ligand that can form three or more coordinate bonds.

Multiplet
A split peak on a proton spectrum. (General term for a doublet, triplet, quartet, quintet etc.)

***n* + 1 rule**
Peaks on a proton NMR spectrum always split into the number of non-equivalent hydrogens on the neighbouring carbon, plus one.

Nitration
A reaction in which a nitro group ($-NO_2$) is added to a molecule.

Nitrile
An organic compound containing a -C≡N functional group.

Nuclear magnetic resonance (NMR) spectroscopy
An analytical technique which uses the absorption of low-energy radio waves to determine the relative environment of an atom within a compound.

Nucleophile
An electron-pair donor. Nucleophiles are electron rich, so they are attracted to areas of positive charge.

Nucleophilic addition
A reaction mechanism where a nucleophile adds on to the δ^+ carbon atom of a carbonyl group.

Optical isomer
A molecule that has the same structural formula as another molecule but is a non-superimposable mirror image of the other molecule.

Orbital
A region of a subshell that contains a maximum of two electrons.

Overall order (of reaction)
The sum of the orders of each reactant in a reaction.

Oxidation
Loss of electrons.

Oxidation state
The total number of electrons an element has donated or accepted. (Also called oxidation number.)

Oxidising agent
Something that gains electrons and gets reduced.

Paper chromatography
A technique for testing the purity of an organic mixture. The mixture is separated into its component parts by a solvent moving up a plate made of paper.

Partial pressure
The pressure exerted by an individual gas in a mixture of gases.

pH
A measure of the hydrogen ion concentration in a solution.
$pH = -\log_{10} [H^+]$

pH chart
A chart to show the colour of an indicator at different pHs.

pH curve
A graph used to follow the progress of an acid-base titration. You make a pH curve by plotting the pH against the volume of acid (or alkali) added.

pH meter
An electronic gadget used to measure pH, made up of a probe connected to a digital display.

Phenol
An aromatic organic compound with the formula C_6H_5OH.

Phenolphthalein
A pH indicator that changes colour between pH 8.3 and 10.

Plane polarised light
Light where the waves all vibrate in the same direction.

Polyamide
A polymer that has amide links between the monomers.

Polyester
A polymer that has ester links between the monomers.

Polymer
A long molecule formed from lots of repeating units (called monomers).

Polymerisation
The process of forming a polymer from monomers.

Precipitate
A solid that forms in a solution.

Rate constant (*k*)
A constant in the rate equation. The larger it is, the faster the rate of reaction.

Rate-determining step
The slowest step in a reaction mechanism which determines the overall rate of a reaction.

Rate equation
An equation of the form rate = $k[A]^m[B]^n$ which tells you how the rate of a reaction is affected by the concentration of the reactants.

Reaction order
A number that tells you how the concentration of a particular reactant affects the reaction rate.

Reaction rate
The change in the amount of reactants or products per unit time.

Recrystallisation
A technique used to purify an organic solid. The solid is dissolved in a minimal amount of a hot solvent, and then the solution is cooled. As the solution cools, the pure solid becomes insoluble in the solvent and crystallises out.

Redox potential
The voltage measured when a half-cell is connected to a standard hydrogen electrode.

Redox reaction
A reaction where reduction and oxidation happen simultaneously.

Redox titration
A titration that can be performed to determine how much reducing agent is needed to exactly react with a known quantity of oxidising agent, or vice versa.

Reducing agent
Something that donates electrons and gets oxidised.

Reduction
Gain of electrons.

Reflux
An organic technique where a mixture is heated in such a way that volatile compounds can't evaporate from the reaction apparatus, but instead condense and fall back into the mixture.

Repeat unit
A part of a polymer that repeats over and over again.

Retention time
The time taken from the injection of a sample to the moment when a substance is detected in gas chromatography.

R_f value
The ratio of the distance travelled by a spot to the distance travelled by the solvent in thin-layer chromatography.

Salt bridge
A connection between two half-cells that ions can flow through, used to complete the circuit in an electrochemical cell. Often a piece of filter paper soaked in a salt solution.

Sand bath
A piece of equipment used to heat a chemical mixture. Made up of a container filled with sand that can be heated to a set temperature. The vessel containing the reaction mixture is submerged in the sand and so is heated.

Second electron affinity
The energy needed to change 1 mole of gaseous 1– ions into 1 mole of gaseous 2– ions.

Second ionisation energy
The energy needed to change 1 mole of gaseous 1+ ions into 1 mole of gaseous 2+ ions.

Splitting pattern
Peaks on proton NMR spectra may be split into further peaks. The resultant group of peaks is called a splitting pattern.

Standard conditions
A temperature of 298 K (25 °C), a pressure of 100 kPa and all ion solutions having a concentration of 1.00 mol dm^{-3}.

Standard electrode potential
The voltage measured under standard conditions when a half-cell is connected to a standard hydrogen electrode.

Standard hydrogen electrode
An electrode where hydrogen gas is bubbled through a solution of aqueous H^+ ions under standard conditions.

Standard redox potential
The voltage measured under standard conditions when a half-cell is connected to a standard hydrogen electrode.

Stereoisomer
A molecule that has the same structural formula as another molecule but with the atoms arranged differently in space.

Strong acid/base
An acid or base that dissociates almost fully in water.

Subshell
A subdivision of an energy level (shell). Subshells may be s, p, d or f subshells.

Substitution reaction
A reaction in which one functional group is swapped for another.

Synthesis
A method detailing how to create a chemical.

Synthetic route
A step-by-step pathway of how to get from one organic compound to another, showing the reagents, catalysts and conditions needed, as well as any intermediate products.

Thin-layer chromatography (TLC)
A type of chromatography where a solvent moves over a glass or plastic plate, which is covered in a thin layer of solid, resulting in the separation of a mixture of substances.

Titration
An analytical technique that allows you to calculate the concentration of a species in solution.

Tollens' reagent
A colourless solution of silver nitrate dissolved in aqueous ammonia which can be used to distinguish between aldehydes and ketones.

Toxic substance
A substance that can cause illness or even death.

Transition element
A metal that can form one or more stable ions with a partially filled d-subshell.

Tribasic acid
An acid that can release three H^+ ions per molecule.

Water bath
A piece of equipment used to heat a chemical mixture. Made up of a container filled with water that can be heated to a set temperature. The vessel containing the reaction mixture is submerged in the water and so is heated.

Weak acid/base
An acid or base that only partially dissociates in water.

IR Data

Bond	Where it's found	Wavenumber (cm^{-1})
C–C	alkanes, alkyl chains	750 – 1100
C–X	haloalkanes (X = Cl, Br, I)	500 – 800
C–F	fluoroalkanes	1000 – 1350
C–O	alcohols, esters, carboxylic acids	1000 – 1300
C=C	alkenes	1620 – 1680
C=O	aldehydes, ketones, carboxylic acids, esters, amides, acyl chlorides, acid anhydrides	1630 – 1820
aromatic C=C	arenes	several peaks in range 1450 – 1650 (variable)
C≡N	nitriles	2220 – 2260
C–H	most organic molecules	2850 – 3100
O–H	carboxylic acids	2500 – 3300 (broad)
N–H	amines, amides	3300 – 3500
O–H	alcohols, phenols	3200 – 3600

Acknowledgements

Cover Photo **Andrew Lambert Photography**/Science Photo Library, p 2 Science Photo Library, p 3 **NASA/Goddard Space Flight Center**/Science Photo Library, p 4 **Robert Brook**/Science Photo Library, p 7 © **Ecelop**/iStockphoto.com, p 8 **Andrew Lambert Photography**/Science Photo Library, p 12 (top) **Martin Shields**/Science Photo Library, p 12 (bottom) **Andrew Lambert Photography**/Science Photo Library, p 14 **GIPhotoStock**/Science Photo Library, p 16 **Andrew Lambert Photography**/Science Photo Library, p 18 **Andrew Lambert Photography**/Science Photo Library, p 24 **Andrew Lambert Photography**/Science Photo Library, p 25 **Andrew Lambert Photography**/Science Photo Library, p 32 **Martyn F. Chillmaid**/Science Photo Library, p 35 **Andrew Lambert Photography**/Science Photo Library, p 40 **Charles D. Winters**/Science Photo Library, p 42 **Emilio Segre Visual Archives/American Institute of Physics**/Science Photo Library, p 49 **Charles D. Winters**/Science Photo Library, p 55 Science Photo Library, p 58 **Molekuul**/Science Photo Library, p 59 Science Photo Library, p 60 (top) **Martyn F. Chillmaid**/Science Photo Library, p 60 (bottom) **Martyn F. Chillmaid**/Science Photo Library, p 65 **Martyn F. Chillmaid**/Science Photo Library, p 67 **Martyn F. Chillmaid**/Science Photo Library, p 68 Science Photo Library, p 69 © **photongpix**/iStockphoto.com, p 70 **Richard J. Green**/Science Photo Library, p 72 **Martyn F. Chillmaid**/Science Photo Library, p 75 **Martyn F. Chillmaid**/Science Photo Library, p 79 **Charles D. Winters**/Science Photo Library, p 80 © **Eraxion**/iStockphoto.com, p 84 © **angelblue1**/iStockphoto.com, p 86 **Andrew Lambert Photography**/Science Photo Library, p 93 **David Taylor**/Science Photo Library, p 95 Science Photo Library, p 96 **Emilio Segre Visual Archives/American Institute of Physics**/Science Photo Library, p 97 **Andrew Lambert Photography**/Science Photo Library, p 100 **Andrew Lambert Photography**/Science Photo Library, p 101 **Martyn F. Chillmaid**/Science Photo Library, p 103 **Adam Hart-Davis**/Science Photo Library, p 106 Science Photo Library, p 116 (top) **Andrew Lambert Photography**/Science Photo Library, p 116 (bottom) **Andrew Lambert Photography**/Science Photo Library, p 118 **Andrew Lambert Photography**/Science Photo Library, p 121 **Andrew Lambert Photography**/Science Photo Library, p 123 **Charles D. Winters**/Science Photo Library, p 125 **Martyn F. Chillmaid**/Science Photo Library, p 133 (top) **Martyn F. Chillmaid**/Science Photo Library, p 133 (bottom) **Cordelia Molloy**/Science Photo Library, p 134 © **rocksolidlunchkids**/iStockphoto.com, p 141 **Klaus Guldbrandsen**/Science Photo Library, p 143 **Astrid & Hanns-Frieder Michler**/Science Photo Library, p 144 **Andrew Lambert Photography**/Science Photo Library, p 147 **Dr Mark J. Winter**/Science Photo Library, p 148 **Andrew Lambert Photography**/Science Photo Library, p 152 **Power And Syred**/Science Photo Library, p 154 (left) **Andrew Lambert Photography**/Science Photo Library, p 154 (right) **Andrew Lambert Photography**/Science Photo Library, p 155 (left) **Andrew Lambert Photography**/Science Photo Library, p 155 (right) **Charles D. Winters**/Science Photo Library, p 157 **Andrew Lambert Photography**/Science Photo Library, p 158 (top) **Andrew Lambert Photography**/Science Photo Library, p 158 (bottom) **Charles D. Winters**/Science Photo Library, p 165 **Clive Freeman, The Royal Institution**/Science Photo Library, p 166 **Laguna Design**/Science Photo Library, p 170 **Ria Novosti**/Science Photo Library, p 172 Science Photo Library, p 175 **Martyn F. Chillmaid**/Science Photo Library, p 182 **Tek Image**/Science Photo Library, p 183 **Andrew Lambert Photography**/Science Photo Library, p 184 **Andrew Lambert Photography**/Science Photo Library, p 186 **Martyn F. Chillmaid**/Science Photo Library, p 187 **Andrew Lambert Photography**/Science Photo Library, p 192 Science Photo Library, p 198 **Martyn F. Chillmaid**/Science Photo Library, p 201 **Laguna Design**/Science Photo Library, p 203 **Klaus Guldbrandsen**/Science Photo Library, p 207 **Martyn F. Chillmaid**/Science Photo Library, p 210 (top) © **fotokostic**/iStockphoto.com, p 210 (middle) **Eye of Science**/Science Photo Library, p 210 (bottom) © **monkeybusinessimages**/iStockphoto.com, p 211 **GIPhotoStock**/Science Photo Library, p 227 **Andrew Lambert Photography**/Science Photo Library, p 228 **Andrew Lambert Photography**/Science Photo Library, p 234 © **ErikaMitchell**/iStockphoto.com, p 239 **Trevor Clifford Photography**/Science Photo Library, p 240 **Andrew Lambert Photography**/Science Photo Library, p 241 **Andrew Lambert Photography**/Science Photo Library, p 242 **Sinclair Stammers**/Science Photo Library, p 245 **Massimo Brega, The Lighthouse**/Science Photo Library, p 248 **Hank Morgan**/Science Photo Library, p 255 **Mark Sykes**/Science Photo Library, p 257 **Friedrich Saurer**/Science Photo Library, p 258 **Hank Morgan**/Science Photo Library, p 261 **Stephen Ausmus/US Department of Agriculture**/Science Photo Library, p 274 (top) © **Achim Prill**/iStockphoto.com, p 274 (bottom) **Martyn F. Chillmaid**/Science Photo Library, p 275 © **Valdore**/iStockphoto.com, p 280 © **AtomStudios**/iStockphoto.com

Index